Lecture Notes in Computer Science

Lecture Notes in Computer Science

Vol. 117: Fundamentals of Computation Theory. Proceedings, 1981. Edited by F. Gécseg. XI, 471 pages. 1981.

Vol. 118: Mathematical Foundations of Computer Science 1981. Proceedings, 1981. Edited by J. Gruska and M. Chytil. XI, 589 pages. 1981.

Vol. 119: G. Hirst, Anaphora in Natural Language Understanding: A Survey. XIII, 128 pages. 1981.

Vol. 120: L. B. Rall, Automatic Differentiation: Techniques and Applications. VIII, 165 pages. 1981.

Vol. 121: Z. Zlatev, J. Wasniewski, and K. Schaumburg, Y12M Solution of Large and Sparse Systems of Linear Algebraic Equations. IX, 128 pages. 1981.

Vol. 122: Algorithms in Modern Mathematics and Computer Science. Proceedings, 1979. Edited by A. P. Ershov and D. E. Knuth. XI, 487 pages. 1981.

Vol. 123: Trends in Information Processing Systems. Proceedings, 1981. Edited by A. J. W. Duijvestijn and P. C. Lockemann. XI, 349 pages. 1981.

Vol. 124: W. Polak, Compiler Specification and Verification. XIII, 269 pages. 1981.

Vol. 125: Logic of Programs. Proceedings, 1979. Edited by E. Engeler. V, 245 pages. 1981.

Vol. 126: Microcomputer System Design. Proceedings, 1981. Edited by M. J. Flynn, N. R. Harris, and D. P. McCarthy. VII, 397 pages. 1982.

Voll. 127: Y.Wallach, Alternating Sequential/Parallel Processing. X, 329 pages. 1982.

Vol. 128: P. Branquart, G. Louis, P. Wodon, An Analytical Description of CHILL, the CCITT High Level Language. VI, 277 pages. 1982.

Vol. 129: B. T. Hailpern, Verifying Concurrent Processes Using Temporal Logic. VIII, 208 pages. 1982.

Vol. 130: R. Goldblatt, Axiomatising the Logic of Computer Programming. XI, 304 pages. 1982.

Vol. 131: Logics of Programs. Proceedings, 1981. Edited by D. Kozen. VI, 429 pages. 1982.

Vol. 132: Data Base Design Techniques I: Requirements and Logical Structures. Proceedings, 1978. Edited by S.B. Yao, S.B. Navathe, J.L. Weldon, and T.L. Kunii. V, 227 pages. 1982.

Vol. 133: Data Base Design Techniques II: Proceedings, 1979. Edited by S.B. Yao and T.L. Kunii. V, 229–399 pages. 1982.

Vol. 134: Program Specification. Proceedings, 1981. Edited by J. Staunstrup. IV, 426 pages. 1982.

Vol. 135: R.L. Constable, S.D. Johnson, and C.D. Eichenlaub, An Introduction to the PL/CV2 Programming Logic. X, 292 pages. 1982.

Vol. 136: Ch. M. Hoffmann, Group-Theoretic Algorithms and Graph Isomorphism. VIII, 311 pages. 1982.

Vol. 137: International Symposium on Programming. Proceedings, 1982. Edited by M. Dezani-Ciancaglini and M. Montanari. VI, 406 pages. 1982.

Vol. 138: 6th Conference on Automated Deduction. Proceedings, 1982. Edited by D.W. Loveland. VII, 389 pages. 1982.

Vol. 139: J. Uhl, S. Drossopoulou, G. Persch, G. Goos, M. Dausmann, G. Winterstein, W. Kirchgässner, An Attribute Grammar for the Semantic Analysis of Ada. IX, 511 pages. 1982.

Vol. 140: Automata, Languages and programming. Edited by M. Nielsen and E.M. Schmidt. VII, 614 pages. 1982.

Vol. 141: U. Kastens, B. Hutt, E. Zimmermann, GAG: A Practical Compiler Generator. IV, 156 pages. 1982.

Vol. 142: Problems and Methodologies in Mathematical Software Production. Proceedings, 1980. Edited by P.C. Messina and A. Murli. VII, 271 pages. 1982.

Vol. 143: Operating Systems Engineering. Proceedings, 1980. Edited by M. Maekawa and L.A. Belady. VII, 465 pages. 1982.

Vol. 144: Computer Algebra. Proceedings, 1982. Edited by J. Calmet. XIV, 301 pages. 1982.

Vol. 145: Theoretical Computer Science. Proceedings, 1983. Edited by A.B. Cremers and H.P. Kriegel. X, 367 pages. 1982.

Vol. 146: Research and Development in Information Retrieval. Proceedings, 1982. Edited by G. Salton and H.-J. Schneider. IX, 311 pages. 1983.

Vol. 147: RIMS Symposia on Software Science and Engineering. Proceedings, 1982. Edited by E. Goto, I. Nakata, K. Furukawa, R. Nakajima, and A. Yonezawa. V. 232 pages. 1983.

Vol. 148: Logics of Programs and Their Applications. Proceedings, 1980. Edited by A. Salwicki. VI, 324 pages. 1983.

Vol. 149: Cryptography. Proceedings, 1982. Edited by T. Beth. VIII, 402 pages. 1983.

Vol. 150: Enduser Systems and Their Human Factors. Proceedings, 1983. Edited by A. Blaser and M. Zoeppritz. III, 138 pages. 1983.

Vol. 151: R. Piloty, M. Barbacci, D. Borrione, D. Dietmeyer, F. Hill, and P. Skelly, CONLAN Report. XII, 174 pages. 1983.

Vol. 152: Specification and Design of Software Systems. Proceedings, 1982. Edited by E. Knuth and E. J. Neuhold. V, 152 pages. 1983.

Vol. 153: Graph-Grammars and Their Application to Computer Science. Proceedings, 1982. Edited by H. Ehrig, M. Nagl, and G. Rozenberg. VII, 452 pages. 1983.

Vol. 154: Automata, Languages and Programming. Proceedings, 1983. Edited by J. Díaz. VIII, 734 pages. 1983.

Vol. 155: The Programming Language Ada. Reference Manual. Approved 17 February 1983. American National Standards Institute, Inc. ANSI/MIL-STD-1815A-1983. IX, 331 pages. 1983.

Vol. 156: M.H. Overmars, The Design of Dynamic Data Structures. VII, 181 pages. 1983.

Vol. 157: O. Østerby, Z. Zlatev, Direct Methods for Sparse Matrices. VIII, 127 pages. 1983.

Vol. 158: Foundations of Computation Theory. Proceedings, 1983. Edited by M. Karpinski, XI, 517 pages. 1983.

Vol. 159: CAAP'83. Proceedings, 1983. Edited by G. Ausiello and M. Protasi. VI, 416 pages. 1983.

Vol. 160: The IOTA Programming System. Edited by R. Nakajima and T. Yuasa. VII, 217 pages. 1983.

Vol. 161: DIANA, An Intermediate Language for Ada. Edited by G. Goos, W.A. Wulf, A. Evans, Jr. and K.J. Butler. VII, 201 pages. 1983.

Vol. 162: Computer Algebra. Proceedings, 1983. Edited by J.A. van Hulzen. XIII, 305 pages. 1983.

Vol. 163: VLSI Engineering. Proceedings. Edited by T.L. Kunii. VIII, 308 pages. 1984.

Vol. 164: Logics of Programs. Proceedings, 1983. Edited by E. Clarke and D. Kozen. VI, 528 pages. 1984.

Vol. 165: T.F. Coleman, Large Sparse Numerical Optimization. V, 105 pages. 1984.

Vol. 166: STACS 84. Symposium of Theoretical Aspects of Computer Science. Proceedings, 1984. Edited by M. Fontet and K. Mehlhorn. VI, 338 pages. 1984.

Lecture Notes in Computer Science

Edited by G. Goos and J. Hartmanis

197

Seminar on Concurrency

Carnegie-Mellon University
Pittsburgh, PA, July 9–11, 1984

Edited by S. D. Brookes, A. W. Roscoe and G. Winskel

Springer-Verlag
Berlin Heidelberg New York Tokyo

Editors

Stephen D. Brookes
Computer Science Department, Carnegie-Mellon University
Pittsburgh, PA 15213, USA

Andrew William Roscoe
Programming Research Group
Oxford University, Oxford, OX1 3QD England

Glynn Winskel
Computer Science Department, Cambridge University
Cambridge, CB2 3QG England

CR Subject Classification (1985): C.2.4, D.1.3, F.3, D.3.1, D.3.3, D.2.4, F.4.1

ISBN 3-540-15670-4 Springer-Verlag Berlin Heidelberg New York Tokyo
ISBN 0-387-15670-4 Springer-Verlag New York Heidelberg Berlin Tokyo

Printed in Germany

Printing and binding: Beltz Offsetdruck, Hemsbach/Bergstr.
2145/3140-543210

Seminar on Semantics of Concurrency
Carnegie-Mellon University
Pittsburgh
Pennsylvania
July 9-11, 1984

Acknowledgements.

Sponsorship and partial financial support of this joint US-UK seminar was provided by the National Science Foundation of the United States (NSF) and the Science and Engineering Research Council of Great Britain (SERC). The seminar was held at Carnegie-Mellon University on July 9-11, 1984, and was organized by S. D. Brookes (Carnegie-Mellon University), A. W. Roscoe (Oxford University) and G. Winskel (Cambridge University). We would like to thank Elizabeth Grgurich and Lydia Defilippo for their assistance with the organization.

Note. The following introductory sections have been adapted from the text of the proposal originally submitted by the organizers to the NSF and the SERC. We include them here to provide some idea of the aims of the seminar, and to set the papers of this volume in context. The references cited in the papers contained in this volume provide a fuller survey of current research.

1. Introduction.

Programming languages such as Ada, CSP and CCS, involving some form of parallel composition of commands, are becoming prominent as computer science moves to take advantage of the opportunities of distributed processing. It is well known that allowing concurrent execution may lead to undesirable behaviour, for example *deadlock* or *starvation.* It is of crucial importance to be able to reason effectively about programs written in such languages; to prove, for instance, absence of deadlock. Of course, a formal method of proof will require a formal model as a basis for justifying the proofs.

At present there is no widely accepted method for modelling concurrent processes. There is instead a proliferation of semantics for such languages. Some use widely applicable methods and are based on, for example, Petri nets, labelled transition systems or powerdomains, while some are more specialised and are designed with an idea of detecting and proving rather specific properties of programs.

This seminar was intended to provide a forum in which to discuss and examine the different approaches, their relationships to each other and how they support proofs of properties of programs. A major aim of this project has been to attempt to link up and unify the different methods of providing semantic descriptions and analysis of concurrent programming languages, and to clarify some of the issues in proving properties of concurrent programs. We hope that the papers published in this volume contribute to this goal.

2. Background.

Programming languages involving some form of parallel execution are emerging as the languages of the 80's, in line with the decreasing costs of computer systems and the increased opportunities for speed and efficiency offered by distributed computing. Most recently, the Ada programming language has been put forward in this guise. This language, by virtue of its concurrent features, falls into the general category of "CSP–like" languages, in which concurrently active processes interact by some form of synchronized communication: the so-called *handshake* in CSP or the Ada *rendezvous*.

As is well known, programs written in parallel languages may exhibit pathological behaviour, such as *deadlock*. Deadlock occurs typically when each of a group of concurrent processes is waiting for another process in the group to initiate a communication; since no process is able to make the first move, no communication can occur and the system is stuck. The classical example of this phenomenon is provided by the Dining Philosophers, where the possibility of deadlock means that the philosophers may starve to death. The essence of this example is that several more or less independent machines are competing for use of a small number of shared resources; this type of situation arises frequently in practical computer science, and ways of solving and understanding problems such as deadlock are of paramount importance.

Much work has been done in specifying and reasoning about properties of concurrent systems, and there is much interest, both theoretical and practical, in so-called *safety* and *liveness* properties. Of course, it is of vital importance to be able to reason *effectively* about the behavioural properties of programs. Moreover, if any proof system is to be useful, it must be shown to be *consistent*. This requires a mathematical model of the processes with which the proof system purports to deal, and an understanding of how the model reflects the semantic properties of processes.

In the case of sequential programming languages, where one wants to reason about sequential programs, the situation is much simpler: in general, programs can be taken to denote *input-output* functions or *state-transformations,* and logical systems based on Hoare-style proof rules can be built which are transparently related to the standard denotational semantics of the language in question. Unfortunately, there is no widely accepted method of assigning meanings to concurrent programs; there is not even agreement on what class of mathematical entities are suitable for modelling processes. On the contrary, the situation is somewhat confusing. Many different semantic models have been proposed, and in the main each model seems to have arisen in an attempt to capture precisely a particular type of behavioural property. Typically, in one model it is relatively easy to treat one type of semantic property, but difficult to reason about others. This is not to say, of course, that no successful proof systems have been constructed for parallel languages; the point we are making is that there is a lack of agreement at the basic level of what kind of mathematical object a process is, and this makes it difficult to justify a preference for one semantics or proof system over another.

In view of the proliferation of semantic models for concurrency, and the central importance of the issues introduced by parallelism, we feel that serious effort should be expended in relating the various approaches. This was the basic motivation of the seminar, because it is hoped that clarifying the inter-relationships between alternative approaches to the semantics of parallelism will improve our understanding of the problems associated with concurrency.

Much of the research reported in this seminar considers the particular types of concurrency inherent in systems where individual processes interact by synchronized communication, such as CSP, CCS and Ada, or in other models of parallel computation where the communication discipline follows different lines.

Much work on the semantics of concurrency has been carried out on Milner's language CCS (Calculus of Communicating Systems) or Hoare's language CSP (Communicating Sequential Processes). Both are used widely in theoretical research and have been provided with a variety of semantics, both operational and denotational. Some proofs of equivalence between different semantics have been given, and there are several proof systems for the various semantics. Lately Milner has introduced another class of languages closely related to CCS. They are called the synchronous calculi, abbreviated to SCCS, and have been equipped with a semantics which makes them suitable for modelling synchronous processes. The work on the languages CSP, CCS, and SCCS incorporates many techniques of the following sections, which outline some of the main approaches which have been taken in modelling concurrency.

Labelled transition systems and synchronization trees. These form a basic model of processes, and have been extensively used (as by Plotkin) to give structural operational semantics to a variety of programming languages. A process can move from one configuration to another by making a transition. The transitions (or events) are labelled to show how they synchronize with events in the environment. Labelled transition systems unfold quite naturally to labelled trees—called synchronization trees. Generally the transitions are indivisible, so the processes modelled are thought of as performing only one event at a time—the actions are *interleaved*— in which case it can be argued that they do not handle concurrency in a natural way. Transition systems are widely applicable and widely used and can serve as basic models on which to build more abstract semantics. They are fundamental to much of the work on CCS and SCCS.

Term models. These arise by placing some natural equivalence relation on terms (parts of programs), generally by specifying the operational behaviour of terms with a labelled transition system and then putting some operationally meaningful equivalence relation on these. A notable example is Milner's observational equivalence on CCS programs. Often the equivalence on terms can be generated by a set of proof rules. One is then able to prove a property of a program by establishing its equivalence to some suitably chosen term.

Labelled Petri nets. Petri nets model processes in terms of causal relations between local states and events. They model a process's behaviour by simulating it dynamically through a pattern of basic moves called the "token game". Several people, notably Lauer and Campbell, have given semantics to synchronizing processes as labelled Petri nets. Again, the labels specify how events synchronize with events in the environment. Nets handle concurrency in a natural way—concurrency exhibits itself as causal independence—and are not committed to an interleaving approach. Although intuitive structures, they are difficult to manage mathematically because of the dynamic nature of the token game; in a sense they need their own semantics if we are to reason about them successfully.

Labelled event structures. Roughly, an event structure specifies the possible sets of event occurrences of a process. Forms of event structures have appeared in a variety of work, in foundational work on denotational semantics, in work on distributed computing, and in the theory of Petri nets. Labelled event structures can be used to give a denotational semantics to a wide range of languages like CCS and CSP based on synchronized communication. A Petri net determines an event structure; thus, event structures can be used to give a semantics to nets. Although event structures, like nets, are not committed to interleaving, a semantics in terms of labelled event structures does translate neatly to a semantics in terms of synchronization trees, as demonstrated for instance in the work of Winskel.

Powerdomains. Powerdomains occur in denotational semantics as the domain analogue of powersets; they were introduced by Plotkin, and important foundational work has been carried out by Smyth and Plotkin. Powerdomains are the domains arising naturally when trying to give a semantics to languages in which execution can proceed nondeterministically. Powerdomains were used quite early by Milne and Milner to give a semantics to the language CCS, by reducing concurrency to nondeterministic interleaving. Hennessy and Plotkin gave a powerdomain semantics to a simple parallel programming language with shared variables. Until recently many have tended to avoid their use in giving semantics to languages where the emphasis has been on getting the operational ideas straight. Now they are understood better and reappear as denotational counterparts of natural operational ideas, notably in the work of Hennessy and de Nicola.

Failure-set semantics. Failure-set semantics (Hoare, Brookes, Roscoe) arose as a generalization of the so-called *trace* semantics of CSP, which identified a process with its set of possible sequences of communications (the traces). In addition, a failure set specifies what synchronizations a process can refuse after following a particular trace, the idea being to capture precisely the situations in which a deadlock may occur. Links have been made between failure sets and various other approaches, notably synchronization trees and transition systems. The failures model can also be constructed as the term algebra generated by an axiom system, and a complete proof system exists for this algebra. Attempts to clarify the relationship of failure-sets with other forms of semantics have yielded some interesting results: the failures model turns up in another guise as the model determined by a natural set of axioms on the CSP term algebra, and is closely related to the models developed by Hennessy and de Nicola.

Logics of programs. This area is concerned with the formal expression and proof of properties of programs and has often been brought to bear on CSP-like languages. Generally formal reasoning is conducted in some modal logic such as temporal logic, as in the work of Owicki and Lamport, although some Hoare-style proof systems have been suggested, notably by Owicki and Gries for shared variable concurrency, and by Apt, Francez and de Roever for CSP. Sometimes it is possible to decide automatically whether or not a program satisfies a modal assertion in a particular formal language, as in work of Clarke, Emerson and Sistla. The validity of modal assertions begs the question of what basic models should be used. (Most models do not handle the phenomenon of divergence, or non-termination, adequately.) This is a rich area for investigation, especially as recent results show that many equivalences on CCS and CSP programs are induced by the modal assertions they satisfy. This suggest a possible connection with the Dynamic Logics of Pratt and others. The orderings on powerdomains have a similar modal characterisation too. "Fairness" is an important property of programs which is often best expressed in terms of modalities though at present it is not clear how to deal with it in the most satisfying way; there is a variety of approaches in the current literature.

So far we have mentioned mainly models in which synchronous communication was the method of interaction between concurrently active processes. We now sketch the connections with two other models of parallel computation which exemplify alternative communication disciplines.

The Actor model of computation. The actor model of computation has been developed by Hewitt and associates at MIT. It is based on communication by message-passing between objects or processes of computation called Actors. Although communication is asynchronous the Actor model incorporates many features in common with models of synchronized communication. Receipt of a message by an actor is called an event and together a network of actors determines a causal structure on events—a form of event structure; their axioms have been studied by Hewitt and Baker. Recently Clinger has provided an actor language with a powerdomain semantics which has also addressed to some extent the fairness problem for actors; implementations of actor languages have assumed that a message sent is always received eventually and this fairness property has been difficult to capture in denotational semantics. This work is quite new and its relationship with other work, for example Plotkin's powerdomain for countable nondeterminism, do not seem to be well understood.

Kahn–MacQueen networks. This model is based on the idea that processes communicate by channels; processes read in from input channels and write to output channels. It is one of the earliest models with potential parallelism to have been given a denotational semantics, relatively simple because as originally proposed, Kahn–MacQueen networks computed in a determinate manner—any nondeterminism in the network did not affect the final result. The model is well understood and is often used in theoretical work, when it is extended by theoretically awkward constructs such as a "fair merge" operator; here the work of Park is notable.

This completes our summary of the state of the art as we saw it at the time of the conference. It is admittedly a rather narrowly focussed account, and we apologize to any researchers whose work has not been explicitly mentioned in this brief section. The models described here and many other current research areas are represented to some extent in this volume.

Table of Contents

ON THE AXIOMATIC TREATMENT OF CONCURRENCY

Stephen D. Brookes
Carnegie-Mellon University
Department of Computer Science
Schenley Park
Pittsburgh

0. Abstract.

This paper describes a semantically–based axiomatic treatment of a simple parallel programming language. We consider an imperative language with shared variable concurrency and a critical region construct. After giving a structural operational semantics for the language we use the semantic structure to suggest a class of assertions for expressing semantic properties of commands. The structure of the assertions reflects the structure of the semantic representation of a command. We then define syntactic operations on assertions which correspond precisely to the corresponding syntactic constructs of the programming language; in particular, we define sequential and parallel composition of assertions. This enables us to design a truly compositional proof system for program properties. Our proof system is sound and relatively complete. We examine the relationship between our proof system and the Owicki-Gries proof system for the same language, and we see how Owicki's parallel proof rule can be reformulated in our setting. Our assertions are more expressive than Owicki's, and her *proof outlines* correspond roughly to a special subset of our assertion language. Owicki's parallel rule can be thought of as being based on a slightly different form of parallel composition of assertions; our form does not require *interference-freedom*, and our proof system is relatively complete without the need for auxiliary variables. Connections with the "Generalized Hoare Logic" of Lamport and Schneider, and with the Transition Logic of Gerth, are discussed briefly, and we indicate how to extend our ideas to include some more programming constructs, including conditional commands, conditional critical regions, and loops.

1. Introduction.

It is widely accepted that formal reasoning about program properties is desirable. Hoare's paper [12] has led to attempts to give axiomatic treatments for a wide variety of programming languages. Hoare's paper treated partial correctness properties of commands in a sequential programming language, using simple assertions based on pre- and post-conditions; the axiom system given in that paper is sound and relatively complete [8]. The proof system was *syntax-directed*, in that axioms or rules were given for each syntactic construct. The assertions chosen by Hoare are admirably suited to the task: they are concise in structure and have a clear correlation with a natural state transformation semantics for the programming language; this means that fairly straightforward proofs of the soundness and completeness of Hoare's proof system can be given [1,8].

When we consider more complicated programming languages the picture is not so simple. Many existing axiomatic treatments of programming languages have turned out to be either unsound or incomplete [25]. The task of establishing soundness and completeness of proof systems for program properties can be complicated by an excessive amount of detail used in the semantic description of the programming language. This point seems to be quite well known, and is made, for instance in [1]. Similar problems can be caused by the use of an excessively intricate or poorly structured assertion language, or by overly complicated proof rules. Certainly for sequential languages with state-transformation semantics the usual Hoare-style assertions with pre- and post-conditions are suitable. But for more complicated languages which require more sophisticated semantic treatment we believe that it is inappropriate to try to force assertions to fit into the pre- and post-condition mould; such an attempt tends to lead to pre- and post-conditions with a rather complex structure, when it could be simpler to use a class of assertions with a different structure which more accurately corresponds to the semantics. The potential benefits of basing an axiomatic treatment directly on a well chosen semantics has been argued, for instance, in [7], where an axiomatic treatment of aliasing was given. Parallel programming languages certainly require a more sophisticated semantic model than sequential languages, and this paper attempts to construct a more sophisticated axiomatic treatment based on the *resumption* model of Hennessy and Plotkin [22].

Proof systems for reasoning about various forms of parallelism have been proposed by several authors, notably [2,3,4,11,15,16,17,18,19,20,21]. Owicki and Gries [20,21] gave a Hoare-style axiom system for a simple parallel programming language in which parallel commands can interact through their effects on shared variables. Their proof rule for parallel composition involved a notion of *interference-freedom* and used *proof outlines* for parallel processes, rather than the usual Hoare-style assertions. In order to obtain a complete proof system Owicki found it necessary to use *auxiliary variables* and to add proof rules for dealing with them. These features have been the subject of considerable discussion in the literature, such as [5,16]. Our approach is to begin with an appropriate semantic model, chosen to allow compositional reasoning about program properties. We use the structure of this model more directly than is usual in the design of an assertion language for program properties, and this leads to proof rules with a very simple structure, although (or rather, because) our assertions are more powerful than conventional Hoare-style assertions; Owicki's proof outlines emerge as special cases of our assertions. The soundness and completeness of our proof system are arguably less difficult to establish, as the proof system is closely based on the semantics and the semantics has been chosen to embody as little complication as possible while still supporting formal reasoning about the desired properties of programs.

The programming language discussed here is a subset of the language considered by Owicki [20,21], and by Hennessy and Plotkin [22]. Adopting the structural operational semantics of [22,26] for this language, we design a class of assertions for expressing semantic properties of commands. We then define *syntactic* operations on assertions which correspond to the *semantics* of the various syntactic constructs in the programming language; in particular, we define sequential and parallel composition for assertions. This leads naturally to *compositional*, or syntax-directed, proof rules for the syntactic constructs. We do not need an interference-freedom condition in our rule for parallel composition, in contrast to Owicki's system. Similarly, we do not need an auxiliary variables rule in order to obtain completeness. We show how to construct Owicki's rule for parallel composition and the need for her interference-freedom condition, using our methods. Essentially, Owicki's system uses a restricted subset of our assertions and a variant form of parallel composition of assertions.

We compare our work briefly with that of some other authors in this field, discuss some of its present limitations, and the paper ends with a few suggestions for further research and some conclusions. In particular, we indicate that our ideas can be extended to cover features omitted from the body of the paper, such as conditional critical regions, loops and conditionals. We also believe that with a few modifications in the assertion language we will be able to incorporate guarded commands [9,10], and with an appropriate definition of parallel composition for assertions we will be able to treat CSP-like parallel composition [13], in which processes do not share variables but instead interact solely by means of synchronized communication.

2. A Parallel Programming Language.

We begin with a simple programming language containing assignment and sequential composition, together with a simple form of parallel composition, and a "critical region" construct. Parallel commands interact solely through their effects on shared variables. For simplicity of presentation we omit conditionals and loops, at least for the present, as we want to focus on the problems caused by parallelism. We will return briefly to these features later. As usual for imperative languages, we distinguish the syntactic categories of identifiers, expressions, and commands. The abstract syntax for expressions and identifiers will be taken for granted.

Syntax.

$$I \in \mathbf{Ide} \quad \text{identifiers,}$$
$$E \in \mathbf{Exp} \quad \text{expressions,}$$
$$\Gamma \in \mathbf{Com} \quad \text{commands,}$$
$$\Gamma ::= \mathbf{skip} \mid I{:=}E \mid \Gamma_1 ; \Gamma_2 \mid [\Gamma_1 \parallel \Gamma_2] \mid \langle \Gamma \rangle.$$

The notation is fairly standard. The command **skip** is an atomic action having no effect on program variables. An assignment, denoted $I{:=}E$, is also an atomic action; it sets the value of I to the (execution-time) value of E. Sequential composition is represented by $\Gamma_1; \Gamma_2$. A parallel composition $[\Gamma_1 \parallel \Gamma_2]$ is executed by interleaving the atomic actions of the component commands Γ_1 and Γ_2. A command of the form $\langle \Gamma \rangle$ is a *critical region*; this construct converts a command into an atomic action, and corresponds to a special case of an *await* statement in [20], where the notation **await true do** Γ would have been used.

In describing the semantics of this language, we will focus mainly on commands. The set S of *states* consists simply of the (partial) functions from identifiers to values:

$$S = [\mathbf{Ide} \rightarrow_p V],$$

where V is some set of expression values (typically containing integers and truth values). We use s to range over states, and we write $s + [I \mapsto v]$ for the state which agrees with s except that it gives identifier I the value v. As usual, the value denoted by an expression may depend on the values of its free identifiers. Thus, we assume the existence of a semantic function

$$\mathcal{E} : \mathbf{Exp} \rightarrow [S \rightarrow V].$$

We specify the semantics of commands in the structural operational style [26], and our presentation follows that of [22], where identical program constructs were considered. We define first an abstract machine which specifies the computations of a command. The abstract machine is given by a *labelled transition system*

$$\langle \mathbf{Conf}, \mathbf{Lab}, \rightarrow \rangle,$$

where **Conf** is a set of *configurations*, **Lab** is a set of *labels* (ranged over by α, β and γ), and $\rightarrow$ is a family

$$\{ \xrightarrow{\alpha} \mid \alpha \in \mathbf{Lab} \}$$

of *transition relations* $\xrightarrow{\alpha} \subseteq \mathbf{Conf} \times \mathbf{Conf}$ indexed by elements of **Lab**. An atomic action is either an assignment, or **skip**, or a critical region. We use labels for atomic actions, and assume from now on that all atomic actions of a command have labels: in other words, we deal with *labelled commands*. For precision, we give the following syntax for labelled commands, in which α ranges over **Lab**:

$$\Gamma ::= \alpha\!:\!\mathbf{skip} \mid \alpha\!:\!I\!:=\!E \mid \Gamma_1;\Gamma_2 \mid [\Gamma_1 \parallel \Gamma_2] \mid \alpha\!:\!\langle\Gamma\rangle.$$

For convenience we introduce a term **null** to represent termination, and we specify (purely for notational convenience) that

$$[\mathbf{null} \parallel \Gamma] = [\Gamma \parallel \mathbf{null}] = \Gamma,$$
$$\mathbf{null}; \Gamma = \Gamma.$$

We will use **Com**$'$ for the set containing all labelled commands and **null**. The set of configurations is **Conf** $=$ **Com**$' \times S$. A configuration of the form $\langle\Gamma, s\rangle$ will represent a stage in a computation at which the remaining command to be executed is Γ, and the current state is s. A configuration of the form $\langle\mathbf{null}, s\rangle$ represents termination in the given state. A *transition* of the form

$$\langle\Gamma, s\rangle \xrightarrow{\alpha} \langle\Gamma', s'\rangle$$

represents a step in a computation in which the state and remaining command change as indicated, and in which the atomic action labelled α occurs. We write $\langle\Gamma, s\rangle \rightarrow \langle\Gamma', s'\rangle$ when there is an α for which $\langle\Gamma, s\rangle \xrightarrow{\alpha} \langle\Gamma', s'\rangle$. And we use the notation $\rightarrow^*$ for the reflexive transitive closure of this relation. Thus $\langle\Gamma, s\rangle \rightarrow^* \langle\Gamma', s'\rangle$ iff there is a sequence of atomic actions from the first configuration to the second.

The transition relations are defined by the following syntax-directed transition rules; the transition relations are to be the smallest satisfying these laws. This means that a transition is possible if and only if it can be deduced from the rules.

Transition Rules

$$\langle\alpha\!:\!\mathbf{skip}, s\rangle \xrightarrow{\alpha} \langle\mathbf{null}, s\rangle \tag{A1}$$

$$\langle\alpha\!:\!I\!:=\!E, s\rangle \xrightarrow{\alpha} \langle\mathbf{null}, s + [I \mapsto \mathcal{E}[\![E]\!]s]\rangle \tag{A2}$$

$$\frac{\langle\Gamma_1, s\rangle \xrightarrow{\alpha} \langle\Gamma_1', s'\rangle}{\langle\Gamma_1;\Gamma_2, s\rangle \xrightarrow{\alpha} \langle\Gamma_1';\Gamma_2, s'\rangle} \tag{A3}$$

$$\frac{\langle\Gamma_1, s\rangle \xrightarrow{\alpha} \langle\Gamma_1', s'\rangle}{\langle[\Gamma_1 \parallel \Gamma_2], s\rangle \xrightarrow{\alpha} \langle[\Gamma_1' \parallel \Gamma_2], s'\rangle} \tag{A4}$$

$$\frac{\langle\Gamma_2, s\rangle \xrightarrow{\alpha} \langle\Gamma_2', s'\rangle}{\langle[\Gamma_1 \parallel \Gamma_2], s\rangle \xrightarrow{\alpha} \langle[\Gamma_1 \parallel \Gamma_2'], s'\rangle} \tag{A5}$$

$$\frac{\langle\Gamma, s\rangle \rightarrow^* \langle\mathbf{null}, s'\rangle}{\langle\alpha\!:\!\langle\Gamma\rangle, s\rangle \xrightarrow{\alpha} \langle\mathbf{null}, s'\rangle} \tag{A6}$$

From our definition of the transition system, we see that we have specified that a parallel composition terminates only when both components have terminated. This is because of our conventions about **null**: we have $\langle[\Gamma_1 \parallel \Gamma_2], s\rangle \xrightarrow{\alpha} \langle\Gamma_2, s'\rangle$ whenever $\langle\Gamma_1, s\rangle \xrightarrow{\alpha} \langle\mathbf{null}, s'\rangle$, for instance. It is also clear from the definitions that all computations eventually terminate in this transition system, and that no computation gets "stuck": the only configurations in which no further action is possible are the terminal configurations. These properties would not hold if we add guarded commands or loops to the language. This point will be mentioned again later; for now we will concentrate on the language as it stands.

Examples.

Example 1. Let s be a state and let $s_i = s+[x \mapsto i]$ for $i \geq 0$. Let Γ be the labelled command

$$[\alpha : x{:=}x + 1 \parallel \beta : x{:=}x + 1].$$

Then we have

$$\langle\Gamma, s_0\rangle \xrightarrow{\alpha} \langle\beta : x{:=}x + 1, s_1\rangle \xrightarrow{\beta} \langle\mathbf{null}, s_2\rangle,$$

and a similar sequence in which the order of the two actions is reversed:

$$\langle\Gamma, s_0\rangle \xrightarrow{\beta} \langle\alpha : x{:=}x + 1, s_1\rangle \xrightarrow{\alpha} \langle\mathbf{null}, s_2\rangle.$$

These are the only possible computations from this initial configuration. ∎

Example 2. Let Γ be the command $[\alpha : x{:=}2 \parallel (\beta : x{:=}1; \gamma : x{:=}x + 1)]$. Using the s_i notation of the previous example, we have:

$$\langle\Gamma, s\rangle \xrightarrow{\alpha} \langle\beta : x{:=}1; \gamma : x{:=}x + 1, s_2\rangle \xrightarrow{\beta} \langle\gamma : x{:=}x + 1, s_1\rangle \xrightarrow{\gamma} \langle\mathbf{null}, s_2\rangle,$$
$$\langle\Gamma, s\rangle \xrightarrow{\beta} \langle[\alpha : x{:=}2 \parallel \gamma : x{:=}x + 1], s_1\rangle \xrightarrow{\alpha} \langle\gamma : x{:=}x + 1, s_2\rangle \xrightarrow{\gamma} \langle\mathbf{null}, s_3\rangle,$$
$$\langle\Gamma, s\rangle \xrightarrow{\beta} \langle[\alpha : x{:=}2 \parallel \gamma : x{:=}x + 1], s_1\rangle \xrightarrow{\gamma} \langle\alpha : x{:=}2, s_2\rangle \xrightarrow{\alpha} \langle\mathbf{null}, s_2\rangle.$$

This command sets x to 2 or 3, depending on the order in which its atomic actions are executed. ∎

Example 3. Let Γ be the command $[\alpha : x{:=}1 \parallel \beta : y{:=}1]$. Then we have:

$$\langle\Gamma, s\rangle \xrightarrow{\alpha} \langle\beta : y{:=}1, s + [x \mapsto 1]\rangle \xrightarrow{\beta} \langle\mathbf{null}, s + [x \mapsto 1, y \mapsto 1]\rangle,$$
$$\langle\Gamma, s\rangle \xrightarrow{\beta} \langle\alpha : y{:=}1, s + [y \mapsto 1]\rangle \xrightarrow{\alpha} \langle\mathbf{null}, s + [x \mapsto 1, y \mapsto 1]\rangle.$$

This command sets both x and y to 1. ∎

Semantics.

Using the transition system we may now extract a semantics. For a partial correctness semantics, we should examine the (terminating) computations of a command and extract the initial and final states. Of course, in the present language there is no need to distinguish between total and partial correctness because all computations terminate, but this issue will arise in treatments of an extended language containing loops (for example). For uniformity, we still refer to partial correctness, as the definition we give adapts even to the extended language and does then correspond to partial correctness.

Definition 1. The semantic function $\mathcal{M} : \mathbf{Com} \to [S \to \mathcal{P}(S)]$ is

$$\mathcal{M}[\![\Gamma]\!]s = \{\, s' \mid \langle\Gamma, s\rangle \to^* \langle\mathbf{null}, s'\rangle \,\}. \quad \blacksquare$$

Examples. We have already seen that

1. $\mathcal{M}[\![\alpha\!:\!x\!:=\!x+1 \parallel \beta\!:\!x\!:=\!x+1]\!]s_i = \{\, s_{i+2} \,\}$,
2. $\mathcal{M}[\![\alpha\!:\!x\!:=\!2 \parallel (\beta\!:\!x\!:=\!1; \gamma\!:\!x\!:=\!x+1)]\!]s = \{\, s_2, s_3 \,\}$,
3. $\mathcal{M}[\![\alpha\!:\!x\!:=\!1 \parallel \beta\!:\!y\!:=\!1]\!]s = \{\, s + [x \mapsto 1, y \mapsto 1] \,\}$.

Reasoning about commands.

In conventional Hoare logics for sequential imperative programs, assertions of the form

$$\{\, P \,\}\Gamma\{\, Q \,\}$$

are used, with P and Q being called the pre- and post-condition. These conditions are typically drawn from a simple first order language, and are interpreted as predicates of the state. Given a satisfaction relation $\models$ on conditions and states, we say that $\{\, P \,\}\Gamma\{\, Q \,\}$ is *valid*, written $\models \{\, P \,\}\Gamma\{\, Q \,\}$, iff

$$\forall s, s'[s \models P \;\&\; s' \in \mathcal{M}[\![\Gamma]\!]s \quad \Rightarrow \quad s' \models Q].$$

In other words, a Hoare assertion of this type describes the relationship between an initial state and the possible final states of a computation of a command. However, it is well known [20,22,23] that in a language involving parallel composition it is not possible to reason about partial correctness properties of a command in isolation: account must be taken of the context in which the command is to be run. This is exemplified by the commands

$$x\!:=\!2, \qquad \text{and} \qquad x\!:=\!1; x\!:=\!x+1,$$

which clearly have the same partial correctness properties in isolation, *i.e.*

$$\mathcal{M}[\![x\!:=\!2]\!] = \mathcal{M}[\![x\!:=\!1; x\!:=\!x+1]\!],$$

but which exhibit different partial correctness properties in some programming language contexts; for instance, the commands

$$[x{:=}2 \parallel x{:=}2] \qquad \text{and} \qquad [(x{:=}1; x{:=}x+1) \parallel x{:=}2]$$

do not have the same partial correctness properties, as the latter command may set x to 3. Thus, the $\mathcal{M}$ semantics does not always distinguish between pairs of commands if there is a program context in which they exhibit different partial correctness behaviour. Technically, the relational semantics $\mathcal{M}$ fails to be *fully abstract* [22,23] with respect to partial correctness; it makes too few distinctions between commands, and is therefore "too abstract". In order to reason about the correctness of a parallel combination of commands in a manner independent of the context in which the command appears, we need to know more about the individual commands than simply their relational semantics $\mathcal{M}$. Similarly, we cannot axiomatize partial correctness of commands solely on the basis of partial correctness properties of components: conventional pre- and post-condition assertions are not going to suffice.

Hennessy and Plotkin [22] showed that the transition system above can be used to define a semantics which will distinguish between terms if there is a context in which they can exhibit different partial correctness properties. This semantics uses the notion of a *resumption*. For our subset of the language, we may adapt these ideas slightly to define the following semantics for labelled commands:

$$\mathcal{R} : \mathbf{Com}' \to R,$$
$$R = [S \to \mathcal{P}(\mathbf{Lab} \times R \times S)],$$

with the definition being

$$\mathcal{R}[\![\Gamma]\!]s = \{\langle \alpha, \mathcal{R}[\![\Gamma']\!], s' \rangle \mid \langle \Gamma, s \rangle \xrightarrow{\alpha} \langle \Gamma', s' \rangle \}.$$

Justification for this use of a recursively defined domain R of resumptions can be given if we interpret $\mathcal{P}$ as a powerdomain construct, and the interested reader should consult [22] for details.

Note that according to this definition we have $\mathcal{R}[\![\mathbf{null}]\!]s = \emptyset$ for all states s. Note also that for any state s, $\mathcal{R}[\![\Gamma]\!]s$ will be a finite set. This can be represented as a tree structure as follows, with a branch for each member of the set, labelled by the corresponding atomic action label, with a son consisting of a resumption-state pair.

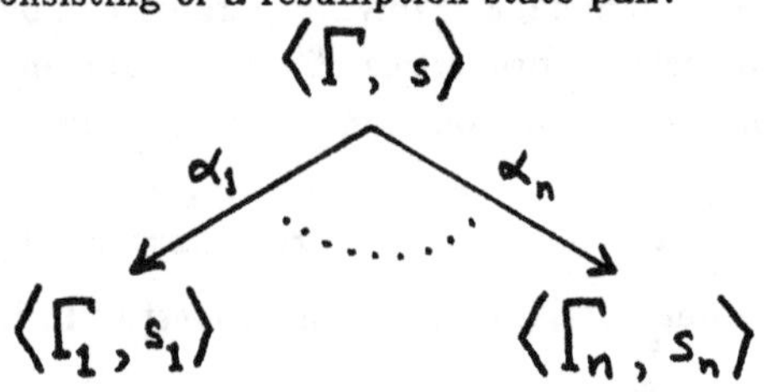

The tree structure suggests a class of assertions with components representing the branch structure of trees. We therefore introduce a class of assertions of the form

$$\phi ::= P \sum_{i=1}^{n} \alpha_i P_i \phi_i,$$

where as before P and the P_i are drawn from some *condition* language, and where the α_i are labels. This notation obviously corresponds with Milner's linear notation for *synchronization trees* [24]; in addition to labelling the arcs with action labels, we also incorporate conditions at nodes. We make no distinction between assertions which differ only in the order in which their branches are written. A tree representation of such a ϕ will often be preferable to the linear notation; for example, the assertion $P \sum_{i=1}^{n} \alpha_i P_i \phi_i$ may be represented as:

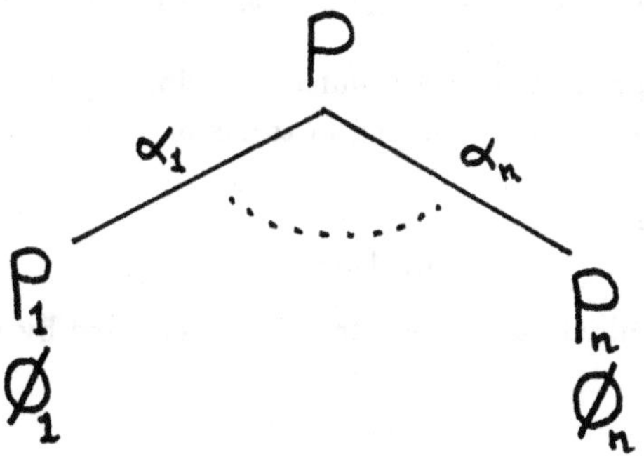

We will feel free to use set braces to delimit conditions as an aid to the eye, and we use NIL for the tree with no branches (this corresponds to termination, since in this language inability to perform any action coincides with termination). Thus, an assertion in which $n = 0$ will be written $\{P\}$NIL; we also introduce the special notation $\bullet$ to stand for the assertion $\{\textbf{true}\}$NIL. Finally, it will be convenient to adopt the convention that $\{P\}\alpha\{Q\}$ (which does not conform to the syntax above) abbreviates the assertion $\{P\}\alpha\{Q\}\{Q\}$NIL (which does).

Note that there is an obvious definition of the *depth* of an assertion ϕ, and that all assertions have finite depth. The terminal assertions are those with zero depth.

In order to express the property that a command Γ *satisfies* an assertion ϕ we write

$$\Gamma \textbf{ sat } \phi.$$

This type of formal property will be the subject of our proof system, and we will see later that we have a generalization of conventional Hoare-style assertions.

When ϕ is the assertion $P\sum_{i=1}^{n}\alpha_i P_i \phi_i$ we interpret Γ **sat** ϕ in the following way. If the command is started in a state satisfying P, then its initial action must be an α_i drawn from the set of initial labels of the assertion, and these labels are precisely the initial actions possible for the command. If the command starts with an α_i action it reaches a state where P_i is true and where the remaining command satisfies ϕ_i. Specifically, we write

$$\models \Gamma \ \mathbf{sat}\ \phi$$

to indicate that Γ satisfies ϕ. This means that, with the above notation,

$$\forall s \forall \alpha.\,(s \models P \ \&\ \langle \Gamma, s\rangle \xrightarrow{\alpha} \langle \Gamma', s'\rangle \quad \Rightarrow \quad \exists i \leq n.\, \alpha = \alpha_i \ \&\ s' \models P_i \ \&\ \Gamma' \models \phi_i), \qquad (1)$$

and, in addition, that

$$\forall s. \forall i.\,(s \models P \Rightarrow \exists \Gamma_i, s_i.\, \langle \Gamma, s\rangle \xrightarrow{\alpha_i} \langle \Gamma_i, s_i\rangle), \qquad (2)$$

so that all of the actions specified in ϕ are indeed possible for Γ when the initial state satisfies P. These definitions can be rephrased in terms of the semantic function $\mathcal{R}$.

Note that we always have

$$\models \mathbf{null}\ \mathbf{sat}\ \bullet,$$

and indeed (non-trivial) terminal assertions can only be satisfied by **null**.

Examples.

Example 1. The command $[\alpha{:}x{:=}x+1 \parallel \beta{:}x{:=}x+1]$ satisfies the assertion

$$\{x=0\}(\alpha\{x=1\}\{x=1\}\beta\{x=2\}$$
$$+\beta\{x=1\}\{x=1\}\alpha\{x=2\}).$$

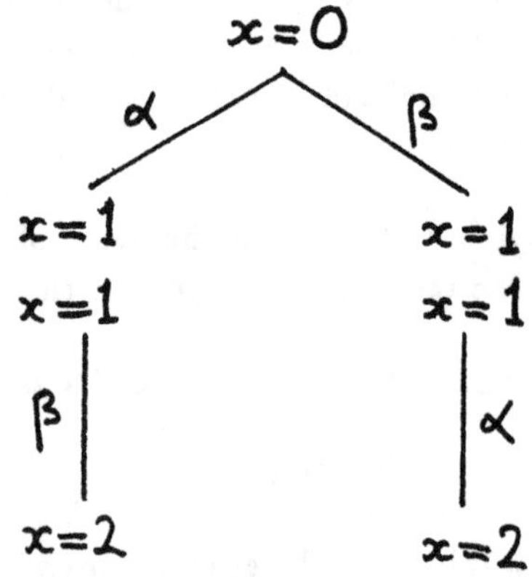

Example 2. The command $[\alpha : x{:=}2 \parallel (\beta : x{:=}1; \gamma : x{:=}x+1)]$ satisfies the assertion

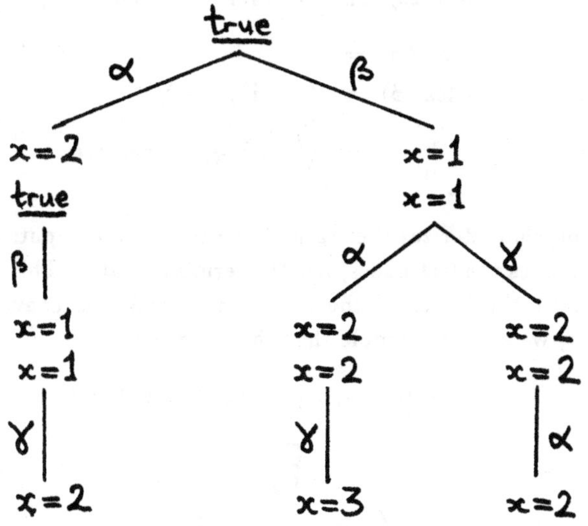

Example 3. The command $[\alpha : x{:=}1 \parallel \beta : y{:=}1]$ satisfies the assertion

$$\{\,\mathbf{true}\,\}(\alpha\{\,x=1\,\}\{\,x=1\,\}\beta\{\,x=1\,\&\,y=1\,\} \\ +\beta\{\,y=1\,\}\{\,y=1\,\}\alpha\{\,x=1\,\&\,y=1\,\}).$$

Note also that the command does *not* satisfy the assertion

$$\{\,\mathbf{true}\,\}(\alpha\{\,x=1\,\}\{\,\mathbf{true}\,\}\beta\{\,x=1\,\&\,y=1\,\} \\ +\beta\{\,y=1\,\}\{\,\mathbf{true}\,\}\alpha\{\,x=1\,\&\,y=1\,\}).$$

Example 4. The assertion

$$\{\,x=0\,\}\alpha\{\,x=1\,\}\{\,x=1\,\}\beta\{\,x=2\,\}$$

is satisfied by the labelled command

$$\alpha : x{:=}x+1; \beta : x{:=}x+1,$$

and so is the assertion

$$\{\,x=0\,\}\alpha\{\,x=1\,\}\{\,x=99\,\}\beta\{\,x=100\,\}. \quad \blacksquare$$

Let ϕ be the assertion $P\sum_{i=1}^{n} \alpha_i P_i \phi_i$. Tree structure suggests the use of the following notation. Define the *root* and *leaf* conditions for ϕ as follows:

$$\begin{aligned} \mathrm{root}(\phi) &= P, \\ \mathrm{leaf}(\phi) &= P \qquad \text{if } n = 0, \\ &= \bigvee_{i=1}^{n} \mathrm{leaf}(\phi_i) \quad \text{otherwise.} \end{aligned}$$

The root condition characterizes the state at the root of a computation tree, and the leaf condition characterizes the leaf nodes, i.e. the terminal states. This is just the disjunction of the conditions at the leaves of the assertion. Using the conventional abbreviations introduced earlier, we see for example that the assertion

$$\{P_0\}(\alpha\{P_1\} + \beta\{P_2\}\{P_3\}\gamma\{P_4\})$$

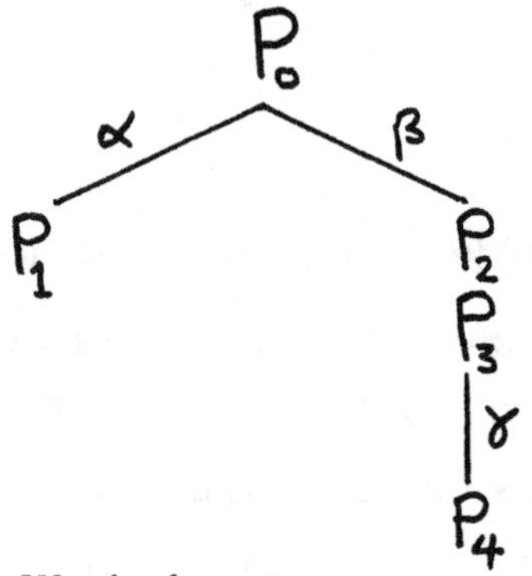

has leaf condition $P_1 \vee P_4$. We also have

$$\begin{aligned} \mathrm{leaf}(\{P\}\alpha\{Q\}) &= Q, \\ \mathrm{leaf}(\{P\}\alpha\{Q\}\bullet) &= \mathbf{true}. \end{aligned}$$

Note that in the syntactic definition of the class of assertions, we have not required that any logical connection exist between adjacent "intermediate" conditions inside an assertion. Although in Example 4 the condition $x = 1$ appears as an intermediate condition, we do not insist that the "following" condition $x = 99$ be a logical consequence. Assertions in which this constraint is satisfied correspond very closely with computation trees and proof outlines. There are good semantic reasons for not making this constraint on the syntax of our assertion language, since assertions satisfying the constraint describe the behaviour of a command in isolation and we know that in general this information is insufficient to characterize the behaviour of a command in all parallel contexts.

Proof System.

Now that we have designed an assertion language for our programming language, let us build a proof system. We will find that we can give a set of syntax-directed proof rules, by constructing syntactic operations on assertions to correspond to the syntactic operations of the programming language. The important point is that we are going to use the semantics directly to suggest how to design our rules.

Atomic assertions.

A terminal assertion $\{P\}$NIL represents termination. An *atomic assertion* has the form $\{P\}\alpha\{Q\}\{R\}$NIL, and the special abbreviated forms $\{P\}\alpha\{Q\}$ and $\{P\}\alpha\{Q\}\bullet$ are thus atomic. Atomic commands satisfy atomic assertions, and the axioms expressing this fact for skip and assignment are simple:

$$\alpha\text{:}\,\mathbf{skip}\ \mathbf{sat}\ \{P\}\alpha\{P\}\bullet \tag{B1}$$

$$\alpha\text{:}\,I\text{:=}E\ \mathbf{sat}\ \{[E\backslash I]P\}\alpha\{P\}\bullet. \tag{B2}$$

We use the notation $[E\backslash I]P$ for the result of replacing every free occurrence of I in P by E, with suitable name changes to avoid clashes.

A *critical region* also creates an atomic action out of a command. In order to axiomatize this construct we need to single out a class of assertions which state properties of a command when run in isolation as an indivisible atomic action, since the effect of the critical region construct is to run a command without allowing interruption. Define safe(ϕ) for ϕ of the form $P\sum_{i=1}^{n}\alpha_i P_i \phi_i$ by

$$\text{safe}(\phi) \quad \Leftrightarrow \quad \bigwedge_{i=1}^{n}(P_i \Rightarrow \text{root}(\phi_i)) \ \& \ \bigwedge_{i=1}^{n}\text{safe}(\phi_i).$$

This is precisely the constraint mentioned earlier: at each node of the tree the post-condition established by the previous atomic action is required to imply the root condition of the remaining subtree. When $n = 0$ this is trivially true, and the two abbreviated forms of atomic assertion $\{P\}\alpha\{Q\}$ and $\{P\}\alpha\{Q\}\bullet$ are always safe.

Intuitively, if Γ satisfies ϕ and ϕ is safe, then ϕ describes a possible execution of Γ in which no non-trivial interruption is allowed or assumed. Thus, a safe assertion gives information about the command's behaviour in isolation. We can therefore use safe assertions in the proof rule for critical regions:

$$\frac{\Gamma\ \mathbf{sat}\ \phi, \quad \text{safe}(\phi)}{\alpha\text{:}\langle\Gamma\rangle\ \mathbf{sat}\ \{\text{root}(\phi)\}\alpha\{\text{leaf}(\phi)\}\bullet}. \tag{B3}$$

The soundness of this rule is easy to establish.

Parallel composition.

It is possible to define a parallel composition for assertions. The definition is given inductively. For the base case, when one of the assertions has zero depth, we specify that

$$[\{P\}\mathrm{NIL} \parallel Q \sum_{j=1}^{m} \beta_j Q_j \psi_j] = \{P \,\&\, Q\} \sum_{j=1}^{m} \beta_j Q_j \psi_j,$$

and similarly when the two terms are exchanged. In particular, it follows that

$$[\bullet \parallel \psi] = [\psi \parallel \bullet] = \psi.$$

(Strictly speaking, these are logical equivalences rather than syntactic identities). The inductive clause is an extension of the well known *interleaving* operation on synchronization trees [6,24,28] which handles the node conditions in an appropriate manner. For assertions ϕ and ψ of the form

$$\phi = P(\sum_{i=1}^{n} \alpha_i P_i \phi_i),$$
$$\psi = Q(\sum_{j=1}^{m} \beta_j Q_j \psi_j),$$

we define

$$[\phi \parallel \psi] = \{P \,\&\, Q\}(\sum_{i=1}^{n} \alpha_i P_i [\phi_i \parallel \psi] + \sum_{j=1}^{m} \beta_j Q_j [\phi \parallel \psi_j]).$$

Note that as far as the action sequences are concerned the operation corresponds to the interleaving of trees.

For example, if ϕ and ψ are the atomic assertions

$$\{\mathbf{true}\}\alpha\{x=1\}\bullet, \quad \{\mathbf{true}\}\beta\{y=1\}\bullet,$$

we get

$$\begin{aligned}[\phi \parallel \psi] = \{\mathbf{true}\}(&\alpha\{x=1\}\{\mathbf{true}\}\beta\{y=1\}\bullet \\ &+\beta\{y=1\}\{\mathbf{true}\}\alpha\{x=1\}\bullet \\ &)\end{aligned}$$

In tree form, this is represented as follows:

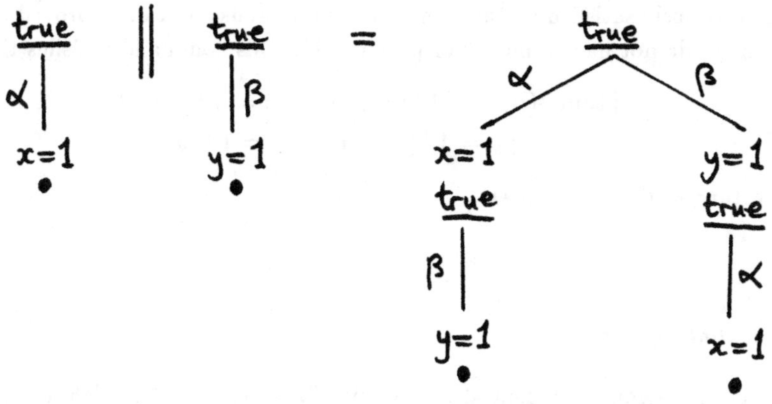

In general, for the abbreviated form of atomic assertion we have:

$$[\{P\}\alpha\{P'\} \,\|\, \{Q\}\beta\{Q'\}] = \{P \,\&\, Q\}(\alpha\{P'\}\{P' \,\&\, Q\}\beta\{Q'\} + \beta\{Q'\}\{P \,\&\, Q'\}\alpha\{P'\})$$

$$[\{P\}\alpha\{P'\}\bullet \,\|\, \{Q\}\beta\{Q'\}\bullet] = \{P \,\&\, Q\}(\alpha\{P'\}\{Q\}\beta\{Q'\}\bullet + \beta\{Q'\}\{P\}\alpha\{P'\}\bullet).$$

Of course, this composition is not guaranteed to produce *safe* assertions, even if the component assertions are safe. Nevertheless, the following result shows that parallel composition of assertions does indeed have the correct effect: if Γ_1 satisfies ϕ and Γ_2 satisfies ψ then $[\Gamma_1 \,\|\, \Gamma_2]$ satisfies $[\phi \,\|\, \psi]$. This is true regardless of the structure of ϕ and ψ.

Theorem 1. If $\models \Gamma_1$ **sat** ϕ and $\models \Gamma_2$ **sat** ψ then $\models [\Gamma_1 \,\|\, \Gamma_2]$ **sat** $[\phi \,\|\, \psi]$. ∎

Thus we are led to the proof rule:

$$\frac{\Gamma_1 \textbf{ sat } \phi \qquad \Gamma_2 \textbf{ sat } \psi}{[\Gamma_1 \,\|\, \Gamma_2] \textbf{ sat } [\phi \,\|\, \psi]}. \tag{B4}$$

As an example, we can show that the command $[\alpha : x{:=}1 \,\|\, \beta : y{:=}1]$ satisfies the assertion

$$\{\textbf{true}\}(\alpha\{x=1\}\{\textbf{true}\}\beta\{y=1\}\bullet + \beta\{y=1\}\{\textbf{true}\}\alpha\{x=1\}\bullet),$$

by forming the parallel composition of the assertions

$$\{\textbf{true}\}\alpha\{x=1\}\bullet, \qquad \{\textbf{true}\}\beta\{y=1\}\bullet,$$

which are obviously satisfied by the component commands and can be proved by (B2). Note that so far we do not have a means of proving that this command satisfies the assertion

$$\{\,\textbf{true}\,\}(\alpha\{\,x=1\,\}\{\,x=1\,\}\beta\{\,x=1\,\&\,y=1\,\}$$
$$+\beta\{\,y=1\,\}\{\,y=1\,\}\alpha\{\,x=1\,\&\,y=1\,\}).$$

We will return to this point later.

Sequential composition.

We may also define a sequential composition for assertions. The definition is straightforward, again by induction on depth. The operation grafts ψ on to the leaf nodes of the tree corresponding to ϕ. In the base case, we put

$$(\{\,P\,\}\mathrm{NIL}); Q\sum_{j=1}^{m}\beta_j Q_j\psi_j \;=\; \{\,P\,\&\,Q\,\}\sum_{j=1}^{m}\beta_j Q_j\psi_j,$$

so that $\bullet;\psi \;=\; \psi$. When ϕ is $P(\sum_{i=1}^{n}\alpha_i P_i\phi_i)$ and $n>0$ we put

$$\phi;\psi \;=\; P\sum_{i=1}^{n}\alpha_i P_i(\phi_i;\psi).$$

Again we can show that the operation has the desired effect: if Γ_1 satisfies ϕ and Γ_2 satisfies ψ then $\Gamma_1;\Gamma_2$ satisfies $\phi;\psi$.

Theorem 2. If $\models \Gamma_1 \,\mathbf{sat}\, \phi$ and $\models \Gamma_2 \,\mathbf{sat}\, \psi$ then $\models (\Gamma_1;\Gamma_2)\,\mathbf{sat}\,(\phi;\psi)$. ∎

This suggests the proof rule:

$$\frac{\Gamma_1\,\mathbf{sat}\,\phi \qquad \Gamma_2\,\mathbf{sat}\,\psi}{(\Gamma_1;\Gamma_2)\,\mathbf{sat}\,(\phi;\psi)}. \tag{B5}$$

As an example, we can now prove that the command $\alpha{:}x{:=}x+1;\beta{:}x{:=}x+1$ satisfies the assertion

$$\{\,x=0\,\}\alpha\{\,x=1\,\}\{\,x=99\,\}\beta\{\,x=100\,\},$$

by forming the sequential composition of the assertions

$$\{\,x=0\,\}\alpha\{\,x=1\,\}, \qquad \{\,x=99\,\}\beta\{\,100\,\}.$$

In summary, the rules so far introduced are:

PROOF RULES

$$\alpha\!:\!\mathbf{skip}\ \mathbf{sat}\ \{\,P\,\}\alpha\{\,P\,\}\ \bullet \tag{B1}$$

$$\alpha\!:\!I\!:=\!E\ \mathbf{sat}\ \{\,[E\backslash I]P\,\}\alpha\{\,P\,\}\ \bullet \tag{B2}$$

$$\frac{\Gamma\ \mathbf{sat}\ \phi \quad \mathrm{safe}(\phi)}{\alpha\!:\!\langle\Gamma\rangle\ \mathbf{sat}\ \{\,\mathrm{root}(\phi)\,\}\alpha\{\,\mathrm{leaf}(\phi)\,\}\ \bullet} \tag{B3}$$

$$\frac{\Gamma_1\ \mathbf{sat}\ \phi_1 \quad \Gamma_2\ \mathbf{sat}\ \phi_2}{[\Gamma_1 \parallel \Gamma_2]\ \mathbf{sat}\ [\phi_1 \parallel \phi_2]} \tag{B4}$$

$$\frac{\Gamma_1\ \mathbf{sat}\ \phi_1 \quad \Gamma_2\ \mathbf{sat}\ \phi_2}{(\Gamma_1;\Gamma_2)\ \mathbf{sat}\ (\phi_1;\phi_2)} \tag{B5}$$

The system presented above is sound but not complete. One reason for incompleteness is rather trivial: every command satisfies an assertion ϕ whose root is false, but we have no way of proving this from the above rules. One solution is to add a rule to this effect:

$$\frac{\neg\mathrm{root}(\phi)}{\Gamma\ \mathbf{sat}\ \phi} \tag{B0}$$

Even this does not guarantee completeness by itself. We saw earlier (Examples 2 and 3) that we were unable to prove some assertions about parallel commands. Example 2, for instance, showed that there is no proof from these rules alone that the command

$$[\alpha\!:\!x\!:=\!x+1 \parallel \beta\!:\!x\!:=\!x+1]$$

satisfies the assertion

$$\{\,x=0\,\}(\alpha\{\,x=1\,\}\{\,x=1\,\}\beta\{\,x=2\,\}\ +\ \beta\{\,x=1\,\}\{\,x=1\,\}\alpha\{\,x=2\,\}).$$

Rule (B0) does not help in these examples. Essentially, the reason for this is that we really need to use *two* assertions about each component command here: we need to be able to say that $x{:=}x+1$ will change the value of x from 0 to 1, and that it will equally well change the value of x from 1 to 2. Of course, in general the number of separate assertions required may be more than two. We will therefore allow *conjunction* of assertions and include a natural rule which expresses an appropriate notion of *implication* for our assertions. For conjunction we simply add to the syntax of our assertion language the clause

$$\phi ::= (\phi_1 \oplus \phi_2).$$

We use $\oplus$ rather than & merely to keep a distinction between conjunction at this level and conjunction in the condition language. The interpretation is simple:

$$\models \Gamma\,\mathbf{sat}\,(\phi_1 \oplus \phi_2) \quad \Leftrightarrow \quad \models \Gamma\,\mathbf{sat}\,\phi_1 \quad \& \quad \models \Gamma\,\mathbf{sat}\,\phi_2.$$

Conjunction is clearly associative, and we may therefore omit parentheses and write

$$\phi_1 \oplus \phi_2 \oplus \phi_3,$$

for example. We then extend the definitions of our syntactic operations to cover conjunctions. The definition of parallel composition of assertions is a straightforward generalization of the earlier definition. When ϕ and ψ are conjunctions, $[\phi \parallel \psi]$ is defined to be a conjunction: for each conjunct $P\sum_{i=1}^{n} \alpha_i P_i \phi_i$ of ϕ and each conjunct $Q\sum_{j=1}^{m} \beta_j Q_j \psi_j$ of ψ we include in $[\phi \parallel \psi]$ a conjunct of the form:

$$\{P \,\&\, Q\}(\sum_{i=1}^{n} \alpha_i P_i[\phi_i \parallel \psi] + \sum_{j=1}^{m} \beta_j Q_j[\phi \parallel \psi_j]).$$

When ϕ and ψ are simple assertions this is exactly the same definition as before. For an example, when ϕ and ψ are the assertions

$$\begin{aligned}\phi &= (\{x=0\}\alpha\{x=1\}) \oplus (\{x=1\}\alpha\{x=2\}),\\ \psi &= (\{x=0\}\beta\{x=1\}) \oplus (\{x=1\}\beta\{x=2\}),\end{aligned}$$

the parallel composition has four conjuncts:

$$\begin{aligned}&\{x=0\}(\alpha\{x=1\}\psi + \beta\{x=1\}\phi),\\ &\{x=1\}(\alpha\{x=2\}\psi + \beta\{x=2\}\phi),\\ &\{\mathbf{false}\}(\alpha\{x=1\}\psi + \beta\{x=2\}\phi),\\ &\{\mathbf{false}\}(\alpha\{x=2\}\psi + \beta\{x=1\}\phi).\end{aligned}$$

For sequential composition we merely put $(\phi_1 \oplus \phi_2); \psi \;=\; (\phi_1; \psi) \oplus (\phi_2; \psi)$ and similarly when we have a conjunction in the second place: in other words, sequential composition distributes over conjunction. With these additions, the axioms and rules given earlier remain sound, with (B3) applicable for conjunction-free assertions as we have not specified a definition of safe(ϕ) when ϕ is a conjunction.

We add rules for conjunction introduction and elimination:

$$\frac{\Gamma\ \mathbf{sat}\ \phi \qquad \Gamma\ \mathbf{sat}\ \psi}{\Gamma\ \mathbf{sat}\ (\phi \bigoplus \psi)} \tag{B6}$$

$$\frac{\Gamma\ \mathbf{sat}\ (\phi \bigoplus \psi)}{\Gamma\ \mathbf{sat}\ \phi, \quad \Gamma\ \mathbf{sat}\ \psi} \tag{B7}$$

Implication between assertions is defined as follows for simple assertions without conjunction; the definition extends in the obvious way to conjunctions: we certainly want to have $(\phi \bigoplus \psi) \Rightarrow \phi$ and $(\phi \bigoplus \psi) \Rightarrow \psi$ for example. For

$$\begin{aligned} \phi &= P(\sum_{i=1}^{n} \alpha_i P_i \phi_i), \\ \psi &= Q(\sum_{i=1}^{n} \alpha_i Q_i \psi_i), \end{aligned}$$

$$(\phi \Rightarrow \psi) \quad \Leftrightarrow \quad (Q \Rightarrow P) \ \& \ \bigwedge_{i=1}^{n} (P_i \Rightarrow Q_i) \ \& \ \bigwedge_{i=1}^{n} (\phi_i \Rightarrow \psi_i).$$

In the case when $n = 0$ this merely requires that $Q \Rightarrow P$. Also, when ϕ is $\{P\}\alpha\{Q\}$ and ψ is $\{P'\}\alpha\{Q'\}$ we have $\phi \Rightarrow \psi$ iff $P' \Rightarrow P$ and $Q \Rightarrow Q'$; this is analogous to the usual Rule of Consequence of conventional Hoare logic [1,12]:

$$\frac{P' \Rightarrow P, \quad \{P\}\Gamma\{Q\}, \quad Q \Rightarrow Q'}{\{P'\}\Gamma\{Q'\}} \tag{C}$$

Our rule for implication is a form of *modus ponens*:

$$\frac{\Gamma\ \mathbf{sat}\ \phi \quad \phi \Rightarrow \psi}{\Gamma\ \mathbf{sat}\ \psi}. \tag{B8}$$

From the definitions above it follows, for example, that

$$\{P\}\alpha\{Q\}\bullet \quad \Rightarrow \quad \{P\}\alpha\{Q\},$$

because $Q \Rightarrow \mathbf{true}$. This means, in particular, that we may derive the following assertion schemas for assignment and skip, by using the axioms (B1) and (B2) together with (B8):

$$\alpha{:}\mathbf{skip}\ \mathbf{sat}\ \{P\}\alpha\{P\}, \tag{B1'}$$

$$\alpha{:}I{:=}E\ \mathbf{sat}\ \{[E\backslash I]P\}\alpha\{P\}. \tag{B2'}$$

These forms resemble the usual Hoare axioms for these constructs [12].

Examples.

Consider again the problematic examples introduced earlier.

Example 1. We wish to prove that Γ **sat** θ, where

$$\Gamma = [\alpha{:}x{:}{=}x+1 \parallel \beta{:}x{:}{=}x+1],$$
$$\theta = \{x=0\}(\alpha\{x=1\}\{x=1\}\beta\{x=2\} + \beta\{x=1\}\{x=1\}\alpha\{x=2\}).$$

We have the following assertions (by rules B2 and B6):

$$\alpha{:}x{:}{=}x+1 \ \textbf{sat}\ \phi$$
$$\phi = (\{x=0\}\alpha\{x=1\}) \oplus (\{x=1\}\alpha\{x=2\}),$$
$$\beta{:}x{:}{=}x+1 \ \textbf{sat}\ \psi$$
$$\psi = (\{x=0\}\beta\{x=1\}) \oplus (\{x=1\}\beta\{x=2\}).$$

We have already seen that $[\phi \parallel \psi]$ is a conjunction of four terms, one of which is

$$\{x=0\}(\alpha\{x=1\}\psi + \beta\{x=1\}\phi).$$

But $\psi \Rightarrow \{x=1\}\beta\{x=2\}$ and $\phi \Rightarrow \{x=1\}\alpha\{x=2\}$. Hence, $[\phi \parallel \psi] \Rightarrow \theta$, and the result follows by (B4) and (B8). ∎

Example 2. In the composition $[\alpha{:}x{:}{=}2 \parallel (\beta{:}x{:}{=}1;\gamma{:}x{:}{=}x{+}1)]$ the two component commands satisfy the assertions

$$\{\textbf{true}\}\alpha\{x=2\},$$
$$\{\textbf{true}\}\beta\{x=1\}((\{x=1\}\gamma\{x=2\}) \oplus (\{x=2\}\gamma\{x=3\})).$$

The parallel composition of these assertions implies the desired assertion:

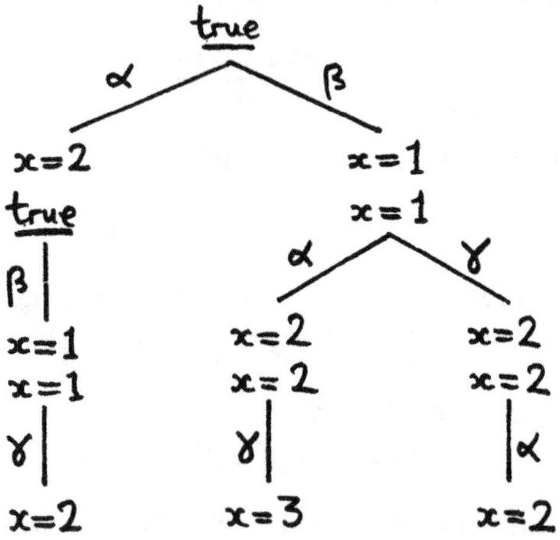

Example 3. Let $\Gamma = [\alpha : x{:=}1 \parallel \beta : y{:=}1]$. We wish to prove that Γ **sat** θ, where

$$\theta = \{\textbf{true}\}(\alpha\{x=1\}\{x=1\}\beta\{x=1 \,\&\, y=1\} \\ +\beta\{y=1\}\{y=1\}\alpha\{x=1 \,\&\, y=1\}).$$

To this end, let ϕ and ψ be the following assertions:

$$\phi = \{\textbf{true}\}\alpha\{x=1\} \oplus \{y=1\}\alpha\{x=1 \,\&\, y=1\},$$
$$\psi = \{\textbf{true}\}\beta\{y=1\} \oplus \{x=1\}\beta\{x=1 \,\&\, y=1\}.$$

Then we have $\alpha : x{:=}1$ **sat** ϕ and $\beta : y{:=}1$ **sat** ψ. And

$$[\phi \parallel \psi] \Rightarrow \{\textbf{true}\}(\alpha\{x=1\}\psi + \beta\{y=1\}\phi)$$

By choosing the appropriate conjuncts in ϕ and ψ we see that this assertion implies θ. That completes the proof. ∎

Soundness and Completeness.

Although we do not provide a proof in this paper, the proof system formed by (B0)–(B8) is sound: all provable assertions are valid. The system is also relatively complete in the sense of Cook [8]: every true assertion of the form Γ **sat** ϕ is provable, given that we can prove all of the conditions necessary in applications of the critical region rule and of *modus ponens*. Both of these rules require assumptions which take the form of implications between conditions. Let Th be the set of valid conditions (including implications between conditions). Write Th $\vdash \Gamma$ **sat** ϕ if this can be proved from (B0)–(B8) using assumptions from Th. The soundness result is:

Theorem 3. If Th $\vdash \Gamma$ **sat** ϕ then $\models \Gamma$ **sat** ϕ. ∎

Relative completeness is expressed as follows:

Theorem 4. If $\models \Gamma$ **sat** ϕ then Th $\vdash \Gamma$ **sat** ϕ. ∎

We omit the proof of this result.

3. Deriving Owicki's proof rules.

In Owicki's proof system, conventional Hoare-style assertions of the form

$$\{P\}\Gamma\{Q\}$$

are used, although the parallel composition rule requires the use of a *proof outline* above the inference line. A proof outline is a command text annotated with conditions, one before and one after each syntactic occurrence of an atomic action. At least for sequential commands, *safe* assertions in our assertion language correspond precisely with such proof outlines because computations of sequential commands follow the syntactic structure of the command. The analogy can be extended to parallel commands too, although the syntactic structure of a proof outline is no longer so close to that of the corresponding safe assertion. The following proof rule forms a connection between our proof system and that of Owicki. Above the line, we have a safe assertion of our form, and below we have a Hoare-style partial correctness assertion. The rule states that a safe assertion implies the partial correctness of the command with respect to its root and leaf conditions. The rule is:

$$\frac{\Gamma \textbf{ sat } \phi, \qquad \text{safe}(\phi)}{\{\text{root}(\phi)\}\Gamma\{\text{leaf}(\phi)\}} \tag{R}$$

To see why Owicki's proof rule for parallel composition required an extra constraint, that of *interference-freedom*, let us see how to model her rule in our notation.

Owicki's parallel composition rule essentially corresponds to a slightly different form of parallel composition of assertions. This may be defined as follows. For $\phi = P\sum_{i=1}^{n}\alpha_i P_i \phi_i$ and $\psi = Q\sum_{j=1}^{m}\beta_j Q_j \psi_j$ with n and m non-zero, we put

$$[\phi \parallel_O \psi] = \{P \,\&\, Q\}(\sum_{i=1}^{n} \alpha_i\{P_i \,\&\, Q\}[\phi_i \parallel_O \psi] + \sum_{j=1}^{m} \beta_j\{P \,\&\, Q_j\}\beta_j[\phi \parallel_O \psi_j]).$$

We also specify that

$$[\{P\}\text{NIL} \parallel_O Q\sum_{j=1}^{m}\beta_j Q_j \psi_j] = \{P \,\&\, Q\}\sum_{j=1}^{m}\beta_j\{P \,\&\, Q_j\}[\{P\}\text{NIL} \parallel_O \psi_j],$$

and a similar definition when the terms are exchanged. In particular,

$$[\bullet \parallel_O \psi] = [\psi \parallel_O \bullet] = \psi.$$

The essential difference between this operation and our earlier one is that this one carries pre-conditions through into post-conditions. For example,

$$[\{P\}\alpha\{P'\} \parallel_O \{Q\}\beta\{Q'\}] = \{P \,\&\, Q\}(\alpha\{P' \,\&\, Q\}\{P' \,\&\, Q\}\beta\{P' \,\&\, Q'\}$$
$$+\beta\{P \,\&\, Q'\}\{P \,\&\, Q'\}\alpha\{P' \,\&\, Q'\}).$$

Unfortunately, this form of composition does not always produce an assertion which correctly describes the behaviour of a parallel composition of commands. We need the notion of *interference-freedom* to guarantee this.

Define the set atoms(ϕ) of *atomic sub-assertions* of ϕ by induction on the depth of ϕ. For the assertion $\phi = P\sum_{i=1}^{n} \alpha_i P_i \phi_i$ we put

$$\text{atoms}(\phi) = \{\{P\}\alpha_i\{P_i\} \mid 1 \leq i \leq n\} \cup \bigcup_{i=1}^{n} \text{atoms}(\phi_i).$$

A terminal assertion $\{P\}$NIL has no atomic sub-assertions. The interference-free condition is defined as follows:

Definition 2. Two assertions ϕ and ψ are interference-free, written int-free(ϕ, ψ), iff for every pair of atomic assertions

$$\{p\}\alpha\{p'\} \in \text{atoms}(\phi), \qquad \{q\}\beta\{q'\} \in \text{atoms}(\psi),$$

the (ordinary Hoare-style assertions)

$$\begin{array}{l} \{p \,\&\, q\}\alpha\{q\} \\ \{p \,\&\, q\}\beta\{p\} \\ \{p \,\&\, q'\}\alpha\{q'\} \\ \{p' \,\&\, q\}\beta\{p'\} \end{array}$$

are valid. ∎

Theorem 5. If ϕ and ψ are interference-free then

$$\models \Gamma_1 \,\textbf{sat}\, \phi, \quad \models \Gamma_2 \,\textbf{sat}\, \psi \quad \Rightarrow \quad \models [\Gamma_1 \parallel \Gamma_2] \,\textbf{sat}\, [\phi \parallel_O \psi]. \quad ∎$$

In view of the above theorem we may include the following rule in our system:

$$\frac{\Gamma_1 \,\textbf{sat}\, \phi, \quad \Gamma_2 \,\textbf{sat}\, \psi, \quad \text{int-free}(\phi, \psi)}{[\Gamma_1 \parallel \Gamma_2] \,\textbf{sat}\, [\phi \parallel_O \psi]}. \tag{B9}$$

Note that this theorem and the proof rule are stated in a form applicable to *all* assertions, not just to safe assertions. This can, therefore, be regarded as a slight extension of Owicki's ideas to encompass a more expressive assertion language. The following result shows that interference-feedom guarantees the preservation of safeness.

Theorem 6. If ϕ and ψ are safe and interference-free, then $[\phi \parallel_O \psi]$ is safe. ∎

The root and leaf conditions of this form of parallel composition satisfy the following logical equivalences:

$$\mathrm{root}(\phi \parallel_O \psi) \equiv \mathrm{root}(\phi) \,\&\, \mathrm{root}(\psi)$$
$$\mathrm{leaf}(\phi \parallel_O \psi) \equiv \mathrm{leaf}(\phi) \,\&\, \mathrm{leaf}(\psi).$$

This may be shown by an inductive argument. The fact that roots and leaves fit together in this composition simply by conjunction provides us with an obvious link with Owicki's proof rule for parallel composition. This rule, taken from [20], is:

$$\frac{\text{proofs of } \{P_1\}\Gamma_1\{Q_1\},\ \{P_2\}\Gamma_2\{Q_2\} \text{ interference-free}}{\{P_1 \,\&\, P_2\}[\Gamma_1 \parallel \Gamma_2]\{Q_1 \,\&\, Q_2\}} \qquad \text{(O)}$$

Now proof outlines for the Hoare assertions $\{P_i\}\Gamma_i\{Q_i\}$ correspond to safe assertions ϕ_i such that Γ_i **sat** ϕ_i, with $\mathrm{root}(\phi_i) = P_i$ and $\mathrm{leaf}(\phi_i) = Q_i$. The interference-freedom of these proof outlines corresponds to interference-freedom of ϕ_1 and ϕ_2. Then $[\phi_1 \parallel_O \phi_2]$ is a safe assertion satisfied by $[\Gamma_1 \parallel \Gamma_2]$, and has root $P_1 \,\&\, P_2$ and leaf $Q_1 \,\&\, Q_2$. Thus, a proof using Owicki's rule can be represented in our system, if we allow the use of (R) and (B9).

Interestingly, the analogy between safe assertions and proof outlines also yields some other connections with conventional Hoare logic. For instance, the sequential composition rule (B5) together with the following property can be used to derive Hoare's rule for sequential composition [12]:

Theorem 7. If ϕ and ψ are safe and $(\mathrm{leaf}(\phi) \Rightarrow \mathrm{root}(\psi))$ then $\phi;\psi$ is safe. ∎

Hoare's rule was:

$$\frac{\{P\}\Gamma_1\{Q\} \qquad \{Q\}\Gamma_2\{R\}}{\{P\}\Gamma_1;\Gamma_2\{R\}}.$$

The derivation relies on the facts that for non-trivial ϕ and ψ we have

$$\mathrm{root}(\phi;\psi) \equiv \mathrm{root}(\phi), \qquad \mathrm{leaf}(\phi;\psi) \equiv \mathrm{leaf}(\psi).$$

Auxiliary variables and auxiliary critical regions.

It is well known [20] that the proof system based on (B0), (B1), (B2), (B3), (C), (B9), (B5) and (R) is not complete for partial correctness assertions. As a simple example, it is impossible even to prove the obviously valid assertion

$$\{x = 0\}[x{:=}x + 1 \parallel x{:=}x + 1]\{x = 2\}$$

using these rules alone. We chose to avoid this problem by introducing conjunctions and implication. This particular assertion, for instance, can be proved by using rule (R) on the assertion discussed in Example 1 earlier. Owicki achieved completeness by adding "auxiliary variables" to programs and adding new proof rules to allow their use. We can formalise this as follows. We say that a set X of identifiers is *auxiliary* for a command Γ if all free occurrences of identifiers from this set in Γ are inside assignments to identifiers also in X. Thus, for instance, for the command

$$x{:=}x+1;\ y{:=}z;\ a{:=}x$$

the sets $\{y\}, \{y, z\}, \{a, x\}$ and $\{x, y, z, a\}$ are auxiliary, but $\{x\}$ is not. Let us write

$$\Gamma \text{ aux } X$$

when X is an auxiliary set of identifiers for Γ. Given any set X of identifiers and any command Γ, we can define a command $\Gamma \backslash X$ resulting from the deletion in Γ of all assignments to identifiers in X. The definition is syntax-directed:

$$\begin{aligned}
\mathbf{skip}\backslash X &= \mathbf{skip} \\
(I{:=}E)\backslash X &= \mathbf{skip} \qquad \text{if } I \in X \\
&= (I{:=}E) \quad \text{otherwise} \\
(\Gamma_1; \Gamma_2)\backslash X &= (\Gamma_1\backslash X); (\Gamma_2\backslash X) \\
[\Gamma_1 \parallel \Gamma_2]\backslash X &= [(\Gamma_1\backslash X) \parallel (\Gamma_2\backslash X)] \\
\langle\Gamma\rangle\backslash X &= \langle\Gamma\backslash X\rangle.
\end{aligned}$$

With this definition, it is clear (and provable) that if X is auxiliary for Γ then $\Gamma\backslash X$ has the same partial correctness effect on identifiers outside X as Γ does, and $\Gamma\backslash X$ leaves the values of all identifiers in X fixed.

Let free$[\![P, Q]\!]$ stand for the set of identifiers having a free occurrence in either P or Q. Owicki's auxiliary variables rule is:

$$\frac{\{P\}\Gamma\{Q\} \qquad \Gamma \text{ aux } X \qquad \text{free}[\![P,Q]\!] \cap X = \emptyset}{\{P\}\Gamma\backslash X\{Q\}}. \tag{AV}$$

In addition to this rule, for completeness of the Owicki proof system we also need a rule for eliminating "unnecessary" critical regions and irrelevant atomic actions which have been inserted merely to cope with auxiliary variables. The following command equivalences are valid with respect to partial correctness in all contexts:

$$\begin{aligned}
\mathbf{skip}; \Gamma &\equiv \Gamma \\
\Gamma; \mathbf{skip} &\equiv \Gamma \\
(\Gamma_1; \Gamma_2); \Gamma_3 &\equiv \Gamma_1; (\Gamma_2; \Gamma_3) \\
\langle\langle\Gamma\rangle\rangle &\equiv \langle\Gamma\rangle \\
\langle\mathbf{skip}\rangle &\equiv \mathbf{skip} \\
\langle I{:=}E\rangle &\equiv I{:=}E \\
[\mathbf{skip} \parallel \Gamma] &\equiv \Gamma \\
[\Gamma \parallel \mathbf{skip}] &\equiv \Gamma
\end{aligned}$$

Owicki's proof system uses a rule based on these equivalences, which we may formalise as follows:

$$\frac{\{P\}\Gamma\{Q\} \quad \Gamma \equiv \Gamma'}{\{P\}\Gamma'\{Q\}}. \tag{EQ}$$

As an example, we can now prove (as in [20]) the assertion

$$\{x = 0\}[x{:=}x + 1 \parallel x{:=}x + 1]\{x = 2\}$$

by first introducing auxiliary variables a and b to tag the two assignments and establishing the assertion

$$\{x = 0\}a{:=}0;\ b{:=}0;\ [\langle a{:=}1;\ x{:=}x + 1\rangle \parallel \langle b{:=}1;\ x{:=}x + 1\rangle]\{x = 2\}.$$

Then we eliminate the auxiliary variables and the extra critical regions. This augmented assertion can be proved by first proving the following assertions for the two parallel components:

$$\begin{aligned}
&\{P_a\}\langle a{:=}1;\ x{:=}x + 1\rangle\{Q_a\},\\
P_a &= (b = 0 \,\&\, x = 0) \vee (b = 1 \,\&\, x = 1),\\
Q_a &= (b = 0 \,\&\, x = 1 \,\&\, a = 1) \vee (b = 1 \,\&\, x = 2 \,\&\, a = 1),\\
&\{P_b\}\langle b{:=}1;\ x{:=}x + 1\rangle\{Q_b\},\\
P_b &= (a = 0 \,\&\, x = 0) \vee (a = 1 \,\&\, x = 1),\\
Q_b &= (a = 0 \,\&\, x = 1 \,\&\, b = 1) \vee (a = 1 \,\&\, x = 2 \,\&\, b = 1).
\end{aligned}$$

These two proof outlines are interference-free (this requires the verification of four conditions), and their use in the parallel rule enables us to conclude

$$\{P_a \,\&\, P_b\}[\langle a{:=}1;\ x{:=}x + 1\rangle \parallel \langle b{:=}1;\ x{:=}x = 1\rangle]\{Q_a \,\&\, Q_b\}.$$

Since we have

$$\begin{aligned}
&\{x = 0\}a{:=}0;\ b{:=}0\{x = 0 \,\&\, a = 0 \,\&\, b = 0\},\\
&x = 0 \,\&\, a = 0 \,\&\, b = 0 \Rightarrow P_a \,\&\, Q_a,\\
&Q_a \,\&\, Q_b \Rightarrow x = 2,
\end{aligned}$$

the desired result follows by the usual Hoare rules for sequential composition and the Rule of Consequence.

The Owicki–Gries proof system can, then, be thought of as built from the rules (B0), (B1), (B2), (B3), (B9), (B5), (AV), (EQ) and (C). It is arguable whether or not our proof system, which does not require the use of auxiliary variables in proofs, is preferable to Owicki's. The reader might like to compare the styles of proof in the two systems for the example above. Just as it is necessary to exercise skill in the choice and use of auxiliary variables in Owicki's system, our system requires a judicious choice of conjunctions. However, the details of auxiliary variables and reasoning about their values can be ignored in our system. At least we are able to demonstrate that there are alternatives to the earlier proof rules of [18,19] which do not explicitly require the manipulation of variables purely for proof-theoretical purposes and which do not require a notion of interference-freedom to guarantee soundness.

4. Extensions.

In this section we discuss briefly some effects of extending the programming language. We add the *await* statement (conditional critical region), conditional command, and *while* loop, thus bringing the language more fully into line with the programming language covered in [20].

The syntax for the new constructs will be:

$$\Gamma ::= \textbf{await}\ \beta\!:\!B\ \textbf{do}\ \gamma\!:\!\Gamma \ \mid\ \textbf{while}\ \beta\!:\!B\ \textbf{do}\ \Gamma\ \mid\ \textbf{if}\ \beta\!:\!B\ \textbf{then}\ \Gamma_1\ \textbf{else}\ \Gamma_2,$$

with B drawn from a syntactic category **BExp** of *boolean expressions* whose syntax will be ignored. We have inserted labels to indicate that the tests are regarded as atomic actions, as is the body of an await statement.

For the semantics of these constructs we add to the transition system the following rules:

$$\frac{s \models \neg B}{\langle \textbf{await}\ \beta\!:\!B\ \textbf{do}\ \gamma\!:\!\Gamma, s\rangle \xrightarrow{\beta} \langle \textbf{await}\ \beta\!:\!B\ \textbf{do}\ \gamma\!:\!\Gamma, s\rangle} \qquad \text{(A7)}$$

$$\frac{s \models B, \quad \langle \Gamma, s\rangle \rightarrow^{*} \langle \textbf{null}, s'\rangle}{\langle \textbf{await}\ \beta\!:\!B\ \textbf{do}\ \gamma\!:\!\Gamma, s\rangle \xrightarrow{\gamma} \langle \textbf{null}, s'\rangle} \qquad \text{(A8)}$$

$$\frac{s \models B}{\langle \textbf{if}\ \beta\!:\!B\ \textbf{then}\ \Gamma_1\ \textbf{else}\ \Gamma_2, s\rangle \xrightarrow{\beta} \langle \Gamma_1, s\rangle} \qquad \text{(A9)}$$

$$\frac{s \models \neg B}{\langle \textbf{if}\ \beta\!:\!B\ \textbf{then}\ \Gamma_1\ \textbf{else}\ \Gamma_2, s\rangle \xrightarrow{\beta} \langle \Gamma_2, s\rangle} \qquad \text{(A10)}$$

$$\frac{s \models B}{\langle \textbf{while}\ \beta\!:\!B\ \textbf{do}\ \Gamma, s\rangle \xrightarrow{\beta} \langle \Gamma; \textbf{while}\ \beta\!:\!B\ \textbf{do}\ \Gamma, s\rangle} \qquad \text{(A11)}$$

$$\frac{s \models \neg B}{\langle \textbf{while}\ \beta\!:\!B\ \textbf{do}\ \Gamma, s\rangle \xrightarrow{\beta} \langle \textbf{null}, s\rangle} \qquad \text{(A12)}$$

We assume given the semantics of boolean expressions, so that a satisfaction relation $\models \subseteq S \times \textbf{BExp}$ is known.

Note that these definitions give loops and conditionals the ability to be interrupted after evaluation of the test and before beginning the selected command. Later we will give a non-interruptible version.

With the extended transition system formed by (A1)–(A12), the old proof rules (B0)–(B8) are still valid. The following proof rules correspond to the new constructs, and are closely connected with the new semantic clauses.

$$\frac{\Gamma \text{ sat } \phi, \quad \text{safe}(\phi)}{\text{await } \beta : B \text{ do } \gamma : \Gamma \text{ sat } \{\text{root}(\phi) \,\&\, B\}\gamma\{\text{leaf}(\phi)\}\bullet} \tag{C7}$$

$$\frac{\text{await } \beta : B \text{ do } \gamma : \Gamma \text{ sat } \phi}{\text{await } \beta : B \text{ do } \gamma : \Gamma \text{ sat } \{P \,\&\, \neg B\}\beta\{P\}\phi} \tag{C8}$$

$$\frac{\Gamma_1 \text{ sat } \phi_1}{\text{if } \beta : B \text{ do } \Gamma_1 \text{ else } \Gamma_2 \text{ sat } \{P \,\&\, B\}\beta\{P\}\phi_1} \tag{C9}$$

$$\frac{\Gamma_2 \text{ sat } \phi_2}{\text{if } \beta : B \text{ do } \Gamma_1 \text{ else } \Gamma_2 \text{ sat } \{P \,\&\, \neg B\}\beta\{P\}\phi_2} \tag{C10}$$

$$\text{while } \beta : B \text{ do } \Gamma \text{ sat } \{P \,\&\, \neg B\}\beta\{P\}\bullet \tag{C11}$$

$$\frac{\text{while } \beta : B \text{ do } \Gamma \text{ sat } \theta, \quad \Gamma \text{ sat } \phi}{\text{while } \beta : B \text{ do } \Gamma \text{ sat } \{P \,\&\, B\}\beta\{P\}(\phi; \theta)} \tag{C12}$$

The soundness of these rules is easy to establish. Note the fact that our earlier rule for an unconditional critical region $\langle\Gamma\rangle$ can be derived from the new rule by making the test **true**.

For a non-interruptible version of loops and conditional, in which there is no interruption point between test and body, we change the semantics as follows:

$$\frac{s \models B, \quad \langle \Gamma_1, s\rangle \xrightarrow{\alpha} \langle \Gamma', s'\rangle}{\langle \text{if } \beta : B \text{ then } \Gamma_1 \text{ else } \Gamma_2, s\rangle \xrightarrow{\alpha} \langle \Gamma', s'\rangle} \tag{A9'}$$

$$\frac{s \models \neg B, \quad \langle \Gamma_2, s\rangle \xrightarrow{\alpha} \langle \Gamma', s'\rangle}{\langle \text{if } \beta : B \text{ then } \Gamma_1 \text{ else } \Gamma_2, s\rangle \xrightarrow{\alpha} \langle \Gamma', s'\rangle} \tag{A10'}$$

$$\frac{s \models B, \quad \langle \Gamma, s\rangle \xrightarrow{\alpha} \langle \Gamma', s'\rangle}{\langle \text{while } \beta : B \text{ do } \Gamma, s\rangle \xrightarrow{\alpha} \langle \Gamma'; \text{while } \beta : B \text{ do } \Gamma, s'\rangle} \tag{A11'}$$

$$\frac{s \models \neg B}{\langle \text{while } \beta : B \text{ do } \Gamma, s\rangle \xrightarrow{\beta} \langle \text{null}, s\rangle} \tag{A12'}$$

The appropriate proof rules are:

$$\frac{\Gamma_1 \ \mathbf{sat}\ P\sum_{i=1}^{n}\alpha_i P_i \phi_i}{\mathbf{if}\ \beta{:}B\ \mathbf{do}\ \Gamma_1\ \mathbf{else}\ \Gamma_2\ \mathbf{sat}\ \{P\ \&\ B\}\sum_{i=1}^{n}\alpha_i P_i\phi_i} \qquad (C9')$$

$$\frac{\Gamma_2 \ \mathbf{sat}\ P\sum_{i=1}^{n}\alpha_i P_i \phi_i}{\mathbf{if}\ \beta{:}B\ \mathbf{do}\ \Gamma_1\ \mathbf{else}\ \Gamma_2\ \mathbf{sat}\ \{P\ \&\ \neg B\}\sum_{i=1}^{n}\alpha_i P_i\phi_i} \qquad (C10')$$

$$\mathbf{while}\ \beta{:}B\ \mathbf{do}\ \Gamma\ \mathbf{sat}\ \{P\ \&\ \neg B\}\beta\{P\}\bullet \qquad (C11)$$

$$\frac{\mathbf{while}\ \beta{:}B\ \mathbf{do}\ \Gamma\ \mathbf{sat}\ \theta, \quad \Gamma\ \mathbf{sat}\ P\sum_{i=1}^{n}\alpha_i P_i\phi_i}{\mathbf{while}\ \beta{:}B\ \mathbf{do}\ \Gamma\ \mathbf{sat}\ \{P\ \&\ B\}\sum_{i=1}^{n}\alpha_i P_i(\phi_i;\theta)} \qquad (C12')$$

We believe that even with these extensions to the programming language the proof system remains sound and relatively complete. Soundness is straightforward, since the proof rules are based so closely on the operational semantics.

5. Conclusions.

We have described a syntax-directed proof system for semantic properties of commands in a simple parallel programming language. The assertions were chosen to correspond in form to the semantic structure, which itself was chosen to be powerful enough to allow reasoning about partial correctness properties to be carried out by manipulating assertions in a context-independent manner. We discussed some connections with more conventional logics such as the Owicki-Gries proof system.

Various proof systems for concurrent languages proposed by Lamport and others can also be related to our work. Lamport [16] proposed using assertions of the form $\{P\}\Gamma\{Q\}$ with the interpretation that in every execution which starts somewhere inside Γ with P true, P remains true until Γ terminates, when Q will be true. Such an assertion corresponds to one of our assertions $P\sum_{i=1}^{n}\alpha_i P_i\phi_i$ in which each P_i (and all other intermediate conditions) are identical to P and all leaf conditions are identical to Q. The proof rule for parallel composition given in [16] was:

$$\frac{\{P\}\Gamma_1\{Q\} \quad \{P\}\Gamma_2\{Q\}}{\{P\}[\Gamma_1 \parallel \Gamma_2]\{Q\}}.$$

But our definition of parallel composition of assertions preserves this uniformity property: the parallel composition of (the assertions representing) $\{P\}\Gamma_1\{Q\}$ and $\{P\}\Gamma_2\{Q\}$ will again have leaf Q and each intermediate condition will be P. (In fact, this uniformity property is preserved both by our $\|$ and by the other form $\|_O$). Thus, either our proof rule (B4) or (O) suffices to derive Lamport's rule. Instead of adding auxiliary variables, Lamport suggested the addition of program labels and simple assertions about them. He suggested using labels λ_i for the control points (or interruption points) of a program, and including in the condition language expressions of the form at(λ), inside(λ), after(λ). Lamport's system requires reasoning about control points and the relationship between them. Since in a Lamport-style assertion the same P has to represent more than one control point at a time, the conditions can get rather large. Indeed, it can be argued that since the same P is serving a multitude of purposes it is more natural to split it up into its components and to attach these components to the control points at which they are intended to hold; this is more in line with our notation, with control points corresponding to nodes in a tree.

The Generalized Hoare Logic of Lamport and Schneider [17] used a similar type of assertion to those of [16], except that they insisted that the post-condition coincide with the pre-condition: they used invariant assertions $\{P\}\Gamma\{P\}$. The interpretation is as before, that whenever an execution begins somewhere inside Γ with P true, P will remain true until termination. Again, their proof rule for parallel composition (essentially, a special case of the one from [16], given above) is representable in our system. Again, control conditions are used inside invariants, so that an invariant is really serving a multitude of purposes and could profitably be split up and distributed to the separate control points.

The *Transition Logic* of Gerth [11] is also has some connection with our work. Gerth's assertions, written $[P]\Gamma[Q]$, are interpreted: every transition that begins somewhere in Γ from a state satisfying P ends in a state satisfying Q. Again, the conditions may involve control assertions. Gerth's rule for parallel composition is:

$$\frac{[P]\Gamma_1[Q] \quad [P]\Gamma_2[Q]}{[P][\Gamma_1 \parallel \Gamma_2][Q]}.$$

But the assertion $[P]\Gamma[Q]$ can again be rendered in our assertion language as an assertion with a simple structure (alternating P and Q along each branch), and again our parallel composition of assertions has the required effect, producing an assertion representating $[P][\Gamma_1 \parallel \Gamma_2][Q]$ from representations of $[P]\Gamma_1[Q]$ and $[P]\Gamma_2[Q]$. This again means that Gerth's rule can be derived in our system.

The proof methodology and program development method advocated by Jones [14] uses *rely* and *guarantee* conditions in addition to pre- and post-conditions. Although we have not yet investigated the connection in any detail, it appears that these ideas are somewhat related to ours; roughly speaking, a rely condition might correspond to a pre-condition assumed by every atomic action in an assertion, and a guarantee condition would then be implied by all post-conditions of atomic actions.

Other authors have proposed compositional proof systems for concurrent programs in which the underlying assertions are temporal in nature. In particular, we refer to [4] and [19]. In contrast to these methods, we have avoided temporal assertions at the expense of using conjunction and implication as operations on more highly structured assertions built from conventional pre- and post-conditions. We still obtained a compositional proof system. In fact, our assertions do have some similarity with temporal logic in the sense that an assertion has built into it a specification of the possible atomic actions and the behaviour of the command after each of them, so that one might be able to represent one of our assertions ϕ in a more conventional temporal or dynamic logic.

We also believe that similar ideas to those used in this paper may be adopted in an axiomatic treatment of other forms of parallel programming. In particular, CSP [13] may be axiomatized if we modify the class of assertions to represent the potential for communication and if we design a suitable parallel composition of assertions. In CSP, the inclusion of guarded commands will necessitate a distinction between deadlock (a stuck configuration) and successful termination, but this may be handled by an appropriate choice of assertion language. We plan to investigate this topic in a future paper, and we hope that some connections with earlier work [2,18,27] will become apparent when this is done.

Another possibility for future development is to investigate an appropriate generalization of predicate transformers, weakest pre-conditions and strongest post-conditions (see [10], for example) for parallel commands, using our more general assertions instead of Hoare-style assertions. For instance, there is a reasonable notion of *strongest safe assertion* for a (labelled) command and an initial condition, provided we have *strongest post-conditions* of conventional type for atomic actions. If $\mathbf{sp}[\![\alpha]\!](P)$ is the strongest post-condition of atomic action α with respect to the pre-condition P, we may build a safe assertion $\Phi(\Gamma, P)$ as follows. If the initial actions for Γ (from states satisfying P) are $\{\alpha_1, \ldots, \alpha_n\}$, and if Γ_i is the remaining command after α_i, we put

$$\begin{aligned} \Phi(\Gamma, P) &= P \sum_{i=1}^{n} \alpha_i P_i \phi_i, \\ \text{where} \quad P_i &= \mathbf{sp}[\![\alpha_i]\!](P), \\ \phi_i &= \Phi(\Gamma_i, P_i). \end{aligned}$$

For convenience we put $\Phi(\mathbf{null}, P) = P$. For example, the assertion built in this way from the command $[\alpha{:}x{:=}x+1 \parallel \beta{:}x{:=}x+1]$ and the initial condition $x = 0$ is:

$$\{x=0\}(\alpha\{x=1\}\{x=1\}\beta\{x=2\} + \beta\{x=1\}\{x=1\}\alpha\{x=2\}).$$

Of course, when we include loops and conditionals we should be more careful in our definitions, but at least for finite commands this type of strongest safe assertion seems to be of interest. We plan to investigate this topic further.

Another point we should mention is that our assertions described above are all finite, and have been given a rather rigid interpretation: they not only describe the potential computations of a command as beginning with one of a given set of actions, but also specify that each of the actions mentioned in the assertion is indeed possible. It is, of course, possible to relax this interpretation; we are not sure if there would be any benefit to doing so, but it may be worth investigating. Similarly, we would like to try the effect of a different choice of assertions. It is clearly possible to model infinite computations by using recursively defined assertions, perhaps with a version of the μ notation often used for this purpose. Thus, if θ is a variable understood to range over assertions, we might write $\mu\theta.[\{P \,\&\, \neg B\}\beta\{P\}\theta]$ for an assertion which would be satisfied by the command **await** $\beta{:}B$ **do** $\gamma{:}\Gamma$. Recursive assertions could then be used to build proof rules for loops and conditional critical regions.

Acknowledgements. The author is grateful for discussions with Eike Best, Ed Clarke, Rob Gerth, Jay Misra, and Glynn Winskel.

6. References.

[1] Apt, K. R., Ten Years of Hoare's Logic: A Survey, ACM TOPLAS, vol. 3 no. 4 (October 1981) 431–483.

[2] Apt, K. R., Francez, N., and de Roever, W. P., A proof system for communicating sequential processes, ACM TOPLAS, vol. 2 no. 3 (July 1980), 359-385.

[3] Ashcroft, E. A., Proving assertions about parallel programs, J. Comput. Syst. Sci. 10 (Jan. 1975), 110-135.

[4] Barringer, H., Kuiper, R., and Pnueli, A., Now You May Compose Temporal Logic Assertions, Proc. 16th ACM Symposium on Theory of Computing, Washington, May 1984.

[5] Best, E., A relational framework for concurrent programs using atomic actions, Proc. IFIP TC2 Conference (1982).

[6] Brookes, S. D., On the Relationship of CCS and CSP, Proc. ICALP 83, Springer LNCS (1983).

[7] Brookes, S. D., A Fully Abstract Semantics and Proof System for An ALGOL-like Language with Sharing, CMU Technical Report (1984).

[8] Cook, S., Soundness and Completeness of an Axiom System for Program Verfification SIAM J. Comput. vol 7. no. 1 (February 1978) 70–90.

[9] Dijkstra, E. W., Cooperating Sequential Processes, in: Programming Languages, F. Genuys (Ed.), Academic Press, NY (1968) 43-112.

[10] Dijkstra, E. W., A Discipline of Programming, Prentice-Hall, New Jersey (1976).

[11] Gerth, R., Transition Logic, Proceedings of the 16th ACM STOC Conference, 1983.

[12] Hoare, C. A. R., An axiomatic basis for computer programming, CACM 12, 10 (Oct. 1969), 576-580.

[13] Hoare, C. A. R., Communicating Sequential Processes, CACM 21, 8 (Aug. 1978), 666-677.

[14] Jones, C. B., Tentative Steps Towards a Development Method for Interfering Programs, ACM TOPLAS vol. 5 no. 4, (October 1983) 596–619.

[15] Keller, R. M., Formal verification of parallel programs, CACM 19,7 (July 1976), 371-384.

[16] Lamport, L., The 'Hoare Logic' of concurrent programs, Acta Informatica 14 (1980), 21-37.

[17] Lamport, L., and Schneider, F., The "Hoare Logic" of CSP, and All That, ACM TOPLAS 6, 2 (April 1984), 281-296.

[18] Levin, G. M., and Gries, D., A proof technique for communicating sequential processes, Acta Informatica 15 (1981), 281-302.

[19] Manna, Z., and Pnueli, A., Verification of Concurrent Programs: The Temporal Framework, in: "The Correctness Problem in Computer Science", ed. R. S. Boyer and J. S. Moore, Academic Press, London (1982).

[20] Owicki, S. S., and Gries, D., An Axiomatic proof technique for parallel programs, Acta Informatica 6 (1976), 319-340.

[21] Owicki, S. S., Axiomatic proof techniques for parallel programs, Ph. D. dissertation, Cornell University (Aug. 1975).

[22] Hennessy, M., and Plotkin, G. D., Full Abstraction for a Simple Parallel Programming Language, Proc. MFCS 1979, Springer LNCS vol. 74, pp. 108–120.

[23] Milner, R., Fully Abstract Models of Typed Lambda-Calculi, Theoretical Computer Science (1977).

[24] Milner, R., A Calculus of Communicating Systems, Springer LNCS vol. 92 (1980).

[25] O' Donnell, M., A Critique of the Foundations of Hoare-Style Programming Logic, CACM vol. 25 no. 12 (December 1982) 927–934.

[26] Plotkin, G. D., A Structural Approach to Operational Semantics, DAIMI Report FN-19, Aarhus University (1981).

[27] Plotkin, G. D., An Operational Semantics for CSP, Proceedings of the W. G. 2.2 Conference, 1982.

[28] Winskel, G., Synchronisation Trees, Proc. ICALP 1983, Springer LNCS vol. 154. (1983).

Hierarchical Development of Concurrent Systems in a Temporal Logic Framework

Howard Barringer and Ruurd Kuiper

Department of Computer Science
University of Manchester
Oxford Road
Manchester M13 9PL
England.

ABSTRACT

This paper presents a formal specification and hierarchic development method for concurrent systems. The approach is based on a temporal logic to enable the specification of both safety and liveness properties in a single uniform framework. Two main problems are addressed, firstly, the reconciliation of temporal logic and compositionality in a structured specification approach, and secondly, to possess natural and easy to use proof rules for justifying parallel decomposition steps. To solve the first, we use a simple modification to the usual temporal logic model; to solve the second, we advocate the use of past time temporal operators in a new systematic and structured style for writing specifications.

1. Introduction

The more important criteria which have directed the design of the hierarchic specification and development approach presented in this paper can be summarised as follows.

Modularity

The independent development of subcomponents of some system, in particular parallel subcomponents, should be possible. This necessitates that formal justification of development steps, for example parallel decomposition, occurs at the specification level and does not require the implementation of the subspecifications.

Expressivenenss

In specifications all desired properties of a system should be expressible; for example, liveness (responsiveness, fairness, etc.) properties as well as safety or invariant properties should be covered.

Abstractness

It should be possible to give fully abstract specifications at every level of development, therefore achieving freedom from implementation bias.

Usability

Proof rules used in the justification of development steps should be natural and easy to use.

Adaptability

The specification approach should be, to a certain extent, implementation strategy independent, for example, allow development towards both shared variable and message based communication mechanisms from a single specification.

In general, extant methods for formal specification and development fall short on some of the above criteria. The traditional state assertion based verification methods, e.g. [OG76, LG81] lack at least in the expressibility and modularity criteria. Normally, safety and only limited liveness properties, like termination, freedom from deadlock, etc., can be treated. Furthermore, the justification that parallel subcomponents achieve some overall specification requires a proof of non-interference between the proofs of the subcomponents considered in isolation; such non-interference proofs can only be given when the subcomponents have been, in a sense, implemented. Temporal logic has been advocated as a useful tool for expressing both safety and liveness properties, especially for concurrent programs [OL82, MP82b, HO83]. However, although the expressibility requirements are handled well, the approaches have some difficulty with general modularity and compositionality criteria; again, proofs about parallel composition usually require the "code" of the individual processes. In a shared variables system, Jones [Jo83], although successfully achieving the modularity criteria, falls short on expressiveness (only safety and termination properties are handled without the introduction of auxiliary history variables into the state). The stream based assertion approaches, e.g. [Ho81, MC81, ZH80], are also successful with respect to the modularity criteria but fall short on general liveness; the paper [MCS82] extends the earlier work of [MC81] with some limited expression of liveness constraints. In [La83] an approach to specifying concurrent program modules is presented that, being based on temporal logic, handles both safety and general liveness properties; furthermore, the approach achieves modular composition of parallel modules. The main differences between Lamport's approach and that presented here is in the way a specification of a component refers to actions other than its own; the distinction here is explicitly restricted to just component and environment actions.

The specification approach presented here, developed using ideas from the above methods as guidance, meets, in our view, the above criteria. The remainder of this paper is structured as follows. Section 2 gives the underlying computational model and section 3 presents a past time temporal language used in writing formal specifications in the structured style presented in section 4. Section 5 gives parallel composition proof rules and an example of their use, then section 6 concludes with some discussion of the approach. The appendix contains an axiomatisation of the past time logic and derivation of some useful (temporal) inference rules.

2. The Basic Computation Model

To achieve the modularity criteria described above, we recognise the need to specify interference as introduced by Jones in [Jo83]. In our approach, this notion of interference is captured by specifying a component in an environment. At each level of development, the behaviour of a component in its environment is given by describing the changes that component can make to the interface with its environment and the changes its environment can make to that interface. Thus, at each level of development, only the observable behaviour is specified. The key to obtaining composable specifications is the ability to distinguish a change made by a component from one made by its environment; such distinction is achieved by labelling transitions in the computation model. In this paper we restrict the specification approach to shared variables communication mechanisms and, hence, the interface between a component and its environment is represented by shared variables. The state of a system provides values for these interface variables and system behaviour consists of a set of infinite labelled state sequences. Given an execution sequence over an interface variable set, Σ,

$$\sigma_0 \rightarrow \sigma_1 \rightarrow \ldots . \rightarrow \sigma_n \rightarrow \sigma_{n+1} \rightarrow \ldots .$$

it is first extended to infinity, if finite, by replicating the final state. Additionally, the transitions are labelled by e (transition made by the environment), c (transition made by the component) or r (transitions which replicate the final state). Thus, the sequences ρ in our computation model are of the form

$$\sigma_0 \xrightarrow{l_0} \sigma_1 \xrightarrow{l_1} \ldots . \xrightarrow{l_{n-1}} \sigma_n \xrightarrow{l_n} \sigma_{n+1} \xrightarrow{l_{n+1}} \ldots .$$

where each label may be e,c or r.

Definition 2.1

The semantics of a component P with interface Σ is defined as a set of extended, labelled, computation sequences, and is denoted by $[\![P,\Sigma]\!]$. The transitions labelled c are according to a given interpretation for the language in which P is expressed, e.g. a suitable operational semantics, however, no restrictions are placed on the transitions labelled e.

This definition complies with the intuitive notion that the semantics of P is the set of execution sequences obtained from running P in any environment.

Example 2.2

Consider the behaviour, i.e. the semantics, of the following component P,

$$P \triangleq x := 1; \quad x := x + 1 \quad ,$$

that has just the variable x as interface to its environment. Typically, in a finite environment, the sequences have the following form.

$$\sigma_0 \xrightarrow{e} \sigma_1 \xrightarrow{e} \ldots\ldots \sigma_m \xrightarrow{c} \sigma_{m+1} \xrightarrow{e} \ldots\ldots \xrightarrow{e} \sigma_n \xrightarrow{c} \sigma_{n+1} \xrightarrow{e} \ldots\ldots \xrightarrow{e} \sigma_f \xrightarrow{r} \sigma_{f+1} \xrightarrow{r} \ldots$$

with $x=a$ at σ_m, $x=1$ at σ_{m+1}, $x=b$ at σ_n, $x=b+1$ at σ_{n+1}.

finite no. of arbitrary e actions (≥0) | 1st step of P setting x to 1 | finite no. of arbitrary e actions (≥0) | 2nd step of P incrementing x | finite no. of arbitrary e actions (≥0) | final state replication

In the remainder of this section, we provide the semantics for the parallel composition of two components with identical interface variable sets; in section 5 proof rules for parallel composition are developed, and an example demonstrates how to handle non-identical interfaces. We use an interleaved model of parallel execution and adopt a convention that indexing a component induces the same indexing on the states and labels. Following ideas of Aczel [Ac83], the meaning of parallel composition of components P_1 and P_2, $[\![P_1 || P_2, \Sigma]\!]$, is taken as the set of conjoined compatible sequences from $[\![P_1,\Sigma]\!]$ and $[\![P_2,\Sigma]\!]$. Essentially, two sequences are compatible if they are identical with respect to states, and can be seen as being generated by P_1 and P_2 working in parallel but labelled from the viewpoint of P_1, respectively P_2. Conjoining two compatible sequences then produces the sequence labelled from the viewpoint of $P_1 || P_2$ considered as a single component.

Definition 2.3

Two extended, labelled, state sequences

$$\ldots \sigma_n{}^1 \xrightarrow{l_n{}^1} \sigma_{n+1}{}^1 \ldots \quad \text{and} \quad \ldots \sigma_n{}^2 \xrightarrow{l_n{}^2} \sigma_{n+1}{}^2 \ldots$$

are compatible if and only if

i) the state sequences are identical, i.e. for all i, $\sigma_i{}^1=\sigma_i{}^2$

ii) the labelling agrees, i.e. for all i

either a) $l_i{}^1 = e_1$ and $l_i{}^2 = e_2$

or b) $l_i{}^1 = e_1$ and $l_i{}^2 = c_2$

or c) $l_i{}^1 = c_1$ and $l_i{}^2 = e_2$

or d) $l_i{}^1 = r_1$ and $l_i{}^2 = r_2$

Definition 2.4

Two compatible sequences

$$\ldots \sigma_n{}^1 \xrightarrow{l_n{}^1} \sigma_{n+1}{}^1 \ldots \quad \text{and} \quad \ldots \sigma_n{}^2 \xrightarrow{l_n{}^2} \sigma_{n+1}{}^2 \ldots$$

are conjoined to produce one sequence

$$\ldots.\ \sigma_n \xrightarrow{l_n} \sigma_{n+1}\ \ldots.$$

where $\sigma_i = \sigma_i^1 = \sigma_i^2$ and l_i is given by

if $l_i^1 = e_1$ and $l_i^2 = e_2$		then $l_i = e$
if $l_i^1 = e_1$ and $l_i^2 = c_2$		
or $l_i^1 = c_1$ and $l_i^2 = e_2$		then $l_i = c$
if $l_i^1 = r_1$ and $l_i^2 = r_2$		then $l_i = r$

assuming e, c and r are the labels associated with $P_1||P_2$ viewed as a single component.

Definition 2.5

The conjoinment of two sets of extended labelled sequences S_1 and S_2, conjoin(S_1,S_2), is the set of conjoined compatible sequences from S_1 and S_2.

The meaning of parallel composition of two components P_1 and P_2 is thus:-

Definition 2.6

$$[\![P_1||P_2,\Sigma]\!] \triangleq \text{conjoin}([\![P_1,\Sigma]\!],[\![P_2,\Sigma]\!]).$$

Example 2.7

Consider the following two components P_1 and P_2

$$P_1 \triangleq x{:=}1;\ x{:=}x+1 \qquad P_2 \triangleq x{:=}2;\ x{:=}x+2$$

run in an environment which can only decrement the interface variable x. Typically, we see in $P_1||P_2$ considered as a single component sequences such as:-

```
P1 view        e1      e1      c1      c1      e1      e1      r1
P1||P2      σ -c→ [2] -e→ [1] -c→ [1] -c→ [2] -e→ [1] -c→ [3] -r→ [3] .....
P2 view        c2      e2      e2      e2      e2      c2      r2
               |       |       |       |       |       |       |
          P2(x:=2)     |   P1(x:=1) P1(x:=x+1) |  P2(x:=x+2)   |
                       |                       |               |
                 environment             environment      final state
                 decrementing x          decrementing x   replication
```

where, for example, [2] represents the state with the value 2 mapped to x.

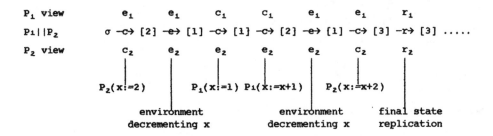

3. Past Time Temporal Logic

A specification of a component must single out a set of allowed sequences (behaviours) and as we desire to specify, in a uniform manner, both safety and liveness aspects of a component, a temporal logic based language is a natural choice as the basis of our specification language. For proving concurrent programs correct, linear future time temporal logic was introduced by Pnueli [Pn79], and further developed by Manna and Pnueli [MP82a, MP82b], Owicki and Lamport [OL82] and Lamport [La83]. In their approaches, program locations are used to infer the future behaviour of a program from only the present state. However, in our approach, to achieve freedom from bias, we use only the interface variables and labels (discerning environment from component actions), and do not introduce location predicates or other auxiliary, e.g. history, variables. As future behaviour can depend upon information now not encoded in the present state, we use a linear time logic equipped with past time operators, [Pr67], to retain access to that information.

3.1 Basic Alphabet

The basic symbols of the language are divided as three groups.

i) local symbols, i.e. symbols whose values are state or transition dependent

$p \in P$	state propositions
$l \in L$	transition propositions
$y \in Y$	state variables

ii) global symbols, i.e. symbols whose values are fixed for the complete sequence

$x \in X$	global variables

iii) constant symbols, i.e. symbols whose values are the same for all sequences

$f \in F$	function symbols
$q \in Q$	predicate symbols

Terms are constructed in the usual way from state and global variables, or by the application of appropriate function symbols to terms. Atomic formulae can then be built from state or transition propositions or by the application of predicates to terms.

The logical constants are the standard truth constants,

true, false

the standard first order logical operators,

$\neg$, $\wedge$, $\vee$, $\rightarrow$, $\leftrightarrow$, $\forall$, $\exists$,

the unary future temporal operators

○ (next time) , ◇ (eventually) , □ (always),

the unary past temporal operators

● (previously), ◆ (sometime in the past), ■ (always in the past),

the binary future temporal operators

$\underline{U}$ (strong until), U (weak until)

and the binary past temporal operators

$\underline{S}$ (strong since), S (weak since).

Temporal formulae are then constructed from atomic formulae by the appropriate application of logical operators.

3.2 Interpretation over Labelled Sequences

Assuming a fixed domain, D, and fixed interpretations for the function and predicate symbols, a model, over which a temporal formula is interpreted, is a 4-tuple,

$$M = (\alpha, \sigma, I, J)$$

where

α assigns D-values to the global variables,

σ is an infinite sequence of states and transitions

$$\sigma \triangleq s_0 \xrightarrow{t_0} s_1 \xrightarrow{t_1} s_2 \xrightarrow{t_2} \ldots\ldots$$

I is a state interpretation assigning D-values to each state variable and truth values {T, F} to state propositions,

J is a transition interpretation assigning truth values to transition propositions.

Given a model $M=(\alpha,\sigma,I,J)$ it is possible to define, inductively, the interpretation of temporal formulae over M. In general, this interpretation only involves change to the sequence σ and in the following $\phi|_\sigma n$ $(t|_\sigma n)$ abbreviates the value of the formula ϕ (term t) over the model M treating the index n as giving the present time.

Terms

$x|_\sigma n \triangleq \alpha(x)$	global variables
$y|_\sigma n \triangleq I(s_n,y)$	state variables
$f(t_1,..,t_m)|_\sigma n \triangleq F_f(t_1|_\sigma n,..,t_m|_\sigma n)$	function applications where F_f is the fixed function value for f
$\bigcirc t|_\sigma n \triangleq t|_\sigma n{+}1$	the next time operator applied to a term is the term evaluated in the sequence with origin as n+1.
$\bullet t|_\sigma n \triangleq t|_\sigma n{-}1$	the previous time operator applied to a term is the term evaluated in the sequence with origin as the previous state, n-1.

Atomic Formulae

$P|_\sigma n \triangleq I(s_n,P)$	state propositions
$\iota|_\sigma n \triangleq J(t_n,\iota)$	transition propositions
$q(t_1,..,t_m)|_\sigma n \triangleq Q_q(t_1|_\sigma n,..,t_m|_\sigma n)$	predicate applications where Q_q is the fixed predicate value for q

Now assuming the standard interpretation for the standard logical symbols (i.e. for **true**, **false**, $\neg,\wedge,\vee,\Rightarrow,\Leftrightarrow,\exists,\forall$), formulae ϕ constructed using the temporal operators are interpreted over $\sigma=s_0\to s_1\to\ldots$ as follows.

$\bigcirc\phi|_\sigma n$ if and only if $\phi|_\sigma n{+}1$

$\bullet\phi|_\sigma n$ if and only if $\phi|_\sigma n{-}1$

Note that if n is 0 then $\bullet\phi|_\sigma n$ is F and hence the formula $\neg\bullet$**true** is true only at the beginning of the sequence σ, in fact, we define the symbol **beg** to denote $\neg\bullet$**true**.

$\Box\phi|_\sigma n = T$ iff for all $i\geq 0$ $\phi|_\sigma n{+}i = T$.

$\Diamond\phi|_\sigma n = T$ iff there is some $i\geq 0$ such that $\phi|_\sigma n{+}i = T$.

$\phi\underline{\mathcal{U}}\psi|_\sigma n = T$ iff there is some $i\geq 0$ such that

a) $\psi|_\sigma n{+}i = T$.

and b) for all j, $0\leq j<i$, $\phi|_\sigma n{+}j = T$.

$\phi\mathcal{U}\psi|_\sigma n = T$ iff $((\phi\underline{\mathcal{U}}\psi)\vee\Box\phi)|_\sigma n = T$.

$\blacksquare\phi|_\sigma n = T$ iff for all i, $n \geq i > 0$, $\phi|_\sigma n-i = T$.

$\blacklozenge\phi|_\sigma n = T$ iff there is some i, $n \geq i > 0$, such that $\phi|_\sigma n-i = T$.

$\phi \underline{S} \psi|_\sigma n = T$ iff there is some i, $n \geq i > 0$, such that
a) $\psi|_\sigma n-i = T$.
and b) for all j, $i > j > 0$, $\phi|_\sigma n-j = T$.

$\phi S \psi|_\sigma n = T$ iff $((\phi \underline{S} \psi) \vee \blacksquare\phi)|_\sigma n = T$.

Note that the past time operators are strict past in that the present time is not included as part of the past.

We define a formula ϕ to be true for a model $M=(\alpha,\sigma.I.J)$ if $\phi|_\sigma n = T$ for all n (≥ 0). Then a formula ϕ is valid, written as $\models \phi$, if the formula ϕ is true in all models.

Finally, we define a formula to be true for a set of models, *M*, if and only if it is true for every model M in *M*.

$\mathcal{M} \models \phi$ iff for all $M \in \mathcal{M}$ and for all $n \geq 0$ $\phi|_\sigma n = T$.

This notion of validity has the equivalent effect to closure under suffix in the usual models, thus allowing $\Box$ (and $\blacksquare$) introduction, etc., cf. [MP82a].

3.3 Some Past Time Temporal Properties

We give here a few temporal properties of the past time language. The appendix contains an axiomatisation of the propositional part of this logic together with derivation of some of the properties given here.

●-Generalisation: If $\models \phi$ then $\models \neg beg \Rightarrow \bullet\phi$

Clearly, if ϕ holds (at any time) then, in particular, if there is a previous moment, it will hold at that moment as well.

●●-Introduction: If $\models \phi \Rightarrow \psi$ then $\models \bullet\phi \Rightarrow \bullet\psi$

Similarly, if $\phi \Rightarrow \psi$ holds at any time, then, in particular, if ϕ holds in the previous moment then so will ψ.

●-Distr1: $\models \bullet(\phi \wedge \psi) \Leftrightarrow (\bullet\phi \wedge \bullet\psi)$

●-Distr2: $\models \bullet(\phi \vee \psi) \Leftrightarrow (\bullet\phi \vee \bullet\psi)$

$\bullet$-Distr3: $\models \neg beg \Rightarrow (\bullet(\phi \Rightarrow \psi) \Leftrightarrow (\bullet\phi \Rightarrow \bullet\psi))$

The above properties reflect the distributive nature of $\bullet$. The latter property has to be guarded as the distribution does not hold in the $\leftarrow$ direction at the beginning of time.

$\blacksquare$-Generalisation: If $\models \phi$ then $\models \blacksquare\phi$

This rule states that as ϕ is valid and hence holds at all times, it is always the case that ϕ has held in the past.

$\blacksquare\blacksquare$-Introduction: If $\models \phi \Rightarrow \psi$ then $\models \blacksquare\phi \Rightarrow \blacksquare\psi$

This rule is similar to $\bullet\bullet$-Introduction.

$\blacksquare$-Distr1: $\models \blacksquare(\phi \wedge \psi) \Leftrightarrow (\blacksquare\phi \wedge \blacksquare\psi)$

Clearly, $\blacksquare$ distributes over conjunctions.

$\blacksquare$-Distr2: $\models (\blacksquare\phi \vee \blacksquare\psi) \Rightarrow \blacksquare(\phi \vee \psi)$

However $\blacksquare$ only distributes over disjunctions in one direction.

The following properties are useful in eliminating certain occurrences of $\bigcirc$.

$$\models \blacksquare\blacksquare\bigcirc\phi \Leftrightarrow \blacksquare\phi$$
$$\models \blacksquare\bigcirc\blacksquare\phi \Leftrightarrow \blacksquare\phi$$
$$\models \bigcirc\blacksquare\blacksquare\phi \Leftrightarrow \blacksquare\phi$$

Finally, we include a useful property characterising a form of induction.

Induction: $\models \blacksquare(\blacksquare\phi \Rightarrow \phi) \Rightarrow \blacksquare\phi$

Initially, i.e. at the beginning of time, $\blacksquare\phi$ is vacuously true and therefore for $\blacksquare\phi \Rightarrow \phi$ to be true ϕ must be true at the start. Now, by inductive arguments, if $(\blacksquare\phi \Rightarrow \phi)$ has been true in all previous moments, ϕ has been true also in all previous moments.

4. Formal Specifications and their Interpretation

As indicated at the start of the previous section a specification of a component will single out a set of allowed sequences. Rather than just use an unstructured temporal formula over the interface variables and transition propositions, as in [BKP84a] and the sequel [BKP84b], we introduce a systematic and structured presentation approach for formal specifications.

A specification of a system is structured as a 6-tuple,

$$\langle \Sigma, T, env_a, comp_a, comp_l, init \rangle,$$

where

- Σ is the set of interface variables,
- T is a triple giving the environment, component and replication transition propositions,
- env_a and $comp_a$ are temporal formulae which describe, respectively, the possible environment and component actions on the interface,
- $comp_l$ describes the component liveness properties, and
- init describes the initial conditions of the system.

The formula env_a is always written in a standard form, $\bigvee_{i \in E} act_i$.

The act_i are temporal formulae which characterise the possible environment transitions, i.e. the disjunction describes the possible state changes that can be made to the interface by the environment. The $comp_a$ formula is of a similar form. The liveness formula $comp_l$ is allowed to be any temporal formula over the transition propositions and interface variables. The initial conditions are just state properties.

The meaning of a specification and the meaning of a component (implementation) satisfying a specification (**sat**) are defined as follows.

<u>Definition 4.1</u>

Given $S = \langle \Sigma, T, env_a, comp_a, comp_l, init \rangle$ then the characteristic formula of the specification, denoted by $F(S)$, is defined as the temporal formula

$$\blacksquare\Box(\mathbf{beg} \Rightarrow init) \Rightarrow ((\blacksquare(e \Rightarrow env_a) \Rightarrow (c \Rightarrow comp_a)) \wedge (\Box\blacksquare(e \Rightarrow env_a) \Rightarrow comp_l)).$$

The characteristic formula requires that, under the assumption that the initial conditions were satisfied, if all the environment actions made so far are correct then the component makes a correct action, and if the environment actions are always correct then the component will be live (according to $comp_l$).

Definition 4.2

The sequences described by a specification, $[\![S]\!]$, are those from all models which satisfy the characteristic formula, i.e.

$$[\![S]\!] \mathrel{\hat{=}} \{ \sigma \mid \text{for all } n,\ F(S)|_{\sigma}n \}.$$

Definition 4.3

A component P satisfies a specification S, written as P **sat** S, if and only if $[\![P,\Sigma]\!] \subseteq [\![S]\!]$.

Example 4.4 Specification of an Unbounded, Unordered Live Buffer

We view a buffer as interacting with its environment through two interface variables, in and out. These interface varibales may be either empty ($\emptyset$) or may contain some message $m \in M$. We assert that the environment does not produce duplicate messages.

Spec BUFFER (in, out: $M \cup \{\emptyset\}$) $\hat{=}$ $\langle \{in,out\}, \langle e,c,r \rangle, env_a, comp_a, comp_l, init \rangle$

where

$$\begin{array}{lll} send(m) & \hat{=}\ in=\emptyset \wedge \bigcirc(in=m) \wedge I_{\neg in} & \text{used to abbreviate send and} \\ receive(m) & \hat{=}\ out=m \wedge \bigcirc(out=\emptyset) \wedge I_{\neg out} & \text{receive actions by the environment} \\ acc(m) & \hat{=}\ in=m \wedge \bigcirc(in=\emptyset) \wedge I_{\neg in} & \text{used to abbreviate accept and} \\ del(m) & \hat{=}\ out=\emptyset \wedge \bigcirc(out=m) \wedge I_{\neg out} & \text{deliver actions by the component} \end{array}$$

in

$$env_a \ \hat{=}\ \exists m \in M.(\ send(m) \wedge \neg \blacklozenge send(m) \ \vee \ receive(m)\ )$$

$$comp_a \ \hat{=}\ \exists m \in M.(\ acc(m) \ \vee \ del(m) \wedge \blacklozenge acc(m) \wedge \neg \blacklozenge del(m)\ )$$

$$comp_l \ \hat{=}\ \forall m \in M.(send(m) \Rightarrow \Diamond acc(m)) \ \wedge \ (out=\emptyset \wedge \exists m \in M.(\blacklozenge acc(m) \wedge \neg \blacklozenge (del(m)) \Rightarrow \exists m \in M.\Diamond del(m))$$

$$init \ \hat{=}\ in=\emptyset \wedge out=\emptyset$$

where the notation $I_{\neg x}$ means all variables apart from x are preserved over the "current" transition, here, for example, $I_{\neg in}$ stands for $\exists a \in M \cup \{\emptyset\}.out=a \wedge \bigcirc(out=a)$.

The environment and component action formulae can easily be seen to capture the desired properties of this buffer. The expected environment actions can either place a unique message, i.e. one that has not already been sent, on the input or remove a message from the output. The desired component actions either accept a message from the input or deliver a message that has been previously taken in but not yet been delivered. An implementation that meets the specification is only committed to make a correct action if the environment has, always in the past of that particular action, not contravened the assumptions placed upon it by, for example, removing messages from the input or putting messages on the output. The liveness aspects of the system require that the component will always accept a message placed on the input and will guarantee delivery of a message providing there does exist some message in the buffer and, of course, the environment is willing to take it. The initial conditions require that both the interface variables are empty ($\emptyset$).

5. Inference Rules for Parallel Composition

Given two components P_1 and P_2 with specifications S_1 and S_2, we develop necessary conditions, in the logic, to derive that the parallel composition of P_1 and P_2, $P_1||P_2$, will satisfy some "overall" specification S. We start by considering components with identical interfaces and develop appropriate conditions with respect to the semantic model. Note that we adopt a similar indexing convention for specifications as for components. Conjoinment is defined for arbitrary sets and is monotone with respect to set inclusion. Thus, given

$$[\![P_1,\Sigma]\!] \subseteq [\![S_1]\!] \quad \text{and}$$
$$[\![P_2,\Sigma]\!] \subseteq [\![S_2]\!] \quad \text{and}$$
$$[\![P_1||P_2,\Sigma]\!] = \mathrm{conjoin}([\![P_1,\Sigma]\!],[\![P_2,\Sigma]\!]) \quad ,$$

we have

$$[\![P_1||P_2,\Sigma]\!] \subseteq \mathrm{conjoin}([\![S_1]\!],[\![S_2]\!]) \quad .$$

Hence, if we can show

$$(*) \qquad \mathrm{conjoin}([\![S_1]\!],[\![S_2]\!]) \subseteq [\![S]\!]$$

then we have shown

$$[\![P_1||P_2,\Sigma]\!] \subseteq [\![S]\!]$$

i.e. $\qquad P_1||P_2$ **sat** S.

Now to capture the condition (*) in terms of the logic, notice that conjoinment is just intersection under certain label matching rules. These matching rules are reflected in the following formulae.

C1. $\qquad \Box\blacksquare(\ e_1 \wedge e_2 \Leftrightarrow e\ )$

C2. $\qquad \Box\blacksquare(\ (e_1 \wedge c_2) \vee (e_2 \wedge c_1) \Leftrightarrow c\ )$

C3. $\square\!\blacksquare(\ r_1 \wedge r_2 \Leftrightarrow r\ )$

C4. $\square\!\blacksquare(\ (e_1+c_1+r_1=1) \wedge (e_2+c_2+r_2=1) \wedge (e+c+r=1)\ )$

C5. $\square\!\blacksquare(\ r \Rightarrow I\ )$

With reference to the conjoinment definition 2.4, axiom C1 corresponds to the first condition, C2 corresponds to the second and C3 corresponds to the last condition. Axiom C4, where by an abuse of notation truth values are treated as integers, states that exactly one of e, c or r, etc., is true at any time. Axiom C5 states that nothing changes over an r action. Hence the following rule is obtained for two process parallel composition.

Rule 5.1

$$\frac{\begin{array}{l} P_i \ \textbf{sat} \ S_i\ ,\quad i=1,2 \\ C1..5 \ \vdash\ F(S_1) \wedge F(S_2) \Rightarrow F(S) \end{array}}{P_1 || P_2 \ \textbf{sat} \ S}$$

Theorem 5.2

The parallel composition rule, 5.1, is sound and relatively complete with respect to the expressive power of the specifications.

This result follows easily as a consequence of the conjoinment construction employed. Such a rule, however, is difficult to use, and a derived version of the rule can be obtained by utilising the particular structure of the specifications S.

Rule 5.3

$$\frac{\begin{array}{l} P_i \ \textbf{sat} \ S_i\ ,\ i=1,2 \\ C1..5 \ \vdash \blacksquare\!\square(beg \Rightarrow init) \wedge \blacksquare(e \Rightarrow env_a) \wedge \bigcirc\!\blacksquare((c_1 \Rightarrow comp_{a1}) \wedge (c_2 \Rightarrow comp_{a2})) \Rightarrow (c \Rightarrow comp_a) \\ C1..5 \ \vdash \blacksquare\!\square(beg \Rightarrow init) \wedge \bigcirc\!\blacksquare(e \Rightarrow env_a) \wedge \bigcirc\!\blacksquare(c_i \Rightarrow comp_{ai}) \Rightarrow (e_j \Rightarrow env_{aj})\ ,\ i=1,2,i \neq j \\ C1..5 \ \vdash (\blacksquare\!\square(beg \Rightarrow init) \wedge \square\!\blacksquare(e \Rightarrow env_a) \wedge \square\!\blacksquare((c_1 \Rightarrow comp_{a1}) \wedge (c_2 \Rightarrow comp_{a2})) \\ \qquad\qquad \wedge\ comp_{l1} \wedge comp_{l2}) \Rightarrow comp_l \\ \vdash init \Rightarrow (init_1 \wedge init_2) \end{array}}{P_1 || P_2 \ \textbf{sat} \ S}$$

where $S_i \triangleq \langle \Sigma, \langle e_i, c_i, r_i \rangle, env_{ai}, comp_{ai}, comp_{li}, init_i \rangle$ and
$S \triangleq \langle \Sigma, \langle e, c, r \rangle, env_a, comp_a, comp_l, init \rangle$

Theorem 5.4

The derived parallel composition rule, 5.4, is sound.

This result is obtained by showing that the premises of the former rule, 5.2, are derivable, via induction in the temporal logic framework, from the premises of this latter rule. The intuition underlying this rule is simply that the second premise ensures that the overall component committments are fulfilled by the subcomponents, the third premise ensures that the environment assumptions of the subcomponents are met, the fourth premise ensures that liveness is obtained, and the fifth premise ensures that initial conditions are met.

The following diagram conveys the interaction between parts of the specification for the safety (action) parts.

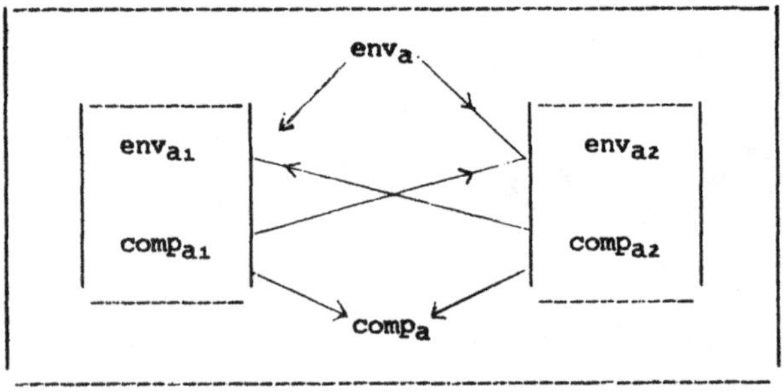

Proof of theorem 5.4

This proof is given in two parts, safety part and liveness part.

Safety Part. Here it must be shown that:-

$$C1..5 \vdash F(S_1) \wedge F(S_2)$$
$$C1..5 \vdash \blacksquare\Box(beg \Rightarrow init) \wedge \blacksquare(e \Rightarrow env_a) \wedge \bigcirc\blacksquare((c_1 \Rightarrow comp_{a1}) \wedge (c_2 \Rightarrow comp_{a2})) \Rightarrow (c \Rightarrow comp_a)$$
$$C1..5 \vdash \blacksquare\Box(beg \Rightarrow init) \wedge \bigcirc\blacksquare(e \Rightarrow env_a) \wedge \bigcirc\blacksquare(c_i \Rightarrow comp_{ai}) \Rightarrow (e_j \Rightarrow env_{aj}),\ i=1,2,\ i \neq j$$
$$\vdash init \Rightarrow (init_1 \wedge init_2)$$

$$C1..5 \vdash (\blacksquare\Box(beg \Rightarrow init) \wedge \blacksquare(e \Rightarrow env_a)) \Rightarrow (c \Rightarrow comp_a)$$

Proof:

0) $\vdash (\blacksquare\Box(beg \Rightarrow init) \wedge \blacksquare(e_1 \Rightarrow env_{a1})) \Rightarrow (c_1 \Rightarrow comp_{a1})$ PR, 1st Premise.

1) $\vdash \blacksquare((c_1 \Rightarrow comp_{a1}) \wedge (c_2 \Rightarrow comp_{a2})) \Rightarrow \blacksquare(c_1 \Rightarrow comp_{a1})$ $\blacksquare\blacksquare$-Intro on PT.

2) $\vdash \blacksquare\Box(beg \Rightarrow init) \wedge \bigcirc\blacksquare(e \Rightarrow env_a) \wedge \bigcirc\blacksquare(c_2 \Rightarrow comp_{a2}) \Rightarrow (e_1 \Rightarrow env_{a1})$
3rd Premise, i=2, j=1.

3) $\vdash (\blacksquare\Box(beg \Rightarrow init) \wedge \bigcirc\blacksquare(e \Rightarrow env_a)) \Rightarrow (\bigcirc\blacksquare(c_2 \Rightarrow comp_{a2}) \Rightarrow (e_1 \Rightarrow env_{a1}))$
PR, 2).

4) $\vdash \blacksquare(\blacksquare\Box(beg \Rightarrow init) \wedge \bigcirc\blacksquare(e \Rightarrow env_a)) \Rightarrow (\blacksquare\bigcirc\blacksquare(c_2 \Rightarrow comp_{a2}) \Rightarrow \blacksquare(e_1 \Rightarrow env_{a1}))$
$\blacksquare\blacksquare$-Intro, 3), twice.

5) $\vdash (\blacksquare\blacksquare\Box(beg \Rightarrow init) \wedge \blacksquare\bigcirc\blacksquare(e \Rightarrow env_a)) \Rightarrow (\blacksquare\bigcirc\blacksquare(c_2 \Rightarrow comp_{a2}) \Rightarrow \blacksquare(e_1 \Rightarrow env_{a1}))$
$\blacksquare$-Distr1, 4).

6) $\vdash (\blacksquare\Box(beg \Rightarrow init) \wedge \blacksquare(e \Rightarrow env_a)) \Rightarrow (\blacksquare(c_2 \Rightarrow comp_{a2}) \Rightarrow \blacksquare(e_1 \Rightarrow env_{a1}))$
PR, $\blacksquare\blacksquare \Rightarrow \blacksquare$, $\blacksquare\bigcirc\blacksquare \Rightarrow \blacksquare$, 5).

7) $\vdash (\blacksquare\Box(beg \Rightarrow init) \wedge \blacksquare(e \Rightarrow env_a)) \Rightarrow$
$(\blacksquare((c_1 \Rightarrow comp_{a1}) \wedge (c_2 \Rightarrow comp_{a2})) \Rightarrow \blacksquare(e_1 \Rightarrow env_{a1}))$ MP, 1), 6).

8) $\vdash (\blacksquare\Box(beg \Rightarrow init) \wedge \blacksquare(e \Rightarrow env_a)) \Rightarrow$
$(\blacksquare((c_1 \Rightarrow comp_{a1}) \wedge (c_2 \Rightarrow comp_{a2})) \Rightarrow (\blacksquare\Box(beg \Rightarrow init_1) \wedge \blacksquare(e_1 \Rightarrow env_{a1})))$ PR,MP,4thPremise,7).

9) $\vdash (\blacksquare\Box(beg \Rightarrow init) \wedge \blacksquare(e \Rightarrow env_a)) \Rightarrow$
$(\blacksquare((c_1 \Rightarrow comp_{a1}) \wedge (c_2 \Rightarrow comp_{a2})) \Rightarrow (c_1 \Rightarrow comp_{a1}))$ MP, 0), 8).

10) $\vdash \blacksquare(\blacksquare\Box(beg \Rightarrow init) \wedge \blacksquare(e \Rightarrow env_a)) \Rightarrow$
$\blacksquare(\blacksquare((c_1 \Rightarrow comp_{a1}) \wedge (c_2 \Rightarrow comp_{a2})) \Rightarrow (c_1 \Rightarrow comp_{a1}))$ $\blacksquare\blacksquare$-Intro, 11)

11) $\vdash \blacksquare(\blacksquare\Box(beg \Rightarrow init) \wedge \blacksquare(e \Rightarrow env_a)) \Rightarrow$
$\blacksquare(\blacksquare((c_1 \Rightarrow comp_{a1}) \wedge (c_2 \Rightarrow comp_{a2})) \Rightarrow (c_2 \Rightarrow comp_{a2}))$ similar to 0)..12).

12) $\vdash \blacksquare(\blacksquare\Box(beg \Rightarrow init) \wedge \blacksquare(e \Rightarrow env_a)) \Rightarrow$
$\blacksquare(\blacksquare((c_1 \Rightarrow comp_{a1}) \wedge (c_2 \Rightarrow comp_{a2})) \Rightarrow ((c_1 \Rightarrow comp_{a1}) \wedge (c_2 \Rightarrow comp_{a2})))$ PR, 10), 11).

13) $\vdash \blacksquare(\blacksquare\Box(beg \Rightarrow init) \wedge \blacksquare(e \Rightarrow env_a)) \Rightarrow \blacksquare((c_1 \Rightarrow comp_{a1}) \wedge (c_2 \Rightarrow comp_{a2}))$ MP, Induction, 12).

14) $\vdash \bigcirc\blacksquare(\blacksquare\Box(beg \Rightarrow init) \wedge \blacksquare(e \Rightarrow env_a)) \Rightarrow \bigcirc\blacksquare((c_1 \Rightarrow comp_{a1}) \wedge (c_2 \Rightarrow comp_{a2}))$ $\bigcirc\bigcirc$-Intro, 13).

15) $\vdash (\bigcirc\blacksquare\blacksquare\Box(beg \Rightarrow init) \wedge \blacksquare(e \Rightarrow env_a)) \Rightarrow \bigcirc\blacksquare((c_1 \Rightarrow comp_{a1}) \wedge (c_2 \Rightarrow comp_{a2}))$ $\bigcirc\blacksquare$-Distr, $\bigcirc\blacksquare\blacksquare \Rightarrow \blacksquare$,14).

16) $\vdash (\blacksquare\Box(beg \Rightarrow init) \wedge \blacksquare(e \Rightarrow env_a)) \Rightarrow \bigcirc\blacksquare((c_1 \Rightarrow comp_{a1}) \wedge (c_2 \Rightarrow comp_{a2}))$ $\bigcirc\blacksquare\blacksquare \Leftrightarrow \blacksquare$, 15).

17) $\vdash (\blacksquare\Box(beg \Rightarrow init) \wedge \blacksquare(e \Rightarrow env_a)) \Rightarrow$
$(\bigcirc\blacksquare((c_1 \Rightarrow comp_{a1}) \wedge (c_2 \Rightarrow comp_{a2})) \Rightarrow (c \Rightarrow comp_a))$ PR, 2nd Premise.

18) $\vdash (\blacksquare\Box(beg \Rightarrow init) \wedge \blacksquare(e \Rightarrow env_a)) \Rightarrow (c \Rightarrow comp_a)$ MP, 16), 17).

Liveness Part. Here it must be shown that:-

$$\frac{\begin{array}{l} Cl..5 \ \vdash \ F(S_1) \wedge F(S_2) \\ Cl..5 \ \vdash \ (\blacksquare\Box(beg \Rightarrow init) \wedge \bigcirc\blacksquare(e \Rightarrow env_a) \wedge \bigcirc\blacksquare(c_i \Rightarrow comp_{ai})) \Rightarrow (e_j \Rightarrow env_{aj}) \quad ,i=1,2,i \neq j \\ Cl..5 \ \vdash \ (\blacksquare\Box(beg \Rightarrow init) \wedge \Box\blacksquare(e \Rightarrow env_a) \wedge \Box\blacksquare((c_1 \Rightarrow comp_{a1}) \wedge (c_2 \Rightarrow comp_{a2})) \\ \qquad \wedge \ comp_{l1} \wedge comp_{l2}) \ \Rightarrow \ comp_l \end{array}}{Cl..5 \ \vdash \ (\blacksquare\Box(beg \Rightarrow init) \wedge \Box\blacksquare(e \Rightarrow env_a)) \ \Rightarrow \ comp_l}$$

The proof of this follows in a similar manner to the proof given above and is left to the interested reader.

Clearly, from the above, the overall result is now obtained, as:-

$$\frac{\begin{array}{l} Cl..5 \ \vdash \ (\blacksquare\Box(beg \Rightarrow init) \wedge \blacksquare(e \Rightarrow env_a)) \Rightarrow (c \Rightarrow comp_a) \\ Cl..5 \ \vdash \ (\blacksquare\Box(beg \Rightarrow init) \wedge \Box\blacksquare(e \Rightarrow env_a)) \Rightarrow comp_l \end{array}}{Cl..5 \ \vdash \ F(S)}$$

It is a simple matter to obtain versions of the rules for the parallel composition of n components. The generalised version of rule 5.1 follows.

Rule 5.5

$$\frac{\begin{array}{l} P_i \ \ sat \ \ S_i \quad , \quad i=1,n \\ Cl..5 \ \vdash \ (\bigwedge_{i=1,n} F(S_i)) \Rightarrow F(S) \end{array}}{\mathop{||}_{i=1,n} P_i \ \ sat \ \ S}$$

Rule 5.3 also generalises in the obvious manner and is included in the Appendix 2.

<u>Example 5.7</u>

To demonstrate application of the derived parallel inference rule we show that the behaviour of two unbounded unordered live buffers, each specified as in example 4.4, coupled by making the output of the first the input of the second, is, indeed that of an unbounded unordered live buffer.

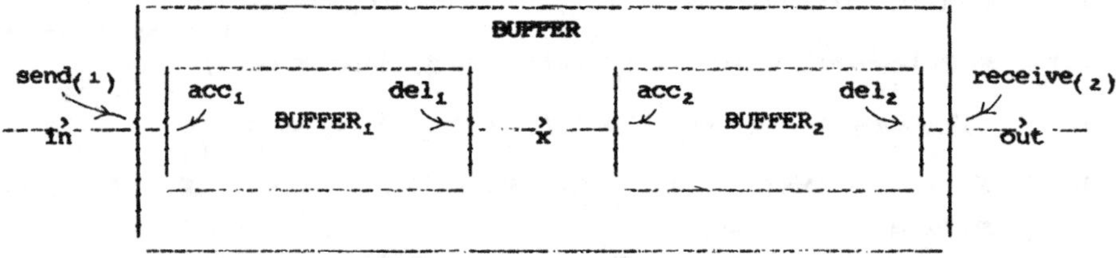

The buffers are connected by an internal shared variable x; thus making the interfaces of $BUFFER_1$, $BUFFER_2$ and BUFFER all different. The rules for parallel composition given so far all require the interfaces to be identical. To enable the rules to be applied in this situation, the specifications of the components are "completed" in that the interfaces of the components are extended to be identical and appropriate assumptions and commitments on the extra variables are added. This completion proceeds as follows in this double buffer example.

Spec BUFFER (in,x,out: $\mathbf{M} \cup \{\emptyset\}$) $\triangleq$ $\langle\{in,x,out\},\langle e,c,r\rangle,env_a,comp_a,comp_l,init\rangle$

where

$send(m) \triangleq .....$

......

$internal \triangleq I_{\neg x}$

in

$$env_a \triangleq \exists m\in\mathbf{M}.(\,send(m) \wedge \neg\blacklozenge send(m) \vee receive(m)\,)$$

$$comp_a \triangleq \exists m\in\mathbf{M}.(\,acc(m) \vee del(m) \wedge \blacklozenge acc(m) \wedge \neg\blacklozenge del(m) \vee internal\,)$$

$$comp_l \triangleq \forall m\in\mathbf{M}.(send(m) \rightarrow \Diamond acc(m)) \wedge (out{=}\emptyset \wedge \exists m\in\mathbf{M}.(\blacklozenge acc(m) \wedge \neg\blacklozenge(del(m)) \rightarrow \exists m\in\mathbf{M}.\Diamond del(m))$$

$$init \triangleq in{=}\emptyset \wedge x{=}\emptyset \wedge out{=}\emptyset$$

The overall BUFFER specification allows internal actions to occur on x, the internal clause in $comp_a$, but assumes the environment does not change x, by the fact that only sends and receives are mentioned in env_a. The specification for BUFFER1 is altered so that the environment is assumed to make any change to out, but the component commits not to change out.

$$\text{Spec BUFFER1 } (in,x,out\colon M \cup \{\emptyset\}) \triangleq \langle \{in,x,out\}, \langle e,c,r\rangle, env_a, comp_a, comp_1, init\rangle$$

where

$$\begin{array}{ll}
send_1(m) & \triangleq in=\emptyset \wedge \bigcirc in=m \wedge I_{\neg in} \\
receive_1(m) & \triangleq x=m \wedge \bigcirc x=\emptyset \wedge I_{\neg x} \\
acc_1(m) & \triangleq in=m \wedge \bigcirc in=\emptyset \wedge I_{\neg in} \\
del_1(m) & \triangleq x=\emptyset \wedge \bigcirc x=m \wedge I_{\neg x} \\
external_1 & \triangleq I_{\neg out}
\end{array}$$

in

$$\begin{array}{lll}
env_a & \triangleq & \exists m\in M.(\ send_1(m) \wedge \neg\blacklozenge send_1(m) \\
 & & \qquad \vee \\
 & & \quad receive_1(m) \\
 & & \qquad \vee \\
 & & \quad external_1\ ) \\
comp_a & \triangleq & \exists m\in M.(\ acc_1(m) \\
 & & \qquad \vee \\
 & & \quad del_1(m) \wedge \blacklozenge acc_1(m) \wedge \neg\blacklozenge del_1(m)\ ) \\
comp_1 & \triangleq & \forall m\in M.(send_1(m) \Rightarrow \Diamond acc_1(m)) \\
 & & \ \wedge \\
 & & (out=\emptyset \wedge \exists m\in M.(\blacklozenge acc_1(m) \wedge \neg\blacklozenge(del_1(m)) \Rightarrow \exists m\in M.\Diamond del_1(m)) \\
init & \triangleq & in=\emptyset \wedge x=\emptyset \wedge out=\emptyset
\end{array}$$

The specification for BUFFER2 is changed in a similar manner.

$$\text{Spec BUFFER2 } (in,x,out\colon M \cup \{\emptyset\}) \triangleq \langle \{in,x,out\}, \langle e,c,r\rangle, env_a, comp_a, comp_1, init\rangle$$

where

$$\begin{array}{ll}
send_2(m) & \triangleq x=\emptyset \wedge \bigcirc x=m \wedge I_{\neg x} \\
receive_2(m) & \triangleq out=m \wedge \bigcirc out=\emptyset \wedge I_{\neg out} \\
acc_2(m) & \triangleq x=m \wedge \bigcirc x=\emptyset \wedge I_{\neg x} \\
del_2(m) & \triangleq out=\emptyset \wedge \bigcirc out=m \wedge I_{\neg out} \\
external_2 & \triangleq I_{\neg in}
\end{array}$$

in

$$\begin{array}{lll}
env_a & \triangleq & \exists m\in M.(\ send_2(m) \wedge \neg\Diamond send_2(m) \\
 & & \qquad \vee \\
 & & \quad receive_2(m) \\
 & & \qquad \vee \\
 & & \quad external_2\ ) \\
comp_a & \triangleq & \exists m\in M.(\ acc_2(m) \\
 & & \qquad \vee \\
 & & \quad del_2(m) \wedge \blacklozenge acc_2(m) \wedge \neg\blacklozenge del_2(m)\ ) \\
comp_1 & \triangleq & \forall m\in M.(send_2(m) \Rightarrow \Diamond acc_2(m)) \\
 & & \ \wedge \\
 & & (out=\emptyset \wedge \exists m\in M.(\blacklozenge acc_2(m) \wedge \neg\blacklozenge(del_2(m)) \Rightarrow \exists m\in M.\Diamond del_2(m)) \\
init & \triangleq & in=\emptyset \wedge x=\emptyset \wedge out=\emptyset
\end{array}$$

As the interfaces are now identical, it is now necessary to establish the 2nd to 4th premises of the rule 5.4 hold. Consider first the second premise. In expanded form it is sufficient to prove

$$
\begin{array}{lll}
(1) & C1..5 \vdash & \blacksquare(\mathrm{beg} \Rightarrow (\mathrm{in}=\emptyset \wedge x=\emptyset \wedge \mathrm{out}=\emptyset)) \wedge \\
& & \quad \blacksquare(e \Rightarrow \exists m \in M.(\mathrm{send}(m) \wedge \neg\blacklozenge \mathrm{send}(m) \vee \mathrm{receive}(m))) \wedge \\
& & \quad \blacksquare(c_1 \Rightarrow \exists m \in M.(\mathrm{acc}_1(m) \vee \mathrm{del}_1(m) \wedge \blacklozenge \mathrm{acc}_1(m) \wedge \neg\blacklozenge \mathrm{del}_1(m)) \wedge \\
& & \quad\;\; c_2 \Rightarrow \exists m \in M.(\mathrm{acc}_2(m) \vee \mathrm{del}_2(m) \wedge \blacklozenge \mathrm{acc}_2(m) \wedge \neg\blacklozenge \mathrm{del}_2(m))) \wedge \\
& & \quad (\exists m \in M.(\mathrm{acc}_1(m) \vee \mathrm{del}_1(m) \wedge \blacklozenge \mathrm{acc}_1(m) \wedge \neg\blacklozenge \mathrm{del}_1(m)) \vee \\
& & \quad\; \exists m \in M.(\mathrm{acc}_2(m) \vee \mathrm{del}_2(m) \wedge \blacklozenge \mathrm{acc}_2(m) \wedge \neg\blacklozenge \mathrm{del}_2(m))) \\
& & \Rightarrow \\
& & \exists m \in M.(\mathrm{acc}(m) \vee \mathrm{del}(m) \wedge \blacklozenge \mathrm{acc}(m) \wedge \neg\blacklozenge \mathrm{del}(m) \vee I_{\neg x})
\end{array}
$$

as the transition proposition c is only true if either c_1 or c_2 is true. Now as $\mathrm{acc}(m) \Leftrightarrow \mathrm{acc}_1(m)$ and $\mathrm{del}(m) \Leftrightarrow \mathrm{del}_2(m)$, the above will be provable if

$$
\begin{array}{lll}
(2) & C1..5 \vdash & \exists m \in M.\blacksquare(\mathrm{beg} \Rightarrow (\mathrm{in}=\emptyset \wedge x=\emptyset \wedge \mathrm{out}=\emptyset)) \wedge \\
& & \quad \blacksquare(e \Rightarrow \exists m \in M.(\mathrm{send}(m) \wedge \neg\blacklozenge \mathrm{send}(m) \vee \mathrm{receive}(m))) \wedge \\
& & \quad \blacksquare(c_1 \Rightarrow \exists m \in M.(\mathrm{acc}_1(m) \vee \mathrm{del}_1(m) \wedge \blacklozenge \mathrm{acc}_1(m) \wedge \neg\blacklozenge \mathrm{del}_1(m)) \wedge \\
& & \quad\;\; c_2 \Rightarrow \exists m \in M.(\mathrm{acc}_2(m) \vee \mathrm{del}_2(m) \wedge \blacklozenge \mathrm{acc}_2(m) \wedge \neg\blacklozenge \mathrm{del}_2(m))) \wedge \\
& & \quad \mathrm{acc}_2(m) \\
& & \quad \Rightarrow \\
& & \quad \blacklozenge \mathrm{acc}_1(m))
\end{array}
$$

To prove (2) notice that

$$
\begin{array}{lll}
(3) & C1..5 \vdash & \exists m \in M.\blacksquare(\mathrm{beg} \Rightarrow (\mathrm{in}=\emptyset \wedge x=\emptyset \wedge \mathrm{out}=\emptyset)) \wedge \\
& & \quad \blacksquare(e \Rightarrow \exists m \in M.(\mathrm{send}(m) \wedge \neg\blacklozenge \mathrm{send}(m) \vee \mathrm{receive}(m))) \wedge \\
& & \quad \blacksquare(c_1 \Rightarrow \exists m \in M.(\mathrm{acc}_1(m) \vee \mathrm{del}_1(m) \wedge \blacklozenge \mathrm{acc}_1(m) \wedge \neg\blacklozenge \mathrm{del}_1(m)) \wedge \\
& & \quad\;\; c_2 \Rightarrow \exists m \in M.(\mathrm{acc}_2(m) \vee \mathrm{del}_2(m) \wedge \blacklozenge \mathrm{acc}_2(m) \wedge \neg\blacklozenge \mathrm{del}_2(m))) \wedge \\
& & \quad \mathrm{acc}_2(m) \\
& & \quad \Rightarrow \\
& & \quad \blacklozenge \mathrm{del}_1(m))
\end{array}
$$

which holds as initially $x=\emptyset$ and as $x=m$ currently there was a previous moment which changed x from $\emptyset$ to m. Similarly, it can be shown that

$$
\begin{array}{lll}
(4) & C1..5 \vdash & \exists m \in M.\blacksquare(\mathrm{beg} \Rightarrow (\mathrm{in}=\emptyset \wedge x=\emptyset \wedge \mathrm{out}=\emptyset)) \wedge \\
& & \quad \blacksquare(e \Rightarrow \exists m \in M.(\mathrm{send}(m) \wedge \neg\blacklozenge \mathrm{send}(m) \vee \mathrm{receive}(m))) \wedge \\
& & \quad \blacksquare(c_1 \Rightarrow \exists m \in M.(\mathrm{acc}_1(m) \vee \mathrm{del}_1(m) \wedge \blacklozenge \mathrm{acc}_1(m) \wedge \neg\blacklozenge \mathrm{del}_1(m)) \wedge \\
& & \quad\;\; c_2 \Rightarrow \exists m \in M.(\mathrm{acc}_2(m) \vee \mathrm{del}_2(m) \wedge \blacklozenge \mathrm{acc}_2(m) \wedge \neg\blacklozenge \mathrm{del}_2(m))) \wedge \\
& & \quad \mathrm{del}_1(m) \\
& & \quad \Rightarrow \\
& & \quad \blacklozenge \mathrm{acc}_1(m))
\end{array}
$$

and hence (2) will hold, and consequently (1). We have omitted the formal steps of the proof but the reader should note that they rely heavily on the assumptions C1..5.

Considering now the third premise, that the environment assumptions of the subcomponents are fulfilled, we must show the following holds (and the similar requirement given by i=2 and j=1). We have used that the transition proposition e_2 is true iff either e or c_1 is true.

$$
\begin{aligned}
(5) \qquad C1..5 \;\vdash\; & \blacksquare\Box(beg \Rightarrow (in=\emptyset \wedge x=\emptyset \wedge out=\emptyset)) \wedge \\
& \quad \blacksquare(e \Rightarrow \exists m \in M.(send(m) \wedge \neg\blacklozenge send(m) \vee receive(m))) \wedge \\
& \quad \blacksquare(c_1 \Rightarrow \exists m \in M.(acc_1(m) \vee del_1(m) \wedge \blacklozenge acc_1(m) \wedge \neg\blacklozenge del_1(m))) \wedge \\
& \quad \exists m \in M.(send(m) \wedge \neg\blacklozenge send(m) \vee receive(m) \vee \\
& \qquad\quad acc_1(m) \vee del_1(m) \wedge \blacklozenge acc_1(m) \wedge \neg\blacklozenge del_1(m)) \\
& \Rightarrow \\
& \exists m \in M.(send_2(m) \wedge \neg\blacklozenge send_2(m) \vee receive_2(m) \vee I_{\neg in})
\end{aligned}
$$

This follows straightforwardly as $del_1(m) \Leftrightarrow send_2(m)$ and $receive(m) \Leftrightarrow receive_2(m)$. Note that $send(m)$ or $acc_1(m)$ infer the clause $I_{\neg in}$.

The liveness requirements are also as easily proven from the subcomponents specifications.

Finally, the initial conditions of the subcomponent specs are trivially satisfied.

6. Discussion

We have presented the framework underlying a formal specification and development method for concurrent systems, for which tentative ideas were discussed at a workshop in Cambridge [BK83]. Because it is based on a temporal logic, it allows a uniform treatment of both safety and liveness properties. Because our specifications make a clear separation between component and environment behaviour, thus recognising the notion of interference, the method is truly hierarchical. Furthermore, the structured form of specifications enables pragmatic parallel composition rules. Extension to complete formal proof systems is possible, as can be seen from the techniques employing unstructured specifications in [BKP84a,BKP84b].

Various notions of completeness, observable equivalence and bias arise in connection with specifications. For instance, the buffer example used in section 4 and 5 requires unique messages; this is due to an incompleteness in expressibility of linear time temporal logic [SCFG82]. This incompleteness can be overcome in various ways. For example, internal components to the state can be allowed, as is advocated by Lamport [La83]; in our system this can be achieved by the addition of auxiliary and/or internal state variables [SJ84]. However, one then has to be most careful that bias is not introduced into the specifications. Another way is to strengthen the logic. Wolper extends linear time temporal logic with regular expressions [Wo81]; this gives greater but still not full expressiveness. An extension which, in our opinion, might well give full expressiveness is the inclusion of temporal operators like $\Diamond^k$, where $\Diamond^k$ is defined by $\Diamond(\phi \wedge \Diamond(\phi \wedge \Diamond(\phi \ldots)))$ k-times, allowing quantification over k. With such extensions to the logic the buffer, handling possibly non-unique messages, can be specified using just the visible variables of a component as its interface.

Acknowledgements

We are sincerely grateful to Amir Pnueli for the keen interest he has shown in our work. An early version of our parallel composition rule was mentioned at the STL/SERC Workshop on the Analysis of Concurrent Systems in Cambridge, September 1983; Amir kindly pointed out some flaws with that version at Cambridge. We also thank Willem Paul de Roever for helpful comments and many interesting discussions about compositional proof systems. Useful comments and stimuli have also been received from Cliff Jones, Leslie Lamport, Jay Misra, Zhou Chao Chen.

This work has been supported under S.E.R.C. grant GR/C/05670; both authors acknowledge their support.

References

[Ac83] P.Aczel
On an Inference Rule for Parallel Composition
Internal Memo
Department of Mathematics, University of Manchester, 1983.

[BK83] H.Barringer and R.Kuiper
Towards the Hierarchical, Temporal Logic, Specification of Concurrent Systems
Proc. of the STL/SERC Workshop on the Analysis of Concurrent Systems
Cambridge, September 1983.

[BKP84a] H.Barringer, R.Kuiper and A.Pnueli
Now You May Compose Temporal Logic Specifications
Proc. of the 16th ACM Symposium on the Theory of Computing
Washington, May 1984.

[BKP84b] H.Barringer, R.Kuiper and A.Pnueli
A Compositional Temporal Approach to a CSP-like Language
Internal Report
Department of Computer Science, University of Manchester, Oct. 1984.

[Go84] G.D.Gough
Decision Procedures for Temporal Logic
M.Sc. Dissertation
Department of Computer Science, University of Manchester, Oct. 1984.

[HO83] B.T.Hailpern and S.S.Owicki
Modular Verification of Computer Communication Protocols
IEEE Trans. on Commun. COM-31, 1, Jan. 1983, pp56-68.

[Ho81] C.A.R.Hoare
A Calculus of Total Correctness for Communicating Processes
Science of Computer Programming, 1, 1981, pp49-72.

[Jo83] C.B.Jones
Specification and Design of (Parallel) Programs
Proc. IFIP 83, Paris, North Holland, 1983, pp321-332.

[La83] L.Lamport
Specifying Concurrent Program Modules
ACM TOPLAS, Apr 1983, Vol. 5, No. 2, 1983, pp190-222.

[LG81] G.M.Levin and D.Gries
A Proof Technique for Communicating Sequential Processes
Acta Informatica 15, 1981, pp281-302.

[MC81] J.Misra and K.M.Chandy
Proofs about Networks of Processes
IEEE TOSE Vol SE-7, No. 4, July 1981.

[MCS82] J.Misra, K.M.Chandy and T.Smith
Proving Safety and Liveness of Communicating Processes with Examples
Proc. 1st ACM SIGACT/SIGOPS Symp. on PODC, Ottawa, Aug. 1982.

[MP82a] Z.Manna and A.Pnueli
Verification of Concurrent Programs: The Temporal Framework
in "The Correctness Problem in Computer Science"
ed. R.S.Boyer and J.S.Moore
International Lecture Notes in Computer Science, pp215-273
Academic Press, London, 1982.

[MP82b] Z.Manna and A.Pnueli
Verification of Concurrent Programs: A Temporal Proof System
Computer Science Report, Stanford University, 1983.

[OG76] S.S.Owicki and D.Gries
An Axiomatic Proof Technique for Parallel Programs 1
Acta Informatica 6, 1976, pp319-340.

[OL82] S.S.Owicki and L.Lamport
Proving Liveness Properties of Concurrent Programs
ACM TOPLAS, Vol. 4, No. 3, July 1982, pp455-495.

[Pn79] The Temporal Semantics of Concurrent Computation
Proc. of the Symp. on Semantics of Concurrent Compoutation
Evian, France, July 1979
Springer-Verlag, LNCS Vol. 70, pp1-20.

[Pr67] A.Prior
Past, Present and Future
Oxford University Press, 1967.

[SCFG82] A.P.Sistla , E.M.Clarke, N.Francez and Y.Gurevich
Can Buffers be Specified in Linear Temporal Logic?
Proc. 1st ACM SIGACT/SICOPS Symp. on PODC, Ottawa, Aug. 1982.

[SJ84] Sa Jin
Temporal Logic Specification of Communication Protocols
Ph.D. Transfer Report
Department of Computer Science, University of Manchester, Sep. 1984.

[Wo81] P.Wolper
Temporal Logic can be more Expressive
Proc. of the 22nd Symp. on FOCS, Oct. 1981.

[ZH80] Zhou Chao Chen and C.A.R.Hoare
Partial Correctness of Communicating Processes and Protocols
Proc. of 2nd Int. Conf. on Distributed Computing Systems, 1981.

Appendix 1: Derivation of Propositional Past Time Logic Formulae

The axiomatisation presented here follows in the style and spirit of Manna and Pnueli's axiomatisation of future time temporal logic. An axiomatisation of an unbounded past time logic is presented in [Go84]; a decision procedure is given from which completeness of the system can be obtained. In the following, axiom schemata 0, 1, 2 and 6 are axioms from the future time axiomatisation. Axiom schema 3 is the past time counterpart to 2. Note the necessity for the $\bullet\mathbf{true}$ guard; this is because at the beginning there is no previous state and therefore the equivalence does not hold. Axiom schema 5 states that there does exist a beginning. Axiom schema 7 defines the Since operator, and schema 8 and 9 give the relationship between $\bigcirc$ and $\bullet$.

Axioms

A0.	$\vdash \phi$	where ϕ is a propositional tautology
A1.	$\vdash \bigcirc\neg\phi \Leftrightarrow \neg\bigcirc\phi$	
A2.	$\vdash \bigcirc(\phi\Rightarrow\psi) \Rightarrow (\bigcirc\phi\Rightarrow\bigcirc\psi)$	
A3.	$\vdash \bullet\mathbf{true} \Rightarrow (\bullet\neg\phi \Leftrightarrow \neg\bullet\phi)$	
A4.	$\vdash \bullet(\phi\Rightarrow\psi) \Rightarrow (\bullet\phi\Rightarrow\bullet\psi)$	
A5.	$\vdash \bigcirc\neg((\bullet\phi)\mathcal{S}\mathbf{false})$	
A6.	$\vdash (\phi\mathcal{U}\psi) \Leftrightarrow (\psi \vee \phi\wedge\bigcirc(\phi\mathcal{U}\psi))$	
A7.	$\vdash (\phi\mathcal{S}\psi) \Leftrightarrow (\bullet\mathbf{true} \Rightarrow (\bullet\psi \vee \bullet\phi\wedge\bullet(\phi\mathcal{S}\psi)))$	
A8.	$\vdash \phi \Leftrightarrow \bigcirc\bullet\phi$	
A9.	$\vdash \bullet\mathbf{true} \Rightarrow (\phi \Leftrightarrow \bullet\bigcirc\phi)$	

The following inference rules are taken as primitive. IR1,2 and 4 are as in the future time axiomatisation; IR3 and IR4 are the past time counterparts.

Inference Rules

IR1. Modus Ponens (MP)
If $\vdash \phi$ and $\vdash \phi\Rightarrow\psi$ then $\vdash \psi$

IR2. Next Genralisation ($\bigcirc$-Gen)
If $\vdash \phi$ then $\vdash \bigcirc\phi$

IR3. Previous Generalisation ($\bullet$-Gen)
If $\vdash \phi$ then $\vdash \bullet\mathbf{true} \Rightarrow \bullet\phi$

IR4. Unless Introduction ($\mathcal{U}$-Intro)
If $\vdash \omega \Rightarrow (\psi \vee \phi\wedge\bigcirc\omega)$ then $\vdash \omega \Rightarrow (\phi\mathcal{U}\psi)$

IR5. Since Introduction ($\mathcal{S}$-Intro)
If $\vdash \omega \Rightarrow (\bullet\mathbf{true} \Rightarrow (\bullet\psi \vee \bullet\phi\wedge\bullet\omega))$ then $\vdash \omega \Rightarrow (\phi\mathcal{S}\psi)$

Derived Rules

It is useful to obtain various derived rules, to make the proof system rather more useful. We do not give a large collection here, but sample a few necessary to establish some of the properties claimed in section 3. The proofs of the future time rules are omitted.

DR0. Propositional Reasoning (PR)

If $\vdash (\phi_1 \wedge \phi_2 \wedge \ldots \wedge \phi_n) \Rightarrow \psi$ and

$\vdash \phi_1$ and $\vdash \phi_2$ and .... $\vdash \phi_n$

then $\vdash \psi$

Proof follows from the propositional tautology

$$\vdash ((\phi_1 \wedge \phi_2 \wedge \ldots \wedge \phi_n) \Rightarrow \psi) \Rightarrow (\phi_1 \Rightarrow (\phi_2 \Rightarrow (\ldots \Rightarrow (\phi_n \Rightarrow \psi)\ldots))))$$

and application of modus ponens n+1 times.

DR1. Next next Introduction ($\bigcirc\bigcirc$-Intro)

If $\vdash \phi \Rightarrow \psi$ then $\vdash \bigcirc\phi \Rightarrow \bigcirc\psi$

DR2. Previous previous Introduction ($\bullet\bullet$-Intro)

If $\vdash \phi \Rightarrow \psi$ then $\vdash \bullet\phi \Rightarrow \bullet\psi$

$\vdash \phi \Rightarrow \psi$	Assumption
$\vdash \bullet true \Rightarrow \bullet(\phi \Rightarrow \psi)$	$\bullet$-Gen
$\vdash \bullet(\phi \Rightarrow \psi) \Rightarrow (\bullet\phi \Rightarrow \bullet\psi)$	A4
$\vdash \bullet true \Rightarrow (\bullet\phi \Rightarrow \bullet\psi)$	PR, -1, -2
$\vdash \neg\bullet true \vee \neg\bullet\phi \vee \bullet\psi$	PR
$\vdash \bullet true \vee \neg\bullet\phi$	T1 (see below)
$\vdash \bullet\phi \Rightarrow \bullet\psi$	PR, -1, -2

DR3. If $\vdash \phi \Leftrightarrow \psi$ then $\vdash \bigcirc\phi \Leftrightarrow \bigcirc\psi$

DR4. If $\vdash \phi \Leftrightarrow \psi$ then $\vdash \bullet\phi \Leftrightarrow \bullet\psi$

$\vdash \phi \Leftrightarrow \psi$	Assumption
$\vdash \phi \Rightarrow \psi$	PR
$\vdash \bullet\phi \Rightarrow \bullet\psi$	$\bullet\bullet$-Intro
$\vdash \psi \Rightarrow \phi$	PR, -3
$\vdash \bullet\psi \Rightarrow \bullet\phi$	$\bullet\bullet$-Intro
$\vdash \bullet\phi \Leftrightarrow \bullet\psi$	PR, -1, -3

DR5. If $\vdash \phi \Leftrightarrow \phi'$ and $\vdash \psi \Leftrightarrow \psi'$

then $\vdash (\phi \mathcal{U} \psi) \Leftrightarrow (\phi' \mathcal{U} \psi')$

DR6. If $\vdash \phi \Leftrightarrow \phi'$ and $\vdash \psi \Leftrightarrow \psi'$

then $\vdash (\phi \mathcal{S} \psi) \Leftrightarrow (\phi' \mathcal{S} \psi')$

$\vdash \phi \Leftrightarrow \phi'$	Assumption
$\vdash \bullet\phi \Leftrightarrow \bullet\phi'$	DR4
$\vdash \bullet\phi \wedge \bullet(\phi\mathcal{S}\psi) \Leftrightarrow \bullet\phi' \wedge \bullet(\phi\mathcal{S}\psi)$	PR
$\vdash \psi \Leftrightarrow \psi'$	Assumption
$\vdash \bullet\psi \Leftrightarrow \bullet\psi'$	DR4
$\vdash (\neg\bullet true \vee \bullet\psi \vee \bullet\phi \wedge \bullet(\phi\mathcal{S}\psi)) \Leftrightarrow (\neg\bullet true \vee \bullet\psi' \vee \bullet\phi' \wedge \bullet(\phi\mathcal{S}\psi))$	PR, -1, -3

$\vdash (\phi S \psi) \Rightarrow (\neg\bullet \mathbf{true} \vee \bullet\psi' \vee \bullet\phi' \wedge \bullet(\phi S \psi))$ A7, PR, -1
$\vdash (\phi S \psi) \Rightarrow (\phi' S \psi')$ Since-Intro
$\vdash (\phi' S \psi') \Rightarrow (\phi S \psi)$ as steps -8 to -1
$\vdash (\phi S \psi) \Leftrightarrow (\phi' S \psi')$ PR, -1, -2

The above derived rules DR3 - DR6 together with the substitutvity of equivalents in PC system are sufficient to establish the substitutivity of equivalents in this bounded past time logic. The result is established by induction on the structure of the formulae. In the following, $\omega[\psi/\phi]$ denotes the formula ω with some occurrence of the subformula ϕ replaced by the formula ψ.

DR7. If $\vdash \phi \Leftrightarrow \psi$ and $\vdash \omega$ then $\vdash \omega[\psi/\phi]$

A useful extension of this derived rules is when the equivalence holds under some hypothesis.

DR8. If $\vdash \eta \Rightarrow (\phi \Leftrightarrow \psi)$ and $\vdash \omega$ then $\vdash \eta \Rightarrow \omega[\psi/\phi]$

<u>Definitions</u>

The other temporal operators, $\Box$, $\Diamond$, $\blacksquare$ and $\blacklozenge$ are now defined in terms of U and S operators.

D1. $\Box\phi \triangleq \phi U \mathbf{false}$
D2. $\Diamond\phi \triangleq \neg\Box\neg\phi$
D3. $\blacksquare\phi \triangleq \phi S \mathbf{false}$
D4. $\blacklozenge\phi \triangleq \neg\blacksquare\neg\phi$

<u>Theorems</u>

We supply two simple theorems about the beginning of time!. The first was necessary to establish the above general substitutivity rule. It does rely upon $\bigcirc$-distributivity which follows straightforwardly from the axioms and rules given.

T1. $\vdash \neg\bullet\phi \vee \bullet\mathbf{true}$

$\vdash \neg\bigcirc((\bullet\phi) S \mathbf{false}) \Leftrightarrow \neg\bigcirc(\bullet\mathbf{true} \Rightarrow (\bullet\mathbf{false} \vee \bullet\bullet\phi \wedge \bullet(\bullet\phi S \mathbf{false})))$
A7, DR3, PR
$\vdash \neg\bigcirc(\bullet\mathbf{true} \Rightarrow (\bullet\mathbf{false} \vee \bullet\bullet\phi \wedge \bullet(\bullet\phi S \mathbf{false})))$
PR, -1, A5
$\vdash \neg(\bigcirc\bullet\mathbf{true} \Rightarrow (\bigcirc\bullet\mathbf{false} \vee \bigcirc\bullet\bullet\phi \wedge \bigcirc\bullet((\bullet\phi) S \mathbf{false})))$
PR, $\bigcirc\bigcirc$-Intro, $\bigcirc$-Distr2,1
$\vdash \neg(\bullet\phi \wedge (\bullet\phi) S \mathbf{false})$ PR, -1
$\vdash \neg\bullet\phi \vee \neg((\bullet\phi) S \mathbf{false})$ PR, -1
$\vdash \neg\bullet\phi \vee \neg(\bullet\mathbf{true} \Rightarrow (\bullet\mathbf{false} \vee \bullet\bullet\phi \wedge \bullet((\bullet\phi) S \mathbf{false})))$
A7, PR, -1
$\vdash (\neg\bullet\phi \vee \bullet\mathbf{true}) \wedge (\neg\bullet\phi \vee \neg(\bullet\mathbf{false} \vee \bullet\bullet\phi \wedge \bullet((\bullet\phi) S \mathbf{false})))$
PR, -1
$\vdash \neg\bullet\phi \vee \bullet\mathbf{true}$ PR, -1

T2. $\vdash \neg @false$

$\vdash @true \Rightarrow (@false \Leftrightarrow \neg @true)$	A3, PR
$\vdash \neg @true \vee \neg @false$	PR, -1
$\vdash \neg @false$	PR, T3, -1

Appendix 2. Generalised Version of Parallel Composition

We present here, without justification, a generalised version of the parallel composition rule Rule 5.3.

$$P_i \ \mathbf{sat} \ S_i \ , \ i=1,n$$

$$\text{C1..5} \quad \vdash \blacksquare\square(beg \Rightarrow init) \wedge \blacksquare(e \Rightarrow env_a) \wedge \bigcirc\blacksquare(\underset{i}{\Delta}(c_i \Rightarrow comp_{ai})) \Rightarrow (c \Rightarrow comp_a)$$

$$\text{C1..5} \quad \vdash \bigwedge_j \left(\blacksquare\square(beg \Rightarrow init) \wedge \bigcirc\blacksquare(e \Rightarrow env_a) \wedge \bigcirc\blacksquare(\underset{i \neq j}{\Delta}(c_i \Rightarrow comp_{ai})) \Rightarrow (e_j \Rightarrow env_{aj})\right)$$

$$\text{C1..5} \quad \vdash \blacksquare\square(beg \Rightarrow init) \wedge \square\blacksquare(e \Rightarrow env_a) \wedge \square\blacksquare(\underset{i}{\Delta}(c_i \Rightarrow comp_{ai})) \wedge comp_{l_1} \wedge comp_{l_2}) \Rightarrow comp_l$$

$$\vdash init \Rightarrow \underset{i}{\Delta} init_i$$

$$P_1 || P_2 \ \mathbf{sat} \ S$$

where $S_i \triangleq \langle \Sigma, \langle e_i, c_i, r_i \rangle, env_{ai}, comp_{ai}, comp_{li}, init_i \rangle$ and
$S \triangleq \langle \Sigma, \langle e, c, r \rangle, env_a, comp_a, comp_l, init \rangle$

On the Composition and Decomposition of Assertions.

by
Glynn Winskel
University of Cambridge,
Computer Laboratory,
Corn Exchange Street,
Cambridge CB2 3QG.

0. Motivation.

Recently there has been a great deal of interest in the problem of how to compose modal assertions, in order to deduce the truth of an assertion for a composition of processes, in a parallel programming language, from the truth of certain assertions for its components *e.g.* [BKP], [St1,2].

This paper addresses that problem from a theoretical standpoint. I wish to focus on the essential issues and so have not been concerned with whether or not the programming language and assertions are "realistic". The programming language is Robin Milner's Synchronous Calculus of Communicating Systems (called SCCS—see [M3] for an introduction and motivation) and the language of assertions is a fragment of dynamic logic brought to the fore because, despite its simplicity, it is expressive enough to characterise observational equivalence, central to the work of Milner et al—see the papers [HM, M2, St1,2, P]. Colin Stirling has tackled the problem of a proof theory for SCCS and CCS with modal assertions and I have been strongly influenced by his approach in spirit, if not in detail.

It is shown how, with respect to each operation op in SCCS, every assertion has a *decomposition* which reduces the problem of proving the assertion holds of a compound process built-up using op to proving assertions about its components. These results provide the foundations of a proof system for SCCS with assertions. For lack of space the proofs are merely indicated at most; full proofs appear in a report of the Computer Laboratory, Cambridge.

While preparing this paper another approach to such proof systems parallel languages occurred to me. The approach uses a mix of the syntax of the programming language with the syntax of assertions. For lack of space, and time, and because this approach fits best with a different notation I shall write it up in another paper [W2]. That will include a full treatment of the relationship of the operational semantics here with a denotational semantics appropriate to observational equivalence.

I have intended the work of these two papers to be a pilot study, to prepare my way towards a clearer understanding of the proof theory of more general languages and assertions. I believe many of the results and connections made will carry through and be useful in a more general setting.

1. The language SCCS.

Assume a set of process variables $x \in \text{Var}$. Assume a set of elementary actions $\alpha \in Act$ forming a *finite* Abelian group $(Act, \bullet, 1, \bar{\ })$ with *composition* $\bullet$, *identity* 1 and *inverse* $\bar{\ }$.

The language of SCCS consists of the following terms

$$p ::= \mathbf{O} \mid x \mid \alpha p \mid p + p \mid p \otimes p \mid p \lceil \Lambda \mid rec\, x.p \mid rec^n x.p \mid \Omega$$

where $x \in \text{Var}$, $\alpha \in Act$, Λ is a subset of Act containing 1 and n is a positive integer.

For convenience we have extended SCCS to include numbered terms of the form $rec^n x.p$ and the completely undefined term Ω. Intuitively the label on such a term bounds the number of calls to the recursive definition. This will be useful later when we come to give proofs involving induction on this number. As a useful convention we shall regard $rec^0 x.p$ as being Ω, and sometimes use $rec^\infty x.p$ to mean $recx.p$.

We say a recursive definition $recx.p$ is *well-guarded* when p has the form αq for some term q and action $\alpha \in Act$. However we shall not assume that recursive definitions are well-guarded in general.

Write $\mathbf{P}$ for the set of SCCS terms, and $\mathbf{P}_C$ for the set *closed* of SCCS terms which we shall call *processes*. We call a numbered term a SCCS term in which *all* occurrences of *rec* are labelled by numbers, and write the set of numbered terms as $\mathbf{P}_N$ and the set of closed numbered terms as $\mathbf{P}_{CN}$.

We explain informally the behaviour of the constructs in the language SCCS. The **O** term represents the *nil* process which has stopped and refuses to perform any action. The behaviour of Ω will be the same as that of $recx.x$ which is busily doing nothing of interest. A *guarded* process αp first performs the action α to become the process p. A *sum* $p+q$ behaves like p or q. Which branch of a sum is followed will often be determined by the context and what actions the process is restricted to; only in the case when both component processes p and q are able to perform an identity action 1 can the process $p+q$ always choose autonomously, no matter what the context, to behave like p or q. A *product* process $p \otimes q$ behaves like p and q set in parallel but in such a way that they perform their actions synchronously, in "lock-step", together performing the $\bullet$-product of their respective actions. (To avoid confusion later, we have chosen a notation different from Milner's, using $\otimes$ instead of $\times$.) The *restriction* $p\lceil \Lambda$ behaves like the process p but with its actions restricted to lie in the set Λ. Restriction is a surprisingly powerful construction; it is what determines what kind of communications are allowed between processes, and without it two processes in parallel would behave in a manner completely independent of eachother. We present the formal definition of behaviour in the next section.

Write $\mathrm{FV}(p)$ for the set of free variables of a term p.

A *substitution* is a map $\sigma : \mathrm{Var} \to \mathbf{P}$ assigning SCCS terms to variables. Given SCCS term p and a substitution σ the term $p[\sigma]$ is the result of substituting $\sigma(x)$ for each free occurrence of x in p—we assume changes are made in the naming of bound variables to avoid the binding of free variables in the substituted terms. We use $[p_0/x_1, \cdots, p_m/x_m, \cdots]$ as an abbreviation for the substitution which replaces free occurrences of the variables x_m by the terms p_m while leaving the other free variables the same.

Let p be a term. A *valuation* is a substitution $\vartheta : \mathrm{Var} \to \mathbf{P}_C$ which assigns a *closed* SCCS term to each variable. So, of course, $p[\vartheta]$ is a closed SCCS term.

2. The behaviour of SCCS.

Following Milner [M1,2,3], the behaviour of a process is represented as a labelled transition system. Its states are processes and so the transition system can be given in a syntax-directed way by defining inductively those transitions which are possible from each process term.

2.1 Definition.

Define the labelled transition relation $\xrightarrow{\alpha}$ between closed SCCS terms to be the least relation closed under the following rules:

$$\alpha p \xrightarrow{\alpha} p$$

$$\frac{p \xrightarrow{\alpha} p'}{p+q \xrightarrow{\alpha} p'} \qquad \frac{q \xrightarrow{\alpha} q'}{p+q \xrightarrow{\alpha} q'}$$

$$\frac{p \xrightarrow{\alpha} p' \quad q \xrightarrow{\beta} q'}{p \otimes q \xrightarrow{\alpha \bullet \beta} p' \otimes q'}$$

$$\frac{p \xrightarrow{\lambda} q}{p\lceil\Lambda \xrightarrow{\lambda} q\lceil\Lambda} \text{ if } \lambda \in \Lambda$$

$$\frac{p[recx.p/x] \xrightarrow{\alpha} q}{recx.p \xrightarrow{\alpha} q} \qquad \frac{p[rec^n x.p/x] \xrightarrow{\alpha} q}{rec^{n+1} x.p \xrightarrow{\alpha} q}$$

Notice there are no rules for **O** or Ω because we do not wish there to be any transitions from such terms.

A process *diverges* if it can be forever busy performing internal events. In the case of SCCS this can only arise through a process unwinding its recursive definition continually. A diverging process has a somewhat dubious status. In the absence of communication with the environment, it never settles down into a stable state, or settles on the full set of actions it is prepared to do. Viewed behaviourally, from the outside so to speak, it continues to "click and whir" and it never becomes clear whether an action not accepted now will continue to not be accepted later. Mathematically it is the complementary notion of *convergence* which has the more basic definition, by induction.

2.2 Definition. For $n \in \omega$, define the predicate $\downarrow$ on $\mathbf{P}_C$ to be the least predicate such that

$$\mathbf{O}\downarrow, \quad \alpha p\downarrow,$$
$$p\downarrow \;\&\; q\downarrow \Rightarrow (p+q)\downarrow,$$
$$p\downarrow \;\&\; q\downarrow \Rightarrow (p\otimes q)\downarrow,$$
$$p\downarrow \Rightarrow (p\lceil A)\downarrow,$$
$$(p[recx.p/x])\downarrow \Rightarrow (recx.p)\downarrow,$$
$$(p[rec^l x.p/x])\downarrow \Rightarrow (rec^{l+1} x.p)\downarrow .$$

where p and q are closed SCCS terms and l is an non-negative integer. Say a closed SCCS term p is *convergent* iff $p\downarrow$. Say a closed term p *diverges*, and write $p\uparrow$, when p does not converge.

Intuitively a divergent term is one whose transitions are not completely specified by a finite stage in the recursion. If all recursions were assumed to be well-guarded then all closed terms but Ω would be convergent.

3. Approximation and numbered term induction.

The number attached to occurrences of *rec* specifies how many times the recursive definition can be unwound when determining the transition system associated with a term. Roughly, the larger the numbers the larger the transition system associated with the term. There corresponds an approximation relation between terms which we write as $\leq$.

3.1 Definition. Define $\leq$ to be the least binary relation on **P** such that

$$\Omega \leq p, \qquad p \leq p$$
$$p \leq q \Rightarrow \alpha p \leq \alpha q$$
$$p \leq p' \;\&\; q \leq q' \Rightarrow p + q \leq p' + q'$$
$$p \leq p' \;\&\; q \leq q' \Rightarrow p \otimes q \leq p' \otimes q'$$
$$p \leq q \Rightarrow p\lceil A \leq q\lceil A$$
$$p \leq q \;\&\; m \leq n \Rightarrow rec^m x.p \;\leq\; rec^n x.q$$
$$p \leq q \Rightarrow rec^n x.p \;\leq\; recx.q.$$

3.2 Lemma. *The relation $\leq$ is a partial order on* **P** *such that*

$$|\{q \in \mathbf{P} \mid q \leq p\}| \leq \infty$$

for all $p \in \mathbf{P}_N$. It has as least element Ω, and satisfies the property that any subset X of **P** *which is bounded above by an element of* **P** *has a least upper bound $\bigsqcup X$ in* **P**. *A bounded finite set of (closed) numbered terms has as least upper bound a (closed) numbered term.*

The order $\leq$ on terms **P** respects the language of SCCS, as expressed in the following lemma.

3.3 Lemma. *Let σ and σ' be substitutions in the relation $\sigma \leq \sigma' \Leftrightarrow_{def} \forall x \in Var.\ \sigma[x] \leq \sigma'[x]$. Let p, q be terms in the relation $p \leq q$. Then $p[\sigma] \leq q[\sigma']$.*

Proof. By structural induction on q. ∎

Many proofs which can be tackled using structural induction together with induction on the numbering on terms can be handled more conveniently by combining the subterm relation with the approximation relation $\leq$. This produces a new well-founded ordering $\preceq$ on which to do the induction "all in one go".

3.4 Definition.
Let p and q be numbered terms, in $\mathbf{P}_N$. Define

$$p \preceq q \Leftrightarrow p \leq q' \text{ for some subterm } q' \text{ of } q.$$

Define $p \prec q \Leftrightarrow p \preceq q\ \&\ p \neq q$.

3.5 Lemma. *The relation $\preceq$ is a partial order on $\mathbf{P}_N$ such that*

$$|\{q \in \mathbf{P}_N \mid q \preceq p\}| \leq \infty$$

for all $p \in \mathbf{P}_N$.

Consequently we can do well-founded induction on $\preceq$:

3.6 Proposition. *(Numbered term induction)*
Let Q be a predicate on $\mathbf{P}$. Then $\forall p \in \mathbf{P}.\ Q(p)$ iff

$$\forall p \in \mathbf{P}((\forall q \prec p.\ Q(q)) \Rightarrow Q(p)).$$

Most of our proofs using numbered term induction will follow a similar pattern. We would like to prove that a predicate R holds for all closed numbered terms $\mathbf{P}_{CN}$, but in order to do so we extend the predicate R to a predicate R_o on all open numbered terms in the following way:

$$R_o(p) \Leftrightarrow_{def} \forall \text{ valuations } \vartheta.\ (\forall x \in \mathbf{FV}(p).\ R(\vartheta[\![x]\!])) \Rightarrow R(p[\vartheta])$$

for open numbered terms p. If it can be shown that $R_o(p)$ holds for all numbered terms, then in particular, by taking ϑ to be any valuation, we have that $R(p)$ holds for all closed terms p.

As an example one can show that the the labelled transition relation $\xrightarrow{a}$ is Noetherian on closed numbered terms, *i.e.* there are no infinite chains

$$p_0 \xrightarrow{\alpha_0} p_1 \xrightarrow{\alpha_1} \cdots \xrightarrow{\alpha_{n-1}} p_n \xrightarrow{\alpha_n} \cdots$$

with $p_0, p_1, \ldots, p_n, \ldots$ in $\mathbf{P}_{CN}$.

3.7 Theorem. *The relation $\xrightarrow{a}$ is Noetherian on $\mathbf{P}_{CN}$.*

Proof.

Let N be the predicate on closed numbered terms given by

$$N(p) \text{ iff there are no infinite chains } p_0 \xrightarrow{\alpha_0} p_1 \xrightarrow{\alpha_1} \cdots \xrightarrow{\alpha_{n-1}} p_n \xrightarrow{\alpha_n} \cdots$$

with $p = p_0, p_1, \ldots, p_n, \ldots$ in $\mathbf{P}_{CN}$. Extend N to all numbered terms by defining

$$N_0(q) \Leftrightarrow \forall \text{ valuations } \vartheta(\forall x \in \mathbf{FV}(p).\ N(\vartheta[\![x]\!])) \Rightarrow N(q[\vartheta]).$$

and prove $N_0(q)$ holds for all numbered terms q by numbered term induction on q. ∎

4. The assertion language.

Hennessy and Milner defined an equivalence relation between processes called *observational equivalence* in [HM, M1]. For our language of SCCS, two processes are observationally equivalent iff whenever one can do an action to become a process then so can the other do the same action to become an equivalent process. They found an alternative characterisation so that processes were observationally equivalent iff they satisfied the same assertions in a simple language of modal assertions [HM]. However there are inadequacies with this treatment of processes because it does not take proper account of divergence. So Milner, in [M2], generalised the definition of observational equivalence and the definition of a process satisfying a modal assertion in order to cope with divergence. (See [HP] for a closely related but different extension of observational equivalence to diverging processes.) In this way Milner extended the result he had obtained with Hennessy, so that in SCCS, for example, two processes are observationally equivalent iff they satisfy the same assertions in the modal language of Hennessy and Milner. In future, "observational equivalence" shall refer to the more refined equivalence of [M2]. Following [P, St1,2] we have simplified the modal language of Hennessy and Milner a little.

4.1 Definition.
The *assertion language* consists of simple modal expressions built up according to:

$$A ::= true \mid false \mid \bigwedge_{i\in I} A_i \mid \bigvee_{i\in I} A_i \mid \langle\alpha\rangle A \mid [\alpha]A$$

where I is a finite indexing set and $\alpha \in Act$.

We shall call elements of this language *assertions*, and write the set of assertions as **Assn**.

By convention we understand $\bigwedge_{i\in I} A_i$ to be *true* and $\bigvee_{i\in I} A_i$ to be *false* when the indexing set I is null. When the indexing set is $I = \{0,1\}$ we can write $\bigwedge_{i\in I} A_i$ as $A_0 \wedge A_1$, and $\bigvee_{i\in I} A_i$ as $A_0 \vee A_1$.

The meaning of an assertions is given by specifying the subset $\Pi[\![A]\!]$ of SCCS processes $\mathbf{P}_C$ which satisfy A:

4.2 Definition. Define

$$\begin{aligned}
\Pi[\![true]\!] &= \mathbf{P}_C \\
\Pi[\![false]\!] &= \emptyset \\
\Pi[\![\bigwedge_{i\in I} A_i]\!] &= \bigcap_{i\in I} \Pi[\![A_i]\!] \\
\Pi[\![\bigvee_{i\in I} A_i]\!] &= \bigcup_{i\in I} \Pi[\![A_i]\!] \\
\Pi[\![\langle\alpha\rangle A]\!] &= \{p \in \mathbf{P}_C \mid \exists q. p \xrightarrow{\alpha} q \ \&\ q \in \Pi[\![A]\!]\} \\
\Pi[\![[\alpha]A]\!] &= \{p \in \mathbf{P}_C \mid p\downarrow \ \&\ \forall q. p \xrightarrow{\alpha} q \Rightarrow q \in \Pi[\![A]\!]\}
\end{aligned}$$

Write $\models p{:}A \Leftrightarrow_{def} p \in \Pi[\![A]\!]$, where p is a SCCS process and A is an assertion, and say *p satisfies A*.

We call an element $p{:}A$ a *correctness assertion*, for p an SCCS term and A an assertion.

So $\models p{:}A$ means the correctness assertion $p{:}A$ is true. Clearly $\models p{:}\langle\alpha\rangle A$ means the process p can do an α-action to become a process satisfying A, and $\models p{:}[\alpha]false$ means the process p refuses to do an α-action. The latter kind of properties are important for detecting deadlock. Notice that $\not\models \Omega{:}[\alpha]true$ and $\not\models \Omega{:}[\alpha]false$ because we insist diverging processes, like Ω, cannot satisfy any assertion of the form $[\alpha]A$.

4.3 Proposition. *Let $p \in \mathbf{P}_C$. Then $p\downarrow \Leftrightarrow \models p{:}[\alpha]true$, for any action α.*

Because we insist that a process satisfying a modal assertion $[\alpha]A$ must converge, satisfaction will be effective; if a process p in $\mathbf{P}_C$ satisfies an assertion A then it can be approximated by a numbered version p' which also satisfies the assertion. To show this we must first see how the transition system associated with a term $p' \leq p$ approximates, and simulates, the transition system associated with p.

4.4 Lemma. *For SCCS processes*

(*i*) For $p, p', q' \in \mathbf{P}_C$
$p' \xrightarrow{\alpha} q' \ \&\ p' \leq p \Rightarrow \exists q.\, q' \leq q \ \&\ p \xrightarrow{\alpha} q.$

(*ii*) For $p, q \in \mathbf{P}_C, q_0 \in \mathbf{P}_{CN}$
$p \xrightarrow{\alpha} q \ \&\ q_0 \leq q \Rightarrow \exists p', q' \in \mathbf{P}_{CN}.\, p' \leq p \ \&\ p' \xrightarrow{\alpha} q' \ \&\ q_0 \leq q'.$

(*iii*) For $p, p' \in \mathbf{P}_C$
$p'\downarrow \ \&\ p' \leq p \Rightarrow p\downarrow \ \&\ (\forall q.\, p \xrightarrow{\alpha} q \Rightarrow \exists q' \leq q.\, p' \xrightarrow{\alpha} q').$

(*iv*) For $p \in \mathbf{P}_C, Y \subseteq \mathbf{P}_{CN}$

$$\begin{aligned} & p\downarrow \ \&\ (\forall q.\, p \xrightarrow{\alpha} q \Rightarrow \exists q_0 \in Y.\, q_0 \leq q) \\ \Rightarrow\ & \exists p' \in \mathbf{P}_{CN}.\, p' \leq p \ \& \\ & p'\downarrow \ \&\ (\forall q.\, p' \xrightarrow{\alpha} q \Rightarrow \exists q_0 \in Y.\, q_0 \leq q). \end{aligned}$$

Proof. The proofs follow by induction on the inductive construction of $\xrightarrow{\alpha}$ and $\downarrow$. ∎

Note that part (iv) above specialises to the result

$$p\downarrow \Rightarrow \exists p' \in \mathbf{P}_{CN}.\, p' \leq p \ \&\ p'\downarrow$$

when we take $Y = \{\Omega\}$.

4.5 Theorem. *Let $p \in \mathbf{P}_C$. Then*

$$\models p{:}A \Leftrightarrow \exists p' \in \mathbf{P}_{CN}.\, p' \leq p \ \&\ \models p'{:}A.$$

Proof. The proof is by structural induction on A using the above lemma parts (i), (ii) for the modality $\langle\alpha\rangle$ and (iii), (iv) for the modality $[\alpha]$. ∎

A topology on processes: There is a natural topology on $\mathbf{P}_C$ which is the Scott–topology, seen in a slightly more general setting than usual.

4.6 Proposition. *The family of sets of the form $\{p \in \mathbf{P}_C \mid q \leq p\}$ for q a closed numbered term are the basis of a topology on $\mathbf{P}_C$. So the open sets have the form*

$$U = \{p \in \mathbf{P}_C \mid \exists p_0 \in X.\, p_0 \leq p\}$$

for a subset X of numbered terms.

The open sets of $\mathbf{P}_C$ are those subsets $U \subseteq \mathbf{P}_C$ which are

(*i*) $\forall p, q.\, p \geq q \in U \Rightarrow p \in U,$
(*ii*) $\forall$ directed $S \subseteq \mathbf{P}_C.\, \bigsqcup S \in U \Rightarrow \exists p \in S.\, p \in U.$

Then theorem 4.4 says each assertion determines an open set of $\mathbf{P}_C$ *i.e.* $\Pi[\![A]\!]$ is open for each assertion A. In fact 4.4 can be made more general, and more useful if we were to extend our present language of assertions.

4.7 Lemma. *Let $\alpha \in Act$. If U is an open set in the topology on processes then so are the sets*

$$\langle\alpha\rangle U =_{def} \{p \in \mathbf{P}_C \mid \exists q \in U.\, q \xrightarrow{\alpha} p\} \quad \text{and}$$
$$[\alpha]U =_{def} \{p \in \mathbf{P}_C \mid p\downarrow \ \&\ \forall q.\, p \xrightarrow{\alpha} q \Rightarrow q \in U\}.$$

Proof. The proof uses lemma 4.4 in the same way as the proof of theorem 4.4. ∎

This topological view is in line with Dana Scott's development of the theory of domains from neighbourhood systems [S1] and with the ideas of Mike Smyth in [Sm], where he proposes that computational properties of a topological space be identified with effective open sets. In the approach to domains using neighbourhood systems, to know more information about a process is to know a smaller neighbourhood in which it is contained. Similar topological ideas have been applied by Gordon Plotkin in [P] to extend the language of assertions by intuitionistic negation and implication; their interpretation are those standard for topological models of intuitionistic logic, so in this extension of **Assn**, for our toplogy, one could take $\Pi[\![A \supset B]\!] = ((\mathbf{P}_C \setminus \Pi[\![A]\!]) \cup \Pi[\![B]\!])^o$ where X^o is the topological interior of the set X (Plotkin's topology is not that here however). One advantage of intuitionistic logic over classical logic is that satisfaction is still effective even for this extended set of assertions. We shall say more on denotational semantics in [W2].

A word on equivalences on programs: The work of Milner et al (see *e.g.* [M1]) shows how much can be done with the observational and bisimulation equivalence, those equivalences induced by the assertions; recall we can take two processes to be equivalent iff they satisfy the same assertions. This argues that the assertions are sufficiently rich to capture a great many of the properties of interest. This should not seem so surprising. Remember a process denotes the set of assertions it satisfies so is essentially modelled as an (infinite) conjunction of these assertions; only for a finite process would a single assertion in **Assn** capture its full behaviour.

Although the assertions may make it possible to distinguish all the processes one could wish, this is not to say the logic is as expressive as one would like from all points of view. Clearly it is rather primitive. For example one would like the ability to specify infinite behaviours by finite assertions.

Quite possibly there are other properties of interest to which the language of assertions is blind. However it is interesting that two other well-known notions of equivalence can be induced by taking fragments of the assertion language **Assn**. They are *trace equivalence* and *failure-set equivalence.* Strictly speaking the failure-set equivalence has not been defined on SCCS but the definition that follows has been based on the work of [HBR] modified to take proper account of divergence. The use of traces and their associated equivalence is widespread, see *e.g.* [H] and [HdeN]. As far as these two equivalences are concerned **Assn** is certainly expressive enough. The assertions which suffice to induce the *trace-equivalence* take the form

$$\langle \alpha_0 \rangle \langle \alpha_1 \rangle \cdots \langle \alpha_{j-1} \rangle \mathit{true},$$

while the assertions for *failure-set-equivalence* take the form

$$\langle \alpha_0 \rangle \langle \alpha_1 \rangle \cdots \langle \alpha_{j-1} \rangle \bigwedge_{\beta \in I} [\beta] \mathit{false}).$$

5. The decomposition of assertions.

We are interested in how the goal of proving an assertion holds of a process reduces to the subgoals of proving assertions about its subprocesses, and in the converse problem, of how assertions about subprocesses combine to yield assertions about the compound process. It is clear for example that an assertion $\langle \alpha \rangle A$ holds of a process αp iff A holds of p. Similarly $[\alpha]A$ holds of a process $p + q$ iff $[\alpha]A$ holds of both components p and q. However $\models p + q : \langle \alpha \rangle A$ iff $\models p : \langle \alpha \rangle A$ or $\models q : \langle \alpha \rangle A$; there is not a unique subgoal. Similarly ther are many possible ways in which $\models p \otimes q : \langle \alpha \rangle \mathit{true}$; this holds whenever $\models p : \langle \beta \rangle \mathit{true}$ and $\models q : \langle \gamma \rangle \mathit{true}$ with $\beta \bullet \gamma = \alpha$.

For each unary operation op of SCCS we show how for an assertion A there is an assertion $D_{op}[\![A]\!]$ so that

$$\models \mathrm{op}(p) : A \Leftrightarrow \models p : D_{op}[\![A]\!].$$

For each binary operation op of SCCS we show how for an assertion A there is a finite set of pairs of assertions $\mathcal{D}_{op}[\![A]\!]$ so that

$$\models p \otimes q : A \quad \text{iff} \quad \exists (B,C) \in \mathcal{D}_{op}[\![A]\!].\ \models p : B \ \&\ \models q : C.$$

Thus we see how, with respect to each operation op in SCCS, every assertion has a *decomposition* which reduces the problem of proving the assertion holds of a compound process built-up using op to proving assertions about its components. These results provide the foundations of our proof systems for SCCS with assertions **Assn**, both here and in [W2].

The guarded-decomposition of assertions:

5.1 Definition. Let $\alpha \in Act$. Define the assertion $\mathcal{D}_\alpha[\![A]\!]$, for an assertion A, by the structural induction:

$$\mathcal{D}_\alpha[\![true]\!] = true$$
$$\mathcal{D}_\alpha[\![false]\!] = false$$
$$\mathcal{D}_\alpha[\![\bigwedge_{i \in I} A_i]\!] = \bigwedge_{i \in I} \mathcal{D}_\alpha[\![A_i]\!]$$
$$\mathcal{D}_\alpha[\![\bigvee_{i \in I} A_i]\!] = \bigvee_{i \in I} \mathcal{D}_\alpha[\![A_i]\!]$$
$$\mathcal{D}_\alpha[\![\langle\beta\rangle A]\!] = \begin{cases} A & \text{if } \beta = \alpha \\ false & \text{if } \alpha \neq \alpha \end{cases}$$
$$\mathcal{D}_\alpha[\![[\beta]A]\!] = \begin{cases} A & \text{if } \beta = \alpha \\ true & \text{if } \beta \neq \alpha. \end{cases}$$

The following result is essentially contained in [St1,2].

5.2 Theorem. *Let $\alpha \in Act$. Let A be an assertion.*

$$\forall p \in \mathbf{P}_C.\ \models \alpha p : A \Leftrightarrow \models p : \mathcal{D}_\alpha[\![A]\!].$$

Proof. By structural induction on A. ∎

The sum-decomposition of assertions:

5.3 Definition. Define $\mathcal{D}_+[\![A]\!]$ by structural induction on the assertion A:

$$\mathcal{D}_+[\![true]\!] = \{(true, true)\}$$
$$\mathcal{D}_+[\![false]\!] = \{(true, false), (false, true)\}$$
$$\mathcal{D}_+[\![\bigwedge_{i \in I} A_i]\!] = \{(\bigwedge_{i \in I} A_{i0}, \bigwedge_{i \in I} A_{i1}) \mid \forall i \in I.(A_{i0}, A_{i1}) \in \mathcal{D}_+[\![A_i]\!])\}$$
$$\mathcal{D}_+[\![\bigvee_{i \in I} A_i]\!] = \bigcup_{i \in I} \mathcal{D}_+[\![A_i]\!]$$
$$\mathcal{D}_+[\![\langle\alpha\rangle A]\!] = \{(\langle\alpha\rangle A, true), (true, \langle\alpha\rangle A)\}$$
$$\mathcal{D}_+[\![[\alpha]A]\!] = \{([\alpha]A, [\alpha]A)\}.$$

The following result is essentially contained in [St1,2].

5.4 Theorem. *For all p and q in $\mathbf{P}_C$*

$$\models p + q : A \Leftrightarrow \exists (B,C) \in \mathcal{D}_+[\![A]\!].\ \models p : B \ \&\ \models q : C.$$

Proof. By structural induction on A. ∎

The parallel decomposition of assertions: The problem of decomposition for $\otimes$ is a little more difficult.

5.5 Definition. Define $\mathcal{D}_\otimes[\![A]\!]$ by structural induction on the assertion A:

$$\mathcal{D}_\otimes[\![true]\!] = \{(true, true)\}$$
$$\mathcal{D}_\otimes[\![false]\!] = \{(true, false), (false, true)\}$$
$$\mathcal{D}_\otimes[\![\bigwedge_{i\in I} A_i]\!] = \{(\bigwedge_{i\in I} A_{i0}, \bigwedge_{i\in I} A_{i1}) \mid \forall i \in I.(A_{i0}, A_{i1}) \in \mathcal{D}_\otimes[\![A_i]\!]\}$$
$$\mathcal{D}_\otimes[\![\bigvee_{i\in I} A_i]\!] = \bigcup_{i\in I} \mathcal{D}_\otimes[\![A_i]\!]$$
$$\mathcal{D}_\otimes[\![\langle\alpha\rangle A]\!] = \{(\langle\beta\rangle B, \langle\gamma\rangle C) \mid \beta \bullet \gamma = \alpha \ \& \ (B, C) \in \mathcal{D}_\otimes[\![A]\!]\}$$
$$\mathcal{D}_\otimes[\![[\alpha]A]\!] = \text{ the set of pairs}$$
$$(\bigwedge_{\beta\in Act} [\beta] \bigvee_{i\in I_\beta} \bigwedge_{j\in J_{\alpha\bullet\overline{\beta}}} B_{\beta ij}, \quad \bigwedge_{\gamma\in Act} [\gamma] \bigvee_{j\in J_\gamma} \bigwedge_{i\in I_{\alpha\bullet\overline{\gamma}}} C_{\gamma ij})$$
$$\text{such that}$$
$$\beta \bullet \gamma = \alpha \Rightarrow (B_{\beta ij}, C_{\gamma ij}) \in \mathcal{D}_\otimes[\![A]\!].$$

5.6 Theorem. *For all p and q in $\mathbf{P}_C$*

$$\models p \otimes q : A \Leftrightarrow \exists (B, C) \in \mathcal{D}_\otimes[\![A]\!]. \ \models p : B \ \& \models q : C.$$

Proof. By structural induction on A. ∎

The restriction-decomposition of assertions: We can associate with any assertion A an *assertion* $\mathcal{D}_{\lceil\Lambda}[\![A]\!]$ so that A is satisfied by $p\lceil\Lambda$ iff $\mathcal{D}_{\lceil\Lambda}[\![A]\!]$ is satisfied by p.

5.7 Definition. Let Λ be a subset of Act containing 1. Define $\mathcal{D}_{\lceil\Lambda}[\![A]\!]$, for an assertion A, by the structural induction:

$$\mathcal{D}_{\lceil\Lambda}[\![true]\!] = true$$
$$\mathcal{D}_{\lceil\Lambda}[\![false]\!] = false$$
$$\mathcal{D}_{\lceil\Lambda}[\![\bigwedge_{i\in I} A_i]\!] = \bigwedge_{i\in I} \mathcal{D}_{\lceil\Lambda}[\![A_i]\!]$$
$$\mathcal{D}_{\lceil\Lambda}[\![\bigvee_{i\in I} A_i]\!] = \bigvee_{i\in I} \mathcal{D}_{\lceil\Lambda}[\![A_i]\!]$$
$$\mathcal{D}_{\lceil\Lambda}[\![\langle\alpha\rangle A]\!] = \begin{cases} \langle\alpha\rangle \mathcal{D}_{\lceil\Lambda}[\![A]\!] & \text{if } \alpha \in \Lambda \\ false & \text{if } \alpha \notin \Lambda \end{cases}$$
$$\mathcal{D}_{\lceil\Lambda}[\![[\alpha]A]\!] = \begin{cases} [\alpha] \mathcal{D}_{\lceil\Lambda}[\![A]\!] & \text{if } \alpha \in \Lambda \\ [\alpha] true & \text{if } \alpha \notin \Lambda. \end{cases}$$

One clause of the above definition may be puzzling. Why do we take $\mathcal{D}_{\lceil\Lambda}[\![[\alpha]A]\!] = [\alpha]true$ if $\alpha \notin \Lambda$ rather than taking it to be simply the assertion *true*? The answer: because of divergence. For example, because Ω diverges, $\not\models \Omega\lceil\Lambda : [\alpha]A$ while $\models \Omega : true$.

5.8 Theorem. *Let $p \in \mathbf{P}_C$ and A be an assertion. Then*

$$\models p\lceil\Lambda : A \Leftrightarrow \models p : \mathcal{D}_{\lceil\Lambda}[\![A]\!].$$

Proof. By structural induction on A. ∎

6. Proof rules.

We present a style of proof rules which makes essential use of process variables. By using variables we can capture the decomposition results of section 5 in the proof system. See [W2] for another way.

There is an obvious generalisation of the truth predicate $\models$ to a relation between correctness assertions.

6.1 Definition. Let X be a finite subset of correctness assertions and let $p:A$ be a correctness assertion. Define $X \models p:A$ iff

$$\forall \text{ valuations } \vartheta.\ (\forall (q:B) \in X.\ \models q[\vartheta]:B) \Rightarrow \models p[\vartheta]:A.$$

In other words, $X \models p:A$ iff all the valuations which make every correctness assertions in X true also make the correctness assertion $p:A$ true.

We present a proof system for *sequents* of the form $X \vdash p:A$ where X is a finite set of correctness assertions, $p:A$ is a correctness assertion. It will be sound in the sense that

$$X \vdash p:A \Rightarrow X \models p:A,$$

and satisfy a form of completeness.

6.2 Notation. Let X be a set of correctness assertions. Let σ be a substitution for X. By $X[\sigma]$ we mean the set of correctness assertions $\{p[\sigma]:A \mid p:A \in X\}$.

When X is a set of correctness assertions $\{p_0:A_0,\cdots,p_{n-1}:A_{n-1}\}$ we sometimes write $X \models p:A$ as

$$p_0:A_0,\cdots,p_{n-1}:A_{n-1} \models p:A$$

and $X \vdash p:A$ as

$$p_0:A_0,\cdots,p_{n-1}:A_{n-1} \vdash p:A$$

omitting the set-brackets and, for example, abbreviate $\emptyset \vdash p:A$ to $\vdash p:A$.

6.3 Definition. Proof rules.

In the following let $X, Y, \cdots$ be a finite set of correctness assertions, $p, q, \cdots$ be SCCS terms, $x, y, \cdots$ process variables, and $A, B, \cdots$ assertions. Let $\vdash$ be the least relation between correctness assertions closed under the following rules:

Structural rules

refl. rule $\quad X \vdash p:A \quad$ if X contains $p:A$

tran. rule
$$\frac{\{X \vdash p:A \mid (p:A) \in Y\},\ Y \vdash q:B}{X \vdash q:B}$$

subs. rule
$$\frac{X \vdash p:A}{X[\sigma] \vdash p[\sigma]:A}$$

Logical rules

true r. rule $\quad \vdash x:\mathit{true}$

false l. rule $\quad x:\mathit{false} \vdash p:A \quad$ for any term p and assertion A

$\bigwedge$*r.* rule $\quad \{x:A_i \mid i \in I\} \vdash x:\bigwedge_{i\in I} A_i$

$\bigwedge$*l.* rule $\quad x:\bigwedge_{i\in I} A_i \vdash x:A_i \quad$ for any $i \in I$

$\bigvee$*r.* rule $\quad x:A_i \vdash x:\bigvee_{i\in I} A_i$

$\bigvee$*l.* rule
$$\frac{\{X,\ p:A_i \vdash q:B \mid i \in I\}}{X,\ p:\bigvee_{i\in I} A_i \vdash q:B}$$

Correctness rules

$\mathbf{O}$–$[\alpha]$ rule	$\vdash \mathbf{O}:[\alpha]A$
α–$\langle\alpha\rangle$ rule	$x:A \vdash \alpha x:\langle\alpha\rangle A$
α–$[\alpha]$ rule	$x:A \vdash \alpha x:[\alpha]A$
α–$[\beta]$ rule	$\vdash \alpha x:[\beta]A$ if $\beta \neq \alpha$
$+$–$\langle\alpha\rangle$ rule	$x:\langle\alpha\rangle A \vdash x+y:\langle\alpha\rangle A$ $y:\langle\alpha\rangle A \vdash x+y:\langle\alpha\rangle A$
$+$–$[\alpha]$ rule	$x:[\alpha]A, y:[\alpha]A \vdash x+y:[\alpha]A$
$\otimes$–$\langle\alpha\rangle$ rule	$\dfrac{x:B,\ y:C \vdash x\otimes y:A}{x:\langle\beta\rangle B,\ y:\langle\gamma\rangle C \vdash x\otimes y:\langle\alpha\rangle A}$ provided $\beta \bullet \gamma = \alpha$
$\otimes$–$[\alpha]$ rule	$\dfrac{\{x:B_\beta,\ y:C_\gamma \vdash x\otimes y:A \mid \beta\bullet\gamma=\alpha\}}{x:\bigwedge_{\beta\in Act}[\beta]B_\beta,\ y:\bigwedge_{\gamma\in Act}[\gamma]C_\gamma \vdash x\otimes y:[\alpha]A}$
$\lceil\Lambda$–$\langle\lambda\rangle$ rule	$\dfrac{x:A \vdash x\lceil\Lambda:B}{y:\langle\lambda\rangle A \vdash y\lceil\Lambda:\langle\lambda\rangle B}$ if $\lambda\in\Lambda$
$\lceil\Lambda$–$[\lambda]$ rule	$\dfrac{x:A \vdash x\lceil\Lambda:B}{y:[\lambda]A \vdash y\lceil\Lambda:[\lambda]B}$ if $\lambda\in\Lambda$
$\lceil\Lambda$–$[\mu]$ rule	$x:[\mu]true \vdash x\lceil\Lambda:[\mu]A$ if $\mu\notin\Lambda$
rec. rule	$p[recx.p/x]:A \vdash recx.p:A$ $p[rec^n x.p/x]:A \vdash rec^{n+1}x.p:A$ for $n\in\omega$

6.4 Theorem. *(Soundness) Let X be a finite set of correctness assertions and $p:A$ be a correctness assertion. Then $X \vdash p:A \Rightarrow X \models p:A$.*

Proof. As usual one checks the soundness of each rule. ∎

The following lemmas, 6.6–6.10, show how the decomposition rules of section 5 are captured in the proof system. The results 6.6–6.8 are essentially contained in [St1].

6.5 Lemma. *If $\models \Omega:A$ then $\vdash \Omega:A$. Moreover $\vdash \Omega:A \Leftrightarrow\ \vdash x:A$ for any variable x.*

Proof. By structural induction on A using the structural rules and logical rules only which treat Ω and x alike. ∎

6.6 Lemma. *If $\models \mathbf{O}:A$ then $\vdash \mathbf{O}:A$.*

Proof. By structural induction on A using the structural rules, logical rules and $\mathbf{O}$–$[\alpha]$ rule only. ∎

6.7 Lemma. *For an assertion A, $x:\mathcal{D}_\alpha[\![A]\!] \vdash \alpha x:A$*

Proof. This is proved by structural induction on A using the structural and logical rules and the α–$\langle\alpha\rangle$ rule, α–$[\alpha]$ rule and α–$[\beta]$ rule. ∎

6.8 Lemma. *If $(B,C)\in\mathcal{D}_+[\![A]\!]$ then $x:B, y:C \vdash x+y:A$.*

Proof. This is proved by structural induction on A using the structural and logical rules and the +–$\langle\alpha\rangle$ rule and +–$[\alpha]$ rule . ∎

6.9 Lemma. *If* $(B,C) \in \mathcal{D}_{\otimes}[\![A]\!]$ *then* $x{:}B, y{:}C \vdash x \otimes y{:}A$.

Proof. By structural induction on A using all the structural and logical rules and the rules for $\otimes$. ∎

6.10 Lemma. *For an assertion* A, $x{:}\mathcal{D}_{\lceil\Lambda}[\![A]\!] \vdash x\lceil\Lambda{:}A$.

Proof. By structural induction on A using all the structural and logical rules with the rules for $\lceil\Lambda$. ∎

6.11 Theorem. *(Completeness)*
Let p *be SCCS term and* A *an assertion. Then* $\models p{:}A \Leftrightarrow \vdash p{:}A$.

Proof.

" $\Leftarrow$" By soundness.

" $\Rightarrow$"

Let Q be the predicate on closed numbered terms given by

$$Q(p) \Leftrightarrow_{def} \forall A.\ (\models p{:}A \Rightarrow \forall p' \geq p.\ \vdash p'{:}A).$$

Extend Q to all numbered terms by taking

$$Q_0(p) \Leftrightarrow_{def} (\forall \vartheta : \text{Var} \to \mathbf{P}_{CN}.\ (\forall x \in \mathbf{FV}(p).\ Q(\vartheta[\![x]\!])) \Rightarrow Q(p[\vartheta])).$$

Then show by numbered term induction using lemmas 6.5—6.10 that Q_0 holds for all numbered terms. The implication " $\Rightarrow$" follows. ∎

We do not have the strong form of completeness $X \models p{:}A \Leftrightarrow X \vdash p{:}A$, but the relation $X \models p{:}A$ is probably not recursively enumerable. One could strengthen the proof system by including rules to express modal tautologies, including *e.g.* the rule

$$\frac{x{:}A \vdash x{:}B}{x{:}[\alpha]A \vdash x{:}[\alpha]B}$$

and perhaps by including such rules and insisting recursions be well–guarded one could obtain a strongly complete proof system.

7. Conclusion, related work, future work.

Colin Stirling has produced a related proof system for SCCS but without restriction and in the case where recursive definitions are guarded. His proof system captures the concept *relative satisfaction*, so he has proof rules which generate the relation $p \models^{St}{}_{B} A$ with this interpretation: if a process q satisfies B then $p \otimes q$ satisfies A; so relative satisfaction takes account of the environment. Clearly we can translate relative satisfaction into our notation by noting that $p \models^{St}{}_{B} A \Leftrightarrow x{:}B \models p \otimes x : A$. Our proof system suffers from the defect that we do not have a strong form of completeness, but his suffers from the same fault. I suspect that it may be very difficult to extend his proof system to restriction.

We have seen how a range of different equivalences can be captured by restricting to subsets of the assertion language. An interesting problem is that of how to turn proof systems for processes with assertions into proof systems for equivalences of processes, a more common approach in the theory of CCS, SCCS and CSP. There is the attractive possibility that there is a proof system which includes proof systems for the multitude of equivalences there are. One would need a suitable metatheory in which to embed proof systems for assertions. Such metatheories are being developed for domain theory underlying denotational semantics and it may not be too hard to adopt, for example, the ideas of Abramsky, in [Ab], to this end.

Certainly, although the presentation here has been based on an operational semantics for SCCS, the work can be seen from the viewpoint of denotational semantics. This is followed through in [W2] which recasts the semantics of SCCS, in the traditional framework of Scott–Strachey denotational semantics and one sees the translation between different semantics for *e.g.* Milner's *bisimulation equivalence* and Hoare's *failure-set equivalence* expressed as an *embedding–projection* pair between domains. This approach will make clearer the relation with the ideas of Scott [S, S1, LW], with the work of Golson and Rounds [GR], Plotkin and Smyth [P,Sm], and Hoare and Olderog [H, OH].

Future work: more complicated programming languages and logics of assertions; the relations with intuitionistic logic are intriguing too.

References

[Ab] Abramsky, S., Domain theory as a theory of experiments. In this proceedings (1984).

[Ac] Aczel, P., An introduction to inductive definitions. In the handbook of Mathematical Logic, Ed. Barwise, J., North–Holland (1983).

[BKP] Barringer H., Kuiper R. and Pnueli A., Now you may compose temporal logic specifications. In the proceedings of STOC 84 (1984).

[deNH] de Nicola, R. and Hennessy, M.C.B., Testing Equivalences for Processes, Lecture Notes in Comp. Sc. vol. 154 (1983). To appear in JACM.

[GR] Golson, W. and Rounds W., In this proceedings (1984).

[H] Hoare, C.A.R., A model for communicating sequential processes. Monograph of the Programming Research Group, Oxford University (1981).

[HBR] Hoare, C.A.R., Brookes, S.D., and Roscoe, A.W., A Theory of Communicating Processes, Technical Report PRG-16, Programming Research Group, University of Oxford (1981); appears also in JACM (1984).

[HM] Hennessy, M.C.B. and Milner, R., On observing nondeterminism and concurrency, Springer LNCS Vol. 85. (1979).

[HP] Hennessy, M.C.B. and Plotkin, G. D., A term model for CBL. Springer LNCS Vol. 88. (1980).

[LW] Larsen, K. and Winskel, G., Using Information Systems to solve Recursive Domain Equations Effectively. Springer Lecture Notes in Comp. Sc., vol. 173 (1984).

[M1] Milner, R., A Calculus of Communicating Systems. Springer Lecture Notes in Comp. Sc. vol. 92 (1980).

[M2] Milner, R., A modal characterisation of observable machine–behaviour. Springer Lecture Notes in Comp. Sc. vol. 112 (1981).

[M3] Milner, R., Calculi for synchrony and asynchrony, Theoretical Computer Science, pp.267–310 (1983).

[OH] Olderog, E–R. and Hoare, C.A.R., Specification–oriented semantics for communicating processes. Monograph of the Programming Research Group, Oxford University (1984).

[P] Plotkin, G. D., Some comments on Robin's "A modal characterisation of observable machine–behaviour". Handwritten notes, Comp. Sc. Dept., University of Edinburgh (1983).

[S] Scott, D. S., Domains for Denotational Semantics. ICALP 1982.

[S1] Scott, D. S., Lectures on a mathematical theory of computation. Oxford University Computing Laboratory Technical Monograph PRG-19 (1981).

[Sm] Smyth, M.B., Power domains and predicate transformers: a topological view. Proc. of ICALP 83, Springer Lecture Notes in Comp. Sc. vol. 154 (1983).

[St1] Stirling, C., A complete modal proof system for a subset of SCCS. Research report, Dept. of Comp. Sci., Edinburgh University (1984).

[St2] Stirling, C., A proof theoretic characterisation of observational equivalence. Research report, Dept. of Comp. Sci., Edinburgh University, CSR-132-83 (1983). A version also appears in the proceedings of the Bangalore conference, India (1983) and is to appear in Theoretical Computer Science.

[W1] Winskel, G., Synchronisation trees. Technical Report, Comp. Sc. Dept., Carnegie-Mellon University (1983).To appear in Theoretical Computer Science.

[W2] Winskel, G., A complete proof system for SCCS with modal assertions. In preparation.

PROCESS ALGEBRA WITH ASYNCHRONOUS COMMUNICATION MECHANISMS

J.A. BERGSTRA, J.W. KLOP
Centre for Mathematics and Computer Science, Kruislaan 413,
1098 SJ Amsterdam, The Netherlands.

J.V. TUCKER
Department of Computer Studies, University of Leeds
Leeds, LS2 9JT, England.

INTRODUCTION

In this paper we present an algebraic analysis of concurrent processes with three types of asynchronous communication. Our starting point is an algebraic axiomatisation PA_δ (for *P*rocess *A*lgebra) of concurrent processes without communication, in which the concurrency is that of the free merge, or arbitrary interleaving, of atomic actions. Such concurrent cooperation of processes is *asynchronous cooperation*, as each process may operate in connection with its own clock. The system PA_δ was first introduced in [7] together with an extension to an axiomatisation ACP (for *A*lgebra of *C*ommunicating *P*rocesses) of concurrent processes with a communication mechanism.

The laws for communication in ACP, like those in Milner's CCS, concern *synchronous communication*, requiring the synchronisation or simultaneous execution $a|b$ of so-called communication actions a,b. In research on laws for concurrency, while concurrent cooperation has been examined in its asychronous and synchronous cases, concurrent process communication in the asynchronous case has been neglected. In this paper we take up the idea of *asynchronous communication* wherein a communication by actions a,b is consistent with b being performed after a (say). We have devised algebraic treatments of this idea based upon three models :

(i) mail via a queue-like channel;
(ii) mail via a bag-like channel;
(iii) causality in systems.

The plan of the paper is this : Section 1 introduces the axiom system PA_δ describing the free merge of processes; here δ is a constant for process failure or deadlock. This axiom system underlies the three axiom systems we present. Section 2 is devoted to the distinctions been cooperation/communication and synchronous/asychronous, and attempts a classification of formalisms such as CCS, CSP, MEIJE, SCCS, CHILL and so forth. Section 3 presents the algebraic systems for (i) and (ii) above; and Section 4 presents the system for (iii) together with an involved example on the control of a printer.

This paper is part of a long series of reports on process algebra and its applications, including [6,7]. The paper can be read independently, though knowledge of part of [7] may be helpful; in addition, [7] contains a discussion of related approaches to the algebraic theory of concurrency, including CCS and SCCS in Milner [23,24].

We thank Ms. Judith Thursby for her preparation of this typescript.

1. PROCESS ALGEBRA WITHOUT COMMUNICATION

As a point of departure we consider an algebraic axiom system PA_δ that analyses concurrent processes without communication. The system PA_δ is derived from [7] where a system PA was introduced for concurrent process algebra without communication, and the δ-laws for process deadlock were introduced in a system ACP for concurrent process algebra with synchronous communication.

Process algebra is concerned with concurrent processes made from a finite set A of atomic processes or *actions*, including a special failed or deadlocked process $\delta \in A$. There are four process generating binary operations,

$+$ *alternative composition (sum)*
$\cdot$ *sequential composition (product)*
$\|$ *parallel composition (merge)*
$\lfloor\!\lfloor$ *left-merge*

and these components satisfy a set PA_δ of axioms given below.

1.1 Signature More formally, let Σ_{PA_δ} be the following signature :

S	:	P	*sorts*
F	:	$+: P \times P \rightarrow P$	*functions*
		$\cdot: P \times P \rightarrow P$	
		$\|: P \times P \rightarrow P$	
		$\lfloor\!\lfloor: P \times P \rightarrow P$	
C	:	a for all $a \in A$	*constants*

1.2 Axioms Let PA_δ be the set of equations over Σ_{PA_δ} in Table 1.

$x + y = y + x$	A1
$(x + y) + z = x + (y + z)$	A2
$x + x = x$	A3
$(x + y)z = xz + yz$	A4
$(xy)z = x(yz)$	A5
$x + \delta = x$	A6
$\delta x = \delta$	A7
$x \| y = x \lfloor\!\lfloor y + y \lfloor\!\lfloor x$	M1
$a \lfloor\!\lfloor x = ax$	M2
$(ax) \lfloor\!\lfloor y = a(x \| y)$	M3
$(x+y) \lfloor\!\lfloor z = x \lfloor\!\lfloor z + y \lfloor\!\lfloor z$	M4

Table 1

1.3 Semantics A Σ_{PA_δ}-structure P satisfying the axioms in PA_δ is a *process algebra with deadlock*; the class of all such algebras we denote $ALG(\Sigma_{PA_\delta}, PA_\delta)$.

In analogy with the theory of data type specifications, it is useful to consider the equational axiomatisation $(\Sigma_{PA_\delta}, PA_\delta)$ in two ways :

(i) as an *initial algebra specification* (in the sense of ADJ[1]) for the special structure A_ω of all finite processes with deadlock i.e. the initial algebra semantics of the specification is $I(\Sigma_{PA_\delta}, PA_\delta) \cong A_\omega$

(ii) as a general axiomatic specification of such concurrent process algebras with semantics $ALG(\Sigma_{PA_\delta}, PA_\delta)$.

These views rest on the distinction between finite and infinite processes, which requires technical elaboration :

Let $P \models PA_\delta$ be any process algebra. For $p \in P$ and $\alpha \in A^* \cup A^\omega$, the set of finite or infinite sequences of actions from A, we will define what it means for α to be a *trace* of p:

Definition. (i) If $\alpha = a_1 * a_2 * \ldots * a_n$, where $a_i \in A$ $(i=1,\ldots,n)$ and * denotes concatenation, then α is a *trace* of p if there are $p_1,\ldots,p_n, q_1,\ldots,q_n,q_{n+1} \in P$ such that

$$p = p_1,\ p_i = a_i p_{i+1} + q_i \quad (i=1,\ldots,n-1)$$

$$p_n = a_n + q_n$$

(ii) If $\alpha = a_1 * a_2 * \ldots$ then we call α a *trace* of p if there are p_i, q_i such that

$$p = p_1,\ p_i = a_i p_{i+1} + q_i \quad (i \geq 1).$$

If $p \in P$ has an infinite trace, it is an *infinite* process; otherwise it is *finite*. The initial algebra $I(\Sigma_{PA_\delta}, PA_\delta)$ contains finite processes only.

There are various ways to construct process algebras that contain infinite processes, most of which have been developed for the more general case of communicating processes. The synchronisation trees (modulo observational equivalence or bisimulation) from Milner [23] (see also Winskel [31]) constitute such a model if one considers the degenerate case of the absence of synchronisation primitives. In De Bakker & Zucker [3,4] a topological construction is given via metric spaces, and in Bergstra & Klop [7] an equivalent algebraic construction using projective limits. Bergstra, Klop & Tucker [8] describes a direct algebraic construction by means of adjoining solutions of suitable fixed point equations. The solution of recursion equations is important in the theory because such equations constitute an important specification tool for process definition; these equations require infinite processes for their solution. The projective limit constructions and the topological constructions lead to models *in which all guarded systems of equations can be solved.*

2. COOPERATION AND COMMUNICATION

2.1 A Classification of Concurrency Informally, one thinks of processes as logical configurations of atomic acts. A process p is executed as follows : choose a first action, perform it; then choose a second action that is possible after the first action (according to the definition of the process), perform it; and so on. On thinking of the parallel execution of processes one involves notions to do with time and clocks. Informally, in the parallel execution of two processes p,q, two basic kinds of *process cooperation* can be distinguished:

Synchronous Cooperation : the regime of synchronous cooperation allows p,q to be executed in parallel with the same speed as measured by the same clock; this idea is encorporated in SCCS [14,24], ASP [7], MEIJE [2,28].

Asynchronous Cooperation : the regime of asynchronous cooperation allows p,q to proceed in parallel with their own speeds, as measured by their own independent clocks; this idea is encorporated in CSP [15-17], CCS [23], ACP [7], with restrictions determined by possible mutual interactions between processes, and in the system PA_δ, where there are no interactions.

Now, in the interaction between the atomic actions of two processes p,q two basic kinds of *process communication* can be distinguished :

Synchronous Communication : the regime of synchronous communication requires that communication between actions a,b can take place only if both are performed simultaneously; this type of communication is sometimes called *handshaking* and is encorporated in CSP, CCS, ACP, and Ada.

Asynchronous Communication : the regime of asynchronous communication allows communication between actions a,b to be consistent with b being performed after a;

this idea is encorpoated in CHILL [9].

Combining the above regimes one arrives at four categories which can be used to classify models of concurrent processes, namely :

SS *synchronous cooperation + synchronous communication*
SCCS, MEIJE, ASP, ASCCS

SA *synchronous cooperation + asynchronous communication*
No example known to us.

AS *asynchronous cooperation + synchronous communication*
CCS, CSP, ACP, Ada, Petri nets,
uniform processes of [3,4]

AA *asynchronous cooperation + asynchronous communication*
CHILL, data flow networks
restoring circuit logic

2.2 Comments on Examples The combinations SS and AS have been extensively studied in process theory; we refer to Austry & Boudol [2] and De Simone [28] for a comparison between MEIJE and SCCS, to Milner [23,24] and Hennessy [14] for CCS and SCCS, to Bergstra & Klop [7] for ACP and ASP, to De Bakker & Zucker [3,4] for uniform processes, and to Brookes [11,12], Winskel [30] for discussions about and comparisons between CSP and CCS. For CSP see Hoare [15,16] and Hoare, Brookes & Roscoe [17].

It might be puzzling why ASCCS, which gives according to Milner [24] a framework for "asychronous processes", is classified under SS. The reason is that it is a subcalculus of SCCS, and hence also employs synchronous cooperation and synchronous communication - even though asynchronously cooperating processes may be *interpreted* in ASCCS.

The combination AA in studied for instance using temporal logic in Pnueli [26], Lamport [21] and Koymans, Vytopil & de Roever [19], Kuiper & de Roever [20]. Moreover, trace theories are used to describe the semantics of data flow networks (see Kahn [18], Brock & Ackerman [10]) and the semantics of restoring circuit logic (see Ebergen [13], Rem [27] and Van de Snepscheut [29]. Restoring circuit logic is intended to describe the behaviour of circuits regardless of delays in the connecting wires. This delay insensitivity leads to the classification under AA.

A discussion of the case AA in an algebraic setting is absent to our knowledge. In Milne [22] and Bergstra & Klop [6] the AA case is reduced to the AS case for switching circuits and data flow networks respectively. We are not aware of any "direct" algebraic descriptions of the AA case.

2.3 The AA Case One may imagine a wild variety of different mechanisms for asynchronous communication. We will now proceed to describe three mechanisms for asynchronous communication that are consistent with asynchronous cooperation.

The mechanisms are closely related to one another :

(i) Mail via an order-preserving channel (cf a queue)

(ii) Mail via a non-order-preserving channel (cf a bag)

(iii) A causal mechanism wherein one action causes another.

For each of these mechanisms we will present an algebraic notation based upon

(a) a special purpose *alphabet of atomic actions*;

(b) an appropriate *encapsulation operator*; and

(c) a set of axioms to specify the semantics of the mechanism.

In each case the axiom system is an extension of PA_δ; cases (i) and (ii) we will complete in the next section while case (iii) we will treat in Section 4. It may be helpful to make a comparision with the construction of ACP as an extension of PA_δ.

3. MAIL VIA A CHANNEL

We will treat the cases of mail via an order-preserving channel and mail via a non-order-preserving channel together since the syntax and axioms proposed for these mechanisms coincide to a large extent.

3.1 The alphabet. Let B be a finite set of actions. Let D be a finite set of *data*, and c a special symbol for *channel*. For all $d \in D$ there are actions

$c \uparrow d$	*send data* d *via channel* c *considered as a potential action*
$c \boldsymbol{\uparrow} d$	*send data* d *via channel* c *considered as an actual action*
$c \downarrow d$	*receive data* d *via channel* c *considered as a potential action*
$c \boldsymbol{\downarrow} d$	*receive data* d *via channel* c *considered as an actual action*

The distinction between $c \uparrow d$ and $c \boldsymbol{\uparrow} d$ may be slightly unusual $c \uparrow d$ indicates an *internal, intended, potential,* or *future* action while $c \boldsymbol{\uparrow} d$ denotes an *external, realised, actual,* or *past* action; and similarly for $c \downarrow d$ and $c \boldsymbol{\downarrow} d$.

This distinction is implicit in the synchronous communication operator $|$ of ACP where a communication takes the form $a|b = c$ for atomic acts a,b,c. By virtue of the equation, a,b can be seen as potential actions giving rise to the communication c as an actual action.

Let $c{\uparrow}D = \{c{\uparrow}d \mid d \in D\}$ and likewise for $c\boldsymbol{\uparrow}D$, etc.

Now we define the alphabet to be

$$A = B \cup \{\delta\} \cup (c{\uparrow}D) \cup (c\boldsymbol{\uparrow}D) \cup (c{\downarrow}D) \cup (c\boldsymbol{\downarrow}D).$$

Note that the cardinality $|A| = |B| + 4|D| + 1$.

The actions $b \in B$ are not related to channel c. Although we specify syntax and axioms for one channel c only, the presence of several channels, c,c',... is entirely unproblematic; in that case, B may also contain actions $c'{\uparrow}d$ etc. since these are not related to channel c.

3.2 Encapsulation Operator. Here the situation divides into the cases of mail via an order-preserving channel (3.2.1) and mail via an non-order-preserving channel (3.2.2).

3.2.1 *Queue-like Channel.* Let D* be the set of *sequences* σ of data $d \in D$. The empty sequence is denoted by ε. Concatenation of sequences α,τ is denoted as $\alpha*\tau$; especially if $\alpha = <d_1,\ldots,d_n>$ $(n\geq 0)$ then $d*\sigma = <d,d_1,\ldots,d_n>$ and $\sigma*d = <d_1,\ldots,d_n,d>$. Further, if $n\geq 1$, last $(\sigma) = d_n$.

Now for each $\sigma \in D^*$ there is an *encapsulation operator* $\mu_c^\sigma : P\to P$ where P is a domain of processes (i.e. the elements of a process algebra satisfying the axioms below). Informally, if x is a process, then $\mu_c^\sigma(x)$ denotes *the process obtained by requiring that the channel* c *initially contains a data sequence* σ *and that no communications with* c *are performed outside* x. Thus, x and $\mu_c^\sigma(x)$ correspond to internal and external views of a system's behaviour, in some sense.

There are other relevant intuitions about encapsulation. The process $\mu_c^\sigma(x)$ can be viewed as the result of the *partial execution* of x with respect to c with initial contents σ. By execution we mean the transformation of internal or potential actions like $c\uparrow D$ into an external or actual actions like $c\Uparrow d$, and their effect on processes (cf Remark 4.6). Encapsulation is formally defined by axioms MO1-9 below.

3.2 *Bag-like Channel.* For the bag-like channel the situation is very much the same except that a data sequence σ is now a *multiset* of data. We denote a finite multiset of $d\in D$ by M. Now for all finite multisets M over D we introduce again an encapsulation or partial execution operator

$$\mu_c^M : P\to P$$

3.3 The signature. Although the various ingredients of the signature, both for th cases of mail via a queue-like channel and via a bag-like channel, have now all been introduced, we will display these signatures once more in Table 2.

3.4 Axioms. Suppose a set B of actions, a set D of data and a channel name c are given. Then we have the following axiom systems :

$PA_\delta(\mu_c^\sigma,B,D)$ in Table 3

$PA_\delta(\mu_c^M,B,D)$ in Talbe 4

for mail via a queue-like channel and mail via a bag-like channel, respectively. Here a varies over the alphabet $A = B \cup \{\delta\} \cup c\uparrow D \cup c\Uparrow D \cup c\downarrow D \cup c\Downarrow D$, and e varies over $E = B \cup \{\delta\} \cup c\uparrow D \cup c\downarrow D$.

$+$	*alternative composition (sum)*
$\cdot$	*sequential composition (product)*
$\|\|$	*parallel composition (merge)*
$\lfloor\!\lfloor$	*left-merge*
δ	*dead-lock or failure*
b	*atomic action* ε B, *independent from* c
$c\uparrow d$	*send* d *via channel* c; *internal view*
$c\Uparrow d$	*send* d *via channel* c; *external view*
$c\downarrow d$	*receive* d *via* c; *internal view*
$c\Downarrow d$	*receive* d *via* c; *external view*
μ_c^σ	*encapsulation w.r.t. queue-like channel* c
μ_c^M	*encapsulation w.r.t. bag-like channel* c

Table 2.

3.5 Semantics. The axiom systems $PA_\delta(\mu_c^\alpha,B,D)$ and $PA_\delta(\mu_c^M,B,D)$ determine initial algebras

$$A_\omega(+,\cdot,\|,\lfloor\!\lfloor,\delta,\mu_c^\sigma,B,D)$$

$$A_\omega(+,\cdot,\|,\lfloor\!\lfloor,\delta,\mu_c^M,B,D)$$

respectively. These are just enrichments of the initial algebra I(PA) denoted A_ω or

$$A_\omega(+,\cdot,\|,\lfloor\!\lfloor,\delta)$$

of PA_δ. Using a projective limit construction as with ACP in [7], or a topological completion as in [3,4], it is possible to construct larger models

$$A^\infty(+,\cdot,\|,\lfloor\!\lfloor,\delta,\mu_c^\alpha,B,D)$$

$$A^\infty(+,\cdot,\|,\lfloor\!\lfloor,\delta,\mu_c^M,B,D)$$

with infinite processes, *in which all guarded systems of equations can be solved.*

3.6 Examples. We will now give some examples both for the case of an order-preserving channel and the case of non-order-preserving channel.

3.6.1 *Example for a queue-like channel.* Consider the following very simple data flow network :

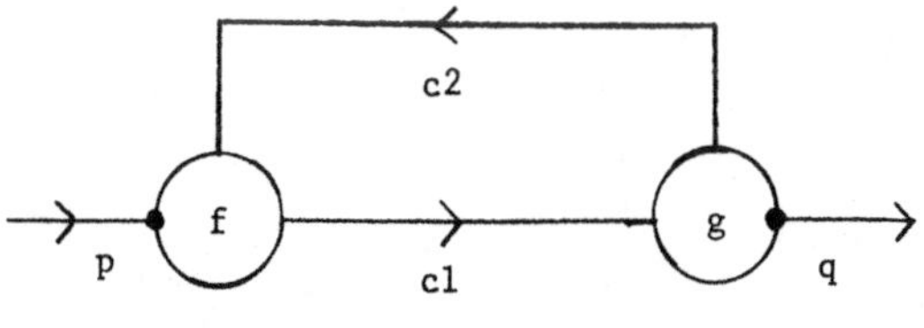

Figure 1.

$PA_\delta(\mu_c^\sigma, B, D)$

$x + y = y + x$	A1
$(x + y) + z = x + (y + z)$	A2
$x + x = x$	A3
$(x + y)z = xz + yz$	A4
$(xy)z = x(yz)$	A5
$x + \delta = x$	A6
$\delta x = \delta$	A7
$x \| y = x \mathbin{\|\!\lfloor} y + y \mathbin{\|\!\lfloor} x$	M1
$a \mathbin{\|\!\lfloor} x = ax$	M2
$ax \mathbin{\|\!\lfloor} y = a(x \| y)$	M3
$(x + y) \mathbin{\|\!\lfloor} z = x \mathbin{\|\!\lfloor} z + y \mathbin{\|\!\lfloor} z$	M4
$\mu_c^\sigma(e) = e$	MO1
$\mu_c^\sigma(ex) = e.\mu_c^\sigma(x)$	MO2
$\mu_c^\sigma(c\uparrow d) = c\Uparrow d$	MO3
$\mu_c^\sigma(c\uparrow d.x) = c\Uparrow d.\mu_c^{d*\sigma}(x)$	MO4
$\mu_c^{\sigma*d}(c\downarrow d) = c\Downarrow d$	MO5
$\mu_c^{\sigma*d}(c\downarrow d.x) = c\Downarrow d.\mu_c^\sigma(x)$	MO6
$\mu_c^\sigma(c\downarrow d) = \delta$ if $d \neq last(\sigma)$ or $\sigma = \varepsilon$	MO7
$\mu_c^\sigma(c\downarrow d.x) = \delta$ if $d \neq last(\sigma)$ or $\sigma = \varepsilon$	MO8
$\mu_c^\sigma(x + y) = \mu_c^\sigma(x) + \mu_c^\sigma(y)$	MO9

<u>Table 3</u> $(a \in A,\ e \in E,\ \sigma \in D^*)$

$PA_{\delta}(\mu_c^M, B, D)$

$x + y = y + x$	A1
$(x+y) + z = x + (y+z)$	A2
$x + x = x$	A3
$(x+y)z = xz + yz$	A4
$(xy)z = x(yz)$	A5
$x + \delta = x$	A6
$\delta x = \delta$	A7
$x \parallel y = x \lfloor\!\lfloor y + y \lfloor\!\lfloor x$	M1
$a \lfloor\!\lfloor x = ax$	M2
$ax \lfloor\!\lfloor y = a(x \parallel y)$	M3
$(x+y) \lfloor\!\lfloor z = x \lfloor\!\lfloor z + y \lfloor\!\lfloor z$	M4
$\mu_c^M(e) = e$	MNO1
$\mu_c^M(ex) = e.\mu_c^M(x)$	MNO2
$\mu_c^M(c{\uparrow}d) = c\boldsymbol{\uparrow}d$	MNO3
$\mu_c^M(c{\uparrow}d\ .\ x) = c\boldsymbol{\uparrow}d.\ \mu_c^{M\cup\{d\}}(x)$	MNO4
$\mu_c^{M\cup\{d\}}(c{\downarrow}d) = c\boldsymbol{\downarrow}d$	MNO5
$\mu_c^{M\cup\{d\}}(c{\downarrow}d.x) = c\boldsymbol{\downarrow}d\ .\ \mu_c^M(x)$	MNO6
$\mu_c^M(c{\downarrow}d) = \delta$ if $d \notin M$	MNO7
$\mu_c^M(c{\downarrow}d.x) = \delta$ if $d \notin M$	MNO8
$\mu_c^M(x+y) = \mu_c^M(x) + \mu_c^M(y)$	MNO9

Table 4. ($a \in A$, $e \in E$, M a multiset over D)

with actions

rp(d)	*processor* f *reads value* d *at port* p
wq(d)	*processor* g *writes* d *at port* q

There are two order-preserving channels c1 and c2. Internally, the node f satisfies

$$f = \sum_{d \in D} (rp(d) + c2{\downarrow}d) \cdot c1{\uparrow}d \cdot f.$$

So, node f merges the inputs from p and c2 and emits these through c1. The node g is defined by

$$g = \sum_{d \in D} c1{\downarrow}d \cdot (i \cdot c2{\uparrow}\alpha(d) + i \cdot wq(d)) \cdot g$$

The effect of the internal step i is to make the choice nondeterministic, and $\alpha : D \to D$ is a transformation of the data; thus g obtains d from c1 and then chooses whether to 'recycle' $\alpha(d)$ via c2 or to output d via port q.

The network N is now externally described by

$$N = \mu^{\varepsilon}_{c1}\mu^{\varepsilon}_{c2}(f \| g).$$

Note that the actions c1↓d, c1↑d, c1⇓d and c1⇑d are unrelated to c2 and thereby work as b's in the definition for μ^{α}_{c2}. Conversely, the send and receive actions for c2 are unrelated to c1.

3.6.2 *Example for a queue-like channel.* Consider the very simple communication protocol as in Figure 2 :

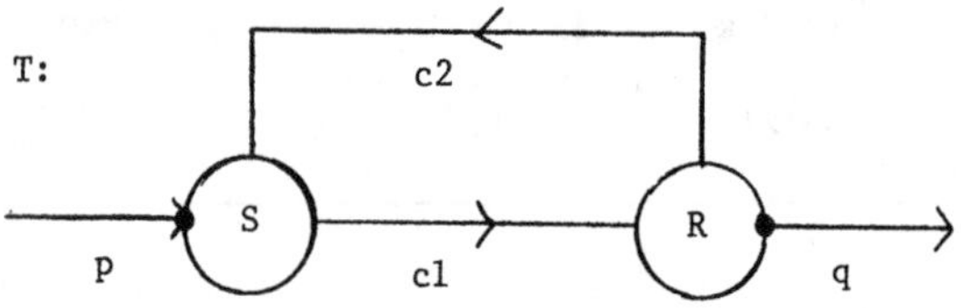

Figure 2

$$S = \sum_{d \in D} rp(d) \cdot c1{\uparrow}d \cdot c2{\downarrow}ack \cdot S$$

$$R = \sum_{d \in D} c1{\downarrow}d \cdot wq(d) \cdot c2{\uparrow}ack \cdot R$$

$$T = \mu^{\varepsilon}_{c1}\ \mu^{\varepsilon}_{c2}\ (S \| R).$$

In fact the protocol T satisfies the following recursion equation (as one easily computes from the axioms in $PA_{\delta}(\mu^{\alpha}_{c},B,D)$) :

$$T = \sum_{d \in D} rp(d) \cdot c1{\Uparrow}d \cdot c1{\Downarrow}d \cdot wq(d) \cdot c2{\Uparrow}ack \cdot c2{\Downarrow}ack \cdot T.$$

This recursion equation constitutes an external *specification* of T.

3.6.3 *Example for a bag-like channel* :

(i) $\mu_c^{\emptyset}(c{\uparrow}d \cdot c{\downarrow}d) = c\boldsymbol{\uparrow}d \cdot c\boldsymbol{\downarrow}d$

(ii) $\mu_c^{\emptyset}(c{\uparrow}d \cdot \sum_{u \in D} c{\downarrow}u) = c\boldsymbol{\uparrow}d \cdot c\boldsymbol{\downarrow}d$

(iii) $\mu_c^{\emptyset}(c{\uparrow}d \,\|\, c{\downarrow}d) = c\boldsymbol{\uparrow}d \cdot c\boldsymbol{\downarrow}d$

(iv) $\mu_c^{\emptyset}(c{\uparrow}d1 \cdot c{\uparrow}d2 \cdot \sum_{u \in D} c{\downarrow}u \cdot \sum_{u \in D} c{\downarrow}u) =$

$$c\boldsymbol{\uparrow}d1 \cdot c\boldsymbol{\uparrow}d2 \cdot (c\boldsymbol{\downarrow}d1 \cdot c\boldsymbol{\downarrow}d2 + c\boldsymbol{\downarrow}d2 \cdot c\boldsymbol{\downarrow}d1)$$

(v) Let $D = D1 \cup D2$, $D1 \cap D2 = \emptyset$, and

$$H = \left[\sum_{d \in D1} c1{\downarrow}d \cdot c2{\uparrow}d + \sum_{d \in D2} c1{\downarrow}d \cdot c3{\uparrow}d \right] \cdot H$$

Then H separates the D1 messages from the D2 messages.

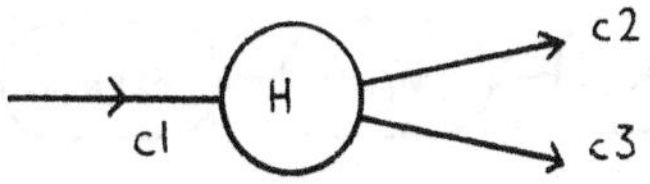

Figure 3.

(vi) Let $d1 \neq d2$. Then :

$\mu_c^{\emptyset}\ (c{\uparrow}d1 \cdot c{\downarrow}d2) = c{\uparrow}d1 \cdot \delta$

$\mu_c^{\emptyset}\ (c{\uparrow}d1 \,\|\, c{\downarrow}d2) = c{\uparrow}d1 \cdot \delta$

$\mu_c^{\emptyset}\ (c{\downarrow}d2 \,⌊\!⌊\, c{\uparrow}d1) = \delta.$

3.7 Remarks Notice that there is no guarantee that after a send action $c{\uparrow}d$ the corresponding receive action $c{\downarrow}d$ will ever be performed. Thus the send action *enables* the receive action but does not *force* its execution. This holds for both mechanisms.

In the tele-communications area the design language SDL, used by CCITT, is quite popular. SDL mainly consists of a format for graphical notations for concurrent system descriptions with a send and receive mechanism. SDL leaves open the nature of the transmission protocol that supports the send and receive instructions. In SDL, example 3.6.2 can be depicted as follows :

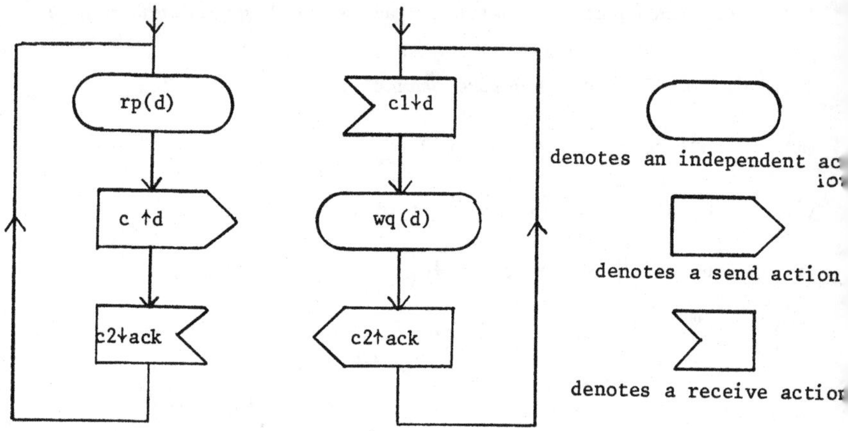

Figure 4

Here it is assumed that in each cycle d receives a value at rp(d) and $c1\downarrow d$ respectively. The μ-encapsulation of the protocol leads to the following SDL description :

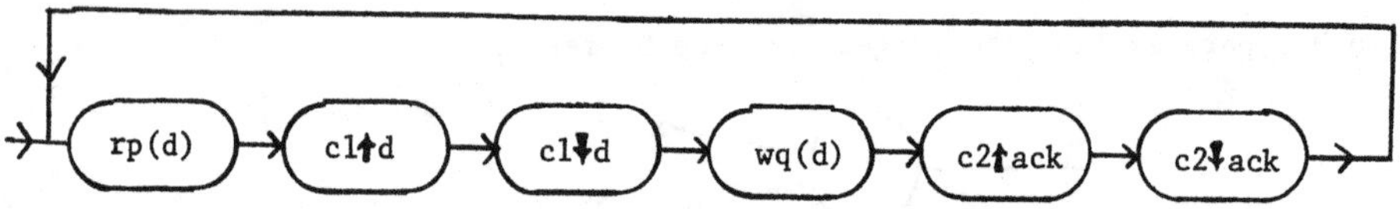

Figure 5

3.8 Remark on synchronous communication.

A syntax for synchronous communication along a channel c, inspired by CSP and CCS, would be :

c!d	*send* d
c?d	*receive* d
c#d	*communicate* d

In ACP [7] one introduces a communication function | on actions. In this particular example, | would work as follows :

$$c!d \mid c?d = c\#d$$

Notice that we do not use variables : for example, $c?x\cdot P$ is modelled by $\sum_{d\in D} c?d\cdot P[d/x]$ This differs from CCS where one would have

$$c(d) \mid \bar{c}(d) = \tau.$$

4. CAUSALITY

In the previous section, the action $c\Uparrow d$ is the executed or actualised form of $c\uparrow d$ and likewise $c\Downarrow d$ is $c\downarrow d$ after execution or actualisation. Moreover, in some sense a casual effect is involved : c↑d causes c↓d. These concepts will be made explicit in the present section.

4.1 Actualisation. On the alphabet A we postulate an operator $\hat{}:A \to A$, such that $\hat{\delta} = \delta$ and $\hat{\hat{a}} = \hat{a}$ for all $a \in A$. The action $\hat{a}$ is called the *actualisation* of a. Writing $B = A-\hat{A}$, where $\hat{A} = \{\hat{a} \mid a \in A\}$, A is partitioned as follows :

$$A = B \cup \hat{A} .$$

4.2 Causal relations On the set B of not yet completed actions we have a binary relation R encoding the casual relations between such actions. Instead of $(a,b) \in R$ we write :

$$a \Vdash b ,$$

in words : "a causes b". Further notations are :

Dom(R) for the *domain* of R, i.e. $Dom(R) = \{b \mid \exists b' \;\; b \Vdash b'\}$, and
Ran(R) for the *range* of R, i.e. $Ran(R) = \{b \mid \exists b' \;\; b' \Vdash b\}$.

So Dom(R) contains the *causes* or *stimuli* and Ran(R) the *effects* or *responses*. Note that an action can be both a cause and an effect. Finally, write $R(b) = \{b' \mid b \Vdash b'\}$ for the set of effects of b.

4.3 Encapsulation Operator. Let $b \in B$. Performing b has two consequences : b is now changed into $\hat{b}$, and all $b' \in R(b)$, actions caused by b are now *enabled*. The operator which takes care of the execution of b (or, in another phrasing which changes the view from "internal" to "external") and which takes into account which actions are enabled, is the *encapsulation operator* γ^E where $E \subseteq B$. The intuitive meaning of γ^E is : $\gamma^E(x)$ is *the process where initially all actions of* E *are enabled and all casual effects take place within* x, *i.e. actions within* x *are neither enabled or disabled by actions outside* x *and conversely*.

4.4 Axioms and Semantics. The axioms for the operations γ^E are given in Table 5 below. Semantically, as with the previous axiomatisations, the equations specify an enrichment of the initial algebra $I(PA_\delta)$. And again it is possible to enrich the important model constructions for infinite processes to permit the solution of guarded systems of equations.

4.5 Examples (i) Suppose $a \Vdash d$, $c \Vdash b$ (see Figure 6(a)).

$$\gamma^{\emptyset}(ab \| cd) = \gamma^{\emptyset}(a(b \| cd)) + \gamma^{\emptyset}(c(d \| ab)) = \hat{a}\gamma^{\{d\}}(b \| cd) + \ldots =$$

$$\hat{a}\gamma^{\{d\}}(bcd + c(d \| b)) + \ldots = \hat{a}(\delta + \hat{c}\gamma^{\{d,b\}}(db+bd) + \ldots =$$

$$\hat{a}\hat{c}(\hat{d}\hat{b} + \hat{b}\hat{d}) + \hat{c}\hat{a}(\hat{b}\hat{d} + \hat{d}\hat{b}) = (\hat{a} \| \hat{c})(\hat{b} \| \hat{d}).$$

$PA_\delta(\gamma,\hat{\ })$ over atoms A with causality relation R

$x + y = y + x$	A1
$(x + y) + z = x + (y + z)$	A2
$x + x = x$	A3
$(x + y)z = xz + yz$	A4
$(xy)z = x(yz)$	A5
$x + \delta = x$	A6
$\delta x = \delta$	A7
$x \| y = x \lfloor\!\lfloor y + y \lfloor\!\lfloor x$	M1
$a \lfloor\!\lfloor y = ay$	M2
$ax \lfloor\!\lfloor y = a(x \| y)$	M3
$(x + y) \lfloor\!\lfloor z = x \lfloor\!\lfloor z + y \lfloor\!\lfloor z$	M4
$\hat{\delta} = \delta$	G1
$\hat{\hat{a}} = \hat{a}$	G2
$\gamma^E(a) = \hat{a}$ if $a \in E$ or $a \notin Ran(R)$	G3
$\gamma^E(a) = \delta$ if $a \notin E$ and $a \in Ran(R)$	G4
$\gamma^E(ax) = \gamma^E(a) \cdot \gamma^{(E-\{a\}) \cup R(a)}(x)$	G5
$\gamma^E(x + y) = \gamma^E(x) + \gamma^E(y)$	G6

Table 5.

(ii) Suppose $d \| \!\!- a$, $b \| \!\!- c$ (see Figure 6(b)). Then $\gamma^\emptyset(ab \| cd) = \delta$.

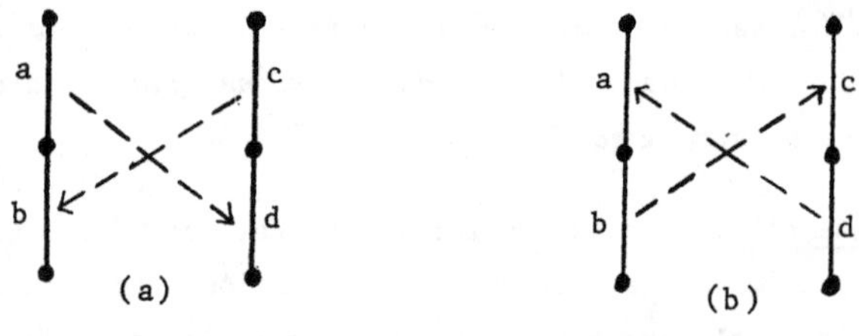

Figure 6.

Note that circular causal relations, such as in this example (ii), yield deadlock. Here an action a must be considered to cause the actions accessible from a or 'later' than a. (Indeed, we have $a \cdot b = \gamma^\emptyset(a \| b)$ for $a \| \!\!- b$)

(iii) Let X and Y be the two infinite processes recursively defined by X = abX and Y = cdY; so $X = (ab)^\omega$ and $Y = (cd)^\omega$. Suppose $a \| \!\!- c$ and $d \| \!\!- b$. Then

$$\gamma^\emptyset(X \| Y) = \gamma^\emptyset(a(bX \| Y) + c(dY \| X)) = \hat{a}\gamma^{\{c\}}(bX \| Y) + \delta =$$

$$\hat{a}\gamma^{\{c\}}(b(X \| Y) + c(dY \| bX)) = \hat{a}(\delta + \hat{c}\gamma^\emptyset(dY \| bX)) =$$

$$\hat{a}\hat{c}(\hat{d}\gamma^{\{b\}}(Y \| bX) + \delta) = \hat{a}\hat{c}\hat{d}\gamma^{\{b\}}(b(X \| Y) + Y \mathbin{⌊\!⌊} bX) =$$

$$\hat{a}\hat{c}\hat{d}\hat{b}\gamma^{\emptyset}(X \| Y).$$

Hence $\gamma^{\emptyset}(X \| Y) = (\hat{a}\hat{c}\hat{d}\hat{b})^{\omega}$.

4.6 Remarks It should be noted that *however often an action* b *has been enabled, after being performed it is again disabled.* For instance if $b \Vdash c$, then

$$\gamma^{\emptyset}(bbcc) = \hat{b}\gamma^{\{c\}}(bcc) = \hat{b}\hat{b}\gamma^{\{c\}}(cc) = \hat{b}\hat{b}\hat{c}\gamma^{\emptyset}(c) = \hat{b}\hat{b}\hat{c}\delta.$$

Thanks to the interpretation of causality as introducing an obligation (which has no multiplicity), the mail via an unordered channel mechanism differs from the present mechanism. For, in the setting of Section 3, we have

$$\mu_c^{\emptyset}(c\uparrow d \cdot c\uparrow d \cdot c\downarrow d \cdot c\downarrow d) = c\uparrow d \cdot c\uparrow d \cdot c\downarrow d \cdot c\downarrow d .$$

It is, however, easy to specify the variant of the causality mechanism above such that the obligations form a multiset rather than a set: axioms G1-6 from Table 5 carry over to that case unaltered, with only the stipulation that E is a multiset.

It is also simple to generalise the above causality relation to the case where an effect b may have several causes $a_1,\ldots,a_n$:

$$a_1,\ldots,a_n \Vdash b,$$

meaning that all the a_i $(i=1,\ldots,n)$ have to be executed in order to enable b.

Finally, let us remark that there is an interesting connection between the "spatial" notion of encapsulation (as represented by the operators ∂_H in ACP; μ_c^{σ}, μ_c^{M} in the mail mechanisms of Section 3; and the present γ^{E} for causality) and the "temporal" notion of execution. In some sense, one could say :

encapsulation = execution

Indeed, an encapsulated process can be thought to be already executed since no further interactions with an environment are possible.

4.7 Printer Example As a finale we will examine a somewhat involved example. This example of the control of a printer constitutes an abstract version of the highest level of a specification case study reported in [5]. Henk Obbink [25] (Philips Research) suggested we should use a stimulus-response or causality mechanism at the highest specification level. An important motivation for the present paper is to present a proper foundation for such a causality mechanism in process algebra. In fact, mail via order-preserving or non-order-preserving channels turn out to be modifications of this same idea (with the advantage of having better syntax).

Let us consider a configuration of three components :

CM	*command module*
P	*printer*
D	*display*

The only command that CM can issue is to start the printer; the printer will stop by itself. If the printer runs out of paper, a message to this effect must be displayed where upon new paper will be provided, and printing proceeds. When printing has finished this is reported to CM.

The behaviour of the components is defined by equations and depicted in the diagrams in Figure 7(a), (b), (c). From now on, we adopt the following

Convention. We will use the following typographical convention : instead of denoting actions as b, $\hat{b}$ we will write, respectively, *b* and b. So *italicized actions* are in B and are not yet completed, and *completed actions* are in $\hat{B}$ are in $\hat{B}$ are in usual print.

CM

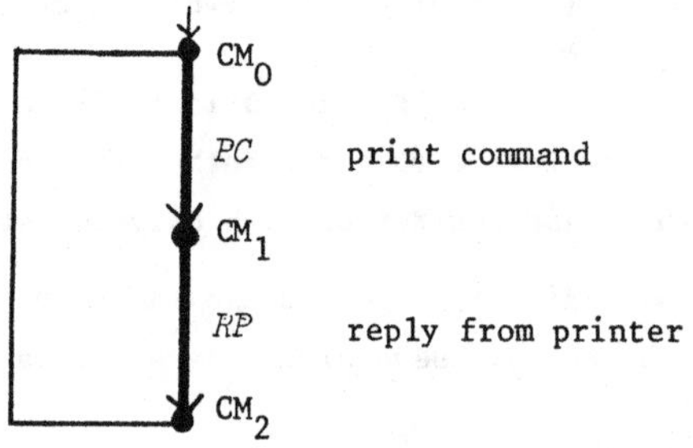

Figure 7(a).

$$CM = CM_0 \qquad CM_0 = PC.CM_1$$

$$CM_1 = RP.CM_2 \qquad CM_2 = CM_0$$

$$CM = PC.RP.CM$$

P

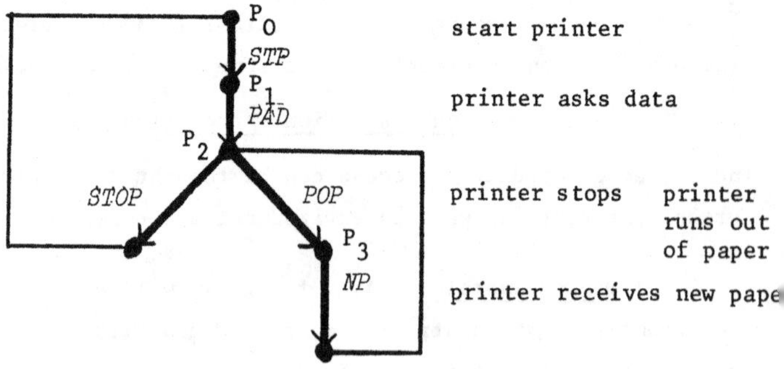

Figure 7(b).

$$P = \mathit{STP}.\mathit{PAD}.P_2$$

$$P_2 = \mathit{STOP}.P + \mathit{POP}.\mathit{NP}.P_2$$

D

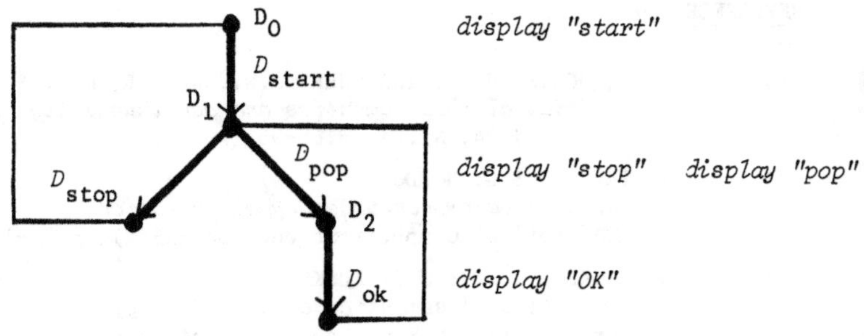

Figure 7(c).

$$D = D_{start} . D_1$$
$$D_1 = D_{stop} . D + D_{pop} \; D_{ok} . D_1$$

In these diagrams, fat arrows represent actions; the other lines identify control points and have no direction.

The casual relations in R are listed below :

$$\begin{array}{llllll} PC & \Vdash & STP & STP & \Vdash & D_{start} \\ STOP & \Vdash & D_{stop} & D_{stop} & \Vdash & RP \\ POP & \Vdash & D_{pop} & D_{pop} & \Vdash & NP \\ NP & \Vdash & D_{ok} & & & \end{array}$$

The entire system $\mathcal{S}$ is now described externally by :

$$\mathcal{S} = \gamma^{\emptyset}(CM_0 \| P_0 \| D_0) \; .$$

Further, let $\mathcal{S}^*$ be the subsystem that starts with the exceptional case of no paper :

$$\mathcal{S}^* = \gamma^{\{NP\}}(CM_1 \| P_3 \| D_2) \; .$$

It can be shown that $\mathcal{S}$ and $\mathcal{S}^*$ satisfy the following specification by means of recursion equations :

$$\begin{aligned} \mathcal{S} = \; & PC \cdot STP \cdot [D_{start} \cdot PAD \cdot \{STOP \cdot D_{stop} \cdot RP \cdot \mathcal{S} + POP \cdot D_{pop} \cdot \mathcal{S}^*\} \\ & + PAD \, . \, \{D_{start} \cdot (STOP \, . \, D_{stop} \, . \, RP \, . \, \mathcal{S} + POP \cdot D_{pop} \cdot \mathcal{S}^*) + \\ & + STOP \cdot D_{stop} \cdot RP \cdot \mathcal{S} + POP \cdot D_{pop} \cdot \mathcal{S}^*\}] \end{aligned}$$

$$\begin{aligned} \mathcal{S}^* = \; & NP \cdot [STOP \cdot D_{OK} \cdot D_{stop} \cdot RP \cdot \mathcal{S} + POP \cdot D_{OK} \cdot D_{pop} \cdot \mathcal{S}^* \\ & + D_{OK} \cdot (STOP \cdot D_{stop} \cdot RP \cdot \mathcal{S} + POP \cdot D_{pop} \cdot \mathcal{S}^*)] \end{aligned}$$

REFERENCES

[1] ADJ (GOGUEN, J.A., THATCHER, J.W., WAGNER, E.G. & J.B. WRIGHT), *Initial algebra semantics and continuous algebras,* JACM Vol.24, Nr. 1, p.68-95 (1975).

[2] AUSTRY, D. & G. BOUDOL, *Algèbre de processus et synchronisation,* Theoretical Computer Science 30 (1984), p.91-131.

[3] DE BAKKER, J.W. & J.I. ZUCKER, *Denotational semantics of concurrency,* Proc. 14th ACM Symp. on Theory of Computing, p.153-158, 1982.

[4] DE BAKKER, J.A. & J.I. ZUCKER, *Processes and the denotational semantics of concurrency,* Information and Control, Vol. 54, No.1/2, p.70-120, 1982.

[5] BERGSTRA, J.A., HEERING, J., KLINT, P. & J.W. KLOP, *Een analyse van de case-study HμP,* mimeographed notes, Centrum voor Wiskunde en Informatica, Amsterdam 1984.

[6] BERGSTRA, J.A. & J.W. KLOP, *A process algebra for the operational semantics of static data flow networks,* Report IW 222/83, Mathematisch Centrum, Amsterdam 1983.

[7] BERGSTRA, J.A. & J.W. KLOP, *Process algebra for communication and mutual exclusion. Revised version,* Report CS-R8409, Centrum voor Wiskunde en Informatica, Amsterdam 1984.

[8] BERGSTRA, J.A., KLOP, J.W. & J.V. TUCKER, *Algebraic tools for system construction,* in : Logics of Programs, Proceedings 1983 (eds. E. Clarke and D. Kozen), Springer LNCS 164, 1984.

[9] BRANQUART, P., LOUIS, G. & P. WODON, *An analytical description of CHILL, the CCITT High Level Language,* Springer LNCS 128, 1982.

[10] BROCK, J.D. & W.B. ACKERMAN, *Scenarios : A model of non-determinate computation,* in : Proc. Formalization of Programming Concepts (eds. J. Diaz and I. Ramos), p.252-259, Springer LNCS 107, 1981.

[11] BROOKES, S.D., *On the relationship of CCS and CSP,* Proc. 10th ICALP, Barcelona 1983 (ed. J. Diaz), Springer LNCS 154, p.83-96, 1983.

[12] BROOKES, S.D. & W.C. ROUNDS, *Behavioural equivalence relations induced by programming logics,* Proc. 10th ICALP, Barcelona 1983, Springer LNCS 154 (ed. J. Diaz), p.97-108, 1983.

[13] EBERGEN, J., *On VLSI design,* NGI-SION Proceedings 1984, p.144-150, Nederlands Genootschap voor Informatica, Amsterdam 1984.

[14] HENNESSY, M., *A term model for synchronous processes,* Information and Control 51, p.58-75 (1981).

[15] HOARE, C.A.R., *Communicating Sequential Processes,* C. ACM 21 (1978), p.666-677.

[16] HOARE, C.A.R.,
A model for Communicating Sequential Processes
in : "On the construction of programs" (eds. R.M. McKeag and A.M. McNaughton), Cambridge University Press (1980), p.229-243.

[17] HOARE, C., BROOKES, S. & W. ROSCOE,
A theory of communicating sequential processes,
Programming Research Group, Oxford University (1981). To appear in JACM.

[18] KAHN, G.,
The semantics of a simple language for parallel programming,
in : PROC. IFIP 74, North-Holland, Amsterdam 1974.

[19] KOYMANS, R., VYTOPIL, J. & W.P. DE ROEVER,
Real-time programming and asynchronous message passing,
in : Proc. of the Second Annual ACM Symposium on Principles of Distributed Computing, Montreal, 1983.

[20] KUIPER, R. & W.P. DE ROEVER,
Fairness assumptions for CSP in a temporal logic framework,
TC2 Working Conference on the Formal Description of Programming Concepts, Proc., Garmisch 1982.

[21] LAMPORT, L.
'Sometime' is sometimes 'NOT never',
Tutorial on the temporal logics of programs, SRI International CSL-86, 1979.

[22] MILNE, G.J.,
CIRCAL : A calculus for circuit description,
Integration, Vol.1, No. 2 & 3, 1983, p.121-160.

[23] MILNER, R.,
A Calculus of Communicating Systems,
Springer LNCS 92, 1980.

[24] MILNER, R.,
Calculi for synchrony and asynchrony,
Theor. Comp. Sci. 25 (1983), p.267-310.

[25] OBBINK, H., personal communication, April 1984.

[26] PNUELI, A.,
The temporal logic of programs,
in : Proc. 19th Ann. Symp. on Foundations of Computer Science, IEEE, p.46-57, 1977.

[27] REM, M.,
Partially ordered computations, with applications to VLSI design,
Proc. 4th Advanced Course on Foundations of Computer Science, Part 2 (eds. J.W. de Bakker and J. van Leeuwen), Mathematical Centre Tracts 159, p.1-44, Mathematisch Centrum, Amsterdam 1983.

[28] DE SIMONE, R.,
On MEIJE and SCCS : infinite sum operators vs. non-guarded definitions,
Theoretical Computer Science 30 (1984), p.133-138.

[29] VAN DE SNEPSCHEUT, J.L.A.,
Trace Theory and VLSI Design,
Ph.D. Thesis, Eindhoven University of Technology, 1983.

[31] WINSKEL, G.,
Event structure semantics for CCS and related languages,
Proc. ICALP 82, Springer LNCS 140, p.561-576, 1982.

[32] WINSKEL, G.,
Synchronisation trees,
Proc. 10th ICALP (ed. J. Diaz), Barcelona 1983, Springer LNCS 154, p.695-711.

Axioms for Memory Access in Asynchronous Hardware Systems *

J. Misra

Department of Computer Science

The University of Texas at Austin

Austin, Texas 78712

Absract

The problem of concurrent accesses to memory registers by asynchronous components is considered. A set of axioms about the values in a register during concurrent accesses is proposed. It is shown that if these axioms are met by a register then concurrent accesses to it may be viewed as nonconcurrent, thus making it possible to analyze asynchronous algorithms without elaborate timing analysis of operations. These axioms are shown, in a certain sense, to be the weakest. Motivation for this work came from analyzing low level hardware components in a VLSI chip which concurrently access a flip-flop.

1. Introduction

This paper is motivated by issues in hardware design. It addresses the problem of concurrent accesses to memory registers by asynchronous components. Any system in which concurrent accesses are permitted can be proven correct only if some assumptions are made about the behaviors of the registers, particularly under concurrent reads and writes. Unfortunately, physical behaviors of registers are so complex that a direct analysis of the physical behavior cannot be employed in any reasonable correctness argument. Therefore, we propose an axiomatic basis for the study of memory registers. We show that if certain axioms are obeyed by any register, then it may be analyzed as a "serial device" and hence any correctness issue involving the register is considerably simplified. We also show that our axioms are the weakest ones enjoying this property. Discussions with hardware designers lead us to believe that devices, satisfying these axioms, can be realized in current hardware technology.

* This work was supported by a grant from the IBM Corporation.

In analyzing concurrent systems [7], it has generally been assumed that memory references are nonconcurrent, i.e. all accesses to a memory register are equivalent to those accesses made in some sequence. Thus if two or more processes simultaneously attempt to access a memory register, then the accesses will be made in some arbitrary sequential order: the effect of concurrent accesses *op*1||*op*2 is equivalent to the sequence *op*1;*op*2 or *op*2;*op*1. It follows then that if two write operations are simultaneously attempted, then one of the values appears in the memory register upon completion of both operations. Also, if a read and a write overlap in time then the read will either receive the value before the write or the value after the write.

Nonconcurrency of accesses to a memory register can be established either by locking the register such that a write operation is never executed concurrently with any other operation or by building the register in such a way that concurrent accesses appear nonconcurrent to an external observer. This paper is motivated by questions of asynchronous hardware design. At the lowest hardware level, a flip-flop is a memory register which is capable of storing one bit. Locking a flip-flop requires implementing a lock bit, which again has to be implemented as a flip-flop with similar kinds of constraints on accesses. Also, the overhead of locking and consequent loss of concurrency makes such an approach unattractive for very low level hardware implementation. Therefore, we consider the problem of building a register such that concurrent accesses appear nonconcurrent and also nonconcurrent accesses appear to preserve their order.

It is by no means obvious what value gets deposited in a register if two writers are simultaneously writing into it. See [1,5,8,10] for descriptions of some of the complexities associated with a flip-flop operation. Therefore we propose to study registers axiomatically. We postulate a set of axioms about the properties of a register which make intuitive sense. We then show that any register obeying these axioms can be viewed as one for which accesses are nonconcurrent.

Figure 1 depicts certain concurrent accesses to a register pictorially.

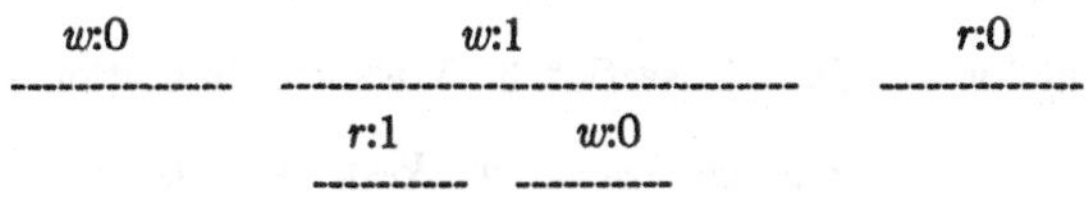

Figure 1. Concurrent Accesses to a Register.

Each horizontal line denotes a time interval in which an operation executes. *w*:0 denotes a write operation that writes a "0" into the register; similarly *w*:1. *r*:0 denotes a read operation that returns a value 0; similarly *r*:1. In Figure 1, operations *w*:1, *r*:1 are *concurrent*, because they overlap in time and so do *w*:1 and *w*:0.

If the register behaves in the manner depicted in Figure 1, we may assume that the operations take place one at a time in a sequential manner as follows.

```
w:0        w:1        r:1        w:0        r:0
--------   --------   --------   --------   --------
```

Figure 2. Operations in Figure 1 Ordered Logically.

In this case processes which access the register can be analyzed as if concurrent memory references are arbitrarily ordered. Consider, however, the situation depicted in Figure 3, which is identical with Figure 1 except that the last read returns a value 1.

```
w:0                  w:1                    r:1
---------   -------------------------------   -------
                r:1          w:0
             ---------    ---------
```

Figure 3. Another Set of Concurrent Accesses to a Register.

Assume for this example that a process *P* sequentially executes *w*:0, *r*:1, *w*:0 and *r*:1 and a process *Q* executes *w*:1. Then it is impossible to analyze processes *P*, *Q* assuming that concurrent accesses to the common register are arbitrarily ordered. This is because if concurrent accesses are arbitrarily ordered, then process *P* can guarantee that both its reads will return different values, contradicting the actual operation as given in Figure 3. The question then is: what properties of the register will make it behave as in Figure 1 and not as in Figure 3.

We formally state the problem in the next section. We define valid schedules, a set of concurrent operations whose effect is equivalent to some sequential (nonconcurrent) executions of these operations. We suggest axioms for a register in section 3. We show, in section 4, that these axioms define only valid schedules and, in a sense, are the weakest. We also give a simple, necessary and sufficient condition for the validity of a schedule.

The example in Figure 3 is from Mills and Lounsbery [6]. They showed that elaborate timing analysis is needed if a register indeed behaves in this manner. Work reported here began after reading that paper and as an attempt to derive conditions under which a register will not display such pathological behavior.

Lamport [2,3] has considered the problem of concurrent reading and writing on a register which may hold more than one atomic data item; therefore, the possibility of an inconsistent read exists. In [2,3] he proposes protocols for reading and writing which guarantee consistency of every read. We do not consider the problem of receiving an inconsistent value in a read operation. In [4] he treats a problem similar to the one treated here for the special case of one writer, i.e. there are no overlapping write operations. It is then shown that a schedule is valid if and only if a write operation overlaps with at most one read operation. This result holds under very weak assumptions about the change in register value during a write.

A problem, similar to the one addressed here, appears in concurrent database access and is called the serializability problem [9]. In that problem, a number of transactions—analogous to processes—each having several atomic steps, concurrently read from and write into a database. It is assumed that truly concurrent steps, i.e. those happening at exactly the same time, are arbitrarily ordered and therefore the result of concurrent access is an interleaved sequence of steps accessing the database. It is required to develop conditions which guarantee that any interleaved sequence of transaction steps is equivalent to some serial executions of the transactions. Therefore each transaction may assume that it is executing alone, even if that is not the case, when these conditions are met. Our problem is different in several respects. Our notion of serial execution is much weaker: we merely observe the accesses made to a register without knowing which process made an access. Therefore, our problem is to devise conditions under which concurrency is equivalent to interleaving; database concurrency problem assumes this equivalence and asks when interleaving is equivalent to sequential execution.

2. Basic Concepts

A *schedule* is any set of concurrent or nonconcurrent reads and writes on a register. We consider only those schedules in which every operation that has started has also ended. A schedule may be depicted pictorially as in Figure 1. We propose an algebraic notation to describe a schedule. This notation captures all relevant details of a schedule except the actual amount of time used in the execution of an operation. In the following, *op* denotes either a read or a write operation. We use $|op{:}x$ to denote the beginning of *op* with associated value x (if *op* is a write operation then x is the value it is writing; if *op* is a read operation, then the value returned by the read is x). We will omit x when this value is irrelevant to the discussion. $op{:}x|$ denotes the end of the operation *op* with associated value x.

Precede denotes that some event (start or end of an operation) happens before another event. Thus, $|op1{:}x$ *precedes* $|op2{:}y$ means that *op*1 starts before *op*2. We write *op*1 *precedes* *op*2 to denote that *op*1$|$ *precedes* $|$*op*2, i.e. *op*1 ends before *op*2 begins. Operations *op*1, *op*2 are *concurrent* if neither *precedes* the other; they are *nonconcurrent* otherwise.

A *valid schedule* S is one for which it is possible to rearrange the operations so that all operations are nonconcurrent, all nonconcurrent operations in S preserve their orders, and the values received by the read operations are consistent with the write operations. Formally, S is a valid schedule iff there exists a permutation S' of S such that:

VC1::

For every *op*, $|op$ *precedes* $op|$ in S' and

VC2::

Every pair of operations in S' is nonconcurrent and

VC3::

If *op*1 *precedes* *op*2 in S then *op*1 precedes *op*2 in S' and

VC4::

If $w{:}x$ is the closest preceding write operation for $r{:}y$ in S' then $y{=}x$.

Figure 1 depicts a valid schedule because the permutation of it given by Figure 2 satisfies the four conditions given above. Figure 3 depicts an invalid schedule, i.e. a schedule that is not valid.

If a set of processes access a register in such a manner that their access schedule S is valid, then we can analyze these processes using the familiar assumption that memory references are nonconcurrent. We can then imagine that the register is being accessed in a sequential manner as given by S' . Conversely, if any access schedule is invalid, then such an assumption cannot be made about access schedules in general and therefore analyses of concurrent programs become far more formidable.

Valid schedules constitute a rich class. For instance, $|w{:}x \ \ |w{:}y \ \ w{:}x| \ \ |r{:}y \ \ |r{:}x \ \ w{:}y| \ \ r{:}y|$ $r{:}x|$ is valid even though the two read operations $r{:}x$ and $r{:}y$ may start and end nearly simultaneously and still return different values.

3. Axioms for Register Operation

The following axioms about the behavior of a register reflect our understanding about the value held by a register, how it is manipulated by writes and how it affects the results of reads. We assume that a register has a unique value at some time instants and its value is undefined at other time instants. The undefined value may correspond to the point where a component, such as a flip-flop, may be undergoing state transition.

In the rest of the paper we will use variables x, y, z... instead of constants 0,1,... to denote values associated with operations. It is important to distinguish between variables and their values. All variables appearing in the write operations are distinct even though their values may be identical. We will distinguish between two identical values which correpsond to two different variables; we will treat them as different values. Therefore, in our terminology, $r{:}x$, $r{:}y$ receive the same value if and only if variables x and y are identical. In the following description "value x" is an abbreviation for "value corresponding to variable x."

We first present the axioms and then provide the rationale. In the following, ***point*** is a time instant. If $t1$, $t2$ are points then $t1 < t2$ denotes that $t1$ is a time instant before $t2$ and $t2$ is a time instant after $t1$. When there can be no confusion, we will use $|op$ and $op|$ to denote the start and end times of operation op. t is ***within*** op means, $|op \leq t \leq op|$.

3.1. Axioms

A1:: For every $r{:}x$, there is some point within r where the register value is x.

A2:: If register value is x at point t and a write operation, $w{:}y$ starts after t and ends before t', $t < t'$, then the register value at t' is different from x (it could be undefined).

A3:: If register value is x at point t' then there exists t, $t \leq t'$, such that t is within $w{:}x$ and register value at t is x.

A4:: If register value is x at t and t' then it is x at all points between t and t'.

3.2. Rationale for the axioms

Axiom A1 says that it is impossible to return a value x if the register never has the value x during a read. Note that the register may have several different values during a read and the axiom does not specify which value will be returned by the read.

Axiom A2 says that a write operation will definitely affect the value of the register. Upon completion of a write operation, $w{:}y$, it may be asserted that the register no longer has its former value. Note however that we do not require the register value to be y upon completion of $w{:}y$. It is likely that the register never has value y if $w{:}y$ is concurrent with other write operations.

Axiom A3 says that any register value x at t' must be written by a write operation that starts at or before t' ; i.e., the register can't change its value miraculously. In this case, the write operation $w{:}x$ deposits the value x at some point within w, at or before t' .

Axiom A4 implies that $w{:}x$ writes the value only once and does not try to rewrite if the value changes, presumably as a result of another write. Therefore once the value changes, the register never regains its former value. This requirement is realistic in the way hardware typically changes values in a register. Multiple writing of the same value by one write will only overwrite the value of a competing write; in a pathological situation, this could lead to nonterminating operations if, for instance, two writes alternately overwrite each other's values.
Notation: We use (x) within a schedule to denote that the register value is x at that point and remains x until some other (y) appears in the schedule.

Example 1

It can be verified that the following schedule is valid and it satisfies all the axioms.

$|w{:}p \ \ (p) \ \ w{:}p| \ \ |w{:}z \ \ |r{:}y \ \ |w{:}y \ \ |w{:}x \ \ |r{:}x \ \ (x) \ \ (y) \ \ r{:}y| \ \ w{:}x| \ \ r{:}x| \ \ w{:}z| \ \ w{:}y| \ \ |r{:}y \ \ r{:}y|$

Register value is never z even though $w{:}z$ is an operation in the schedule. Now consider a modification of the above schedule, $|w{:}p \ \ (p) \ \ w{:}p| \ \ |r{:}y \ \ |w{:}y \ \ |w{:}x \ \ |r{:}x \ \ (x) \ \ (y) \ \ r{:}y| \ \ |w{:}z \ \ w{:}x| \ \ r{:}x| \ \ w{:}z| \ \ w{:}y| \ \ |r{:}y \ \ r{:}y|$. This schedule can be shown to be invalid. Axiom A2 is violated for this schedule.

3.3. Notes on the Axioms

[1] It follows from A1 and A3 that a read operation receives value x only if there is a $w{:}x$ in the schedule. To avoid pathological situations, we assume that initially there is a write operation in every schedule which ends before any other operation starts. We have also assumed that every read returns a value, and not undefined, as the result.

[2] It is possible to combine A3 and A4: if the register value is x at t' then there exists $t \leq t'$ such that t is within $w{:}x$ and the register value is x at all t'', $t \leq t'' \leq t'$. We have kept the two axioms separate to emphasize the distinct assumptions embodied in each one.

[3] Axiom A4 may be weakened to read: if register value is x at t and t' then for all t'', $t \leq t'' \leq t'$, the value is either x or undefined. All the theorems in this paper are satisfied when this weak version is substituted for A4. It should be noted, however, that this weakening is without much merit; under the assumption that every read returns a value, and not undefined, as its result, no set of experiments can establish whether a register obeys A4 or the weak version of A4.

4. Properties of Valid Schedules

We now show that all schedules on a register satisfying these axioms are valid. We will also show that these axioms are, in a sense, the weakest axioms guaranteeing validity. We first give a necessary and sufficient condition for the validity of a schedule.

Given any schedule S, define a relation *before* on the values associated with the operations, as follows.

[1] x *before* x, if some $r{:}x$ *precedes* $w{:}x$.

[2] x *before* y, $y \neq x$, if $op1{:}x$ *precedes* $op2{:}y$ for some $op1$, $op2$.

Example 2

Consider the schedule,

$$|w{:}x \quad w{:}x| \quad |w{:}y \quad |w{:}z \quad |r{:}y \quad |r{:}z \quad w{:}z| \quad w{:}y| \quad r{:}y| \quad r{:}z|$$

x *before* y, because $w{:}x$ *precedes* $r{:}y$ and x *before* z, because $w{:}x$ *precedes* $r{:}z$.

Theorem 1. A schedule is valid if and only if *before* is an irreflexive partial order relation.

Proof: Let *before* be an irreflexive partial order for some schedule S. For each value x_i, construct the subsequence, $|w{:}x_i \;\; w{:}x_i| \;\; |r_1{:}x_i \;\; r_1{:}x_i| \;\; |r_2{:}x_i \;\; r_2{:}x_i|\ldots$, where the write operation $w{:}x_i$ appears first followed by all the read operations whose associated value is x_i; if $r_j{:}x_i$ *precedes* $r_k{:}x_i$ in S, then r_j appears prior to r_k in this subsequence.

Let x_0, $x_1\ldots$ be a total order of all values in S consistent with the partial order *before*; such a total order can be obtained by a topological sort of the values with respect to *before*. Now construct the desired permutation S' from S by appending the subsequences, corresponding to x_0, x_1, ... We claim that S' is a permutation of S which satisfies the conditions VC1, VC2, VC3 and VC4. VC1 is trivially satisfied. Every pair of operations in S' is nonconcurrent, by construction. If $op1{:}x$ *precedes* $op2{:}x$ in S then, from the irreflexivity of *before*, $op2$ is a read and hence the relative order of $op1$, $op2$ is preserved by the construction. If $op1{:}x$ *precedes* $op2{:}y$, $x \neq y$, then x *before* y holds. The subsequence corresponding to x appears before that of y and hence the order is preserved. Every read receives the value of the closest preceding write, by construction.

Conversely, we show that if S is a valid schedule then *before* is an irreflexive partial order. Since S is valid, there exists a permutation S' satisfying VC1, VC2, VC3 and VC4. In S', all operations with associated value x must appear contiguously and $w{:}x$ *precedes* all $r{:}x$; otherwise some read will not receive the value of the closest preceding write. Therefore S' defines a total order of the values. This total order must be consistent with the relation *before*. Hence *before* must be a partial order, otherwise no total order would be consistent with it. Irreflexivity of *before* follows trivially. □

Example 3

Schedule S of Example 2 has the following associated S', constructed by the procedure given in Theorem 1. A total order consistent with *before* is,

$x \;\; z \;\; y.$

From this we construct S' :

$$|w{:}x \quad w{:}x| \quad |w{:}z \quad w{:}z| \quad |r{:}z \quad r{:}z| \quad |w{:}y \quad w{:}y| \quad |r{:}y \quad r{:}y|$$

Example 4

Consider the following schedule which is similar to the one given pictorially in Figure 3 and given below in algebraic notation.

$|w{:}x\ w{:}x|\quad |w{:}y\quad |r{:}y\quad r{:}y|\quad |w{:}z\quad w{:}z|\quad w{:}y|\quad |r{:}y\quad r{:}y|$

before is not a partial order because *y before z* and *z before y*. Therefore, this schedule is not valid.

Theorem 2. Any schedule satisfying axioms A1, A2, A3 and A4 is valid.

Proof: We show that *before* is an irreflexive partial order for such a schedule and hence using Theorem 1 the result follows.

Let S be a schedule satisfying the axioms. Define,

$$R_x = \{t \mid \text{value of register at point } t \text{ is } x\}$$

Either R_x is empty or from A4, R_x is an *interval*, i.e., if t_1, t_2 are in R_x then any t, $t_1 < t < t_2$, is also in R_x. No $r{:}x$ can *precede* $w{:}x$ in S, because from A1, there is some point t' within a read where the register value is x and from A3, there is some point t within $w{:}x$, such that $t \leq t'$. Therefore *before* is irreflexive.

Observation: If R_x is nonempty, for every $op{:}x$ there is some point within op which is in R_x. This follows from A1 if op is a read. If op is a write, the result follows by picking any point t from R_x and then applying A3.

We now show that *before* is a partial order. Consider any two values, x, y, $x \neq y$, for which R_x is nonempty and R_y is nonempty. For $op1{:}x$, $op2{:}y$, some point t_1 within $op1$ is in R_x and some point t_2 within $op2$ is in R_y. $t_1 < t_2$, if $op1$ *precedes* $op2$. Since R_x, R_y are intervals, then every point in R_x is prior to every point in R_y. Hence *before* is a partial order on values x for which R_x is nonempty.

Now consider some y for which R_y is empty. There can be no $r{:}y$ in the schedule because A1 then requires that at some point the register value be y. Therefore, there is only a $w{:}y$ in S. The only way *before* is not a partial order is if there is some value x for which $op1{:}x$ *precedes* $w{:}y$, which *precedes* some $op2{:}x$. We show that this is impossible. Since there are at least two operations involving x, there is at least one $r{:}x$ in S and hence R_x is nonempty. From the previous observation, some t_1 within $op1$ and some t_2 within $op2$ are both in R_x. $t_1 < |w{:}y$ and $w{:}y| < t_2$. Hence, $w{:}y$ is completely within R_x; this violates A2.

Therefore, *before* is an irreflexive partial order. □

Theorem 2 shows that in any schedule if the register values satisfy A1 through A4, then the schedule is valid. We prove the converse in Theorem 3: for every valid schedule it is possible to specify register values at certain points such that axioms A1 through A4 are satisfied. While it is difficult to define precisely the notion of weakest axioms, we can reasonably claim—based on Theorems 2 and 3—that our proposed axioms are the weakest. Theorem 4 shows that the axioms are all independent, i.e., no axiom is implied by the other three.

Theorem 3. It is possible to assign register values at certain points in a valid schedule such that axioms A1 through A4 are satisfied.

Proof: For a valid schedule S, there is a permutation S' satisfying VC1, VC2, VC3, VC4. We use S' to assign register values at certain points in S. Let op_1, op_2, ... , op_n be the sequence of operations in S' and let v_i be the value associated with op_i. As before, the notation (v_i) within a schedule means that the register has value v_i at that point and continues to have the value v_i until there is some (v_j), $v_j \neq v_i$, in the schedule. We use the following algorithm to assign (v_i), $1 \leq i \leq n$, to some points in the schedule S.

[1] (v_1) is assigned immediately following $|op1$ in S.

[2] (v_i), $1 < i$, is assigned immediately following $|op_i$ or $(v_{(i-1)})$ whichever comes later in S.

For instance, if

S is $|op2$ $|op1$ $|op3$ $op1|$ $op3|$ $op2|$, for which

S' is $|op1$ $op1|$ $|op2$ $op2|$ $|op3$ $op3|$,

we assign

$|op2$ $|op1$ (v_1) (v_2) $|op3$ (v_3) $op1|$ $op3|$ $op2|$

Note:

[1] (v_1), (v_2), ... appear in this order in the schedule.

[2] Values associated with reads may be deleted from the assignment constructed, because the same value is also associated with a write. We prefer retaining all (v_i) because it simplifies the following proof.

We sketch a proof that this assignment of values satisfies the axioms. We first show that (v_i) will lie between $|op_i$ and $op_i|$, for all i in S, according to our construction. (v_i) is assigned after $|op_i$ according to our construction. We will now show, using induction, that (v_i) *precedes* $op_j|$ in S, $j \geq i$. In the proof we use the fact that $|op_i$ *precedes* $op_j|$ in S if $j \geq i$, because otherwise, S' does not preserve order among op_i, op_j. Now (v_1) *precedes* $op_j|$, $j \geq 1$, by construction and the fact that $|op_1$ *precedes* $op_j|$. (v_i), $i > 1$, either comes immediately after $v_{(i-1)}$—and since according to induction, $v_{(i-1)}$ *precedes* $op_j|$, $j \geq i\text{-}1$, the result holds—or (v_i) comes immediately after $|op_i$ which *precedes* $op_j|$, $j \geq i$.

Axiom A1 is satisfied because within each operation, and hence within each read, the register has the associated value. Axiom A2 is satisfied because:

[1] $v_i \neq v_j$ means $v_i \neq v_k$, for any $k \geq j$ (this follows from S');

[2] for a write operation op_j, let register value be v_i prior to the write; register value is v_j some point during the write (from the previous paragraph) and $v_i \neq v_j$; any point after the write has a value v_k, $k \geq j$, and since $v_i \neq v_j$, $v_i \neq v_k$, $k \geq j$.

Axiom A3 holds because in S' , if $op_i{:}x$ is a write and $op_j{:}x$ is a read, then $i < j$; according to our construction (v_i) appears before (v_j) and (v_i) appears within op_i. Axiom A4 holds trivially. □

Corollary: For any schedule, there exist register values satisfying axioms A1 through A4, if and only if the schedule is valid. □

We now show that the axioms are independent: if we drop any of the axioms we can find an invalid schedule with a set of register values which satisfy the remaining axioms.

Theorem 4: Any three axioms (from A1 to A4) are satisfied by some assignment of register values to some invalid schedule.

Proof: For each combination of three axioms we show an invalid schedule and specify register values satisfying these axioms.

A1, A2, A3: $|w{:}y \;\; |w{:}x \;\; |r{:}x \;\; (x) \;\; r{:}x| \;\; (y) \;\; w{:}y| \;\; |r{:}y \;\; r{:}y| \;\; |r{:}x \;\; (x) \;\; w{:}x| \;\; r{:}x|$

This schedule is invalid because, from the read operations alone, it follows that x *before* y and y *before* x.

A1, A2, A4: $|r{:}x\ \ (x)\ \ r{:}x|\ \ |w{:}x\ \ w{:}x|$

This schedule is invalid because a read *precedes* a write and hence x *before* x.

A1, A3, A4: $|w{:}x\ \ (x)\ \ |r{:}x\ \ r{:}x|\ \ |w{:}y\ \ w{:}y|\ \ w{:}x|\ \ |r{:}x\ \ r{:}x|$

This schedule is invalid because x *before* y and y *before* x.

A2, A3, A4: $|w{:}x\ \ (x)\ \ w{:}x|\ \ |w{:}y\ \ (y)\ \ w{:}y|\ \ |r{:}x\ \ r{:}x|$

This schedule is invalid because x *before* y and y *before* x. □

We now derive certain properties of valid schedules.

Property 1. If the register value is x at all points during a read then the read returns a value x.

Proof: Using A1, no other value can be returned. □

Property 2. In a schedule S, let $w{:}x_1$, $w{:}x_2$, .. be a set of write operations and $r{:}y$ be a read operation such that every $w{:}x_i$ *precedes* this $r{:}y$ and for any other write operation *op* in S, either *op precedes* all these w's or r *precedes op*. Then $y \in \{x_1, x_2, ...\}$.

Proof: Since the schedule S is valid, some $w{:}x_i$ and r will appear adjacent in any S' satisfying VC1, VC2. The result follows by applying VC3 to S' . □

Corollary: If $w{:}x$ *precedes* $r{:}y$ and for every write operation *op*, either *op precedes* w or r *precedes op*, then $x = y$. □

Note: The above corollary gives a condition under which a write is successful in depositing its value in the register; the write operation executes nonconcurrently with every other write. As we have seen earlier, not all writes need be successful.

Property 3. In a schedule S, let $r{:}x_1$, $r{:}x_2$,... be a set of read operations. Suppose for every write operation *op* in S, either *op precedes* all these r or every r *precedes op*. Then $x_1 = x_2 =$ ...

Proof: Since the schedule is valid, all these read operations will appear adjacent in any permutation S' of S satisfying VC1, VC2. Result follows by applying VC3 to S' . □

5. Summary and Conclusion

Advances in VLSI technology have now made it possible to place over 100,000 devices on a chip. Design methodology for dense chips, however, has still remained largely ad hoc. It is believed [6,10] that designing a chip as a set of asynchronous modules will simplify the design process. There has been a considerable amount of research on asynchronous concurrent programming in the last fifteen years. This paper is an effort to study the applicability of this research in hardware design. We have studied a fundamental assumption—nonconcurrency of simultaneous access—which is basic to most concurrent programming work. We have shown how this assumption can be met by designing memory registers which meet certain axioms. The axioms seem quite basic and are usually met in practice, at least for flip-flops. The most nonintuitive is axiom A4, which says that the implementation of a write operation must attempt to write its value only once. We have shown that these axioms are sufficient and, in a sense, necessary.

Acknowledgement

Dr. Harlan D. Mills, of IBM, has pointed out the necessity of elaborate timing analysis if nonconcurrency assumption is not met [6]. I am indebted to him for suggesting the problem and for his enthusiasm, encouragement and advice. I am grateful to other members of the Provable Hardware Design Group (Jim Aylor, Ray Hookway, Norm Pleszkoch, John Saunders) of IBM, Federal System Division, for interaction and constructive criticism during the course of this work. Professor Doug Jensen has pointed out that the proposed axioms may be viewed as design rules for constructions of registers. I am thankful to Professor Charles Molnar for his comments. Dr. Leslie Lamport has kindly brought some of his early unpublished work to my attention.

References

[1] Chaney, T. and Molnar, C., "Anomalous Behavior of Synchronizer and Arbiter Circuits," *IEEE Trans. on Computers*, April 73, pp. 421-422.

[2] Lamport, L., "Concurrent Reading and Writing," *CACM*, Vol. 20, No. 11 (November 77), pp. 806-811.

[3] Lamport, L., "A New Approach to Proving the Correctness of Multiprocess Program," *ACM TOPLAS*, Vol. 1, No. 1, July 79.

[4] Lamport, L., "A Theorem on Multiprocess Algorithms," Technical Report CA-7503-2011, Massachusetts Computer Associates, March 1975.

[5] Marino, L.P., "General Theory of Metastable Operation," *IEEE Trans. on Computers*, Vol. C-30, No.2, February 81.

[6] Mills, H.D. and Lounsbery, J.M., "Combinatorial Analyses of Process Synchronization," IBM, FSD (internal memo), August 1983.

[7] Owicki, S. and Gries, D., "An Axiomatic Proof Technique for Parallel Programs," *Acta Informatica* 6, 4 (1976), pp. 319-340.

[8] Saunders, J.M., "Engineering Description of a Flip Flop Reader and Writer," IBM, FSD (internal memo), January 1984.

[9] Ullman, Jeffrey D., *Principles of Database Systems*, Computer Science Press, 1980.

[10] Wann, D. and Franklin, M., "Asynchronous and Clocked Control Structures for VLSI Based Interconnection Networks," *IEEE Trans. on Computer*, Vol. C-32, No. 3, March 1983, pp. 264-293.

Executing Temporal Logic Programs

(preliminary version)

Ben Moszkowski

Computer Laboratory, University of Cambridge,
Corn Exchange Street, Cambridge CB2 3QG, England

24 August 1984

Abstract

Over the last few years, temporal logic has been investigated as a tool for reasoning about computer programs, digital circuits and message-passing systems. In the case of programs, the general feeling has been that temporal logic is an adjunct to existing languages. For example, one might use temporal logic to specify and prove properties about a program written in, say, CSP. This leads to the annoyance of having to simultaneously use two separate notations.

In earlier work we proposed that temporal logic itself directly serve as the basis for a programming language. Since then we have implemented an interpreter for such a language called *Tempura*. We are developing Tempura as a tool for directly executing suitable temporal logic specifications of digital circuits and other discrete-time systems. Since every Tempura statement is also a temporal formula, we can use the entire temporal logic formalism for our assertion language and semantics. Tempura has the two seemingly contradictory properties of being a logic programming language and having imperative constructs such as assignment statements.

The presentation given here first describes the syntax and semantics of a first-order temporal logic having the operators $\bigcirc$ (*next*) and $\Box$ (*always*). This serves as the basis for the Tempura programming language. The lesser known temporal operator *chop* is subsequently introduced, resulting in *Interval Temporal Logic*. We then show how to incorporate *chop* and related constructs into Tempura.

1. Introduction

Temporal logic [12,20] has been recently put forward as a useful tool for reasoning about concurrent programs and hardware. Within temporal logic, one can express logical operators for reasoning about time-dependent concepts such as "*always*" and "*sometimes.*" Consider, for example, the English sentence

"*If the propositions P and Q are always true, then P is always true.*"

This can be represented in temporal logic by the formula

$$\Box(P \wedge Q) \supset \Box P.$$

Here the operator $\Box$ corresponds to the notion "*always.*" Thus, the subformula $\Box(P \wedge Q)$ can be understood as "*P and Q are always true.*"

Typically, temporal logic has been thought of as a tool for specifying and proving properties of programs written in, say, CSP [11] or variants of Pascal with concurrency [10]. This distinction between temporal logic and programming languages has troubled us since it has meant that we must simultaneously use two separate notations. Programming formalisms such as Hoare logic [9], dynamic logic [6,19], and process logic [4,7] also reflect this dichotomy. One way to bridge the gap is to find ways of using temporal logic itself as a tool for programming and simulation. With this in mind, we have developed *Tempura*, an imperative programming language based on subsets of temporal logic. Every Tempura statement is a temporal logic formula. This lets us specify and reason about Tempura programs without the need for two notations.

Another aspect of the current usage of temporal logic is the restriction of temporal constructs to such propositional operators as □ (*always*), ○ (*next*), ◇ (*sometimes*) and $\mathcal{U}$ (*until*). In fact, there are quite a few other useful propositional and first-order temporal operators for treating such programming concepts as iteration, assignment and scoping. We explore these constructs within *Interval Temporal Logic*, a formalism having the operators □, ○ and the lesser known temporal operator *chop*. This also serves as the underlying notation for Tempura programs and their specifications and properties.

1.1. Organization of Paper

We start off by reviewing the syntax and semantics of a temporal logic having the operators □ (*always*) and ○ (*next*). A number of temporal constructs are then presented and later used to build legal Tempura statements and expressions. This is followed by a description of an interpreter for executing such statements and a discussion of some of the trade-offs made in implementing the system. Subsequently, we extend the logic to include the temporal operator *chop*. Within the resulting Interval Temporal Logic we derive some Algol-like constructs which are subsequently incorporated into Tempura and the interpreter. We conclude with a look at some related work. The Tempura examples given here have been intentionally kept simple. However, in the full version of this paper we plan to discuss Tempura programs that have been implemented for such tasks as parallel quicksorting and simulation of a hardware multiplier.

2. Basic Features of the Temporal Logic

Before describing Tempura, it is necessary to have an understanding of the underlying temporal logic. Some of the constructs described here will be later used in Tempura programs. Others will facilitate reasoning about program behavior. Rather than presenting the entire logic at once, we will first introduce some basic operators and derive others from them. In a later section, some additional operators will be considered.

2.1. Syntax of the Logic

The initial set of constructs includes conventional logical operators such as = (*equality*) and ∧ (*logical-and*). In addition, there are the two temporal operators ○ (*next*) and □ (*always*).

2.1.1. Syntax of Expressions

Expressions are built inductively as follows:

- Individual variables: $A, B, C, \ldots$
- Functions: $f(e_1, \ldots, e_k)$, where $k \geq 0$ and $e_1, \ldots, e_k$ are expressions. In practice, we use functions such as + and *mod*. Constants such as 0 and 1 are treated as zero-place functions.

- Next: $\bigcirc e$, where e is an expression.

Here are two examples of syntactically legal expressions:

$$I + (\bigcirc J) + 1, \qquad (\bigcirc I) + J - \bigcirc\bigcirc(I + \bigcirc J).$$

2.1.2. Syntax of Formulas

Formulas are built inductively as follows:

- Predicates: $p(e_1, \ldots, e_k)$, where $k \geq 0$ and $e_1, \ldots, e_k$ are expressions. Predicates include $\leq$ and other basic relations.
- Equality: $e_1 = e_2$, where e_1 and e_2 are expressions.
- Logical connectives: $\neg w$ and $w_1 \wedge w_2$, where w, w_1 and w_2 are formulas.
- Next: $\bigcirc w$, where w is an formula.
- Always: $\Box w$, where w is an formula.

Here are some syntactically legal ITL formulas:

$$(J = 2) \wedge \bigcirc(I = 3), \quad \big(\bigcirc\Box[I = 3]\big) \wedge \neg\big([\bigcirc J] = 4\big), \quad \bigcirc\big(\Box[I = 3] \wedge \bigcirc\bigcirc[J = 4]\big).$$

Note that the operator $\bigcirc$ can be used both for expressions (e.g., $\bigcirc J$) and for formulas (e.g., $\bigcirc(I = 3)$).

2.2. Models

A model is a triple $(\mathcal{D}, \Sigma, \mathcal{M})$ containing a data domain $\mathcal{D}$, a set of states Σ and a interpretation $\mathcal{M}$ giving meaning to every function and predicate symbol. For the time being, we take the data domain $\mathcal{D}$ to be the integers. A state is a function mapping variables to values in $\mathcal{D}$. We let Σ be the set of all such functions. For a state $s \in \Sigma$ and a variable A, we let $s[\![A]\!]$ denote A's value in s. Each k-place function symbol f has an interpretation $\mathcal{M}[\![f]\!]$ which is a function mapping k elements in $\mathcal{D}$ to a single value:

$$\mathcal{M}[\![f]\!] \in (\mathcal{D}^k \to \mathcal{D}).$$

Interpretations of predicate symbols are similar but map to truth values:

$$\mathcal{M}[\![p]\!] \in (\mathcal{D}^k \to \{\mathit{true}, \mathit{false}\}).$$

We assume that $\mathcal{M}$ gives standard interpretations to operators such as $+$ and $<$.

The semantics given here keep the interpretations of function and predicate symbols independent of intervals. The semantics can however be extended to allow for functions and predicates that take into account the dynamic behavior of parameters.

Using the states in Σ, we construct *intervals* of time from the set Σ^+. An interval is thus any nonempty, finite sequence of states. If s, t and u are states $\in \Sigma$, then the following are possible intervals:

$$\langle s \rangle, \quad \langle sttsus \rangle, \quad \langle tttt \rangle.$$

Note that an interval always contains at least one state.

We now introduce some basic notation for manipulating intervals. Given an interval σ, we let $|\sigma|$ be the *length* of σ. Our convention is that an interval's length is the number of states *minus one*. Thus the intervals above have respective lengths 0, 5 and 3. The individual states of an interval σ are denoted by $\sigma_0, \sigma_1, \ldots, \sigma_{|\sigma|}$. For instance, the following equality is true iff the variable A has the value 5 in σ's final state:

$$\sigma_{|\sigma|}[A] = 5.$$

The model described here views time as being discrete and is not intended to be a realistic representation of the world around us. Nonetheless, it provides a sound basis for reasoning about many interesting dynamic phenomena involving timing-dependent and functional behavior. Furthermore, a discrete-time view of the world often corresponds to our mental model of digital systems and computer programs. In any case, we can always make the granularity of time arbitrarily fine.

2.3. Interpretation of Expressions and Formulas

We now extend the interpretation $\mathcal{M}$ to give meaning to expressions and formulas on intervals. The construct $\mathcal{M}_\sigma[\![e]\!]$ will be defined to equal the value in $\mathcal{D}$ of the expression e on the interval σ. Similarly, $\mathcal{M}_\sigma[\![w]\!]$ will equal the truth value of the formula w on σ.

At first glance, the following definitions may seem somewhat arbitrary. We therefore suggest that an initial reading be rather cursory since the subsequent discussion and examples provide motivation. The definitions can then be referenced as needed.

- $\mathcal{M}_\sigma[\![v]\!] = \sigma_0[\![v]\!]$, where v is a variable.
  Thus, a variable's value on an interval equals the variable's value in the interval's initial state.
- $\mathcal{M}_\sigma[\![f(e_1, \ldots, e_k)]\!] = \mathcal{M}[\![f]\!](\mathcal{M}_\sigma[\![e_1]\!], \ldots, \mathcal{M}_\sigma[\![e_k]\!])$.
  The interpretation of the function symbol f is applied to the interpretations of $e_1, \ldots, e_k$.
- $\mathcal{M}_\sigma[\![\bigcirc\, e]\!] = \mathcal{M}_{\langle\sigma_1 \ldots \sigma_{|\sigma|}\rangle}[\![e]\!]$, if $|\sigma| \geq 1$.
  We leave the value of $\bigcirc\, e$ unspecified on intervals having length 0.
- $\mathcal{M}_\sigma[\![p(e_1, \ldots, e_k)]\!] = \mathcal{M}[\![p]\!](\mathcal{M}_\sigma[\![e_1]\!], \ldots, \mathcal{M}_\sigma[\![e_k]\!])$.
- $\mathcal{M}_\sigma[\![e_1 = e_2]\!] = \textit{true}$ iff $\mathcal{M}_\sigma[\![e_1]\!] = \mathcal{M}_\sigma[\![e_2]\!]$.
- $\mathcal{M}_\sigma[\![\neg w]\!] = \textit{true}$ iff $\mathcal{M}_\sigma[\![w]\!] = \textit{false}$.
- $\mathcal{M}_\sigma[\![w_1 \wedge w_2]\!] = \textit{true}$ iff $\mathcal{M}_\sigma[\![w_1]\!] = \textit{true}$ and $\mathcal{M}_\sigma[\![w_2]\!] = \textit{true}$.
- $\mathcal{M}_\sigma[\![\bigcirc\, w]\!] = \textit{true}$ iff $|\sigma| \geq 1$ and $\mathcal{M}_{\langle\sigma_1 \ldots \sigma_{|\sigma|}\rangle}[\![w]\!] = \textit{true}$.
- $\mathcal{M}_\sigma[\![\square\, w]\!] = \textit{true}$ iff for all $i \leq |\sigma|$, $\mathcal{M}_{\langle\sigma_i \ldots \sigma_{|\sigma|}\rangle}[\![w]\!] = \textit{true}$.

Examples

We will now illustrate the use of $\mathcal{M}$ by considering the semantics of the sample temporal formulas given earlier. Let s, t and u be states in which the variables I and J have the following values:

	I	J
s	1	2
t	3	4
u	3	1

The formula

$$(J = 2) \wedge \bigcirc(I = 3)$$

is true on an interval σ iff σ has length ≥ 1, the value of J in the state σ_0 is 2 and the value of I in the state σ_1 is 3. Thus, the formula is true on the interval $\langle stu \rangle$. On the other hand, the formula is false on the interval $\langle ttu \rangle$ because J's initial value on this interval is 4 instead of 2.

The formula

$$(\circ\Box[I=3]) \wedge \neg([\circ J]=4)$$

is true on any interval σ having length ≥ 1 and in which I equals 3 in the states $\sigma_1, \ldots, \sigma_{|\sigma|}$ and J does not equal 4 in σ_1. Thus the formula is true on the interval $\langle sutut \rangle$ but is false on $\langle t \rangle$ and $\langle stutu \rangle$.

The formula

$$\circ(\Box[I=3] \wedge \circ\circ[J=4])$$

is true on an interval σ having length ≥ 3 and in which the variable I equals 3 in the states σ_1, $\ldots$, $\sigma_{|\sigma|}$ and the variable J equals 4 in the state σ_3. Thus this formula is true of the interval $\langle suutu \rangle$ but is false on $\langle s \rangle$ and $\langle sutuu \rangle$.

2.4. Satisfiability and Validity

A formula w is *satisfied* by an interval σ iff the meaning of w on σ equals *true*:

$$\mathcal{M}_\sigma[\![w]\!] = \mathit{true}.$$

This is denoted as follows:

$$\sigma \models w.$$

If all intervals satisfy w then w is *valid*, written $\models w$.

Example (Validity):

The following formula is true on an interval σ iff $|\sigma| \geq 1$, the variable I always equals 1 and in the state σ_1, I equals 2:

$$\Box(I=1) \wedge \circ(I=2).$$

No interval can have all of these characteristics. Therefore the formula is false on all intervals and its negation is always true and hence valid:

$$\models \quad \neg[\Box(I=1) \wedge \circ(I=2)].$$

3. Deriving Other Operators

The kinds of interval behavior one can describe with the constructs so far introduced may seem rather limited. In fact, this is not at all the case since we can develop quite a variety of derived operators. We will now present some derived operators that have proved useful in reasoning about simple computations.

3.1. Boolean Operators

The conventional boolean constructs $w_1 \vee w_2$ (logical-or) , $w_1 \supset w_2$ (implication) and $w_1 \equiv w_2$ (equivalence) can be expressed in terms of $\neg$ and $\wedge$. We can define logical-or as shown below:

$$w_1 \vee w_2 \quad \equiv_{\mathrm{def}} \quad \neg(\neg w_1 \wedge \neg w_2).$$

We then express implication and equivalence as follows:

$$w_1 \supset w_2 \quad \equiv_{\mathrm{def}} \quad \neg w_1 \vee w_2, \qquad w_1 \equiv w_2 \quad \equiv_{\mathrm{def}} \quad (w_1 \supset w_2) \wedge (w_2 \supset w_1).$$

The boolean constructs *true* and *false* can also be derived.

Example (Implication):

If in an interval σ, the variable I always equals 1 and in the state σ_1 the variable J equals 2 then it follows that the expression $I + J$ equals 3 in σ_1. This fact can be expressed by the following valid formula:

$$\models \quad [\Box(I=1) \land \bigcirc(J=2)] \supset \bigcirc(I+J=3).$$

Example (Equivalence):

The formula

$$\bigcirc([I=1] \land [J=2])$$

is true on an interval σ iff σ has length ≥ 1 and in the state σ_1, the variable I has the value 1 and the variable J has the value 2. It turns out that the conjunction

$$\bigcirc(I=1) \land \bigcirc(J=2)$$

has the same meaning. The equivalence of these two formulas is expressible as follows:

$$\bigcirc([I=1] \land [J=2]) \;\equiv\; [\bigcirc(I=1) \land \bigcirc(J=2)].$$

This formula is true on all intervals and is therefore valid. In general, if two formulas w_1 and w_2 have the same meaning on all intervals, then the equivalence $w_1 \equiv w_2$ is valid.

3.2. The Operator *empty*

The formula ***empty*** is true on an interval iff the interval has length 0:

$$\sigma \models \textit{empty} \quad \text{iff} \quad |\sigma| = 0.$$

We can define ***empty*** as follows:

$$\textit{empty} \quad \equiv_{\text{def}} \quad \neg\bigcirc\,\textit{true}.$$

Example (Testing the length of an interval):

We can use the constructs $\bigcirc$ and ***empty*** to test the length of an interval. For example, the formula

$$\bigcirc\bigcirc\bigcirc\,\textit{empty}$$

is true on an interval σ iff σ has length 3.

3.3. The Operators *gets* and *stable*

It is useful to say that over time one expression e_1 equals another expression e_2 but with a one-unit delay. We use the construct e_1 ***gets*** e_2 to represent this and define it as follows:

$$e_1 \;\textit{gets}\; e_2 \quad \equiv_{\text{def}} \quad \Box(\neg\textit{empty} \supset [(\bigcirc e_1) = e_2]).$$

The test $\neg$***empty*** ensures that we do not "run off" the edge of the interval by erroneously attempting to examine e_1's value in the nonexistent state $\sigma_{|\sigma|+1}$.

For instance, the formula K ***gets*** $2K$ is true on an interval σ iff the variable K is repeatedly doubled from each state to its successor:

$$\sigma \models \quad K \;\textit{gets}\; 2K \quad \text{iff} \quad \text{for all } i < |\sigma|,\ \sigma_{i+1}[\![K]\!] = 2 \cdot \sigma_i[\![K]\!].$$

The construct ***stable*** e is true iff the value of the expression e remains unchanged. We can readily define ***stable*** in terms of ***gets***:

$$\textit{stable}\; e \quad \equiv_{\text{def}} \quad e \;\textit{gets}\; e.$$

Example (Expressing an invariant condition):

The following formula is true on an interval σ in which I and J are both initially 0 and I repeatedly increases by 1 and J repeatedly increases by 2:

$$(I = 0) \wedge (J = 0) \wedge (I \; gets \; I + 1) \wedge (J \; gets \; J + 2).$$

In any interval for which this is true, J always equals $2I$. Below is a valid property that formalizes this:

$$\models \quad \big[(I = 0) \wedge (J = 0) \wedge (I \; gets \; I + 1) \wedge (J \; gets \; J + 2)\big] \;\supset\; \Box(J = 2I).$$

This shows how the operator $\Box$ can express an invariant condition.

Example (Stability):

The formula

$$(I = 1) \wedge stable \; I$$

is true iff I initially equals 1 and its value remains unchanged. This is the same as saying that I always equals 1. The following valid property expresses this equivalence:

$$\models \quad \big[(I = 1) \wedge stable \; I\big] \equiv \Box(I = 1).$$

3.4. The Operator *halt*

We can specify that a formula w becomes true only at the end of an interval σ by using the formula *halt* w:

$$halt \; w \quad \equiv_{\text{def}} \quad \Box(w \equiv empty).$$

Thus w must be false until the last state at which time w is true. For example, the formula

$$halt(I > 100)$$

is true on σ iff the value of the variable I exceeds 100 in exactly the last state of σ.

Example (Repeatedly doubling a number):

From what we have so far presented, it can be seen that the formula

$$(I = 1) \wedge halt(I > 100) \wedge (I \; gets \; 2I)$$

is true on an interval where the variable I is initially 1 and repeatedly doubles until it exceeds 100. The following valid implication states that intervals on which this formula is true will terminate upon I equalling the value 128:

$$\models \quad \big[(I = 1) \wedge halt(I > 100) \wedge (I \; gets \; 2I)\big] \supset halt(I = 128).$$

```
Output = 1
State #0 ready.

Output = 2
State #1 ready.

Output = 4
State #2 ready.

Output = 8
State #3 ready.

Output = 16
State #4 ready.

Done!  Computation length = 4.
```

Figure 1: Execution of Formula (1)

4. A Temporal Programming Language

Consider now the formula

$$(M = 4) \wedge (N = 1) \wedge \mathit{halt}(M = 0) \wedge (M \mathrel{\mathit{gets}} M - 1) \wedge (N \mathrel{\mathit{gets}} 2N).$$

This holds true of intervals of length 4 in which M successively runs through the values 4, 3, 2, 1 and 0 and N simultaneously runs through the values 1, 2, 4, 8, and 16. Let us now explore how to automate the process of taking such a temporal formula and finding an interval satisfying it. One way to do this is to develop a procedure that analyzes the formula and either terminates with the length of some acceptable interval and values of the relevant variables in all the interval's states or else fails.

We will use another technique which we call ***interval generation***. This approach takes the original formula and scans it once for each state of the interval being generated. We introduce the predicates ***input*** and ***output***. In any state where the predicate $\mathit{input}(v)$ is true, the user can input a value for the variable v. Whenever the predicate $\mathit{output}(e)$ is encountered, the expression e is evaluated and its value is displayed to the user. The net effect is that the temporal formula is "executed" with the predicates ***input*** and ***output*** providing communication to the user. For example, the formula given below includes a subformula that always outputs the value of N to the user:

$$\begin{aligned}&(M = 4) \wedge (N = 1) \wedge \mathit{halt}(M = 0)\\ &\quad \wedge (M \mathrel{\mathit{gets}} M - 1) \wedge (N \mathrel{\mathit{gets}} 2N) \wedge \Box\, \mathit{output}(N).\end{aligned} \tag{1}$$

As the overall formula is processed, the successive values of N are displayed. Figure 1 shows a sample session in which this is executed.

When the following formula is executed, the user is continually asked for the values of I:

$$\Box\, \mathit{input}(I) \wedge \mathit{halt}(I = 0) \wedge (J = 0) \wedge \Box\, \mathit{output}(J) \wedge (J \mathrel{\mathit{gets}} J + I). \tag{2}$$

These values are summed into J and J itself is displayed. The interval terminates upon I equalling 0. An execution of this is given in figure 2. Numbers in boxes (e.g., $\boxed{6}$) are input by

```
Input = [6]
Output = 0
State #0 ready.

Input = [2]
Output = 6
State #1 ready.

Input = [5]
Output = 8
State #2 ready.

Input = [0]
Output = 13
State #3 ready.

Done!  Computation length = 3.
```

Figure 2: Execution of Formula (2)

the user.

The general problem of finding an interval that satisfies a temporal formula is unsolvable. However, there are subsets of temporal logic for which the task is managable. We now present *Tempura*, a programming language based on one such subset.

4.1. Syntax of Tempura

The main syntactic categories in Tempura are locations, expressions and statements. Let us look at each of these separately:

4.1.1. Locations

A *location* is a place into which values can be stored and later retrieved. Variables such as I, J and K are permissible locations. In addition, if l is a location, so is the temporal construct $\bigcirc l$.

4.1.2. Expressions

Expressions can be either arithmetic or boolean. All numeric constants and variables are legal arithmetic expressions. In addition, if e_1 and e_2 are arithmetic expressions, so are operations such as the following:

$$e_1 + e_2, \quad e_1 - e_2, \quad e_1 \cdot e_2, \quad e_1 \div e_2, \quad e_1 \; mod \; e_2.$$

In addition, if e is an arithmetic expression then so is the temporal construct $\bigcirc e$.

Relations such as $e_1 = e_2$ and $e_1 \geq e_2$ are boolean expressions. If b, b_1 and b_2 are boolean expressions, then so are the following:

$$\neg b, \quad b_1 \wedge b_2, \quad b_1 \vee b_2, \quad b_1 \supset b_2, \quad b_1 \equiv b_2.$$

The constants *true* and *false* and the construct *empty* are boolean expressions as well.

4.1.3. Statements

Certain temporal formulas are legal statements in Tempura. A statement is either *simple* or *compound*. Simple statements are built from the constructs given below. Here l is a location, e an arithmetic expression and b a boolean expression:

$l = e$	(equality)
empty	(terminate)
$\neg$*empty*	(do not terminate)
input(l)	(input into a location)
output(e)	(output an expression).

The statement $l = e$ stores the value of the arithmetic expression e into the location l.

Compound statements are built from the constructs given below. Here w, w_1 and w_2 are themselves statements and b is a boolean expression:

$w_1 \wedge w_2$	(parallel composition)
$b \supset w$	(conditional execution)
$\bigcirc w$	(next)
$\Box w$	(always)

Note that certain temporal formulas can be used as both boolean expressions and statements. Here are three examples:

$$I = 3, \quad (J = 2) \wedge (K = J + 3), \quad (I = 0) \supset \textit{empty}.$$

On the other hand, the following legal boolean expressions are not Tempura statements even though they are semantically equivalent to the respective formulas given above:

$$3 = I, \quad (2 = J) \wedge (J + 3 = K), \quad \neg(I = 0) \vee \textit{empty}.$$

4.2. Some Other Statements

Other constructs such as *gets*, *stable* and *halt* can be readily added to Tempura. One way to do this is to expand these to statements already described. Here are some possible equivalences:

$$\begin{aligned} l \textit{ gets } e &\equiv \Box\big(\neg \textit{empty} \supset [(\bigcirc l) = e]\big), \\ \textit{stable } l &\equiv l \textit{ gets } l, \\ \textit{halt } b &\equiv \Box\big([b \supset \textit{empty}] \wedge [\neg b \supset \neg \textit{empty}]\big). \end{aligned}$$

Once we include these statements, programs such as the following can be readily processed:

$$\textit{input}(I) \wedge (J = 1) \wedge \Box\, \textit{output}(J) \wedge \textit{halt}(I = 0) \wedge (I \textit{ gets } I - 1) \wedge (J \textit{ gets } 2J).$$

This statement initially requests the input of a value for I and then repeatedly outputs the first few powers of 2 until I is decreased to 0.

4.3. An Interpreter for Tempura

We now briefly outline an interpreter for executing Tempura statements. The interpreter takes a statement and generates an acceptable interval by repeatedly scanning and modifying the statement until the final state of the interval is reached. A flag named ***done*** is used to indicate termination. Each iteration of the interpreter corresponds to one state of the interval being generated. In addition to the flag ***done***, an environment called ***env*** maintains each variable's current and next values. Over time, as the statement is executed, the entries in the environment are updated to reflect changes to the variables. The full version of this paper will discuss the implementation of the interpreter in more detail.

As we mentioned earlier, Tempura statements are limited to a subset of temporal formulas. So far we have only mentioned syntactic restrictions. Let us consider some limitations that the interpreter itself imposes on Tempura programs. This will give some idea of the design trade-offs we have made.

4.3.1. Determinism

The interpreter expects the user to completely specify the behavior of variables and to indicate when termination should occur. For example, the statement

$$I \; \textit{gets} \; I+1$$

lacks information on I's initial value and does not specify when to stop. Thus other details must be included for the interpreter to properly operate. Of course, we could be more lenient by using backtracking and related techniques to resolve such omissions. However, for the sake of the simplicity and efficiency of the interpreter, it seems reasonable at the moment to require explicit, unambiguous information on all aspects of variable behavior.

4.3.2. Left-to-right processing

The interpreter scans statements from left to right. Therefore the statement

$$(J = I + 3) \wedge (I = 0)$$

is not properly handled since the value of I is not yet known during the evaluation of the expression $I + 3$. This can be remedied by reordering the two equalities as follows:

$$(I = 0) \wedge (J = I + 3).$$

4.3.3. Restrictions on *empty*

The construct *empty* as implemented by the interpreter is also subject to restrictions. Consider the following statement for running I through the values 10, 9, ..., 0:

$$(I = 10) \wedge (I \; \textit{gets} \; I - 1) \wedge \textit{halt}(I = 0).$$

This does not execute properly since the definition of the *gets* construct involves a test of the value of *empty*, but this in not determined until the *halt* construct is encountered and processed. The solution here is to simply exchange the two operations, thus yielding the following:

$$(I = 10) \wedge \textit{halt}(I = 0) \wedge (I \; \textit{gets} \; I - 1).$$

4.3.4. Restrictions on the operator ○

The environment only maintains the current and next values of variables. Therefore, an attempt to store in a location such as $\bigcirc\bigcirc\bigcirc I$ does not work properly because this looks too far into the future.

4.3.5. Why these restrictions?

The limitations outlined here could to some extent be avoided by automated static analysis, by repeated scanning of statements during each state and by modifying the environment to store more values for each variable. Nevertheless, the current interpreter seems to be a reasonable compromise. More experience is needed before a firm conclusion is reached on these matters.

5. Further Temporal Constructs

In addition to the constructs already presented, temporal logic contains various useful operators such as existential quantification ($\exists$) and the temporal operator *chop*. Some of these constructs are rather similar to certain kinds of statements found in Algol and related programming languages. We first extend the syntax and semantics of the temporal logic to include $\exists$ and *chop*. The resulting formalism is called Interval Temporal Logic. Within it we define a number of interval-dependent operators. Tempura is subsequently expanded to include some of these.

5.1. Syntax of *chop* and $\exists$

In addition to the constructs previously introduced, we now permit formulas of the following two forms:

- Chop: $w_1; w_2$, where w_1 and w_2 are formulas.
- Existential quantification: $\exists v.\ w$, where v is a variable and w is a formula.

The following are two simple formulas:

$$(\mathit{stable}\ I); (\mathit{stable}\ J), \qquad \exists I.\ \Box(J = 2I).$$

5.2. Semantics of *chop* and $\exists$

The semantics of these operators are as follows:

- $\mathcal{M}_\sigma[\![w_1; w_2]\!] = \mathit{true}$ iff
  for some $i \le |\sigma|$, $\mathcal{M}_{(\sigma_0 \dots \sigma_i)}[\![w_1]\!] = \mathit{true}$ and $\mathcal{M}_{(\sigma_i \dots \sigma_{|\sigma|})}[\![w_2]\!] = \mathit{true}$.
- $\mathcal{M}_\sigma[\![\exists v.\ w]\!] = \mathit{true}$ iff
  for some interval $\sigma' \in \Sigma^+$, $\sigma \sim_v \sigma'$ and $\mathcal{M}_{\sigma'}[\![w]\!] = \mathit{true}$.
  Here the relation $\sigma \sim_v \sigma'$ is defined to be true iff the intervals σ and σ' have the same length and agree on the behavior of all variables except possibly the variable v.

Examples

Consider the following states and their assignments to the variables I and J:

	I	J
s	2	4
t	0	4
u	2	3

We assume that s, t and u agree on assignments to all other variables.

The following formula is true any interval on which I is stable for a while and then J is stable for the remainder of the interval:

$$(\textit{stable}\ I);(\textit{stable}\ J).$$

The interval $\langle sustst \rangle$ satisfies the formula since I is always 2 on the subinterval $\langle sus \rangle$ and J is always 4 on $\langle stst \rangle$. The formula is also true on the intervals $\langle s \rangle$ and $\langle uuu \rangle$ but it is false on the interval $\langle stuu \rangle$.

The formula

$$\exists I.\ \Box(J = 2I)$$

is intuitively true on any interval on which we can construct an I such that J always equals $2I$. This is the same as saying that J is always even. For example, the interval $\langle ttt \rangle$ satisfies the formula. From the semantics of $\exists$ given previously it follows that to show this we need to construct an interval σ' for which the relation $\langle ttt \rangle \sim_I \sigma'$ is true and which satisfies the subformula $\Box(J = 2I)$. The interval $\langle sss \rangle$ achieves both of these constraints. Therefore $\langle ttt \rangle$ satisfies the original formula. Other intervals satisfying the formula include $\langle sss \rangle$ itself and $\langle sst \rangle$ but not $\langle u \rangle$ or $\langle stut \rangle$. Existential quantification is a tricky concept and the reader should not necessarily expect to grasp it immediately.

5.3. Discussion of the Operator *chop*

The construct *chop* is rather different from the conventional temporal operators $\Box$ and $\bigcirc$. The later examine an interval's suffix subintervals whereas *chop* splits the interval and tests both parts. This facilitates looking at arbitrary subintervals of time.

Harel, Kozen and Parikh [7] appear to be are the first to mention *chop* as a temporal construct. It is considered in more detail by Chandra, Halpern, Meyer and Parikh [4]. In [5] and [16] we use *chop* to facilitate reasoning about timing-dependent digital hardware. Our subsequent work in [18] and [17] uses *chop* to give specifications and properties of simple algorithms and message-passing systems. In the rest of this section we examine *chop* and other ITL constructs and then extend Tempura to include them.

5.4. The Operator *fin*

The formula *fin* w is true on an interval σ iff w is itself true on the final subinterval $\langle \sigma_{|\sigma|} \rangle$. We express *fin* w as follows:

$$\textit{fin}\ w \quad \equiv_{\text{def}} \quad \Box(\textit{empty} \supset w).$$

The formula *fin* w is weaker than *halt* w since *fin* w only looks at the last state but *halt* w tests behavior throughout.

An Example

The following formula is true on an interval σ iff $|\sigma| = 3$ and I is initially 1 and repeatedly doubles:

$$(\bigcirc\bigcirc\bigcirc\, \textit{empty}) \wedge (I = 1) \wedge (I\ \textit{gets}\ 2I).$$

One effect is that I ends up equal to 8. This is expressed by the valid implication given below:

$$\models \quad [(\bigcirc\bigcirc\bigcirc\, \textit{empty}) \wedge (I = 1) \wedge (I\ \textit{gets}\ 2I)] \supset \textit{fin}(I = 8).$$

5.5. Assignment

The formula $e_1 \rightarrow e_2$ is true for an interval if the expression e_1's initial value equals the expression e_2's final value. We define this as follows:

$$e_1 \rightarrow e_2 \quad \equiv_{\text{def}} \quad \exists A.\ \big[(\textit{stable } A) \land (A = e_1) \land \textit{fin}(e_2 = A)\big],$$

where the variable A does not occur free in either e_1 or e_2. The stability of A is used to compare the values of e_1 and e_2 at different times. We call this construct ***temporal assignment***. For example, the formula $I+1 \rightarrow I$ is true on an interval σ iff the value of $I+1$ in the initial state σ_0 equals the value of I in the final state $\sigma_{|\sigma|}$. If desired, we can reverse the direction of the arrow:

$$I \leftarrow I+1.$$

The formula

$$(I \leftarrow I+1) \land (J \leftarrow J+I)$$

is then true in an interval iff I increases by 1 and in parallel J increases by I. Similarly, the following specifies that the values of the variables A and B are exchanged:

$$(A \rightarrow B) \land (B \rightarrow A).$$

Unlike assignment in conventional programming languages, temporal assignment only affects variables explicitly mentioned; the values of other variables do not necessarily remain fixed. For example, the formulas

$$I \leftarrow I+1$$

and

$$(I \leftarrow I+1) \land (J \leftarrow J)$$

are not equivalent since the first formula does not require J's initial and final values to be equal.

Example (Sequential composition of assignments):

The formula

$$(K+1 \rightarrow K);(K+2 \rightarrow K)$$

is true on an interval σ iff there is some $i \leq |\sigma|$ such that the subformula $K+1 \rightarrow K$ is true on the subinterval $\langle \sigma_0 \ldots \sigma_i \rangle$ and the subformula $K+2 \rightarrow K$ is true on remaining subinterval $\langle \sigma_i \ldots \sigma_{|\sigma|} \rangle$. The net effect is that K increases by 3. This is expressed by the following property:

$$\models \quad \big[(K+2 \rightarrow K);(K+1 \rightarrow K)\big] \supset (K+3 \rightarrow K).$$

5.6. Conditional Formula

We let the boolean construct ***if*** w_1 ***then*** w_2 ***else*** w_3 be true on an interval if either w_1 and w_2 are true or $\neg w_1$ and w_3 are true. This can be formalized by the following definition:

$$\textit{if } w_1 \textit{ then } w_2 \textit{ else } w_3 \quad \equiv_{\text{def}} \quad (w_1 \supset w_2) \land (\neg w_1 \supset w_3).$$

Example (In-place computation of the maximum of two numbers):

The temporal formula

$$\textit{if } I \geq J \textit{ then } (I \leftarrow I) \textit{ else } (I \leftarrow J)$$

is true in any interval where I's value in the final state equals the maximum of the values of I and J in the initial state. This can be seen by case analysis on the test $I \geq J$.

Let the function $\max(i, j)$ equal the maximum of the two values i and j. The following temporal formula also places the maximum of I and J into I:

$$I \leftarrow \max(I, J)$$

The equivalence of the two approaches is expressed by the following property:

$$\models \quad [I \leftarrow \max(I, J)] \equiv [\textit{if } I \geq J \textit{ then } (I \leftarrow I) \textit{ else } (I \leftarrow J)].$$

5.7. While-Loops

Within temporal logic, various kinds of iterative constructs can be introduced as formulas. One of the most important is the ***temporal while-loop***. The basic form is similar to that for a while-loop in Algol:

$$\textit{while } w_1 \textit{ do } w_2,$$

where w_1 and w_2 are themselves formulas.

The while-loop obeys the following general expansion property:

$$\textit{while } w_1 \textit{ do } w_2 \quad \equiv \quad \textit{if } w_1 \textit{ then } \big(w_2; [\textit{while } w_1 \textit{ do } w_2]\big) \textit{ else empty}.$$

Thus, if w_1 is true, the body of the loop, w_2, is examined after which the loop is repeated. If w_1 is false, the interval must have length 0. It is possible to express while-loops using operators presented earlier. For-loops and other iterative constructs can also be handled.

Example (Computing the greatest common divisor):

Consider the following assignment which specifies that N's final value equals the initial value of the greatest common divisor of M and N:

$$N \leftarrow \textit{gcd}(M, N).$$

The formula below implies this:

$$\textit{while } (M \neq 0) \textit{ do } \big([M \leftarrow N \textit{ mod } M] \wedge [N \leftarrow M]\big).$$

5.8. The Construct *skip*

The construct ***skip*** is true on an interval σ iff σ has length 1. We can express ***skip*** as follows:

$$\textit{skip} \quad \equiv_{\text{def}} \quad \bigcirc \, \textit{empty}.$$

Example (Measuring the length of an interval):

An interval's length can be tested using ***skip*** and ***chop***. For example, the formula

$$\textit{skip}; \textit{skip}; \textit{skip}$$

is true on intervals having length 3. Since ***chop*** is associative, we can omit parentheses without being ambiguous.

Example (Unit-length iterations):

The following while-loop repeatedly decrements I and sums I into J over each unit of time until I equals 0:

$$\textit{while}\,(I = 0)\;\textit{do}\,\big(\textit{skip} \wedge [I \leftarrow I - 1] \wedge [J \leftarrow J + I]\big).$$

The body of the loop contains the ***skip*** operator in order that the length of each iterative step be 1. The behavior can also be expressed using ***halt*** and ***gets***. Here is a semantically equivalent way of doing this:

$$\textit{halt}(I = 0) \wedge (I\;\textit{gets}\;I - 1) \wedge (J\;\textit{gets}\;J + I).$$

5.9. Incorporating ITL Constructs into Tempura

We now extend Tempura to include statements based on the ITL constructs just introduce. The set of simple statements is now expanded to include the following:

$l \leftarrow e$	(assignment)
skip	(unit interval)

Compound statements are extended to include the following:

$w_1; w_2$	(sequential composition)
if b *then* w_1 *else* w_2	(conditional statement)
while b *do* w	(while-loop)
$\exists v.\ w$	(existential quantification).

Example (Hiding a variable):

The following toy program has two distinct variables both called I:

$$(I = 0) \wedge (I\;\textit{gets}\;I + 1) \wedge \textit{halt}(I = 5) \wedge \exists I.\ \big[(I = 1) \wedge (I\;\textit{gets}\;3I) \wedge \Box\,\textit{output}(I)\big].$$

The first I runs from 0 to 5 and in parallel the second I is repeatedly tripled from 1 to 243. The use of existential quantification ($\exists$) keeps the two I's separate and in effect hides the second one. As this example illustrates, we can use $\exists$ to create locally scoped variables.

Example (Computing sums):

The following Tempura program uses a while-loop to compute a sum:

$$\begin{aligned} &\textit{input}(I) \wedge (J = 0) \wedge \Box\,\textit{output}(J) \\ &\quad \wedge \big[\textit{while}\;I \neq 0\;\textit{do}\,\big(\textit{skip} \wedge [I \leftarrow I - 1] \wedge [J \leftarrow J + I]\big)\big]. \end{aligned} \tag{3}$$

The user inputs a value and the program then determines the sum of the numbers up to that value. Figure 3 shows a sample session in which the user requests the sum of the values up to 4.

```
Input = [4]
Output = 0
State #0 ready.

Output = 4
State #1 ready.

Output = 7
State #2 ready.

Output = 9
State #3 ready.

Output = 10
State #4 ready.

Done!  Computation length = 4.
```

Figure 3: Execution of Formula (3)

Example (Computing powers):

Consider the problem of finding the value of the expression I^J and placing this in another variable K. We can specify this using the temporal assignment

$$K \leftarrow I^J.$$

The following Tempura program achieves this by looking at J's binary structure:

$$(K = 1) \wedge \left[\textit{while}\,(J > 0)\;\textit{do}\,(\textit{skip} \wedge w)\right],$$

where the statement w has the form

$$\begin{array}{l} \textit{if}\;(J\;\textit{mod}\;2 = 0) \\ \quad \textit{then}\;\left[(I \leftarrow I \cdot I) \wedge (J \leftarrow J \div 2) \wedge (K \leftarrow K)\right] \\ \quad \textit{else}\;\left[(I \leftarrow I) \wedge (J \leftarrow J - 1) \wedge (K \leftarrow K \cdot I)\right]. \end{array}$$

6. Experience and Further Work

Based on the ideas discussed here, we have implemented a Tempura interpreter in Lisp. Tempura programs for such tasks as parallel quicksorting, fast fourier transforms, and simulation of a hardware multiplier have been written and successfully run. We intend to discuss some of this work in the full version of this paper. Together with Roger Hale, a PhD student, we are experimenting with the system and are trying out further programming examples. Another Tempura interpreter has been developed as a programming project by Nigel Beckwith.

Tempura contains various other features including for-loops, arrays and procedures. All of these can be fitted into the framework of temporal logic (see [5] and [16] for more details). The main change to the interpreter is the addition of a memory for maintaining the values of variables and array elements. The environment entries no longer store values themselves but instead point to cells in the memory. This approach is very similar to that used in executing conventional block-structured languages.

7. Some Related Work

The functional programming language *Lucid* [2,3] developed by Ashcroft and Wadge is similar to parts of Tempura. For example, the Lucid program

$$I = 0 \ fby \ (I + 1); \quad J = 0 \ fby \ (J + I)$$

roughly corresponds to the temporal formula

$$(I = 0 \wedge J = 0) \wedge (I \ gets \ I + 1) \wedge (J \ gets \ J + I).$$

This illustrates how the operator ***gets*** can be handled in Lucid. On the other hand, Algol-like temporal constructs such as $\leftarrow$, ***chop*** and ***while*** do not have direct analogs in Lucid. Thus, a Tempura construct such as

$$\textit{while}\ (M \neq 0)\ \textit{do}\ \big(\textit{skip} \wedge [M \leftarrow M - 1] \wedge [N \leftarrow 2N]\big)$$

cannot be readily translated. In [1], a calculus is developed for reasoning about Lucid programs.

Hehner [8] views programs as logical predicates over input-output behavior of variables. Various Algol-based constructs such as assignment (":="), sequencing (";") and while-loops are treated in this manner. Time is introduced by means of an explicit clock variable. Hehner then goes on to introduce concurrency through CSP-like channels. It seems too early to compare this approach with temporal logic.

Manna and Wolper [14] investigate techniques for synthesizing CSP synchronization code from temporal logic specifications. Examples include a reader-writer system and the dining philosphers' problem. Mishra and Clarke [15] use temporal logic to describe asynchronous digital circuits and then generate corresponding finite-state automata. Tang [21] and Manna and Pneuli [13] discuss ways of translating conventional programming constructs into transition systems described in temporal logic. The resulting temporal descriptions can then be used to reasoning about the original programs. In contrast to these approaches, we have worked on developing a set of temporal operators that facilitate programming directly in temporal logic. This bypasses the need for two notations and omits any synthesis from specifications.

8. Conclusions

The present work has investigated Tempura, a program language based on Interval Temporal Logic. The ITL formalism provides a way to treat such programming concepts as assignment and loops as formulas about intervals of time. Therefore, Tempura programs, their specifications and their properties can all be expressed in the same formalism. In the future, we hope to use Tempura for simulating various hardware devices and message-passing systems. In addition, we plan to explore the feasibility of using it as a general-purpose programming language.

Acknowledgements

We wish to thank Mike Gordon, Roger Hale and Edmund Ronald for stimulating conversations and suggestions. Funding from the British Science and Engineering Research Council is gratefully acknowledged.

9. References

[1] E. A. Ashcroft and W. W. Wadge. *Lucid: A formal system for writing and proving programs. SIAM Journal of Computing 5*, 3 (September 1976), 336-354.

[2] E. A. Ashcroft and W. W. Wadge. "Lucid, a nonprocedural language with iteration." *Communications of the ACM 20*, 7 (July 1977), 519-526.

[3] E. A. Ashcroft and W. W. Wadge. *Lucid, the Data Flow Programming Language*, to be published.

[4] A. Chandra, J. Halpern, A. Meyer, and R. Parikh. Equations between regular terms and an application to process logic. *Proceedings of the 13-th Annual ACM Symposium on Theory of Computing*, Milwaukee, Wisconsin, May, 1981, pages 384–390.

[5] J. Halpern, Z. Manna and B. Moszkowski. A hardware semantics based on temporal intervals. *Proceedings of the 10-th International Colloquium on Automata, Languages and Programming*, Barcelona, Spain, July, 1983.

[6] D. Harel. *First-Order Dynamic Logic*. Number 68 in the series *Lecture Notes in Computer Science*, Springer-Verlag, Berlin, 1979.

[7] D. Harel, D. Kozen, and R. Parikh. "Process logic: Expressiveness, decidability, completeness." *Journal of Computer and System Sciences 25*, 2 (October 1982), pages 144–170.

[8] E. C. R. Hehner. "Predicative programming (parts I and II)." *Communications of the ACM 27*, 2 (February 1984), pages 134–151.

[9] C. A. R. Hoare. "An axiomatic basis for computer programming." *Communications of the ACM 12*, 10 (October 1969), pages 576–580, 583.

[10] C. A. R. Hoare. Towards a theory of parallel programming. In C. A. R. Hoare and R. H. Perrott, editors, *Operating Systems Techniques*, pages 61–71. Academic Press, London, 1972.

[11] C. A. R. Hoare. "Communicating sequential processes." *Communications of the ACM 21*, 8 (August 1978), pages 666–677.

[12] Z. Manna and A. Pnueli. Verification of concurrent programs: The temporal framework. In R. S. Boyer and J. S. Moore, editors, *The Correctness Problem in Computer Science*, pages 215–273, Academic Press, New York, 1981.

[13] Z. Manna and A. Pnueli. How to cook your favorite programming language in temporal logic. *Proceedings of the Tenth Annual ACM Symposium on Principles of Programming Languages*, Austin, Texas, January, 1983, pages 141–154.

[14] Z. Manna and P. L. Wolper. "Synthesis of computing processes from temporal logic specifications." *ACM Transactions on Programming Languages and Systems 6*, 1 (January 1984), pages 68–93.

[15] B. Mishra and E. M. Clarke, Automatic and hierarchical verification of asynchronous circuits using temporal logic. Technical report CMU-CS-83-155, Department of Computer Science, Carnegie-Mellon University, September, 1983.

[16] B. Moszkowski. *Reasoning about Digital Circuits*. PhD Thesis, Department of Computer Science, Stanford University, 1983.

[17] B. Moszkowski. A temporal analysis of some concurrent systems. To appear in the proceedings of the STL Workshop on Concurrency, Cambridge, England, September, 1983.

[18] B. Moszkowski and Z. Manna. Reasoning in interval temporal logic. Technical report STAN-CS-83-969, Department of Computer Science, Stanford University, July, 1983.

[19] V. R. Pratt, Semantical considerations on Floyd-Hoare logic. *Proceedings of the 17-th Annual IEEE Symposium on Foundations of Computer Science*, Houston, Texas, October, 1976, pages 109–121.

[20] N. Rescher and A. Urquart. *Temporal Logic*. Springer-Verlag, New York, 1971.

[21] C. Tang. Toward a unified logic basis for programming languages. *Proceedings of IFIP Congress 83*, Elsevier Science Publishers B.V. (North-Holland), Amsterdam, 1983, pages 425–429.

The Static Derivation of Concurrency and Its Mechanized Certification

Christian Lengauer
Chua-Huang Huang
Department of Computer Sciences
The University of Texas at Austin
Austin, Texas 78712-1188

Abstract

This is an attempt to combine the two research areas of programming methodology and automated theorem proving. We investigate the potential for automation of a programming methodology that supports the compile-time derivation of concurrency in imperative programs. In this methodology, concurrency is identified by the declaration of certain semantic properties (so-called "semantic relations") of appropriate program parts. Semantic declarations can be exploited to transform the sequential execution of the program into a parallel execution. We make observations about the automation of correctness proofs of such transformations for a limited domain of programs: sorting networks.

1. Introduction

This paper is about the feasibility of a research area: *programming methodology*, or the formal derivation of programs. Like the formal proof of programs, the formal derivation of programs will be feasible in a software production environment only if it is mechanically supported. Program logics in their present form are technically too intricate to be efficiently and reliably applied by hand on a large scale, and it is doubtful that they will become simpler in the future. (This is not to say that the formal derivation and proof of programs by hand is not of considerable academic interest.) The research area that deals with the automation of formal logics is *automated theorem proving*. We would like to contribute to the currently emerging and very important link between programming methodology and automated theorem proving.

Automating or, more exactly, mechanically certifying the derivation of programs helps both the programmer and the customer who uses the program. The programmer will find an automated derivation more difficult and tedious than a derivation by hand. This is to be expected: an automated derivation does not permit any informal steps; each ever so little detail has to be formalized. However, what is gained, is the near-to-complete confidence that the derivation rules have been applied correctly. The customer reaps most of the reward of an automated derivation. All he has to believe in order to be convinced of the correctness of the programmer's product is:

(a) that the program's specification meets his needs, and

(b) that the theorem which states that the program satisfies the specification is correctly represented in the mechanized programming calculus.

He does not have to be concerned with any aspects of the proof at all. However, both the programmer and the customer must believe one more thing: that the programming calculus has been implemented correctly, i.e., that no faulty programs can be certified.

The methodology in whose automation we are interested focusses on the static derivation of concurrency in imperative programs [9]. In this methodology, the derivation of concurrency proceeds by a successive compression of the program's executions based on the declaration of certain useful program properties. Most interesting programs contain recursions or loops. The most effective and practical transformations of such programs will also be recursive, and their proofs of correctness will require induction. We are therefore interested in the mechanical treatment of recursion and induction.

The following section reviews our methodology. Sect. 3 introduces the class of programs that we explore: sorting networks. After some general observations about the mechanical support of trace transformations and a justification why we view them as theorems (Sect. 4), we describe a mechanically supported "proof methodology" of trace transformations and illustrate it on several sorting networks (Sect. 5). We conclude the paper with a discussion of the challenges in the automation of this proof methodology (Sect. 6).

A more detailed account of our mechanized semantic theory and the full description of a mechanical proof can be found in [12].

2. A Methodology for the Static Derivation of Concurrency

Our goal is to mechanize parts of a particular methodology for the derivation of concurrency in programs [9]. This section describes that methodology.

Two different motives may lead to the application of concurrency:

(1) The desire for a specific program *behavior*.

For instance, one might wish to run an experiment which involves certain processes executed by designated processors that communicate and synchronize with each other in some fashion. Such applications are to ensure the correct functioning of some machine configuration with a specific concurrency structure. Examples are distributed or operating systems.

(2) The desire for fast program *results*.

For instance, one might wish to execute a numerical or data processing algorithm with concurrency in order to obtain a result faster. Such applications do not refer to a specific machine configuration or concurrency structure, but only to some relation of input and output values. Examples are numerical and sorting algorithms.

The programming methodology described here takes the second approach: concurrency is viewed as a tool for accelerating the acquisition of results, not as a basic characteristic of a program. Consequently, concurrency will not be part of the problem specification, but will be derived after the development of the program. We would like to certify this derivation mechanically.

This methodology can be applied to every programming problem that is completely specified by an input/output assertion pair. A terminating solution must exist, i.e., the output assertion must not be false. An execution time limit in form of a function of the input variables may or may not be added. One could conceive also the addition a storage space limit but, in its present from, the methodology does not provide for that.

The methodology cannot be applied to a programming problem with additional constraints like a specific concurrent behavior. Programs with a specific behavior can be derived (see, for instance, the Producer/Consumer and the Dining Philosophers in [9]), but the correctness of such behavior has to be argued informally.

Thus, we permit the specification of a programming problem in three parts:

(a) the input constraints under which the program shall operate,

(b) the results which the program is supposed to achieve, and

(c) an optional time limit imposed on the program's execution.

The program development then proceeds along the following lines:

(1) Perform a formal stepwise refinement of a program that achieves the desired result under the given input constraints. The program does not address the question of execution order. It may not require a total order of its operations, but an easy, sequential execution can, at this point, serve as a first execution time estimate.

(2) Declare simple relations between program components, so-called "semantic relations", that allow relaxations in sequencing, e.g., concurrency. Do so until the execution time of the program satisfies the specified time limit.

A refinement of program S is, for instance, S: S1;S2. The semicolon denotes "application". It may be implemented by executing S1 and then S2, but need not be in all cases.

Semantic relations are, for instance, the commutativity of the components S1 and S2 (written S1&S2), and the independence of S1 and S2 (written S1||S2). S1 and S2 are commutative, i.e., S1&S2 may be declared if the execution of S1 and then S2 has the same effect as the execution of S2 and then S1. If S1&S2 is declared, S1;S2 may also be implemented by executing S2 and then S1. S1 and S2 are independent, i.e., S1||S2 may be declared if the execution of S1 and S2 in parallel has the same effect as their execution in order. If S1||S2 is declared, S1;S2 may also be implemented by executing S1 and S2 in parallel. A third semantic relation is the idempotence of some component S (written !S). S is idempotent, i.e., !S may be declared if S has the same effect as S;S. If !S is declared, we may add to or delete from a sequence of consecutive calls of S.

Idempotence helps eliminate superfluous parts of an execution, or duplicate parts of an execution for commutation to appropriate places. Commutativity helps distribute program components to places in the execution where they can be executed in concurrence with others. Independence helps add concurrency. Independence implies commutativity.

To declare semantic relations for some program, one does not need to understand the program as a whole. A local understanding of the components appearing in the declared relation is sufficient. The concurrency that is induced by semantic declarations is of a very simple nature: there is no need for synchronization (other than at the point of termination) or mutual exclusion, as is required for conventional concurrent processes. Most semantic declarations come easily to mind and have a simple proof.

But the foremost benefit of this approach to the derivation of fast programs is that the more important and better understood question of program refinement is resolved before the less important and more complex question of concurrency arises. Concurrency is later added in isolated steps (by invoking semantic relations) without changing the approved meaning of the program.

For concurrency to be correct, a program has to fulfill intricate requirements. That is what makes concurrency so hard to understand. It is easier to derive concurrency on an informed basis (as the last step of the program derivation) than on an uninformed basis (as the first step of the program derivation). The correctness proof of concurrency is easier at a refinement level where concurrency is simple, e.g., between two independent program parts than at a refinement level where concurrency is complicated, e.g., between two processes that require synchronization and mutual exclusion.

Thus, in our methodology, the development of programs with concurrency is divided into two stages:

Stage 1: The development and formal semantic description of a *program* that achieves the desired result. This requires a formal refinement and the declaration of semantic relations. Programs are composed by the usual program combinators, e.g., composition: **S1;S2** (read: "**S2** is applied to the results of **S1**").

Stage 2: The derivation of a fast *execution* of the program produced at Stage 1. (An execution of a program is also called a *trace*.) This is conceptually simple but computationally complex. It involves the computation of execution times and the invocation of semantic relations to transform traces and improve execution time. There are two trace combinators: **S1→S2** (read: "execute S1 and then S2"), and **<S1 S2>** (read: "execute S1 and S2 in parallel").

We call Stage 1 the *refinement calculus* and Stage 2 the *trace calculus*. Either of the two stages has the potential for automation. Automation of Stage 1 would yield a mechanical system for program refinement. Research along these lines is under way elsewhere [2, 13]. Automation of Stage 2 would yield a very powerful optimizing compiler (since we view concurrency as optimization). Early work in this area [8] has been without a formal semantic basis. At that time, formal semantics was in its infancy. Our interest is the mechanical support of Stage 2 on a formal semantic basis.

The most common approach to programming in which the derivation of concurrency is divorced from the derivation of the program is data flow programming [1]. A data flow program makes no explicit reference to the order of execution. It is executed on a special machine architecture that follows the sequencing imposed by the data dependencies of the program's variables. Data flow languages are "referentially transparent": they do not permit the re-assignment of variables. This simplifies the identification of data independencies so much that, commonly, no programmer assistance is needed to identify concurrency. Our approach is "referentially opaque", i.e., permits the re-assignment of variables and, consequently, requires a more complicated data flow analysis. We have to explicitly declare and subsequently exploit data independencies (in our formalism, semantic relations).

The vast majority of software that exists today and is currently being produced is referentially opaque. The vast majority of today's machine architectures support the referentially opaque programming style. While we must strive for new programming styles and machine architectures, we must also continue to increase our understanding of the present technology.

3. Expository Domain: Sorting Networks

Semantic relations can be declared for programs in any imperative programming language that has a weakest precondition semantics. For the purpose of our investigation we choose a very simple language. We do not want to complicate our mechanical proofs of trace transformations by unduly complicated semantics of programs and traces. We define the language of *sorting networks* [7]. The general problem that we pursue is to sort an array $a_{0..n}$ of numbers into ascending order in no more time than O(n). The linear time requirement forces us to consider a concurrent execution. In the language of sorting networks, refinements can have the following structure:

(1) The *null statement* skip does nothing.

(2) The *comparator module* `cs(i,j)` accesses an array **a** of numbers. It compares elements a_i and a_j and, if necessary, swaps them into order. A simpler version of comparator module with only one argument, `cs(i)`, deals with adjacent elements a_{i-1} and a_i. We call sorting networks that are composed of simple comparator modules *simple sorting networks*. The comparator module is of imperative nature, i.e., its implementation requires assignment.

(3) The *composition* `S1;S2` of refinements S1 and S2 applies S2 to the results of S1.

Sorting networks are well-suited for our methodology because they terminate and only their results, not their behaviors matter. They also have a wide range of applications and are extensively researched. It is important to realize that we are not trying to do research in sorting networks. We chose them as a well-understood first domain in which to test our ideas of automation.

Since we are concerned with the trace calculus of the methodology, we do not dwell on the refinement of programs but accept the particular sorting network whose trace transformations we want to study as given. So far, we have studied three sorting networks: the insertion sort, the odd-even transposition sort, and the bitonic sort [7]. The insertion sort and the odd-even transposition sort can be expressed as simple sorting networks. The bitonic sort expects array **a** already presorted in bitonic order. Let us describe each of the three sorting networks in turn.

3.1. Insertion Sort

The following refinement describes the insertion sort:

```
insertion-sort(n):  sort(n)

                sort(0):  skip
(i>0)           sort(i):  sort(i-1); S(i)

                S(0):     skip
(i>0)           S(i):     cs(i); S(i-1)
```

Comparator modules may be declared idempotent. Consecutive applications of the same comparator module do not yield any new results. For `|i-j|>1`, i.e., if `i` and `j` are not "neighbors", `cs(i)` and `cs(j)` are disjoint: they do not share any variables. Components that do not share variables may be declared independent.

```
          !cs(i)
|i-j|>1  ⇒  cs(i)||cs(j)
```

Note that the prerequisite `|i-j|>1` makes `cs(i)||cs(j)` a semantic rather than syntactic condition. (Semantic declarations can also be qualified with respect to a postcondition. For the underlying theory see [11].)

For, say, a six-element array (n=5), the refinement has the following sequential execution, if we interpret composition ';' as execution in order '→' and expand components `sort(i)` and `S(i)` (i≤5) of `sort(5)`:

```
tau(5) = cs(1)→cs(2)→cs(1)
                    →cs(3)→cs(2)→cs(1)
                           →cs(4)→cs(3)→cs(2)→cs(1)
                                  →cs(5)→cs(4)→cs(3)→cs(2)→cs(1)
```

If we count the number of comparator modules `cs`, `tau(5)` has length 15. In general, `tau(n)` has length `n(n+1)/2`, i.e., is quadratic in `n`. To derive a linear execution, we have to exploit the independence declaration for `sort(n)` and compress `tau(n)` into a trace with concurrency. We have already laid out the sequential trace `tau(5)` in a form which suggests how this can be done. We commute comparator modules in `tau(5)` left, and then merge adjacent modules whose indices differ by 2 into a parallel command:

$$\mathtt{tau}^{\sim}(5) = \mathtt{cs(1)}\rightarrow\mathtt{cs(2)}\rightarrow\left\langle\begin{array}{c}\mathtt{cs(1)}\\ \mathtt{cs(3)}\end{array}\right\rangle\rightarrow\left\langle\begin{array}{c}\mathtt{cs(2)}\\ \mathtt{cs(4)}\end{array}\right\rangle\rightarrow\left\langle\begin{array}{c}\mathtt{cs(1)}\\ \mathtt{cs(3)}\\ \mathtt{cs(5)}\end{array}\right\rangle\rightarrow\left\langle\begin{array}{c}\mathtt{cs(2)}\\ \mathtt{cs(4)}\end{array}\right\rangle\rightarrow\left\langle\begin{array}{c}\mathtt{cs(1)}\\ \mathtt{cs(3)}\end{array}\right\rangle\rightarrow\mathtt{cs(2)}\rightarrow\mathtt{cs(1)}$$

If we assume instantaneous initiation and termination of parallel commands (instantaneous forks and joins), this execution is of length 9. In general, `tau~(n)` is of length 2n−1, i.e., linear in `n`. The degree of concurrency increases as we add inputs. This is a property of all three sorting networks. They are not limited to a fixed number of concurrent actions. However, if only a fixed number `k` of processors is available, the independence declaration may be exploited only to generate a concurrency degree of `k` or less.

Note that the idempotence declaration of comparator modules does not help in the derivation of concurrency for the insertion sort. As we shall see in the next section, array $a_{0..n}$ can be sorted faster than by `tau~(n)`, but not when we start with the refinement of the insertion sort.

3.2. Odd-Even Transposition Sort

The odd-even transposition sort is the simplest possible example of the transformation of a sorting network. Here is the refinement:

```
odd-even-sort(n):      sort(n+1,n)

          sort(0,j):   skip
          sort(1,j):   S(j-1)
(i>1)     sort(i,j):   S(j-1); S(j); sort(i-2,j)

          S(0):        skip
          S(1):        cs(1)
(i>1)     S(i):        cs(i); S(i-2)
```

As a simple sorting network like the insertion sort, the odd-even transposition sort adopts the semantic declarations of the previous section:

$$!\mathtt{cs(i)}$$

$$|\mathtt{i}-\mathtt{j}|>1 \;\Rightarrow\; \mathtt{cs(i)}\,||\,\mathtt{cs(j)}$$

The sequential trace of this refinement for a five-element array (n=4) is:

$$\mathtt{tau(4)} = \mathtt{cs(3)}\rightarrow\mathtt{cs(1)}\rightarrow\mathtt{cs(4)}\rightarrow\mathtt{cs(2)}\rightarrow\mathtt{cs(3)}\rightarrow\mathtt{cs(1)}\rightarrow\mathtt{cs(4)}\rightarrow\mathtt{cs(2)}\rightarrow\mathtt{cs(3)}\rightarrow\mathtt{cs(1)}$$

The number of comparator modules in tau(4) is 10. In general, tau(n) has length n(n+1)/2. In every S(i), the indices of all comparator modules differ at least by 2. Thus we can convert each S(i) into one parallel command. The resulting parallel trace is:

$$\mathtt{tau^{-}(4)} = \left\langle \begin{matrix}\mathtt{cs(1)}\\ \mathtt{cs(3)}\end{matrix} \right\rangle \rightarrow \left\langle \begin{matrix}\mathtt{cs(2)}\\ \mathtt{cs(4)}\end{matrix} \right\rangle \rightarrow \left\langle \begin{matrix}\mathtt{cs(1)}\\ \mathtt{cs(3)}\end{matrix} \right\rangle \rightarrow \left\langle \begin{matrix}\mathtt{cs(2)}\\ \mathtt{cs(4)}\end{matrix} \right\rangle \rightarrow \left\langle \begin{matrix}\mathtt{cs(1)}\\ \mathtt{cs(3)}\end{matrix} \right\rangle$$

tau⁻(4) is of length 5. In general, tau⁻(n) is of length n+1.

3.3. Bitonic Sort

An array $a_{0..n}$ is in *bitonic order* if $a_0 \geq \ldots \geq a_i \leq \ldots \leq a_n$ for some $0 \leq i \leq n$. Let us write array $a_{0..n}$ as a sequence $\langle a_0, a_1, \ldots, a_n \rangle$. The bitonic sorting algorithm sorts an array a that is already in bitonic order into ascending order by sorting the subsequences $\langle a_0, a_2, \ldots \rangle$ and $\langle a_1, a_3, \ldots \rangle$ independently, and then comparing and interchanging (a_0, a_1), (a_2, a_3),... . Since the subsequences of a bitonic sequence are also bitonic, $\langle a_0, a_2, \ldots \rangle$ and $\langle a_1, a_3, \ldots \rangle$ can be sorted by the same algorithm, until all subsequences have length 1. The bitonic sort is not a simple sorting network. It requires the general comparator module cs(i,j).

The refinement of the bitonic sort is:

```
          bitonic-sort(n):              sort(0,1,n+1)

          sort(base, step, 0):          skip
          sort(base, step, 1):          skip
(leng>1)  sort(base, step, leng):       sort(base, step*2, ⌈leng/2⌉);
                                        sort(base+step, step*2, ⌊leng/2⌋);
                                        S(base, step, step*2, ⌊leng/2⌋)

          S(base, dist, step, 0):       skip
(leng>0)  S(base, dist, step, leng):    cs(base, base+dist);
                                        S(base+step, dist, step, leng-1)
```

Refinement **sort** performs the bitonic sort as described. It is qualified by three parameters, **base**, **step**, and **leng**, that identify a subsequence of **a**: **base** is the index of the first element, **step** is the difference of the indices of any two adjacent elements, and **leng** is the number of elements in the subsequence. Refinement **S** performs the step of comparisons and interchanges. It is qualified by four parameters, **base**, **dist**, **step**, and **leng**, that identify a sequence of comparator modules that access array **a**: **base** is the index of the left array element accessed by the first comparator module, **dist** is the distance of the left and right elements accessed by any comparator module, **step** is the distance of the left elements (or right elements) of any two adjacent comparator modules, and **leng** is the number of comparator modules in sequence.

Like simple comparator modules, general comparator modules may be declared idempotent. Also, disjoint comparator modules may be declared independent. General comparator modules $cs(i_1,i_2)$ and $cs(j_1,j_2)$ are disjoint if they do not overlap, i.e., if $i_1 \neq j_1$, $i_1 \neq j_2$, $i_2 \neq j_1$, and $i_2 \neq j_2$.

$$!cs(i_1,i_2)$$

$$i_1 \neq j_1 \wedge i_1 \neq j_2 \wedge i_2 \neq j_1 \wedge i_2 \neq j_2 \quad \Rightarrow \quad cs(i_1,i_2) \,||\, cs(j_1,j_2)$$

Let us construct a binary tree of bitonic sequences whose root is the entire array **a**, and whose left and right subtrees are recursively constructed by splitting the root into subsequences as prescribed by the bitonic sorting algorithm. We call this tree the *sequence tree* of **a**. The sequence tree of an eight-element array (n=7) is:

```
                 ⟨a0,a1,a2,a3,a4,a5,a6,a7⟩
                      /            \
            ⟨a0,a2,a4,a6⟩      ⟨a1,a3,a5,a7⟩
              /       \          /       \
         ⟨a0,a4⟩   ⟨a2,a6⟩   ⟨a1,a5⟩   ⟨a3,a7⟩
          /   \     /   \     /   \     /   \
        ⟨a0⟩ ⟨a4⟩ ⟨a2⟩ ⟨a6⟩ ⟨a1⟩ ⟨a5⟩ ⟨a3⟩ ⟨a7⟩
```

At each node $\langle a_{i_1}, a_{i_2}, a_{i_3}, a_{i_4}, \ldots \rangle$, the bitonic sorting algorithm requires an application of comparator modules **cs**(i_1, i_2);**cs**(i_3, i_4);..., which we shall call a *segment*. The following *segment tree* corresponds to the previous sequence tree:

```
            cs(0,1);cs(2,3);cs(4,5);cs(6,7)
                   /              \
       cs(0,2);cs(4,6)        cs(1,3);cs(5,7)
         /          \           /          \
   cs(0,4)      cs(2,6)    cs(1,5)      cs(3,7)
```

Segments of leaves in the sequence tree are null and are not represented in the segment tree.

Note that, in the refinement of the bitonic sort, segments are represented by calls of **S**. We can now view the sequential trace **tau** of the bitonic sort as the post-order traversal of segments in the segment tree:

```
tau(7) = cs(0,4)→cs(2,6)→cs(0,2)→cs(4,6)
                        →cs(1,5)→cs(3,7)→cs(1,3)→cs(5,7)
                                        →cs(0,1)→cs(2,3)→cs(4,5)→cs(6,7)
```

tau(7) has length 12. In general, **tau**(2^k-1) has length $2^{k-1}k$. (The refinement works for all bitonic arrays, but we choose to consider only arrays whose length is a power **k** of 2. Such arrays yield complete sequence and segment trees.) Observe that any two distinct segments **x** and **y** in the segment tree which are not in an ascendant/descendant relationship have no common elements. Such **x** and **y** are independent, and we can commute them or make them parallel. For instance, we can commute all segments that are on the same level in the tree (i.e., that have the same distance from the root) into adjacency:

```
tau'(7) = cs(0,4)→cs(2,6)→cs(1,5)→cs(3,7)
                        →cs(0,2)→cs(4,6)→cs(1,3)→cs(5,7)
                                        →cs(0,1)→cs(2,3)→cs(4,5)→cs(6,7)
```

Then we can merge each level into one parallel command:

```
tau~(7) = <cs(0,4) cs(2,6) cs(1,5) cs(3,7)>
                        →<cs(0,2) cs(4,6) cs(1,3) cs(5,7)>
                                        →<cs(0,1) cs(2,3) cs(4,5) cs(6,7)>
```

tau~(7) is of length 3, with a concurrency degree of 4. In general, **tau~**(2^k-1) is of length **k**, with a concurrency degree of 2^{k-1}.

4. On the Mechanical Support of Trace Transformations

Given a sequential trace that we know to be correct, we would like to derive an equivalent but faster parallel trace. Let us assume a recursive sequential trace. We can prove its equivalence with the parallel trace by a recursive application of a sequence of trace transformations. Although such trace transformations are in many cases quite simply described in informal English, their formal application is extremely tedious (as is effectively demonstrated by our manually derived proof of the insertion sort transformation in Sect. 5.4 of [11]). We do not want to rely on an informal description but would like some mechanical aid in the formal application.

We might be tempted to view the trace transformation as a recursive algorithm. Say, algorithm **trans(n)** transforms sequential trace **tau(n)** into parallel trace **tau~(n)** by appropriately commuting and ravelling **tau**'s comparator modules. The computational complexity of **trans(n)** will depend on the particular transformation it performs. For instance, [12] contains a cubic algorithm for the transformation of the insertion sort. If we intend to sort frequently it is very reasonable to "buy" a linear execution with cubic compilation. However, the algorithmic approach to transformation has one fundamental problem: an unbounded trace can never be completely transformed in finite time - and recursive or looping programs yield unbounded traces.

A better approach is to treat trace transformations as theorems, not algorithms. A trace transformation theorem states the semantic equivalence of a sequential trace and its parallel transformation:

```
semantics of parallel trace = semantics of sequential trace
```

In particular, recursive transformations are inductive theorems. Transformation theorems of sorting networks are of the form:

```
TAU.MAIN:   For all n>0,
            semantics of tau~(n) = semantics of tau(n)
```

The proof essentially rewrites one side of the equation into the other. Because it uses induction (on n), it can deal with unbounded traces in finite time. In other words, the length of the proof does not depend on the length of the trace.

Our current focus is the automation of such proofs. For this purpose, we use a powerful induction prover [4] that is based on a mechanized functional logic particularly suitable for program verification [3]. The prover is designed to prove theorems about recursive functions but is not an expert on sorting networks and their trace transformations. Our attempts to turn it into such an expert are described in the following section.

Ultimately we would like the mechanical support not only in the *proof* but also in the *discovery* of transformation theorems. We imagine a set of mechanized heuristics that transform sequential traces correctly into equivalent parallel traces, using induction. A formal correctness proof of these heuristics would save us from proving the transformation of every single trace separately. However, for the time being, we prefer to deal with the simple semantics of traces, not with the more complicated semantics of heuristics for the transformation of traces.

5. The Mechanical Correctness Proof of Trace Transformations

We are applying Boyer & Moore's mechanical treatment of recursion and induction [3]. All the reader has to know about Boyer & Moore's mechanized logic to understand this paper is that terms in first-order predicate logic are expressed in a LISP-like functional form. (We will here actually keep basic logic and arithmetic operations in infix notation.) Predicates are functions with a boolean range. There are no quantifiers. A variable that appears free in a term is taken as universally quantified. For example, the term

$$\texttt{(NUMBERP X)} \quad \Rightarrow \quad \texttt{X < X+1}$$

expresses the fact that any number is smaller than the same number incremented by 1. Functions can be declared (without a function body) or defined (with a function body), and facts can be asserted (introduced as an "axiom") or proved (introduced as a "lemma").

This section sketches the implementation of the semantic theory that is necessary to prove trace transformation theorems for sorting networks in Boyer & Moore's logic. We shall gloss over a lot of details. For instance, we shall not display the bodies of the defined functions that we introduce.

5.1. Trace Representation

We represent a trace by a LISP list. The elements of the list are executed in sequence. If a list element is itself a list, it is called a *parallel command* and its elements are executed in parallel. If an element of a parallel command is again a list, its elements are executed in sequence, etc. Thus, a trace is a multi-level list whose odd levels reflect sequential execution, and whose even levels reflect parallel execution. In the realm of simple sorting networks, we can represent traces by multi-level lists of integers. For example, traces **tau(5)** and **tau~(5)** of the insertion sort,

$$\begin{aligned}\texttt{tau(5)} = \ & \texttt{cs(1)}\rightarrow\texttt{cs(2)}\rightarrow\texttt{cs(1)}\\ & \rightarrow\texttt{cs(3)}\rightarrow\texttt{cs(2)}\rightarrow\texttt{cs(1)}\\ & \rightarrow\texttt{cs(4)}\rightarrow\texttt{cs(3)}\rightarrow\texttt{cs(2)}\rightarrow\texttt{cs(1)}\\ & \rightarrow\texttt{cs(5)}\rightarrow\texttt{cs(4)}\rightarrow\texttt{cs(3)}\rightarrow\texttt{cs(2)}\rightarrow\texttt{cs(1)}\end{aligned}$$

$$\texttt{tau\~{}(5)} =$$

$$\texttt{cs(1)}\rightarrow\texttt{cs(2)}\rightarrow\left\langle\begin{array}{c}\texttt{cs(1)}\\ \\ \texttt{cs(3)}\end{array}\right\rangle\rightarrow\left\langle\begin{array}{c}\texttt{cs(2)}\\ \\ \texttt{cs(4)}\end{array}\right\rangle\rightarrow\left\langle\begin{array}{c}\texttt{cs(1)}\\ \texttt{cs(3)}\\ \texttt{cs(5)}\end{array}\right\rangle\rightarrow\left\langle\begin{array}{c}\texttt{cs(2)}\\ \\ \texttt{cs(4)}\end{array}\right\rangle\rightarrow\left\langle\begin{array}{c}\texttt{cs(1)}\\ \\ \texttt{cs(3)}\end{array}\right\rangle\rightarrow\texttt{cs(2)}\rightarrow\texttt{cs(1)}$$

are represented by

```
(TAU 5)   =  '(1  2 1  3 2 1  4 3 2 1  5 4 3 2 1)
(TAU~ 5)  =  '(1 2 (3 1) (4 2) (5 3 1) (4 2) (3 1) 2 1)
```

In our formalism [10], parallel commands are binary, i.e., can have at most two parallel components. An n-ary parallel command is expressed as nested binary parallel commands. This coincides with LISP's (and Boyer & Moore's) representation of a list as a nesting of pairs. E.g., the parallel command `'(5 3 1)` of trace `(TAU~ 5)` is really `'(5 . (3 . (1 . NIL)))`.

In the realm of general sorting networks, traces are represented as multi-level lists of pairs of integers.

5.2. Trace Semantics

Traces have weakest precondition semantics [10]. Since a weakest precondition is a function from programs and predicates to predicates [5], the weakest precondition calculus can be directly implemented in Boyer & Moore's logic.

Our methodology divides the development of programs into two stages. Stage 1, the refinement calculus, is concerned with the *derivation* of program semantics, i.e., the derivation of a refinement. Stage 2, the trace calculus, is concerned with the *preservation* of program semantics, i.e., the transformation of sequential executions into concurrent executions. Consequently, we need not implement a complete weakest precondition generator in order to implement Stage 2. We are only interested in the equality of weakest preconditions, not in their actual values. A weakest precondition that is not affected by the trace transformations need not be spelt out but may be provided as a "black box". In Boyer & Moore's logic, a black box is represented by a function that has been *declared* (without a function body) rather than *defined* (with a function body). The primitive components of sorting networks are comparator modules. For the purpose of trace transformations, we are not interested in the inside of a comparator module. Therefore we declare the weakest precondition of a comparator module **cs** as a function

Declared Function: `(CS I S)`

where `I` represents an integer if **cs** is simple and a pair of integers if **cs** is general, and `S` denotes the postcondition (or "poststate"). Since function `CS` is declared, not defined, we must provide by axiom some essential information about `CS` that is not evident from the declaration. We add two axioms. One restricts the domain of simple comparator modules to numbers:

Axiom CS.TAKES.NUMBERS: (NOT (NUMBERP I)) ⇒ ((CS I S) = F)

Axiom CS.TAKES.NUMBERS states that the prestate of CS for any non-number and poststate is false, i.e., that such a CS is not permitted. A respective axiom for general comparator modules tests for pairs of numbers rather than numbers. The other axiom expresses the "rule of the excluded miracle" (Dijkstra's first healthiness criterion [5]) for comparator modules:

Axiom CS.IS.NOT.MIRACLE: (CS I F) = F

Axiom CS.IS.NOT.MIRACLE states that the prestate of any CS with false poststate is false, i.e., comparator modules cannot establish "false".

To determine the weakest precondition of some trace L that is composed of comparator modules CS for poststate S, we define a "cs-machine", a function

Defined Function: (M.CS FLAG L S)

that composes calls to CS as prescribed by trace L. Beside L and S, M.CS takes a FLAG that signals whether the trace is to be executed in sequence (FLAG='SEQ) or in parallel (FLAG='PAR). In accordance with our trace representation, FLAG='SEQ in top-level calls and FLAG alternates with every recursive call.

When FLAG='PAR, the trace represents a parallel command and its elements must be checked for independence. We can make use of the semantic declarations provided at Stage 1. The smallest component that a semantic declaration for a sorting network will mention is the comparator module. We may therefore, from Stage 1, assume knowledge about the independence of comparator modules and may express this knowledge by a declared function

Declared Function: (IND.CS I J)

that evaluates the independence of comparator modules I and J. Again, look at I and J as integers or pairs of integers, as appropriate. We then define a function

Defined Function: (ARE.IND.CS L1 L2)

that uses IND.CS to determine the mutual independence of all comparator modules of trace L1 with all comparator modules of trace L2. If the two members of a parallel command (remember the restriction to binary parallel commands) pass test ARE.IND.CS their execution has identical semantics in parallel as in sequence - only their execution time differs.

The execution time of traces plays a role in the selection of proper transformation theorems. At present, we take transformation theorems as given and only prove them by mechanical means. Therefore, execution time is left out of the current implementation.

The semantic equivalence of **tau~** and **tau** for any of the three previously described transformations is formally expressed as

```
Lemma TAU.MAIN:    0<N  ⇒  (  (M.CS 'SEQ (TAU~ N) S)
                            = (M.CS 'SEQ (TAU  N) S) )
```

5.3. Trace Transformations

Independence declarations are exploited via transformation rules that express commutations and parallel merges of independent program components.

The theorem for parallel merges corresponds to transformation rule (G3i) of Sect. 5.2 of [10]:

```
Lemma G3i:     (ARE.IND.CS L1 L2)
                  ⇒  (  (M.CS 'SEQ <L1 L2> S)
                      = (M.CS 'SEQ  L1+L2  S))
```

For clarity, we return here to our previous notation for traces. Traces must, of course, be fully represented in the mechanized logic.

To express commutations, we must be more specific about the meaning of "independence". The declaration of IND.CS does not provide any clues. We do not need to know everything about independence; otherwise we would define, not declare IND.CS. But we must be able to conclude that independent comparator modules may be commuted. As we did with CS, we characterize IND.CS by axiom:

```
Axiom GLOBAL.IND.CS:
               (IND.CS I J)
                  ⇒  ((CS J (CS I S)) = (CS I (CS J S)))
```

If we instantiate both FLAG1 and FLAG2 to 'SEQ, the following theorem enables commutations:

```
Lemma ARE.IND.CS.IMPLIES.COMMUTATIVITY:
               (ARE.IND.CS L1 L2)
                  ⇒  (  (M.CS FLAG1 L1 (M.CS FLAG2 L2 S))
                      = (M.CS FLAG2 L2 (M.CS FLAG1 L1 S)) )
```

5.4. Independence Criteria

For simple sorting networks, we have introduced the concept of "non-neighbors" to declare independence. Two simple comparator modules are *non-neighbors* if their indices differ by at least 2. We may provide this known fact by axiom:

```
Axiom NON.NEIGHBORS.ARE.IND.CS:
                    (NON.NEIGHBORS I J)  ⇒  (IND.CS I J)
```

where function NON.NEIGHBORS identifies non-neighbors. NON.NEIGHBORS is defined while IND.CS is declared. With IND.CS alone we could not decide the independence of anything; with this axiom we can decide the independence of simple comparator modules. We may, for example, apply theorem G31 with cs(5) for L1 and cs(3)→cs(1) for L2, since cs(5) is not neighbor of cs(3) and cs(1):

```
(M.CS 'SEQ <cs(5) cs(3) cs(1)> S)  =  (M.CS 'SEQ <cs(5) cs(3)→cs(1)> S)
```

Two more applications of G31, exploiting also the non-neighborhood of cs(3) and cs(1), yield:

```
(M.CS 'SEQ <cs(5) cs(3) cs(1)> S)  =  (M.CS 'SEQ cs(5)→cs(3)→cs(1) S)
```

This formula expresses the equivalence of the parallel and sequential execution of comparator modules cs(5), cs(3), and cs(1).

For general sorting networks, we characterize independence by the concept of "non-overlap". Two general comparator modules *do not overlap*, if they do not touch the same array element. This fact is provided by axiom:

```
Axiom NO.OVERLAP.ARE.IND.CS:
                    (NO.OVERLAP I J)  ⇒  (IND.CS I J)
```

where function NO.OVERLAP establishes non-overlap.

5.5. Application Theorems

Ideally, we would like to submit to the prover nothing else but an application theorem - ours are of the form:

```
TAU.MAIN:    0<N  ⇒  (  (M.CS 'SEQ (TAU~ N) S)
                      = (M.CS 'SEQ (TAU  N) S) )
```

where TAU and TAU~ are defined appropriately - and have it certified without any further input. However, no existing prover is expert enough in the theory of trace transformations of sorting networks to accomplish such a proof on its own. To educate the prover, we must implement our theory on it, i.e., express the theory in the mechanized logic, and have it certified and at disposal for further proofs.

Up to this point, we have described the implementation of the basic semantic theory, the part that applies to all simple, resp., general sorting networks. It consists of the semantics of traces of comparator modules, a set of trace transformation theorems, and an independence criterion for comparator modules. The semantic theory is not fully represented in the mechanized logic: we introduced two declared (not defined) functions. The theory is also not fully certified: we made four axiomatic assumptions. They reflect the knowledge that is presumed in the theory.

Even with the basic semantic theory in place and after proper definition of the initial trace TAU and the final trace TAU$^{\sim}$, the work required to make the proof of an application TAU.MAIN succeed is substantial. Essentially, we have to communicate our proof strategy to the prover. Where the transformation consists of several steps, the prover may have to be informed about each individual step. For instance, since we can commute at any place where we can merge (remember that independence implies commutativity), we must tell the prover about the transformation that we prefer: commutation or merge. Our transformations of the insertion sort and the bitonic sort each consist of two steps: one of commutations and one of merges. The transformation of the odd-even sort consists of only one step of merges. For every step of the transformation, the trace parts that are manipulated must be identified, and their independence must be established. This generally involves educating the prover about useful facts of number theory. For our simple sorting networks, we had to tell the prover about properties of maximization, for our general sorting network about properties of division. Establishing these prerequisites before the proof of the application theorem is the most tedious aspect of a mechanized certification. For an effective use of a mechanized theory in many applications, clean and widely applicable proof strategies are of central importance.

BASIC THEORY		*all comparator modules*		
		trace semantics trace transformation rules		
		simple comp. mods.		*general comp. mods.*
	independence criterion	non-neighbors		no overlap
		insertion sort	*odd-even sort*	*bitonic sort*
APPLICATION	*algebraic prerequisites*	maximization	maximization	division
	transformation strategy	1st step: commute 2nd step: merge	one step: merge	1st step: commute 2nd step: merge
	auxiliary lemmas	see [12]		see [6]
	main theorem	TAU.MAIN	TAU.MAIN	TAU.MAIN

We shall provide no further details of the individual proofs of our three applications. The previous table displays the overall proof structure. The proof of the insertion sort is documented in [12], that of the bitonic sort in [6].

While the basic theory may contain some declared functions and axioms (and our's does), the application part of the proof should not (and ours do not). That is, with respect to the basic theory, applications should be completely certified. It is important that every axiomatic assumption is fully understood. An inconsistency in an axiom is not recognized by the prover and puts the entire mechanized theory into jeopardy!

6. Conclusions

By its very name, the area of automated theorem proving invites high expectations: the hope is kindled that, whenever the human prover seems lost or uncertain in a proof, the mechanism will take over and guide him along. A presently more fitting name would be *automated proof checking*: the human has to conceive and carry out the proof; but he can count on a mechanized certification of his proof steps, if these steps are chosen appropriately. In order to make the mechanized certification succeed, the human prover has to be familiar not only with the abstract theory on which his proof relies but also with its mechanized counterpart. Like it is the crux of numerical analysis that floating point numbers do not have the nice properties of real numbers, it is the dilemma of automated theorem proving that the mechanization of a logic does not preserve many of its desirable properties. Therefore, a proof certified by a mechanism is actually more difficult than a proof certified by a human. But it is also more reliable.

Let us summarize some of the difficulties that we encountered in the automated as opposed to human certification of trace transformations.

Automated provers work by a set of heuristics. The human who develops the proof is best advised to follow these heuristics. Good heuristics are, of course, those that are naturally followed in many proofs. When the heuristics fail, the human has to document his proof strategy with "proof hints". If a proof is loaded with proof hints, it is probably not tailored very well to the automated prover. (This could indicate a bad proof or a bad prover.) We have spent considerable effort on minimizing and structuring proof hints.

A proof assertion may have many different representations. For instance, all of the formulas below represent the same assertion about a, b, and c:

(a) $a^2+b^2 = c^2$

(b) $a^2+b^2-c^2 = 0$

(c) $c^2-a^2-b^2 = 0$

(d) $aa+bb = cc$

An automated prover may not recognize an assertion in all representations - unless it happens to be an expert on this particular class of assertions. Boyer & Moore's prover, for instance, is not enough of an expert in algebra to treat representations (a) to (d) equivalently. The human has to make sure that the proof uses only representations that the prover can treat as is desired. This can be accomplished by either disciplining the proof or educating the prover, i.e., making it aware of equivalent representations. Education of the prover is a two-edged sword. With too much knowledge, it may spend a long time searching for appropriate facts or even apply at points inappropriate proof rules.

One major concern of automated certification is execution efficiency. The most fundamental efficiency requirement is termination. An inappropriate choice of proof steps may lead to an infinite computation. For instance, many automated provers, like Boyer & Moore's, rewrite equalities only in one direction in order to avoid infinite looping. E.g., with the knowledge of A=B, Boyer & Moore's prover will substitute B for A in proofs, but not vice versa. This has immediate consequences for the implementation of our theory: semantic declarations may be exploited only in one direction. In any particular proof, we may commute left or commute right, but not both; we may use idempotence to compress traces or expand traces, but not both; we may increase or decrease the parallelism in a trace, but not both. Even if we stick with one direction, we may have termination problems if our transformation sequence is not well-founded. For instance, decreasing parallelism is always well-founded, while increasing parallelism is not. Therefore, we actually let the prover transform traces "backwards", from parallel to sequential.

When solving a programming problem, a programmer has the choice of programming in an existing language, or designing a new language which is particularly suited for the class of problems that he is investigating. A new "special purpose" language may permit him to write more natural programs and may yield more efficient executions. An existing "general purpose" language may grant him more flexibility in reformulating the problem or moving to a different problem class altogether. The same choice presents itself in mechanizing certification. One might use an existing general purpose prover, or one might build a new special purpose prover. In choosing Boyer & Moore's mechanized logic, we have taken the "general purpose" option, exactly for the reasons stated: we prefer general certification power for the development of our mechanized theory of trace transformations and, in the long run, we do not want to confine ourselves to the language of sorting networks. Boyer & Moore's prover is a suitable and user-friendly tool for the implementation of specialized theories.

Acknowledgements

We are grateful to J Moore and Bob Boyer who patiently answered our countless questions about their prover.

References

1. Ackerman, W. B. "Data Flow Languages." *Computer 15*, 2 (Feb. 1982), 15-25.

2. Bates, J. L., and Constable, R. L. Proofs as Programs. Tech. Rept. TR 82-530, Cornell University, 1982.

3. Boyer, R. S., and Moore, J S. *A Computational Logic*. Academic Press, 1979.

4. Boyer, R. S., and Moore, J S. A Theorem Prover for Recursive Functions, a User's Manual. Computer Science Laboratory, SRI International, 1979.

5. Dijkstra, E. W. *A Discipline of Programming*. Series in Automatic Computation, Prentice-Hall, 1976.

6. Huang, C.-H., and Lengauer, C. The Automated Proof of a Trace Transformation for a Bitonic Sort. Tech. Rept. TR-84-30, Department of Computer Sciences, The University of Texas at Austin, 1984.

7. Knuth, D. E. *The Art of Computer Programming, Vol. 3: Sorting and Searching*. Addison-Wesley, 1973. Sect. 5.3.4.

8. Kuck, D. J. "A Survey of Parallel Machine Organization and Programming." *Computing Surveys 9*, 1 (Mar. 1977), 29-59.

9. Lengauer, C., and Hehner, E. C. R. "A Methodology for Programming with Concurrency: An Informal Presentation." *Science of Computer Programming 2*, 1 (Oct. 1982), 1-18:

10. Lengauer, C. "A Methodology for Programming with Concurrency: The Formalism." *Science of Computer Programming 2*, 1 (Oct. 1982), 19-52.

11. Lengauer, C. A Methodology for Programming with Concurrency. Tech. Rept. CSRG-142, Computer Systems Research Group, University of Toronto, Apr., 1982.

12. Lengauer, C. "On the Role of Automated Theorem Proving in the Compile-Time Derivation of Concurrency." *Journal of Automated Reasoning 1* (1985). To appear. Earlier version: On the Mechanical Transformation of Program Executions to Derive Concurrency. Tech. Rept. TR-83-20, Department of Computer Sciences, The University of Texas at Austin, Oct., 1983.

13. Manna, Z., and Waldinger, R. "A Deductive Approach to Program Synthesis." *ACM TOPLAS 2*, 1 (Jan. 1980), 90-121.

Semantic Considerations in the Actor Paradigm of Concurrent Computation

Gul Agha
The Artificial Intelligence Laboratory
Massachussetts Institute of Technology
Cambridge, Ma 02139
and
Dept. of Computer and Communication Science
University of Michigan
Ann Arbor, Mi 48109

Abstract

This paper discusses the theory of concurrent processing in the context of the actor paradigm. The basic precepts of the actor paradigm are explained. We develop a new formalism to describe the behavior of actors and the evolution of systems of actors. It is hoped that the structure of concurrent computation and the intuitions behind the actor paradigm will be better understood in terms of this model. In particular, we define certain relations between the configurations an actor system may be in and explain how the behavior of actor systems can be understood in terms of these relations. We also define an actor-based language, called *Sal*, which has a simple syntax but nevertheless embodies the concepts involved.

Several examples of simple actor systems are presented. Two kinds of actors are defined and their relevance to spawning concurrency is noted. The low level detail inherent in the transition systems we define retains some purely operational information. The usefulness of our constructs, beside the obvious pedagogic one, will be in the ability to abstract higher level principles to express and prove properties of actor systems, without the combinatorial explosion implied by all the possible inter-leavings of events. We suggest some directions for future research in this area.

1 Introduction

The actor paradigm of concurrent computation is a foundational theory of parallel processing by a distributed system. At the same time, the actor paradigm is pragmatically strong enough to provide the foundations for powerful and expressive programming languages. The paradigm is based on a message-passing semantics between independent computational agents called *actors*. The order of arrival of messages is indeterminate leading to a naturally inherent nondeterminism in the evolution of the system. This nondeterminism is due to the different possible arrival orderings for the messages. The message-passing discipline is constrained so that the eventual delivery of all communications sent is guaranteed. The paradigm also provides for the dynamic creation and reconfiguration of actors in the system. In this paper we describe a model for actor systems that enables us to describe the behavior and abstract significant properties of actor systems.

The early development of the actor paradigm can be traced to two seminal papers: *Laws for Parallel Communicating Processes* [Hewitt and Baker 77] and *Viewing Control Structures as Patterns of Passing Messages* [Hewitt 77]. The first paper stated some of the axioms which must be obeyed by any group of independent agents performing computations in parallel. These axioms can be derived from first principles. In the second paper, Hewitt showed how various control structures could be understood in terms of specific patterns of message-passing between self–contained computational agents. Since these agents function in parallel, message-passing provides a natural method for spawning concurrency by replacing sequential control structures.

Clinger[81] proposed a fixed-point semantics for actors using power domains. The elements of the domain in the semantics are sets of *augmented event diagrams* first proposed in Grief[75]. Augmented event diagrams are behavioral representations of the history of computation by the concurrent computational agents. Each diagram is a collection of life-lines representing the linear order of events in the life of each actor. These individual life-lines are connected by causal links when an event in the life of one actor causes an event at another actor. Pending events are used to label each life line and represent events that are going to happen at the actor in its future (*i.e.*, events caused by communications that have been sent to that actor but have not been recieved). In Clinger's model, the description of an actor system carries the entire history of the computation; this tends to obscure the underlying abstract equivalencies between different actor systems.

The actor paradigm exploits the object-oriented methodology of programming which has shown increasing promise in programming language design as witnessed by recent development of object-based languages such as CLU [Liskov 77] and SMALLTALK [Goldberg 83]. Actor theory differentiates between objects whose behavior changes over their life-time and those that are behaviorally constant. Thus, on the one hand, it shares with Milner's *Calculus of Communicating Systems* [Milner 80] the use of recursively defined behaviors, and on the other, it extracts the maximum possible concurrency from the concept of immutable and permanent objects which are the backbone of *functional programming* [Backus 78]. Actor theory allows explicit consideration of causality and causal reasoning in contradistinction to models such as *Petri Nets* [Peterson 77] and *data flow* [Fosseen 72] where the relationship between the elements of the system is static.

There are two primary differences between the actor paradigm and other proposed models of concurrent computation: firstly, synchronization of different agents in the system is not a primitive; and secondly, the system of agents as a whole is dynamically reconfigurable. Our claim is that this makes the actor paradigm more elemental than other models of concurrent computation as it assumes fewer restrictions on the relations between agents in the system over time. In particular, synchronization between agents can be built by suitably designing a system. The paradigm also is more general in that it does not assume that all actors exist at the genesis of the system: instead, actors may be created in the course of the computation.

2 Actor Systems

Conceptually, an actor system is a network of computational agents called *actors*. The only means by which an actor may affect the behavior of another actor is by sending it a communication. All computation is carried out in response to communications recieved. Each actor performs its computations independently of, and concurrently with, all other actors. Physically, several actors may time-share on a single processor, or alternately, be on different processors, but in any case this is of little consequence to the actor model because each actor is a distinct agent. Simply making these assumptions about actors implies that several intuitive properties of parallel systems must be obeyed by all actor systems. These are the so-called laws of parallel processing.

To exploit the inherent concurrency in actors, one must understand how control structures can be generalized to patterns of message-passing. When a single communication activates several other communications, concurrency is rapidly spawned in the system. We briefly review these basic precepts of the actor paradigm below.

2.1 Laws of Parallel Processing

The concept of a unique global clock is not meaningful in the context of a distributed system of self-contained parallel agents. The reasoning here is exactly analogous to that in special relativity: information in each computational agent is localized within that agent and must be communicated before it is known to any other agent. As long as one assumes that there are limits as to how fast information may travel from one computational agent to another, the local states of one actor as recorded by another relative to its own local states, will be discordant with the observations done the other way round. One can, of course, build synchronization mechanisms between the processors but that is exactly what these are: methods of restricting the effects of a fundamental epistemological limitation by constricting the available independence.

To take a simple example, suppose two processors, x and y are 3×10^3 *km* apart, and each one processes $\sim 10^9$ *instructions/sec*. Assuming the speed of light as the maximum speed at which information can be transmitted, the local state of processor x as recorded by processor y will be off by at least 10^7*instructions*.

In any real network of computational agents, one can not predict precisely when a communication sent by one agent will arrive at another. This is particularly true in actor systems since actors are virtual computational agents, and will, in general be time-sharing a processor with numerous other actors. Therefore a realistic model must assume that the arrival order of communications sent is both arbitrary and entirely unknown. In particular, the use of the ***arbiter*** as the hardware element for serialization implies that the arrival order is physically indeterminate.

We may conclude that, for an actor system, a linear global time is not (uniquely) definable. Instead, each actor has a local time which linearly orders the events as they occur at that actor, or alternately, orders the local states of that actor. These local orderings of events are related to each other by the *activation ordering.* The activation ordering represents the causal relationships between events happening at different actors. Thus the global ordering of events is a partial order in which events occurring at different actors are unordered unless they are connected, directly or indirectly, because of one or more causal links.

The set of actors a particular actor may communicate with defines an interconnection topology of actors. In actor systems, this topology is dynamic, because for one new actors are created and, for another an actor may communicate with different actors at different points in its local times. The interconnection topology of actors is constrained by the *locality laws* which specify the possible configurations any physically realizable distributed system may have. For example, the *law of finite acquaintances* states that an actor may know about only finitely many other actors at any given point in its local time.

A detailed discussion of the laws of parallel processing can be found in [Hewitt and Baker 77] where they were first proposed or in [Clinger 81] where they are formalized and in terms of an actor model and shown to be consistent. Although we will not do so here, it is easy to show that the model for actors described here satisfies the laws of parallel processing.

2.2 Patterns of Message-Passing

Message-passing provides an effective method of spawning concurrency. Various control structures, such as recursion and iteration, can be translated into specific patterns of message-passing [Hewitt 77]. For example, consider the recursive factorial function. The desired behavior of a recursive factorial actor is that it responds to a communication containing a natural number n, and the address of a *customer* ε, by eventually sending a communication containing the number $n!$ to the given customer, ε. The recursive factorial actor may be defined as follows: if $n \neq 0$, the factorial actor creates a new customer ψ and sends itself a communication containing the number $n - 1$ and the address of this newly created actor ψ. The behavior of ψ will be to multiply the number it receives by n and send the result to the address of ε which was specified when it was created by the factorial actor. If $n = 0$ in the communication received by the factorial actor, it simply sends a communication containing 1.

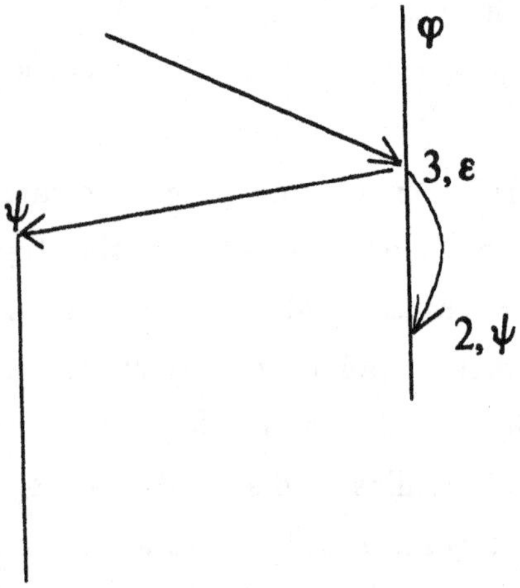

Figure 1: Request to a Recursive Factorial Actor

Suppose the factorial actor is sent a communication containing $(3, \hat{\varepsilon})$, where $\hat{\varepsilon}$ is the mail address of some actor ε. The behavior of factorial actor can be illustrated as in figure 1. Subsequently, the factorial actor creates another customer (which will be integral in continuing the computation), and sends itself another communication, so that the figure, at the of all the activations done by the original request, looks like Fig. 2.

The above example illustrates how a recursive control structure can be unfolded as a chain of *customers*. Notice that if a different communication was sent to the factorial actor, that request would activate its own chain of customers and communications to these customers would be processed concurrently. The two

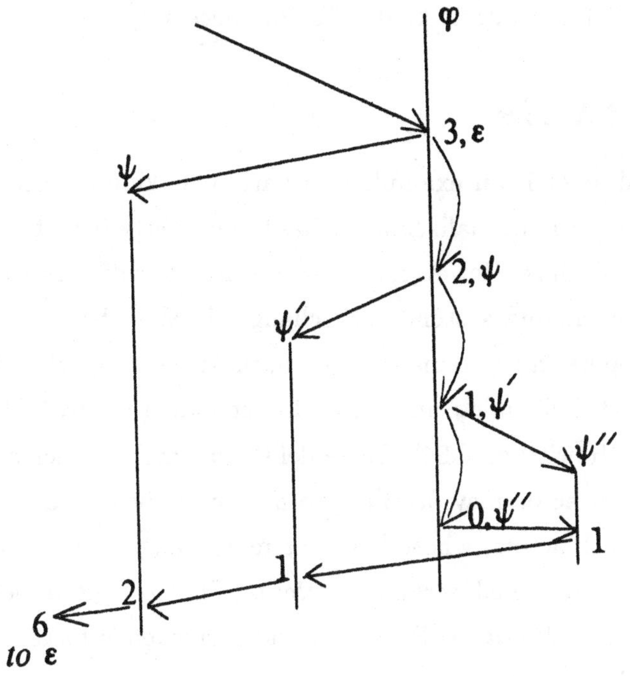

Figure 2: Completion of the computation of 3!

chains would not interfere with one another.

3 The Behavior of an Actor

An actor is a computational agent that can compute arbitrarily complex recursive functions. The reason for restricting the space of functions is simply that an actor always has a computable behavior. An actor carries out its computations in response to receiving a communication. Since it always has a well-defined behavior, we assume that it responds to any communications recieved after a finite interval. We do not have to deal with any conflicts in the timing of the arrival of communications. One can think of the mail system as putting the communications sent to each actor in it's *mail queue.* An actor processes a pending communication whenever it's through with the one it is currently processing. However, there is no need to explicitly model the behavior of a mail queue since arrival order nondeterminism already implies that there is no assumption about when a message is processed. To define the behavior of an actor precisely we must understand the two basic kinds of actors necessary.

3.1 Kinds of Actors

The factorial actor is an example of a particular kind of actor, namely, the *unserialized actor*. An unserialized actor has the property that its behavior never changes over its life-time. However, such actors are not sufficient to model shared resources in a distributed system. The changes in shared objects, such as employee records, operating systems, and so on, must be encapsulated within these objects because of their indeterminate and open-ended nature of their usage by different sources [Hewitt, et al 84]. To model the behavior of such actors, we have the notion that an actor may *become* another actor, i.e., an actor may change its local state. Such actors, whose behavior may change as a result of receiving a communication are called *serialized actors*. The concept of serialized actor evolved from that of *Monitors* [Hoare 78] and corresponds to that of *serializers* in [Atkinson and Hewitt 79].

Thus an actor may, as a result of receiving a communication, make simple decisions or computations, and, consequentially,

- Send more communications to specific actors
- Create new actors
- Specify a replacement behavior

A mail address is where a particular actor resides. To send an actor a communication, the sender must know the mail address associated with that actor. Communications may be sent to actors that have been newly created since their mail addresses are known (to their creator) upon their creation. Note that the number of communications sent and the number of new actors created must both be finite. Whenever a new actor is created, it gets a mail address which is distinct from all other mail addresses in existence. When the behavior of an actor is replaced, it nevertheless retains its old mail address.

Identifiers are necessary to represent the mail addresses of newly created actors because several actors with identical behaviors may be created at the same time by an actor. These identically behaving actors may, however, be sent differing communications. For example, one needs to be able to specify whether the communications should go to the same actor, or to different actors. The difference can be profound if the actors in question happen to be serialized. The scope of the identifiers is completely local.

Formally, if β is a behavior of an actor, β is a function defined as follows

$$\beta : \mathcal{K} \longrightarrow (N \longrightarrow \mathcal{T}) \times (I \longrightarrow \mathcal{A}) \times \mathcal{R}$$

where $\mathcal{K}$ is the universe of *possible communications*, N is a finite set of *positive integers*, $\mathcal{T}$ represents the *tasks* to be created (explained below), I is a finite set of *identifiers*, $\mathcal{A}$ represents the *actors* that may be created and $\mathcal{R}$ represents the specification of the *replacement behavior*. The elements of N simply distinguish between identical communications sent to the same target, so that there may be more than one such communication (this is in place of using multisets).

The elements of $\mathcal{T}$ are pairs of targets and communications. The targets of communications may be either actors that already exist (hence their mail addresses are known), or actors that are newly created (represented by the local identifiers which are to be replaced by the mail addresses when these actors are created). Therefore, the targets are elements of $(\mathcal{M} \cup I)$. An actor may communicate the mail addresses of any newly created actor, therefore the communications to be sent are a function of the mail addresses, represented as $(I^* \longrightarrow \mathcal{K})$.

Simultaneously created actors may know about each other's mail address: thus the behavior of a newly created actor is a function of the mail addresses of the other actors created. This is specified by representing $\mathcal{A}$ as $(I^* \longrightarrow \mathcal{B})$, where $\mathcal{B}$ is the universe of *possible behaviors*. Finally, an actor may know the mail addresses of the actors it creates: *i.e.* the replacement behavior is also a function of the mail addresses of newly created actors. Thus $\mathcal{R}$ represents $(I^* \longrightarrow \mathcal{B})$. In section 5, we specify how the behaviors, and the communications, are derived in any system of actors by specifying suitable mail addresses to replace the identifiers.

Remark. Note that if the behavior of an actor is not dependent on the mail address of newly created actors, we do not write it as a function but simply as a behavior. The same notational convenience is used for communications. If we wish to emphasize the fact that we really have a function of the free variables that are determined once the mail addresses are known, we will write a behavior as $\beta[id_1, \ldots, id_j]$ where j is the number of new actors created.

Definition 3.1 Serialized and Unserialized Actors. *Let α be an actor with behavior β. α is called an unserialized actor if*

$$\forall \overline{k} \in \mathcal{K} \; (\beta(\overline{k}) = (T, A, \beta') \implies \beta = \beta')$$

where T represents the newly created tasks, and A represents the newly created actors. Otherwise, α is called a serialized actor and β' is called the replacement behavior for β in response to communication $\overline{k}$.

Example 3.1 Recursive Factorial. The recursive factorial discussed in section 2 is an example of an unserialized actor. Fig. 4 gives the code for such an actor. The behavior of a recursive factorial, φ, can be described as follows: [1]

$$\varphi[k_1, k_2] = \begin{cases} \{(1, k_2, [1]\} \times \emptyset \times \varphi & \text{if } k_1 = 0 \\ \\ \{(1, \widehat{self}, [k_1 - 1, \widehat{c}])\} \times \{(c, \psi^{k_1}_{k_2})\} \times \varphi & \text{otherwise} \end{cases}$$

where $\psi^{k_1}_{k_2}[n] = \{(1, k_2, [n * k_1])\} \times \emptyset \times \beta_\perp$ and $\widehat{c}$ is the mail address of the newly created customer, represented by identifier c, and $\widehat{self}$ is the mail address of the factorial actor. $\beta_\perp$ is the behavior of *an undefined actor*, which essentially never processes its communications again.

3.2 Insensitive Actors

When an actor accepts a communication and proceeds to carry out its computations, other communications it may have received must be buffered until the replacement behavior is computed. When such a replacement actor is known, it processes the buffered communications, as well as any new ones received. The time it takes for an actor to respond to a communication is not significant because no assumption is made about the arrival order of communications in the first place.

---

[1] We use $\times$ delimiter instead of giving a tuple simply for ease of reading. We also write a task as a 3-tuple instead of a 2-tuple with the second element as a 2-tuple.

However, the desired replacement for a serialized actor may depend on communication with other actors. For example, suppose a checking account has overdraft protection from a corresponding savings account. When a withdrawal request results in an overdraft, the balance in the checking account after processing the withdrawal, would depend on the balance in the savings account. Thus the checking account actor would have to communicate with the savings account actor, and *vice-versa* before the new balance (and hence the replacement behavior) is determined. The relevant communication from savings account can *not* therefore be buffered until a replacement is specified!

There are several possible ways of modeling the above situation. One could differentiate between scanning a communication and processing it, and then allow the actor to scan a communication in order to decide whether to process it. With this model, an actor would scan all communications and decide to process only communications bearing some "signature", *i.e.*, satisfying a particular pattern. A second approach would be to have such actors internally buffer all communications they do not want to "process" immediately. A third model would allow an actor to create, and kill, an additional mailbox (or mailboxes) with a higher priority. An actor would then have levels of readiness (and deadlock).

In this paper, we deal with this problem simply by defining the concept of an *insensitive* behavior which processes only a type of communication called a *become communication*. A become communication tells an actor its replacement behavior. The behavior of an insensitive actor may be (loosely) described as

$$\beta_i(\overline{k}) = \begin{cases} \emptyset \times \emptyset \times \alpha & if\ \overline{k} \simeq \text{become } \alpha \\ \\ (1, \widehat{self}, \overline{k}) \times \emptyset \times \beta_i & otherwise \end{cases}$$

Example 3.2 Checking Account. Consider the checking account actor α_1 whose local state is parameterized by the balance b in the account. Suppose that the account the actor represents allows an automatic transfer of funds from a corresponding savings account. Let the savings account be represented by the actor α_2. Suppose α_1 receives a communication to withdraw an amount a for a customer v such that $a > b$. It must communicate with α_2 to determine its new balance. Since a savings account can hardly be expected to send a "become communication", α_1 creates a customer, α_3, which will do so by packaging the reply from α_2 appropriately. α_3 also sends a response to the customer of the withdrawal request. (See figure 3).

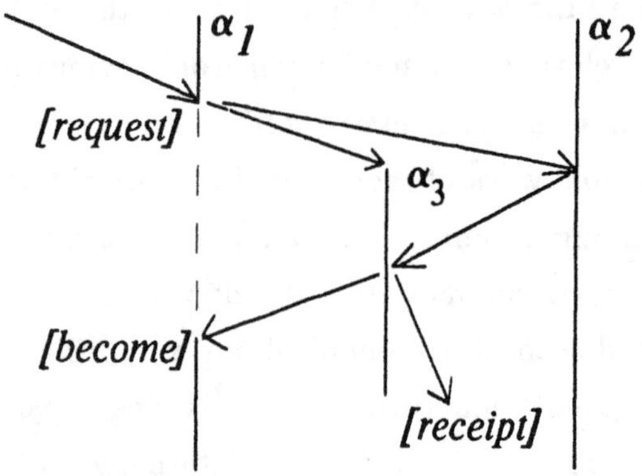

Figure 3: Insensitive Actors. The dotted life-line of α_1 represents the time it is *insensitive.*

Remark. Notice that insensitive actors introduce the possibility of ***deadlock.*** If in a system the targets of all the communications tasks are insensitive and none of the communications is *become* communication then no further evolution is really possible (all transitions are to "behaviorally" equivalent systems).

4 A Simple Actor Language

A series of languages has been developed to exploit the actor paradigm and provide higher level linguistic constructs to support programming in concurrent systems. The programming language *Act2* is such a actor-based language [Theriault 82].

The family of *Actn* languages is rich in its exploitation of ideas either derived from, or developed for, the field of Artificial Intelligence. For example, they provide an elaborate description system for reasoning which serves to substitute *type-checking* with generalized *pattern-matching*. The expressive power of *Act3* results from the synergistic effect of integrating varied areas of research endeavor in computer science. However, these "realistic" features also tend to obscure some essential principles of the actor paradigm which we would like to emphasize. We will instead use a simple actor language, called *Sal*, to show some examples.

4.1 Sal

The purpose of *Sal* is simply to illustrate how the basic concepts expressed in our model can be embodied in a programming language. The behavior of an actor in *Sal* is specified by a *script*. A program in *Sal* is an expression that defines certain scripts (using *def expressions*), uses these scripts in *new expressions* and sends communications to actors created by such new expressions. All identifiers are lexically scoped and the mail addresses of actors is bound to the identifiers representing them.

The syntax of a script σ is as follows:

$$\sigma ::= \quad \text{def } \delta\ (\overline{a})\ \odot\ [\overline{k}]\ \ S \text{ end def}$$

$$\begin{aligned} S ::= \quad & (\, S' \,) \ \mid\ S_1 \,;\, S_2 \ \mid\ S_1 \,//\, S_2 \ \mid\ \text{send } e \text{ to } P \ \mid \\ & \text{if } b \text{ then } S_1 \text{ fi} \ \mid\ \text{become } \delta\,\langle \overline{d} \rangle \ \mid \\ & \text{let } x = e_1\ \{S'\} \ \mid\ \sigma_1 \bullet \cdots \bullet \sigma_n \ \mid \\ & \text{new } P_1 : \delta_1\langle\, \overline{d}_1 \,\rangle \bullet \cdots \bullet P_n : \delta_n\langle\, \overline{d}_n \,\rangle \end{aligned}$$

$\overline{a}$ is a list of parameters in the script which must be instantiated to some value when an (new or replacement) actor is created. $\overline{k}$ represents values bound from the incoming communication. e_1 is an arbitrary expressions and P is an identifier that represents an actor. b is an arbitrary boolean expression. σ_i's represent scripts, and S, S', S_1, S_2, are statements. The precedence order for disambiguating statements (from highest to lowest priority) is: ( ) , ; , // .

The intended meaning of the script can be informally described as follows. The behavior of an actor is defined using a script σ when the actor is created. The behavior is a function of local parameters, $a_1, \ldots, a_i$, and a sequence of variables, $k_1, \ldots, k_j$. The values of of the parameters a_p, for $1 \leq p \leq i$, are set by d_p in the corresponding array of values. When an actor accepts a communication, it binds the identifiers $k_1, \ldots, k_j$ to the corresponding values in the sequence specifying the accepted communication. The actor then executes the statement S with the closure thus being defined by the local parameters and the communication accepted. Note that all identifiers follow lexical scoping rules and are always local to the environment.

The meaning of the statements is for the most part quite obvious. The statement **send** e **to** P causes the expression e to be evaluated and and the result sent to the mail address bound to the identifier P. (Note that e may evaluate to a sequence of values and not necessarily a single value). The statement **if** b **then** S' **fi** causes S' to be executed if the boolean expression b is true. **let** $x = e_1$ $\{S'\}$ binds the identifier x to the expression e_1 in the scope of expression S'.

The command **become** $\delta\langle\overline{d'}\rangle$ specifies the replacement behavior for the actor by providing values to instantiate parameters of some script. There may be at most one executable *become* command in any actor given any communication. New actors may be simultaneously created by the *new* statement and these actors may know each other's the mail addresses. The mail address of the actor defined using the script tagged by δ_i is bound to the local identifiers P_i in a *new* expression.

4.2 Example Behavior Specifications

Instead of formalizing the meaning of a script, we simply provide some examples to illustrate the actor definitions in *Sal* . In any event, the behavior of an actor is quite simple. The complexity of actor systems is an emergent property of the patterns of communication in a "organization" of actors.

Example 4.1 Recursive Factorial. The script of the recursive factorial actor may be specified in *Sal* as in Fig. 4. It's behavior is mathematically specified as a function in example 3.1 and illustrated in figures 1 and 2.

Example 4.2 A Bank Account. A bank account is a simple example of a serialized actor. The behavior of this actor is parameterized by a single variable, namely the balance in the account. The script of a bank account is given below.

```
def φ ( ) ⊙ [n, m]
 become φ ⟨ ⟩ //
 if n = 0 then send [1] to m fi //
 if n ≠ 0 then
   def ψ ( ) ⊙ [k]
     send n * k to m
   end def
   new c : ψ⟨ ⟩ ;
  send [n − 1 , c] to φ
 fi
end def
```

Figure 4: `A Recursive Factorial.`

New bank accounts can be freely created by new expressions instantiating the balance parameter appropriately. What's significant is that the mail address of newly created bank accounts may be freely communicated (initially by the actor creating it). This bank account, α_1 has overdraft protection from another account α_2. It becomes *insensitive* if there is an overdraft as described in Example 3.2. We assume that the script of the savings account is similar. The script for an insensitive bank account, β_i is given in figure 6 and that for a customer, α_3, which will appropriately package the response from the savings account is in figure 7.

5 Configurations

A *configuration* is a description of an actor system in some frame of reference (there is no implied uniqueness of the configuration of an actor system). A configuration represents a fragment of the picture and not necessarily the totality of actors. A actor system may be described in terms of the possible configurations that it may be in. While we will require each configuration to be a finitary element, the set of possibilities will, in general, be countably infinite.

```
def α1 (a) ⊙ [r, d , m]
  if r = deposit then
    become α1 ⟨a + d⟩ //
    send ["deposited"] to m
  fi
  //
  if r = withdrawal then
     if a ≥ d then
       become α1 ⟨a − d⟩ //
       send ["withdrawn"] to m
     fi //
     if a < d then
       become βi ⟨⟩ //
       new P : α3⟨a, m, α1⟩ ;
       send ["withdrawal", a − d, P] to α2
     fi
  fi  end def
```

Figure 5: A Bank Account with Overdraft Protection

```
def βi () ⊙ [k1 , k2 , k3]
  if k1 = become then
    become α1 ⟨k2⟩
  fi//
  if k1 ≠ become then
    become βi ⟨⟩ //
    send [k1 , k2 , k3] to βi
  fi  end def
```

Figure 6: An Insensitive Bank Account

```
def α3 (a , m1 , m2 ) ⊙ [ k1 , k2 , k3]
    if k1 = withdrawn then
        send ["withdrawn"] to m1 //
        send ["become" , 0] to m2
    fi //
    if k1 = complaint then
        send ["complaint"] to m1 //
        send ["become" , a] to m2
    fi end def
```

Figure 7: A Customer to Process Overdrafts

Relations between configurations are the basic unit of analysis for actor systems because different descriptions of an actor system do not affect each other in any manner whatsoever. Thus sets of configurations inherit properties derived point-wise from their elements. We will define configurations and a fundamental transition relation between them. A configuration is defined in terms of a local states function and a set of unprocessed tasks.

5.1 Local States Function

A local states function, l, is a partial function from the set of mail addresses, $\mathcal{M}$, to a set of behaviors, $\mathcal{B}$, i.e.,

$$l : \mathcal{M} \longrightarrow \mathcal{B}$$

$\mathcal{M}$ is a countably infinite set which we will map to the set of integers with the $<$ relation defined between mail addresses. $\mathcal{B}$ is the set of behaviors defined in the section 3. An actor will be thought of as residing at a specific mail address. The mail address an actor has at its creation is the mail address with which it will be permanently identified. We make local states function a total function by extending its range to $\mathcal{B} \cup \{\bot\}$, where $\bot$ is an undefined element. The local states function now maps all previously undefined elements to $\bot$.

In any configuration, only a finite number of actors may exist. This is simply a statement about the nature of our universe! Since it is intended that actors be "real" objects, this restriction must be obeyed by any physically realizable configuration. Note that this is a stronger condition than the *law of finite acquaintances* proposed in [Hewitt and Baker 1977]. The law of finite acquaintances only required that any individual actor have only finitely many *acquaintances*. One can derive the law as a corollary of the stronger condition assumed here.

Now we can formalize the notion that there are at most finitely many actors in a given configuration: if l is a local states function in a configuration then

$$\exists i, i' \in \mathcal{M} \ \forall j \in \mathcal{M} \ (j \geq i \lor j < i' \implies l(j) = \perp)$$

Remark. The motivation for using mail addresses less than i' is that these are never set in any configuration to "defined" mail addresses: they represent actors that are *external* to the configuration.

5.2 Tasks

An actor sending a communication is required to specify the mail address of the recipient. The recipient's mail address is called the *target* to which the communication is being sent. The object composed of the communication and the target is called *task*. In our model each task is considered distinct because it is initiated by a unique actor at a unique point in its existence. Thus two tasks with equal communications and targets are equivalent but **not** equal.

Why discriminate between tasks that are equivalent? Recall that the delivery of all communications sent is guaranteed. This is simply a statement of a finite, albeit indeterminate, conceptual distance between two actors. Since the sender must specify a (valid) mail address, the communication sent must be eventually received, although after an arbitrarily long delay. Thus, if behaviorally equivalent tasks were considered equal, one could not express any properties of the system relying on a particular task being delivered after a finite amount of delay. Of course, equivalent properties could be expressed in terms of multisets but our model is somewhat simpler.

Definition 5.1 Task. *A task is an element of* $\mathcal{T}$ *such that*

$$\mathcal{T} = \mathcal{N} \times \mathcal{M} \times \mathcal{K}$$

where $\mathcal{N}$ *is the universal set of tags,* $\mathcal{M}$ *is the set of all mail addresses, and* $\mathcal{K}$ *is the set of all communications.* $\mathcal{N}$ *is isomorphic to the set of natural numbers under the* $<$ *relation.*

Communications are arbitrary finite sequences of values where the set of values is isomorphic to the set of natural numbers. There may only be a finite number of tasks in any given configuration. This is again a statement of the finiteness property of the universe. We can express this property as follows: Let T be the set of tasks in any configuration, then

$$\exists i \in \mathcal{N}\ \forall j \in \mathcal{N}\ \forall m \in \mathcal{M}\ \forall \overline{k} \in \mathcal{K}(\ (j, m, \overline{k}) \in T \implies j \leq i\ )$$

We can now define a configuration as follows:

Definition 5.2 Configurations. *A configuration is a two tuple* (l, T)*, where* l *is a local states function and* T *is a finite set of tasks.*

5.3 Transitions between Configurations

We now discuss how actor systems may evolve in terms of their descriptions. We will follow the convention that the mail addresses and tags will be represented by the set of integers and the set of natural numbers, respectively, with which they are isomorphic. Let *states* and *tasks* be two functions defined on configurations that extract the first and second component of a configuration. Thus the range of *states* is the set of local states functions and the range of *tasks* is the power set of tasks. A transition relation specifies how a configuration may possibly evolve into another by processing some task.

The following definition essentially shows how an interpreter for an actor language would, in theory, work. It thus specifies an operational semantics for an abstract actor language. Note that this is the so-called semantics by reduction. The definition is justified by the finiteness properties stated above.

Definition 5.3 Transitions. *Let c_1 and c_2 be two configurations, then c_1 is said to have a transition to c_2 by processing a task $t = (i, m, \overline{k})$, symbolically,*

$$c_1 \xrightarrow{t} c_2$$

if $t \in tasks(c_1)$ and furthermore, if $states(c_1)(m) = \beta$ where

$$\beta(\overline{k}) = \{(n_1, m_1, \overline{k}_1), \ldots, (n_j, m_j, \overline{k}_j)\} \times \{(id_1, \widetilde{\beta_1}), \ldots, (id_q, \widetilde{\beta_q})\} \times \widetilde{\beta}'$$

and $\overline{m}$ is the minimal mail address such that $\forall m' > \overline{m}$, $states(c_1)(m')$ is undefined, and $\overline{i}$ be the minimal tag such that $\forall (i', m', \overline{k}') \in tasks(c_1)$ $(i' \leq \overline{i})$ then the following hold:

$$states(c_2)(m') = \begin{cases} states(c_1)(m') & \text{if } m' \neq m \text{ and } m' \leq \overline{m} \\ \beta_p & \text{if } m' = \overline{m} + p \text{ and } 1 \leq p \leq q \\ \beta' & \text{if } m' = m \end{cases}$$

$$tasks(c_2) = (tasks(c_1) - t) \cup \{(\overline{i} + 1, m_1, \overline{k}_1), \ldots, (\overline{i} + j, m_1, \overline{k}_j)\}$$

where β' and each of β_p are derived from $\widetilde{\beta}'$ and $\widetilde{\beta_p}$ by substituting the appropriate mail addresses, namely, $\overline{m} + i$ for id_i.

Example 5.1 Recursive Factorial. We consider the simple case of the factorial being sent a single communication. Let c_1 be a configuration such that

$$c_1 = \langle \{ (-1, \varepsilon), (1, \varphi) \}, \{ (1, 1, [3, -1]) \} \rangle$$

where φ is the recursive factorial actor defined in example 3.1, and ε is the behavior of an *external actor* which for our purposes now is identical to the behavior of an *undefined actor* except that its mail address will never be set inside the configuration. The intuition here is that communications to ε are like outputs in classical models. We can describe the transition from c_1 as below. Note that instead of labeling each transition with the communication, we simply label it with the tag of the transition. Since the behavior of ε is $\perp$ we do not list it in the local states function.

$$c_1 \xrightarrow{1} \langle \{(1,\varphi)\,,\,(2,\psi^3_{-1})\,\}\,,\,\{(2,1,[2,2])\}\rangle$$

Since there is only one task, the transition above is the only one possible and thus this example is deterministic. This remains true in later transitions of the configurations. If we call RHS above c_2 then the transitions from it look like

$$c_2 \xrightarrow{2} \langle \{(1,\varphi)\,,\,(2,\psi^3_{-1})\;(3,\psi^2_2)\,\}\,,\,\{(3,1,[1,3])\}\,\rangle$$

$$\xrightarrow{3} \langle \{(1,\varphi)\,,\,(2,\psi^3_{-1})\,,\,(3,\psi^2_2)\,,\,(4,\psi^1_3)\}\,,\,\{(3,1,[1,3])\}\,\rangle$$

$$\ldots \quad \ldots\ldots\ldots$$

$$\xrightarrow{7} \langle \{(1,\varphi)\,\}\,,\,\{(8,-1,[6])\}\,\rangle$$

Note that we follow the convention that all the mail address not specified by the local states function are assumed to be ***undefined mail addresses.***

If one had started with a configuration where the task was to evaluate the factorial of an arbitrary natural number, we could establish the analogous result by induction on the number.

5.4 Behavioral Equivalence of Configurations

Although each configuration is a contemporaneous description of an actor system, and therefore does not explicitly carry its history, there is nevertheless some operational information inherent in each configuration. This is because, in each configuration, both the mail addresses in the local states function, and the tag of every task, depend on the details of the history of that configuration. Such details are not really relevant to the potential evolution of its future behavior.

Definition 5.4 Behavioral Equivalence. *Two configurations c_1 and c_2 are considered behaviorally equivalent, symbolically, $c_1 \approx c_2$, if there exists a relabeling of all the mail addresses and tags in c_1 such that $c_1 = c_2$.*

Note that it is **not** sufficient to relabel the mail addresses in the tasks and the domain of the local states function. The relabeling must be followed through in the domain and the range of the behaviors as well.

Example 5.2 Insensitive Actors. Let c_1 and c_2 be two configurations, and $m \in \mathcal{M}$ be such that $states(c_1)(m) = \beta_i$, where β_i is the behavior of an insensitive actor. Then $c_1 \xrightarrow{(i,m,\bar{k})} c_2$ implies that $c_1 \approx c_2$ Conversely, if $c_1 \xrightarrow{(i,m,\bar{k})} c_2$ and $states(c_1)(m) \neq \beta_i$ then $c_1 \not\approx c_2$.

The concept of unserialized actors is extremely useful. In particular, unserialized actors may be copied arbitrarily. For example, suppose c_1 and c_2 are two configurations such that the local states function of c_2 differs from that of c_1 only in so far as it assigns an extra mail address to an unserialized actor whose behavior is identical to that of another unserialized actor in the configuration, and furthermore, the sets of tasks are identical except that some of the tasks going to the particular unserialized actor in c_1 go to the extra actor in c_2. Then from a semantic point of view, one would like the behavior of the two configurations to be represented identically. Computations in c_2 may proceed a little faster, but that is really an issue for the efficiency of the algorithm in the context of a parallel system.

Unfortunately, the definition of behavioral equivalence we have specified is not extensional enough for this purpose. One can refine the notion of behavioral equivalence by changing the definition of a configuration to require the explicit specification of actors that are *receptionists, i.e.*, actors in a given configuration that may receive communications from actors outside the configuration. Such actors constitute the "input ports" for any given configuration. The "output ports" are already implicitly known as the external actors. The significant difference between the other models using the notion of ports and actors is that the actor model explicitly considers the dynamic evolution of the "ports" as new receptionists may become known to the external actors, and *vice-versa*. One can then view the configuration only in terms of communications to these ports. We will not delve in this direction here.

6 Nondeterminism and Fairness

The transition relation between configurations defines a *computation tree* where the various possible transitions on a configuration define a partial order. In the simple example of the configuration with the recursive factorial actor discussed in the previous section, the possible computational structure was linear. This case is, of course, the degenerate one involving sequential programming. In general, a configuration has many possible transitions stemming from the arrival order nondeterminism inherent in the relation.

Of particular interest in actor systems is the fact that all communications sent are subsequently delivered. This guarantee of delivery is a particular form of fairness, and there are many other forms of fairness, such as fairness over arbitrary predicates. We will not go into the merits of the different forms here but consider the implications of guaranteeing the delivery of any particular communication even when there is an infinite sequence of transitions which does not involve the delivery of a particular communication sent. To deal with this guarantee of mail delivery, it is not sufficient to consider the transition relation we defined in the last section. We will instead develop a second kind of transition relation which we call the *subsequently transition.*[2] We first define a partial order using the transition relation and then use it to define the subsequently transition.

6.1 Possibility Relation

Suppose the "initial" configuration in example 4.1 had been

$$c_{fact} = \langle \{ (1, \varphi) \} , \{ (1, 1, [n, -1]) , (2, 1, [m, -2]) \} \rangle$$

where n and m are some nonnegative integers, and we do not list the external actors in the local states function.

Since in this configuration, there are two tasks to be processed, there are two possible transitions from it. Thus there two *possible* configurations that can follow "next". Each of these has several possible transitions, and so on. This

[2]Milner brought to our attention that the relation we define here is similar to that developed independently in [Costa and Sterling 84] for a *fair CCS*.

motivates the definition of a fundamental partial order between configurations which can be used to give actors a fixed-point semantics.

Definition 6.1 Possibility Relation. *A configuration c is said to possibly evolve into a configuration c', symbolically, $c \longrightarrow^* c'$, if there exists a sequence of tasks, $t_1, \ldots, t_n$, and a sequence of configurations, $c_0, \ldots, c_n$, for some n, a non-negative integer, such that,*

$$c = c_0 \xrightarrow{t_1} c_1 \xrightarrow{t_2} \cdots \xrightarrow{t_n} c_n = c'$$

Remark 1. If $n = 0$ above, we simply mean the identity relation.

Remark 2. It is easy to see why the above relation is reflexive and transitive. It is a little trickier to show that it is indeed anti-symmetric. The proof of that property follows by observing the way in which unprocessed tasks are tagged. If some configuration c has tasks with tags $i_1, \ldots, i_p$, and if $c \longrightarrow^* c'$ then there must be at least one tag between i_1 and i_p that is used in c but not used in c'. This is can be shown by induction on p and we leave it as an exercise.

One could show, by straight forward induction, that the configuration c_{fact} possibly goes to one in which a $n!$ communication is sent to the mail address -1. For example, there exists some j such that

$$c_{fact} \longrightarrow^* \langle \{(1, \varphi)\}, \{(j, -1, [n!]), (2, 1, [m, -2])\} \rangle$$

Similarly, there exists some j and j' such that

$$c_{fact} \longrightarrow^* \langle \{(1, \varphi)\}, \{(j, -1, [n!]), (j', -2, [m!])\} \rangle$$

Of course, one can make a stronger statement than the one above: considering that the computation structure is finite, one can show that there is a set of configurations, C that c_{fact} necessarily goes to such that

$$c' \in C \implies c' \approx \langle \{(1, \varphi)\}, \{(j, -1, [n!]), (j', -2, [m!])\} \rangle$$

We can't uniquely define the configuration because the tags j and j' depend on the precise arrival order of the incoming communications. The configuration on the RHS of the relation above has the interesting property that no further evolution is possible from it. We call such a configuration *quiescent* (cf. termination of a computation).

6.2 Subsequently Relation

Consider the following example which requires concurrent processing of two requests. Suppose the factorial actor recieved two communications, one of which was to evaluate the factorial of -1, *i.e.*, the configuration defined was:

$$\langle \{ (1, \varphi) \} , \; \{ (1, 1, [n, -1]) , (2, 1, [-1, -2]) \} \rangle$$

where n is some nonnegative integer. The way we defined the factorial actor, this implies that it would embark on the equivalent of a non-terminating computation. More precisely it would send itself a communication with $-k$ in response to a communication with $-k-1$, and so on, and therefore it will not possibly evolve to any configuration which is quiescent.

Recall that in the actor model the delivery of all communications sent is guaranteed. This implies that despite the continual presence of a communication with a negative number in every configuration this configuration possibly goes to, it must at some point process the task with the request to evaluate the factorial of n.[3] We can express this sort of a result by defining the following relation on sets of configurations.

Definition 6.2 Subsequently Relation. *We say a configuration, c subsequently goes to c′, symbolically,* $c \overset{t}{\hookrightarrow} c'$, *if*

$$\begin{aligned} & (\, t \in tasks(c) \implies (\, c \longrightarrow^* c' \,\wedge\, t \notin tasks(c') \,\wedge \\ & \qquad\qquad \nexists c'' \,(t \notin tasks(c'') \,\wedge\, c \longrightarrow^* c'' \,\wedge\, c'' \longrightarrow^* c')) \,\vee \\ & (\, t \notin tasks(c) \,\wedge\, c = c') \end{aligned}$$

Basically, the subsequent transition represents the first configuration which does not contain the task in question. If we defined the set of configurations, C, as follows

$$C = \{c' \,|\, c \overset{t}{\hookrightarrow} c'\}$$

then the guarantee of mail delivery implies that the configuration c must pass through C. We can define a necessity relation based on the subsequently relation

[3] This in turn results in the request to evaluate the factorial of $n-1$. Thus by induction we can establish that at some point in its life, this factorial actor will (indirectly) activate a communication $[n!]$ to the mail address -1.

but will not digress here to do so. The subsequently transition thus provides a way of defining a fair semantics by derivation for an actor model. The model is assumed to have these two transition relations as primitives.

Remark. The subsequently relation defines what may be considered locally infinite transitions. This is due to the nature of nondeterminism in the actor model. The relation captures the unbounded nondeterminism inherent in the actor paradigm. For a discussion of this phenomenon, see [Clinger 81]. Some authors have found unbounded nondeterminism to be rather distressing. In particular, it has been claimed that unbounded nondeterminism could never occur in a real system [Dijkstra 77]. Actually unbounded nondeterminism is ubiquitous due to the quantum physical nature of our universe. For example, it is found in meta-stables states in VLSI [Mead and Conway 80].

7 Conclusions

The purpose of this paper has been to clarify some of the issues in the semantics of the actor paradigm of concurrent computation. We have attempted to define, in somewhat formal terms, what the behavior of an actor is. It needs to be reiterated that the complexity of computations in actor systems stems from the patterns of communications between individual actors, and not from the behavior of these actors alone. It is our conjecture that every model of concurrent computation can be derived as a special case of the actor model. Other models tend to make additional assumptions that do not necessarily follow from first principles. Our contention is that assumptions such as universal synchronization between different agents in the system will only serve to restrict the amount of concurrency in the system.

We have discussed how a fair semantics may be built on the subsequently relation between the configurations. However, it should be observed that configurations, in some sense, are too primitive to a unit for analysis of actor systems. This is because there is still too much operational information in a configuration. A basic goal of any model should be that it should not discriminate between configurations that seem intuitively equivalent. This is not true for the model we defined. One step in this direction would be to take equivalence classes of configurations as the primitive elements in the model. Interestingly enough, doing so would imply that the anti-symmetry property may not hold for either the subsequently or the possibility relation.

It should be observed that the definition of behavioral equivalence we provided is not sufficiently strong: it still allows one to discriminate between configurations that seem equivalent in the sense that their behavior is not distinguishable except in terms of the operational details essentially unobservable from the "outside" of the configuration. We discussed the example of an arbitrary number of copies of an unserialized actor. This problem is, however, not limited to unserialized actors. For example, suppose an actor creates another actor but does not send that actor a communication, or send its mail address to any other actor, or even retain the mail address in any actors it creates. By the locality laws, we know that the created actor will never be sent a communication because no one will possibly know its mail address. Since this actor will never receive a communication, it can never do anything (recall that in the actor paradigm, all behavior is in response to processing a communication). We would like a configuration with this actor to be behaviorally equivalent to a configuration that is identical all other respects except that it does not have the actor in question.

The general solution to this problem is in perhaps in the direction of using the locality laws to mask information inside the configuration, provided that such information is neither relevant nor potentially relevant to the external environment. We did not explicitly use the locality laws to restrict the class of functions that may be validly used to specify the behavior of new actors and changes in local states. This is not difficult to do. The locality laws are also valid in the specification of the actor-based language, *Sal* .

It is interesting to consider the nature of mail addresses in actor systems. While information about mail addresses is purely local, the mail address itself is a "global entity" in the sense that once communicated, it refers to the same actor. Mail addresses can be created locally despite the fact we do so globally in our operational semantics. For example, a distributed operating system does this. In essence, it is only the objects are real; the tags we provide are purely arbitrary means of keeping track of them. The tags may indeed be defined locally in terms of the actor creating the object.

In the final analysis, the various competing models of concurrent computation may be judged on the basis of how efficiently they exploit parallelism in distributed architectures. It is probably a truism that no single model will be the basis of an optimal architecture for all conceivable applications. At the same time, the chances are that the more restrictive a model is, the more circumscribed its domain of applicability is likely to be. In this regard, it should be noted that the actor paradigm assumes little more than the laws of parallel processing.

Acknowledgments

Much of the development of the actor paradigm has been inspired by the work of Carl Hewitt at M.I.T., who has also contributed, by his encouragement and constructive criticism, to the development of many ideas in this paper. I am also indebted to William Rounds for his suggestions, including the suggestion that I should define an actor-based language with an easy to follow syntax. I would like to thank John Holland for providing both intellectual impetus and moral support over the years. Conversations with Robin Milner, Vaughn Pratt, and Paul Scott, and Joe Stoy have provided critical feedback. Members of the Semantics Group at M.I.T. have created an atmosphere which made the work described here possible. In particular, Carl Manning, Chunka Mui and Thomas Reinhardt provided helpful comments on the drafts of this paper.

The work described in here was made possible by generous funding from the System Development Foundation.

References

[Atkinson and Hewitt 79] Atkinson, R. and Hewitt, C. Specification and Proof Techniques for Serializers. IEEE Transactions on Software Engineering SE-5 No. 1, IEEE, January, 1979.

[Backus 78] Backus, J. Can Programming be Liberated from the von Neumann Style? A Functional Style and Its Algebra of Programs. *Communications of the ACM 21*, 8 (August 1978), 613-641.

[Clinger 81] Clinger, W. D. Foundations of Actor Semantics. AI-TR- 633, MIT Artificial Intelligence Laboratory, May, 1981.

[Dijkstra 77] Dijkstra, E. W. *A Discipline of Programming.* Prentice-Hall, 1977.

[Fosseen 72] Fosseen, J.B. Representation of Algorithms by Maximally Parallel Schemata. Master Th., Massachusetts Institute of Technology, 1972.

[Goldberg 83] Goldberg, A. and Robson, D. *Smalltalk-80: The Language and Its Implementation.* Addison-Wesley Publishing Company, 1983.

[Greif 75] Greif, I. Semantics of Communicating Parallel Processes. Technical Report 154, MIT, Project MAC, 1975.

[Hewitt 77] Hewitt, C.E. Viewing Control Structures as Patterns of Passing Messages. *Journal of Artificial Intelligence 8-3* (June 1977), 323-364.

[Hewitt and Baker 77] Hewitt, C. and Baker, H. Laws for Communicating Parallel Processes. 1977 IFIP Congress Proceedings, IFIP, August, 1977, pp. 987-992.

[Hewitt, et al 84] Hewitt, C., Reinhardt, T., Agha, G. and Attardi, G. Linguistic Support of Receptionists for Shared Resources. Memo Forthcoming , MIT Artificial Intelligence Laboratory, 1984.

[Hoare 78] Hoare, C. A. R. Communicating Sequential Processes. *CACM 21*, 8 (August 1978), 666-677.

[Liskov, Snyder, Atkinson, and Schaffert 77] Liskov B., Snyder A., Atkinson R., and Schaffert C. Abstraction Mechanism in CLU. *Communications of the ACM 20*, 8 (August 1977).

[Mead and Conway 80] Mead, C. and Conway, L. *Introduction to VLSI Systems.* Addison-Wesley, Reading, MA, 1980.

[Milner 80] Milner, R. *Lecture Notes in Computer Science. Vol. 92: A Calculus of Communicating Behavior.* Springer-Verlag, 1980.

[Peterson 77] Peterson, J.L. Petri Nets. *Comput. Survey* (Sept. 1977).

[Smyth 78] Smyth, M.B. Petri Nets. *J. of Comput. Survey Science* (Feb. 1978).

[Theriault 83] Theriault, D. Issues in the Design and Implementation of Act2. Technical Report 728, MIT Artificial Intelligence Laboratory, June, 1983.

The Pomset Model of Parallel Processes: Unifying the Temporal and the Spatial

Vaughan Pratt
Stanford University
Stanford, CA 94305

1. Temporal Theory - Qualitative Scheduling

1.1. Background

The progenitor of our pomset model is Kahn's history-transformer model of nets [Kah74, KaM77], in which a process is viewed as a function from n-tuples of histories to histories, where a history is a sequence of values. Each connection or channel of the net is associated with such a history. Kahn's model, being functional rather than relational, only caters for determinate processes. This has the advantage of permitting a straightforward least-fixed-point analysis, and the disadvantage of excluding such basic processes as the merge process. The Brock-Ackerman anomaly [BA81] demonstrates the need for something more than histories in extending Kahn's model to treat nondeterminate processes. Brock and Ackerman show how to extend Kahn's model by inclusion of ordering information between events on different channels.

The pomset model was introduced by the present author [Pra82]. It is intended as a theoretical framework for the Brock-Ackerman extension of Kahn's model. However the topic of models of concurrency has been particularly active in recent years, with the inevitable consequence that any given viewpoint ages rapidly. Thus the present paper describes our original model but from a more current perspective.

The basic idea of the model remains unchanged: a process is a set of pomsets, networks are defined in terms of events as channel-data pairs, and real-time is modelled by extending partial orders to more general semirings (only hinted at near the end of the paper [Pra82]).

A major change is the symmetrization of input and output. Our channels are no longer directed; instead they are just places to share information. Communication is by consensus: information is shared simply when the communicating parties agree to share it. This both simplifies the model and makes it more useful and less oriented to any particular communication protocol, a goal of our original paper that was not as well met as now.

With this improvement to our model has come the ability to model bus communication, in which several processes all have both read and write access to a single channel. We can model quite complex bus protocols on even a single wire on which handshakes and data in both directions are represented simultaneously by appropriate combinations of say voltages and impedances. We also can model continuous as well as discrete systems. Indeed cooperating physical laws like $F = ma$ and $E = mv^2/2$ may be modelled as continuous communicating processes, permitting physical and information systems to be modelled not only in the same style but even in the same model. This opens up the possibility of proving correct a discrete flip-flop starting from the continuous equivalent-circuit model of its constituent transistors, an exercise we hope to engage in on some future occasion.

By far the most extensive work on pomsets to date is Jay Gischer's thesis [Gis84]. Although his thesis concentrates on axiomatizability questions for theories of pomsets under several different combinations of pomset operations, it also makes a number of other contributions to the subject of pomsets and their algebras. The material in this first section on pomsets is within the scope of Gischer's thesis, and we take the opportunity to advertise some of his results. The two following sections, on spatial processes and real time, are topics not addressed in the thesis. We adopt Gischer's notation throughout.

There are strong connections between our pomsets and Glynn Winskel's event structures [W84]. One difference is in the conflict relation that is a part of event structures but is absent from the pomset model.

1.2. Variety, Sequence, and Concurrency

In this section we build up to the pomset model by starting with what we feel are quite basic notions for any process-oriented model of computation. By "process" we have in mind either event-oriented or state-oriented computation, with a contrast being intended with say the applicative style of functional programming, where one emphasizes functions, their application, and their types. On the other hand we see less of a contrast with some models of imperative programs - we view the binary-relation-on-states model advocated by de Bakker [deB72] and used for dynamic logic as a special case of the current study.

A fundamental concept in a process-oriented model of computation is variety of behavior. A popular way to model variety is with sets: a program or process is modelled as the set of its possible behaviors.

If the program exhibits only stimulus-response behavior, as with the binary-relation-on-states model, each behavior may consist of a stimulus-response pair. In this case a program consisting of a set of such pairs may be considered a binary relation from stimuli to responses. If the program is determinate (same stimulus yields same response every time) and total (every stimulus yields a response), this relation will then be a function from stimuli to responses. Stimuli and responses may be either events or states - we will not attempt here to distinguish these two concepts.

A second fundamental concept is course of events, or thread of control, a concept that is important in the context of "ongoing" processes. The stimulus-response model admits only a limited notion of course of events, namely an initial event followed by a final event. A richer model would include intermediate events as well, generalizing behaviors from pairs of events to sequences of events. The concept of variety of behavior continues however to be modelled as a set of alternative such behaviors, making variety of behavior a notion more basic than, or at least independent of, course of events.

Whereas a set of pairs is a binary relation, a set of sequences is a language (possibly with infinite strings), and so languages constitute an appropriate model for ongoing processes. The language model is made particularly attractive by the extensive work done on formal languages over the past two decades in response to the needs of both programming and natural languages. The word "trace" is used by some authors to denote a sequence used in this application.

A third fundamental concept is concurrency: two events happening at the same time, or overlapping in time, or in the weakest sense of "concurrency," just having no specific temporal relationship to each other. One approach to modelling concurrency is to treat it in terms of variety in course of events, that is, as a derived concept utilizing both variety of behavior and course of events. A basic example of this is to represent the concurrent execution of two processes, modelled as languages L and M, as the language L||M consisting of all interleavings or shuffles of strings one from each of L and M. This is the approach adopted in language or trace models.

An alternative approach to modelling concurrency is to consider it a primitive notion in its own right, independent of both of the notions of variety of behavior and course of events. One argument for this goes as follows.

For two atomic (indivisible) processes L and M, modelled as languages each consisting of one unit-length string, their concurrent execution L||M is simply LM∪ML. For arbitrary languages however there is no such convenient expression for L||M in terms of course of events (concatenation) and variety of behavior (union). If L and M are given as built up with concatenation and union (and possibly other operations, e.g. Kleene star) from atomic processes then one may derive an expression for L||M in terms of the atoms and the other operations. However to require this decomposition into atoms represents a serious handicap for a model or logic of concurrent programs.

Consider for example the situation where a software engineer needs to verify the operation of a system containing two concurrently executing programs. He is provided with specifications of the behavior of the programs, but not to a sufficient level of detail that he can say what the interleavings of the atomic commands are. This situation can arise either because the atomic behavior is far too complex to be reckoned with, or because the supplier of the programs does not want the user depending on implementation details that go beyond the specifications, in order to preserve the supplier's flexibility in subsequently improving the software, or because the granularity of interleaving varies between applications.

If sets primitively model variety and strings primitively model sequentiality, what primitively models concurrency? We propose the pomset, or partially ordered multiset.

A string s of length n on alphabet Σ is commonly defined as a function $s:\{0,1,2,\ldots,n-1\}\rightarrow\Sigma$. In order to lead up to pomsets we shall adopt a different definition: s is a totally ordered multiset of n elements drawn from Σ. To be a multiset means that the drawing is performed with replacement. If sets were used rather than multisets, the alphabet {0,1} would yield only five strings, namely the empty string, 0, 1, 01, and 10. The distinction between multiset and set is whether sampling is with or without replacement. The distinction remains when the set or multiset is equipped with an order to make it a pomset or poset respectively.

Informally, a partially ordered multiset is a string with the requirement removed that its order be total. The phrase "partially ordered set" abbreviates to "poset", so by analogy we shall abbreviate "totally ordered multiset" to "tomset" and "partially ordered multiset" to "pomset." We now formalize the notion of pomset.

A *partial order* is a set $(V,<)$ where $<$ is an irreflexive transitive binary relation on a vertex set V. A *labelled partial order* or lpo is a 4-tuple $(V,\Sigma,\mu,<)$ where $(V,<)$ is a partial order and $\mu:V\rightarrow\Sigma$ labels the vertices of V with symbols from an alphabet Σ.

Two lpo's $[V,\Sigma,<,\mu]$ and $[V',\Sigma,<',\mu']$ are *isomorphic* when there exists a bijection $\tau:V\rightarrow V'$ such that for all u in V, $\mu(u) = \mu'(\tau(u))$, and for all u,v in V, $u<v$ just when $\tau(u) <' \tau(v)$.

A *pomset* $[V,\Sigma,<,\mu]$ is the isomorphism class of the lpo $(V,\Sigma,<,\mu)$.

The reason for defining pomsets only up to isomorphism is to suppress the identities of the elements of V, so that only the cardinality of V counts, leaving Σ as the only important set underlying a pomset, just as the alphabet is the only important set underlying a string. The motivation is the same as in graph theory, where the identity of graphs is normally defined only up to isomorphism. See the appendix for further discussion of isomorphism.

The carrier V may be considered the events of a behavior. The symbols of the alphabet Σ are the actions associated with those events. In the context of operating systems the distinction is that between job and program: the job is an *execution* of the program and the program *controls* the job. A job is a particular event, and the program controlling the job determines the action taking place. One job executes only one program, but one program may control many jobs, even concurrently. In the context of communication the distinction is that between message and contents: a message contains its contents and its contents appear in the message. One message has only one contents, but the same contents may appear in many messages. The word "event" is intended to be interpreted broadly to cover jobs, messages, experimental observations, etc.

Applications. We make no assumptions concerning the atomicity, temporal extent, or spatial extent of events. Events may be atomic, or may have a structure that can itself be represented as a pomset. An event may represent a point in time, or an interval of time. An event may represent the momentary occurrence of a voltage at a point in an integrated circuit, or the formation of the Rocky Mountains. Our emphasis is on keeping the model simple rather than forcing attributes of certain types of events on it. Applications are to be fitted to the model, not the model to any particular application.

Related structures. Multisets, sets, tomsets, strings, n-tuples, and posets may be considered particular kinds of pomsets. A multiset is a pomset with the empty order, that is, an unordered pomset. A poset (partially ordered set) is a pomset with an injective labelling. A set is a multiset that is also a poset (unordered, injective labelling). A tomset is at the other extreme from a multiset: it is totally ordered. A string is a finite tomset. An n-tuple is a string of length n. An ordered pair is a 2-tuple, written either ab or (a,b) depending on context.

In the case of a set (and hence also poset), the labels uniquely determine the elements of V. In this case it is sometimes convenient to identify V with the range of μ and to consider $<$ to partially order that range rather than V itself. Sets and posets may then be treated merely as subsets and posets of Σ, and V and μ dispensed with. The ordered sets Z and R of integers and reals respectively are particularly useful pomsets; they provide a basis for discrete and dense time. In the case of R time forms an ordered set of points, but without a metric for distance.

The (unique) empty or unit pomset, denoted ε, meets our definition of string and therefore must be our old friend the empty string. It is also a multiset, a set (the empty set), and a poset.

An atom, or atomic pomset, has just one element. Atoms also satisfy our definitions of string, multiset, set, and poset. The atoms are in one-to-one correspondence with Σ, and so just as in language theory we shall feel free to make the usual identification between atoms and symbols.

1.4. Algebras of Pomsets

Like most mathematical objects, pomsets do not make good hermits, but thrive when allowed to gather together into algebras. As in any society a certain degree of conformity is demanded of its members: an algebra of pomsets has a base consisting of an ordinal β, and an alphabet Σ consisting of an arbitrary set. Only $\beta\Sigma$-pomsets may join such an algebra, namely those having the form $[V,\Sigma,<,\mu]$ where V is an element of β. (As usual we identify each ordinal with the set of those ordinals less than it.)

The finite pomsets are those with base ω, the countable ones those with base ω_1 (the least uncountable ordinal, which consists of exactly the countable ordinals). The binary pomsets are those with alphabet $2 = \{0,1\}$, the finite decimal tomsets are decimal numerals.

Algebras come with operations. Among the more elementary operations are shuffle and concatenation. (Since no actual shuffling takes place one might prefer in place of shuffle a more neutral name; "co" for concurrency suggests itself, as in the pronunciation of a||b as "a co b.")

Definition. Let $p = [V,\Sigma,<,\mu]$ and $p' = [V',\Sigma,<',\mu']$ be pomsets with V and V' disjoint. Then their *shuffle* $p||p'$ is $[V\cup V',\Sigma,<\cup<',\mu\cup\mu']$ and their *concatenation* p.p', or just pp', is $[V\cup V',\Sigma,<\cup<'\cup(V\times V'),\mu\cup\mu']$.

No loss of generality is entailed by the assumption of disjointness since pomsets are only defined up to isomorphism. If we regard pomsets as graphs then shuffling merely juxtaposes them, placing them side by side to form one graph, while concatenation not only juxtaposes them but adds additional edges to the order, one from each element of V to each element of V'. It is easily verified that the ordering relation remains irreflexive and transitive even with the additional edges introduced by concatenation. Both operations generalize to more arguments; any *string* of pomsets may be concatenated, while any *multiset* of pomsets may be shuffled.

Both concatenation and shuffle are associative, and shuffle is commutative. Neither distributes over the other. The unit pomset ε serves as a two-sided identity for both concatenation and shuffle: $p\varepsilon = \varepsilon p = \varepsilon||p = p$. These laws completely axiomatize the equational theory of pomsets under concatenation and shuffle [Gis84].

Concatenation preserves strings, and indeed is just what is normally meant by concatenation of strings in formal language theory. Shuffle on the other hand does not preserve strings. Gischer defines a function from pomsets to languages that amounts to the completion of a pomset to a set of tomsets. This function, or functor if we were describing all this categorically, maps shuffle to the usual notion of language shuffle.

One might ask what is special about concatenation and shuffle as pomset operations. Here they form a natural introduction to a more general class of operations, the *pomset-definable* operations. Gischer [Gis84] defines both these and the notion of substitution or pomset homomorphism at the same time as follows, with an operation that we shall call expansion.

1.5. Expansion: Pomset-definable Operations and Substitution Homomorphisms

Let P,P' be algebras of pomsets with respective alphabets Σ,Σ', let $p = [V,\Sigma,<,\mu]$ be a pomset of P, and let $\alpha:\Sigma\rightarrow P'$ be a "Σ-tuple" of pomsets of P'. Informally the expansion of p via α transforms p into a pomset p' in P' by expanding each v in p into a whole pomset $p_v = \alpha(\mu(v))$, preserving order both within and between the p_v's.

More formally, let $p'' = [V',\Sigma,<'',\mu']$ be the shuffle (juxtaposition, or disjoint union) of the pomsets $p_v = \alpha(\mu(v))$ for v in V. Let $<^*$ partially order V' such that for each pair u',v' in V' drawn from p_u,p_v respectively, $u'<^*v'$ just when $u<v$ in p. Let $<'$ be the union of $<''$ and $<^*$. Then the *expansion of* p *via* α is just $p' = [V',\Sigma',<',\mu']$.

Thus in an expansion p' two elements of V' may be comparable for one of two reasons: they came from a common element v of V, in which case they were comparable in the pomset p_v that replaced v, or they came from different elements u and v which were comparable in p.

For example let $\Sigma = 2 = \{0,1\}$, let C = 01, S = 0||1 be two-element pomsets (taking 0 and 1 as atoms as explained above), and let $\langle C,C \rangle$ and $\langle S,S \rangle$ be pairs (2-tuples, i.e. functions with domain 2). Then the expansion of one of C or S via one of $\langle C,C \rangle$ or $\langle S,S \rangle$ leads to one of four pomsets: C and $\langle C,C \rangle$ yield the string 0101, C and $\langle S,S \rangle$ yield (0||1)(0||1), S and $\langle C,C \rangle$ yield (01)||(01), and S and $\langle S,S \rangle$ yield 0||1||0||1.

The expansion of C via a pair (p,q) is just pq, the concatenation of the pair. Thus the pomset C defines the binary operation of pomset concatenation. Similarly the expansion of S via (p,q) is p||q, so the pomset S defines the binary shuffle operation. More generally, any pomset with alphabet $n = \{0,1,2,...,n-1\}$ defines some n-ary operation in an algebra of pomsets on some (other) alphabet Σ' mapping n-tuples of pomsets to pomsets. When the defining pomset is infinite the significance of such operations is not clear, so it is natural to consider the pomset-definable operations to be restricted to those defined by finite pomsets.

If we regard a Σ-tuple α as a function from atomic pomsets to pomsets, then the pomset function mapping p to the expansion of p via α may be regarded as the natural extension of α to pomsets. This situation is very common in algebra. Suppose we are given some set of free generators, say the variables in some term language, or the symbols of an alphabet used to form strings. Then a function f from the generator set to some algebra has a unique extension f^+ to a homorphism from the algebra that the generators generate. In the case of variables occurring in terms, such a homomorphism is called a substitution. In the case of symbols in strings it is the notion of string homomorphism encountered in language theory. (There also exist language homomorphisms, which further extend string homomorphisms to homomorphisms on sets of strings.) As with terms and strings, pomsets are freely generated by their atomic constituents.

It is natural to identify the homomorphism itself with the generator-mapping function that it extends, since the extension always exists and is unique. Thus we may consider a Σ-tuple to define, or more simply to be, a pomset homomorphism. We shall follow the terminology that goes with terms and call such homomorphisms *substitutions*.

To summarize: expansion takes one pomset from an algebra P with alphabet Σ and a Σ-tuple of pomsets from an algebra P' with alphabet Σ', and yields a pomset from P'. Fixing the one pomset determines a Σ-ary operation on the algebra P'; when Σ is the ordinal n and P is finite, this operation is an n-ary pomset-definable operation. Fixing the Σ-tuple of pomsets yields a function f that in turn determines a substitution f^+ from P to P'.

The notion of tomset is a potentially useful generalization of the notion of string. The concatenation of two tomsets is defined and a tomset, even when the tomsets are uncountable.

The operations of concatenation and shuffle are obviously of considerable interest. One may ask whether any of the other operations are of interest, or even whether any of them are not already expressible directly in terms of concatenation and shuffle. The latter question is answered positively in Gischer's thesis - concatenation and shuffle do not constitute a basis for all the finitary pomset-definable operations. Gischer proves the much stronger result that those operations have no finite basis - no finite set of operations forms a basis. This is in contrast say to the set of finitary Boolean operations, for which a single operation may serve as a basis.

One operation that is of some interest is the quaternary operation N(p,q,r,s). This is the operation defined by the poset {0,1,2,3} with 0<2, 1<2, and 1<3. This operation is not expressible using shuffle and concatenation.

Substitutions are of interest wherever there is structure. In the purely temporal theory of this section, as opposed to the spatial theory below, the structure is in the events. What may be an atomic event from one perspective may be revealed as a more complex event closer up. A substitution may expand a point into a hive of scheduled activity.

We will also find substitutions useful in developing the spatial theory, where they allow us to describe the effect on behavior of connecting a component into a system.

1.7. Discrete vs. Continuous Pomsets

Functions may map reals to integers or integers to reals or reals to reals just as readily as integers to integers. By the same token we may have pomsets with either the base or the alphabet or both being a continuum.

In the pomset model time appears only as an order; there is no measure. For a discrete order (every element but the last has a well-defined successor) one may use the successor relation to infer a measure: each element follows its predecessor one unit later. But in a dense order there is no such obvious measure. Thus if we take (V,<) to be the set of reals with its standard order, we have an unmeasured time dimension in which there is no way to detect the speeding up or slowing down of time, either locally or globally.

1.8. Example: Modelling the Two-way Channel with Disconnect

At an STL/SERC workshop on the analysis of concurrent systems, held in Cambridge, UK, in August 1983, the participants were asked to specify each of ten information systems. The first system, a two-way channel with disconnect, was probably the simplest; it also got the lion's share of the participants' attention. It was presented thus. "The 'channel' between endpoints 'a' and 'b' can pass messages in both directions simultaneously, until it receives a 'disconnect' message from one end, after which it neither delivers nor accepts messages at that end. It continues to deliver and accept messages at the other end until the 'disconnect' message arrives, after which it can do nothing. The order of messages sent in a given direction is preserved."

Here is a solution to this problem within the pomset framework. The solution emphasizes formality at the expense of succinctness; we have an approach to achieving both at once that we shall describe elsewhere.

The desired channel is the set of all its possible behaviors. Each such behavior is a pomset which is constructed, in a way specified below, from a structure $(V,<,m,port,contents,erase)$ satisfying conditions 1-8 below. V is a finite set of events (either transmissions or receipts of messages), $<$ is a partial ordering of V indicating necessary temporal precedences, $m:V \rightarrow V$ is a function giving, for each transmission or receipt, its matching receipt or transmission, $port:V \rightarrow \{0,1\}$ is a function giving for each event v the port (0 or 1) at which v occurs, erase is a predicate holding for those events to be erased by the construction, and $contents:V \rightarrow M$ maps each event to its contents, drawn from the set M of possible message contents, among which is the message D for disconnect. We write $u \lessgtr v$ to denote comparability of u and v, namely $u<v$ or $v<u$.

For all u and v:

1. $u = m(m(u))$	m is a pairing function
2. $u \lessgtr m(u)$	transmission-receipt pairs linearly ordered
3. $(port(u) = port(v)) \rightarrow u=v$ or $u \lessgtr v$	ports linearly ordered
4. $port(u) + port(m(u)) = 1$	matching spans ports
5. $u<m(u)$ & $u<v$ & $v<m(v) \rightarrow m(u)<m(v)$	channel is order preserving
6. $contents(u) = contents(m(u))$	channel is noiseless
7. $u<v$ & $erase(u) \rightarrow erase(v)$	erasure is suffix-closed
8. $contents(u)=D$ & $u<v \rightarrow erase(v)$	D forces erasure of all subsequent events

Events come in matched pairs u,m(u) (1), with one preceding the other (2). Whichever comes first is the transmission event, the other is then the matching receipt. The set of events at each port is linearly ordered in time (3). Transmission and receipt occur at opposite ports (4). Messages are received in the order transmitted (5). Message contents are received as transmitted (no noise on the channel) (6). The predicate "erase" specifying which events did not really happen is suffix-closed: any event following a non-happening is itself a non-happening (7). Nothing happens after transmission of a disconnect message (including the matching receipt of that disconnect message) (8). Note that this does not preclude two nonerased concurrent transmissions of disconnect messages from the two ports.

Now from each structure satisfying these conditions construct a pomset $(H,\Sigma,<',\mu)$ where H is that subset of V for which erase does not hold, $<'$ is the restriction of $<$ to H, $\Sigma = (2 \times 2) \times M$ (where $2 = \{0,1\}$), and $\mu(u) = ((port(u),m(u)<u),contents(u))$ where $m(u)<u$ is 0 or 1 depending on whether that predicate fails or holds respectively. Then the process consisting of all possible such pomsets is the

desired two-way channel with disconnect.

The label ((p,t),x) on each event in each such pomset indicates the port p at which that event occurred, the type of event - 0 is transmission, 1 is receipt - and the message x received or transmitted.

It will be noted that the function m that pairs up events is absent from the label. The idea is that this information, though visible during our construction of the process, should not be visible in the finished process on the ground that it is not an "observable" of that process. We can see messages being transmitted and others being received, but the problem did not require that we be able to keep track of the connection between transmissions and receipts. Accordingly the connection is deleted from the final specification.

The construction of the pomsets may be viewed as their implementation, and the connection between transmissions and receipts as an implementation detail. The implementation style of specifying things, where a structure is built up and then partially discarded, is widely used in mathematics. Consider for example the construction of the integers as the quotient of sets of pairs (a,b) of natural numbers with the equivalence relation $(a,b) \equiv (a+c,a+c)$, interpreting each equivalence class [(a,b)] as the integer $a-b$; the rationals may be constructed similarly as pairs (a,b), reduced modulo the relation $(a,b) \equiv (ac,bc)$.

2. Spatial Theory - Communication in Nets

2.1. Projection and Net Behaviors

We have viewed a process behavior thus far as a collection of events distributed only in time, with the distribution being determined by the order. The term "endogenous," applied by A. Pnueli to distinguish temporal logic from an "exogenous" logic like dynamic logic, seems to be equally applicable to this purely temporal notion of process. In an endogenous model the universe is viewed as a single process. An exogenous model has distinct processes each with its own identity independent of other processes, yet able to coexist and communicate with other processes. We now wish to be more exogenous, that is, to distinguish between independent communicating processes.

Definition. A *translation* is a function $t:\Sigma \rightarrow \Sigma'$ between two alphabets.

As an example of translation, suppose we are given a module with two channels (ports) 0 and 1 on each of which may appear values from a set D, and suppose we wish to use this module in a context having connections 2,3,4 by attaching 0 to 3 and 1 to 4. Then the event (0,d) denoting the appearance of value $d \in D$ on channel 0 is translated to the event (3,d) in the 2,3,4 context. Similarly an event (1,d) is translated to (4,d). In this example Σ is $2 \times D$ and Σ' is $\{2,3,4\} \times D$, and translation affects channel names but not data values.

As another example we may have for Σ the real interval [0,5] and for Σ' the set {0,X,1} with X denoting invalid, and a translation mapping all elements of the interval [0,2] to 0, the (open) interval (2,3) to X, and [3,5] to 1. This translation would correspond to the interpretation of analog signals, perhaps voltages, as digital signals in a three-valued system. The obvious application is in using an analog module in a digital context.

The above two examples can be combined into a single example which translates both the channels and the data values, translating (c,d) to (f(c),g(d)) where f and g are the respective translations of those examples.

Definition. Given a translation $t:\Sigma\rightarrow\Sigma'$, the *projection induced by* t is the substitution $t^{-+}:\Sigma'\dagger\rightarrow\Sigma\dagger$ mapping pomsets on Σ' to pomsets on Σ.

In more detail, the inverse of an arbitrary function $t:\Sigma\rightarrow\Sigma'$ is not $t^{-}:\Sigma'\rightarrow\Sigma$ but rather $t^{-}:\Sigma'\rightarrow 2^{\Sigma}$, a function mapping symbols to sets of symbols. Any symbol not in the range of t will be mapped by t^{-} to the empty set; we can think of this as being "projected out" by t^{-}. Any symbol in Σ' hit only once by t will be mapped by t^{-} to exactly one symbol in Σ; we can think of this as a coordinate transform, or renaming, from Σ' back to Σ. Any symbol in Σ' hit more than once by t will be mapped to a set of two or more symbols in Σ; we can think of those symbols as needed for labelling simultaneous events in Σ that are mapped by t to a single event in Σ'. (Consider a translation which attaches two pins of an integrated circuit to the same printed circuit board wire. A single event on that wire can happen only if the corresponding events on each of those two pins can happen simultaneously.)

Since a set of symbols is also a pomset of symbols with the empty order, t^{-} is therefore a function mapping symbols to pomsets. In the temporal section we saw how such a function had a unique extension to a substitution, so let us form that extension, t^{-+}, to yield a mapping from pomsets to pomsets. We call this a projection because a major use of it is to project out some of the events of a pomset. However as noted just above it may also duplicate some events, so its function really goes beyond the normal notion of projection. We have not thought of a better word than projection to describe this action.

The action of a projection on a process P is the set of pomsets resulting from applying the projection to each of the pomsets of P, a process, so projection maps not only pomsets to pomsets but processes to processes.

A net N of processes P_i each with associated translation t_i embedding it in that net is the set N of those behaviors p such that, for all i, $t_i^{-+}(p) \in P_i$.

Such a net includes all its internal behaviors. Where a translation t defines an embedding in the net of its external connections, the external behavior of the net N is just $t^{-+}(N)$, the projection of N induced by t. The effect of this projection is to hide the internal behavior and provide the appropriate external port names for the externally visible portion of the behavior.

At this point the whole procedure probably looks quite mysterious. Let us dispel some of the mystery by showing how it works in the familiar context of composition of binary relations.

2.2. Example: Composition of Binary Relations

Let us begin with a familiar operation, the composition MN of two binary relations M and N on a set A. Using the representation of binary relations called for by our approach, we shall exhibit their composition as a projection of the set of behaviors projecting to behaviors of M and N.

The usual way this can be done for binary relations is to have three projections $\mu(a,b,c) = (a,b)$, $\nu(a,b,c) = (b,c)$, and $\kappa(a,b,c) = (a,c)$. Then the net behavior MN is $K = \{(a,b,c) | \mu(a,b,c) \in M \ \& \ \nu(a,b,c) \in N\}$, the set of all behaviors whose projections under μ and ν are in M and N respectively. The composition itself is then the projection $\kappa(K)$.

To fit this into our scheme we shall show how to represent μ,ν,κ as inverses of translations. We take $\Sigma = \{0,1\} \times A$ and $\Sigma' = \{0,1,2\} \times A$ for the domain and codomain of all three translations. We shall regard the pair (a,b) as the ordered multiset $(0,a)<(1,b)$, and the triple (a,b,c) as $(0,a)<(1,b)<(2,c)$. The appropriate translations are then $m(c,x) = (c,x)$, $n(c,x) = (c+1,x)$, and $k(c,x) = (-c,x) \pmod 3$. (That is, $m(0,x)=(0,x)$, $m(1,x)=(1,x)$, $n(0,x)=(1,x)$, $n(1,x)=(2,x)$, $k(0,x)=(0,x)$, $k(1,x)=(2,x)$.)

Now $m^{-}(0,x) = \{(0,x)\}$, $m^{-}(1) = \{(1,x)\}$, and $m^{-}(2) = \{\}$. Hence the behaviors mapped by m^{-+} to behaviors of M will be just those pomsets having an event (0,a), an event (1,b), and any number of events (2,c) for various values of c, with the order arbitrary except that $(0,a)<(1,b)$, and with $(a,b) \in M$. Of these, the ones mapped by m^{-+} to behaviors of N will have one event (1,b) and one event (2,c), where $(b,c) \in N$ and $(1,b)<(2,c)$, but with no constraints on events of the form (1,a). But this then limits the possible behaviors of the net to just $(0,a)<(1,b)<(2,c)$ where $(a,b) \in M$ and $(b,c) \in N$.

The most noteworthy difference from the standard construction $\{(a,b,c) | \mu(a,b,c) \in M \ \& \ \nu(a,b,c) \in N\}$ is that our construction does not assume at the outset that the result will consist only of triples. Instead the construction "discovers" this for itself.

It should now be clear how the projection k^{-+} discards the middle element of each triple to yield the desired composition.

Had we removed the order in defining binary relations, we would have hit a small snag.. Net behaviors would still have only three events, (0,a), (1,b), (2,c), this time with (0,a) and (1,b) being incomparable and similarly for (1,b) and (2,c). However the ordering between (0,a) and (2,c) would be unconstrained. Hence for each triple (0,a), (1,b), (2,c) we would have *three* pomsets, one for each of the possible order relationships between (0,a) and (2,c): incomparable, $(0,a)<(2,c)$, and $(2,c)<(0,a)$. We avoided this variety by forcing $(0,a)<(1,b)<(2,c)$, which by transitivity of $<$ forces $(0,a)<(2,c)$.

An alternative and acceptable approach would have been to consider the set of all three pomsets representing all possible orderings of a pair to be an acceptable encoding of that pair. Then we would have pomsets coming in threes in M and N as well as in the projection of their intersection, and in 13's for the net behaviors (1 completely unordered, 6 with one element incomparable to the other two, 6 linearly ordered).

It is fair to ask what influence the choice of Σ' had on this example. What if it had been taken to be {0,1,2,3}×A instead of {0,1,2}×A? Would the fourth channel have confused matters? The answer is that the net behaviors would contain, in addition to the three events (0,a)<(1,b)<(2,c), a cloud of events (3,d) related arbitrarily by < to these three and to each other. However the final projection would project out not only (1,b) but the whole of this cloud. Thus although {0,1,2,3}×A is a less elegant choice of Σ' than {0,1,2}×A, in the end it does not affect the outcome. The physical interpretation of all this is that the fourth channel is a loose wire whose behavior is unknown but irrelevant.

Note that nowhere in our notions of translation and projection do we make any assumptions about either the structure of the network or the type of constituent. This method of describing the behavior of a network of processes works equally well for any processes connected in any fashion.

3. Real-Time Theory - Quantitative Scheduling

3.1. Semirings

So far our notion of temporal relationship has been qualitative, namely whether one event precedes another. We would now like to extend the theory to deal with a richer notion of temporal relationship. One obvious notion is that of time as a number: by how many femtoseconds or teracenturies did one event precede another. Other notions of time, or even only marginally timelike relationships between events, may also suggest themselves.

Our thesis is that the appropriate algebraic structure for supplying the elements of a temporal relationship is the semiring. Semirings cater for parallel and serial composition of relationships in a suitably general way, providing one binary operation for each of these two concepts.

A semiring is an algebra (A,+,.,0) such that (A,+,0) is a monoid (+ is associative and has 0 as left and right identity) and . is associative and distributes over +, and has 0 as left and right annihilator ($a.0 = 0.a = 0$). The + operation caters for parallel composition of relationships and the . operation for their serial composition.

Up to now we have built into our theory the assumption of a particular semiring that we shall call the Boolean semiring. It consists of two values 0 and 1, with + interpreted as disjunction and . as conjunction. The idea is that every pair of events is related by either 0, meaning no temporal order, or 1, meaning that the first precedes the second. The operation + deals with variety of behavior: given several sources of information about whether one event precedes another, if any is a 1 then the upshot is a 1, otherwise it is 0. The operation . deals with course of events: if a precedes b *and* b precedes c then a precedes c. This is transitivity, a conjunctive concept.

A semiring that we shall call the *taxidriver's semiring* consists of the nonnegative reals with + interpreted as max, . as addition, and 0 as the number 0. The numbers can be thought of as the cost of getting from one event to another. When there are competing costs, the highest is always chosen. The cost of getting from a via b to c is the sum of the costs of getting from a to b and from b to c. The discrete version of this semiring substitutes the natural numbers for the nonnegative reals.

The *taxi passenger's semiring* is similar but includes infinity in the algebra, interprets . as min (the passenger prefers the cheapest route), and 0 as infinity (the least identity for min). To satisfy the semiring identity $a.0 = 0$ we need to take the product of numeric 0 with semiring 0 (here infinity) to be infinity. This semiring too has a discrete version, consisting of the natural numbers and infinity.

The taxidriver's semiring is useful in dealing with times between events that may not be reduced, e.g. for preventing events from interfering with each, meeting specifications for integrated circuits, etc. . Dually the taxi passenger's semiring is good for times that may not be exceeded, e.g. for preventing timeouts, or establishing upper bounds on the running time of processes.

3.3. General Theory

We may now generalize our theory of processes from the Boolean semiring to arbitrary semirings. We begin with the idea that a binary relation from A to B is an A×B Boolean matrix. The interior and exterior operations of matrix multiplication are respectively conjunction and disjunction; that is, the dot product of two vectors is formed as the disjunction of pairwise conjunctions, and the matrix product MN of matrices M and N is the matrix of dot products whose ik-th entry is the dot product of the i-th row of M with the k-th column of N.

A binary relation M from A to A is a partial order when it is irreflexive (leading diagonal of M is all zeroes) and transitive ($M^2 \leq M$).

Now these interior and exterior operations associated with binary relations are respectively the . and + operations of the Boolean semiring. If we substitute for that semiring any other semiring, our definitions of irreflexive and transitive need not be changed since they are expressed in terms of semiring operations independently of any particular semiring such as the Boolean semiring.

Thus we may generalize the structure $[V,\Sigma,<,\mu]$ to $[V,\Sigma,S,M,\mu]$ where S is a semiring (no longer necessarily the Boolean semiring {0,1}) and M is an irreflexive transitive matrix over S. Such a structure is no longer a pomset; one might call it a measured multiset, where M provides the measurements between elements of the multiset. A process then becomes a set of measured multisets.

The notion of substitution does not generalize smoothly. Suppose we have events $e<f<g$ and we map f to $f1<f2$ and then extend that map to take $e<f<g$ to $e<f1<f2<g$. Now if $<$ is replaced by some measure of the delay between events, we have a problem relating $e<f<g$ and $e<f1<f2<g$. The problem is that whatever delay there is between f1 and f2 does not appear in $e<f<g$, where the event f itself is treated as having no delay of its own. Thus if there were at least a 2-microsecond delay between e and f and at least a 3-microsecond delay between f and g, then there would be a 5-microsecond delay between e and g. But this assumes that f itself involves no delay, which may contradict the expansion of f to $f1<f2$, in which there may be a nonzero delay.

This problem does not arise however for the special case of "length-preserving" homomorphisms, ones that map atoms only to sets, that is, pomsets with the empty order. This special case is all that is used in defining the notion of projection, which therefore remains unchanged when more general semirings are used. Thus the spatial theory does extend gracefully to general semirings.

However we do not see how to integrate this semiring approach with general substitutions. Some adjustment is needed to our temporal model to cater for this. We would be interested in hearing reasonable solutions.

3.4. Applications

A typical requirement in designing hardware is to achieve minimum delay times between certain events. For this the taxidriver's semiring is appropriate. Whenever there are two separate delay requirements for the same pair of events, the larger is taken, corresponding to semiring + being numeric max. Whenever there must be a delay of at least m between events e1 and e2, and a delay of at least n between e2 and e3, there must be a delay of at least $m+n$ between e1 and e3, corresponding to semiring being numeric addition.

4. Appendix

Since strings (finite tomsets) may be defined very simply as a function from $\{0,1,2,...,n-1\}$, it is natural to ask why pomsets should not have an equally simple definition. The basic obstacle, as we shall see, is that partial orders have nontrivial automorphisms.

In the case of a pomset that is a string of length n, V has n elements and the order $<$ is total. In this case the set $n = \{0,1,...,n-1\}$ with its standard order may serve as a canonical representative of the isomorphism class of (V,<). That is, the function μ:n$\rightarrow\Sigma$ is for our purposes equivalent to the tomset [n,Σ,<,μ]. This establishes the connection between our isomorphism-based definition of tomsets and the simpler definition as a function.

More generally, any "womset" (well-ordered multiset) may be defined as a function from the appropriate ordinal to Σ. For the usual notion of an infinite string $s_0s_1s_2$... the appropriate ordinal is ω. An ordinal serves as a canonical representative of an isomorphism class of well ordered sets.

A well-ordered set (V,<) has no non-trivial automorphisms (isomorphisms from the set to itself). Another way to say this is that each element of a well-ordered set (V,<) uniquely determines an element of the corresponding ordinal. Hence an ordinal may be used as a representative of an isomorphism class of a well-ordered set without contributing any additional information not already present in the class.

In general however, ordered sets, whether ordered totally or partially, may have nontrivial automorphisms. For example the function x+5 is an automorphism of the structure (Z,<) of integers with their standard order. In general therefore the function μ:Z$\rightarrow\Sigma$ and its composition with x+5 will be distinct functions mapping the integers to Σ, yet they will both be representatives of the isomorphism class [Z,Σ,<,μ] with no way of telling which is the canonical representative. Hence such functions overspecify the classes they represent.

Therefore, rather than attempt to base the theory of pomsets on canonical representatives of isomorphism classes we just base it on the classes themselves.

5. Bibliography

[BA81] Brock, J.D. and W.B. Ackerman, Scenarios: A Model of Non-Determinate Computation. In LNCS 107: Formalization of Programming Concepts, J. Diaz and I. Ramos, Eds., Springer-Verlag, New York, 1981, 252-259.

[deB72] de Bakker, J.W., and W.P. de Roever, A calculus for recursive program schemes, in **Automata, Languages and Programming**, (ed. Nivat), 167-196, North Holland, 1972.

[Gis84] Gischer, J., **Partial Orders and the Axiomatic Theory of Shuffle**, Ph.D. Thesis, Computer Science Dept., Stanford University, Dec. 1984.

[Kah74] Kahn, G., The Semantics of a Simple Language for Parallel Programming, IFIP 74, North-Holland, Amsterdam, 1974.

[KaM77] Kahn, G. and D.B. MacQueen, Coroutines and Networks of Parallel Processes, IFIP 77, 993-

998, North-Holland, Amsterdam, 1977.

[Pr82] Pratt, V.R., On the Composition of Processes, Proceedings of the Ninth Annual ACM Symposium on Principles of Programming Languages, Jan. 1982.

[W84] Winskel, G., Categories of Models for Concurrency, this volume.

Lectures on a Calculus for Communicating Systems

Robin Milner

Edinburgh University
Department of Computer Science
King's Buildings
Mayfield Road
Edinburgh, U.K.

1. THE CALCULUS CCS AND ITS EVALUATION RULES

1.1 Introduction

Sequential computation, which until quite recently was the only mode of computation available in well-known programming languages, has a well-established model theory. This fact owes much to the lambda-calculus, which existed long before any notion of implementing a programming language. Yet the primary purpose of the lambda calculus was to study evaluation or execution; it was (and is) a paradigm for evaluation, in the same way that the predicate calculus is a paradigm for deduction. More recently, and largely due to Dana Scott, the model theory of the lambda calculus has grown and has been harmonised with its evaluation theory.

CCS is an attempt to provide an analogous paradigm for concurrent computation, conducted by communication among independent agents. It arose after several unsuccessful attempts by the author to find a satisfactory generalisation of the lambda calculus, to admit concurrent computation; it also came to be based upon evaluation rules, after unsuccessful attempts to find mathematical spaces (based upon Scott's work, for example) which would self-evidently provide the correct model theory of concurrency.

The relationship between a calculus for communication and the lambda calculus is far from clear. There is a temptation to claim that, since sequential computation is 'just a special case' of concurrent computation, so the lambda calculus should be a sub-calculus of whatever calculus we adopt for concurrent computation. On the other hand the notion of higher-order function, which fits so well with the lambda calculus, seems to find no *obvious* generalisation in the setting of concurrent communicating systems. For the present, it seems best to treat concurrency on its own terms, without trying at the same time to generalise any known treatment of sequential computation.

The plan of these lectures is to begin with rules of evaluation, noting that evaluation and communication become almost the same thing, and then to proceed to an abstract notion of behaviour which is based firmly upon evaluation. We shall look at some mathematical properties of this notion of behaviour, and we shall also explore the expressive power of the calculus.

We begin in this lecture with an example, presented in terms of some derived combinators, and we then give the complete (basic) calculus with its evaluation rules.

1.2 An example

To illustrate how communication works in CCS, we take a little example from Milner (1980), Section 8.4. It illustrates how a pushdown store can be built from a chain of identical cells, each capable of holding zero, one or two values. The end cell, at the 'bottom' of the pushdown store, can either die (to shrink the store), or split into two cells (to expand the store). Also, a cell can become the end cell if its lower neighbour dies.

A single cell, holding the value y, may be drawn thus:

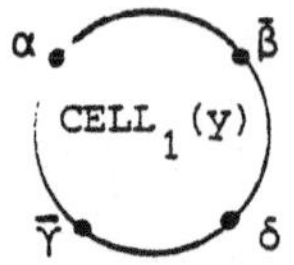

and a pushdown store holding values $x_1,\dots,x_n$ (from top down), one per cell, may be drawn thus:

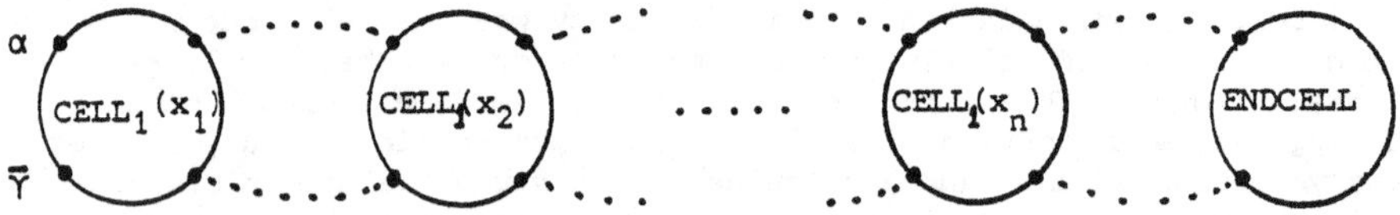

Note that values *enter* an agent at ports with unbarred names (α,δ) and *leave* an agent at ports with barred names ($\bar\beta,\bar\gamma$); when such ports are linked (always an unbarred to a barred name) then it is understood that the emission of a value from one agent and its entry to the other constitute a single indivisible action - a communication.

Now to describe the behaviour of a single cell, we need only define what transitions may occur among its four possible states: $CELL_0$ holding no value, $CELL_1(y)$ holding one value y, $CELL_2(x,y)$ holding two values x and y, and ENDCELL. These transitions may be given by a set of equations, in which each right-hand side is a sum of alternatives, and each alternative is a single potential action prefixed to the 'state' which will follow it. A potential action is either an unbarred port-name, signifying a potential input (and qualifying a variable to be bound to the input value), or a barred port name, signifying a potential output (and qualifying a particular output value).

$$CELL_1(y) = \alpha x.CELL_2(x,y) + \bar\gamma y.CELL_0$$
$$CELL_2(x,y) = \bar\beta y.CELL_1(x)$$
$$CELL_0 = \delta x.(\mathit{if}\ x = \$\ \mathit{then}\ ENDCELL\ \mathit{else}\ CELL_1(x))$$
$$ENDCELL = \alpha x.(CELL_1(x) \frown ENDCELL) + \bar\gamma\ \$.NIL$$

The last equation needs further explanation. In its second alternative, NIL represents the dead agent; ENDCELL has surrendered its rôle as endmarker to its upper neighbour. In its first alternative, the derived combinator $\frown$ links the two cells into which ENDCELL has subdivided upon receiving a pushed-down value x ; and this is the very combinator which we use to express the complete pushdown store, holding n values, as in our diagram:

$$CELL_1(x_1) \frown CELL_1(x_2) \frown \dots \frown CELL_1(x_n) \frown ENDCELL$$

If the reader refers to Milner (1980) he or she can find the detailed proof that the system works as intended; there should even be enough clues above to get an idea of how it functions.

Having given a flavour of the calculus we are now ready to set it out precisely, in its basic form. The notations used above will be derived from the basic calculus in Lecture 5.

1.3 The Basic Calculus

The notations of the foregoing example are rich enough for programming, at least for systems which are not too large, but still too rich for a formal basis. For the latter purpose we prefer a more basic form, in which value variables and value expressions have all but vanished. In Lecture 5 we shall see that the richer notations of our example can all, without exception, be derived from those of the basic form; indeed the expressive power is greater than the example may suggest.

We presuppose a set Δ of *names*, $\alpha,\beta,\gamma,\ldots$ range over Δ. Let $\bar{\Delta}=\{\bar{\alpha}|\alpha\in\Delta\}$ be disjoint from Δ and in bijection with it, under the map $\alpha\mapsto\bar{\alpha}$; we call $\bar{\Delta}$ the *conames*. We define a *label* to be a member of $\Lambda=\Delta\cup\bar{\Delta}$, and we shall use λ to range over Λ. Further, we extend the map $(\bar{\ })$ to Λ by defining $\bar{\bar{\alpha}}=\alpha$; we shall refer to $\lambda,\bar{\lambda}$ as *complements*.

The labels apparently serve a dual purpose, though the two purposes are strongly related. First, they are the names - or conames - of actions which an agent may perform; second, in static or spatial diagrams of systems they are used to label the ports (peripheral regions) at which such actions may occur.

With these purposes particularly in mind, we define a *sort* to be any subset L of Λ; we shall say that an agent P has sort L, and write P::L, when any visible action which P may perform in the future must lie in L. Indeed, in a full exposition (see Milner (1980)) we can ascribe to each agent P a distinguished sort L(P) for which it is clear that P::L(P). We also define a *relabelling* to be any function $S:\Lambda\to\Lambda$ which respects complement; that is, $\overline{S(\lambda)}=S(\bar{\lambda})$. Intuitively, the purpose of a relabelling is to change the labels of an agents actions.

We need, for our semantic treatment, a distinguished action τ - the invisible action - which is not a member of Λ. We shall call the set $\Lambda\cup\{\tau\}$ the *actions*, and shall let μ,ν range over the actions. τ has no complement, and we extend any relabelling S by declaring $S(\tau)=\tau$.

Finally, some syntactic matters. We presuppose a set $\mathcal{V}$ of agent *variables*, we use X,Y,.. to range over $\mathcal{V}$. We define below the class of *agent expressions* $\mathcal{E}$, using E,F,... to range over $\mathcal{E}$. Then we take $\mathcal{P}$, the *agents*, to be the agent expressions with no free variables; we use P,Q,... to range over $\mathcal{P}$. We often use I to stand for any countable set, and then use $\langle E_i\rangle_{i\in I}$ for an I-indexed family of agent expressions. In this case, when I is understood, we may also denote the family by $\tilde{E}$.

With this preamble, we can now define $\mathcal{E}$ as the smallest class including $\mathcal{V}$, the variables, and containing the following expressions (where E,E_i are already in $\mathcal{E}$):

(1) $\mu.E$, $\mu\in\Lambda\cup\{\tau\}$, an *action* ;

(2) $\Sigma\langle E_i\rangle_{i\in I}$, a *summation* ;

(3) $E_0|E_1$, a *composition* ;

(4) $E\backslash A$, $A \subseteq \Delta$, a *restriction* ;

(5) $E[S]$, $S:\Lambda \to \Lambda$, a *relabelling* ;

(6) $fix_j \langle X_i \rangle_{i\in I} \langle E_i \rangle_{i\in I}$, $j \in I$, a *recursion* .

Some informal remarks about the meaning of each construction will help in understanding the formal rules which follow.

(1) The behaviour of $\mu.E$ is considered to be the action μ followed by the behaviour of E.

(2) The behaviour of $\Sigma\tilde{E}$ will be the behaviour of any one of the $E_i, i \in I$. We shall write NIL or $E_0 + E_1$ for $\Sigma\tilde{E}$, in the two cases $I = \emptyset$ or $I = 2$.

(3) The composite $E_0|E_1$ allows concurrent behaviour of E_0 and E_1, with communication through complementary actions.

(4) The behaviour of $E\backslash A$ is that of E, but only as far as each action, or its complement, is not in A.

(5) The behaviour of E[S] is that of E, but with the actions relabelled by S.

(6) We write the family $\langle fix_j \tilde{X}\tilde{E} \rangle_{j\in I}$ as fix $\tilde{X}\tilde{E}$, omitting the suffix j. Intuitively the I-indexed family of behaviours of fix $\tilde{X}\tilde{E}$ is a solution of the I-indexed family of equations $\tilde{X} = \tilde{E}$ in $\tilde{X}$.

Our syntax allows expressions with free variables ($fix_j\tilde{X}\tilde{E}$ binds all the variables $\tilde{X}$ in $\tilde{E}$), but it suffices to give formal semantics just to the agents $\mathcal{P}$, i.e. those expressions without free variables. To this end, we introduce a family of *action relations*, indexed by $\Lambda \cup \{\tau\}$, over $\mathcal{P}$;

$$P \xrightarrow{\mu} P'$$

means that P may do μ, and become P' in doing so. In giving *action rules*, we adopt the convention that the action below the horizontal line may be inferred from the action(s) above the line.

The action relations $\xrightarrow{\mu}$, then, are defined to be the smallest which satisfy the following rules:

(1) $\mu.E \xrightarrow{\mu} E$

(2) $$\frac{E_j \xrightarrow{\mu} E'}{\Sigma\tilde{E} \xrightarrow{\mu} E'} \quad (j \in I)$$

(3) $$\frac{E_0 \xrightarrow{\mu} E_0'}{E_0|E_1 \xrightarrow{\mu} E_0'|E_1} \qquad \frac{E_1 \xrightarrow{\mu} E_1'}{E_0|E_1 \xrightarrow{\mu} E_0|E_1'}$$

$$\frac{E_0 \xrightarrow{\lambda} E_0' \qquad E_1 \xrightarrow{\bar{\lambda}} E_1'}{E_0|E_1 \xrightarrow{\tau} E_0'|E_1'}$$

(4) $$\frac{E \xrightarrow{\mu} E'}{E\backslash A \xrightarrow{\mu} E'\backslash A} \quad (\mu, \bar{\mu} \notin A)$$

(5) $$\frac{E \xrightarrow{\mu} E'}{E[S] \xrightarrow{S(\mu)} E'[S]}$$

$$\text{(6)}\quad \frac{E_j\{\widetilde{\text{fix}\,X E}/\widetilde{X}\} \xrightarrow{\mu} E'}{\text{fix}_j\widetilde{X}\widetilde{E} \xrightarrow{\mu} E'} \quad (j \in I)$$

Note: in the final rule, for recursion, we use the convention that $E\{\widetilde{F}/\widetilde{X}\}$ denotes the result of substituting expressions $\widetilde{F}$ for variables $\widetilde{X}$ simultaneously in E, with change of bound variables as necessary to avoid clashes.

1.4 Derivation Trees

From the rules of action, we can infer the entire behaviour of any agent and present it as a tree. For example consider

$$P \equiv \alpha.(\beta.NIL + \tau.\gamma.NIL) + \alpha.\gamma.NIL$$

we can infer $P \xrightarrow{\alpha} P_1$ and $P \xrightarrow{\alpha} P_2$, where $P_1 \equiv \beta.NIL + \tau.\gamma.NIL$ and $P_2 \equiv \gamma.NIL$. Further, we can infer $P_1 \xrightarrow{\beta} NIL$ and $P_1 \xrightarrow{\tau} P_2$, and $P_2 \xrightarrow{\gamma} NIL$. Arranging all these actions in a tree, we get

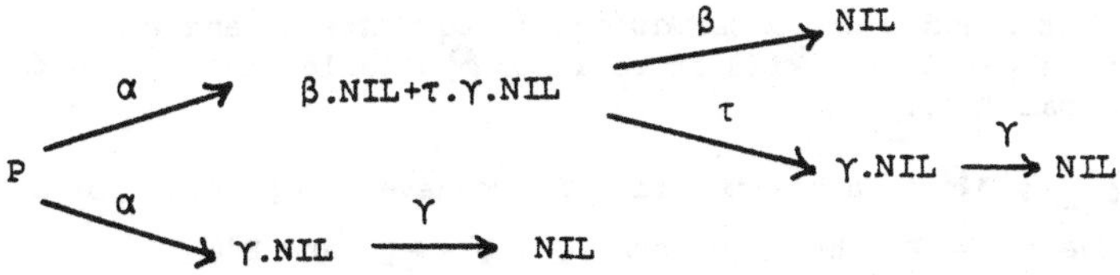

and if we omit the node information, we get the *action tree* of P:

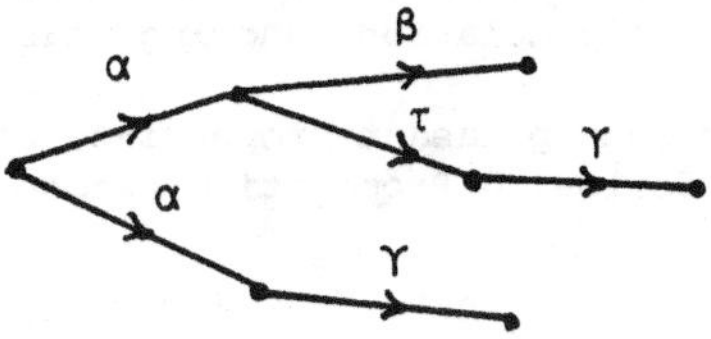

The work of the next lecture is to establish an equivalence relation over agents, in which two agents are equivalent when their action trees are sufficiently 'similar'. We shall wish to ignore the silent actions, represented by arcs labelled τ, to a certain extent in defining this similarity. These arcs cannot be ignored entirely, since a τ-action represents an ability to act autonomously and thereby to preempt alternatives. For example the two trees

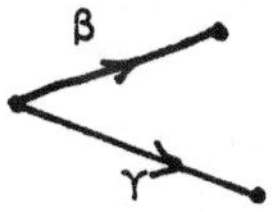

and

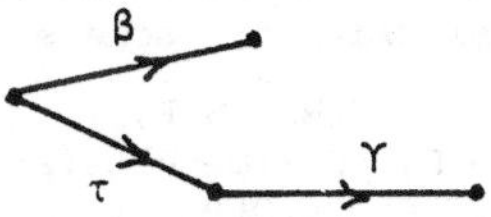

which represent the agents $\beta.NIL + \gamma.NIL$ and $\beta.NIL + \tau.\gamma.NIL$ will *not* be similar; the first agent offers β and γ as alternative actions, while the second can autonomously discard the β alternative by performing its τ action. However, it will turn out that the agent P above will be equivalent to $Q \equiv \alpha.(\beta.NIL + \tau.\gamma.NIL)$ whose tree is

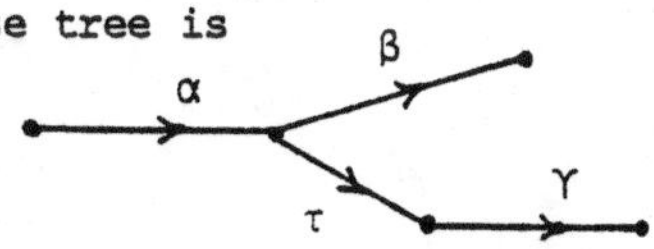

This example shows that our similarity relation will not be a trivial or immediately obvious one.

2. BISIMULATION AND OBSERVATIONAL EQUIVALENCE OF AGENTS

2.1 Bisimulation

What is the extent to which τ-actions may be ignored? We argue that equivalence of agents should be expressed in terms of their visible actions (not τ-actions) only, and to this end we define a family $\overset{s}{\Longrightarrow}$ of relations, where s ranges over Λ^*. In fact, if $s = \lambda_1 \ldots \lambda_n$ $(n \geq 0)$ we define

$$P \overset{s}{\Longrightarrow} P' \text{ iff } P(\overset{\tau}{\longrightarrow})^* \overset{\lambda 1}{\longrightarrow} (\overset{\tau}{\longrightarrow})^* \ldots \overset{\lambda n}{\longrightarrow} (\overset{\tau}{\longrightarrow})^* P'$$

thus allowing an arbitrary number of τ actions to interleave the visible actions. Then we express our equivalence in terms of $\overset{s}{\Longrightarrow}$, not in terms of $\overset{\mu}{\longrightarrow}$. Note that when $s = \varepsilon$ (the empty sequence) then $P \overset{\varepsilon}{\Longrightarrow} P'$ iff $P(\overset{\tau}{\longrightarrow})^* P'$; we shall write just $P \Longrightarrow P'$ in this case.

We shall say that P and Q are *observationally equivalent*, and write $P \approx Q$, if there exists a particular kind of relation $\mathcal{R}$, called a *bisimulation*, containing the pair P,Q.

<u>Definition</u> $\mathcal{R} \subseteq \mathcal{P} \times \mathcal{P}$ is a bisimulation if whenever $P\mathcal{R}Q$ then, for all $s \in \Lambda^*$,

(i) Whenever $P \overset{s}{\Longrightarrow} P'$ then, for some Q', $Q \overset{s}{\Longrightarrow} Q'$ and $P'\mathcal{R}Q'$.

(ii) Whenever $Q \overset{s}{\Longrightarrow} Q'$ then, for some P', $P \overset{s}{\Longrightarrow} P'$ and $P'\mathcal{R}Q'$.

As a simple example, take $P \equiv \lambda.(\beta.NIL + \tau.\gamma.NIL) + \alpha.\gamma.NIL$ and $Q \equiv \alpha.(\beta.NIL + \tau.\gamma.NIL)$, as illustrated in Lecture 1. It can be checked that $\mathcal{R} = Id \cup \langle P,Q \rangle$ is an appropriate bisimulation, showing that $P \approx Q$.

The theory of bisimulations has some pleasant properties, the most elementary of which are summarised in the following Proposition, whose proof we omit.

<u>Proposition 2.1</u>

(1) $Id_{\mathcal{P}}$ is a bisimulation
(2) If $\mathcal{R}$ and $\mathcal{S}$ are bisimulations, so are $\mathcal{R}^{-1}$ (the converse relation) and $\mathcal{R} \circ \mathcal{S}$ (the composition of relations)
(3) $\approx = \bigcup \{\mathcal{R} : \mathcal{R}$ is a bisimulation$\}$
(4) $\approx$ is an equivalence relation. ■

Thus, from (3), observational equivalence is the largest bisimulation. Our example above shows that it is often easy to establish simple results by exhibiting a bisimulation; some such results are as follows:

$$P + P \approx P, \quad P + NIL \approx P,$$
$$P + Q \approx Q + P, \quad P + (Q + R) \approx (P + Q) + R,$$
$$P|NIL \approx P, \quad P|Q \approx Q|P,$$
$$P|(Q|R) \approx (P|Q)|R, \quad \tau.P \approx P$$

and there are many others. We also have

$$P \approx Q \quad \text{implies} \quad P|R \approx Q|R,$$
$$P \approx Q \quad \text{implies} \quad \mu.P \approx \mu.Q$$

and in fact

Proposition 2.2 Observational equivalence is preserved by all combinators of CCS except for summation and recursion. ∎

The exception of summation can be justified as follows. We have $\tau.P \approx P$ (as stated above), but in general it is *false* that $\tau.P+Q \approx P+Q$; we gave an example of this inequivalence at the end of Lecture 1. In the next section we show how observational equivalence may be slightly strengthened so that it is preserved by all combinators.

Before going further, we look at bisimulation in a little more detail. First, it is clear that $\mathcal{R}$ is a bisimulation if $\mathcal{R} \subseteq \mathcal{F}(\mathcal{R})$, where $\mathcal{F}(\mathcal{R})$ is the relation given by the following:

Definition $(P,Q) \in \mathcal{F}(\mathcal{R})$ iff, for all $s \in \Lambda^*$,

(i) Whenever $P \overset{s}{\Longrightarrow} P'$ then, for some Q', $Q \overset{s}{\Longrightarrow} Q'$ and $P' \mathcal{R} Q'$;

(ii) Whenever $Q \overset{s}{\Longrightarrow} Q'$ then, for some P', $P \overset{s}{\Longrightarrow} P'$ and $P' \mathcal{R} Q'$;

Thus a bisimulation is exactly a *pre-fixed-point* of $\mathcal{F}$, and the existence of a largest bisimulation is just an instance of a standard result concerning largest pre-fixed-points, since $\mathcal{F}$ is monotone for relations under inclusion. In fact it is also standard that the largest pre-fixed-point of a monotone function is also the largest fixed-point, hence:

Proposition 2.3 $\approx\; = \mathcal{F}(\approx)$ ∎

We later need a slight refinement of the bisimulation idea:

Definition $\mathcal{R}$ is a *bisimulation up to* $\approx$ iff $\approx\mathcal{R}\approx$ is a bisimulation.

Clearly, to show $P \approx Q$, it is sufficient to show that P and Q are in some bisimulation up to $\approx$. It is often easier to exhibit a bisimulation up to $\approx$ than to exhibit a bisimulation, and moreover it can be established by checking a simple property:

Proposition 2.4 $\mathcal{R}$ is a bisimulation up to $\approx$ iff $\mathcal{R} \subseteq \mathcal{F}(\approx\mathcal{R}\approx)$ ∎

The original notion of observational equivalence, given in Milner (1980), was defined without use of bisimulation. Instead, it was defined as the limit (intersection) of a ω-indexed chain of decreasing equivalence relations; this was adopted since it offered a proof technique (mathematical induction) for results about observational equivalence. Subsequently Park (1981) pointed out the present notion and the proof method (exhibiting a bisimulation) associated with it. This is a clear improvement. In fact (see Lecture 4) it agrees with the previous notion exactly, when the chain of decreasing relations is extended to a sufficiently high ordinal; this indicates that transfinite induction is an alternative method for obtaining properties of observational equivalence.

2.2 Observational Congruence

We now turn to the question of refining observational equivalence to a congruence relation. For this purpose, we must consider equivalences not only over agents $\mathcal{P}$, but over expressions $\mathcal{E}$. First, we extend $\approx$ to $\mathcal{E}$:

Definition Let $\tilde{X}$ be the free variables occurring in E or in F. Then $E \approx F$ iff, for all agents P, $E\{P/X\} \approx F\{\tilde{P}/\tilde{X}\}$

Next, we give a precise definition of congruence over $\mathcal{E}$:

<u>Definition</u> An equivalence relation $\equiv$ over $\mathcal{E}$ is a *congruence* if

(1) $E \equiv F$ implies $\mu.E \equiv \mu F$, $E\backslash A \equiv F\backslash A$ and $E[S] \equiv F[S]$

(2) $E_i \equiv F_i$ $(i=0,1)$ implies $E_0|E_1 \equiv F_0|F_1$

(3) $\tilde{E} \equiv \tilde{F}$ implies $\Sigma\tilde{E} \equiv \Sigma\tilde{F}$ and $fix_j\widetilde{XE} \equiv fix_j\widetilde{XF}$.

We propose to refine $\approx$ as little as possible in forming a congruence; that is, we look for $\approx^c$, the largest congruence over $\mathcal{E}$ such that $\approx^c \subseteq \approx$. We shall obtain three distinct characterisations of this congruence.

<u>Definition</u> The relation $\approx^+$ over $\mathcal{E}$ is defined as follows:

$E \approx^+ F$ iff, for all $R \in \mathcal{P}$, $E + R \approx F + R$

<u>Proposition 2.5</u> Let $\tilde{X}$ be the free variables occurring in E or F. Then $E \approx^+ F$ iff, for all agents $\tilde{P}$, $E\{\tilde{P}/\tilde{X}\} \approx^+ F\{\tilde{P}/\tilde{X}\}$ ∎

This proposition, which is easily proved from the definitions, shows that $\approx^+$ over expressions is reducible, by substitution of agents for free variables, to the same relation over agents.

It will turn out that $\approx^+$ is the congruence that we require, and its definition provides one characterisation - intuitively motivated by the fact that summation is the only combinator (except recursion) which fails to preserve observational equivalence.

To establish that $\approx^+$ is what we require, the first step is to find a second characterisation, showing exactly in what respect it differs from observational equivalence in terms of bisimulation.

<u>Proposition 2.6</u> The following are equivalent for all agents P,Q:

(1) $P \approx^+ Q$

(2) For all $\mu \in \Lambda \cup \{\tau\}$

(i) If $P \xrightarrow{\mu} P'$ then, for some Q', $Q \xrightarrow{\mu}\Rightarrow Q'$ and $P' \approx Q'$

(ii) If $Q \xrightarrow{\mu} Q'$ then, for some P', $P \xrightarrow{\mu}\Rightarrow P'$ and $P' \approx Q'$

<u>Proof</u> (in outline)

(2) $\Rightarrow$ (1): Assume (2), and take any $R \in \mathcal{P}$. We require $P + R \approx Q + R$. To this end, we show that $\{(P+R, Q+R)\} \cup \approx$ is a bisimulation. For this, it is enough to show that whenever $P + R \overset{s}{\Rightarrow} P'$, and this composite action involves at least one action $\xrightarrow{\mu}$, then for some Q' we have $Q + R \overset{s}{\Rightarrow} Q'$ and $P' \approx Q'$. The details are routine using (2).

(1) $\Rightarrow$ (2): Suppose that (2) is false, so that for example $P \xrightarrow{\mu} P'$ but whenever $Q \xrightarrow{\mu}\Rightarrow Q'$ then $P' \not\approx Q'$. It is then easy, if we take R to be λ.NIL where λ is some action for which P and Q are not in the domain of $\overset{\lambda}{\Rightarrow}$, to show that $P + R \not\approx Q + R$. ∎

Our next step is to show that $\approx^+$ is indeed a congruence, and for this purpose the alternative characterisation (2) of Prop 2.6 is useful.

<u>Proposition 2.7</u> $\approx^+$ is a congruence.

Proof

In view of Proposition 2.5, it is enough to establish the conditions of the definition of congruence for agents only. For this purpose, we work directly with the alternative characterisation given by Prop 2.6(2), and the details are routine except in the case of proving

$$\tilde{E} \approx^{+} \tilde{F} \text{ implies } \text{fix}_j\tilde{X}\tilde{E} \approx^{+} \text{fix}_j\tilde{X}\tilde{F}$$

For simplicity of exposition we shall prove this in the case that $\tilde{X}$ is a singleton; that is, we prove

$$E \approx^{+} F \text{ implies } \text{fixXE} \approx^{+} \text{fixXF}$$

and (as noted above) we need only consider the case in which at most X is free in E or in F. Now consider the relation

$$\mathcal{R} = \{(G\{\text{fixXE}/X\}, G\{\text{fixXF}/X\}) \mid \text{at most X is free in G}\}$$

We shall show not just that $\mathcal{R}$ is a bisimulation up to $\approx$ (which will establish fixXE $\approx$ fixXF by taking G to be X) but that for each G

$$\text{If } G\{\text{fixXE}/X\} \xrightarrow{\mu} P' \text{ then, for some } Q', \quad G\{\text{fixXF}/X\} \xrightarrow{\mu} Q' \text{ and } P'\mathcal{R}{\approx}Q'. \qquad (*)$$

For this, and the symmetric property with E and F interchanged, both establishes that $\mathcal{R}_+$ is a bisimulation up to $\approx$ and ensures (by taking G to be X) that fixXE $\approx^{+}$ fixXF, from Prop 2.6.

To prove (*), we use induction on the depth of the inference of $G\{\text{fixXE}/X\} \xrightarrow{\mu} P'$. Assume then that $G\{\text{fixXE}/X\} \xrightarrow{\mu} P'$ and consider the cases for G. Most cases are routine applications of the induction hypothesis; we concentrate on the cases in which G is a variable (which must be X) and in which G is a recursion.

(i) G is X. Then fixXE $\xrightarrow{\mu}$ P', so by a shorter inference $E\{\text{fixXE}/X\} \xrightarrow{\mu} P'$; so by induction

$$E\{\text{fixXF}/X\} \xrightarrow{\mu}\Rightarrow Q' \text{ and } P'\mathcal{R}{\approx}Q'.$$

But $E \approx^{+} F$, so by Props.2.5,2.6 we have

$$F\{\text{fixXF}/X\} \xrightarrow{\mu}\Rightarrow Q'' \text{ with } Q' \approx Q''$$

and hence, by the recursion rule

$$\text{fixXF} \xrightarrow{\mu}\Rightarrow Q'' \text{ with } P'\mathcal{R}{\approx}Q''$$

and this is what we require, since G is X so G{fixXF/X} is fixXF.

(ii) G is $\text{fix}_j\tilde{Y}\tilde{H}$, with at most X and $\tilde{Y}$ free in $\tilde{H}$. If $X \in \tilde{Y}$ then the result is easy, since X is then not free in G, so G{fixXF/X} is identical with G{fixXE/X}. So assume $X \notin \tilde{Y}$. In this case, G{fixXE/X} is $\text{fix}_j\tilde{Y}(\tilde{H}\{\text{fixXE}/X\})$, and from our assumption we know that, by a shorter inference,

$$H_j\{\text{fixXE}/X\}\{\text{fix}\tilde{Y}(\tilde{H}\{\text{fixXE}/X\})/\tilde{Y}\} \xrightarrow{\mu} P'$$

Rewriting, by commuting substitutions, this is to say that

$$H_j\{\text{fix}\tilde{Y}\tilde{H}/\tilde{Y}\}\{\text{fixXE}/X\} \xrightarrow{\mu} P'$$

Hence, by our induction hypothesis, we have

$$H_j\{\text{fix}\tilde{Y}\tilde{H}/\tilde{Y}\}\{\text{fixXF}/X\} \xrightarrow{\mu}\Rightarrow Q'$$

with $P'\mathcal{R}{\approx}Q'$. Rewriting again, by commuting substitutions, and then applying the recursion rule, we obtain

$$G\{fixXF/X\} \overset{\mu}{\Rightarrow}\Rightarrow Q'$$

and we are done. ∎

To complete the work, we need the notion of context.

Definition. A *context* $\mathcal{C}[\ ]$ is an expression with zero or more 'holes', to be filled by an expression. We write $\mathcal{C}[E]$ for the result of placing E in each 'hole'. (Note that free variables of E may thus become bound.)

We now give our third characterisation of the desired congruence.

Definition. $E \approx^c F$ iff, for all contexts $\mathcal{C}[\ ]$, $\mathcal{C}[E] \approx \mathcal{C}[F]$.

Proposition 2.8

(1) $\approx^c = \approx^+$

(2) $\approx^c$ is the largest congruence included in $\approx$.

Proof

(1) Since $\approx^+$ is a congruence, it follows from the definitions of congruence that $E \approx^+ F$ implies $\mathcal{C}[E] \approx^+ \mathcal{C}[F]$ for every context $\mathcal{C}[\ ]$. But $\approx^+ \subseteq \approx$, so it follows that $\approx^+ \subseteq \approx^c$. On the other hand $\approx^c \subseteq \approx^+$, by considering the restricted class of contexts of the form $[\ ] + R$ where R is any agent.

(2) Let $\equiv$ be any congruence included in $\approx$. Then, exactly as in the first part of (1) but using $\equiv$ in place of $\approx^+$, we obtain $\equiv \subseteq \approx^c$.

Another view of what we have done is gained by observing that, on general grounds, the largest congruence included in a given equivalence relation is always guaranteed to exist. But it can be that, for an arbitrary equivalence, this congruence is very much smaller than the equivalence itself. What we have shown is that, since $\approx$ is 'almost' a congruence, the required congruence in this case is not much smaller, and can be characterised in various ways which allow us to work with it. The argument is similar to what was done in Chapter 5 of Milner (1980), and also to the work in Section 8 of Milner (1983).

Having obtained a satisfactory congruence relation, we may decide that the meaning of any agent is just its congruence class; we may then choose to write "=" in place of "$\approx^c$", and interpret P = Q as asserting equality of interpretation. The question then arises: what are the true equations in CCS? Space precludes a detailed presentation. However, we can assert that all the equivalences listed after Prop 2.1 are also valid with "$\approx$" replaced by "=", with one exception: it is not the case that $\tau.P = P$. But - as in Milner (1980) - we can state three properties which are not immediately obvious, but which appear to capture all that can be asserted equationally about the unobservable action τ :

(1) $P + \tau.P = \tau.P$

(2) $\mu.(P + \tau.Q) = \mu.(P + \tau.Q) + \mu.Q$

(3) $\mu.\tau.P = \mu.P$

In fact, as we see in the next section, these laws form the basis of a complete equational theory for finite agents, i.e. those which are written without recursion or infinite summation.

3. EQUATIONAL AXIOMS AND THEIR COMPLETENESS FOR FINITE BEHAVIOURS

3.1 Introduction

Having established a number of properties of observation equivalence and congruence, we now look at their equational characterisation.

There are many equation schemata which are satisfied by observation congruence. For the full calculus, however, there can never be a recursive equational axiomatisation which is complete, i.e. a recursive set of equation schemata from which all and only the valid instances of observational congruence follow by equational reasoning. For then the latter class of valid instances would be recursively enumerable, and this is contradicted by the fact that arbitrary Turing machines may be represented by terms of CCS, and hence their behavioural equivalence represented by CCS equations. A clue to this representation is given by our 'pushdown' example in Lecture 1, since a Turing tape can be modelled by two pushdowns.

But there does exist an axiomisation which is complete for all finite behaviours, i.e. those represented without using recursion or infinite summation (the axioms are sound over *all* behaviours). This lecture is devoted to presenting the axioms and proving their completeness.

The axioms are simple, and are no doubt useful in reasoning about behaviours (not only finite ones). The interest in completeness is not immediately practical, particularly as the behaviours which arise in practice are almost never finite; the interest lies more in the insight which is provided by the proof of completeness, which relies (as do most such proofs) upon reducing terms to a particular normal form. The three axioms involving τ, and their use in normalising terms, reveal the essence of the operator probably more clearly than does the bare definition of observational congruences.

The proof given in this lecture is essentially Theorem 4.2 of Hennessy and Milner (1983); the result was first announced in Hennessy and Milner (1980).

3.2 An Axiomatisation for finitary CCS

We shall consider the following set of axioms for CCS without infinite sums or recursion.

The first seven axioms concern only summation and action-prefix. We take the liberty of replacing finitary summation by the empty sum NIL and binary summation.

(A1) $x + (y + z) = (x + y) + z$ (A3) $x + x = x$

(A2) $x + y = y + x$ (A4) $x + \mathrm{NIL} = x$

(A5) $x + \tau.x = \tau.x$

(A6) $\mu.(x + \tau.y) = \mu.(x + \tau.y) + \mu.y$

(A7) $\mu.\tau.y = \mu.y$

The remaining axioms are represented by three axiom schemata, in which we let u and v stand for arbitrary finite sums $\sum_i \mu_i.x_i$ and $\sum_i \nu_j.y_j$ respectively. In view of (A1) and (A2) these sums can be taken to represent iterated binary summation in which the order and association of terms is immaterial.

(A8) $u|v = \sum_i \mu_i.(x_i|v) + \sum_j \nu_j.(u|y_j) + \sum_{\mu_i=\bar{\nu}_j} \tau.(x_i|y_j)$

(A9) $u\backslash A = \sum_{\mu_i,\bar{\mu}_i \notin A} \mu_i.(x_i\backslash A)$

(A10) $u[S] = \sum_i (S\mu_i).(x_i[S])$

These axioms are easily proved to be sound, when equality is interpreted as observational congruence and the variables x,y,z,x_i,y_j are replaced by arbitrary agents of CCS; in each case it is enough to appeal to the characterisation of observational congruence given in Theorem 2.

It is important for our present purpose to note that, by use of (A8)-(A10), any agent of finitary CCS may be proved equal to one involving only NIL, binary summation and action-prefix. For these axioms allow any finitary agent P to be equated to a form $\Sigma\mu_i.P_i$ in which each P_i has fewer occurrences of operation symbols than P; by iterating this process all occurrences of the composition, restriction and relabelling combinators may be eliminated. Therefore, to prove that the axioms are complete for finitary CCS, it is sufficient to prove that (A1)-(A7) are complete for agents containing only NIL, binary summation and action prefix. We give a name to the latter class of agents:

<u>Definition.</u> An agent P is a *sumform* if it takes the form of a finite sum $\sum_i \mu_i.P_i$ where each P_i is also a sumform.

Note that, in particular, NIL is a sumform.

3.3 Completeness of the Axiomatisation

In this section we are concerned only with sumforms, and we shall allow P,Q (possibly subscripted) to stand only for sumforms. We shall write $\vdash P = Q$ to mean that the equation may be proved from (A1)-(A7) by normal equational reasoning. The section is devoted to proving a single theorem.

<u>Theorem 3.1</u> (Completeness) If $P \approx^c Q$ than $\vdash P = Q$

The proof depends upon a few lemmas, which allow us to deduce that two observationally congruent sumforms can always be proved equal to a single, normal, sumform.

We begin with a few technical details. First, we say that P and Q are *sum-congruent*, and write $\vdash P =_s Q$, when $\vdash P = Q$ may be proved using only axioms (A1) and (A2), which is to say that P and Q differ at most in the order and association of summands (in any subterm). Second, we refer to any term P', for which $P \overset{\mu}{\Rightarrow} P'$, as a *μ-derivative* of P. Thus for example if P is $\tau.(\beta.(\tau.P_1 + P_2) + \tau.P_3)$ then it has as β-derivatives the terms $\tau.P_1 + P_2$ and P_1, and as τ-derivatives the terms $\beta.(\tau.P_1 + P_2) + \tau.P_3$ and P_3. Note that a μ-derivative of P is always a proper subterm of P.

Finally, we shall reserve $P \equiv Q$ to mean that P and Q are identical.

It can be seen that the same subterm P' may occur in P more than once as a μ-derivative; the intuition of our notion of normal form is that this does not happen.

Definition. A term $\Sigma\mu_i.P_i$ is a *proper normal form* if

(i) It does not take the form $\tau.P'$;

(ii) Each P_i is a proper normal form;

(ii) For $k \neq j$, no μ_k-derivative of $\mu_j.P_j$ is sumcongruent to P_k.

A *normal form* is either P or $\tau.P$, where P is a proper normal form.

Thus for example $\alpha.\tau.NIL$ is not normal, since $\tau.NIL$ is not a proper normal form. Also $\alpha.(\tau.P_1 + P_2) + \alpha.P_1$ is not a normal form. As a first step towards reducing terms to normal form, we prove the following:

Absorption Lemma. If P' is a μ-derivative of P, and $\vdash P' = Q$, then $\vdash P + \mu.Q = P$.

Proof By induction on the structure of $P \equiv \Sigma\mu_i.P_i$. We examine three ways in which $P \overset{\mu}{\Rightarrow} P'$ is possible, with $\vdash P' = Q$:

Case 1: $\mu = \mu_i$ and $\vdash P_i = Q$.
Using (A1)-(A3), we have

$$\vdash P + \mu.Q = P + \mu_i.P_i = P$$

Case 2: $\mu = \mu_i$ and $P_i \overset{\tau}{\Rightarrow} P'$, $\vdash P' = Q$.
By induction $\vdash P_i + \tau.Q = P_i$. hence

$$\begin{aligned}\vdash P + \mu.Q &= P + \mu.P_i + \mu.Q \quad \text{by (A1)-(A3)}\\ &= P + \mu.(P_i + \tau.Q) + \mu.Q\\ &= P + \mu.(P_i + \tau.Q) \quad \text{by (A6)}\\ &= P + \mu.P_i\\ &= P\end{aligned}$$

Case 3: $\mu_i = \tau$ and $P_i \overset{\mu}{\Rightarrow} P'$, $\vdash P' = Q$.
By induction $\vdash P_i + \mu.Q = P_i$; hence

$$\begin{aligned}\vdash P + \mu.Q &= P + \tau.P_i + \mu.Q \quad \text{by (A1)-(A3)}\\ &= P + \tau.(P_i + \mu.Q) + \mu.Q\\ &= P + \tau.(P_i + \mu.Q) + (P_i + \mu.Q) + \mu.Q \quad \text{by (A5)}\\ &= P + \tau.(P_i + \mu.Q) + (P_i + \mu.Q) \quad \text{by (A1)-(A3)}\\ &= P + \tau.(P_i + \mu.Q) \quad \text{by (A5)}\\ &= P\end{aligned}$$

∎

From this, it is a short step to show that every sumform can be proved equal to a normal form.

Normal Form Lemma. Every P may be proved equal to a normal form.

Proof By induction on the structure of $P \equiv \Sigma\mu_i.P_i$. First, we may assume by the inductive hypothesis that each P_i is a normal form, and further - by (A7) - that it is a proper normal form. It remains to establish condition(iii) for P to be normal. Suppose then, for $k \neq j$, that some μ_k-derivative of $\mu_j.P_j$ is sumcongruent to P_k. Then from the Absorption

Lemma we have

$$\vdash \mu_j.P_j + \mu_k.P_k = \mu_j.P_j$$

Then, by (A1)-(A3), the summand $\mu_k.P_k$ can be eliminated from P. This elimination can be repeated until no duplicate derivatives remain. ◼

There remains the possibility that two normal forms may be observationally congruent, yet not sumcongruent. As a step towards denying this possibility, we prove the following:

Derivative Lemma. The following are equivalent for normal forms P and P' :

(1) $\vdash P =_s P'$

(2) Each μ-derivative of P is sumcongruent to a μ-derivative of P', and conversely.

Proof It is immediate that (1) implies (2), so we consider the converse. Assume (2), and let

$$P \equiv \sum_h \lambda_h.P_h + \sum_i \tau.Q_i \qquad (\lambda_h \in \Lambda)$$

$$P' \equiv \sum_j \lambda_j'.P_j' + \sum_k \tau.Q_k' \qquad (\lambda_j' \in \Lambda)$$

(a) We first show that each Q_i is sumcongruent to some Q_k', and conversely. Take Q_1. Since $P \overset{\varepsilon}{\Longrightarrow} Q_1$, Q_1 is sumcongruent to some τ-derivative of P', say Q_1' or one of its τ-derivatives. In the former case we are done, so assume the latter. Now Q_1', being a τ-derivative of P', is sumcongruent to Q_i or one of its τ-derivatives for some i, with $i \neq 1$ since Q_1 is (up to sumcongruence) a proper subexpression of Q_1'. But this implies that Q_1 is sumcongruent to a τ-derivative of $\tau.Q_i$, a contradiction since P is a normal form.

(b) Next, we show that each P_h is sumcongruent to some P_j', with $\lambda_h = \lambda_j'$, and conversely. Take P_1. Since $P \overset{\lambda_1}{\Longrightarrow} P_1$, P_1 is sum-congruent to some λ_1-derivative of P'. If this were a λ_1-derivative of some Q_k' then by (a) P_1 would also be sumcongruent to a λ_1-derivative of some Q_i, contradicting the normality of P. Hence, for some j such that $\lambda_1 = \lambda_j'$, P_1 is sumcongruent *either* to P_j', in which case we are done, *or* to a τ-derivative D of P_j'. But in the latter case P_j', being a λ_1-derivative of P', must be sumcongruent to a λ_1-derivative of some summand of P; moreover this summand is different from $\lambda_1.P_1$, else D (hence also P_1) would be sumcongruent to a proper subterm of P_1; P_1 must therefore be sumcongruent to a λ_1-derivative of some other summand of P, contradicting the normality of P.

(c) We deduce from (a) and (b) together that each summand of P is sumcongruent to a summand of P', and conversely. Since no two summands of a normal form may be sumcongruent, we conclude that P and P' have exactly the same summands (up to sumcongruence) and hence $\vdash P =_s P'$. ◼

We are now ready to prove the Completeness Theorem.

Theorem 3.1 (Completeness) If $P \approx^c Q$ then $\vdash P = Q$.

Proof By the Normal Form Lemma, it will be enough to treat the case in which P and Q are normal forms. We consider two main cases.

Case 1: P and Q are proper normal forms.

We prove by induction on the structure of P and Q that

$$P \approx Q \quad \text{implies} \quad \vdash P =_s Q \ .$$

Assume then that this holds for all pairs of agents smaller than P,Q, and assume $P \approx Q$. It will be enough, by the Derivative Lemma, to prove that every μ-derivative of P is sumcongruent to some μ-derivative of Q.

Suppose then that $P \overset{\mu}{\Rightarrow} P'$. Then, because $P \approx Q$, *either* there exists Q' such that $Q \overset{\mu}{\Rightarrow} Q'$ and $P' \approx Q'$, *or* - in the case that $\mu = \tau$ - $P' \approx Q$. In the first case it follows by the induction hypothesis that $\vdash P' =_s Q'$ and we are done. We shall show that the second case contradicts the assumption that P is a proper normal form.

For this purpose, suppose that $P \overset{\tau}{\Rightarrow} P'$ and $P' \approx Q$. By induction, we have $\vdash P' =_s Q$ (since P' is smaller than P). But P is a proper normal form, and therefore possesses a summand $\tau.P_1$ with a τ-derivative sumcongruent to P' and to Q, and possesses at least one other summand, $\nu.P_2$ say. Hence, because $P \approx Q$ and $P \overset{\nu}{\Rightarrow} P_2$, there exists some Q_2 such that *either* $Q \overset{\nu}{\Rightarrow} Q_2$ *or* $\nu = \tau$ and $Q \equiv Q_2$, with $P_2 \approx Q_2$; further, by induction, $\vdash P_2 =_s Q_2$. But since Q is sumcongruent to a τ-derivative of $\tau.P_1$, we have in either case that Q_2 - and hence P_2 also - is sumcongruent to a ν-derivative of $\tau.P_1$, which contradicts the normality of P.

Case 2: P and Q are arbitrary normal forms.

If $P \approx^c Q$ then, for some $\lambda \in \Lambda$ which does not occur in P or Q we have $P + \lambda.NIL \approx Q + \lambda.NIL$. But both the latter agents are proper normal forms, and hence, by Case 1, $\vdash P + \lambda.NIL =_s Q + \lambda.NIL$. It follows immediately that $\vdash P =_s Q$.

This completes the proof of the theorem; note that we have shown also that any pair of normal forms which are observationally congruent are also sumcongruent. ■

4. A CHARACTERISATION IN MODAL LOGIC OF OBSERVATIONAL EQUIVALENCE

4.1 Discussion

In Lecture 2, observational equivalence ($\approx$) was defined as the largest bisimulation relation; that is, the largest relation $\mathcal{R}$ for which

$$\mathcal{R} \subseteq \mathfrak{F}(\mathcal{R})$$

where $\mathfrak{F}$ is a certain function of relations which is monotonic for set inclusion. It follows from standard fixed-point theory that

$$\approx \;=\; \bigcup\{\mathcal{R} \mid \mathcal{R} \subseteq \mathfrak{F}(\mathcal{R})\}$$

and also that $\approx$ is indeed a fixed point of $\mathfrak{F}$, i.e.

$$\approx \;=\; \mathfrak{F}(\approx)$$

Another standard result tells us that $\approx$ can be approximated from above; that is, it is the intersection (limit) of a decreasing chain of relations beginning with the universal relation. This chain may be written $\langle \approx_\kappa \rangle_{\kappa \in O}$, where O is some initial segment of the ordinals (large enough to well-order the relations over $\mathcal{P}$); its elements are given by

$$\approx_0 \;=\; \mathcal{P} \times \mathcal{P}$$

$$\approx_{\kappa+1} = \mathcal{F}(\approx_\kappa)$$

and for a limit ordinal λ :

$$\approx_\lambda = \bigcap_{\kappa<\lambda} \approx_\kappa$$

Then the standard result states that the greatest fixed-point of   , i.e. the observational equivalence relation $\approx$, is given by

$$\approx = \bigcap_{\kappa \in O} \approx_\kappa \qquad .$$

It is clearer to see the definition written out, for the non-limit ordinals:

$P \approx_0 Q$ for all agents P and Q

$P \approx_{\kappa+1} Q$ iff, for every $s \in \Lambda^*$,

(1) Whenever $P \overset{s}{\Rightarrow} P'$ then, for some Q', $Q \overset{s}{\Rightarrow} Q'$ and $P' \approx_\kappa Q'$

(2) Whenever $Q \overset{s}{\Rightarrow} Q'$ then, for some P', $P \overset{s}{\Rightarrow} P'$ and $P' \approx_\kappa Q'$.

It is easy to see, by induction that the chain is decreasing, i.e. that $\approx_\lambda \subseteq \approx_\kappa$ whenever $\lambda > \kappa$ (this is a consequence of the monotonicity of $\mathcal{F}$), and that each $\approx_\kappa$ is an equivalence relation. It is less easy to see that the chain restricted to the finite ordinals $n \in \omega$ is *strictly* decreasing, i.e. that the relations $\approx_n$ are all different, and still less easy to see that the limit $\approx$ is not reached at ω , i.e. we have $\approx_{\omega+1} \neq \approx_\omega$.

We shall not spend long on the latter point. It was mentioned in Milner (1980) Chapter 3 that, while $\approx_{\omega+1}$ and $\approx_\omega$ differ, they agree when restricted to finite agents; in fact they also agree when restricted to agents for which no infinite τ-derivation is possible. In spite of this difference, in Milner (1980) it was chosen to take $\approx_\omega$ as observational equivalence, since its properties could be verified by simple mathematical induction because $\approx_\omega = \bigcap_{n\in\omega} \approx_n$. We have seen however, in Lecture 2, that the technique of bisimulation is appropriate for proving properties of $\approx = \bigcap_{\kappa\in O} \approx_\kappa$, and the latter (being the maximal fixed-point of $\mathcal{F}$) is mathematically a better choice for observational equivalence.

To see that $\langle\approx_n\rangle_{n\in\omega}$ is a strictly decreasing chain of equivalences, we give a sequence $\langle P_n, Q_n\rangle_{n\in\omega}$ of pairs of agents, for which $P_n \approx_n Q_n$ but $P_n \not\approx_{n+1} Q_n$.

$$P_0 = \beta.NIL \ , \quad Q_0 = \gamma.NIL \quad ;$$

$$P_{n+1} = \alpha.(P_n + Q_n) \, , \; Q_{n+1} = \alpha.P_n + \alpha.Q_n \quad .$$

The evaluation trees of these agents, for n = 1 and n = 2, may be pictured:

P_1

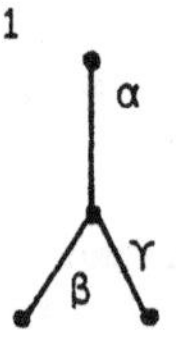

Q_1

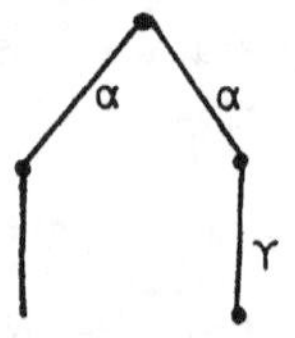

P_2

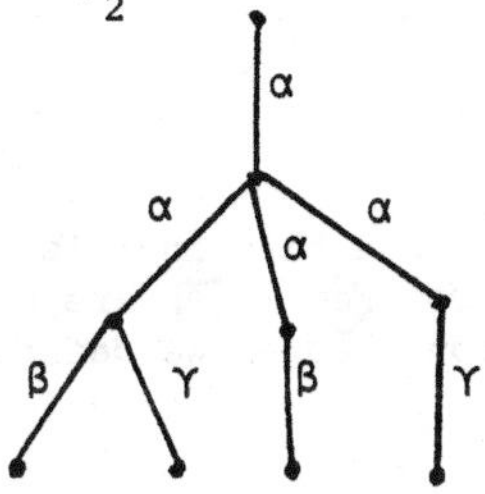

Q_2

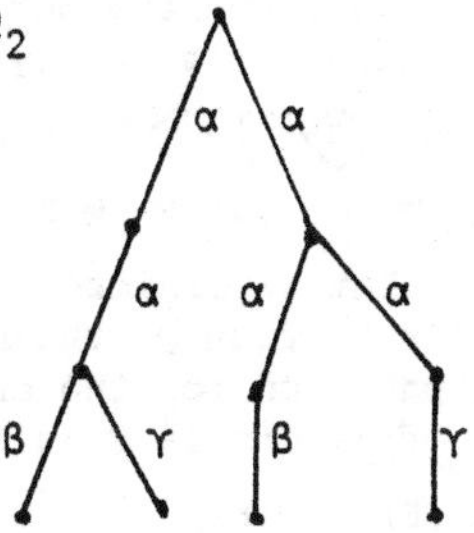

We shall not detail the proof that $P_n \approx_n Q_n$ and $P_n \not\approx_{n+1} Q_n$ for each n, but in preparation for what follows it is instructive to show a property possessed by the behaviour of Q_2, but not by the behaviour of P_2 :

> An α-action is *possible* such that after any further α action it is *necessary* that both a β-action and a γ-action are *possible.*

It is easy to check, from the diagrams of P_2 and Q_2, that the latter possesses the property and the former does not. This alternation of *possibility* and *necessity* of action (to depth 3 in this case) is the key to the logical characterisation which follows.

4.2 A Modal Logic

Let E be a set, called the *experiments*. In our application, we shall take E to be Λ^*, but our results hold for arbitrary E. Let $\mathcal{L}$ be the smallest set of logical formulae such that

(1) If $F \in \mathcal{L}$, then $\neg F \in \mathcal{L}$;

(2) If $F_i \in \mathcal{L}$ for each i in some countable set I, then $\bigwedge_{i \in I} F_i \in \mathcal{L}$;

(3) If $F \in \mathcal{L}$ and $e \in E$, then $\langle e \rangle F \in \mathcal{L}$.

Note that $\mathcal{L}$ is nonempty since, by (2), it always contains the empty conjunction $\bigwedge_{i \in \emptyset} F_i$, which we write TRUE. Now let $\mathcal{P}$ be a set, called the *agents*, and for each $e \in E$ let $\xrightarrow{e} \subseteq \mathcal{P} \times \mathcal{P}$ be a relation (the e-experiment relation) such that for each $P \in \mathcal{P}$ the set $\{P' \mid P \xrightarrow{e} P'\}$ is countable. Again, in our application $\mathcal{P}$ is taken to be the agents of CCS, and for $e = s \in \Lambda^*$ we take $\xrightarrow{e}$ to be $\overset{s}{\Longrightarrow}$.

We interpret $\mathcal{L}$ by defining the *satisfaction* relation $\models \subseteq \mathcal{P} \times \mathcal{L}$ as follows, by induction on the structure of formulae:

(1) $P \models \neg F$ iff not $P \models F$;

(2) $P \models \bigwedge_{i \in I} F_i$ iff $P \models F_i$ for each $i \in I$;

(3) $P \models \langle e \rangle F$ iff, for some P', $P \xrightarrow{e} P'$ and $P' \models F$.

For convenience, we adopt the following abbreviations in $\mathcal{L}$:

FALSE	stands for	$\neg$ TRUE
$F_0 \wedge F_1$	stands for	$\bigwedge_{i \in 2} F_i$
$\bigvee_{i \in I} F_i$	stands for	$\neg \bigwedge_{i \in I} \neg F_i$
$F_0 \vee F_1$	stands for	$\bigvee_{i \in 2} F_i$
$[e]F$	stands for	$\neg \langle e \rangle \neg F$

As an example, we can formulate our statement (at the end of the preceding section) of a property satisfied by Q_2 but not by P_2 :

Let F be $\langle\alpha\rangle[\alpha](\langle\beta\rangle \text{TRUE} \wedge \langle\gamma\rangle \text{TRUE})$;

then $Q_2 \models F$, but $P_2 \not\models F$.

It is no accident that we claimed that $P_2 \not\approx_3 Q_2$, and that in this formula F which distinguishes P_2 from Q_2 the modal operators $\langle e\rangle$, $[e]$ are nested to depth 3. In preparation for the characterisation theorem we define the modal depth D(F) of a formula F as follows:

(1) $D(\neg F) = D(F)$

(2) $D(\bigwedge_{i\in I} F_i) = \sup\{D(F_i) \mid i \in I\}$

(3) $D(\langle e\rangle F) = 1 + D(F)$

Note that D(TRUE) = 0, and indeed D(F) = 0 iff F contains no occurrence of the modal operator $\langle e\rangle$. Also, since we allow infinitary conjunction, the depth of a formula is any countable ordinal. We therefore define $\mathcal{L}_\kappa \subseteq \mathcal{L}$, for each ordinal κ, as follows:

$$\mathcal{L}_\kappa = \{F \mid D(F) \leq \kappa\}$$

Now, for our arbitrary set $\mathcal{P}$ of agents and arbitrary experiment relations $\xrightarrow{e}$, the chain of equivalence relations $\langle \approx_\kappa \rangle$ is defined just as at the start of this lecture but using $\xrightarrow{e}$ in place of $\overset{s}{\Longrightarrow}$; then as before $\approx = \bigcap_\kappa \approx_\kappa$. Our characterisation theorem, which we now prove, states that $P \approx_\kappa Q$ iff no formula in $\mathcal{L}_\kappa$ distinguishes P from Q.

<u>Theorem</u> (1) For each κ , $P \approx_\kappa Q$ iff, for every $F \in$ $_\kappa$,

$$P \models F \iff Q \models F$$

(2) $P \approx Q$ iff, for every $F \in \mathcal{L}$,

$$P \models F \iff Q \models F$$

<u>Proof</u>. (2) follows directly from (1), since $\mathcal{L} = \bigcap_\kappa \mathcal{L}_\kappa$. We prove (1) by induction on κ .

If $\kappa = 0$ then the result is trivial, since formulae of depth 0 distinguish no agent. Otherwise, assume the result for all $\lambda < \kappa$.

(i) Let $P \approx_\kappa Q$, and let $P \models F$. It is easy to see that the critical case is when F has the form $\langle e\rangle F'$, and we treat only this case. Then for some P', $P \xrightarrow{e} P' \models F'$. Also, by assumption, some Q' exists for which $Q \xrightarrow{e} Q'$, and $P' \approx_\lambda Q'$ for some $\lambda < \kappa$.

But by induction, since $P' \models F'$, also $Q' \models F'$. Hence, since $Q \xrightarrow{e} Q'$, $Q \models F$. By a symmetric argument, we have shown that $P \approx_\kappa Q$ implies $P \models F \iff Q \models F$ for each $F \in \mathcal{L}_\kappa$.

(ii) Suppose on the other hand that $P \not\approx_\kappa Q$. We wish to find a formula $F \in \mathcal{L}_\kappa$ such that $P \models F$ and $Q \not\models F$.

Consider first the case that $\kappa = \lambda + 1$. Then without loss of generality, for some e and P' we have $P \xrightarrow{e} P'$ and, for every Q', $Q \xrightarrow{e} Q'$ implies $P' \not\approx_\lambda Q'$. Let $\{Q_i \mid i \in I\}$ be the countable set of agents Q' for which $Q \xrightarrow{e} Q'$. Then for each $i \in I$, since $P' \not\approx_\lambda Q_i$, there exists by induction a formula $F_i \in \mathcal{L}_\lambda$ such that $P' \models F_i$ and $Q_i \not\models F_i$ (negation allows the distinction to take this form in each case). Define F to be $\langle e \rangle \bigwedge_{i \in I} F_i$. Then, since $P \overset{e}{\Rightarrow} P'$, we have $P \models F$. On the other hand, since $Q \overset{e}{\Rightarrow} Q'$ implies $Q' \not\models \bigwedge_{i \in I} F_i$, we have $Q \not\models F$. Thus F is the required formula.

Now consider the case that κ is a limit ordinal. By the definition of $\approx_\kappa$ for limit ordinals it follows from $P \not\approx_\kappa Q$ that $P \not\approx_\lambda Q$ for some $\lambda < \kappa$. Thus, by induction, there exists $F \in \mathcal{L}_\lambda$ such that $P \models F$ and $Q \not\models F$, and we are done since $F \in \mathcal{L}_\kappa$ also. ∎

This theorem was first announced in Hennessy and Milner (1980), but only for a finitary logic (i.e. only finitary conjunctions), which is sufficient in the case that the image of each P under each $\overset{e}{\Rightarrow}$ is finite.

The importance of the result is that it provides an alternative characterisation of observational equivalence.

5. DERIVED OPERATORS AND DYNAMICALLY-CHANGING CONFIGURATIONS

5.1 Value Variables and Value Expressions

The example given in Lecture 1, Section 1.2, illustrates the use of variables over data spaces, and expressions employing the constants and operators appropriate to these spaces. For simplicity, we shall not consider several types of data, and shall assume that data values form a countable set (if larger spaces, e.g. function spaces, are needed then everything can be done by allowing summations and recursions which use uncountable index sets). In what follows, we use x,y,... for value variables and allow e,f,... to range over value expressions.

The example shows that value variables are bound by names $\alpha,\beta,\ldots$, and that co-names $\bar{\alpha},\bar{\beta},\ldots$ are used to qualify value expressions; thus, in the agent expression

$$\alpha x.\mathrm{CELL}_2(x,y) + \bar{\gamma}y.\mathrm{CELL}_0$$

the value variable x is bound, while there are two free occurrences of y. Apart from this, value variables or expressions may appear as parameters to parametric agent identifiers (e.g. CELL_2), and in a form such as the conditional

$$\mathit{if}\ e\ \mathit{then}\ E\ \mathit{else}\ F$$

a (boolean) value expression e may occur. Other forms may be required involving value expressions; it is likely that they can be treated along the lines indicated below.

Our aim is to show how all such value manipulation can be encoded into the basic calculus presented in Section 1.3. The point of this is that, for theoretical purposes, the analyses which we have done thereby extend automatically to richer calculi with value manipulation. This avoids tedious detail in theoretical analysis; much of the semantic discussion, as presented for example in Chapter 5 of Milner (1980) for a richer calculus, thereby exhibits essential features of concurrency and communication more clearly.

The encoding is simple; essentially, it depends only on one device. In place of the name α and co-name $\bar{\alpha}$ which may qualify value variables or expressions over a data space D, we consider the sets Δ and $\bar{\Delta}$ of names and co-names to contain the families $\{\alpha_d \mid d \in D\}$ and $\{\bar{\alpha}_d \mid d \in D\}$ respectively. Now let us represent by $\hat{E}$ the encoding in the basic calculus of an agent expression E of the richer calculus. Then

(1) If E is $\alpha x.F$, then $\hat{E}$ is $\sum_{x \in D} \alpha_x.\hat{F}$

(2) If E is $\bar{\alpha}e.F$, then $\hat{E}$ is $\bar{\alpha}_e.\hat{F}$

(3) If E is if e then F else G, then $\hat{E}$ is

$$\sum_{e} \hat{F} + \sum_{\neg e} \hat{G}$$

(4) If E is $C(e_1,e_2,\ldots)$, where C is a parametric agent identifier, then $\hat{E}$ is $C_{e_1e_2}\ldots$; here we are using a countable family $\{C_{d_1d_2}\ldots \mid d_1,d_2,\ldots \in D\}$ of agent identifiers in the basic calculus.

(5) A defining equation $C(x_1,x_2,\ldots) = E$ is encoded as a family $\{C_{x_1x_2\ldots} = \hat{E} \mid x_1,x_2,\ldots \in D\}$ of defining equations.

It is worth noting that, by these encoding rules, value computation is not represented by actions of CCS; instead, this computation is relegated to the indices of labels λ and agent identifiers C. This point is most clearly observed in the encoding of the conditional expression.

The use of defining equations - even a countably infinite number - in the basic calculus can of course be eliminated by the use of the recursion combinator, at the cost of readability. The family

$$C_j = E_j \qquad (j \in I)$$

of defining equations (in which any of the C_i may occur in any E_j) can be replaced by

$$C_j = \text{fix}_j\langle X_i\rangle_{i\in I}\langle E_i\rangle_{i\in I}$$

which may be abbreviated to $\tilde{C} = \text{fix}\tilde{X}\tilde{E}$. One may even go further, and eliminate all defined agent identifiers in favour of their defining recursion expressions, and thereby the encoding into the basic calculus is complete.

5.2 Derived Composition Combinators

The basic composition combinator "|" is the only means by which communication between independent agents is admitted to CCS. From it, with the help of restriction and relabelling, many others can be derived, and their properties deduced from those of the basic combinators.

As a first example, consider the chaining combinator "⌢" used in Section 1.2. Its purpose was quite particular to the example of that section; it links two ports $\bar{\beta}$ and δ in one agent to two ports α and $\bar{\gamma}$ in another, and restricts these ports.

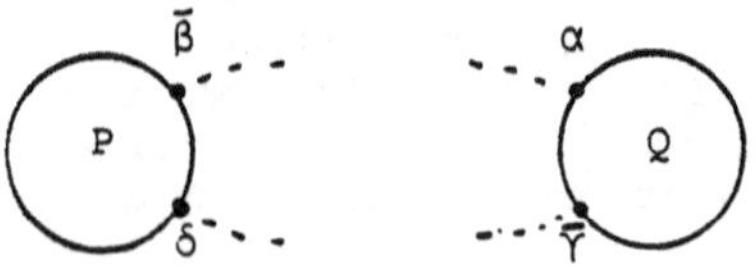

Its definition is quite simple:

$$P \supset Q = (P[\theta/\beta, \eta/\delta] \mid Q[\theta/\alpha, \eta/\gamma]) \setminus \{\theta, \eta\}$$

where θ and η are new names. The associativity of "$\supset$" is easily deduced from equational properties of the basic combinators, and this property is important for the proof that the pushdown store works correctly, as detailed in Milner (1980), Section 8.4.

A combinator of more general use is sequential composition. If we decide to adopt a convention that a certain label $\bar{\delta}$ will always be the last action in any computation in which it occurs, then sequential composition may be defined as follows

$$P\ ;\ Q \;=\; (P[\delta'/\delta] \mid \delta'.Q) \setminus \delta'$$

where δ' is new. Again, the associativity of sequential composition is easily deduced.

How do we ensure that $\bar{\delta}$ is always the last action in any computation in which it occurs? Let us say that an agent P has the δ-*termination property* if whenever

$$P \xrightarrow{\mu_1} P_1 \xrightarrow{\mu_2} \ldots\ldots \xrightarrow{\mu_n} P_n \xrightarrow{\bar{\delta}} P' \qquad (n \geq 0)$$

then P' has no action. In what derived calculus, then, does every agent P have the δ-termination property? We clearly cannot allow unconstrained use of "$|$", since $P|Q$ will not possess the property even when P and Q possess it. But we may adopt another defined composition operator, "$|_\delta$", defined as follows:

$$P \mid_\delta Q \;=\; (P[\delta_1/\delta] \mid Q[\delta_2/\delta] \mid (\delta_1.\delta_2.\bar{\delta}.NIL + \delta_2.\delta_1.\bar{\delta}.NIL)) \setminus \{\delta_1, \delta_2\}$$

where δ_1 and δ_2 are new. Clearly $P \mid_\delta Q$ terminates (by $\bar{\delta}$) only when P and Q have both terminated. Then we may define a derived calculus by adopting the following constraints:

(1) Composition "$|$" is not used, but replaced by "$|_\delta$" and ";" .

(2) δ and $\bar{\delta}$ are never involved explicitly in any restriction or relabelling operation.

(3) δ and $\bar{\delta}$ are never used as action prefixes, with the exception that $\bar{\delta}$.NIL, which may be written *skip*, is allowed.

Then the termination property will be possessed by every definable agent, as may be proved by induction on the length of computations.

Again, we note that many properties of the derived combinators, can be deduced. Some are as follows:

$$P \mid_\delta (Q \mid_\delta R) \;=\; (P \mid_\delta Q) \mid_\delta R$$
$$P\ ;\ skip \;=\; skip$$
$$P \mid_\delta skip \;=\; P$$
$$skip\ ;\ P \;\approx\; P$$

5.3 Dynamically Varying Configurations

Many systems - particularly systems built in hardware - are naturally expressed in the form

$$P = (P_1 | P_2 | \ldots . | P_n) \backslash A$$

where the composition operator "|" does not appear in any P_i. Typically each P_i will be capable of infinite computation, through the use of recursion. Now every computation of P will preserve the structure of P itself, as a restricted composite of exactly n sequential agents. (This should be slightly qualified; any of the P_i may, during computation, reduce to NIL, and - since NIL is a unit for composition - this amounts to P_i dying.) In fact, this fixed structure is obtained by the simple constraint of avoiding the use of composition "|" inside recursion.

In Lecture 1 we saw a very simple example of a dynamically varying structure, the pushdown store, in which the store's ability to grow unboundedly was obtained just by the use of the chaining combinator "$\frown$" inside a (mutual) recursion.

Let us now consider a richer case of dynamically varying configuration. Let us suppose that we are concerned with a *resource* agent R, of sort $\{\alpha,\beta\}$:

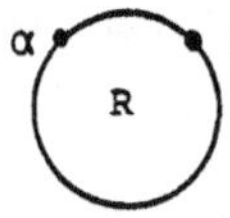

Further, we may imagine a system which at some point in its computational history contains two agents P and Q together with a number of differently labelled instances of R:

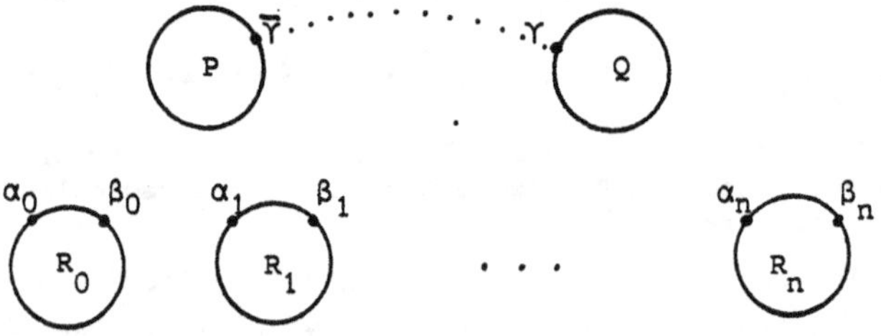

Each R_i is given by $R_i = R[\alpha_i/\alpha,\beta_i/\beta]$, and the system as a whole would be written as

$$(P | Q | R_0 | \ldots | R_n)\backslash A$$

where A includes $\{\alpha_i,\beta_i \mid i \geq 0\}$ as a subset. In the diagram, we have not included all the links which may exist among all the components.

A natural requirement, which often arises in real systems, is for P to delegate to Q - from time to time - the ability to interact with one or other instance of R. For this purpose, P may simple designate the index i of the appropriate instance, by emitting this index at $\bar{\gamma}$. So P may somewhere contain the subexpression $\bar{\gamma}i.P'$. Q, on the other hand, must receive this index and use it to interact with R_i, so it will contain somewhere the subexpression

$$\gamma x.(\ldots\bar{\alpha}_x. \;\ldots\; \bar{\beta}_x. \;\ldots)$$

which of course, using the encoding described in 5.1 above, is equivalent to

$$\sum_{i\in\omega} \gamma_i.(\ldots\bar{\alpha}_i. \;\ldots\bar{\beta}_i. \;\ldots)$$

It may be that, because the number of instances of R in existence is always bounded by n, this summation need only be finite - i.e. indexed by n - rather than infinite. But we may also imagine that unboundedly many instances of R are created - perhaps by P - during computation, and in this case the infinite summation is necessary.

We see thus that the presence of infinite summation in the basic calculus allows the representation of dynamically varying configurations, and - in a sense - the passage of communication links as values between one agent and another. In Milner (1980), Chapter 9, it was pointed out that the original version of CCS was probably defective in this respect; the example studied there was the natural one of allowing unboundedly many concurrent activations of a single procedure in a concurrent programming language. The use of infinite summation to overcome the defect was pointed out in Milner (1983), Section 6. It is quite certain that the slender syntax of our basic calculus, and even the derived notations which we have considered, are not sufficient always to present such applications in a lucid way; but it is rather important that the basic calculus *does* allow them to be encoded, since it is then evident that no essentially new semantic problems arise in handling these applications. The problem of presenting them lucidly is, of course, a problem of programming language design; it is hard, and the problem of devising rigorous but intelligible methods of analysis or verification for such languages is even harder.

References

1. Costa, G. and Stirling, C. (1983). A Fair Calculus of Communicating Systems. Vol. 154, Lecture Notes in Computer Science, Springer-Verlag, pp. 97-108.

2. Hennessy, M. and Milner R. (1983). Algebraice Laws for Nondeterminism and Concurrency. Technical Report CSR-133-83, Computer Science Dept, University of Edinburgh.

3. Hennessy, M. and Stirling, C. (1983). The Power of the Future Perfect in Program Logics. Technical Report CSR-156-83, Computer Science Dept, University of Edinburgh.

4. Hoare, C.A.R., Brookes, S.D. and Roscoe, A.D. (1981). A Theory of Communicating Sequential Processes, Technical Monograph PRG-16, Computing Laboratory, University of Oxford.

5. Milner, R. (1980). <u>A Calculus of Communicating Systems</u>. Vol. 92, Lecture Notes in Computer Science, Springer-Verlag.

6. Milner, R. (1982a). A Complete Inference System for a Class of Regular Behaviours. Technical Report CSR-111-82, Computer Science Dept, University of Edinburgh. (To appear in Journal of Computer and Systems Sciences.)

7. Milner, R. (1982b). A Finite Delay Operator in Synchronous CCS. Technical Report CSR-116-82, Computer Science Dept, University of Edinburgh.

8. Milner, R. (1983). Calculi for Synchrony and Asynchrony. J. Theoretical Computer Science, Vol.25, pp. 267-310.

9. de Nicola, R. and Hennessy, M. (1982). Testing Equivalences for Processes. Technical Report CSR-123-82, Computer Science Dept, University of Edinburgh.

10. Park, D. (1981). Concurrency and Automata on Infinite Sequences. In Vol.104, Lecture Notes in Computer Science, Springer-Verlag.

Acknowledgement I would like to thank Dorothy McKie for her expert typing of a difficult manuscript.

CONCURRENT BEHAVIOUR: SEQUENCES, PROCESSES AND AXIOMS

Eike Best

Gesellschaft für Mathematik und Datenverarbeitung
5205 St. Augustin 1, Postfach 1240, Fed. Rep. Germany

Two ways of describing the behaviour of concurrent systems have widely been suggested: arbitrary interleaving and partial orders. Sometimes the latter has been claimed superior because concurrency is represented in a "true" way; on the other hand, some authors have claimed that the former is sufficient for all practical purposes.

Petri net theory offers a framework in which both kinds of semantics can be defined formally and hence compared with each other. Firing sequences correspond to interleaved behaviour while the notion of a process is used to capture partial order semantics. For most concurrent programming languages such as CSP or shared variable languages, sequence semantics is widely used but little work exists on process semantics.

This paper aims at obtaining formal results about the relationship between processes and firing sequences in net theory. We show that generally speaking, the class of behaviours defined by the two semantics is the same, but that it is difficult to find a "nice" relationship between sequences and processes. We also discuss one of the process axioms which is particularly interesting on intuitive grounds. Finally, we define the notion of a process also for concurrent programming languages, thus providing the basis to do similar analyses as have been done in net theory.

1. INTRODUCTION

Concurrent systems usually involve sets of activities that are causally and temporally unrelated unless the contrary is specified by some means of synchronisation such as communication or mutual exclusion over common variables. The existence of a global clock cannot in general be assumed. Two ways of describing the semantics of concurrent systems have been proposed: arbitrary interleaving of atomic actions and partial orders in which concurrency is represented as the absence of ordering.

Some authors claim the latter approach to be superior to the former because concurrency is represented in a "true" way [e.g. 19]. On the other hand, it is sometimes argued that interleaving semantics is easier to define and is sufficient for all practical purposes (e.g. [18] where it is claimed that sequences suffice for the analysis of safety and liveness properties of concurrent systems).

Virtually all major concurrent system models and description languages have been equipped with interleaving semantics. Referring to some of the recent literature, we may quote firing sequence semantics and step semantics for Petri nets [11] and COSY [20], rewrite semantics for CSP [28], CCS [22] and for shared variable programs [15], and control sequence semantics for the latter [3]. For COSY, a partial order semantics is provided by the vector firing sequence formalism [32]. Partial order semantics have also been suggested for shared variable programs in [6] and for CSP in [30]. For CCS, a partial order semantics may be obtainable via a translation into Petri nets [13]. Net theory, in turn, offers a partial order semantics by means of the process notion developed in [11,14,25].

Net theory is uniform in the sense that the processes of a net describing a concurrent system may again be described by special kinds of nets called occurrence nets (we use the terminology of [12]). Processes are essentially labelled occurrence nets describing the possible behaviours of a system net. Occurrence nets have themselves been the objects of close study [1 , 4 , 9 ,10,17], and as a result, their properties are by now fairly well understood. Processes have been introduced in [11,14] by means of a set of axioms relating the underlying occurrence net, the labelling, and the system net to each other. Thus, net theory offers a framework in which both kinds of semantics have been formalised and can hence be compared with each other. Furthermore, it is possible to relate properties of a system net to properties of its processes in a formal way.

The present paper addresses some of the issues relating to processes and firing sequences in Petri nets and in concurrent programs and has been written with three purpose in mind. Firstly, it is intended to provide an indication of some of the more recent work done in studying the properties of occurrence nets, particularly with respect to their relation to the process axioms [2 ,10,11,14]. Secondly, we aim at obtaining mathematical results to help answer the question put at the beginning: In general, is process semantics inherently superior to sequence semantics? If so, in what particular way? And if not, is there perhaps a "nice" relationship between the two? Thirdly, we hope to show that this work can be of direct relevance for the behavioural description of concurrent system models that, on the face of it, differ from net theory, such as CSP or a shared variable language.

Section 2 contains basic definitions and the firing sequence semantics fo Petri nets. In section 3 we introduce the process axioms as well as a construction by which a process can be derived from a firing sequence. We then prove that for finite system nets, the process axioms are consistent and complete with respect to this construction. This shows that the process axioms give, in a sense, the intuitively expected objects. We then show that the completeness result fails to hold for infinite system nets, but tha it can be retrieved by considering step sequences which are a generalisation of firing sequences first introduced in [11].

One of the process axioms is particularly interesting because it restricts the class of occurrence nets under consideration. We examine this axiom more closely in section 4, showing also connections to several other properties of occurrence nets that have been studied in the literature.

For special classes of nets, it is known that processes can be identified with equivalence classes of sequences, namely such sequences that differ only in the order of adjacent concurrent transition firings. The partial order given by the process then corresponds to the intersection of the orders of the sequences in an equivalence class In general, such a nice relationship cannot be found. In section 5, we will investigat this problem in general and examine how much of the correspondence just mentioned can be salvaged. More specifically, we will prove a theorem which relates equivalence classes of sequences to equivalence classes of processes.

Finally, in section 6 we apply the ideas expounded in the earlier sections to obtain the behavioural semantics, both in terms of interleavings and in terms of processes, of a shared variable language and of CSP. The first part of section 6 essentially reiterates and combines the interleaving approach described in [3] and the partial order approach of [6] for a shared variable language with atomic actions. The second part of section 6 then shows that the behavioural semantics of CSP can be defined in an entirely analogous way which can also be related to the approach of [30].

2. BASIC DEFINITIONS

Net theory stipulates that a concurrent system be described by two kinds of objects, state-like objects S (sometimes called places) and action-like objects T (sometimes called transitions). The idea is that state objects may "hold" (to make up a certain state) and that transitions may "occur" (and thus change the state). Thus, state objects and transitions are interconnected in an alternating fashion, which in net theory is captured by an interconnection relation F (for "flow") defined as a subset of $(S\times T)\cup(T\times S)$.

2.1 Definition.

(S,T,F) is a net iff S and T are disjoint sets, $F \subseteq (S\times T)\cup(T\times S)$ and $T \subseteq \mathrm{dom}(F)\cap\mathrm{cod}(F$

From a formal point of view it is advantageous to interpret the relation F as a functi $F\colon (S\times T\cup T\times S)\to\{0,1\}$ with the convention $(x,y)\in F \Leftrightarrow F(x,y)=1$ and $(x,y)\notin F \Leftrightarrow F(x,y)=0$. We will make use of this view.

2.2 Notation.

Suppose $x \in S \cup T$; $\cdot x = \{y \in S \cup T \mid (y,x) \in F\}$ (the pre-set of x),
$x^{\cdot} = \{y \in S \cup T \mid (x,y) \in F\}$ (the post-set of x).

The reader may notice that definition 2.1 differs slightly from the definition of a net given in [12] which requires $S \cup T = dom(F) \cup cod(F)$ instead of $T \subseteq dom(F) \cap cod(F)$. Thus, we allow isolated places but require that transitions have at least one pre-place and at least one post-place. This accords with the intuition expressed in [14], the idea being that it makes relatively little sense to allow isolated transitions that don't change the state, while it does turn out useful to allow isolated places. However, the author believes that this slight inconsistency does not impinge on the basic idea behind the definitions of a net, which is the distinction between S-elements and T-elements.

Net theory employs the concept of a marking in order to describe state holdings, while the state changes effected by a transition occurrence are described by the transition rule. In general, state objects are allowed to hold several times, for example representing the presence of several similar resources. We shall consider nets with a capacity function K which defines a bound on the possible number of holdings of a state object (including the case of unlimited capacity which is usually considered in the literature).

2.3 Definition.

(i) (S,T,F,K) is a net with capacities iff (S,T,F) is a net and $K: S \to (\mathcal{N} \cup \{\infty\})$ is a capacity function (by definition, $\mathcal{N}$ is the set of positive integers)

(ii) M is a marking of (S,T,F,K) iff $M: S \to \mathcal{Z}$ ($\mathcal{Z}$= the set of integers) such that $\forall s \in S$: $0 \le M(s) \le K(s)$

(iii) $N=(S,T,F,K,M_o)$ is a system net iff (S,T,F,K) is a net with capacities and M_o is a marking (called the initial marking of N).

M_o represents the initial state of the system described by N. Henceforth we will only consider countable system nets (believing that other nets have no practical significance). The transition rule, defined next, specifies under which conditions a marking M enables a transition t, and how the occurrence of t changes M into a new marking M'.

2.4 Definition.

Let (S,T,F,K) be a net with capacities, M a marking and $t \in T$.

(i) M enables t iff $\forall s \in S$: $F(s,t) \le M(s) \le K(s) - F(t,s)$

(ii) M' is produced from M by the occurrence (or firing) of t (in symbols: $M[t>M'$) iff M enables t and $\forall s \in S$: $M'(s) = M(s) - F(s,t) + F(t,s)$.

Note that this definition ensures that M' is again a marking.

2.5 Definition.

Let $N=(S,T,F,K,M_o)$ be a system net, let $M_1, M_2, \ldots$ be markings and let $t_1, t_2, \ldots \in T$.

(i) $\sigma = M_o t_1 M_1 \ldots t_n M_n$ is a (finite) firing sequence of N iff $\forall i$, $1 \le i \le n$: $M_{i-1}[t_i>M_i$;
$\sigma = M_o t_1 M_1 t_2 \ldots$ is an (infinite) firing sequence of N iff $\forall i$, $1 \le i$: $M_{i-1}[t_i>M_i$;

(ii) For finite σ we define the length of σ, $|\sigma|$, by n, that is the number of transitions in σ; this includes the case $\sigma = M_o$, in which case $|\sigma| = 0$.

(iii) $[M_o> = \{M \mid \exists \sigma = M_o \ldots M_n: M = M_n\}$ (the set of markings reachable from M_o by successive firings of single transitions).

Definition 2.5 specifies the firing sequence semantics of Petri nets. The process semantics will be defined in the next section; it uses a special class of nets defined next.

2.6 Definition.

A net (S,T,F) is called occurrence net iff

(i) $\forall s \in S$: $|\cdot s| \le 1 \wedge |s^{\cdot}| \le 1$, and

(ii) F^* is acyclic, i.e. $\forall x,y \in S \cup T$: $(x,y) \in F^* \wedge (y,x) \in F^* \Rightarrow x=y$ (where F^* is the reflexive and transitive closure of F, i.e. $F^o = id$, $F^{n+1} = F \circ F^n$ and $F^* = \bigcup_n F^n$).

The S-elements of an occurrence net are usually called conditions and denoted by B. Conditions will be used to represent state holdings. The T-elements of an occurrence net are usually called events and denoted by E. They will be used to represent transition occurrences. 2.6(i) means that an occurrence net contains no non-deterministic choices, the idea being that all choices are resolved at the behaviour level. 2.6(ii) means that an occurrence net contains no cycles, the idea being that all loops are unfolded at the behaviour level. Because of 2.6(ii), the structure $(X,\le)$ derived from an occurrence net (B,E,F) by putting $X = B \cup E$ and $\le = F^*$ is a partial order (a poset).

2.7 Definition.

Let $(X,\leq)$ be the poset derived from an occurrence net (B,E,F).

(i) $< = (\leq\backslash id_X)$, $li = (\leq\cup\geq)$, $co = (X\times X\backslash li)\cup id_X$

(ii) $l\subseteq X$ is a li-set (chain) iff $\forall x,y\in l\colon (x,y)\in li$
      $l\subseteq X$ is a line iff l is a li-set and $\forall z\in X\backslash l\ \exists x\in l\colon (x,z)\notin li$ (i.e. l is maximal)
      L is the set of lines of $(X,\leq)$ (respectively, of (B,E,F))

(iii) $c\subseteq X$ is a co-set (antichain) iff $\forall x,y\in c\colon (x,y)\in co$
       $c\subseteq X$ is a cut iff c is a co-set and $\forall z\in X\backslash c\ \exists x\in c\colon (x,z)\notin co$
       C is the set of cuts of $(X,\leq)$ (respectively, of (B,E,F))
       a cut $c\subseteq X$ will be called a B-cut iff $c\subseteq B$; BC is the set of B-cuts of (B,E,F).

The relations li and co denote sequentiality (ordering) and concurrency (absence of ordering), respectively. Lines may be interpreted as the "sequential subprocesses" of (B,E,F) while cuts may be interpreted as "states" of (B,E,F). In particular, the B-cuts will be related to the markings of a system net under a process labelling.

2.8 Notation.

Let $N=(B,E,F)$ be an occurrence net and let $(X,\leq)$ be the associated poset.

(i) $^{O}N = \{x\in X \mid \cdot x=\emptyset\}$ (the set of initial elements of N)
     $N^{O} = \{x\in X \mid x\cdot=\emptyset\}$ (the set of final elements of N)
     (Note that 2.1 implies $^{O}N\subseteq B$ and $N^{O}\subseteq B$.)

(ii) For $A_1,A_2\subseteq X$: $[A_1,A_2] = \{z\in X \mid \exists x\in A_1\ \exists y\in A_2\colon x\leq z\leq y\}$ (the interval between A_1 and for $x\in X$ we write $[A_1,x]$ and $[x,A_2]$ instead of, resp., $[A_1,\{x\}]$ and $[\{x\},A_2]$.

Pictorially, the S-elements of a net are represented by circles, the T-elements are represented by boxes, and the F relation is represented by arrows from circles to boxes or the other way round. The capacity function is represented by writing the number K(s) next to the circle representing s; by convention, $K(s)=\infty$ if such a number is absent. Markings M are represented by placing M(s) "tokens" (black dots) on the place s. Figure 1 gives a simple example illustrating all notions introduced so far (as well as anticipating the process notion).

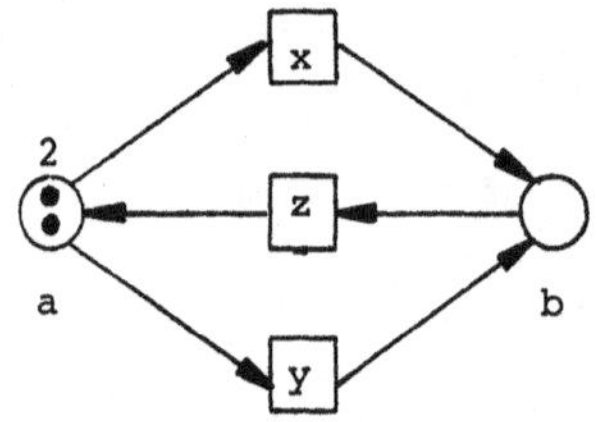

(i) A system net

$$\binom{a}{a} x \binom{a}{b} y \binom{b}{b} z \binom{a}{b} y \binom{b}{b}$$

(ii) A firing sequence
     of (i)

a B-cut

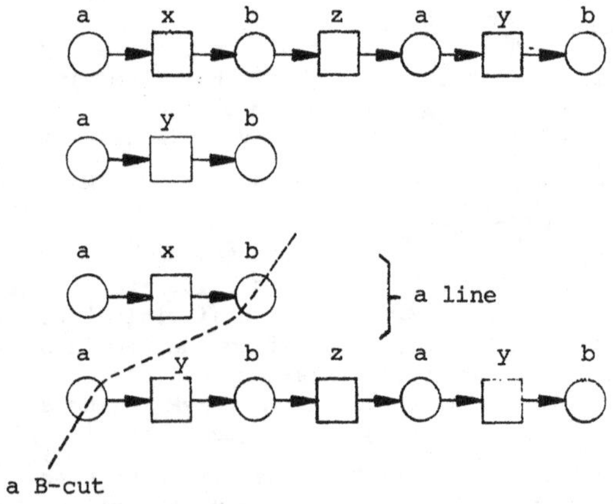

(iii) Two occurrence nets describing
      processes of (i)

Figure 1

For example, the place "a" in Figure 1(i) might represent the "free" state of at most two resources. The place "b" might represent the "used" state of resources. Both x and y then represent the act of claiming a resource for use, while z describes the freeing of a resource. The initial marking indicates that initially two resources are free and none is used. The firing sequence in Figure 1(ii) and the processes 1(iii) describe the (concurrent) claiming of the two resources and the (partly) subsequent freeing and re-claiming of one of them.

We end this preparatory section by introducing the notions of contact-freeness and safeness (often also called boundedness). Contact-freeness means that a transition can fail to be enabled only because of the fact that some of its pre-states fail to hold (rather than because its post-states hold too often).

2.9 Definition.

A system net $N=(S,T,F,K,M_o)$ is contact-free iff
$\forall M\in[M_o\rangle\ \forall t\in T:\ (\forall s\in S:\ M(s)\geq F(s,t)) \Rightarrow (\forall s\in S:\ M(s)\leq K(s)-F(t,s))$.

In particular, all nets with $K(s)=\infty$ for all s are contact-free, and so is the net shown in Figure 1(i). Safeness, on the other hand, means that a bound can be given for the number of tokens on a given place.

2.10 Definition.

Let $N=(S,T,F,K,M_o)$ be a system net and let $s\in S$.
(i) s is n-safe (for $n\in\mathbb{N}$) iff $\forall M\in[M_o\rangle$: $M(s)\leq n$
(ii) N is n-safe iff $\forall s\in S$: s is n-safe; N is safe iff $\exists n$: N is n-safe.

In particular, if $K(s)\neq\infty$ then s is K(s)-safe. Note, however, that all s may be n-safe without N itself being safe (this may be the case for infinite nets). The case $K(s)=1$ for all s is particularly important; the net is then 1-safe (but not necessarily contact-free, see Figure 2).

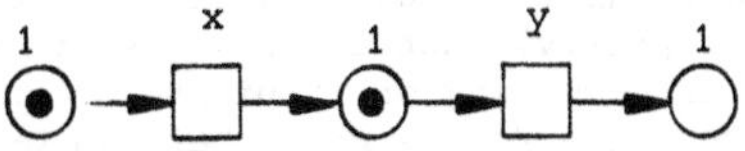

Figure 2: A 1-safe net which is not contact-free

3. THE PROCESS NOTION OF NET THEORY

The idea to describe the behaviour of Petri nets by means of occurrence nets can be traced back at least to [17]. In [25], Petri suggested a set of axioms linking occurrence nets to system nets. Based on this idea, [11] offers the first axiomatisation of the properties of a process. Subsequently these axioms have been generalised and modified because of some counterintuitive problems [10,14]. In this section we examine the process notion closely and define a construction to derive processes from firing sequences. We will also show that the process axioms, essentially as defined in [10,14], are consistent and complete with respect to this more intuitive construction.

Before giving the process axioms, we need to define a property of occurrence nets. Let $N=(B,E,F)$ be an occurrence net and let $c\in C$ be a cut of N. The c-discreteness property requires that all elements of N have a "finite distance" to c:

3.1 Definition.

Let $N=(B,E,F)$ be an occurrence net and let $c\in C(N)$.
N is c-discrete iff $\forall x\in B\cup E\ \exists n=n(x):\ \forall l\in L(N):\ |[c,x]\cap l|\leq n \wedge |[x,c]\cap l|\leq n$.

Figure 3 illustrates this definition. To see that the net shown in Figure 3 is not c_1-discrete, consider the event x; for any $n\in\mathbb{N}$ a line l can be found such that $|[c_1,x]\cap l|>n$.

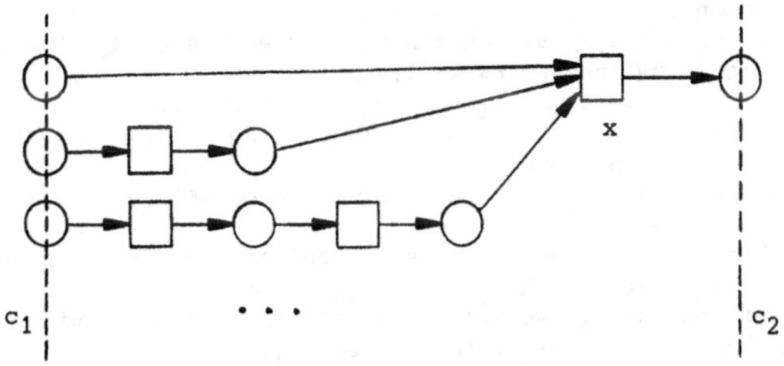

Figure 3: An occurrence net which is c_2-discrete but not c_1-discrete

The next definition gives the process axioms for contact-free system nets. The fact that this definition works only for contact-free nets has been remarked in [11]. This point can be appreciated by considering the net shown in Figure 2: The firing rule specifies that x can occur only strictly after y, but it is not possible to express this ordering by means of the definition that follows.

3.2 Definition.

Let $N=(S,T,F,K,M_o)$ be a contact-free system net, $N'=(B,E,F')$ an occurrence net and $p\colon B\cup E \to S\cup T$ a labelling of N'.

The pair $\pi = (N',p)$ is called a process of N iff

(i) $p(B)\subseteq S$, $p(E)\subseteq T$

(ii) ${}^{o}N' \in BC(N')$

(iii) $\forall s\in S\colon M_o(s)=|p^{-1}(s)\cap {}^{o}N'|$

(iv) N' is ${}^{o}N'$-discrete

(v) $\forall e\in E\ \forall s\in S\colon F(s,p(e))=|p^{-1}(s)\cap {}^{\bullet}e| \wedge F(p(e),s)=|p^{-1}(s)\cap e^{\bullet}|$.

The requirement 3.2(i) means that the conditions of N' represent holdings of the places of N and that the events of N' represent occurrences of the transitions of N. 3.2(ii,iii) mean that N' starts with a B-cut which "corresponds to" the initial marking M_o in the sense that every condition in ${}^{o}N'$ represents some token of M_o. Requirement 3.2(iv) means that all elements of N' are finitely reachable from ${}^{o}N'$, in a sense to be made precise. Finally, 3.2(v) guarantees that transition environments are respected; essentially, this encodes the transition rule 2.4(ii). Actually, the definition given in [14] requires only 3.2(i,ii,iii,v), but it is argued in the last section of [14] that a property like 3.2(iv) is necessary on intuitive grounds. This is further analysed in [10], and we will discuss the relationship between c-discreteness and the properties considered there in section 4 below. As an example, the reader is invited to check that the labelled occurrence nets shown in Figure 1(iii) satisfy the process axioms with respect to the system shown in Figure 1(i).

Before giving the construction associating processes to firing sequences we prove that the countability of N implies the countability of N'.

3.3 Theorem.

Let $(N',p)=(B,E,F,p)$ be a process of a (countable) system net N. Then N' is countable.

Proof: Because of $E\subseteq dom(F)\cap cod(F)$ (definition 2.1) it suffices to prove that B is countable; the countability of E and F then follows.

Define recursively $B_n\subseteq B$ by $B_o={}^{o}N'$, $B_{n+1}=B_n\cup\{b\in B \mid {}^{\bullet}({}^{\bullet}b)\subseteq B_n\}$.

The countability of N implies that all B_n are countable.

Then define $B'_n\subseteq B$ by $B'_n = \{b\in B \mid \max_{l\in L}\{|l\cap[{}^{o}N',b]|\}=(2n+1)\}$.

It is easily proved that $B_n=B'_n$ for all $n\geq 0$.

By ${}^{o}N'$-discreteness, $B = \bigcup_{n\geq 0} B'_n$; hence B is a countable union of countable sets. □3.3

3.4 Construction.

Let $N=(S,T,F,K,M_o)$ be a contact-free system net and let $\sigma=M_o t_1 M_1\ldots$ be a firing sequence of N.

To σ we associate a set $\Pi(\sigma)$ (of, as it will turn out, processes) as follows.

We construct labelled occurrence nets $(N_i,p_i)=(B_i,E_i,F_i,p_i)$, $p_i\colon B_i\cup E_i \to S\cup T$ by induction on i.

i=0. Define $E_o=F_o=\emptyset$ and B_o as containing, for each $s\in S$, $M_o(s)$ new conditions b with $p_o(b)=s$ (this defines p_o as well).

i→i+1. Suppose $(N_i,p_i)=(B_i,E_i,F_i,p_i)$ to be constructed.

By construction, N_i^o is a B-cut corresponding to M_i, i.e. $\forall s\in S\colon M_i(s)=|p_i^{-1}(s)\cap N_i^o|$ (see proposition 3.5 below).

Since M_i enables t_{i+1}, N_i^o contains, for each $s\in {}^{\bullet}t_{i+1}$, at least one condition b with $p_i(b)=s$.

For each $s\in {}^{\bullet}t_{i+1}$ we choose one such condition $b=b(s)$ with $b\in N_i^o\cap p_i^{-1}(s)$; then we add a new event e with $p_{i+1}(e)=t_{i+1}$, such that $(b(s),e)\in F_{i+1}$ for all $s\in {}^{\bullet}t_{i+1}$.

Also, for each $s\in t_{i+1}^{\bullet}$ we add a new condition $b'=b'(s)$ with $p_{i+1}(b')=s$, such that $(e,b'(s))\in F_{i+1}$ for all $s\in t_{i+1}^{\bullet}$.

For $x\in B_i\cup E_i$, of course, $p_{i+1}(x)=p_i(x)$.

If σ is finite, say $|\sigma|=n$ then the construction stops at n, and we put $(N_n,p_n)\in\Pi(\sigma)$.

If σ is infinite then we put $(\cup B_i,\cup E_i,\cup F_i,\cup p_i)\in\Pi(\sigma)$.

3.5 Proposition.

The notation used in construction 3.4 is assumed.
Then $\forall i, 0 \le i$: $\forall s \in S$: $M_i(s) = |p_i^{-1}(s) \cap N_i^{\circ}|$.

Proof: By induction.

i=0. Immediate (notice that ${}^{\circ}N_o = N_o = N_o^{\circ}$).

i→i+1. By 2.4(ii), $\forall s \in S$: $M_{i+1}(s) = M_i(s) - F(s, t_{i+1}) + F(t_{i+1}, s)$.
Hence 3.5 follows immediately by construction. □3.5

The construction is non-deterministic because, in general, there may be more than one $b \in N_i^{\circ} \cap p_i^{-1}(s)$. For example, both processes shown in Figure 1(iii) are in $\Pi(\sigma)$ if σ is the firing sequence shown in Figure 1(ii). However, for 1-safe nets we have:

3.6 Theorem.

Let N be 1-safe, contact-free and let σ be a firing sequence of N. Then $|\Pi(\sigma)| = 1$.

Proof: The construction is in this case deterministic, for suppose $|p_i^{-1}(s) \cap N_i^{\circ}| \ge 2$ for some i and s, then $M_i(s) \ge 2$ by 3.5, contradicting 1-safeness. □3.6

3.7 Theorem. (Consistency of the process axioms w.r.t. construction 3.4)

Let N be contact-free, let σ be a firing sequence of N, and let $\pi = (N', p) \in \Pi(\sigma)$.
Then π satisfies the axioms 3.2.

Proof: It is routine to check the properties 3.2(i,ii,iii,v).
The argument for 3.2(iv) runs as follows.
Suppose σ is infinite (the finite case is easier); then $N' = (B, E, F') = (\cup B_i, \cup E_i, \cup p_i)$.
Suppose $x \in B \cup E$; then $x \in B_i \cup E_i$ for some i.
Define $n = n(x) = \max\{|l| \mid l \in L(N_i)\}$.
First of all, n(x) is well-defined because E_i is a finite set.
Also, the ${}^{\circ}N'$-discreteness condition is satisfied with n=n(x) because in no N_j (j>i) can there be any li-sets between ${}^{\circ}N'$ and x that are larger than n(x). □3.7

3.8 Theorem. (Completeness of the process axioms w.r.t. construction 3.4)

Let N be a finite contact-free system net and let $\pi = (N', p)$ be a process of N.
Then there is a firing sequence σ of N such that $\pi \in \Pi(\sigma)$.

Proof: First we assume $N' = (B, E, F')$ to be finite and we define $n = |E|$.
Because $\le = F^*$ is a partial ordering on E, it is possible to number the elements of E in such a fashion that $E = \{e_1, \ldots, e_n\}$ and $e_j < e_i$ in N' implies j<i.
Now we define sets $c_o, \ldots, c_n \subseteq B$ as follows:
$c_o = {}^{\circ}N'$ and $c_i = (c_{i-1} \setminus {}^{\bullet}e_i) \cup e_i^{\bullet}$ for $1 \le i \le n$. (The pre- and post-sets are w.r.t. F'.)
(The fact that $c_i \subseteq B$ follows by 3.2(ii) and the definition of the c_i.)
Next we claim that the c_i are B-cuts and that ${}^{\bullet}e_{i+1} \subseteq c_i$ for $0 \le i < n$.
This can be done by proving the following auxiliary lemma:

Lemma 1: (i) For $0 \le i \le n$: $c_i \in BC(N')$
(ii) For $0 \le i < n$: (iia) ${}^{\bullet}e_{i+1} \subseteq c_i$
(iib) $\forall j, 1 \le j \le i$: $c_i \cap {}^{\bullet}e_j = \emptyset$
(iic) $\forall j, i < j \le n$: $c_i \cap e_j^{\bullet} = \emptyset$.

Proof: i=0. $c_o \in BC(N')$ by 3.2(ii), whence (i).
${}^{\bullet}e_1 \subseteq c_o$ follows easily because of the numbering of E, whence (iia).
(iib) is vacuously true, and (iic) follows from the definition of $c_o = {}^{\circ}N'$.
i-1→i. This follows in a straightforward way from the definition of c_i together with the induction hypotheses; however, since the proof is slightly tedious we omit it for the sake of brevity. □Lemma 1

Next, define $t_i = p(e_i)$ ($\in T$ because of 3.2(i)).
Further, define markings accordingly as $M_o = M_o$, M_i such that $M_{i-1}[t_i > M_i$ for $1 \le i \le n$.
The M_i are well-defined because of the following:

Lemma 2: For $0 \le i < n$: (i) $\forall s \in S$: $M_i(s) = |p^{-1}(s) \cap c_i|$
(ii) M_i enables t_{i+1}.

Proof: i=0. Then (i) holds because of 3.2(iii).
M_o enables t_1 because of ${}^{\bullet}e_1 \subseteq c_o$ (previous lemma), and by 3.2(v) we have for all $s \in {}^{\bullet}t_1$: $M_o(s) = |p^{-1}(s) \cap c_o| \ge |p^{-1}(s) \cap {}^{\bullet}e_1| = F(s, t_1)$.
i-1→i. The proof is similar, again using 3.2(v). □Lemma 2

This completes the construction of a sequence $\sigma = M_o t_1 \ldots t_n M_n$ such that (as is easily seen) $\pi \in \Pi(\sigma)$.

It remains to settle the case that $\pi = (N', p)$ is infinite; it is here, of course, that property 3.2(iv) comes into play.

First recall that N' is countable (theorem 3.3).

We show that the finiteness of N, together with 3.2(iv), implies that the set E can be numbered such that $E=\{e_1,e_2,...\}$ and $e_j<e_i$ implies j<i.

To show this we need a result on occurrence nets that will be proved later in section 4 (of course, independently of the present theorem).

(The author apologises for some forward references in the remainder in this section, but there was no time to rearrange the paper.)

Because E is countable we may put $E=\{e_1',e_2',...\}$.

Define sets of events E_i (i≥1) by $E_i = E\cap[^{\circ}N',\{e_1',...,e_i'\}]$.

Clearly, $E_i\subseteq E_{i+1}$ and $E = \bigcup_{i\geq 1} E_i$.

Also, the E_i are finite.

To see this, we note that N' is degree-finite (definition 4.5(i)) since N is finite and because of 3.2(v); hence because of 3.2(iv) and theorems 4.6 and 4.7, N' is interval-finite, which implies that [b,e] is finite for all $b\in{}^{\circ}N'$ and $e\in\{e_1',...,e_i'\}$; the finiteness of E_i then follows from $|^{\circ}N'|<\infty$ which is again a consequence of N being finite (and thus having a finite initial marking).

Now the $E_1,E_2,...$ can be numbered successively to give the desired numbering of E.

Finally, the same construction as in the finite case yields an infinite firing sequence $\sigma = M_0t_1M_1...$ with $\pi\in\Pi(\sigma)$. □3.8

Theorems 3.7 and 3.8 give a first answer to the question of relating sequences and processes. They state that, in a sense, the class of objects defined by the process axioms is not principally different from the class of firing sequences. However, note that the completeness theorem relies on the finiteness of the underlying system net N. In fact, it is easily seen that the proof goes through if the finiteness assumption is weakened to degree-finiteness (definition 4.5(i)) and the existence of a finite initial marking. Hence for such nets, there are no processes which satisfy the axioms 3.2 but cannot be derived from firing sequences. For more general infinite system nets, however, the process axioms may well define meaningful objects that are not derivable from firing sequences by construction 3.4. An example is given in Figure

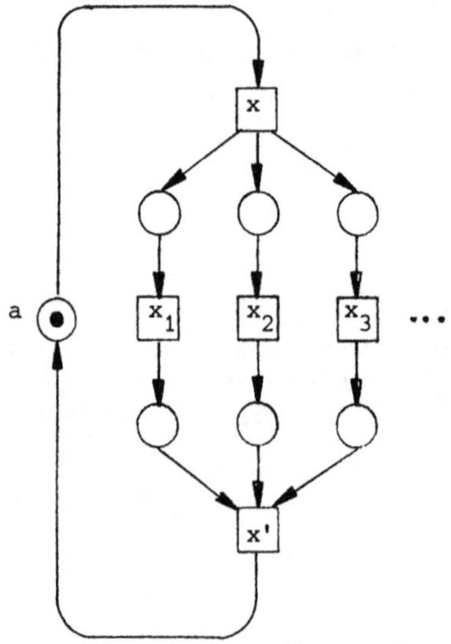

(i) An infinite system net which is not degree-finite

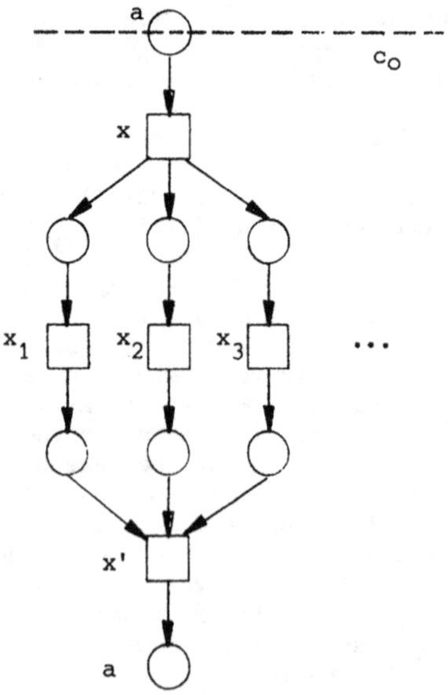

(ii) A process of (i) which is c_o-discrete but neither degree-finite nor interval-finite

Figure 4

There is clearly no firing sequence that can generate the process shown in Figure 4(ii). For example, an attempt $xx_1x_2...$ fails to include transition x'.

Step sequences which have been introduced in [11] as generalisations of firing sequences are able to handle the situation depicted in Figure 4. The idea is that, for example, the set of transitions $\{x_1,x_2,...\}$ in Figure 4 can occur "in one step". The process shown in Figure 4(ii) then consists of (at least) three steps.

3.9 Definition.

Let (S,T,F,K) be a net with capacities, $T_o \subseteq T$ and M a marking of (S,T,F,K).

(i) M concurrently enables the transitions in T_o iff
$\forall s \in S$: $|s^\bullet \cap T_o| \leq M(s) \leq K(s) - |{}^\bullet s \cap T_o|$ (compare 2.4(i))

(ii) M' is produced from M by the concurrent occurrence of all transitions in T_o ("in one step", in symbols: $M[T_o>M'$) iff M concurrently enables T_o and
$\forall s \in S$: $M'(s) = M(s) - |s^\bullet \cap T_o| + |{}^\bullet s \cap T_o|$

(iii) For a system net $N=(S,T,F,K,M_o)$, $M_oT_1M_1...$ is a step sequence iff
$\forall i \geq 1$: $M_{i-1}[T_i>M_i$.

Clearly, every firing sequence is also a step sequence but not vice versa (Figure 4).

In the terminology of [31], 3.9 defines the "simple steps". [31] also introduces a generalised notion of step sequences by allowing transitions to occur concurrently with themselves in one step. It may be conjectured that an analogon of construction 3.4 may be defined for step sequences rather than firing sequences and that the process axioms are essentially complete (in general) with respect to such a construction. However, this question will not be pursued in this paper.

Summarising this section, we have considered a construction by which the concurrent behaviour (the processes) of a Petri net can be associated with the interleaved behaviour of the net (the firing sequences) in an intuitive way. As the main result, we have identified a class of system nets, viz. those that are degree-finite and have a finite initial marking, for which this construction yields exactly the processes as defined by the process axioms 3.2. In a way, this settles the principal question. However, nothing is said about how "nicely" (or not) processes correspond to firing sequences. This question will be returned to in section 5 below. First, however, we will examine the c-discreteness axiom in more detail.

4. C-DISCRETENESS AND OTHER AXIOMS OF OCCURRENCE NETS

We will consider several possible alternatives of the c-discreteness axiom 3.2(iv) that have been considered in the literature, namely E-discreteness [2,4,9] (definition 4.1(i)), b-discreteness [10,27] (definition 4.1(ii)), observability [10,33] (definition 4.2) and generability [10,14] (definition 4.3). Because c-discreteness distinguishes occurrence nets with respect to a cut c, it discriminates the admissible structures slightly differently than does, for example, b-discreteness; e.g., consider Figure 5 below.

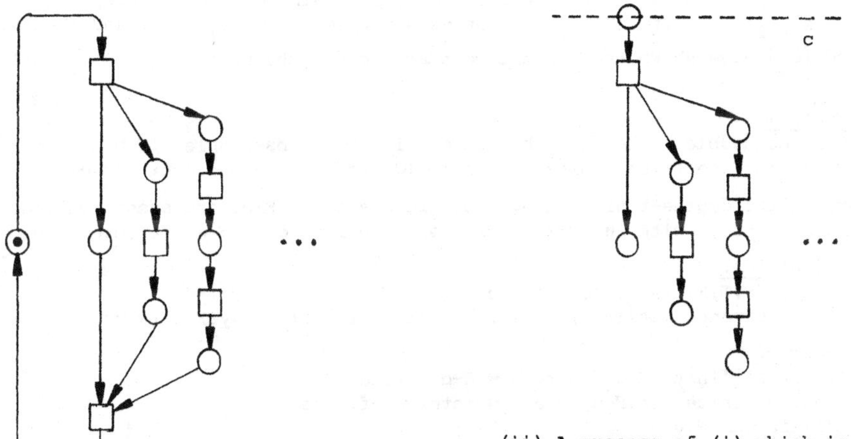

(i) An infinite system net

(ii) A process of (i) which is both b-discrete and c-discrete

Figure 5

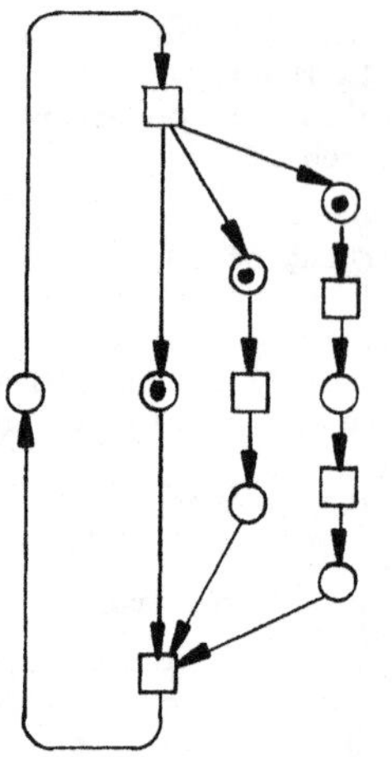

(iii) The same net as (i) with a different initial marking

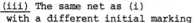

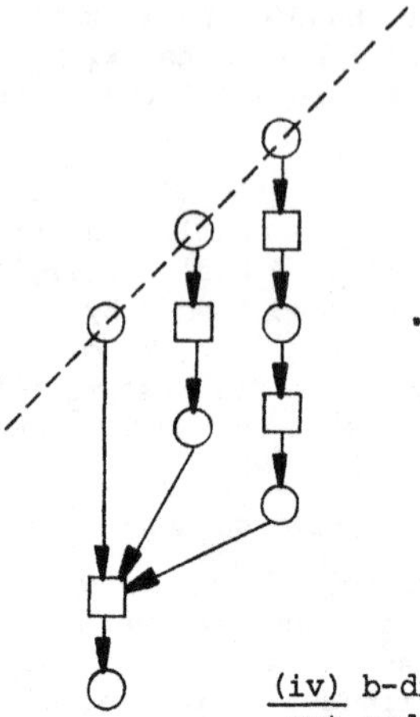

(iv) b-discrete but not c-discrete, hence not a process of (iii)

Figure 5 (continued)

The occurrence nets shown in Figures 5(ii) and 5(iv) are similar. Both are b-discrete (and hence, by theorem 4.4 below, also observable and generable). Yet c-discreteness is so tuned that the first describes a process and the second doesn't.

In the following, let N=(B,E,F) be an occurrence net and let $(X,\leq)$ be the associated poset, i.e. $X=B\cup E$, $\leq=F^*$.

4.1 Definition. [2 ,27]

(i) N is E-discrete iff $\forall x,y\in X\ \forall l\in L: |[x,y]\cap l|<\infty$

(ii) N is b-discrete iff $\forall x,y\in X\ \exists n=n(x,y)\ \forall l\in L: |[x,y]\cap l|\leq n$.

4.2 Definition. [33]

N is observable iff $\exists f: X\to\mathbb{Z}$ such that $\forall x,y\in X$: $x<y$ in N implies $f(x)<f(y)$.

4.3 Definition. [10,14]

(i) $(X',\leq')$ is a sub-poset of $(X,\leq)$ iff $X'\subseteq X$ and $\leq'=\leq\cap(X'\times X')$

(ii) $(X',\leq')$ is chain-bounded iff $\exists n=n(X')\ \forall l\in L(X',\leq'): |l|\leq n$

(iii) $(X',\leq')$ is a convex sub-poset of $(X,\leq)$ iff $(X',\leq')$ is a sub-poset and, in addition, $\forall x,y\in X'\ \forall z\in X$: $x\leq z\leq y$ implies $z\in X'$

(iv) $(X,\leq)$ (and N) is generable iff there are chain-bounded sub-posets $(X_1,\leq_1)$, $(X_2,\leq_2),\ldots$ s.t. $(X_i,\leq_i)$ is convex sub-poset of $(X_{i+1},\leq_{i+1})$ and $(X,\leq)=(\bigcup X_i,\bigcup\leq_i$

[10] and [33] have shown that in the countable case, the properties just mentioned coincide:

4.4 Theorem.

Let N be countable. Then N is b-discrete iff N is observable iff N is generable.

Proof: [33] for the first equivalence and [10] for the second equivalence. □4.4

Further, in the degree-finite case, b-discreteness and E-discreteness coincide. In fact, both coincide with interval-finiteness (definition 4.5 and theorem 4.6).

4.5 Definition.

(i) A net (S,T,F) is degree-finite iff $\forall x\in T: |{}^\bullet x|<\infty \wedge |x^\bullet|<\infty$

(ii) An occurrence net (B,E,F) is interval-finite iff $\forall x,y\in X: |[x,y]|<\infty$.

4.6 Theorem.

(i) Interval-finite ⇒ b-discrete ⇒ E-discrete

(ii) Degree-finite and E-discrete ⇒ interval-finite.

Proof: (i) is immediate.

(ii): Suppose $x,y\in E$ such that the interval between x and y is infinite, then a construction similar to König's lemma yields an infinite li-set between x and y. □4.6

Next we show a connection between c-discreteness and b-discreteness.

4.7 Theorem.

(i) ($\exists c$: N is c-discrete) $\Rightarrow$ N is b-discrete

(ii) N is b-discrete and $|c|<\infty \Rightarrow$ N is c-discrete.

Proof: (i): By contradiction.

If N is not b-discrete then there are $x,y\in X$, $x<y$, such that the li-sets between x and y are of unbounded length.

Assume $c\in C$.

If $y\leq z$ for some $z\in c$ then the c-discreteness condition is violated for x.

If $z\leq x$ for some $z\in c$ then the c-discreteness condition is violated for y.

If $x<z_1$ and $z_2<y$ for $z_1,z_2\in c$ then assume N to be c-discrete and put $n_1=n_1(x)$, $n_2=n_2(y)$ according to definition 3.1.

Since by assumption N is not b-discrete, there is a line l with $|[x,y]\cap l|>n_1+n_2$.

By considering the elements of $[x,y]\cap l$, it is easy to see that either $|[x,c]\cap l|>n_1$ or $|[c,y]\cap l|>n_2$, contradiction.

Hence N is not c-discrete, and no other cases remain.

(ii): It suffices to define $n(x) = \max\{n(x,y) \mid y\in c\}$, where $n(x,y)$ are the numbers that exist by the b-discreteness definition 4.1(ii). □4.7

Together, theorems 4.4, 4.6 and 4.7 show that for system nets which are degree-finite and have a finite initial marking, axiom 3.2(iv) is interchangeable with any of the properties defined in 4.1-4.3. However, it is clear (from the proof of 4.4) how observability and generability can replace c-discreteness even in the general case. For observability, it must be required in addition that the initial cut $^{O}N'$ is assigned a particular number, say 0, by the function f defined in 4.2. For generability, the requirement must be added that $(X_1,\leq_1)=(^{O}N',\emptyset)$ is the first sub-poset defined in 4.3(iv). (These remarks hold only because by 3.3 the occurrence nets in question are countable; [33] contains a tricky example of an uncountable poset that is b-discrete but not observable.)

To start the final part of this section, we draw the reader's attention to the fact that the condition $|c|<\infty$ in 4.7(ii) is not easily replaced. In particular, degree-finiteness is not enough for b-discreteness to imply c-discreteness for all c. A counterexample is shown in Figure 6.

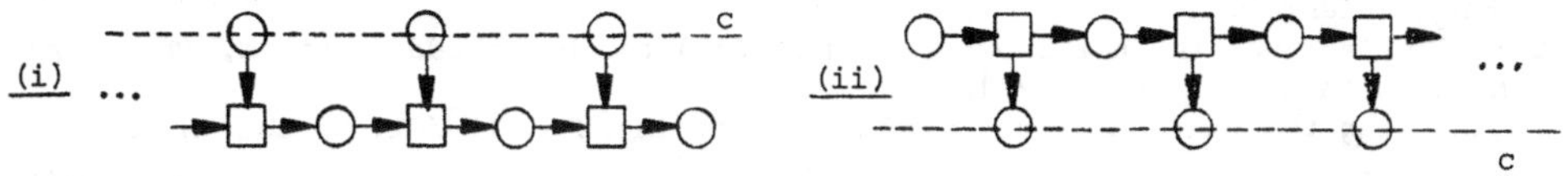

Figure 6: Occurrence nets which are b-discrete and degree-finite but not c-discrete

The nets shown in Figure 6 are not K-dense. K-density has been proposed in [ ] as another meaningful property of occurrence nets. In the remainder of this section we will study its relationship to c-discreteness.

4.8 Definition.

An occurrence net is K-dense iff $\forall c\in C\ \forall l\in L$: $c\cap l \neq \emptyset$.

The idea behind this definition is based on the interpretations of the lines l as the sequential subprocesses, and the cuts c as states, of an occurrence net. K-density requires that every state c determinas a local state $c\cap l$ of every sequential subprocess l (of course, $|c\cap l|\leq 1$ in general).

4.9 Theorem.

If N is K-dense then N is E-discrete.

Proof: See [1]. □4.9

With 4.6, 4.9 implies that K-density is stronger than b-discreteness, provided degree-finiteness is assumed. Hence K-density could conceivably replace c-discreteness in the axiom 3.2(iv), entailing the same consequences. However, Figure 6 shows that the implication is strict. Hence the set of processes resulting if K-density is used in place of 3.2(iv) corresponds to a certain subclass of system nets. [14] have shown that this is exactly the class of (contact-free) safe nets; see Figure 7 and theorem 4.10.

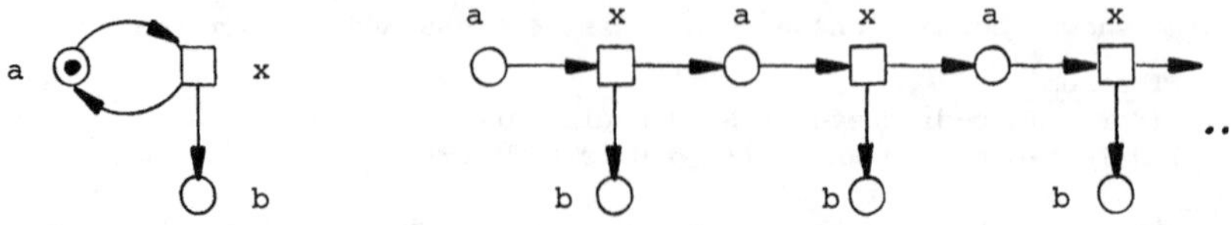

(i) An unsafe system net (ii) A non-K-dense process of (i)

Figure 7

4.10 Theorem.
Let N be a finite contact-free system net.
Then N has only K-dense processes iff N is safe.

Proof: See [14]. □4.10

The connection between K-density and c-discreteness (which so far goes via 4.9, 4.6 and 4.7) can be made stronger as follows:

4.11 Theorem.
Let N=(B,E,F) be degree-finite.
Then N is K-dense iff $\forall c \in C$: N is c-discrete.

Proof: (⇐): Suppose N is not K-dense.
Using the characterisation of K-density proved in [1], one of the nets shown in Figure 6 can be embedded into N.
Hence there is some cut c for which N is not c-discrete.
(Degree-finiteness is not needed for this implication.)
(⇒): Suppose N is not c-discrete for some cut c, and suppose $x \in X$ violates the c-discreteness condition.
Suppose $x<z$ for some $z \in c$; the case $z<x$ for $z \in c$ is analogous.
Put $x=x_o$.
By degree-finiteness, $|{}^{\bullet}x_o|<\infty$, and hence there is some $x_1 \in {}^{\bullet}x_o$ which again violates the c-discreteness condition.
Continuing in this way we find an infinitely descending li-set $\ldots<x_1<x_o$ (again König's lemma).
This implies that the net shown in Figure 6(i) can be embedded into N. (This argument is in detail in [1 ,29].)
Again using the characterisation of K-density in [1], it follows that N is not K-dense. □4.11

Hence requiring c-discreteness for all c in place of 3.2(iv) (which requires c-discreteness only for the initial cut) restricts the class of systems to the safe ones.

To summarise this section, several meaningful axioms of occurrence nets can be defined and shown equivalent to axiom 3.2(iv), at least for countable and degree-finite system nets with finite initial markings. Further, it has been shown that K-density is essentially stronger than 3.2(iv) and corresponds to "nice" system behaviour. Thus, as far as the process axioms themselves are concerned, the overall picture seems to be reasonably clear. It may be mentioned that other process properties properties, notably D-continuity [26], have been studied and their system correlates have been found [5], and that these results have been generalised to posets [29].

5. RELATIONSHIP BETWEEN PROCESSES AND SEQUENCES

In this section we return to examine the question posed at the end of section 3. There we have argued (with theorems 3.7 and 3.8) that it is in principle possible to find a correspondence between processes and firing sequences for system nets that are degree-finite and have a finite initial marking. In this section we restrict ourselves to such nets and we ask the question: Is any more detailed view of this correspondence possible, e.g. by equating processes with equivalence sets of sequences?

The first and obvious answer to this question is to consider the set of linearisations of a process:

5.1 Definition.

Let $N=(S,T,F,K,M_o)$ be contact-free and let $\pi=(N',p)$ be a process of N

$Lin(\pi) = \{\sigma \mid \sigma$ is firing sequence of N and $\pi \in \Pi(\sigma)\}$.

The idea is, of course, that π can be retrieved by intersecting the order of transition occurrences in $Lin(\pi)$. W.Reisig was the first to notice that π may not uniquely be determined by $Lin(\pi)$. His example [31] is given in Figure 9.

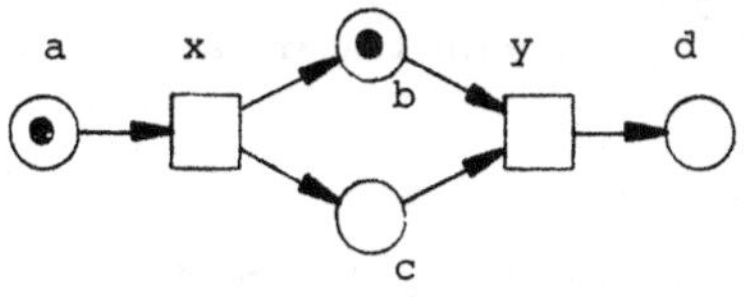

(i) A system net

$$\begin{pmatrix} a \\ b \end{pmatrix} x \begin{pmatrix} bb \\ c \end{pmatrix} y \begin{pmatrix} b \\ d \end{pmatrix} = \sigma$$

(ii) A firing sequence of (i)

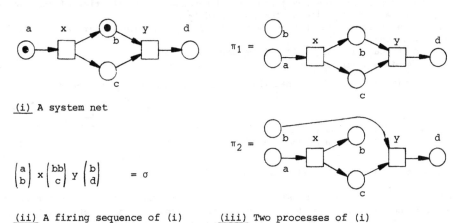

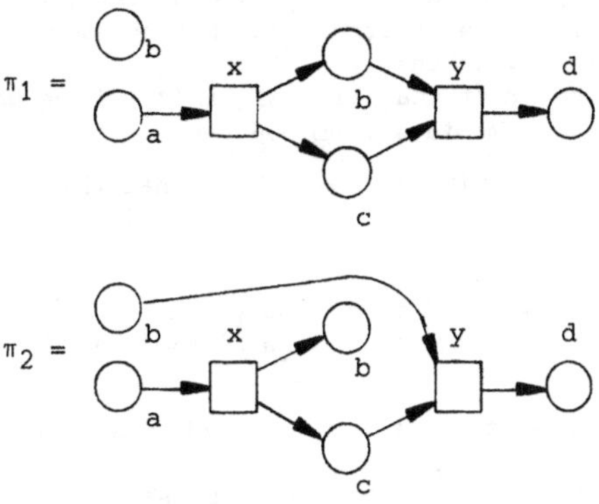

(iii) Two processes of (i)

Figure 9: Two processes with the same Lin-set

For the system shown in Figure 9 we have $\pi_1 \neq \pi_2$ but $Lin(\pi_1)=Lin(\pi_2)=\{\sigma\}$. The problem is that the two tokens on place b are distinguished by the two processes π_1 and π_2 while they are not distinguished in σ. [31] proposes, therefore, to define two processes equivalent if the partial order of event occurrences agrees in both. We denote this equivalence by $\approx$ (definition 5.2). Henceforth N is assumed to be contact-free.

5.2 Definition.

Let $\pi_1=(B_1,E_1,F_1,p_1)$ and $\pi_2=(B_2,E_2,F_2,p_2)$ be processes of N.

Then $\pi_1 \approx \pi_2$ iff $\exists$bijection β: $E_1 \to E_2$ such that (i) $\forall e \in E_1$: $p_1(e)=p_2(\beta(e))$

(ii) $\forall e,e' \in E_1$: $e <_1 e' \Leftrightarrow \beta(e) <_2 \beta(e')$.

Even so, there is only a partial relationship between the Lin-sets 5.1 and the $\approx$-equivalence classes of processes, according to the following theorem:

5.3 Theorem.

Let $\pi_1=(B_1,E_1,F_1,p_1)$ and $\pi_2=(B_2,E_2,F_2,p_2)$ be processes of N.

Then (i) $\pi_1 \approx \pi_2$ implies $Lin(\pi_1)=Lin(\pi_2)$

(ii) If N is 1-safe then $Lin(\pi_1)=Lin(\pi_2)$ implies $\pi_1=\pi_2$.

Before proving this theorem it is necessary to be a bit more precise about firing sequences. In a sequence $\sigma = M_o t_1 M_1 t_2 \ldots$ we call the transition indices, i.e. 1,2,... the "positions" of σ and t_i is the "label" of position i. If $\pi=(B,E,F,p) \in \Pi(\sigma)$ $(E \neq \emptyset)$ then it is clear from construction 3.4 that the events of π and the positions of can be brought into bijective correspondence with each other. For any such correspondence, we denote by $pos(e,\sigma)$ the position in σ that corresponds to $e \in E$; of course, $p(e)$ equals $t_{pos(e,\sigma)}$. Conversely, for a position i in σ $(i \geq 1)$ we denote by $event(i,\pi)$ the event in E that corresponds to position i; again, $t_i=p(event(i,\pi))$. Using this notation we prove an auxiliary lemma:

Lemma: Let $\pi=(B,E,F,p)$ be a process of N and let $e,e' \in E$.

Then $e<e'$ in π iff $\forall \sigma \in Lin(\pi)$: $pos(e,\sigma)<pos(e',\sigma)$ (for all correspondences between π and σ).

Proof: ($\Rightarrow$): Suppose $e<e'$ and $\sigma \in Lin(\pi)$, i.e. $\pi \in \Pi(\sigma)$.

By construction 3.4, clearly, $pos(e,\sigma)<pos(e',\sigma)$.

($\Leftarrow$): Suppose $(e,e') \in co$ in π.

Then the linearisation of E applied in theorem 3.8 can be specified so that $pos(e',\sigma)<pos(e,\sigma)$ in some $\sigma \in Lin(\pi)$. □Lemma

This lemma essentially states that the ordering in π is the intersection of the orderings in the sequences of $Lin(\pi)$; this is noteworthy because for infinite π, $Lin(\pi)$ does not contain all possible linearisations of π (just the ones that are order-isomorphic to $\mathbb{N}$).

Proof of 5.3:

(i): Suppose $\pi_1 \approx \pi_2$ and $\sigma \in Lin(\pi_1)$; we prove that $\sigma \in Lin(\pi_2)$.

By the above lemma, the positions in σ determine a linearisation of the events in π_1, hence by $\pi_1 \approx \pi_2$ also of the events in π_2.

Since the construction in theorem 3.8 works for all such linearisations, $\pi_2 \in \Pi(\sigma)$, i.e. $\sigma \in Lin(\pi_2)$.

The proof that $Lin(\pi_2) \subseteq Lin(\pi_1)$ is symmetric.

(ii): Immediate from 3.6 □5.3

The following example shows that the converse of 5.3(i) does not hold:

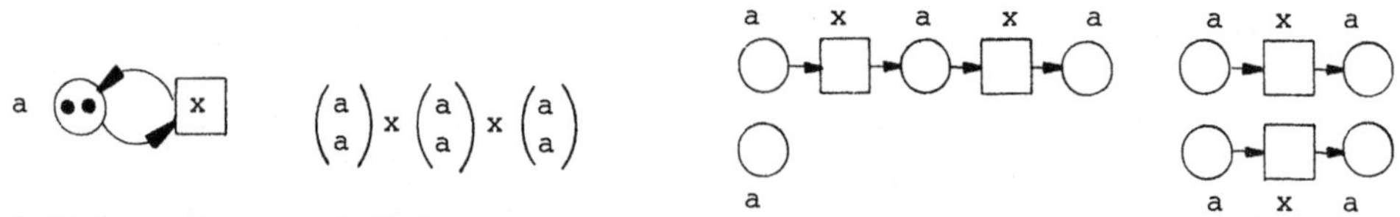

A system net A firing sequence Two processes

There is also a different sense in which 5.3 is unsatisfactory. Since the Lin-sets are presently defined in a roundabout way via the processes, the question arises whether or not there is a more direct way of defining them, say as equivalence classes of a relation defined only on sequences. If so, then the correspondence between sequences and processes would be more clear: $\approx$-classes of processes correspond to independently definable Lin-sets, and vice versa. In the following we will provide a partial answer to this question.

The special case of 1-safe nets points to a possible approach. In 1-safe nets, the Lin-sets define a partitioning of the set of firing sequences, i.e. if $\pi_1 \not\approx \pi_2$ then $Lin(\pi_1) \cap Lin(\pi_2) \neq \emptyset$ (which is not true in general, see Figure 10 below). Furthermore, for finite firing sequences, [21] has shown that every such equivalence class can be generated by a so-called independence relation which can be defined directly on the sequences (even directly on the underlying system net). Below we will retrieve this result and generalise it to infinite sequences. Essentially, the idea is to call two sequences equivalent if they differ only in the order of neighbouring concurrent transition occurrences (this will be called the $\equiv$-equivalence below), and to build the Lin-sets using this equivalence.

The situation is much less clear in the general case. Consider definition 5.4 and Figure 10 for what can go wrong.

5.4 Definition.

Let N be a system net and let σ_1, σ_2 be firing sequences of N.

(i) $\sigma_1 \equiv_o \sigma_2$ iff $\sigma_1 = \sigma_{11} t M_1 t' \sigma_{12}$ and $\sigma_2 = \sigma_{21} t' M t \sigma_{22}$ such that $\sigma_{11} = \sigma_{12}$, $\sigma_{12} = \sigma_{22}$, and the last marking of σ_{11} (and hence also of σ_{21}) concurrently enables $\{t,t'\}$. (See definition 3.9(i).)

(ii) Let σ_1 and σ_2 be finite.
$\sigma_1 \equiv \sigma_2$ iff $(\sigma_1,\sigma_2) \in \equiv_o^*$ (where $\equiv_o^*$ is the reflexive and transitive closure of $\equiv_o$).

Clearly, $\equiv$ is an equivalence relation on the set of finite firing sequences of N. $\equiv_o$ means that σ_1 and σ_2 differ only in the ordering of two adjacent concurrently enabled transitions, and $\equiv$ is the closure of $\equiv_o$ (for finite sequences).

Figure 10 shows two processes which are not $\approx$-equivalent but whose Lin-sets overlap (i.e. do not define a partitioning of the set of firing sequences). Furthermore, the $\equiv$-equivalence class shown in Figure 10(ii) agrees neither with $Lin(\pi_1)$ nor with $Lin(\pi_2)$ where π_1 and π_2 are the processes shown in Figure 10(iii). Hence even modulo $\approx$-equivalence, the process notion distinguishes more finely than does the $\equiv$-equivalence on firing sequences.

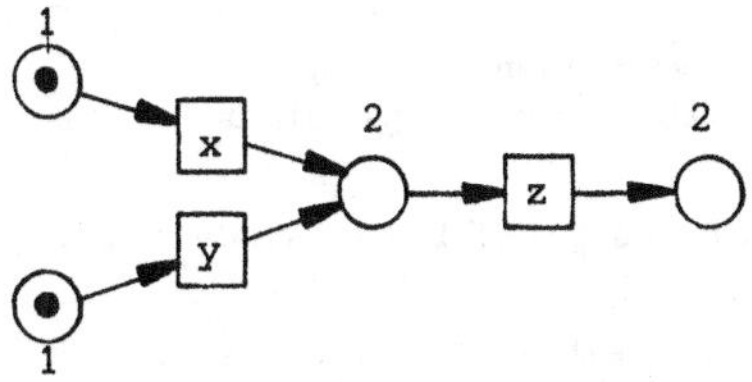

(i) A system net

{ xzy , xyz , yxz , yzx }

(ii) A ≡-equivalence class of firing sequences (markings omitted)

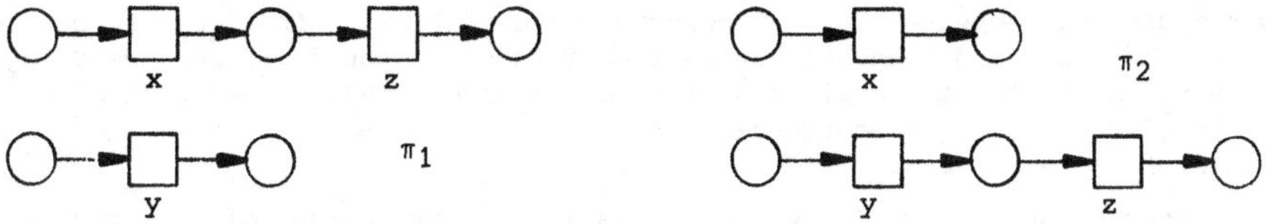

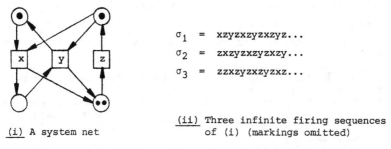

(iii) Two processes of (i)

Figure 10: Processes whose Lin-sets overlap and are not ≡-equivalence classes

If not ≈, what then is the equivalence on processes that corresponds to ≡ (if there is any)? In the remainder of this section we will answer this question. In order to do so in general, we first have to generalise ≡ to infinite sequences. Consider Figure 11 to see that the reflexive transitive closure $\equiv_0^*$ may not work in the infinite case.

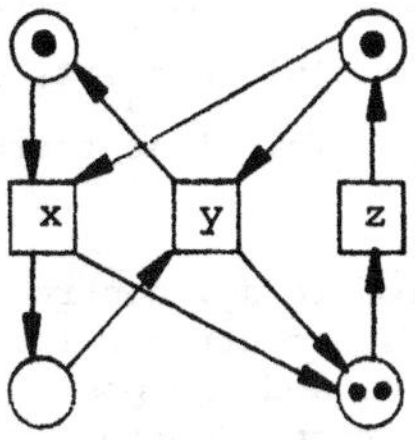

(i) A system net

σ_1 = xzyzxzyzxzyz...

σ_2 = zxzyzxzyzxzy...

σ_3 = zzxzyzxzyzxz...

(ii) Three infinite firing sequences of (i) (markings omitted)

Figure 11: Illustrating the definition of ≡

One would like to define σ_1, σ_2 and σ_3 in Figure 11(ii) to be ≡-related because they can be derived from each other by exchanging neighbouring concurrently enabled transitions; however, a finite number of such exchanges is not enough. Figure 11 also shows the following: Let us attempt to call $\sigma \equiv \sigma'$ if every finite prefix of σ can be extended to a prefix of σ which is $\equiv_0^*$-related to a prefix of σ' (and vice versa). Then in Figure 11(ii), $\sigma_1 \equiv \sigma_2$ and $\sigma_2 \equiv \sigma_3$ but not $\sigma_1 \equiv \sigma_3$. Hence we propose the following definition:

5.5 Definition.

Let σ_1 and σ_2 be infinite firing sequences of N.

(i) Let $n \in N$; then $\sigma_1 \,{}_n\!= \sigma_2$ iff $\exists \sigma, w_1, w_2\colon |\sigma| = n \wedge \sigma_1 = \sigma w_1 \wedge \sigma_2 = \sigma w_2$
(i.e. σ_1 agrees with σ_2 on a prefix of length n)
and $\sigma_1 =_n \sigma_2$ iff $\exists \sigma, \sigma', w\colon |\sigma| = |\sigma'| = n \wedge \sigma_1 = \sigma w \wedge \sigma_2 = \sigma' w$
(i.e. σ_1 agrees with σ_2 from position n onwards)

(ii) $\sigma_1 \equiv \sigma_2$ iff $\forall n \in N \; \exists \sigma_1', \sigma_2'\colon (\sigma_1 \equiv_0^* \sigma_1' \wedge \sigma_1' \,{}_n\!= \sigma_2 \wedge \sigma_2 \equiv_0^* \sigma_2' \wedge \sigma_2' \,{}_n\!= \sigma_1)$.

In other words, $\sigma_1 \equiv \sigma_2$ iff for any arbitrarily long prefix, σ_1 can be $\equiv_0^*$-transformed into another sequence that agrees with σ_2 on that prefix, and vice versa. Clearly, when applied to finite sequences, 5.5(ii) comes to the same as 5.4(ii), i.e. the two definitions are consistent.

5.6 Theorem.

$\equiv$ is an equivalence relation on the set of firing sequences of N.

Proof: Only the transitivity for infinite sequences poses any problems.

Assume $\sigma_1 \equiv \sigma_2$, $\sigma_2 \equiv \sigma_3$ (σ_i infinite) and $n \in \mathbb{N}$.

We prove $\exists \sigma: \sigma_1 \equiv_o^* \sigma \wedge \sigma \;_n{=}\; \sigma_3$ (the other half of the proof being symmetrical).

By $\sigma_2 \equiv \sigma_3$, $\exists \sigma_2'$: $\sigma_2 \equiv_o^* \sigma_2'$ and $\sigma_2' \;_n{=}\; \sigma_3$.

That is, there are sequences $\tau_1, \ldots, \tau_m$: $\sigma_2 = \tau_1 \wedge \tau_m = \sigma_2' \wedge \tau_j \equiv_o \tau_{j+1}$ $(1 \le j < m)$.

Let q be a number such that $\tau_1 =_q \ldots =_q \tau_m$, i.e. that the τ_j differ only at prefixes of length q; clearly, such a number exists and can even be taken $\ge n$.

Because of $\sigma_1 \equiv \sigma_2$, $\exists \sigma_1'$: $\sigma_1 \equiv_o^* \sigma_1'$ and $\sigma_1' \;_q{=}\; \sigma_2$.

Now the desired sequence σ can be constructed as follows: first, σ_1 can be $\equiv_o^*$-transformed into σ_1', and then, σ_1' can be transformed (as could σ_2, because σ_1 agrees with σ_2 on the first q positions) into a sequence σ that agrees with σ_2' on a prefi of length n: $\sigma \;_n{=}\; \sigma_2'$ (because $q \ge n$).

Because of $\sigma_2' \;_n{=}\; \sigma_3$ we also have $\sigma \;_n{=}\; \sigma_3$. □5.6

The next theorem shows that if two sequences are linearisations of a common process then they are $\equiv$-related. Using this result an equivalence relation on processes that corresponds to $\equiv$ may be defined (definition 5.8 below).

5.7 Theorem.

Let σ_1 and σ_2 be two firing sequences of a contact-free system net N.

Then $\Pi(\sigma_1) \cap \Pi(\sigma_2) \neq \emptyset$ implies $\sigma_1 \equiv \sigma_2$.

Proof: Let $\pi = (N', p) = (B, E, F', p)$ be a process that can be derived from both σ_1 and σ_2.

Suppose $\sigma_1 = M_o t_1 M_1 t_2 \ldots$ and $\sigma_2 = M_o' t_1' M_1' t_2' \ldots$

Again we consider σ_1 and σ_2 as sequences of positions i,j etc. with labels t_i, t_j etc. We shall in this proof use "unprimed" indices i,j,... to denote positions in σ_1, and "primed" indices i',j',... to denote positions in σ_2 (thus, $t_{i'} = t_{i'}'$).

We define a correspondence γ between the positions of σ_1 and the positions of σ_2 by

$$(i,i') \in \gamma \quad \text{iff} \quad t_i = t_{i'} \text{ and } |\{j \mid j \le i \wedge t_j = t_i\}| = |\{j' \mid j' \le i' \wedge t_{j'} = t_{i'}\}|$$

(i.e. in σ_1 there are as many positions labelled t_i before i as there are in σ_2 before i').

Clearly, $|\gamma(i)| \le 1$ always.

If $\gamma(i) = \emptyset$ then event(i,π) has no corresponding position in σ_2, contradicting $\sigma_2 \in Lin(\pi)$; similarly, the assumption $\gamma^{-1}(i') = \emptyset$ gives a contradiction.

Hence γ defines a bijection between the positions of σ_1 and the positions of σ_2.

Let (i,j) and (i',j') be pairs of corresponding transition occurrences, i.e. $i' = \gamma(i)$ and $j' = \gamma(j)$; we call these pairs interchanged iff $(i<i' \wedge j>j') \vee (i>i' \wedge j<j')$.

Now fix some number $n \in \mathbb{N}$.

We shall prove that $\exists \sigma: \sigma_1 \equiv_o^* \sigma \wedge \sigma \;_n{=}\; \sigma_2$ (the other half of the proof being analogous

The crucial fact is the following:

Lemma: Suppose $\sigma_1 \;_n{\neq}\; \sigma_2$.

Then there exists an index i in σ_1 such that $(i,i+1)$ and $(\gamma(i),\gamma(i+1))$ are interchanged pairs of indices, M_{i-1} concurrently enables $\{t_i, t_{i+1}\}$, and furthermore, $i+1 \le j$ where $j = \max\{k \mid \gamma(k) \le n\}$.

This lemma states that under the assumption given, one can find, in σ_1, two neighbouring interchangeable transitions whose exchange would bring σ_1 closer to σ_2 on the prefix of length n (because t_{i+1} is the transition that doesn't match with t_j' yet).

The lemma can be proved by choosing i such that $\gamma(i+1) = j'$ where $j' = \min\{k' \mid \sigma_1 \;_{k'}{\neq}\; \sigma_2\}$ j' exists and is smaller than n+1 because of $\sigma_1 \;_n{\neq}\; \sigma_2$.

The proof that M_{i-1} concurrently enables $\{t_i, t_{i+1}\}$ relies on the fact that $\pi \in \Pi(\sigma_1) \cap \Pi(\sigma_2)$; it is slightly lengthy and is therefore omitted. □Lemma

Starting from σ_1, t_{i+1} can be exchanged with its predecessors exactly (i+1-j') times such that the resulting sequence agrees with σ_2 on a prefix of at least length j'+1.

The procedure is repeatable, whence the result. □5.7

Figure 10 shows that the reverse implication of 5.7 does not hold. In Figure 10(ii) we have xzy$\equiv$yzx but $\Pi(xzy) \cap \Pi(yzx) = \{\pi_1\} \cap \{\pi_2\} = \emptyset$.

5.8 Definition.

Let π_1 and π_2 be processes of N.

$\pi_1 \equiv \pi_2$ iff $\exists\sigma_1, \sigma_2: \sigma_1\in Lin(\pi_1) \wedge \sigma_2\in Lin(\pi_2) \wedge \sigma_1\equiv\sigma_2$.

5.9 Corollary.

$\equiv$ is an equivalence relation on the set of processes of N.

Proof: Immediate from 5.6, 5.7, 5.8. □5.9

The next corollary shows that $\approx$ is finer than $\equiv$. The inequality given in 5.10 is strict; e.g. in Figure 10(iii), $\pi_1\equiv\pi_2$ but $\pi_1\not\approx\pi_2$.

5.10 Corollary.

$\approx \subseteq \equiv$.

Proof: $\pi_1 \approx \pi_2 \Rightarrow Lin(\pi_1)=Lin(\pi_2)$ by 5.3 $\Rightarrow \pi_1 \equiv \pi_2$ by definition. □5.10

Further, the $\equiv$-equivalence classes of processes and the $\equiv$-equivalence classes of sequences correspond uniquely to each other. That is, considering Lin (Π, respectively) as relations between processes and sequences (sequences and processes, respectively) we may write $Lin=\Pi^{-1}$, $\Pi=Lin^{-1}$, and furthermore:

5.11 Corollary.

(i) $(\Pi\circ\equiv\circ Lin) \subseteq \equiv$

(ii) $(Lin\circ\equiv\circ\Pi) \subseteq \equiv$

Proof: (i): Suppose $\pi_1\in\Pi(\sigma_1)$, $\pi_1\equiv\pi_2$, $\sigma_2\in Lin(\pi_2)$; we prove $\sigma_1\equiv\sigma_2$.

$\pi_1\equiv\pi_2 \Rightarrow \exists\sigma_1'\in Lin(\pi_1), \sigma_2'\in Lin(\pi_2): \sigma_1'\equiv\sigma_2'$.

$\sigma_1\equiv\sigma_1'$ and $\sigma_2\equiv\sigma_2'$ by 5.7, so $\sigma_1\equiv\sigma_2$ by the transitivity of $\equiv$.

(ii): Immediate from definition 5.8 □5.11

Having proved these results slightly clarifies the overall picture. The equivalence $\equiv$ partitions the set of firing sequences and the set of processes into equivalence classes such that the relations Π and Lin define a bijection on these classes (see Figure 12(i)). Within one such pair of equivalence classes (see Figure 12(ii)) the class of processes can be further partitioned according to the $\approx$ relation; the resulting subclasses correspond to their Lin-sets, but not in a unique way; furthermore, the latter may overlap.

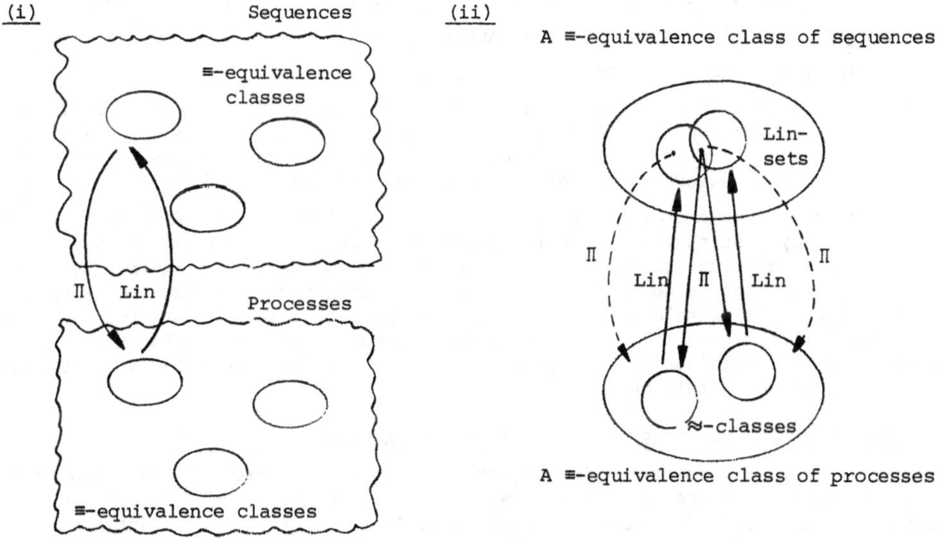

Figure 12: Correspondence between Sequences and Processes

It is not easy to interpret this correspondence. Thinking only in terms of sequences, it does appear that $\equiv$-related sequences should be considered the same. However, thinking in terms of processes, it can be argued that $\equiv$ is too coarse; indeed the processes shown in Figure 10(iii) do describe different behaviour, if only distinguished by distinguishing the two tokens on the same place. Thus ≈, but not necessarily ≡, describes a class of behaviours that should be undistinguishable.

For 1-safe nets, the correspondence just outlined becomes much simpler. In theorem 5.12 below we will show that ≡ (and hence also ≈) reduces to identity for 1-safe nets. This implies that every process corresponds uniquely to its Lin-set, and that the latter, moreover, coincides with a certain ≡-equivalence class of sequences.

5.12 Theorem.

Let N be 1-safe and let π_1,π_2 be processes of N. Then $\pi_1 \equiv \pi_2$ implies $\pi_1 = \pi_2$.

Proof: It is sufficient to prove the converse of 5.7, i.e. $\sigma_1 \equiv \sigma_2 \Rightarrow \Pi(\sigma_1) \cap \Pi(\sigma_2) \neq \emptyset$; the result then follows from 3.6.

So suppose σ_1 and σ_2 are firing sequences of N and $\sigma_1 \equiv \sigma_2$.

Say, $\Pi(\sigma_1) = \{\pi\}$ (cf. 3.6).

We claim that in the construction 3.4 of π from σ_1, whenever a new position i+1 in σ_1 is considered, we always have that $e < event(i+1, \pi_{i+1})$ for $e \in E_i$ implies $pos(e,\sigma_2) < pos(event(i+1, \pi_{i+1}), \sigma_2)$ in σ_2.

Suppose otherwise, then it can easily be seen that E_i contains events e and e' with $p(e)=t$, $p(e')=t'$, $(e,e') \in F_i^2$ and $pos(e,\sigma_2) > pos(e',\sigma_2)$.

However, this means that $t^{\bullet} \cap {}^{\bullet}t' \neq \emptyset$ in N, and by 1-safeness, no reachable marking can concurrently enable {t,t'}.

Hence $pos(e,\sigma_1)$ and $pos(e',\sigma_1)$ cannot be interchanged, and σ_1 is not ≡-related to σ_2, contradiction.

Hence in π we have $e<e' \Rightarrow pos(e,\sigma_2) < pos(e',\sigma_2)$.

By 3.8, $\sigma_2 \in Lin(\pi)$, and the result is proved. □5.12

The preceding proof suggests that for 1-safe nets the ≡ relation can be characterised by a certain relation between the transitions of N. Indeed the independence relation defined next provides such a relation; this is the original relation introduced by [21].

5.13 Definition.

Let $N=(S,T,F,K,M_o)$ be a 1-safe net and let $t,t' \in T$.

Then t indep t' iff $({}^{\bullet}t \cup t^{\bullet}) \cap ({}^{\bullet}t' \cup t'^{\bullet}) = \emptyset$.

5.14 Theorem.

Let N be 1-safe and let $\sigma_1 = \sigma_{11} t M_1 t' \sigma_{12}$, $\sigma_2 = \sigma_{21} t' M_2 t \sigma_{22}$ be as in 5.4(i).

Then $\sigma_1 \equiv_o \sigma_2$ iff $\sigma_{11}=\sigma_{21}$, $\sigma_{12}=\sigma_{21}$ and t indep t'.

Proof: Easy and, therefore, omitted. (See [7] which contains a proof.) □5.14

This fully clarifies the correspondence between processes and sequences for 1-safe nets: Processes correspond to ≡-equivalence classes of sequences, and the latter are generated by the indep relation defined in 5.13. That is, knowing the set of processes is tantamount to knowing the set of sequences and the relation defined in 5.13.

What complicates the matter in the general case is related to the fact that the process notion may distinguish the individualities of several tokens on the same place while the firing sequences don't. Therefore, having some means of explicitly distinguishing tokens might shed more light on the correspondence. One such means might be given by a general translation of arbitrary system nets into system nets with capacity K(s)=1 for all s which is, for example, hinted at in [14]. While such a translation appears possible, it poses problems of its own, the discussion of which falls outside the scope of this paper.

6. SEQUENCES AND PROCESSES IN CONCURRENT PROGRAMMING LANGUAGES

The distinction between state-like objects and transition-like objects plays an important rôle in many programming languages, too. In languages in which variables are used states are built from the values of variables. In the case of concurrent programs, control becomes more important, and the notion of a control state may also be defined. In shared variable languages [e.g. 24], transitions correspond to the atomic actions and to the critical sections of a program. In CSP [16], transitions correspond to the communications of a program and to the internal steps of a program component.

With this correspondence in mind, it is possible to adapt the net theoretic ideas expounded earlier for the semantic description of the (interleaved or partially ordered) behaviour of concurrent programs. For a shared variable language, [3] describes a control sequence semantics which is analogous to the firing sequence semantics (see 2.4 and 2.5) of net theory. In this section, we will show that control sequence semantics can be defined for CSP analogously, giving uniform semantics for both types of programs.

Given that analoga of firing sequence semantics can be defined for concurrent programs, it should then easily be possible to modify construction 3.4 to describe the "true concurrency" semantics of concurrent programs. The main objective of this section is to show how construction 3.4 can be adapted for this purpose. Because of space limitations we must restrict our considerations to (as it were) the simplest non-trivial case, viz. concurrent programs with a fixed number of sequential components and without the nesting of either atomic actions or the parallel operator $\|$. We also neglect all aspects to do with non-termination except through deadlocks or infinite loops.

We start by introducing control sequence semantics as an analogon of firing sequence semantics. In this, the control sequences are defined by means of their projections on the sequential components. This goes back to an idea of Mike Shields in giving firing sequence semantics for COSY [20] and can also be related to the firing rule in a subclass of nets called state net decomposable nets. The effect of the projection requirement is that an action whose name is common to two program components is executed in a synchronised fashion in the parallel composition of the two components. In definition 6.1 and theorem 6.2 we strengthen this motivation by giving the relevant background from net theory.

6.1 <u>Definition.</u>

(i) A net (S,T,F) is called state net iff $\forall t \in T\colon |{}^{\bullet}t| = 1 = |t^{\bullet}|$

(ii) A system net $N=(S,T,F,K,M_o)$ will be called state net decomposable (SND) iff there are n state nets (S_i,T_i,F_i) $(1 \le i \le n)$ such that $S = \biguplus S_i$ ($\uplus$ = disjoint union), $T = \bigcup T_i$, $F = \bigcup F_i$ and $\forall i,\ 1 \le i \le n\colon \exists s \in S_i\colon (M_o(s)=1 \wedge \forall s' \in S_i \backslash \{s\}\colon M_o(s')=0)$ (i.e. each state net component of N has exactly one token under M_o).

(iii) Let $\sigma = M_o t_1 M_1 \ldots$ be a firing sequence of N; then $proj_i(\sigma)$ is defined as the sequence obtained from σ by omitting all t_j and M_j provided $t_j \in T \backslash T_i$.

6.2 <u>Theorem.</u> (Without proof)

σ is a firing sequence of a SND net N iff $\forall i,\ 1 \le i \le n\colon proj_i(\sigma)$ is a firing sequence of (S_i,T_i,F_i,K_i,M_{oi}) (where K_i, M_{oi} are K, M_o restricted to S_i). □6.2

The following definition introduces control programs by analogy with COSY and SND nets.

6.3 <u>Definition.</u>

Let A be a finite set (of action names), let A^* denote the set of finite sequences over A (including the empty sequence ε) and $A^\infty = A^* \cup \{a_1 a_2 a_3 \ldots \mid a_i \in A\}$.

(i) For $X \subseteq A^*$, $Y \subseteq A^\infty$, let X.Y and X^* be defined as usual, e.g. $X.Y = \{xy \mid x \in X,\ y \in Y\}$ where xy denotes ordinary string catenation

(ii) For $A_o \subseteq A$ and $w \in A^\infty$ let $proj(A_o,w)$ denote the sequence in A_o^∞ obtained from w by omitting all elements in $A \backslash A_o$

(iii) k is a control program over A iff $k = \gamma_1 \| \ldots \| \gamma_n$ where the γ_i are derived from the following syntax:

$\gamma\ ::=\ a \mid \gamma;\gamma \mid \gamma \Box \gamma \mid (\gamma|b)^* \quad (a,b \in A)$

Let A(k) denote the set of action names occurring in k.

(iv) To k we associate sets of sequences cs(k) and ccs(k) as follows:

$cs(a) = \{\varepsilon, a\}, \quad ccs(a) = \{a\}$

$cs(\gamma_1;\gamma_2) = cs(\gamma_1) \cup ccs(\gamma_1).cs(\gamma_2), \quad ccs(\gamma_1;\gamma_2) = ccs(\gamma_1).ccs(\gamma_2)$

$cs(\gamma_1 \Box \gamma_2) = cs(\gamma_1) \cup cs(\gamma_2), \quad ccs(\gamma_1 \Box \gamma_2) = ccs(\gamma_1) \cup ccs(\gamma_2)$

$cs((\gamma|b)^*) = ccs(\gamma)^*.(cs(\gamma) \cup \{b\}) \cup ccs(\gamma)^\infty, \quad ccs((\gamma|b)^*) = ccs(\gamma)^*.\{b\}$

$cs(\gamma_1 \| \ldots \| \gamma_n) = \{w \in A^\infty \mid \forall i,\ 1 \le i \le n\colon proj(A(\gamma_i),w) \in cs(\gamma_i)\}$,

$ccs(\gamma_1 \| \ldots \| \gamma_n) = \{w \in A^\infty \mid \forall i,\ 1 \le i \le n\colon proj(A(\gamma_i),w) \in ccs(\gamma_i)\}$.

The sets cs(k) and ccs(k) denote the sets of control sequences and complete control sequences, respectively, of k. They provide a formalism to describe the flow of control in a concurrent program. It is easy to prove that ccs(k) contains exactly the finite maximal elememts of cs(k). In $(\gamma|b)^*$, b denotes a loop termination action; this is necessary because reducing a loop <u>do</u> B→γ <u>od</u> to $(B;\gamma)^*;\overline{B}$ introduces an unwanted control point. The next definition specifies the class of programs that will be considered first, i.e. shared variable programs with atomic actions <...>.

6.4 Definition.

(i) c is a shared variable (SV) program iff $c = \gamma_1 \| \ldots \| \gamma_n$ with the syntax
γ ::= skip | <V:=Expr> | γ;γ | <u>if</u> <BE>→γ □...□ <BE>→γ <u>fi</u> | <u>do</u> <BE>→γ <u>od</u>
(where V, Expr and BE are variables, expressions and Boolean expressions, respectively)

(ii) Let Var(c) be the set of variables of c and S_V the set of values of V∈Var(c)
$S = S(c) = \times\{S_V \mid V \in Var(c)\}$ is the state space of c (spanned by its variables)

(iii) The set A = A(c) of atomic action names of c is defined by giving each syntactically distinguishable action <V:=Expr> or <BE> in c a unique name; furthermore, to describe termination properly, an implicit action <<u>not</u> BE> is introduced for each loop <u>do</u> <BE>→γ <u>od</u> and is given a name, say "b", too

(iv) To each action name a∈A(c) we associate a meaning relation $m(a) \subseteq S \times S$; this is done in the obvious way for actions <V:=Expr>, and for a=<BE>, we put (s',s)∈m(a) iff BE(s')=true and s=s' (states s' with BE(s')=false are mapped to nothing, which will then imply that the <u>if</u> acts like an <u>await</u>)

(v) To c we associate a control program k(c) as follows: replace each <u>if</u> <BE>→γ □...□ <BE>→γ <u>fi</u> by (<BE>;γ)□...□(<BE>;γ); replace each <u>do</u> <BE>→γ <u>od</u> by (<BE>;γ)|b)*; finally, replace each atomic action by its name.

6.5 Definition. (Control Sequence Semantics)

Let c be a program, $s_o, s_1, \ldots \in S(c)$ and $a_1, a_2, \ldots \in A(c)$.

(i) $\sigma = s_o a_1 s_1 a_2 \ldots$ is an execution sequence of c iff
(ia) $a_1 a_2 \ldots \in cs(k(c))$ and (ib) $\forall j, j \geq 1: (s_{j-1}, s_j) \in m(a_j)$

(ii) σ is terminating iff, in addition, $a_1 a_2 \ldots \in ccs(k(c))$.

Now an analogon of construction 3.4 can be defined. The idea in all constructions that follow is to interpret each s_j in an execution sequence σ as a vector and hence to consider σ as a sequence in which vectors and actions alternate, much like firing sequences in nets. Depending how s_j is written in vector form, different derivates of construction 3.4 may be defined. First, we recall from 6.4(ii) that each s_j is a vector of variable values, i.e. $s_j = (s_{j1}, \ldots, s_{jv})$ if v denotes the number of variables in c, i.e. $v = |Var(c)|$. In what follows we will always denote the value of a variable V∈Var(c) in the state s∈S(c) by s_V.

6.6 Construction.

Let $\sigma = (s_{o1}, \ldots, s_{ov}) a_1 (s_{11}, \ldots, s_{1v}) a_2 \ldots$ be an execution sequence of an SV program c.

We construct inductively an occurrence net N=(B,E,F) and a labelling
$p: B \cup E \to (\bigcup_{V \in Var(c)} S_V) \cup A(c)$ as follows:

<u>i=0.</u> $E_o = F_o = \emptyset$ and B_o contains for each V∈Var(c) a condition b with $p_o(b) = s_{oV}$.

<u>i→i+1.</u> Suppose $(N_i, p_i) = (B_i, E_i, F_i, p_i)$ constructed.
By construction, every condition $b \in N_i^o$ corresponds to a variable V and $p_i(b) = s_{iV}$.
For the new event e labelled a_{i+1} we consider the variables in a_{i+1}.
The event e is appended to all conditions b that correspond to variables in a_{i+1}.
Further, we append to this event e $|Var(a_{i+1})|$ new conditions each corresponding to one $V \in Var(a_{i+1})$ and labelled with $s_{i+1,V}$.

Finally, put $(N,p) = (\bigcup^m B_i, \bigcup^m E_i, \bigcup^m F_i, \bigcup^m p_i)$ where $m = |\sigma|$.

Figure 13 illustrates definitions 6.3-6.5 and construction 6.6.

γ₁ = <u>if</u> <x=y>→<x:=0>□<x≠y>→<x:=1> <u>fi</u> ‖ γ₂ = <x:=2>;<y:=3>

<u>(i)</u> A SV program c

$\gamma_1 = ((b_o;a_o)\Box(b_1;a_1)) \;\|\; \gamma_2 = a_2;a_3$ with b_o = <x=y>, a_o = <x:=0>
b_1 = <x≠y>, a_1 = <x:=1>
a_2 = <x:=2>, a_3 = <y:=3>

<u>(ii)</u> A control program k(c)

$\{\varepsilon, b_o, b_1, a_2, \ldots, a_2 b_o a_o a_3, a_2 b_1 a_1 a_3, \ldots\} \subseteq cs(k(c))$

<u>(iii)</u> Some control sequences of k(c)

<u>Figure 13</u>

$$\begin{pmatrix}x=0\\y=0\end{pmatrix} a_2 \begin{pmatrix}x=2\\y=0\end{pmatrix} b_1 \begin{pmatrix}x=2\\y=0\end{pmatrix} a_1 \begin{pmatrix}x=1\\y=0\end{pmatrix} a_3 \begin{pmatrix}x=1\\y=3\end{pmatrix}$$

(iv) An execution sequence of c

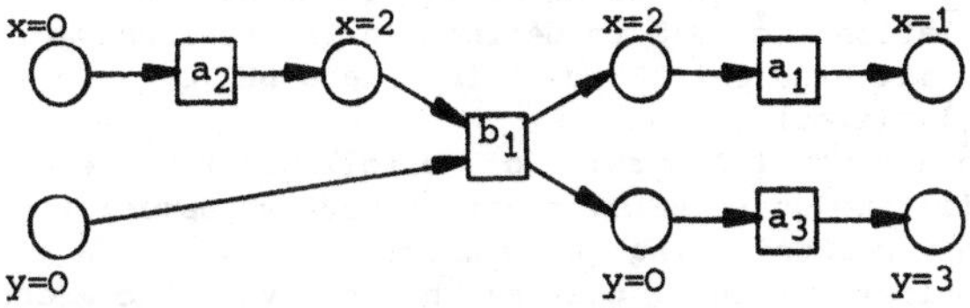

(v) A process associated to (iv) by 6.6

Figure 13 (continued)

As can be seen on this example, the partial order resulting from construction 6.6 describes the data dependencies between the actions in c. Control dependencies disappear unless they are accompanied by data dependencies. Essentially, the construction 6.6 is based on the view of a program as a SND net where the S_i-sets of the state net components are exactly the value sets of the variables of c. In this view, each marking of the SND net corresponds to a state of c in the sense of definition 6.4(ii).

It is possible to model the control dependencies explicitly by extending the state space of c with n new variables (where n is the number of sequential components of c). (The set cs(k(c)) can be used to do so formally, essentially by defining an equivalence on the sequences in cs(k(c)): w is equivalent to v iff $\forall a\in A(c)$: $wa\in cs(k(c)$ iff $va\in cs(k(c))$.) Each state can then be written as $s = (s_1,\dots,s_v,s_1',\dots,s_n')$ where the $s_1,\dots,s_v$ are as before and the $s_1',\dots,s_n'$ denote the n current control locations. Construction 6.6 goes through with the new event labelled a_{i+1} being appended not only to conditions corresponding to variables in a_{i+1} but also to the condition(s) corresponding to the control locations which are changed through the occurrence of a_{i+1}. The resulting partial order reflects control as well as data dependencies. In this paper there is no space to go into the details.

On the other hand, construction 6.6 introduces dependencies even if a common variable is only read but not written to. By being more sophisticated about which variables should be connected to a_{i+1} (e.g. in the trivial example a_{i+1}=<x:=0*y>, variable y need not be connected to a_{i+1}), it is possible to define even more concurrent processes of c than does 6.6. However, "being sophisticated about data dependencies" is a problem of its own and is not dealt with in this paper.

The occurrence net formalism of [6] takes a more detailed view of the executions of concurrent programs based on reads and writes. Essentially, every <V:=Expr> is considered to be split up into a set of concurrent reads (to variables in Expr) followed by a write to V, and every <BE> is considered as a set of reads. From a read/write occurrence net of this form, the collapsing operation defined in [6] produces another occurrence net, and (it is hoped) the atomicity criteria of [6] ensure that the latter is such that it could be a result of construction 6.6. Any more detailed investigation of this connection falls outside the scope of this paper.

The next definition gives the control sequence semantics for CSP.

6.7 Definition.

(i) c is a CSP program iff $c = c_1::\gamma_1 \| \dots \| c_n::\gamma_n$ with the syntax
γ ::= skip | V:=Expr | $\gamma;\gamma$ | io | if $g\to\gamma\square\dots\square g\to\gamma$ fi | do $g\to\gamma$ od , where
io ::= c_j!Expr | c_j?V and g ::= BE | BE;io | io, with the additional requirements that no variables may appear in both γ_i and γ_j ($i\neq j$), that no γ_i may communicate with itself, and that every io command c_j.. in γ_i has at least one matching io command c_i.. in γ_j ($i\neq j$)

(ii) $Var(\gamma_i)$ is the set of variables in γ_i and $S_i = \times\{S_V \mid V\in Var(\gamma_i)\}$ is the state space of γ_i, while $S = S(c) = \times_{i=1,\dots,n} S_i$ is the state space of c.

(iii) The set of action names A = A(c) is defined as follows:
For each skip, V:=Expr and non-communicating guard g=BE in γ_i introduce a

unique name local to γ_i;

For each *pair* of communicating actions introduce a separate name; e.g. if $BE;io$ in γ_i matches with $BE_1;io_1$ and with $BE_2;io_2$ in γ_j then we introduce two different names.

Again each loop do $g \to \gamma$ od requires an extra action called b.

(iv) For $a \in A(c)$ the relation $m(c) \subseteq S \times S$ is defined in the obvious way. E.g. if a is the name of the matching pair $BE;c_j!5$ in γ_i and $BE_1;c_i?x$ in γ_j then $m(a) = m(BE \wedge BE_1) \circ m(x:=5)$.

(v) To c we associate a control program k(c) as follows: replace each skip, V:=Expr and non-communicating guard BE by their respective names; replace every $io = c_j..$ and every communicating guard $BE;c_j..$ by $(a_1 \Box \ldots \Box a_q)$ where q is the number of communications in γ_j that match the given io command ($q \geq 1$ by the assumptions in (i)), and $a_1, \ldots, a_q$ are the names of the respective pairs; finally, replace if $g \to \gamma \Box \ldots \Box g \to \gamma$ fi by $(g;\gamma) \Box \ldots \Box (g;\gamma)$ and do $g \to \gamma$ od by $(g;\gamma|b)^*$.

The control sequence semantics of CSP programs is then defined by 6.5. (We neglect distributed termination which could however easily be accommodated by changing the definition of m(b) or by changing 6.5(ib) slightly.) Note that the handshake rule of a CSP communication is guaranteed by the projection rule in 6.3(iv) combined with the naming convention in 6.7(iii) but that its effect is described by the m relation defined in 6.7(iv). Thus this semantics generalises directly to handshake communications that are more complicated than the assignment.

The process semantics of CSP programs again depends on how states s are viewed as vectors. According to 6.7(ii) $s = (s_1, \ldots, s_n)$ where the $s_i \in S_i$ are the local states spanne by the variables of γ_i. This leads to a component-oriented process construction on which 6.8 is based,

6.8 Construction.

Let $\sigma = (s_{o1}, \ldots, s_{on}) a_1 (s_{11}, \ldots, s_{1n}) \ldots$ be an execution sequence of c $(s_{jk} \in S_k)$.

We may construct an occurrence net N=(B,E,F) and a labelling p: $B \cup E \to (\bigcup_{k=1,..,n} S_k) \cup A($ exactly in the same way as in 6.6, except that a new event labelled a_{i+1} will be appended to those conditions that correspond to γ_k such that $a_{i+1} \in A(\gamma$

An example is given in Figure 14.

c_1 :: if true$\to c_2!(x+1);x:=1 \Box c_2!(x+z) \to z:=4$ fi $\|$ c_2 :: if $c_1?y \to y:=y+1$
$\Box$ true$\to$skip
fi

(i) A CSP program c

$$((b_1;e_1;a_1) \Box (e_2;a_2)) \;\|\; (((e_1 \Box e_2);a_3) \Box (a_4;a_5))$$

with b_1 = true, $e_1 = c_2!(x+1) \| c_1?y$, a_1 = x:=1, $e_2 = c_2!(x+z) \| c_1?y$

a_2 = z:=4, a_3 = y:=y+1, a_4 = true, a_5 = skip

(ii) A control program k(c)

$$\{\varepsilon, \ldots, b_1a_4a_5, e_2a_3a_2, \ldots\} \subseteq cs(k(c))$$

(iii) Some control sequences of k(c) (note that $b_1a_4a_5$ deadlocks)

$$\begin{pmatrix} x=0 \wedge z=2 \\ y=0 \end{pmatrix} e_2 \begin{pmatrix} x=0 \wedge z=2 \\ y=2 \end{pmatrix} a_3 \begin{pmatrix} x=0 \wedge z=2 \\ y=3 \end{pmatrix} a_2 \begin{pmatrix} x=0 \wedge z=4 \\ y=3 \end{pmatrix}$$

(iv) An execution sequence of c

(v) A process associated to (iv) by 6.8

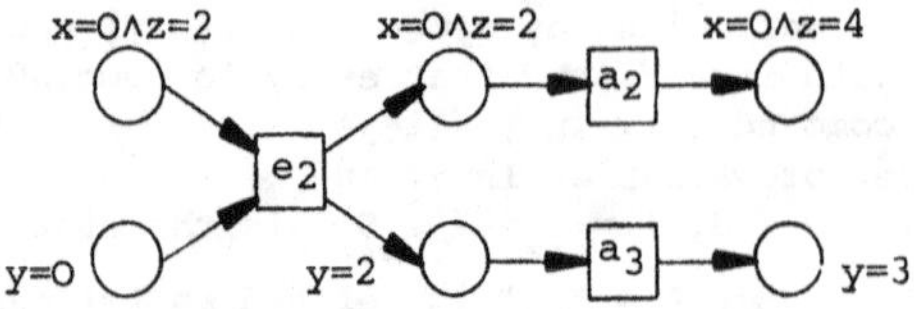

Figure 14

Construction 6.8 reflects the control dependencies of a CSP program via the local states of a sequential component. In order to describe more concurrent processes in which control dependencies that are not accompanied by data dependencies disappear, it is possible to view states s as vectors $(s_1,...,s_n)$ where the s_i $(1 \le i \le n)$ are again vectors $s_i = (s_{i1},...,s_{iv})$ such that $v = |Var(\gamma_i)|$ and $s_{ij} \in S_V$ for the j'th variable V in γ_i, and to define an analogon of 6.8 with this view in mind. However, to do so explicitly would exceed the scope of this paper.

A partial order semantics for CSP has first been defined in [30]. The construction given there differs from the one given here in a few respects. First, it yields a single object (an occurrence net in the sense of [23]) as the semantics of a program, but it may be conjectured that the processes of the latter correspond to the processes as defined in 6.8. Secondly, [30] bases its semantics on Plotkin's rewrite rules [28] which employ the notion of a configuration to denote both the variable state and the control state. Here we have shown that it is unnecessary to add control explicitly to the state, because data dependencies between the atomic actions of a CSP program always go along with control dependencies. Hence it suffices to use the former in order to describe the latter, as done in 6.8.

The careful reader will have noticed that all constructions defined (or sketched) in this section are deterministic, as opposed to construction 3.4. This is no surprise, because the underlying idea has always been to view a program c as an SND net with state components that correspond either to the variables of c or to the sequential components of c or both. Since in any state, each variable has exactly one value and control is at exactly one location, it is clear that the underlying (so far imaginary) SND net is 1-safe, whence the determinacy of the construction (which can be defined even without formally defining the underlying net) follows.

What makes CSP programs particularly nice (and indeed has been a motivation for omitting shared variables) is that there is a structuring of the state net components: each component corresponding to a sequential component of a CSP program can in turn be viewed as made up of state nets of its own corresponding to the local variables. If the nesting of $\|$ is allowed, this may no longer be true and hence the nesting of $\|$ may considerably complicate the theory. A similar remark can be made for the nesting of atomic actions in an SV program. While such nesting is meaningful and is allowed both in the interleaved semantics of [3] and in the partial order semantics of [6], it is not clear how the two are related to each other in the nested case.

Summarising this section, we have attempted to transport construction 3.4 which gives the processes of a Petri net in as simple a way as possible to concurrent programs to give the behavioural semantics of the latter in terms of sequences and processes. No attempt has been made to describe the processes independently by means of axioms, or to investigate the relationship between sequences and processes as has been done in section 5 for nets. To do this will be an interesting topic for future research. However, since the constructions of this section are based on the 1-safe case, it can be hoped that the "nice" relationship between sequences and processes of 1-safe nets can be retrieved in terms of concurrent programs.

7. CONCLUDING REMARKS

In this paper we have investigated the interleaved (sequence) semantics and the partial order (process) semantics of Petri nets and of concurrent programs. With respect to the former, the emphasis was on trying to identify exactly the power of the respective approaches and to study their relationship. We have based our considerations on the process axioms as they are (essentially) defined in [10,14] and we have defined a (perhaps more intuitive) construction by which processes can be associated with firing sequences.

In section 3 we have examined the question under which conditions the axioms are consistent and complete with respect to this construction, and we have identified degree-finite nets with finite initial marking as a class of nets for which a consistency and completeness result holds true. Hence one has to resort to other nets if one wants concurrency to be such that a meaningful partial order behaviour can be defined which cannot be related to firing sequences, an example being the net shown in Figure 4. Incidentally, if one wanted to reconstruct this example in terms of concurrent programs then it is clear from the discussion in section 6 that one would have to consider either infinitely many variables or infinitely many sequential components or both - which may be theoretically interesting but is surely not a very practical proposition.

From the discussion in section 3 this author concludes that to all practical intents and purposes, firing sequences describe essentially the same class of behaviours as do partial orders. Sometimes it has been argued that interleaving semantics is based on the assumption that the activities of a system are synchronised by a global clock. results do not support this argument, because the global clock assumption would entail concurrency being a transitive relation and hence cut out some of the partially ordered behaviours that may be generated from the system structure only, whereas the set of all interleavings does *not* exclude partial orders that fail to be co-transitive. More appropriately, it can be argued that interleaving semantics is based on the assumption of there being a central scheduler. Section 3 can then be interpreted as stating that in practice (i.e. excluding examples like shown in Figure 4), central scheduling is enough to generate all interesting behaviours.

However, what is "lost" if one considers sequences instead of processes is an entirely separate question. Section 5 of this paper shows that the answer is easy only for 1-safe nets (which are, fortunately, an important class of nets). For 1-safe nets, if one considers sequences instead of processes then one loses exactly the $\equiv$-equivalence relation. Since the latter can be retrieved from the <u>indep</u> relation defined in 5.13, the knowledge of all sequences and of <u>indep</u> is sufficient to reconstruct the processes. (Which is, in fact, a known result which has been generalised here for infinite sequences.)

For general nets, the answer to the above question is much less clearly cut. The <u>indep</u> relation cannot be generalised; the Lin-sets of processes have no obvious relationship to the $\equiv$-equivalence classes of sequences, and even if they had, processes may not uniquely be reconstructed from them, not even modulo $\approx$-equivalence. We have provided a partial answer in that we have identified the Π,Lin relationship between sequences and processes as bijective on the $\equiv$-equivalence classes. As to what happens within these classes, however, the feeling is that more can be found out in future research.

In section 6 we have tried to show that net theoretic ideas can be of direct relevance also to the description of the behaviour of concurrent programming languages. We believe to have given a sequence and a partial order semantics of two such languages which are quite simple and close to net theory. Thereby, the construction to derive processes from sequences turns out to be quite flexible. However, this has only laid the groundwork for the interesting questions that may be asked, e.g.: What are the axioms for the processes of concurrent programs, i.e. is there an analogon of 3.2? Is there an analogon of the close relationship between sequences and processes of 1-safe nets in terms of concurrent programs? In particular, what would be an analogon of <u>indep</u>? (The conjecture is, of course, that <u>indep</u> can be formally related to the well-known Reynolds condition on shared variable programs, i.e. no writing to any common variables.) Further, how does nesting and the collapsing rule of [6] fit into the theory? Finally, as pointed out in [30], process semantics may shed some new light on fairness considerations. Any answers to these questions, however, must be left to future work.

<u>ACKNOWLEDGEMENTS</u>

I would like to thank Wolfgang Reisig for discussions on the process axioms, and for pointing out that the <u>indep</u> relation cannot be generalised. Also, I am grateful to César Fernández for persevering in that there should be an intuitively "right" set of process axioms even for infinite nets, and to Yuan Chong Yi who helped me in finding the definition of $\equiv$ for infinite sequences. I am indebted to Einar Smith and Detlef Hillen who detected last-minute mistakes, and particularly to Raymond Devillers who pointed out numerous deficiencies in this paper, particularly the counterexample to the reverse implication of theorem 5.3(i). We conjecture presently that a side-condition with two or more tokens is necessary for the reverse of 5.3(i) to go wrong, and we are working on a proof of this conjecture.

REFERENCES (LNCS denotes Springer Lecture Notes in Computer Science)

1. E.Best: A Theorem on the Characteristics of Non-sequential Processes. Fundamenta Informaticae III.1 (1980), 77-94.
2. E.Best: The Relative Strength of K-density. In: [8], 261-276.
3. E.Best: Relational Semantics of Concurrent Programs (with some Applications). Formal Description of Programming Concepts II (ed.D.Bjørner) (1983), 431-452.
4. E.Best and A.Merceron: Discreteness, K-density and D-continuity in Occurrence Nets. LNCS 145 (1982), 73-83.
5. E.Best and A.Merceron: Frozen Tokens and D-continuity: A Study in Relating System Properties to Process Properties. Århus Workshop on Petri Nets (1984), to appear in: Advances in Net Theory (ed.G.Rozenberg).
6. E.Best and B.Randell: A Formal Model of Atomicity in Asynchronous Systems. Acta Informatica 16 (1981), 93-124.
7. E.Best and K.Voss: Free Choice Systems have Home States. Acta Informatica 21 (1984), 89-100.
8. W.Brauer (ed.): Net Theory and Applications. LNCS 84 (1980).
9. C.Fernández and P.S.Thiagarajan: D-Continuous Causal Nets: A Model of Non-sequential Processes. TCS 28 (1984), 171-196.
10. C.Fernández, M.Nielsen and P.S.Thiagarajan: A Note on Observable Occurrence Nets. Århus Workshop on Petri nets (1984), to appear in: Advances in Net Theory (ed. G.Rozenberg).
11. H.J.Genrich, K.Lautenbach and P.S.Thiagarajan: Elements of General Net Theory. In: [8], 21-163.
12. H.J.Genrich and E.Stankiewicz-Wiechno: A Dictionary of some Basic Notions of Net Theory. In: [8], 519-535.
13. U.Goltz and A.Mycroft: On the Relationship of CCS and Petri Nets. LNCS 172 (1984) 196-208.
14. U.Goltz and W.Reisig: The Non-sequential Behaviour of Petri Nets. Information and Control 57 (1983), 125-147.
15. M.Hennessy and G.Plotkin: Full Abstraction for a Simple Programming Language. LNCS 74 (1979), 108-120.
16. C.A.R.Hoare: Communicating Sequential Processes. CACM 21(8) (1978), 666-677.
17. A.Holt: Final Report on the Project on Information Systems Theory, Applied Data Research ADR6606 (1968).
18. L.Lamport: What Good is Temporal Logic? Inf. Proc. 83, North Holland (1983), 657-667.
19. P.E.Lauer: Synchronisation of Concurrent Processes without Globality Assumptions. ACM SIGPLAN Notices 16(9) (1981), 66-80.
20. P.E.Lauer, M.W.Shields and E.Best: Formal Theory of the Basic COSY Notation. Computing Laboratory, Univ. of Newcastle upon Tyne, TR143 (1979).
21. A.Mazurkiewicz: Concurrent Program Schemes and their Interpretation. Århus Univ. Computer Science Dep. Report DAIMI PB-78 (1977).
22. R.Milner: A Calculus of Communicating Systems. LNCS 92 (1980).
23. M.Nielsen, G.Plotkin and G.Winskel: Petri Nets, Event Structures and Domains I. TCS 13 (1981), 85-108.
24. S.Owicki and D.Gries: An Axiomatic Proof Technique for Parallel Programs I. Acta Informatica 6 (1976), 319-340.
25. C.A.Petri: Non-Sequential Processes. GMD-ISF Report 77.05 (1977).
26. C.A.Petri: Concurrency. In: [8], 251-260.
27. G.Plotkin: In a private discussion, G.Plotkin suggested b-discreteness as an axiom to be satisfied by non-sequential processes. (1979)
28. G.Plotkin: An Operational Semantics for CSP. Formal Description of Programming Concepts II (ed.D.Bjørner) (1983), 199-223.
29. H.Plünnecke: Schnitte in Halbordnungen. GMD-ISF Report 81.09 (1981). Abridged English version to appear in: Advances in Net Theory (ed. G.Rozenberg).
30. W.Reisig: Partial Order Semantics versus Interleaving Semantics for CSP-Like Languages and its Impact on Fairness. LNCS 172 (1984), 403-413.
31. W.Reisig: On the Semantics of Petri Nets. Bericht No.100, FB Informatik, University of Hamburg (1984).
32. M.W.Shields: Adequate Path Expressions. LNCS 70 (1979), 249-265.
33. G.Winskel: Events in Computation. PhD Thesis, Computer Science Department, Edinburgh University (1980).

CATEGORIES OF MODELS FOR CONCURRENCY

by
Glynn Winskel
University of Cambridge,
Computer Laboratory,
Corn Exchange Street,
Cambridge CB2 3QG.

0. Introduction.

The theory of sequential programming language is well understood, making it possible to reason, often in a formal proof system, about the behaviour of programs. However the situation is less settled in the case of parallel programs, where several processes run concurrently to cooperate on a common task. There are concrete models like *Petri nets, event structures, synchronisation trees* and *state-transition systems*, which essentially model a process as moving through states as events occur. These models do not even represent concurrency in the same way. Models like Petri nets and event structures represent concurrent activity in terms of causal independence while most other models simulate concurrency by nondeterministic interleaving of atomic actions. Then there are more abstract models, perhaps based on *powerdomains* or on some reasonable idea of *operational equivalence*, formed with the idea of detecting and proving rather specific properties of processes. Other approaches are based on variants of modal logic but here too similar choices are faced; what is the underlying concrete model and how expressive should the modal logic be?

I am interested in developing a uniform mathematical framework to relate the many different models that exist for parallel computation. At present I have had most success with concrete models for languages in the style of R. Milner's "*Calculus of Communicating Systems*" (CCS) and C.A.R. Hoare's "*Communicating Sequential Process*" (CSP) [W1,2,3]. To give the idea, each kind of concrete model (*e.g.* Petri nets are such a model) carries a notion of morphism appropriate to languages like CCS and CSP, which make it into a category. Then useful constructions within the model, like parallel composition, arise as categorical constructions accompanied by abstract characterisations. Relations between two different kinds of models, say nets and trees, are expressed as an adjunction, between say the category of nets and the category of trees. Because of the way adjunctions preserve categorical constructions this gives a smooth translation between semantics in one model and semantics in another. This technique works for a wide range of parallel programming languages with a wide variety of communication disciplines—they can be expressed in a very general way using the idea of *synchronisation algebra* [W1,2]. Because constructs in the programming languages are modelled by categorical constructions there are accompanying proof rules. But unfortunately because the models are so concrete, the proof rules do not immediately capture aspects of behaviour at the level of abstraction one wants. Still, even the more abstract models and their proof rules have at their basis a concrete model of one sort or another. It is helpful to have a clear understanding of the relationship there is amongst the diversity of such models. Given a modicum of category theory it can be expressed in a surprisingly clean way, as I hope will come across. The basic category theory used here can be found in [AM] or [Mac].

1. Languages for communicating processes—an abstract view.

A host of programming languages CCS, CSP, SCCS, CIRCAL, OCCAM, MEIJE, ESTEREL$\cdots$ are based on the idea that processes communicate by events of synchronisation.

Individually a process P_0 is thought of as capable of performing certain events. Some of them may be communications with the environment and others may be internal actions. Set in parallel with another process P_1 an event e_0 of P_0 might synchronise with an event e_1 of P_1. Whether they do or not will of course depend on what kinds of events e_0 and e_1 are because P_0 and P_1 can only perform certain kinds of synchronisation with their environments. But if they do synchronise we can think of them as forming a synchronisation event (e_0, e_1). The synchronisation event (e_0, e_1) has the same effect on the process P_0 as the component event e_0 and similarly on P_1 has the same effect as the event e_1.

Of course generally not all events of P_0 will synchronise with events of P_1; there might be an internal event of P_0 for example which by its very nature cannot synchronise with any event of P_1. So we cannot expect all events of the parallel composition to have the form (e_0, e_1). Some will have no component event from one process or the other. We can represent these events in the form $(e_0, *)$ if the event e_0 of P_0 occurs unsynchronised with any event of P_1 or $(*, e_1)$ if the event e_1 of P_1 occurs unsynchronised. The $*$ stands for the absence of an event from the corresponding component.

Thus we can view synchronisation as forming compound events from component events; a synchronisation event is viewed as a combination of events from the processes set in parallel.

Whether or not synchronisations can occur is determined by the nature of the events. Right from the start programming languages like CSP and CCS introduce notation to distinguish the different kinds of events. In the early version of CSP [H] the sequential processes are named and events of a sequential process are of the form: send a value v to process P, written $P!v$, or receive a value from process P into variable x, written $P?x$. There is no notation in this language of CSP for the events of synchronisation between processes. In the new version of CSP [HBR] events are distinguished according to the port at which they occur, so processes set in parallel must agree on the occurrence of events at common ports (this goes to back to an early idea of path expressions [CH] and is also at the basis of G. Milne's calculus CIRCAL [Mi]). The idea of ports, places at which processes communicate with the environment, underlies the language of CCS too—see [M1]; originally, apart from τ the labels of CCS $\alpha, \beta, \cdots$ and their complementary labels $\overline{\alpha}, \overline{\beta}, \cdots$ were thought of as port names so in forming the parallel composition of two processes only complementary ports, as indicated by the labels, were connected. So correspondingly in CCS only events carrying complementary labels can synchronise to from an event labelled by τ. In [M1] Value-passing was handled using events labelled αv to represent the input of value v at port α and $\overline{\alpha}v$ to represent the output of value v at port α. Their introduction foreshadowed the liberating step Milner took in the language of synchronous CCS, generally called SCCS. There the labels (called actions) are regarded very abstractly and can be composed according to monoids of actions.

Synchronisation algebras

We take an abstract line inspired by Milner's monoids of actions in SCCS. However synchronisation algebras are more general than monoids of actions because they can express which actions can and cannot occur asynchronously.

We label events of processes to specify how they interact with the environment, so associated with any particular sychronisation algebra is a particular parallel composition. By specialising to particular synchronisation algebras we can obtain a wide range of parallel compositions.

A *synchronisation algebra*, $(L, \bullet, *, 0)$, consists of a binary, commutative, associative operation $\bullet$ on a set of labels which always includes two distinguished elements $*$ and 0. The binary operation $\bullet$ says how labelled events combine to form synchronisation events and what labels such combinations carry. No real events are ever labelled by $*$ or 0. However their introduction allows us to specify the way labelled events synchronise without recourse to partial operations on labels. It is required that $L \setminus \{*, 0\} \neq 0$.

The constant 0 is used to specify when sychronisations are disallowed. If two events labelled λ and λ' are not supposed to synchronise then their composition $\lambda \bullet \lambda'$ is 0. For this reason 0 does indeed behave like a zero with respect to the "multiplication" $\bullet$ *i.e.*

$$\forall \lambda \in L.\ \lambda \bullet 0 = 0.$$

In a synchronisation algebra, the constant $*$ is used to specify when a labelled event can or cannot occur asynchronously. An event labelled λ can occur asynchronously iff $\lambda \bullet *$ is not 0. We insist that the only divisor of $*$ is $*$ itself, essentially because we do not want a synchronisation event to disappear. We require

$$* \bullet * = * \quad \text{and} \quad \forall \lambda, \lambda' \in L.\ \lambda \bullet \lambda' = * \Rightarrow \lambda = *.$$

We present two synchronisation algebras as examples—more can be found in [W1,2].

Example. *The synchronisation algebra for CCS—no value passing:* In CCS [M1] events are labelled by $\alpha, \beta, \cdots$ or by their complementary labels $\bar{\alpha}, \bar{\beta}, \cdots$ or by the label τ. The idea is that only two events bearing complementary labels may synchronise to form a synchronisation event labelled by τ. Events labelled by τ cannot synchronise further; in this sense they are invisible to processes in the environment, though their occurrence may lead to internal changes of state. All labelled events may occur asynchronously. Hence the synchronisation algebra for CCS takes the following form. The resultant parallel composition, of processes p and q say, is represented as $p|q$ in CCS.

$\bullet$	$*$	α	$\bar{\alpha}$	β	$\bar{\beta}$	$\cdots$	τ	0
$*$	$*$	α	$\bar{\alpha}$	β	$\bar{\beta}$	$\cdots$	τ	0
α	α	0	τ	0	0	$\cdots$	0	0
$\bar{\alpha}$	$\bar{\alpha}$	τ	0	0	0	$\cdots$	0	0
β	β	0	0	τ	0	$\cdots$	0	0
.	.	.	.	.	.	$\cdots$	.	.

Example. *The synchronisation algebra for $\|$ in [HBR, B]:* In the new form of CSP events are labelled by $\alpha, \beta, \cdots$ or τ. For the parallel composition $\|$ in [HBR, B] events must "synchronise on" $\alpha, \beta, \cdots$. In other words non-τ-labelled events cannot occur asynchronously. Rather, an α-labelled event in one component of a parallel composition must synchronise with an α-labelled event from the other component in order to occur; the two events must synchronise to form a synchronisation event again labelled by α. The S.A. for this parallel composition takes the following form. We call the algebra L_2.

$\bullet$	$*$	α	β	$\cdots$	τ	0
$*$	$*$	0	0	$\cdots$	τ	0
α	0	α	0	$\cdots$	0	0
β	0	0	β	$\cdots$	0	0
.	.	.	.	$\cdots$	.	.

Using synchronisation algebras one can define a generic programming language, inspired by CCS, SCCS and CSP but parameterised by the synchronisation algebra. For a synchronisation algebra L, the language $\mathbf{Proc}_L$is given by the following grammar:

$$t ::= nil \mid x \mid \lambda t \mid t + t \mid t\lceil\Lambda \mid t[\Xi] \mid t \,Ⓛ\, t \mid rec\ x.t$$

where x is in some set of variables X over processes, $\lambda \in L \setminus \{*, 0\}$, $\Lambda \subseteq L \setminus \{*, 0\}$, and $\Xi : L \to L$ is a relabelling function.

We explain informally the behaviour of the constructs in the language $\mathbf{Proc}_L$. The behaviour can be described accurately by the models presented in the next sections. Roughly, a process of $\mathbf{Proc}_L$determines a pattern of event occurrences over time. The nature of the events, how they interact with the environment, is specified by associating each event with a label from the synchronisation algebra L. The term *nil* represents the *nil* process which has stopped and refuses to perform any event. A *guarded* process λp first performs an event of kind λ to become the process p. A *sum* $p + q$ behaves like p or q; which branch of a sum is followed will often be determined by the context and what kinds of events the process is restricted to. A *parallel composition* process $p \,Ⓛ\, q$ behaves like p and q set in parallel. Their events of synchronisation are those pairs of events (e_0, e_1), one from each process, where e_0 is of kind λ_0 and e_1 is of kind λ_1 so that $\lambda_0 \bullet \lambda_1 \neq 0$; the synchronisation event is then of kind $\lambda_0 \bullet \lambda_1$. The *restriction* $p\lceil\Lambda$ behaves like the process p but with its events restricted to lie in the set Λ. A closed term *rec x.p* recursively defines a process x with body p.

The language **Proc$_L$** is not suited to value–passing. However it can easily be extended to be so, and again the discipline of communication can be handled using synchronisation algebras. Labels are taken to have two components λv; one, λ, can be thought of as a channel name and the other, v, as standing for the value passed or the value received. Processes can be parameterised in the manner of CCS with value–passing (see [M1]).

2. Petri nets, a general model.

Petri nets model processes in terms of how the occurrence of events incur changes in local states called conditions. This is expressed by a causal dependency (or flow) relation between sets of events and conditions, and it is this structure which determines the dynamic behaviour of nets once the causal dependency relation is given its natural interpretation. The most general Petri net we consider has the following form. Here and throughout this paper we refer the reader to the appendix for a treatment of multisets.

Definition. A *Petri net* is a 4–tuple (B, E, F, M_0) where
- (i) B is a non–null set of *conditions*,
- (ii) E is a set of *events*,
- (iii) F is a multiset of $(B \times E) \cup (E \times B)$, called the *causal dependency* relation
- (iv) M_0 is a non–null multiset of conditions, called the *initial marking*

which satisfy the restrictions:

$$\forall e \in E \exists b \in B.\ F_{b,e} > 0 \quad \text{and} \quad \forall e \in E \exists b \in B.\ F_{e,b} > 0.$$

Thus we insist that each event causally depends on at least one condition and has at least one condition which is causally dependent on it.

Nets are often drawn as graphs in which events are represented as boxes and conditions as circles with directed arcs between them, weighted by positive integers, to represent the flow relation. The initial marking is represented by placing "tokens" of the appropriate multiplicity on each weighted condition. Here is an example.

Example.

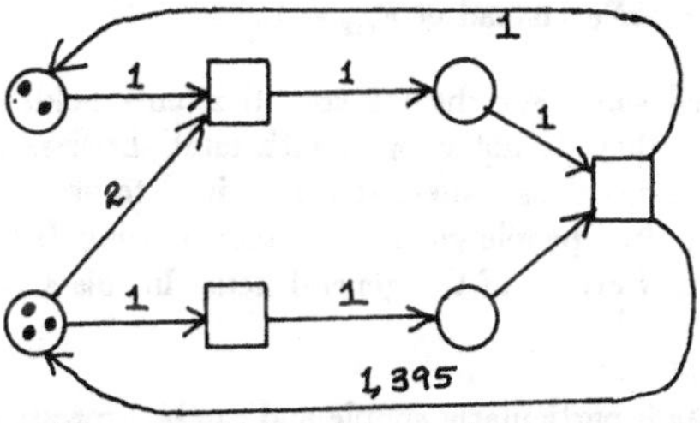

By convention we understand an arc which carries no label to stand for an arc with weight 1.

Later, because we have some problems with both the interpretation and mathematics of such general nets we will restrict to a subclass. But let's be as general as possible for the moment.

Nets viewed as algebras: It is useful, both notationally and conceptually, to regard a Petri net as a 2–sorted algebra on multisets. This view underlies the techniques for finding invariants of nets by linear algebra [Pe, Br, R].

Nets are in 1–1 correspondence with 2–sorted algebras with *sorts* μB a non–trivial multiset of conditions and μE a multiset of events and *operations* the constant $M_0 \in \mu B$, and the unary operations $^\bullet(-) : E \to_\mu B$ and $(-)^\bullet : E \to_\mu B$ which satisfy

$$M_0 \neq \underline{0}\ \&\ ((^\bullet A = \underline{0} \text{ or } A^\bullet = \underline{0}) \Rightarrow A = \underline{0}).$$

The dynamic behaviour of nets

States of a net are represented as *markings* which are simply multisets of conditions. You can think of a condition as a resource and its multiplicity as the amount of the resource. As an event occurs it consumes certain resources and produces others. What and how much is specified by the relation F. Continuing this interpretation, if there are enough resources then more than one event can occur concurrently, and it's even allowed that an event can occur to a certain multiplicity. Now this may be a little hard to swallow, and I'll come clean and admit that very soon we shall specialise to a subclass of nets, called *contact-free*, or *safe*, in which this cannot occur. The reason for specialising to safe nets has mathematical grounds—certain theorems don't go through otherwise—but this may well reflect something unnatural and obscure in the behaviour of the more general nets. I shall say more later.

Let $N = (B, E, F, M_0)$ be a Petri net.

A *marking* M is a multiset of conditions, *i.e.* $M \in \mu B$.

Let M, M' be markings. Let A be a finite multiset of events. Define

$$M \xrightarrow{A} M' \Leftrightarrow {}^\bullet A \leq M \;\&\; M' = (M - {}^\bullet A) + A^\bullet.$$

This gives the *transition relation* between markings. When we wish to stress the net N in which the transition $M \xrightarrow{A} M'$ occurs we write

$$N : M \xrightarrow{A} M'.$$

A *reachable marking* of N is a marking M for which $M_0 \xrightarrow{A_0} M_1 \xrightarrow{A_1} \cdots \xrightarrow{A_{n-1}} M_n = M$ for some markings and multisets of events.

Now we can define the special subclass of nets.

Definition. Say a Petri net $N = (B, E, F, M_0)$ is *contact-free* iff $F \leq \underline{1}$ and $M \leq \underline{1}$ for all reachable markings M.

For contact-free nets we can write xFy instead of $F_{x,y} = 1$.

Remark. Often such nets are called *safe*. For them a condition only holds or fails to hold and an event either occurs or does not occur; they do not happen with multiplicities. For these nets the term "condition" is consistent with its more usual use where it is imagined to assert a state of affairs which either holds or does not hold. In fact, often people go to the extent of using different terms, like "place" and "transition", for the conditions and events of the general nets. In this short exposition there's no need to be so finicky.

The behaviour of contact-free nets is particularly simple and can be expressed just with sets, without the use of multisets. Recall we identify sets with those multisets in which the multiplicity is 1 at greatest.

Proposition. *The behaviour of contact-free nets:*
Let $N = (B, E, F, M_0)$ be a contact-free net.
Let A be a set of events. Then ${}^\bullet A$ and $A^\bullet$ are sets too.
Any reachable marking is a set.
Let M be a reachable marking. Let M' be a marking of N. Then $M \xrightarrow{A} M'$ iff

$$(\forall e \in A. {}^\bullet e \subseteq M) \;\&\; (\forall e, e' \in A.\ {}^\bullet e \cap {}^\bullet e' = \emptyset) \;\&\; M' = (M \setminus {}^\bullet A) \cup A^\bullet.$$

For a contact-free net N, an event e is said to have *concession* at a reachable marking M if ${}^\bullet e \subseteq M$. If two events e and e' have concession at a reachable marking M and share a common precondition, so ${}^\bullet e \cap {}^\bullet e' \neq \emptyset$, the events e, e' are said to be in *conflict* at M. You can see why; if one occurs at M then the other does not. On the other hand, if $M \xrightarrow{A} M'$ the events in A are said to occur *concurrently*.

So much for the objects of our first category. But what are the morphisms? To motivate these let's look at some constructions that are often seen on nets—see [LC] for an early example. They arise when we consider how to give a Petri-net semantics to our generic programming language **Proc**$_L$, for a synchronisation algebra L. Of course when we model a term in **Proc**$_L$by a net, the events of the net will correspond to the actions of communication specifed by the term, so the net carries a little extra structure, a labelling of events by elements of L. Fortunately we can factor the constructions on labelled nets into a construction on the nets proper and an extra construction due to the labelling.

Let us first define the guarding construction in **Proc**$_L$. The guarding construction λp simply precedes the occurrences of events of the net N for p by an event of kind λ. A net construction which achieves this can be drawn in this way:

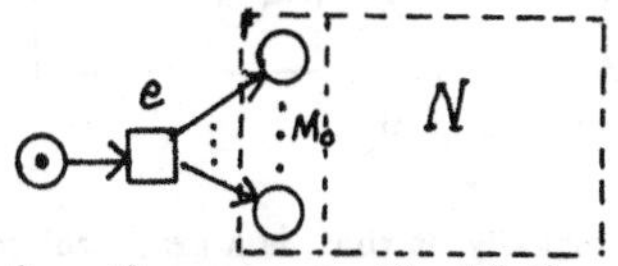

Simply adjoin a new event e, to form the new net eN, with the event e labelled by λ, to the net so that on its occurrence it sets-up the original initial marking.

Now we look at the restriction operation on nets. This simply disallows certain kinds of events from occurring. It can be modelled simply by "deleting" the forbidden events from the net.

Restriction: Let $N = (B, E, F, M_0)$ be a net. Let $E' \subseteq E$. Define the *restriction* of N to E' to be $N\lceil E' = (B, E', F', M_0)$ where F' is F restricted to $(B \times E') \cup (E' \times B)$ *i.e.* $F'_{b,e} = F_{b,e}$ and $F'_{e,b} = F_{e,b}$ for $e \in E'$ and $b \in B$.

Example. Here is a net with its restriction to a subset of events

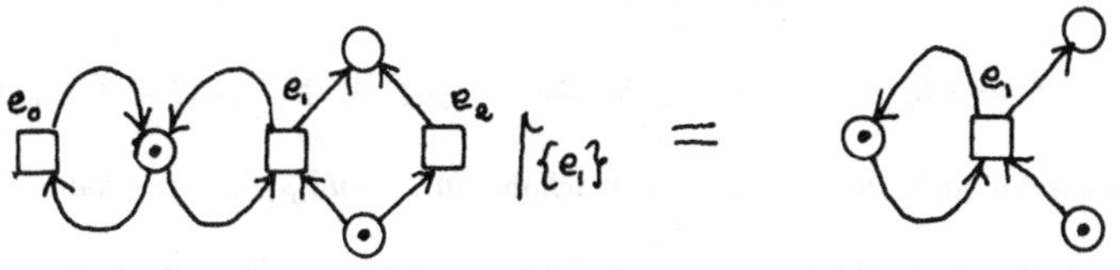

The behaviour of a net restricted to a set of events is a restriction of the behaviour of the original net.

Proposition. *Let $N = (B, E, F, M_0)$ be a net. Let $E' \subseteq E$. Let M and M' be markings of N. Then*

$$N\lceil E' : M \xrightarrow{A} M' \Leftrightarrow N : M \xrightarrow{A} M' \;\&\; A \in \mu E'.$$

Of course if a net is labelled, and so a structure of the form $N = (B, E, F, M_0, l)$ with $l : E \to L \setminus \{*, 0\}$, and $\Lambda \subseteq L$, then we can define restriction to Λ to be the labelled net restricted to those events with labels in Λ. This models the operator $\lceil\Lambda$ in **Proc**$_L$.

Product: Imagine two processes, modelled as nets, set in parallel, side-by-side. Whether or not they communicate, to form events of synchronisation, depends on the what kinds of events they are prepared to do. This can be expressed by labelling the events by elements of a synchronisation algebra. The *product* of two (unlabelled) nets allows arbitrary synchronisations. When they are labelled, forbidden synchronisations can be removed by restriction.

Let $N_0 = (B_0, E_0, F_0, M_0)$ and $N_1 = (B_1, E_1, F_1, M_1)$ be nets. Rather than give a formal definition of their product—which can afterall be found in [W3]—we describe the product construction in graphical terms. Disjoint copies of the two nets N_0 and N_1 are juxtaposed and extra events of synchronisation of the form (e_0, e_1) are adjoined, for e_0 an event of N_0 and e_1 an event of N_1; an extra event (e_0, e_1) has as preconditions those of its components so ${}^\bullet e = {}^\bullet e_0 + {}^\bullet e_1$ and similarly postconditions $e_0{}^\bullet + e_1{}^\bullet$. It is useful to think of the copies of the original events, those which are not synchronised with any companion event of the the other process as having the form $(e_0, *)$ in the copy of N_0 and the form $(*, e_1)$ in the copy of N_1. Then the events of the product have the form $E = \{(e_0, *) \mid e_0 \in E_0\} \cup \{(e_1, *) \mid e_0 \in E_1\} \cup \{(e_0, e_1) \mid e_0 \in E_0 \ \& \ e_1 \in E_1\}$, which is the product of the sets E_0 and E_1 in the category of sets with partial functions. And similarly to be more precise about the conditions we can assume that they have the form $B = B_0 \uplus B_1$ the disjoint union of B_0 and B_1.

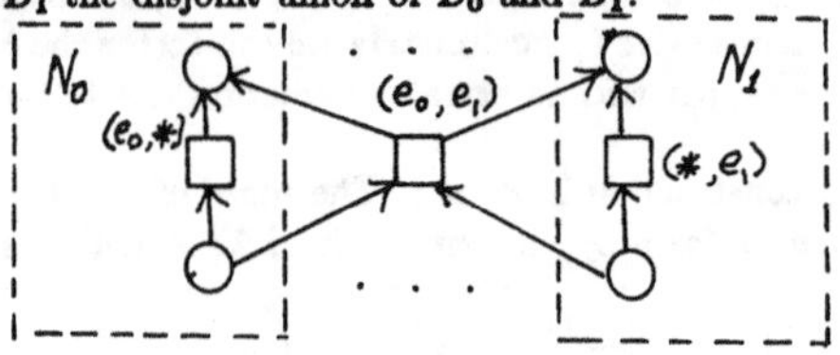

Write $N_0 \times N_1$ for the product of the nets N_0 and N_1.

So far all we have described, and informally at that, is a graphical construction on nets. To justify the construction we must understand the behaviour of the product of two nets in terms of the behaviour of the original nets. For this we need to project the behaviour of the product net to the behaviour of a component net. There are two parts to such a projection, an event part and a condition part. Consider the projection from $N_0 \times N_1$ to N_0. There is an obvious partial function from the events of the product to the events of a component. Define $\pi_0 : E \to E_0$ by $\pi(e_0, e_1) = e_0$—this will be undefined if $e_0 = *$. Define ρ_0 to be the converse relation to the injection $B_0 \to B$. This projects conditions in the product back to the component—again it is a partial function. Now with the help of these two maps we can describe the behaviour of $N_0 \times N_1$.

Proposition. *The behaviour of a product of nets $N_0 \times N_1$ is related to the behaviour of its components N_0 and N_1 by*

$$N_0 \times N_1 : M \xrightarrow{A} M' \quad \text{iff} \quad (N_0 : \rho_0 M \xrightarrow{\pi_0 A} \rho_0 M' \ \& \ N_1 : \rho_1 M \xrightarrow{\pi_1 A} \rho_1 M').$$

A marking M is reachable in $N_0 \times N_1$ iff $\rho_0 M$ is reachable in N_0 and $\rho_1 M$ is reachable in N_1.

Intuitively the behaviour of the product is precisely that allowed when we project into the components. The pair of maps (π_0, ρ_0) specifies how the dynamic behaviour of the product of nets, $N_0 \times N_1$, projects to the dynamic behaviour in the component N_0. The pair (π_1, ρ_1) plays the same role but for the component N_1. They are essential in describing the behaviour of the product of nets.

Parallel composition: Let us look at the parallel composition of two nets. Assume now events of the nets N_0 and N_1 carry labels from a synchronisation algebra L. Let (N_0, l_0) and (N_1, l_1) be labelled nets, so $l_i : E_0 \to L \setminus \{*, 0\}$ for $i = 0, 1$. Their *parallel composition* $(N_0, l_0) \textcircled{L} (N_1, l_1)$ is a labelled net which is the restriction of the product to those events allowed by the synchronisation algebra L *i.e.*

$$\begin{aligned}(N_0, l_0) \textcircled{L} (N_1, l_1) &= ((N_0 \times N_1)\lceil E', l) \quad \text{where} \\ E' &= \{e \in E \mid l_0\pi_0(e) \bullet l_1\pi_1(e) \neq 0\} \\ l(e) &= l_0\pi_0(e) \bullet l_1\pi_1(e).\end{aligned}$$

Of course we want to understand the behaviour of the parallel composition of nets in terms of the behaviour of its components. But this follows from our observations about the restriction and product of nets.

Proposition. *The behaviour of the parallel composition of nets (N_0, l_0) and (N_1, l_1) labelled by a synchronisation algebra is related to the behaviour of its components N_0 and N_1 by*

$$\begin{aligned}N_0 \textcircled{L} N_1 : M \xrightarrow{A} M' \quad \text{iff} \quad & A \in \mu\{e \in E \mid l_0\pi_0(e) \bullet l_1\pi_1(e) \neq 0\} \ \& \\ & N_0 : \rho_0 M \xrightarrow{\pi_0 A} \rho_0 M' \quad \& \quad N_1 : \rho_1 M \xrightarrow{\pi_1 A} \rho_1 M'.\end{aligned}$$

Synchronous product: Another important construction can be derived from the product construction with restriction, that of *synchronous product.* It is the restriction of the product of two nets to events of the form (e_0, e_1) where both e_0 and e_1 must be proper, non-$*$ events. Thus there is a tight synchronisation between the components of a synchronous product; in order to occur within a synchronous product every event of one component must synchronise with an event from the other.

Let $N_0 = (B_0, E_0, F_0, M_0)$ and $N_1 = (B_1, E_1, F_1, M_1)$ be nets. Define their *synchronous product* $N_0 \otimes N_1$ to be the restriction $N_0 \times N_1 \lceil (E_0 \times E_1)$. There are obvious projections got by restricting the projections of the product.

Example. One can represent a ticking clock as the following simple net, call it Ω: 

Given an arbitrary contact-free net N it is a simple matter to serialise, or interleave, its event occurrences; just synchronise them one at a time with the ticks of the clock. This amounts to forming the synchronous product $N \otimes \Omega$ of N with Ω, in a picture:

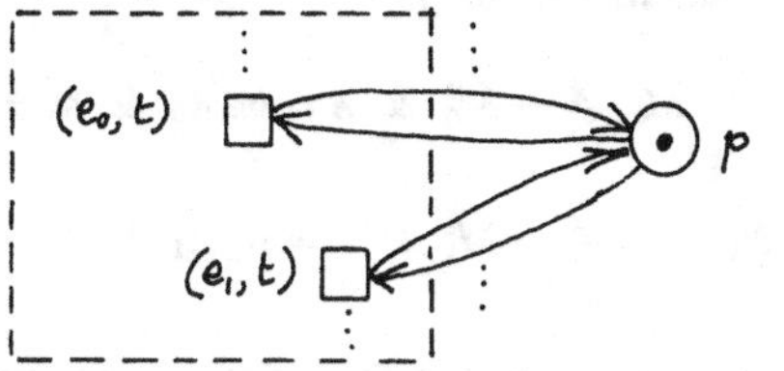

It is easy to check that the synchronous product $N \otimes \Omega$ does serialise the event occurrences of N—just use the properties of restriction and product.

Proposition. *M is a reachable marking of $N \otimes \Omega$ and $M \xrightarrow{A} M'$ in $N \otimes \Omega$ iff $M - p$ is a reachable marking of N and $\exists e.\ A = (e, t)$ & $N : (M - p) \xrightarrow{e} (M' - p)$.*

Sum: We define the sum construction but only for contact-free nets as I'm not sure what the general construction should be. Roughly the sum construction fuses together the initial markings of two nets, so the resulting net either behaves like one component or the other. Again we shall describe the construction graphically—refer to [W3] for a formal definition.

Let $N_0 = (B_0, E_0, F_0, M_0)$ and $N_1 = (B_1, E_1, F_1, M_1)$ be contact-free nets. The two nets N_0 and N_1 are laid side by side and then a little surgery is performed on their initial markings. For each pair of conditions b_0 in the initial marking of N_0 and b_1 in the initial marking of N_1 a new condition (b_0, b_1) is created and made to have the same pre and post events as b_0 and b_1 together. The conditions in the original initial markings are removed and replaced by a new initial marking consisting of these newly created conditions. Here is the picture:

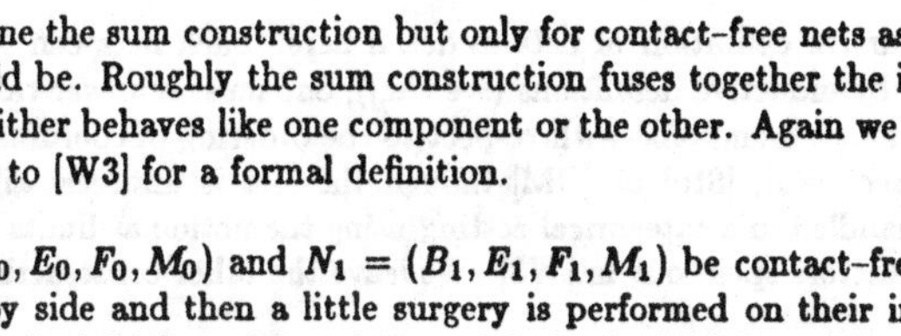

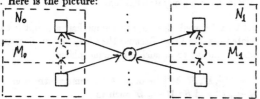

Notice a condition in the initial marking of one component is generally represented by more than one condition in the initial marking of the sum.

Example. The sum of two nets:

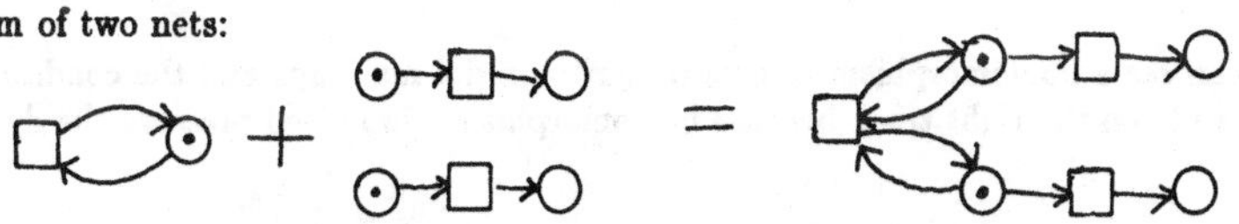

The set of events of the sum E is the disjoint union $E_0 \uplus E_1$ of the events of the components. There are the obvious injections $in_0 : E_0 \to E$ and $in_1 : E_1 \to E$ on events. The initial marking of the sum can be represented by $M = M_0 \times M_1$, and its set of conditions by

$$B = \{(b_0, *) \mid b_0 \in B_0 \setminus M_0\} \cup \{(*, b_1) \mid b_1 \in B_1 \setminus M_1\} \cup M.$$

Then there are the obvious injection relations ι_0 and ι_1 where

$$b_0 \iota_0 b \Leftrightarrow \exists b_1 \in B_1 \cup \{*\}.\ b = (b_0, b_1),$$
$$b_1 \iota_1 b \Leftrightarrow \exists b_0 \in B_0 \cup \{*\}.\ b = (b_0, b_1).$$

Thus the injection relations are opposite to the obvious partial functions taking a condition in B to its first or second component. Using the injections we can express the behaviour of the sum in terms of the behaviour of its components.

Proposition. *Let $N_0 + N_1$ be the sum of contact-free nets with injections (in_0, ι_0) and (in_1, ι_1). Then M is a reachable marking of $N_0 + N_1$ and $M \xrightarrow{A} M'$ iff*

$\exists$ *reachable marking* $M_0, A_0, M_0'.\ N_0 : M_0 \xrightarrow{A_0} M_0'\ \ \&\ \ A = in_0 A_0\ \ \&\ \ M = \iota_0 M_0\ \ \&\ \ M' = \iota_0 M_0'$

or

$\exists$ *reachable marking* $M_1, A_1, M_1'.\ N_1 : M_1 \xrightarrow{A_1} M_1'\ \ \&\ \ A = in_1 A_1\ \ \&\ \ M = \iota_1 M_1\ \ \&\ \ M' = \iota_1 M_1'.$

Those familiar with Milner's work may be a little bothered by our definition of sum. For the + of CCS and SCCS once a component has been selected nondeterministically the choice is stuck to, which is not true in general for our sum—consider the example above. However our construction will agree with Milner's on those contact-free nets for which $\forall b \in M_0\ \not\exists e.\ eFb$ *i.e.* no event leads into the initial marking. If one were to systematically give a net semantics to the languages $\mathbf{Proc}_L$, which include CCS and SCCS, all the nets constructed would be contact-free and satisfy this property.

We do not describe the recursive definition of nets in detail here. Such nets can be defined in the standard way one builds-up sets by inductive definitions (see [Ac]); one must however take a little care to ensure that the operations on nets are monotonic with respect to the ordering of coordinatewise inclusion on nets, but this is not hard (see [W3], [Stu] or [GM] though the last is unnecessarily complicated). Alternatively, recursion can be handled in a categorical setting using the notion ω-limits of chains of *net-embeddings* and ω-continuous functors spelt-out in [W3]. We leave the other constructions for $\mathbf{Proc}_L$ as an exercise.

Projections and injections on nets are examples of a more general notion of morphism between nets. It seems from our examples that a morphism from a net N to a net N' should express how the behaviour of N induces a behaviour in N'. We look for a general definition.

Given that we can regard a net as a 2-sorted algebra, an obvious first attempt is to take morphisms to be *homomorphisms* of the associated net-algebras. Because they are algebras over multisets the maps should be *linear*. Let's spell out what it means to be such a homomorphism.

Let $N = (B, E, F, M)$ and $N' = (B', E', F', M')$ be nets. A *homomorphism* from N to N' is a pair of multifunctions (η, β) with $\eta : E \rightarrow_\mu E'$ and $\beta : B \rightarrow_\mu B'$ such that

$$\beta M = M'\ \ \&\ \ \forall A \in \mu E.\ {}^\bullet(\eta A) = \beta({}^\bullet A)\ \ \&\ \ (\eta A)^\bullet = \beta(A^\bullet).$$

You can see a homomorphism of nets preserves initial markings and the condition-environments of events. We are on the right track because homomorphisms do indeed preserve the dynamic behaviour of nets.

Proposition. *Let $(\eta, \beta) : N \rightarrow N'$ be a homomorphism of nets. If $M \xrightarrow{A} M'$ in N then $\beta M \xrightarrow{\eta A} \beta M'$ in N'.*

If (η, β) is a homomorphism from N to N', as a computation

$$M_0 \xrightarrow{A_0} M_1 \xrightarrow{A_1} \cdots \xrightarrow{A_{n-1}} M_n \xrightarrow{A_n} \cdots$$

is traced-out in N so the computation

$$\beta M_0 \xrightarrow{\eta A_0} \beta M_1 \xrightarrow{\eta A_1} \cdots \xrightarrow{\eta A_{n-1}} \beta M_n \xrightarrow{\eta A_n} \cdots$$

is traced-out in N'. This is not to say that all homomorphisms on nets should be morphisms. But if the morphisms are homomorphisms they will automatically preserve behaviour, a property we certainly require.

Example. A homomorphism:

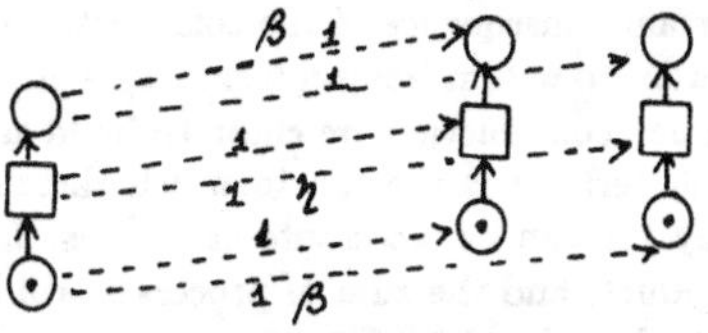

There is a problem with the interpretation of the homomorphism in this example. The occurrence of a single event in the domain of the homomorphism induces the simultaneous or coincident occurrence of 2 events e_0 and e_1 in its range. This goes against a view of Petri nets expressed by Petri that events which are coincident are the same event. Morphisms should be homomorphisms which *preserve* events, in the sense that η should be a partial function, thus fobidding the example above. Note we do not want morphisms to "preserve conditions" in the sense that β should be a partial function; to do so would rule out the injections used to characterise the behaviour of our sum construction.

Definition. A *morphism* of Petri nets is a homomorphism (η, β) in which η is a partial function. A *morphism* (η, β) is *synchronous* when η is a total function.

When nets are contact-free, just as their behaviour can be described using sets and relations instead of multisets and multifunctions, so can morphisms be characterised in a more elementary manner.

Proposition. *Let $N = (B_0, E_0, F_0, M_0)$ and $N_1 = (B_1, E_1, F_1, M_1)$ be contact-free nets. A pair (η, β) is a morphism $N_0 \to N_1$ iff η is a partial function, and β is a relation between B_0 and B_1 such that:*

(i) $M_1 = \beta M_0$ and $\forall b_1 \in M_1 \exists! b_0 \in M_0.\ b_0 \beta b_1$,

(ii) *If $b_0 \beta b_1$ then*

$$\eta \text{ restricts to a total function } {}^\bullet b_0 \to {}^\bullet b_1 \quad \text{and}$$
$$\eta \text{ restricts to a total function } b_0{}^\bullet \to b_1{}^\bullet,$$

(iii) *If $e_0 \eta e_1$ then*

$$\beta^{op} \text{ restricts to a total function } {}^\bullet e_1 \to {}^\bullet e_0 \quad \text{and}$$
$$\beta^{op} \text{ restricts to a total function } e_1{}^\bullet \to e_0{}^\bullet.$$

(We use R^{op} for the opposite relation to R.)

Definition. Let **Net** be the category of nets with net morphisms. Let $\mathbf{Net}^c$ be the full subcategory of nets with objects just the contact-free nets. Let $\mathbf{Net}_{syn}$ and $\mathbf{Net}^c_{syn}$ be their subcategories in which morphisms are synchronous.

The constructions we have seen turn out to be categorical constructions. Recall the definition of product in a category. A product of two objects N_0 and N_1 consists of an object $N_0 \times N_1$ with projection morphisms $\Pi_0 : N_0 \times N_1 \to N_0$ and $\Pi_1 : N_0 \times N_1 \to N_1$ which satisfy the property that given any pair of morphisms $f_0 : N \to N_0$ and $f_1 : N \to N_1$ there is a *unique* morphism $[f_0, f_1] : N \to N_0 \times N_1$ such that $f_0 = \Pi_0 \circ [f_0, f_1]$ and $f_1 = \Pi_1 \circ [f_0, f_1]$. Coproduct is the dual notion got by reversing the arrows. Categorical constructions such as these are unique to within isomorphism.

Proposition.

The product $N_0 \times N_1$, with morphisms (π_0, ρ_0) and (π_1, ρ_1), is a categorical product in **Net**, *the category of nets.*

The synchronous product $N_0 \otimes N_1$, with morphisms the restrictions of the projections is a product in $\mathbf{Net}_{syn}$, *the category of nets with synchronous morphisms.*

The sum $N_0 + N_1$ with injections (in_0, ι_0) and (in_1, ι_1) is a coproduct in both the subcategories of contact-free nets with morphisms and synchronous morphisms.

The fact that parallel composition is so closely related to a product adds mathematical substance to the intuition, often expressed, that parallelism is some kind of "orthogonality".

So what? Well, one important consequence of the constructions being categorical is that each comes accompanied by a characterisation to within isomorphism. This means that we need not worry about the details of the concrete and ad hoc construction we chose to build-up our product, synchronous product and sum. But more important perhaps is the use to which these facts can be put when we translate between different models. They too can be made into categories. In them too parallel compositions are obtained by restricting the product, and the sum of processes will be modelled as a coproduct. And it happens that the categories can be related by functors, passing back and forth, in such a way that the categorical constructions are preserved. We see a typical example of how in the next section. We turn to consider other models, and see how they can be embedded in the category of nets. (For the most part we shall be very sketchy in our treatment of labelled versions of these other models, but because we show how they can be identified with labelled nets it follows how to perform constructions on these other labelled structures.)

3. Occurrence nets—the semantics of Petri nets.

Nets are rather complex objects with an intricate behaviour which so far has been expressed in a dynamic way. We would like to know when two nets have essentially the same behaviour. In this section we propose a more "static" representation of their behaviour as a certain kind of net, a net of condition and event occurrences. This is a generalisation of the familiar unfolding of a state-transition system to a tree [W2]. The theorems of this section only work if we restrict the class of nets and we will assume that the nets are contact-free. The occurrence net we associate with a contact-free net will be built-up essentially by unfolding the net to its occurrences. This unfolding is a canonical representative of the behaviour of the original net. Occurrence nets and the operation of unfolding a net to an occurrence net were first introduced in [NPW, W].

We want to axiomatise those nets in which conditions and events correspond to occurrences (as is the case with Petri's causal nets but we also wish to represent conflict in these nets).

An *occurrence net* is a contact-free net (B, E, F, M) for which the following restrictions are satisfied:

(i) $b \in M \Leftrightarrow {}^\bullet b = \emptyset$, so the initial marking is identified with the set of conditions which are not preceded by any events in the F-relation,

(ii) $\forall b \in B. |{}^\bullet b| \leq 1$, so a condition can be caused to hold through the occurrence of at most one event,

(iii) F^+ is irreflexive and $\forall e \in E.\ \{e' \mid e'F^*e\}$ is finite, so we ban repetitions of the same event and insist the occurrence of an event can only depend on the occurrence of a finite number of events,

(iv) $\#$ is irreflexive where

$$e \#_1 e' \Leftrightarrow_{def} e \in E \ \&\ e' \in E \ \&\ {}^\bullet e \cap {}^\bullet e' \neq \emptyset \text{ and}$$
$$x \# x' \Leftrightarrow_{def} \exists e, e' \in E. e \#_1 e' \ \&\ eF^*x \ \&\ e'F^*x'.$$

In this way we eliminate those events which cannot possibly occur because they depend on the previous occurrence of conflicting events.

Suppose $N = (B, E, F, M)$ is an occurrence net. We call the relation $\#_1$ defined above the *immediate conflict relation* and $\#$ the *conflict relation*. We define the *concurrency relation*, *co*, between pairs $x, y \in B \cup E$ by:

$$x \; co \; y \Leftrightarrow_{def} \neg(xF^+y \text{ or } yF^+x \text{ or } x\#y).$$

Being nets, occurrence nets determine a subcategory of **Net**.

Definition. Write **Occ** for the category of occurrence nets with net morphisms. Write $\mathbf{Occ}_{syn}$ for the subcategory of occurrence nets with synchronous morphisms.

For occurrence nets there is an especially simple definition of a *concurrency relation* and *conflict relation* which was previously only defined with respect to a marking.

Proposition. *Let $N = (B, E, F, M)$ be an occurrence net. Then every event of N has concession at some reachable marking and every condition of N holds at some reachable marking.*

Let e, e' be two events of N. Let b, b' be two conditions of N.

The relations $\#_1 \subseteq E^2$ and $\# \subseteq (B \cup E)^2$ are binary, symmetric, irreflexive relations. The relation of immediate conflict $e\#_1 e'$ holds iff there is a reachable marking of N at which the events e and e' are in conflict.

The relation co is a binary, symmetric, reflexive relation between conditions and events of N. We have $b \; co \; b'$ iff there is a reachable marking of N at which b and b' both hold. We have $e \; co \; e'$ iff there is a reachable marking at which e and e' can occur concurrently.

Proposition. *Let $N = (B, E, F, M)$ be a contact-free net. There is a unique occurrence net $\mathcal{U}N = (B', E', F', M')$ with a folding $f = (\eta, \beta) : \mathcal{U}N \to N$ which satisfies:*

$$B' = \{(\emptyset, b) \mid b \in M\} \cup \{(\{e_0\}, b) \mid e_0 \in E' \;\&\; b \in B \;\&\; \eta(e_0)Fb\},$$
$$E' = \{(S, e) \mid S \subseteq B' \;\&\; e \in E \;\&\; \beta S = {}^\bullet e \;\&\; \forall b_0, b_0' \in S. b_0 \; co \; b_0'\},$$
$$xF'y \Leftrightarrow \exists w, z.\; y = (w, z) \;\&\; x \in z,$$
$$M' = \{(\emptyset, b) \mid b \in M\},$$

and

$$e_0 \eta e \Leftrightarrow \exists S \subseteq B'.\; e_0 = (S, e),$$
$$b_0 \beta b \Leftrightarrow b \in M \;\&\; b_0 = (\emptyset, b) \text{ or } \exists e_0 \in E'.\; b_0 = (\{e_0\}, b).$$

Example. This example illustrates a contact-free net together with its occurrence net unfolding.

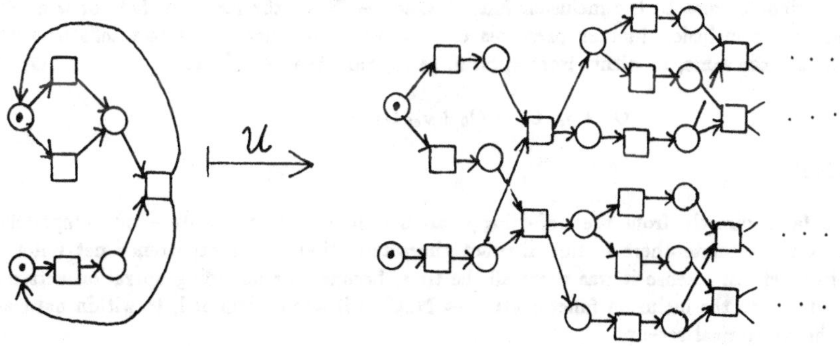

Something is lost in the passage from a net N to the occurrence net $\mathcal{U}N$. For example two non-isomorphic nets like

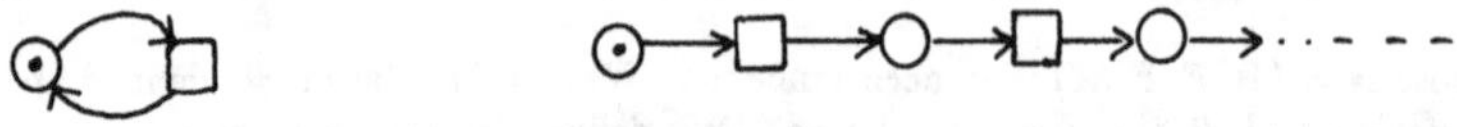

unfold to isomorphic occurrence nets. We have lost information about which events are occurrences of the same repetitive event. Still, $\mathcal{U}N$ is in some sense the natural occurrence net which represents N. We make this precise.

The morphism $f : \mathcal{U}N \to N$ expresses how the conditions and events in $\mathcal{U}N$ are occurrences of conditions and events in the original contact-free net N where events and conditions may occur repeatedly. It is the construction $\mathcal{U}N$ together with the morphism f which possess an abstract characterisation; the pair $\mathcal{U}N$, f is *cofree* over N. Informally this says that $\mathcal{U}N$ is the "best" occurrence net to represent N. Formally it says

Proposition. *If O is any other occurrence net which maps $g : O \to N$ then there is a unique morphism $h : O \to \mathcal{U}N$ such that this diagram commutes:*

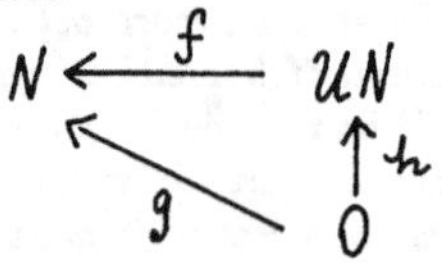

See [W3] for a proof.

Because this can be done for all contact-free nets N this implies by [Mac thm 2, p.81] that the operation of unfolding on nets extends to an operation on morphisms to make $\mathcal{U}$ into a functor $\mathbf{Net}^c \to \mathbf{Occ}$ which is the *right adjoint* to the inclusion functor $\mathbf{Occ} \to \mathbf{Net}^c$. Together the inclusion functor and $\mathcal{U}$ determine an *adjunction* between $\mathbf{Occ}$ and $\mathbf{Net}^c$; the inclusion functor is the *left adjoint* and $\mathcal{U}$ the *right adjoint* of the adjunction. This has some important consequences.

By [Mac thm 1, p. 114] right adjoints preserve limits and in particular products. Thus we know that

$$\mathcal{U}(N_0 \times N_1) \cong \mathcal{U}N_0 \times_{Occ} \mathcal{U}N_1,$$

for contact-free nets N_0 and N_1, *i.e.* that if we take the product of two contact-free nets, and then unfold the result, we obtain the same net to within isomorphism as if we unfold the nets first, and then form their product in the category $\mathbf{Occ}$.

The unfolding of an occurrence net is isomorphic to the occurrence net itself. Formally the morphism $f_O : \mathcal{U}O \to O$ is a *natural isomorphism* for any occurrence net O. This makes the adjunction a bit special; it is a *coreflection* and $\mathbf{Occ}$ is a *coreflective subcategory* of $\mathbf{Net}^c$. Thus we see that the product of two occurrence nets O_0 and O_1 in $\mathbf{Occ}$ is

$$O_0 \times_{Occ} O_1 \cong \mathcal{U}O_0 \times_{Occ} \mathcal{U}O_1 \cong \mathcal{U}(O_0 \times_{Net} O_1).$$

Because $\mathcal{U}$ is a right adjoint to the inclusion functor $\mathbf{Occ} \to \mathbf{Net}^c$, the inclusion functor is a left adjoint to $\mathcal{U}$, and so the inclusion functor preserves colimits like coproduct. This fact tells us that coproducts in $\mathbf{Occ}$ are the same, to within isomorphism, as coproducts in $\mathbf{Net}^c$ *i.e.*

$$O_0 +_{Occ} O_1 \cong O_0 +_{Net} O_1,$$

the coproduct in $\mathbf{Net}^c$.

Proving these facts directly from the unfolding construction is quite unwieldy—and completely uninstructive—so it is fortunate there is this abstract characterisation of the occurrence net unfolding of a contact-free net. In a sense it was there all the time, because the unfolding operation acts on nets as the right adjoint to the inclusion functor $\mathbf{Occ} \to \mathbf{Net}^c$ so it was determined, to within natural isomorphism, by the categorical set-up.

Right adjoints preserve limits; they do not necessarily preserve colimits, and indeed here is a simple example where a coproduct is not preserved by unfolding.

Example. This example is essentially the same as that given in [W2] for a category of transition systems where unfolding yields a tree. Let N be the net . Let Ω be the net representing a clock, as seen before. Then $\mathcal{U}(N+\Omega) \not\cong \mathcal{U}N + \mathcal{U}\Omega$.

Of course we can restrict to subcategories of nets so that unfolding does preserve coproducts. A subcategory, which have already remarked on, for which this is true is that where the nets satisfy: every condition in the initial marking has no pre–events.

The coreflection between **Occ** and **Net**^{c} cuts down to a coreflection between the subcategories of synchronous morphisms with the analogous results.

It is now a simple exercise to define operations on labelled occurrence nets which correspond to constructs of **Proc**$_L$, in the same way as we did for nets. For example, the parallel composition of labelled occurrence nets is the restriction of their product in **Occ** .

Why did we restrict ourselves to contact–free nets in this section? Although there does seem to be a natural occurrence–net unfolding of the more general nets it is easy to see that this cannot be cofree over the original net. Let the net N consist of a single condition b with the initial marking $2b$. Suppose there were an occurrence net O which was cofree over N. The occurrence net would *either* have an initial marking containing two conditions c, d so that in the "folding" $f = (\beta, \eta) : O \to N$ we had $\beta_{d,b} = \beta_{c,b} = 1$ *or* a single condition p such that $\beta_{p,b} = 2$. The latter case is impossible as we would then not have a morphism h making this diagram commute:

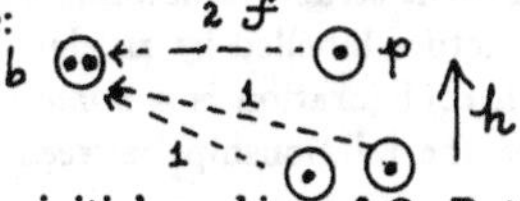

So if anything $\beta_{c,b} = \beta_{d,b} = 1$ for c, d in the initial marking of O. But then of course we do not have a *unique* morphism making this diagram commute, as is shown by these two morphisms:

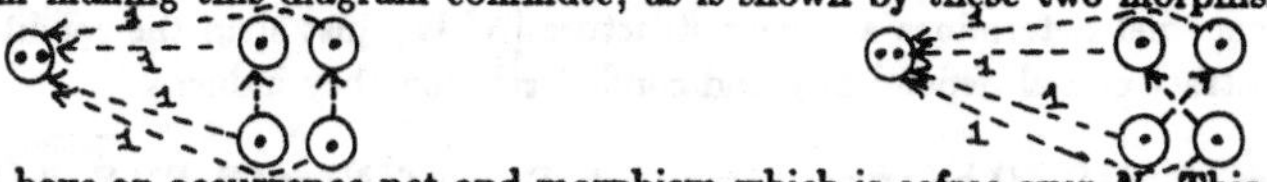

Thus we cannot have an occurrence net and morphism which is cofree over N. This argument works just as well to show there cannot in general be a contact–free net which is cofree over an arbitrary Petri net. The relationship between the categories **Net** and **Net**^{c}, and the categories **Net** and **Occ** does not seem to be as pleasant as that between the other categories we discuss here, and certainly is not understood as well.

4. Event structures.

We show the relationship between a category of event structures and the category of nets. The event structures are of the simple form introduced in [NPW]; they consist of a set of events related by a causal dependency relation and a conflict relation. The paper [NPW] and thesis [W] contain a great deal to motivate event structures. The morphisms on event structures were introduced in [W1] and we refer the reader there and to [W] for the relationship between the event structures used here and more general event structures.

We show that constructions given in [NPW] determine an adjunction between nets and event structures. There is a right adjoint, part of a coreflection, from occurrence nets to event structures. This composes with the right adjoint of unfolding, part of a coreflection, to give a right adjoint from nets to event structures, consequently part of a coreflection. This pleasant categorical set–up makes it easy to relate semantics given in terms of nets to those in terms of event structures, and through them to the *pomset* model of Vaughan Pratt [Pr] and the *behaviour systems* of Mike Shields [Sh1,2].

An event structure can be regarded as an occurrence net with its conditions stripped away leaving the F^* relation as the causal dependency relation and the # relation as conflict.

An *event structure* is a triple $(E, \leq, \#)$ consisting of

(i) E a set of events,

(ii) $\leq$ the *causal dependency relation* a partial order on E and

(iii) $\#$ the *conflict relation* a binary symmetric relation on E

which satisfy $e \# e' \leq e'' \Rightarrow e \# e''$ and $[e] =_{def} \{e' \in E \mid e' \leq e\}$ is finite.

Remark. Notice that here we insist that event structures satisfy a finiteness restriction, $[e] < \infty$, a restriction not enforced in [NPW]. Event structures of the simple form above are called *prime* event structures in [W1, 2].

Event structures are accompanied by a natural idea of *configuration* (or state), the downwards-closed and conflict-free subsets of events with respect to $\leq$ and $\#$. Intuitively a configuration is a set of events that occur in some history of a process; it should only be possible for an event to occur once the events on which it causally depends have occurred and it should be impossible for two events in conflict to occur in the same history.

Let $(E, \leq, \#)$ be an event structure. Let $x \subseteq E$. Say x is *downwards-closed* iff $\forall e, e' \in E. e \leq e' \in x \Rightarrow e \in x$. Say x is *conflict-free* iff $\forall e, e' \in x. \neg(e \# e')$. Write $\mathcal{L}(E, \leq, \#)$ for the set of left-closed conflict-free subsets.

The set of configurations of an event structure determine a *behaviour system* in the sense of [Sh1,2]. Imagine every event of an event structure labelled by an element of a synchronisation algebra, to form a labelled event structure. Then each configuration is a *pomset* and the set of configurations is a *process* in the sense of [Pr]. This indicates the relationship between labelled event structures and the pomset model.

Clearly an occurrence net determines an event structure [NPW]; just strip the conditions away but remember the more abstract causal dependency and conflict relation they induce.

Definition. Let $N = (B, E, F, M)$ be an occurrence net. Define $\mathcal{E}(N) = (E, F^* \lceil E, \# \lceil E)$.

A morphism $(\eta, \beta) : N \to N'$ between occurrence nets N and N' consists in part of a partial function $\eta : E \to E'$ between the associated sets of events. The partial function η always respects the event structures associated with the nets, in this sense:

$$\forall x \in \mathcal{L}(\mathcal{E}N). \ (\eta x \in \mathcal{L}(\mathcal{E}N') \ \ \& \ \ (\forall e, e' \in x. \ \eta(e) = \eta(e') \neq * \Rightarrow e = e')).$$

So, on the event structures the map η preserves configurations and the nature of events. It seems natural to take this as a definition of morphisms on event structures, so a morphism on event structures is a partial function between the sets of events which satisfies the property above.

Definition. Define $\mathbf{P}$ to be the category of event structures obtained by taking morphisms on event structures to be partial functions on the sets of events which preserve configurations and events in the sense above; morphisms are composed as partial functions. Define $\mathbf{P}_{syn}$ to be the subcategory of synchronous morphisms, in which maps are total.

Clearly $\mathcal{E}$ extends to a functor $\mathbf{Occ} \to \mathbf{P}$ from occurrence nets to event structures by defining $\mathcal{E}$ on morphisms (η, β) by

$$\mathcal{E}(\eta, \beta) = \eta.$$

Note we not only have a functor $\mathcal{E} : \mathbf{Occ} \to \mathbf{P}$ from occurrence nets to event structures but also the functor $\mathcal{E} \circ \mathcal{U} : \mathbf{Net}^c \to \mathbf{P}$, translating arbitrary contact-free nets to event structures.

It is natural to ask if, conversely, an event structure can be identified with an occurrence net. Of course we would like every morphism between event structures to correspond to net morphism between the associated nets. We seek a functor $\mathcal{N} : \mathbf{P} \to \mathbf{Occ}$ which "embeds" the category of event structures in the category of occurrence nets, so $\mathcal{E}\mathcal{N}E$ is naturally isomorphic to the original event structure E. Ideally, we would hope that $\mathcal{E}$ would be a right adjoint to $\mathcal{N}$ making a coreflection. This is indeed the case and we have all the benefits explained in the last section. We explain the construction of $\mathcal{N}$, a minor modification of that in [NPW].

An event structure can be identified with a canonical occurrence net. The basic idea is to produce an occurrence net with as many conditions as are consistent with the causal dependency and conflict relations of the event structure. But we do not want more than one condition with the same beginning and ending events—we want an occurrence net which is "condition–extensional" in the terms of [Br]. Thus we can identify the conditions with pairs of the form (e, A) where e is an event and A is a subset of events causally dependant on e and with every distinct pair of events in A in conflict. But not quite, we also want initial conditions with no beginning events.

Definition. Let $(E, \leq, \#)$ be an event structure. Define $\mathcal{N}(E, \leq, \#)$ to be (B, E, F, M) where

$$M = \{(\emptyset, A) \mid A \subseteq E \ \& \ (\forall a, a' \in A.\ a(\# \cup 1)a')\}$$
$$B = M \cup \{(e, A) \mid e \in E \ \& \ A \subseteq E \ \& \ (\forall a, a' \in A.\ a(\# \cup 1)a') \ \& \ (\forall a \in A.\ e < a)\}$$
$$F = \{(e, (e, A)) \mid (e, A) \in B\} \cup \{((c, A), e) \mid (c, A) \in B \ \& \ e \in A\}.$$

This time it is easier to establish the coreflection by showing the freeness of the occurrence net associated with an event structure.

Proposition. *Let $(E, \leq, \#)$ be an event structure.*
Then $\mathcal{N}(E, \leq, \#)$ is an occurrence net. Moreover, $\mathcal{E} \circ \mathcal{N}(E, \leq, \#) = (E, \leq, \#)$.
The net $\mathcal{N}E$ and identity function $1_E : E \to \mathcal{E}\mathcal{N}E$ is free over E with respect to $\mathcal{E}$ i.e. for any morphism $f : E \to \mathcal{E}N$ in $\mathbf{P}$ there is a unique morphism $h : \mathcal{N}E \to N$ in $\mathbf{Occ}$ such that $\mathcal{E}h \circ 1_E = f$ (i.e. $\mathcal{E}h = f$).

Thus there is a coreflection between event structures and occurrence nets with $\mathcal{E}$ as its right adjoint and $\mathcal{N}$ as its left adjoint . This composes with the coreflection between occurrence nets and contact–free nets we saw in the last section to give a coreflection between event structures and contact–free nets.

Reasoning in the same way as we did for the coreflection between $\mathbf{Net}^c$ and $\mathbf{Occ}$, we see, for instance,

$$\mathcal{E}(N_0 \times_{Occ} N_1) \cong \mathcal{E}N_0 \times_P \mathcal{E}N_1$$
$$E_0 \times_P E_1 \cong \mathcal{E}\mathcal{U}(\mathcal{N}E_0 \times_{Net} \mathcal{N}E_1)$$
$$E_0 +_P E_1 \cong \mathcal{E}\mathcal{U}(\mathcal{N}E_0 +_{Net} \mathcal{N}E_1),$$

which translates constructions in one category to constructions in the other, giving the product and coproduct in $\mathbf{P}$ in terms of the product and coproduct in $\mathbf{Net}^c$.

With extra labelling structure one can carry out the construction for parallel compostion pretty much as for nets. More direct definitions of the product, sum and parallel composition of event structures can be found in [W1].

5. Trees and synchronisation trees.

Trees underlie most interleaving models of parallel computation. The nodes represent states and the arcs occurrences of events. When the arcs are labelled by elements of a synchronisation algebra they are generally called *synchronisation trees*, a term introduced by Milner in [M1] for the special case when the synchronisation algebra is that for CCS. Trees can be identified with a special kind of event structure, and so of course with a special kind of net, just applying the results of the previous section.

A *tree* is an event structure in which any two compatible configurations are comparable. In other words, if, when ordered by inclusion, the partial order of the configurations of an event structure form a tree with limit points, we call the event structure a tree. This picks out those event structures $(E, \leq, \#)$ in which pairs of events are either in conflict or related by causal dependency *i.e.*

$$\forall e, e' \in E.\ e \leq e' \text{ or } e' \leq e \text{ or } e \# e'.$$

You can check that in this representation of trees, finite configurations correspond nodes and events to arcs of a tree. We can pick out arcs of the tree by the "covering" relation on finite configurations

$$x \longrightarrow y \Leftrightarrow \exists e.\ e \notin x \ \&\ y = x \cup \{e\}.$$

As event structures, trees inherit a notion of morphism from the category **P** . Let S and T be trees with finite configurations S^0 and T^0, to be thought of as nodes. A morphism $\theta : S \to T$ on trees corresponds to a map $\hat{\theta} : S^0 \to T^0$ on nodes which satisfies these properties which can be easily understood in terms of the more familiar graphical view of trees:

(i) $\hat{\theta}(\emptyset) = \emptyset$ *i.e.* the root-node is preserved,

(ii) $x \longrightarrow y \Rightarrow \hat{\theta}(x) = \hat{\theta}(y)$ or $\hat{\theta}(x) \longrightarrow \hat{\theta}(y)$ *i.e.* either arcs are preserved or collapsed.

Synchronous morphisms θ correspond to those in which (ii) is replaced by the stronger property

$$x \longrightarrow y \Rightarrow \hat{\theta}(x) \longrightarrow \hat{\theta}(y).$$

Definition. Write **Tr** for the category of trees and $\mathbf{Tr}_{syn}$ for the subcategory with synchronous morphisms.

Again, as you'd expect by now, trees form a coreflective subcategory of event structures and this can be got by cutting down a coreflection between the category of contact-free nets $\mathbf{Net}^c$ and **Tr** . We need not look very far for the coreflection. Putting a contact-free net N in synchronous product with the "ticking clock" Ω, of section 2, we obtain the net $N \otimes_{Net} \Omega$ in which the event occurrences are serialised. Unfolding this to an occurrence net and then taking the event structure associated with this we obtain a tree,

$$\mathcal{T}N = \mathcal{E}\mathcal{U}(N \otimes \Omega).$$

Using the property that right adjoints preserve products we derive

$$\begin{aligned} \mathcal{T}N &= \mathcal{E}\mathcal{U}(N \otimes \Omega) \\ &\cong (\mathcal{E}\mathcal{U}N) \otimes_P (\mathcal{E}\mathcal{U}\Omega) \\ &\cong (\mathcal{E}\mathcal{U}N) \otimes_P \Omega_P \end{aligned}$$

where Ω_P is the event structure associated with the "clock"; it consists of events $0 \leq 1 \leq 2 \leq \cdots \leq t \leq \cdots$. Thus $\mathcal{T}N$ puts the event structure associated with N in synchronous product with the event-structure model of a clock. While intuitive it does require a proof that $\mathcal{T}N$ is a tree. We refer to [W1] where it is shown that $(- \otimes_P \Omega_P) : \mathbf{P} \to \mathbf{Tr}$ extends to a right adjoint of the inclusion functor $\mathbf{Tr} \to \mathbf{P}$, identifying trees with a certain kind of event structure. This adjunction is a coreflection. Composing it with the coreflection between contact-free nets and event structures we obtain

Proposition. *$\mathcal{T}$ extends to a functor which is right adjoint to the functor $\mathcal{N} : \mathbf{Tr} \to \mathbf{Net}^c$. They determine a coreflection between* **Tr** *and* $\mathbf{Net}^c$.

Thus there is an interleaving, or serialising, functor $\mathcal{T} = \mathcal{E}\mathcal{U}(-\otimes\Omega) : \mathbf{Net}^c \to \mathbf{Tr}$ which translates the non-interleaving models of Petri nets and event structures into the interleaving model of trees. We know that products are preserved by $\mathcal{T}$ and that coproducts of trees coincide with their coproducts regarded as contact–free nets. Consequently, when we label nets and trees by elements of a synchronisation algebra we have that parallel compositions are preserved by interleaving and that the notion of sum agrees on trees whether we look on it as based on the coproduct of trees or the coproduct of trees regarded as nets.

By carrying out the construction in **Net**^{c}, it is easy to see that the coproduct of trees has the effect of glueing them together at the root. The product has a more interesting characterisation, familiar from the work of Milner on synchronisation trees. Write $\Sigma_{i\in I}T_i$ for the more general coproduct of a set of trees T_i indexed by $i \in I$; this construction glues the set of trees together at their roots. The guarding operation eN on a net N gives a guarding operation on trees; it simply prefixes a tree T by an event e. Note any tree can be represented to within isomorphism as a coproduct of guarded trees $\Sigma_{a\in A}aT_a$ for some set of events A. It is shown in [W1,2] that the product in the category of trees has the following form:

Proposition. *Let S and T be trees. Then*

$$S \cong \sum_{a\in A} aS_a \quad \text{and} \quad T \cong \sum_{b\in B} bT_b$$

for some sets of events A and B and trees S_a and T_b indexed by $a \in A$ and $b \in B$ respectively. We have the following characterisation of the product of S and T in **Tr** *:*

$$S \times T \cong \sum_{a\in A}(a,*)S_a \times T + \sum_{a\in A, b\in B}(a,b)S_a \times T_b + \sum_{b\in B}(*,b)S \times T_b.$$

Restricting the events of the product in accord with *e.g.* the synchronisation algebra for CCS we obtain the recursive characterisation of the parallel composition of synchronisation trees that Milner uses in [M1]. This reassuring fact demonstrates the coherence of the categorical view of constructs in a range of models.

6. Conclusion, loose ends.

There is a criss–cross of coreflections bridging different categories. We have seen some in this paper. I'll summarise those categories of models that have been related by coreflections in a diagram:

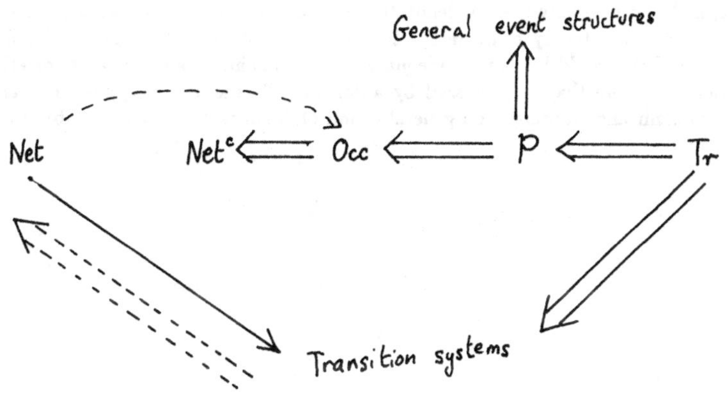

Coreflections are represented by double arrows in the direction of the left adjoint, and single functors by single arrow. Coreflections which are suspected, but not yet worked out are represented by dotted double arrows. As was pointed out there are fundamental obstacles to obtaining an adjunction between general nets and contact-free nets. Still, there does seem to be an obvious unfolding of a general net to an occurrence net. At present I have no idea of its categorical significance. And what about a coreflection between transition systems and nets? A category of transition systems is defined in [W2] and there is an obvious functor from nets in general to transition systems—take markings as states and single occurrences of events as transitions. If there is a left adjoint to that functor—there probably is—it will have to extend that which embeds trees in nets; the "obvious" identification of transition systems with nets in which states are represented as single conditions in a contact-free net cannot be the right adjoint. There is another variety of transition system, those in which transitions correspond to concurrent firings of a set of events; I haven't thought much about that category.

All the categories of models we have considered have been unlabelled. Constructions on labelled objects were derived, though it was never defined what it meant to be a morphism between labelled nets for example. This can be done following the lines of [W2] in which categories of labelled trees (synchronisation trees) and transition systems are introduced. The idea is to restrict the morphisms further in accord with the extra labelling structure; the label of the image of an event should *divide* the label of the original event.

Each category has its own natural notion of equivalence, induced by isomorphism. We started with the Petri net model, our most concrete and least abstract model, with all its detail, and passed to the far abstract model of trees in which the concurrency structure is lost entirely. As far as the synchronisation-tree model is concerned the two CCS terms $(\alpha nil \| \beta nil)$ and $(\alpha\beta nil + \beta\alpha nil)$ are the same—they denote isomorphic synchronisation trees—while as nets or event structures they are distinguished because they are not isomorphic.

There are, of course, many more abstract models yet, *e.g.* powerdomain models, models based on observational equivalence, the failure-set model and traces model, and their relationship is being understood better all the time. It remains to be clarified whether or not the categorical approach here can be generalised in a useful way to more abstract models. (The paper [LP] is an attempt, though I'm not convinced that the approach is useful for relating models and is anything like general enough.) To do so it seems necessary to pass beyond the vocabulary of events and conditions or physical states to properties of the kind captured by temporal or modal logics, and take morphisms which respect these properties. The papers [S, Sm, Ab, LW, W4] portray denotational semantics in this light and to some extent the role of the categories here is taken by domains and the role of coreflections by embedding-projection pairs (see [W5]).

There is an apparent mismatch between the approach used here, with processes represented as objects in a category, and that generally used in denotational semantics where processes are taken to be elements of a domain, itself in a category of domains. Indeed it is hard to see how all the detailed structure of Petri nets, for example, could be caught adequately in a domain. It appears that sometimes we need a finer categorical structure than is possessed by a domain. This issue has appeared in another context, the work of Lehmann and Abramsky on generalisation of domains to categories [Ab1, Le].

Appendix: multisets and multifunctions.

Multisets

Let X be a set.

A *multiset* of X is a function $f : X \to \omega$. Write f_x for the *multiplicity* $f(x)$ of the element x. Write μX for the set of multisets of X.

Let $n \in \omega$. Define $\underline{n}$ of X to be the multiset $\underline{n} : x \mapsto n$. In particular, the *null* multiset $\underline{0}$ of X is the function. $\underline{0} : x \mapsto 0$.

Let $x \in X$. Define the *singleton* multiset $\hat{x}$ to be the function $\hat{x} : y \mapsto \begin{cases} 1 & \text{if } x = y \\ 0 & \text{otherwise.} \end{cases}$
Say a multiset is a singleton if it has this form. Whenever it is clear form the context we shall write x for $\hat{x}$.

By convention, we shall identify subsets of X with those multisets of $f \in \mu X$ such that $f \leq \underline{1}$.

Operations on multisets

Many operations and relations on multisets are induced pointwise by operations and relations on integers.

Let $f, g \in \mu X$. Define

$$(f + g)_x = f_x + g_x,$$
$$(f - g)_x = \begin{cases} f_x - g_x & \text{if } f_x \leq g_x \\ 0 & \text{otherwise} \end{cases}$$
$$(f \vee g)_x = \max\{f_x, g_x\}$$
$$(f \wedge g)_x = \min\{f_x, g_x\}$$

for $x \in X$. Define

$$f \leq g \Leftrightarrow \forall x \in X.\ f_x \leq g_x.$$

Occasionally it might happen that for example f is a multiset over a set X while g is a multiset over another set Y. In such a case we can still make sense of the operations above by simply extending f and g to be multisets over $X \cup Y$.

Let $n \in \omega$ and $f \in \mu X$. Define their *scalar multiplication* nf to be the multiset given by $(nf)_x = nf_x$ for $x \in X$.

Multifunctions

Let X and Y be sets. A *multifunction* from X to Y is a function $\theta : \mu X \to \mu Y$ which is *linear i.e.*

$$\theta(nf + mg) = n(\theta f) + m(\theta g)$$

for all $n, m \in \omega$ and $f, g \in \mu X$. Write $\theta : X \to_\mu Y$ when θ is such a multifunction. Clearly the multifunction θ determines and is determined by the *matrix* $\theta_{x,y} = (\theta x)_y$ for $x \in X, y \in Y$, a multiset of $X \times Y$, and we shall often define a multifunction by giving its matrix.

By convention, we shall identify the *relations* between a set X and a set Y with those multifunctions $\theta : X \to_\mu Y$ for which $\theta_{x,y} \leq 1$. In particular, we shall identify *functions* and *partial functions* with their extensions to multifunctions. We use $*$ as a value to represent when the function is undefined. We shall use standard notation for relations and functions *e.g.* writing xRy when x and y are in relation R. For a relation R we use R^{op} to represent the converse or opposite relation $xR^{op}y \Leftrightarrow_{def} yRx$.

Acknowledgements

I have learnt much from discussions with Mogens Nielsen and Gordon Plotkin, and from working with students on their projects at Aarhus University. I saw the definition of morphisms on general nets, and not just the contact-free ones, in discussion with Ursula Goltz.

References

[Ab] Abramsky, S., Domain theory as a theory of experiments. In this proceedings (1984).

[Ab1] Abramsky, S., Ph. D. thesis, University of London. In preparation.

[Ac] Aczel, P., An introduction to inductive definitions. In the handbook of Mathematical Logic, Ed. Barwise, J., North-Holland (1983).

[AM] Arbib, M.A.,and Manes,E.G., Arrows, Structures and Functors, The categorical imperative. Academic Press (1975).

[B] Brookes, S.D., On the relationship of CCS and CSP, ICALP 1983.

[Br] Brauer, W.(Ed.), Net Theory and Applications, Springer-Verlag Lecture Notes in Comp. Sci., vol.84 (1980).

[CH] Campbell, R. H.,and Habermann, A. N.,, The Specification of Process Synchronisation by Path Expressions. Springer-Verlag Lecture Notes in Comp. Sc. Vol.16 (1974).

[GR] Goltz, U. and Reisig, W., Processes of Place/Transition Nets. Icalp 83 and to appear in Information and Control.

[GM] Goltz, U. and Mycroft, A., On the relationship of CCS and Petri nets. ICALP 84 Springer-Verlag Lecture Notes in Comp. Sc. Vol.172 (1984).

[H] Hoare, C.A.R., Communicating sequential processes. Comm. ACM 21 (1978).

[HBR] Hoare, C.A.R., Brookes, S.D., and Roscoe, A.W., A Theory of Communicating Processes, Technical Report PRG-16, Programming Research Group, University of Oxford (1981); in JACM (1984).

[Le] Lehmann, D., Categories for fixed-point semantics. FOCS 17 (1976).

[LC] Lauer, P. E. and Campbell, R. H., Formal semantics for a class of high-level primitives for coordinating concurrent processes. Acta Informatica 5 pp.297-332 (1974).

[LP] Labella, A., and Peterossi, A., Towards a Categorical Understanding of Parallelism. Report of Istituto di Analisi dei Sistemi ed Informatica del C.N.R., Rome (1983).

[LW] Larsen, K. and Winskel, G., Using Information Systems to solve Recursive Domain Equations Effectively. Springer Lecture Notes in Comp. Sc., vol. 173 (1984).

[Mac] Maclane, S., Categories for the Working Mathematician. Graduate Texts in Mathematics,Springer (1971).

[M1] Milner, R., A Calculus of Communicating Systems. Springer Lecture Notes in Comp. Sc. vol. 92 (1980).

[M2] Milner, R., Calculi for synchrony and asynchrony, Theoretical Computer Science, pp.267-310 (1983).

[Mi] Milne, G., CIRCAL and the representation of communication, concurrency and time. Report of Comp Sc Dept, University of Edinburgh (1983).

[NPW] Nielsen, M., Plotkin, G., Winskel, G., Petri nets, Event structures and Domains, part 1 . Theoretical Computer Science, vol. 13 (1981).

[Pr] Pratt, V. R., On the composition of processes. ACM, Stanford University (1982), and see the paper in this proceedings.

[Pe] Peterson, J. L., Petri Net Theory and the Modelling of Systems. Prentice–Hall (1981).

[R] Reisig, W., Petri nets. Springer Lecture Notes in Comp. Sc., to appear.

[S] Scott, D., Domains for Denotational Semantics, Springer–Verlag Lecture Notes in Comp. Sc. 140 (1982).

[Sh1,2] Shields, M., Non–sequential behaviours: 1 and 2. Reports of the Comp. Sc. Dept., University of Edinburgh (part 1: 1982, part 2: 1983).

[Stu] Student projects for the course "Models for Concurrency", Computer Science Dept., University of Aarhus, Denmark (1980).

[Sm] Smyth, M.B., Power domains and predicate transformers: a topological view. Proc. of ICALP 83, Springer Lecture Notes in Comp. Sc. vol. 154 (1983).

[W] Winskel, G., Events in Computation. Ph.D. thesis, University of Edinburgh (1980).

[W1] Winskel, G., Event structure semantics of CCS and related languages, Springer–Verlag Lecture Notes in Comp. Sc. 140 and as a report of the Computer Sc. Dept., University of Aarhus, Denmark (1982).

[W2] Winskel, G., Synchronisation trees. Technical Report, Comp. Sc. Dept., Carnegie–Mellon University (1983).To appear in Theoretical Computer Science.

[W3] Winskel, G., A New Definition of Morphism on Petri Nets. Springer Lecture Notes in Comp Sc, vol. 166 and also as a report of the Computer Laboratory, University of Cambridge (1984).

[W4] Winskel, G., A note on powerdomains and modality. Springer Lecture Notes in Comp Sc, vol. 158 (1984).

[W5] Winskel, G., A complete proof system for SCCS with modal assertions. In preparation.

MAXIMALLY CONCURRENT EVOLUTION OF NON-SEQUENTIAL SYSTEMS

R.Janicki
Institute of Mathematics,Warsaw Technical University,Poland.
P.E.Lauer
Computing Laboratory,University of Newcastle upon Tyne,UK.
R.Devillers
Universite Libre de Bruxelles,Brussels,Belgium.

ABSTRACT

The semantics expressed intuitively as "execute as much as possible in parallel" is formally defined and analysed. The relation between such a maximally concurrent semantics and "normal" semantics is developed. Some sufficient criteria for the equivalence of these semantics are formulated. As an abstract model of non-sequential systems the COSY path expression formalism is used.

1 INTRODUCTION

There are two widely accepted semantics of executions in non-sequential systems.The first one,standard in the Petri Net approach (cf.[Br80]), may intuitively be expressed as:"execute as possible (i.e. not necessarily maximally concurrent)", whilst the second one is usually expressed as "execute as much as possible in parallel" (cf.[BR81,DLMSS78]). The first semantics is more general but in practice the second one is sometimes more natural and easier to implement.

In the paper we try to answer the question:"when the semantics 'execute as much as possible in parallel' is equivalent to the semantics 'as possible'?".

Concurrent systems may exhibit extremely complicated behaviour and informal reasoning is not reliable enough to establish their properties, so we must use an abstract formal model. As a formal model we will use the COSY path expression formalism (cf.[LSC81]), which is sufficiently wide and has been developed to a great level of sophistication,and provides a respectable number of analytic criteria which are also efficiently mechanisable. Furthermore, a computer based environment, called BCS, and based on the COSY formalism was recently implemented (cf.[L82,LH82,L83]). BCS permits, among other things, the analysis of a COSY system specification by concurrent simulation. In the process of using this simulator it became obvious that systems for which the maximally concurrent behaviour determines the full behaviour are much more easy to analyse.

In the paper we recall a formal description of the semantics "execute as possible", and define a similar formal description of the semantics "execute as much as possible in parallel". A sufficient criterion for the equivalence of both semantics is also formulated and proved.

2 BASIC COSY SYNTAX AND SEMANTICS

COSY (the abbreviation of COncurrent SYstem) is a formalism intended to simplify the study of synchronic aspects of concurrent systems where possible by abstracting away from all aspects of systems except those which have to do with synchronisation.

A basic COSY path program, or generalised path is a collection of single paths enclosed in program and endprogram parentheses.

A single path is a regular expression enclosed by path and end.

For instance:

```
P = program
    path a;b,c end
    path (d;e)*;b end
    endprogram
```

In every regular expression like the above, the semicolon denotes sequence (concatenation), and comma denotes mutually exclusive choice. The comma binds more strongly than semicolon, so that the expression "a;b,c" means "first a, then either b or c". An expression may be enclosed in conventional parentheses with Kleene star appended, as for instance "(d;e)*" which means that the enclosed expression may be executed zero or more times. The expression appearing between path and end is implicitly so enclosed, so a single path describes cyclic sequences of actions. The synchronisation among paths is due to common actions ("b" in the above example). Every single path describes a sequential subsystem. The formal description of the COSY syntax may be found for instance in [LSC81,L82,L83].

The semantics of generalised paths can be described by means of vectors of strings (an approach initiated in [S79]).

With every single path P=path body end, we associate its set of operations Ops(P). As it was pointed out above, "body" may be treated as a standard regular expression. The only difference is replacing "U" by ",", using ";" to denote concatenation, and assuming that mutually exclusive choice binds more strongly than concatenation (in traditional notation the opposite assumption is made). Thus for instance "a;b,c" is equivalent to "a(bUc)" according to traditional notation.

For every regular expression E, let |E| denote the regular language described by E.

For every single path P=path body end the language |body| is called the set of cycles of P and denoted by Cyc(P), i.e. Cyc(P)=|body|. From the set Cyc(P) we construct the set of firing sequences of P, denoted by FS(P), as follows:

$$FS(P)=Pref(Cyc(P)^*),$$

where for every alphabet A and every language $L \subseteq A^*$:

$$Pref(L)=\{x \mid (\exists y \in A^*): xy \in L\}.$$

The set FS(P) is the set of sequences of operation executions permitted by the single path P.

Let us consider a generalised path $P=$ program $P_1 \ldots P_n$ endprogram (or simply $P=P_1 \ldots P_n$), where P_i's are single paths. To model the non-sequential behaviour of $P=P_1 \ldots P_n$, partial orders of executions of operations will be constructed which are represented by vectors of strings.

A vector $(x_1,\ldots,x_n)$ is a possible behaviour of $P=P_1 \ldots P_n$ if each x_i for $i=1,\ldots,n$ is a possible firing sequence of P_i and furthermore, if the x_i's agree about the number and order of executions of operations they share. To formally define the set of possible behaviours or histories of P, vectors of strings are introduced together with a concatenation operation on them.

Let us consider the set $Ops(P_1)^* \times \ldots \times Ops(P_n)^*$. If the vectors $(x_1,\ldots,x_n)$ and $(y_1,\ldots,y_n)$ belong to the above set their concatenation is defined as:

$$(x_1,\ldots,x_n)(y_1,\ldots,y_n)=(x_1y_1,\ldots,x_ny_n).$$

Let $Ops(P)=Ops(P_1) \cup \ldots \cup Ops(P_n)$, and for $i=1,\ldots,n$ let $h_i:Ops(P)^* \longrightarrow Ops(P_i)^*$ be an erasing homomorphism given by:

$$(\forall a \in Ops(P)):h_i(a)=\begin{cases} a & \text{if } a \in Ops(P_i) \\ e & \text{otherwise} \end{cases}$$

where "e" denotes the empty string.

Let $\underline{\ \ }:Ops(P)^* \longrightarrow Ops(P_1)^* \times \ldots \times Ops(P_n)^*$ be the mapping defined as follows:

$$(\forall x \in Ops(P)^*):\underline{x}=(h_1(x),\ldots,h_n(x)).$$

The set $Vops(P)=\{\underline{a} \mid a \in Ops(P)\}$ is called the set of vector operations of P. For every $i=1,\ldots,n$, let $[\ ]_i:Ops(P_1)^* \times \ldots \times Ops(P_n)^* \longrightarrow Ops(P_i)^*$ be a projection defined as:

$$[(x_1,\ldots,x_i,\ldots,x_n)]=x_i.$$

Note that: $(\forall \underline{x} \in Vops(P)^*)(\forall i=1,\ldots,n):[\underline{x}]_i=h_i(x)$.

The set of all possible behaviours or histories of P, the vector firing sequences of P, denoted by VFS(P), is defined by:

$$VFS(P)=(FS(P_1) \times \ldots \times FS(P_n)) \cap Vops(P)^*.$$

The set $FS(P_1) \times \ldots \times FS(P_n)$ in the definition of VFS(P) guarantees that each string component x_i of a history $\underline{x}=(x_1,\ldots,x_n) \in VFS(P)$ is a firing sequence of the path P_i, and the set $Vops(P)^*$ guarantees that all these firing sequences agree about the number and order of executions of operations they share.

The set VFS(P) can be treated as a formal description of the execution semantics: "execute as possible (i.e. not necessarily maximally concurrent)".

Let $ind \subseteq Ops(P) \times Ops(P)$ be the following relation:

$$(\forall a,b \in Ops(P)):(a,b) \in ind :\Longleftrightarrow (\forall P_i)\ a \notin Ops(P_i) \text{ or } b \notin Ops(P_i).$$

The relation ind is called the independency relation.

Note that:

$(a,b)\in ind \Longleftrightarrow a\neq b$ & $\underline{ab}=\underline{ba} \Longleftrightarrow (\forall i)[\underline{a}]i\neq e \Longrightarrow [\underline{b}]i=e$.

The definition of ind implies that only independent operations may execute concurrently. However, indpendent operations may not always execute concurrently or may never execute concurrently at all.

The formal model of behaviour permits us to speak formally of dynamic properties of systems specified by a generalised path P=P1...Pn.

We say that P=P1...Pn is deadlock free if and only if:

$(\forall \underline{x}\in VFS(P))(\exists a\in Ops(P))\ \underline{xa}\in VFS(P)$,

that is every history $\underline{x}$ may be continued.

We say that P=P1...Pn is adequate if and only if:

$(\forall \underline{x}\in VFS(P))(\forall a\in Ops(P))(\exists \underline{y}\in Vops(P)^*)\ \underline{xya}\in VFS(P)$,

that is, if every history $\underline{x}$ of P may be continued eventually enabling every operation in P. Adequacy is a property akin to absence of partial system deadlock.

Considerable work has been done concerning the verification of properties of generalised paths, in particular relating to adequacy, parallel resource releasing mechanisms, and others.For more details the reader is advised to refer to [LSC81,L82,L83]. These papers contain almost complete bibliographies concerning the COSY approach.

3 THE PROBLEM OF MAXIMALLY CONCURRENT EVOLUTION.

Let us start with the following example (see [L82]):

```
P=program
    path a,c;d end
    path b;c,d end
  endprogram
```

At the beginning we are able to perform actions a and b, both concurrently or each of them separately. After the concurrent performance of a and b, only action d is enabled; and after its performance we are again able to perform a and b concurrently or each of them separately one step at a time. Note that in this way we never perform the action c. On the other hand we may start with the performance of the action b only and next we are able to perform c. This example shows that doing two independent and simultaneously enabled actions in one step, is not the same as doing them in either order but sequentially, that is, in two steps.

This example shows that the semantics "execute as much as possible in parallel" may not be equivalent to the semantics "execute as possible".

Let us analyse this problem formally. First of all, we must formally define the semantics "execute as much as possible in parallel".

Let P=P1...Pn be a generalised path, and let Ind(P) $\subseteq 2^{P}$ be the following family of sets of operations:

$$A \in Ind(P) :\iff (\forall a,b \in A)\ (a,b) \in ind.$$

In other words elements of Ind(P) are sets of independent operations. If A={a1,...,ak}∈Ind(P), then $\underline{a1}...\underline{ak}=\underline{ai1}...\underline{aik}$ for any permutation i1,...,ik so we may write $\underline{A}=\underline{a1}...\underline{ak}$.

For every $\underline{x}$∈VFS(P), an operation a∈Ops(P) is said to be <u>enabled</u> at $\underline{x}$ if and only if:

$$(\forall i=1,\dots,n)\ a \in Ops(Pi) \implies [\underline{x}]ia \in FS(Pi).$$

For every $\underline{x}$∈VFS(P), a set of independent operations A∈Ind(P) is said to be <u>concurrently</u> <u>enabled</u> at $\underline{x}$ if and only if every a∈A is enabled at $\underline{x}$.

3.1 <u>COROLLARY</u>

For every $\underline{x}$∈VFS(P):

1. a∈Ops(P) is enabled at $\underline{x}$ <==> $\underline{xa}$∈VFS(P),

2. A∈Ind(P) is enabled at $\underline{x}$ <==> $\underline{xA}$∈VFS(P).[]

For every $\underline{x}$∈VFS(P), let enabled($\underline{x}$) denote the family of all concurrently enabled sets of operations at $\underline{x}$.

A concurrently enabled set at $\underline{x}$, A∈enabled($\underline{x}$), is said to be <u>maximally</u> <u>concurrent</u> if and only if it may not be extended, i.e. iff $(\forall B \in enabled(\underline{x}))\ A \subseteq B \implies A=B$.

For every $\underline{x}$∈VFS(P), let maxenabled($\underline{x}$) denote the family of all maximally concurrent sets enabled at $\underline{x}$. Of course maxenabled($\underline{x}$) $\subseteq$ enabled($\underline{x}$).

3.2 <u>COROLLARY</u>

For every generalised path P the following are equivalent:

1. P is deadlock-free,

2. $(\forall \underline{x} \in VFS(P))\ enabled(\underline{x}) \neq \{\ \}$,

3. $(\forall \underline{x} \in VFS(P))\ maxenabled(\underline{x}) \neq \{\ \}$. []

Let -s>, -c>, -m> $\subseteq$ Vops(P)* x Vops(P)* be the following relations:

$$\underline{x} \text{ -s> } \underline{y} :\iff (\exists a \in Ops(P))\ \{a\} \in enabled(\underline{x})\ \&\ \underline{y}=\underline{xa},$$

$$\underline{x} \text{ -c> } \underline{y} :\iff (\exists A \in enabled(\underline{x}))\ \underline{y}=\underline{xA},$$

$\underline{x}$ -m> $\underline{y}$:<==> $(\exists A \in maxenabled(\underline{x}))\ \underline{y}=\underline{x}A$.

The relations -s>, -c>, -m> are called respectively: the sequential reachability in one step, the concurrent reachabilty in one step , and the maximally concurrent reachability in one step.

3.3 LEMMA

VFS(P) = $\{\underline{x} \mid \underline{e}$-s>*$\underline{x}\}$ = $\{\underline{x} \mid \underline{e}$-c>*$\underline{x}\}$.

Proof:
By the definition we have -s>* = -c>*, then $\{\underline{x} \mid \underline{e}$-s>*$\underline{x}\}$=$\{\underline{x} \mid \underline{e}$-c>*$\underline{x}\}$. Furthermore: VFS(P)=(FS(P1)x...xFS(Pn)) $\cap$ Vops(P)*, and from the definition of -s> we obtain:

1. $\underline{e} \in \{\underline{x} \mid \underline{e}$-s>*$\underline{x}\}$ $\cap$ (FS(P1)x...xFS(Pn)) $\cap$ Vops(P)*,

2. if $\underline{y} \in \{\underline{x} \mid \underline{e}$-s>*$\underline{x}\}$ $\cap$ (FS(P1)x...xFS(Pn)) $\cap$ Vops(P)* then :
$\underline{ya} \in \{\underline{x} \mid \underline{e}$-s>*$\underline{x}\}$<==>$\underline{ya} \in$(FS(P1)x...xFS(Pn)) $\cap$ Vops(P)*.

Thus $\{\underline{x} \mid \underline{e}$-s>*$\underline{x}\}$=(FS(P1)x...xFS(Pn)) Vops(P)*, which ends the proof.

The above lemma states that VFS is fully characterisable by the relation -c>. The computer based environment, BCS, mentioned in the introduction is nothing but an implementation of the relation -c> (see [LJ82,L83]).

The relation -m> is that mathematical object which represents the maximally concurrent evolution, i.e. one step under the rules of the semantics "execute as much as possible in parallel".

Let us define: VMFS(P) = $\{\underline{x} \mid \underline{e}$ -m>* $\underline{x}\}$.

The set VMFS(P) represents all histories that may be reached by a maximally concurrent evolution of the system (the vector maximal firing sequences), so it may be treated as a formal description of the execution semantics:"execute as much as possible in parallel".

For every X $\subseteq$ Vops(P)*, let Pref(X)=$\{\underline{x} \mid (\exists \underline{y} \in$Vops(P)*) $\underline{xy} \in$X$\}$.

3.4 COROLLARY

Pref(VMFS(P)) $\subseteq$ VFS(P). []

We will say that P is completely charaterised by maximally concurrent evolution if and only if:

VFS(P) = Pref(VMFS(P)).

The above equality is a formal expression of the fact that the semantics "execute as much as possible in parallel" and the semantics "execute as possible" are equivalent.

We are now going to elucidate the structure of Pref(VMFS(P)), and to prove formally that the above notion is well defined. We prove that VMFS(P) is a tree and if VFS(P)=Pref(VMFS(P)) then the notions of deadlock-freeness and adequacy may be described in terms of VMFS only.

3.5 LEMMA

(∀x∈VFS(P))(∀y1,y2∈VMFS(P)) (y1-c>*x & y2-c>*x) ==> (y1-m>*y2 or y2-m>*y1).

Proof:
If this is not true, (∃y,y1'≠y2'∈VMFS(P)) such that one has the pattern:

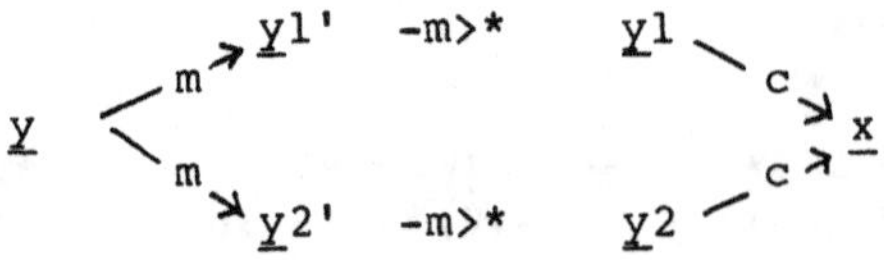

(one may have y1'=y1 and/or y2'=y2), where y1'=yA, y2'=yB and A ≠ B. Assume that a∈A-B. As x=ya...=yB..., therefore a must occur after B in the second expression, i.e. x=ya...=yBc1...cka..., and a must commute with each ci and each b in B. But then B is no longer maximally concurrent at y since one may add {a} to it, hence the lemma. []

As an almost immediate consequence of lemma 3.5 we obtain:

3.6 COROLLARY

1. VMFS(P) is a tree (VFS(P) is not!),
2. Each x∈VFS(P) has a unique greatest prefix in VMFS(P),
3. For every x∈Pref(VMFS(P)), if y is its greatest prefix in VMFS(P) and if y' is any of its least extensions in VMFS(P), then y-m>*y'. []

More details on the structure of VMFS(P) may be found in [De83].

A generalised path P is said to be M-deadlock-free if and only if:

(∀x∈VMFS(P))(∃y≠e) xy∈VMFS(P).

3.7 COROLLARY

P is M-deadlock-free <==> (∀x∈VMFS(P)) maxenabled(x)≠{ }.[]

3.8 THEOREM

If VFS(P)=Pref(VMFS(P)) then:

P is deadlock-free <==> P is M-deadlock-free.

Proof:
(==>).A consequence of corollaries 3.2 and 3.7.
(<==).Let x∈VFS(P). Since VFS(P)=Pref(VMFS(P)) then (∃z) xz∈VMFS(P). Of course xz∈VFS(P), so if z≠e then P is deadlock-free. If z=e then x∈VMFS(P) and there is y such that xy∈VMFS(P) ⊆ VFS(P); thus P is also deadlock-free. []

A generalised path P is said to be M-adequate if and only if:

(∀x∈VMFS(P))(∀a∈Ops(P))(∃y∈Vops(P)*) xya∈VMFS(P).

3.9 THEOREM

If VFS(P)=Pref(VMFS(P)) then:

P is adequate <==> P is M-adequate.

Proof:
(==>).Let x∈VMFS(P) and a∈Ops(P). Since P is adequate, then (∃y∈Vops(P)*) xya∈VFS(P), and since VFS(P)=Pref(VMFS(P)), then (∃z∈Vops(P)*) xyaz∈VMFS(P).If xya∈VMFS(P), we have our result; if it is not true, we have a pattern such as the following:

```
       y1 -m> y2 -m> ... -m>y(k-1)
       ↑m                  |
       |                   m↓
  x -m> yØ  -s>*  xya  -s>*  yk  -m>*  xyaz
```

where for i=1,...,k , yi=y(i-1)Ai.
Because a belongs to one of the Ai we may write yi=y(i-1)...a, where y(i-1) is an extension of x in VMFS(P).
(<==).Let x∈VFS(P), a∈Ops(P). Since VFS(P)=Pref(VMFS(P)) then (∃z∈Vops(P)*) xz∈VMFS(P)). Since P is M-adequate then (∃y) xzya∈VMFS(P) ⊆ VFS(P), and P is adequate. []

4 SUFFICIENT CONDITIONS FOR COMPLETE CHARACTERISATION BY MAXIMALLY CONCURRENT EVOLUTION

In this section we try to characterise the class of generalised paths posessing the property VFS(P)=Pref(VMFS(P)). A full characterisation does not exist so far, but some nice results may be formulated and proved.

We start with a technical lemma.

4.1 LEMMA

Let x∈Pref(VMFS(P)), y is its greatest prefix in VMFS(P), and y' is one of its least extensions in VMFS(P). Then:

(a) they are related by the following pattern:

```
     y1-m>y2-m>...-m>y(k-1)
     ↑m               |
     |                m↓
  y=yØ -c>* x -c>* y'=yk
```

where $(\forall i=1,\ldots,k)\ \underline{y}i=\underline{y}(i-1)\underline{A}i$.

(b) there is a decomposition $Ai=Bi \cup Ci$, for $i=1,\ldots,k$, such that:

1. $\underline{x} = \underline{y}\underline{B1}\underline{B2}\ldots\underline{Bk}$,

2. $\underline{y}' = \underline{x}\underline{C1}\underline{C2}\ldots\underline{Ck}$,

3. if $k>0$ then $\underline{C1}\neq\{\ \}$,

4. $(\forall i=1,\ldots,k)\quad Bi\neq\{\ \}$,

5. $(\forall i=1,\ldots,k)(\forall c\in Ci)(\forall j=1,\ldots,k)(\forall b\in Bj)\quad (c,b)\in ind$,

6. $(\forall i=2,\ldots,k)(\forall b\in Bi)(\exists b'\in B(i-1))\quad (c,b)\notin ind$.

Proof:
(a) results from corollary 4.6(3).
(b) If $\underline{x}\in VMFS(P)$ then $\underline{x}=\underline{y}=\underline{y}'$, $k=0$ and there is no problem.
If $k=1$, the lemma simply expresses that $\underline{y}\neq\underline{x}\neq\underline{y}'$ and that we have

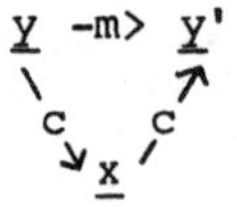

For $k\geq 2$, let $\underline{x}=\underline{y}\underline{z0}$ and $\underline{y}'=\underline{x}\underline{w}$. For $i=1,\ldots,k$, let Bi be the set of all the operations in Ai that occur in $\underline{z}(i-1)$, $Ci=Ai - Bi$ and let us construct $\underline{z}i$ from $\underline{z}(i-1)$ by dropping the first occurrence of each operation in Bi. Properties (1) and (2) then result from the fact that $\underline{y}'=\underline{y}\underline{z0}\underline{w}=\underline{x}\underline{w}=\underline{y}\underline{A1}\ldots\underline{Ak}$. Property (3) results from the fact that if $C1=\{\ \}$, then $\underline{y}\underline{B1}=\underline{y}\underline{A1}=\underline{y}1$ would be a greater prefix of $\underline{x}$ in VMFS(P) than $\underline{y}$. Property (5) results from the fact that: since $\underline{y}'=\underline{y}\underline{A1}\ldots\underline{Ak}=\underline{y}\underline{B1}\ldots\underline{Bk}\underline{C1}\ldots\underline{Ck}$, each operation $c\in C1$ has to commute with all the operations in $B2,\ldots,Bk$; moreover, if $c=b\in Bj$, from the construction of B1, c would belong to B1 and not to C1 since that means that c occurs in $\underline{z}(j-1)$, and thus in $\underline{z0}$; the same argument may then be resumed for $C2,\ldots,Ck$, in that order.
Property (4) results from the fact that:

- if $Bk=\{\ \}$, then $\underline{y}\underline{A1}\ldots\underline{A}(k-1)=\underline{y}(k-1)$ would be an extension of $\underline{x}$ in VMFS(P) smaller than $\underline{y}'$,

- let us suppose that i is the least index in $\{1,\ldots,k-1\}$ such that $Bi=\{\ \}$; from property (5), we know that each $c\in Ci=Ai$ is independent from each operation in $B(i+1)$ $(\neq\{\ \})$; but then , Ai would not be maximally concurrent at $\underline{y}(i-1)$ since we may add $B(i+1)$ to it.

Property (6) results from an argument similar to the one used for (5), namely if $(\exists i\in\{2,\ldots,k\})(\exists b\in Bi)(\forall b'\in B(i-1))\quad (b,b')\in ind$, since from property (5) $(\forall c\in C(i-1))(b,c)\in ind$, then $A(i-1)=B(i-1) \cup C(i-1)$ would not be maximally concurrent at $\underline{y}(i-2)$ since one may add b to it. []

At present we may formulate the most general (as yet) theorem characterising the equality of VFS(P)=Pref(VMFS(P)).

4.2   THEOREM

$VFS(P) \neq Pref(VMFS(P)) \implies (\exists x \in VFS(P))\ (\exists a,b,c \in Ops(P))\ xab \in VFS(P)$ &
$xac \in VFS(P)$ & $a \neq b$ & $b \neq c$ & $(b,c) \notin ind$ & $(a,c) \in ind$.

Proof:
Let $w \in VFS(P) - Pref(VMFS(P))$. Then w has a prefix $v = ub$, where $b \in Ops(P)$, such that $v \in VFS(P) - Pref(VMFS(P))$ but $u \in Pref(VMFS(P))$. Indeed, if $w = a_1 \ldots a_k$, where $(\forall i)\ a_i \in Ops(P)$ and if m is the first index such that $a_1 \ldots a_m \notin Pref(VMFS(P))$, then one may take $v = a_1 \ldots a_m$, $u = a_1 \ldots a_{(m-1)}$, $b = a_m$. As the decomposition of w is not unique, it may happen that u and b are not unique but this will be irrelevant for the rest of the proof.

Note also that $u \notin VMFS(P)$. If this did not hold, b could be extended to a maximally concurrent set B enabled at u, and v would be a prefix of $uB \in VMFS(P)$.

Let y be the greatest prefix of u in $VMFS(P)$, and let y' be one of its least extensions in $VMFS(P)$. From lemma 4.1 and the fact $u \notin VMFS(P)$ we have:

$$
\begin{array}{l}
y_1 \ \overset{\ }{\underset{m}{-m>}}\ \ldots\ -m>\ y_{(p-1)} \\
\ \ \Big|\ m \qquad\qquad\qquad\qquad \Big| \\
\ \ \Big|\qquad\qquad\qquad\qquad\quad \Big|\ m \\
y = y_0\ -c>+\ u\ -c>+\ y_p' = y_p \in VMFS(P) \\
\qquad\quad \Big|\ s \\
\qquad\quad ub \notin Pref(VMFS(P))
\end{array}
$$

where: $u = yA_1 \ldots A_p$, $y' = uC_1 \ldots C_p$, $p \geq 1$, $C_1 \neq \{\ \}$, $A_i \neq \{\ \}$, $A_i \cup C_i$ is maximally concurrent at $y_{(i-1)} \in VMFS(P)$ for $i = 1, \ldots, p$; and for $i = 2, \ldots, p: (\forall a \in A_i)(\exists a' \in A_{(i-1)})\quad (a,a') \notin ind$; and for $i = 1, \ldots, p: (\forall c \in C_i)(\forall a \in A_j$ where $j > i)\ (a,c) \in ind$. Assume that $p = 1$. Then: $u = yA$, $y' = uC$, $A \neq \{\ \} \neq C$, $A \cup C$ is maximally concurrent at y; we also have: $b \notin C$ (otherwise ub would be a prefix of $y' \in VMFS(P)$), and $b \notin A$ (otherwise b would be independent of the C's and would also be enabled at y', but then ub would be a prefix of $ubc = ucb = y'b$, which is a prefix of some $y'B \in VMFS(P)$).

Next we have: $(\exists a \in A)\ (a,b) \notin ind$ (otherwise $A \cup \{b\}$ could be extended to a maximally concurrent set A' enabled at y and ab would be a prefix of $yA' \in VMFS(P)$), and $(\exists c \in C)\ (c,b) \notin ind$ (otherwise b would again be enabled at y' and ub would be a prefix of some $y'B \in VMFS(P)$).

Let $u = xa$. Thus x,a,b,c satisfy the theorem, with the additional property that $(a,b) \notin ind$. If $p > 1$, a similar reasoning can be followed. Let us assume that p is minimal. Then we may assume that $(\exists c \in C_1)\ (c,b) \notin ind$ (otherwise we have uC_1 is a prefix of y', uC_1b is not a prefix $VMFS(P)$ since if $uC_1bz = ubC_1z \in VMFS(P)$ then ub is also a prefix of $VMFS(P)$, so y_1 is a prefix of uC_1 and p is not minimal).

We also have: $b \notin C_1$ (otherwise ub would be a prefix of $y' \in VMFS(P)$), and $b \notin A_p$ (otherwise $(\forall i)(\forall c \in C_i)$ $(b,c) \in ind$, b would be enabled at y' and ub is a prefix of $y'b = uC_1 \ldots C_pb = ubC_1 \ldots C_p$ which is a prefix of some $y'B \in VMFS(P)$).

Let $a \in A_p$ and $u = xa$. Thus x,a,b,c satisfy the theorem. []

Let us consider the example from the beginning of section 4. In this case we have $VFS(P) \neq Pref(VMFS(P))$, because for instance

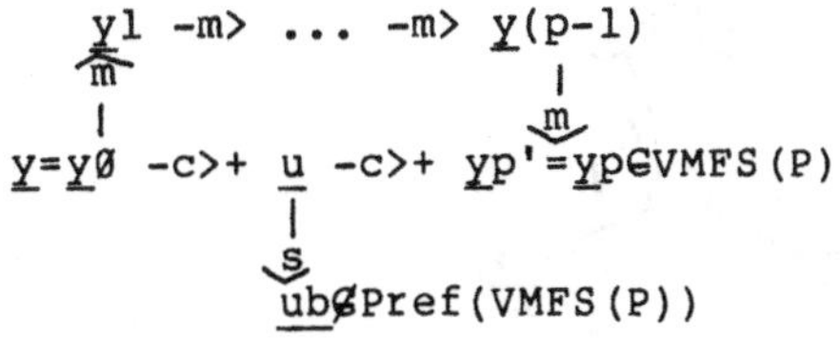

$\underline{bc} \in VFS(P) - Pref(VMFS(P))$. Note that here: $\underline{bc},\underline{ba} \in VFS(P)$, $(c,a) \notin ind$, $(b,a) \in ind$, so $\underline{e},b,c,a$ satisfy the right side of the implication from theorem 5.2.

Let us now define the following relations on Ops(P) x Ops(P):

$(a,b) \in pre :\iff (\exists i)(\exists x \in FS(P_i))\ xab \in FS(P_i)\ \&\ a \neq b$,

$(a,b) \in \underline{pre} :\iff a \neq b\ \&\ (a,b) \notin ind\ \&\ (\exists \underline{x} \in VFS(P))\ \underline{xab} \in VFS(P)$,

$(a,b) \in exc :\iff (\exists i)(\exists x \in FS(P_i))\ xa \in FS(P_i)\ \&\ xb \in FS(P_i)\ \&\ a \neq b$,

$(a,b) \in \underline{exc} :\iff a \neq b\ \&\ (a,b) \notin ind\ \&\ ((\exists \underline{x} \in VFS(P))\ \underline{xa} \in VFS(P)\ \&\ \underline{xb} \in VFS(P))$,

$(a,b) \in con :\iff (a,b) \in ind\ \&\ (\exists \underline{x} \in VFS(P))\ \underline{xab} \in VFS(P)$.

In terms of Petri Nets associated to P (see for instance [LSC81]), the relations pre, exc and con describe the following simple situations:

$(a,b) \in pre$ <==>

$(a,b) \in exc$ <==>

$(a,b) \in con$ <==>

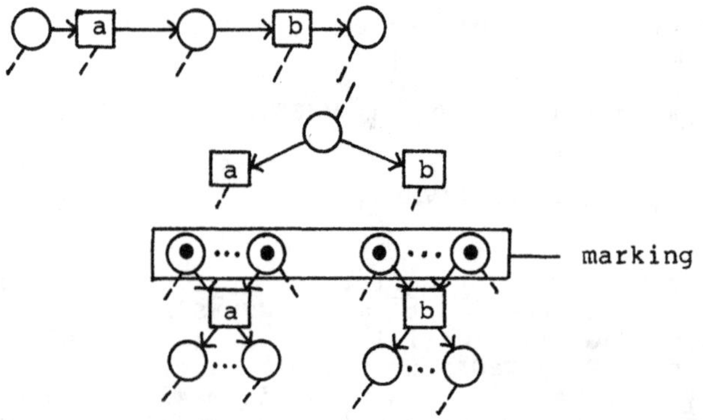

where dashed lines denote context.

Let PDTØ(P), PDT1(P), PDT2(P) $\subseteq$ Ops(P) x Ops(P) x Ops(P) be the following relations:

$(a,b,c) \in PDT\emptyset(P) :\iff (a,b) \in pre \cup ind\ \&\ (b,c) \in exc\ \&\ (a,c) \in ind$,

$(a,b,c) \in PDT1(P) :\iff (a,b) \in pre \cup con\ \&\ (b,c) \in exc\ \&\ (a,c) \in con$,

$(a,b,c) \in PDT2(P) :\iff (a,b) \in \underline{pre} \cup con\ \&\ (b,c) \in \underline{exc}\ \&\ (a,c) \in con$.

The name PDT is an abbreviation of Potentially Dangerous Triple.

4.3 THEOREM

$PDT\emptyset(P) = \{\ \} \implies PDT1(P) = \{\ \} \implies PDT2(P) = \{\ \} \implies VFS(P) = Pref(VMFS(P))$.

Proof:
The first two implications follow from:

$\underline{pre} \subseteq pre$, $\underline{exc} \subseteq exc$, $con \subseteq ind$.

The third implication is equivalent to theorem 5.2, with the additional requirement that the same x may be used for <u>pre</u> and con, and that <u>xa</u> may be used for x in <u>exc</u>. []

A generalised path P=P1...Pn is said to be a GE0-path if and only if each Pi contains no comma, no star and no repeated operation name (cf.[LSC81]).

4.4 COROLLARY

Every GE0-path is completely characterised by maximally concurrent evolution.

The example:

         P=<u>program</u>
            <u>path</u> a;b <u>end</u>
            <u>path</u> c;b <u>end</u>
            <u>path</u> b,c <u>end</u>
            <u>endprogram</u>

shows that PDT1(P)={ } is not a necessary condition for having VFS(P)=Pref(VMFS(P)). In this case we have (a,b,c)∈PDT1(P) and VFS(P)=Pref(VMFS(P)).The condition PDT2(P)={ } is probably also not necessary to that equality, but a counter example is not known so far. But the conditions PDT0(P)={ } and/or PDT1(P)={ } are sufficiently weak to have wide applications (for instance they may be applied to all examples from [L82]). The general necessary conditions for the equality VFS(P)=Pref(VMFS(P)) are an open problem so far, and they seem to be rather complicated.

5   ACKNOWLEDGEMENTS

The work reported in this paper was supported by a grant from the Science and Engineering Council of Great Britain. John Cotronis contributed to the initial formulation of the problem of maximally concurrent evolution.

6   REFERENCES

[Br80] W Brauer (ed.) : Proceedings of the Advanced Course on General Net Theory of Processes and Systems, Hamburg, 1979. <u>Lecture Notes in Computer Science</u> <u>84</u>, Springer Verlag, 1980

[BR81] E Best, B Randell : A Formal Model of Atomicity in Asynchronous Systems, <u>Acta Informatica</u> <u>16</u>, 93-124 (1981).

[De83] R Devillers : On the Maximally Concurrent Evolution of a COSY System, Report ASM/106, Computing Laboratory, University of Newcastle upon Tyne, 1983.

[DLMSS78]
        E W Dijkstra, L Lamport, A J Martin, C S Scholten, E F M Steffens : On the fly garbage collection : an exercise in cooperation,<u>CACM</u> <u>21</u>, 966-975 (1978).

[L82] P E Lauer : Computer System Dossiers, Proc. Int. Seminar on Synchronisation, Control and Communication in Distributed Computing Systems, London, Sept. 20 through 24, 1982. To appear in a Book by Academic Press.

[L83] P E Lauer : Users' introduction to BCS : A computer based environment for specifying analysing and verifying concurrent systems, Report ASM/107, Computing Laboratory, University of Newcastle upon Tyne, June 1983.

[LH82] P E Lauer, B C Hamshere : Project on a Computer Based Environment for the Design and Analysis of Highly Parallel and Distributed Computing Systems, Report ASM/103, Computing Laboratory, University of Newcastle upon Tyne, 1982.

[LJ82] P E Lauer, R Janicki :The role of maximally concurrent simulation in the computer based analysis of distributed systems, Report ASM/96, Computing Laboratory, University of Newcastle upon Tyne, 1982.

[LSC81] P E Lauer, M W Shields, J Y Cotronis: Formal behavioural specification of concurrent systems without globality assumptions, Int. Colloq. on Formalization of Programming Concepts, Lecture Notes in Computer Science V.107, 1981.

[S79] M W Shields : Adequate Path Expressions; Proc. Intern. Symposium on the Semantics of Concurrent Computation, Evians-les-Bains, July 2-4, 1979. Lecture Notes in Computer Science No.70, Springer Verlag, 1979, pp. 249-265.

AN IMPROVED FAILURES MODEL FOR COMMUNICATING PROCESSES

S. D. Brookes
Carnegie-Mellon University
Pittsburgh, Pa.
USA

A. W. Roscoe
Programming Research Group
Oxford University
Oxford
England

0. Abstract.

We extend the failures model of communicating processes to allow a more satisfactory treatment of divergence in addition to deadlock. The relationship between the revised model and the old model is discussed, and we make some connections with various models proposed by other authors.

1. Introduction.

The papers [3,4] introduced the *failure sets* model for communicating sequential processes. This model, an extension of the *traces* model of [13], was able to represent nondeterministic behaviour in a simple but effective way. We showed how to use this model to give a denotational semantics to an abstract version of Hoare's language CSP [14], and used it to prove some theorems about the behaviour of programs. The model enjoyed many elegant mathematical properties, which facilitated formal manipulation and derivation of process properties.

The failures model of processes is able to support a formal treatment of *deadlock* properties. A process is said to *deadlock* if it reaches a stage where it is unable to participate further in events; this property is captured very simply by the failures model, since a potential deadlock corresponds to the ability to refuse all events and this is reflected directly in the structure of the failure set of a process. However, there are problems associated with the treatment in this model of the phenomenon of *divergence*. A process *diverges* when it is engaged in an infinite unbroken sequence of internal actions invisible to its environment, and as a result leaves its environment waiting eternally for a response. It is important to be able to reason about the possibility of divergence, especially when trying to establish a *liveness* property, such as the ability of a process to make some visible response to its environment. The original failures model has certain weaknesses in its treatment of diverging processes, as remarked in [11,12,19,20,2,23], and we will make in this paper suitable alterations to the model which allow a more satisfactory account to be given. The need for these adjustments was originally, independently, suggested by Hennessy and de Nicola in [23] and by Roscoe in [12], and had a direct influence on the development of [2]. The relationship of the new model with the models of Hennessy, de Nicola, and other authors, is discussed in more detail in the final section of this paper. The new model retains the ability to model deadlock, and is thus in a well defined sense an improvement over the original. Again the model possesses an elegant mathematical structure and is well suited to formal manipulation.

A second adjustment, independent of the treatment of divergence, is also suggested in this paper. In the original failures model of processes all refusal sets were finite. This condition is natural when the processes have a finite alphabet of discourse, so that each process is only capable of participation in events drawn from a finite set. However, when processes are allowed to have infinite alphabets it still seems unnatural not to be able to tell explicitly from the semantics of a process whether or not it can refuse an infinite set of events. We will introduce here infinite refusal sets, but with a closure condition making the change from the old model largely cosmetic. In particular, the old model will be seen to "sit inside" the new one in the natural way, so that we are clearly making a reasonable generalization. With this adjustment in place it becomes slightly easier to formulate some of the deadlock properties of processes, since deadlock corresponds explicitly to the refusal of the entire alphabet of events.

We revise the definitions of some of the process compositions from [3,4] to take divergence into account more accurately, and we give examples to show inadequacies in the earlier definitions in their handling of this phenomenon.

Outline.

The first two sections of the paper introduce the old and the new models, and use them to give a semantics to the version of CSP described in [3,4]. Some intuitions are given to justify the changes we have made in building the new model, and the relationship between the old and new models is analysed. The third section gives some examples of applications of the model, defining in the new model the semantics of some interesting forms of process composition which were used in [3,4]. We see that, with care, all of the applications discussed in those papers may be transferred to this more general setting. The same is true of the proof techniques described in the appendix of [4]. The fourth section contains a comparison of the work of this paper with that of other authors, setting our work in a more general context. This section also contains some conclusions and points the way forward to future research.

For obvious reasons the contents of this paper overlaps the material of [3,4] to a substantial degree. In order to avoid too much repetition, and to restrict the length of this paper, much of the material of the earlier papers is assumed.

Notation.

Throughout this paper we will use the following conventions in notation. Given a set Σ of *events*, the set of finite sequences or *traces* over Σ will be denoted Σ^*. We use a, b, c to range over Σ, and s, t, u to range over Σ^*. The empty sequence is $\langle\rangle$, and the sequence with elements $a_1, \ldots, a_n$ in that order is written $\langle a_1, \ldots, a_n \rangle$, although sometimes we may omit the braces and write $a_1 \ldots a_n$. Given traces s and t, we write st for their concatenation. We say $s \leq t$ (s is a *prefix* of t) if there is a trace u such that $su = t$; such a trace u is called a *suffix* of t. The powerset of Σ is denoted $\mathcal{P}(\Sigma)$, while we use $p(\Sigma)$ for the finite powerset (the set of all finite subsets); of course, if Σ itself is finite these two powersets coincide. Finally X, Y, Z range over $\mathcal{P}(\Sigma)$ or $p(\Sigma)$, depending on the context.

2. The failures model.

In this section we begin by recalling the earlier *failures model* of [3,4] and its use to give a semantics to a version of CSP.

A process is regarded as an agent which communicates with its environment by performing actions or *events* drawn from an alphabet Σ. Each event can be thought of as an atomic action. Sequential processes are characterised at least partially by the set of possible sequences of events in which they may participate; this constitutes the so-called *trace set* of a process [13]. However, since we are going to be modelling processes with nondeterministic behaviour, traces are not enough. The trace set of a process does not indicate the possibility that deadlock might occur as the result of a nondeterministic decision by a process. The effect of a nondeterministic decision by a process is to restrict its ability to communicate on the next step, by choosing a set of events which will not be possible on that step. Accordingly, the concept of a *failure* suggests itself as a means of modelling the effects of nondeterministic decisions. A failure has the form

$$(s, X),$$

where s is a finite sequence of events and X is a finite set of events. If a particular failure (s, X) is possible for a process, then the process *may* perform the sequence of events s and then be unable to perform any of the events in the set X; we say the process can do s then refuse X.

Bearing in mind the intuition behind this notion of failures, the failure set of a process satisfies four simple conditions (M1)-(M4) below. We therefore define a failure set to be any subset

$$F \subseteq \Sigma^* \times p(\Sigma)$$

satisfying these conditions:

$$(\langle\rangle, \emptyset) \in F \tag{M1}$$
$$(st, \emptyset) \in F \Rightarrow (s, \emptyset) \in F \tag{M2}$$
$$(s, X) \in F \ \& \ Y \subseteq X \ \Rightarrow \ (s, Y) \in F \tag{M3}$$
$$(s, X) \in F \ \& \ (s\langle c\rangle, \emptyset) \notin F \ \Rightarrow \ (s, X \cup \{c\}) \in F. \tag{M4}$$

We will denote the failures model by M.

For any set F of failures we define

$$\begin{aligned} \text{traces}(F) &= \{\, s \mid \exists X.\, (s, X) \in F \,\} \\ \text{initials}(F) &= \{\, c \mid \langle c\rangle \in \text{traces}(F) \,\} \\ \text{refusals}(F) &= \{\, X \mid (\langle\rangle, X) \in F \,\} \\ F\ \underline{\text{after}}\ s &= \{\, (t, X) \mid (st, X) \in F \,\}. \end{aligned}$$

By condition (M3), s is a trace of F if and only if $(s, \emptyset)$ is a failure of F. Thus, (M1) and (M2) state that the traces of a process form a non-empty, prefix-closed set. (M2) says that if a process can refuse all events in a set Y then it can also refuse all subsets of Y. Finally, (M4) states that an event which is impossible on the next step can be included in a refusal set. It is easy to see that for any trace s of F, the set F after s also satisfies the conditions above; this represents the behaviour of the process once it has performed the sequence s.

Since failures represent the results of nondeterministic decisions made by a process, there is a natural partial ordering on failure sets:

$$F_1 \sqsubseteq F_2 \Leftrightarrow F_1 \supseteq F_2.$$

We read $F_1 \sqsubseteq F_2$ as saying that F_1 is more nondeterministic than F_2. The set of all failure sets, ordered by this relation, forms a complete semi-lattice. This means that every non-empty collection of processes has a greatest lower bound (union) and every directed set of processes has a least upper bound (intersection); in particular, the intersection of a chain of processes is again a process. The least element (called CHAOS in [3,4]) is simply $\Sigma^* \times p(\Sigma)$, the set containing all possible failures. The maximal elements, the so-called *deterministic* processes, are characterised by the condition:

$$(s, X) \in F \ \Leftrightarrow \ X \cap \text{initials}(F\ \underline{\text{after}}\ s) = \emptyset,$$

or, equivalently, that their refusal sets contain only impossible events.

CSP operations.

Next we recall the abstract syntax given in [3,4] for a version of CSP. We use P, Q to range over (syntactic) processes. The following BNF-style grammar defines the syntax of our process language:

$$P ::= \mathrm{STOP} \mid \mathrm{SKIP} \mid (a \to P) \mid P \sqcap Q \mid P \Box Q \mid$$
$$P \| Q \mid P ||| Q \mid P;Q \mid P \backslash a \mid f^{-1}(P) \mid f(P) \mid p \mid \mu p.P$$

STOP represents a deadlocked process, and SKIP represents a process which terminates successfully. Two forms of parallel composition are represented by $P \parallel Q$ and $P|||Q$; the former is known as *synchronous* parallel composition, the latter *asynchronous*. Sequential composition is denoted $P;Q$, and prefixing a single event is denoted $(a \to P)$. Two forms of choice are represented by $P \Box Q$ and $P \sqcap Q$; the first form is "controllable" and the second "uncontrollable" or purely nondeterministic. The hiding operation $P \backslash a$ conceals all occurrences of the event a. We let f range over a set of *alphabet transformations*; these are renaming functions $f : \Sigma \to \Sigma$ satisfying the *finite pre-image property*, i.e. that for every $a \in \Sigma$ the set $f^{-1}(a) = \{ b \in \Sigma \mid f(b) = a \}$ is finite, so that only finitely many events become identified under a renaming. The process $f^{-1}(P)$ can perform an event b whenever P can perform the image event $f(b)$. Conversely, the process $f(P)$ performs $f(a)$ whenever P can perform a. For further explanation of the nature and significance of these syntactic operations see [4]. In the final two clauses p ranges over a set of process identifiers and $\mu p.P$ is a recursive term, corresponding informally to a recursive process definition of the form $p = P$.

We will denote the set of terms defined by this syntax by TCSP. A term is closed if it has no free process identifiers. In order to interpret terms with free process identifiers we will use an *environment*, which we take to be a function ρ from process identifiers to failure sets. Let MEnv be the set of all environments of this type. We use the notation $\rho + [p \mapsto F]$ for the environment which agrees with ρ except that it maps the process identifier p to the failure set F.

The failures semantics of TCSP is summarized below; these clauses are essentially the same as the definitions given in [3,4], except that we have made explicit use of environments in order to treat the semantics of recursive terms rather more rigorously. In the earlier papers we did not make an explicit distinction between syntax and semantics, preferring rather to blur the distinction and use the same notation for the syntactic as well as semantic operations. Here we are forced to emphasise the separation of syntax and semantics, because we will later have another semantics to discuss.

This semantics is denotational, in that the failure sets of compound processes are definable from the failure sets of their components. We assume familiarity with the basic ideas of denotational semantics, as explained for example in [26]. We define the semantic function

$$\mathcal{M} : \mathrm{TCSP} \to [\mathrm{MEnv} \to M]$$

by the clauses:

$$\begin{aligned}
\mathcal{M}[\![p]\!]\rho &= \rho[\![p]\!] \\
\mathcal{M}[\![\mathrm{STOP}]\!]\rho &= \{(\langle\rangle, X) \mid X \in p(\Sigma)\} \\
\mathcal{M}[\![\mathrm{SKIP}]\!]\rho &= \{(\langle\rangle, X) \mid \surd \notin X \ \&\ X \in p(\Sigma)\} \cup \{(\surd, X) \mid X \in p(\Sigma)\} \\
\mathcal{M}[\![(a \to P)]\!]\rho &= \{(\langle\rangle, X) \mid a \notin X \ \&\ X \in p(\Sigma)\} \cup \{(\langle a\rangle s, X) \mid (s, X) \in \mathcal{M}[\![P]\!]\rho\} \\
\mathcal{M}[\![P \sqcap Q]\!]\rho &= \mathcal{M}[\![P]\!]\rho \cup \mathcal{M}[\![Q]\!]\rho \\
\mathcal{M}[\![P \Box Q]\!]\rho &= \{(\langle\rangle, X) \mid (\langle\rangle, X) \in \mathcal{M}[\![P]\!]\rho \cap \mathcal{M}[\![Q]\!]\rho\} \\
&\quad \cup \{(s, X) \mid s \neq \langle\rangle \ \&\ (s, X) \in \mathcal{M}[\![P]\!]\rho \cup \mathcal{M}[\![Q]\!]\rho\} \\
\mathcal{M}[\![P \parallel Q]\!]\rho &= \{(s, X \cup Y) \mid (s, X) \in \mathcal{M}[\![P]\!]\rho \ \&\ (s, Y) \in \mathcal{M}[\![Q]\!]\rho\} \\
\mathcal{M}[\![P|||Q]\!]\rho &= \{(u, X) \mid \exists s, t.\, u \in \mathrm{merge}(s, t) \ \& \\
&\quad (s, X) \in \mathcal{M}[\![P]\!]\rho \ \&\ (t, X) \in \mathcal{M}[\![Q]\!]\rho\} \\
\mathcal{M}[\![P; Q]\!]\rho &= \{(s, X) \mid s \text{ tick-free} \ \&\ (s, X \cup \{\surd\}) \in \mathcal{M}[\![P]\!]\rho\} \\
&\quad \cup \{(st, X) \mid (s\surd, \emptyset) \in \mathcal{M}[\![P]\!]\rho \ \&\ s \text{ tick-free} \ \&\ (t, X) \in \mathcal{M}[\![Q]\!]\rho\} \\
\mathcal{M}[\![P \backslash a]\!]\rho &= \{(s\backslash a, X) \mid (s, X \cup \{a\}) \in \mathcal{M}[\![P]\!]\rho\} \\
&\quad \cup \{((s\backslash a)t, X) \mid \forall n.\, (sa^n, \emptyset) \in \mathcal{M}[\![P]\!]\rho\} \\
\mathcal{M}[\![f^{-1}(P)]\!]\rho &= \{(s, X) \mid (f(s), f(X)) \in \mathcal{M}[\![P]\!]\rho\} \\
\mathcal{M}[\![f(P)]\!]\rho &= \{(f(s), X) \mid (s, f^{-1}(X)) \in \mathcal{M}[\![P]\!]\rho\} \\
\mathcal{M}[\![\mu p.P]\!]\rho &= \mathrm{fix}(\lambda F.\mathcal{M}[\![P]\!](\rho + [p \mapsto F])).
\end{aligned}$$

For an open term the environment explicitly supplies a meaning for free identifiers. In the clause for $P|||Q$, we use the notation merge(s, t) for the set of all traces obtained by interleaving the traces s and t. The special event $\surd$ is used to denote successful termination, and is used in a sequential composition $P; Q$ to signal the starting point of the second process. A trace is tick-free if it does not contain an occurrence of this event, and a trace ending with $\surd$ represents termination. In the definition of $P\backslash a$, we use the notation $s\backslash a$ for the result of removing all occurrences of a from the trace s. Further explanation and intuitions for these definitions will be found in [4].

As mentioned above, the failures model M forms a complete semi-lattice under the superset ordering. This ordering amounts to a measure of the amount of nondeterminism a process can exhibit. All of the failure set operations used in the semantic clauses above are continuous, so we can appeal to the Knaster-Tarski Fixed Point Theorem to justify the existence of least fixed points [26]. We have used the notation *fix* for the least fixed point operator. Thus, the semantics of a recursively defined process is obtained as the least fixed point of the corresponding function from failures to failures. By continuity, this fixed point can be obtained in the usual way as a limit: the failure set of the process $\mu p.P$ in environment ρ is generated as the intersection of the sequence

$$\begin{aligned} F_0 &= \text{CHAOS}, \\ F_{n+1} &= \mathcal{M}[\![P]\!](\rho + [p \mapsto F_n]) \qquad (n \geq 0). \end{aligned}$$

As an example, the term $\mu p.(a \to p)$ denotes a process which has the ability to perform an unlimited number of a events:

$$\mathcal{M}[\![\mu p.(a \to p)]\!]\rho = \{ (a^n, X) \mid n \geq 0 \ \& \ a \notin X \ \& X \in p(\Sigma) \}.$$

This process satisfies the fixed point equation $P = (a \to P)$. The recursion $\mu p.p$ denotes the failure set CHAOS, and is the most nondeterministic of all processes. Mutual recursions can be dealt with in a similar fashion.

We write

$$\begin{aligned} P \sqsubseteq_M Q &\Leftrightarrow \forall \rho.[\mathcal{M}[\![P]\!]\rho \supseteq \mathcal{M}[\![Q]\!]\rho], \\ P \equiv_M Q &\Leftrightarrow \forall \rho.[\mathcal{M}[\![P]\!]\rho = \mathcal{M}[\![Q]\!]\rho]. \end{aligned}$$

In other words, $P \equiv_M Q$ when the two processes have identical failure sets (in this model). When $P \sqsubseteq_M Q$ we say that P is more nondeterministic than Q. This relation induces a pre-ordering on TCSP terms.

In view of the Fixed Point Theorem, a process defined by recursion should satisfy its definition. This is expressed formally in the following way. Let P be a term with free process identifier p. We write $[Q\backslash p]P$ for the term arising by replacing every free occurrence of p in P by Q, with suitable name changes to avoid clashes. Then we have:

$$\mu p.P \equiv_M [(\mu p.P)\backslash p]P.$$

We will often suppress the μ notation and simply define a process by the fixed point equation it is required to satisfy; the implicit understanding when we do this is that we are defining the *least* fixed point.

The following properties of processes will be assumed. Proofs may be found in the earlier papers [3,4] or else in [19,20]. This is not an exhaustive list or a complete set of true equivalences; [19] contains a complete set of axioms for a significant subset of our language (omitting some of the operators).

$$
\begin{aligned}
P \Box P &\equiv_M P \\
P \Box Q &\equiv_M Q \Box P \\
P \Box (Q \Box R) &\equiv_M (P \Box Q) \Box R \\
P \Box (Q \sqcap R) &\equiv_M (P \Box Q) \sqcap (P \Box R) \\
P \sqcap (Q \Box R) &\equiv_M (P \sqcap Q) \Box (P \sqcap R) \\
P \Box \mathrm{STOP} &\equiv_M P \\
(a \rightarrow (P \sqcap Q)) &\equiv_M (a \rightarrow P) \sqcap (a \rightarrow Q) \\
a \rightarrow P) \Box (a \rightarrow Q) &\equiv_M (a \rightarrow P) \sqcap (a \rightarrow Q) \\
P \sqcap P &\equiv_M P \\
P \sqcap Q &\equiv_M Q \sqcap P \\
P \sqcap (Q \sqcap R) &\equiv_M (P \sqcap Q) \sqcap R \\
P \parallel Q &\equiv_M Q \parallel P \\
P \parallel (Q \parallel R) &\equiv_M (P \parallel Q) \parallel R \\
P \parallel (Q \sqcap R) &\equiv_M (P \parallel Q) \sqcap (P \parallel R) \\
(a \rightarrow P) \parallel (b \rightarrow Q) &\equiv_M \mathrm{STOP} \qquad \text{if } a \neq b \\
&\equiv_M (a \rightarrow (P \parallel Q)) \quad \text{if } a = b \\
P \parallel \mathrm{STOP} &\equiv_M \mathrm{STOP} \\
P|||Q &\equiv_M Q|||P \\
(P|||Q)|||R &\equiv_M P|||(Q|||R) \\
P|||(Q \sqcap R) &\equiv_M (P|||Q) \sqcap (P|||R) \\
(a \rightarrow P)|||(b \rightarrow Q) &\equiv_M (a \rightarrow (P|||(b \rightarrow Q))) \Box (b \rightarrow ((a \rightarrow P)|||Q)) \\
P; (Q; R) &\equiv_M (P; Q); R \\
\mathrm{STOP}|||Q &\equiv_M Q \\
\mathrm{SKIP}; Q &\equiv_M Q \\
\mathrm{STOP}; Q &\equiv_M \mathrm{STOP} \\
P; (Q \sqcap R) &\equiv_M (P; Q) \sqcap (P; R) \\
(P \sqcap Q); R &\equiv_M (P; R) \sqcap (Q; R) \\
(a \rightarrow P); Q &\equiv_M (a \rightarrow P; Q) \qquad \text{if } a \neq \surd \\
(P \backslash a) \backslash b &\equiv_M (P \backslash b) \backslash a \\
(P \backslash a) \backslash a &\equiv_M P \backslash a \\
(a \rightarrow P) \backslash b &\equiv_M (a \rightarrow P \backslash b) \qquad \text{if } a \neq b \\
&\equiv_M P \backslash b \qquad \text{if } a = b \\
(P \sqcap Q) \backslash a &\equiv_M (P \backslash a) \sqcap (Q \backslash a)
\end{aligned}
$$

TABLE 1

3. The new model.

The failures model is unable to provide an adequate treatment of the phenomenon of *divergence*. In addition, all refusal sets were taken to be finite. The new model has the same basic structure but with two modifications.

1. Divergence. A process is said to diverge at some stage if it is possible for it to engage in an unbounded sequence of internal actions, invisible to its environment. Such behaviour is introduced when hiding an infinite sequence of events; if such a sequence is rendered invisible to the environment of the process, the resulting process diverges. An example of this is provided by the term

$$(\mu p.(a \to p))\backslash a.$$

Here the recursively defined process is able to perform an unbounded sequence of a events, which become internal actions when the hiding operation is applied. Divergence is also introduced by ill-defined recursive definitions, because we regard the initiation of a recursive call as an internal action; an example is provided by the recursive term $\mu p.p$, whose execution results in an infinite sequence of recursive calls. In the failures model M a divergence caused by hiding was modelled as CHAOS, although another plausible version of the hiding operation regarded this type of divergence as indistinguishable from deadlock. Some of the properties of this version of hiding were investigated in [2]. This alternate form of hiding, which models divergence by STOP and thus identifies divergence with deadlock, does not have such appealing algebraic properties, and the chaotic form was preferred in [3,4]. In particular, the chaotic form of hiding is a continuous operation, unlike the deadlocking version. However, CHAOS is simply the process which can at any stage in its execution *refuse* any set of events; that is, CHAOS *always responds* to its environment by either refusing or performing an event. It can therefore be argued that it is unreasonable to identify divergence with CHAOS, the ability to *fail to respond* at all to the environment, since divergence is more accurately represented by the *inability* to respond in any finite time. Indeed, CHAOS does not possess all of the combinational properties we would like to associate with a diverging process. In particular, the following equivalences do not generally hold in the failures model:

$$\begin{aligned} P \square \text{CHAOS} &\equiv_M \text{CHAOS}, \\ P \parallel \text{CHAOS} &\equiv_M \text{CHAOS}, \\ P|||\text{CHAOS} &\equiv_M \text{CHAOS}, \\ \text{CHAOS}; Q &\equiv_M \text{CHAOS}. \end{aligned}$$

In each of these cases we would expect divergence of the component process to cause the possibility of divergence in the compound process. Similar problems were encountered by Hennessy and de Nicola [12,19], in trying to axiomatize the failures model, and by Roscoe [23] when trying to make connections between the failures semantics and an operational interpretation of process behaviour. The use of CHAOS for the purpose of modelling divergence does not quite fit properly with operational intuitions. Thus, the failures model alone is insufficiently powerful to give a satisfactory or convincing account of divergence. In order to provide a more pleasing treatment of divergence, we introduce an extra component into the semantic description of a process. In addition to a failure set, a process will be associated with a *divergence set*; this will be a set of traces. If s is a divergence trace of a process we interpret this as saying that the process may be diverging once it has performed the sequence s.

2. Infinite refusal sets. Secondly, if Σ is infinite we will allow refusal sets to be infinite; but we also add a closure condition which makes this change largely cosmetic. Specifically, an infinite set will be a possible refusal if and only if all of its finite subsets are refusable. Thus, infinite refusal sets are determined by their finite subsets being refusable.

In this new model, which we will denote N, processes are modelled as pairs

$$\langle F, D\rangle$$

with

$$F \subseteq \Sigma^* \times \mathcal{P}(\Sigma),$$
$$D \subseteq \Sigma^*.$$

In such a pair $\langle F, D\rangle$ the failure set is F and the divergence set is D. We will extract these two components with the functions *failures* and *div*. We require the following conditions on F, which should be compared with (M1)–(M4) of the previous section.

$$(\langle\rangle, \emptyset) \in F \tag{N1}$$
$$(st, \emptyset) \in F \Rightarrow (s, \emptyset) \in F \tag{N2}$$
$$(s, X) \in F \;\&\; Y \subseteq X \Rightarrow (s, Y) \in F \tag{N3}$$
$$(s, X) \in F \;\&\; (\forall c \in Y.\, ((s\langle c\rangle, \emptyset) \notin F)) \Rightarrow (s, X \cup Y) \in F \tag{N4}$$
$$(\forall Y \in p(X).\, (s, Y) \in F) \Rightarrow (s, X) \in F. \tag{N5}$$

The only difference between (N1)–(N4) and the previous conditions is that Y is allowed to be infinite in (N4), whereas from use of (M4) only finite sets of impossible events can be included. (N5) states that a set is refusable if all of its finite subsets are refusable; the converse is implied by (N3).

We also impose a condition on the divergence set, corresponding to the intuition that divergence is a persistent phenomenon: once a process is diverging it diverges forever. Moreover, it is impossible to determine finitely any information about a diverging process, so that we cannot rule out the possibility that it might engage at some stage in some sequence of events. In other words, we regard divergence as *catastrophic*. These considerations lead us to formulate some conditions relating the divergence set D and failure set F

of a process:

$$s \in D \Rightarrow st \in D \tag{D1}$$
$$s \in D \Rightarrow (st, X) \in F. \tag{D2}$$

Condition (D1) states that the divergence set of a process is *suffix-closed.* The other condition states the catastrophic or chaotic nature of divergence. A similar argument was used in [3,4] to suggest that the failure set of a diverging process should be the most nondeterministic.

As in the old model, there is a natural partial order on the set of pairs $\langle F, D \rangle$:

$$\langle F_1, D_1 \rangle \sqsubseteq \langle F_2, D_2 \rangle \Leftrightarrow F_1 \supseteq F_2 \ \& \ D_1 \supseteq D_2.$$

The interpretation of this is that a process P_1 is more nondeterministic than P_2 if it can diverge whenever P_2 can diverge and fail whenever P_2 can fail. Again this ordering produces a complete semi-lattice structure; the least element, the most nondeterministic process, denoted $\perp$, has divergence set Σ^* and failure set $\Sigma^* \times \mathcal{P}(\Sigma)$. Since our model identifies all terms which diverge, we find it convenient to abuse notation slightly and introduce a constant term $\perp$ to the syntax of TCSP, representing divergence explicitly.

We say that a process is *divergence-free* if its divergence set is empty. The divergence-free processes form a semi-lattice which is clearly isomorphic to the old failures model, with bottom element CHAOS. The isomorphism $\Phi : M \to N$, given by

$$\Phi(F) = (\{(s, X) \mid \forall Y \in p(X).(s, Y) \in F\}, \emptyset),$$

merely assumes no divergence and introduces infinite refusal sets when required by (N5). Thus, in this model there is a distinction between the processes

$$\begin{aligned} \perp &= \langle \Sigma^* \times \mathcal{P}(\Sigma), \Sigma^* \rangle, \\ \Phi(\text{CHAOS}) &= \langle \Sigma^* \times \mathcal{P}(\Sigma), \emptyset \rangle. \end{aligned}$$

Note that the *deterministic* processes in the new model (the maximal elements) are precisely the images of deterministic processes in the old model, under this isomorphism. In particular, deterministic processes are divergence-free.

Semantics.

To give a semantics to our TCSP language we define a mapping $\mathcal{N}$ from processes to failure sets and divergence sets, when supplied with an environment for the meanings of free identifiers. Now we need an environment which maps process identifiers to pairs $\langle F, D \rangle$. Thus, an environment e will be a function e : TCSP $\to N$. As remarked earlier, we use the functions *failures* and *div* to extract the two components of a pair $\langle F, D\rangle$. We write $e + [p \mapsto \langle F, D\rangle]$ for the environment which agrees with e except at p, which is mapped to the given pair. Let NEnv be the set of environments of this type. The type of the semantic function is thus

$$\mathcal{N} : \text{TCSP} \rightarrow [\text{NEnv} \rightarrow N].$$

For presentation purposes it is sometimes convenient to factor $\mathcal{N}$ into two component functions, by defining auxiliary semantic functions $\mathcal{F}$ and $\mathcal{D}$ such that

$$\mathcal{N}[\![P]\!]e = \langle \mathcal{F}[\![P]\!]e, \mathcal{D}[\![P]\!]e\rangle.$$

With this notation, $\mathcal{F}[\![P]\!]e$ is the failure set of P and $\mathcal{D}[\![P]\!]e$ is the divergence set. This enables us, when desirable, to define $\mathcal{N}[\![P]\!]$ in terms of the two components. Strictly speaking, the intention is to define both components simultaneously (using mutual recursion). This is illustrated in the definition for recursive terms:

$$\mathcal{N}[\![\mu p.P]\!]e = \text{fix}(\lambda\langle F, D\rangle.\mathcal{N}[\![P]\!](e + [p \mapsto \langle F, D\rangle])).$$

For the other syntactic constructs, we define the divergence semantics first and then give the failure sets. For the other syntactic constructs, the divergence semantics

$$\mathcal{D} : \text{TCSP} \rightarrow [\text{NEnv} \rightarrow \mathcal{P}(\Sigma^*)]$$

is provided by the clauses:

$$\begin{aligned}
\mathcal{D}[\![p]\!]e &= \text{div}(e[\![p]\!])\\
\mathcal{D}[\![\text{STOP}]\!]e &= \emptyset\\
\mathcal{D}[\![\text{SKIP}]\!]e &= \emptyset\\
\mathcal{D}[\![a \rightarrow P]\!]e &= \{\, \langle a\rangle s \mid s \in \mathcal{D}[\![P]\!]e \,\}\\
\mathcal{D}[\![P \sqcap Q]\!]e &= \mathcal{D}[\![P]\!]e \cup \mathcal{D}[\![Q]\!]e\\
\mathcal{D}[\![P \,\Box\, Q]\!]e &= \mathcal{D}[\![P]\!]e \cup \mathcal{D}[\![Q]\!]e\\
\mathcal{D}[\![P \| Q]\!]e &= \{\, st \mid s \in (\mathcal{D}[\![P]\!]e \cap \text{traces}(\mathcal{F}[\![Q]\!]e)) \cup (\mathcal{D}[\![Q]\!]e \cap \text{traces}(\mathcal{F}[\![P]\!]e)) \,\}\\
\mathcal{D}[\![P ||| Q]\!]e &= \{\, u \mid \exists s, t.\, u \in \text{merge}(s,t) \;\&\\
&\qquad (s \in \mathcal{D}[\![P]\!]e \;\&\; t \in \text{traces}(\mathcal{F}[\![Q]\!]e) \vee t \in \mathcal{D}[\![Q]\!]e \;\&\; s \in \text{traces}(\mathcal{F}[\![P]\!]e)) \,\}\\
\mathcal{D}[\![P;Q]\!]e &= \mathcal{D}[\![P]\!]e \cup \{\, st \mid s \text{ is tick-free } \;\&\; s\surd \in \text{traces}(\mathcal{F}[\![P]\!]e) \;\&\; t \in \mathcal{D}[\![Q]\!]e \,\}\\
\mathcal{D}[\![P \backslash a]\!]e &= \{\, (s\backslash a)t \mid s \in \mathcal{D}[\![P]\!]e \,\} \cup \{\, (s\backslash a)t \mid \forall n. sa^n \in \text{traces}(\mathcal{F}[\![P]\!]e) \,\}\\
\mathcal{D}[\![f^{-1}(P)]\!]e &= \{\, s \mid f(s) \in \mathcal{D}[\![P]\!]e \,\}\\
\mathcal{D}[\![f(P)]\!]e &= \{\, f(s)t \mid s \in \mathcal{D}[\![P]\!]e \,\}
\end{aligned}$$

Notice from this definition that STOP and SKIP have empty divergence sets, while a nondeterministic composition $P \sqcap Q$ or $P \,\Box\, Q$ may diverge if one of the components diverges. In a parallel composition $P \| Q$ or $P ||| Q$ divergence can start at some stage if either of the component processes can diverge. A sequential composition $P;Q$ can diverge if either the first component diverges or if the second diverges after the first one has terminated successfully. The hiding operation explicitly introduces divergence in a case where the original process is capable of unboundedly many hidden actions; this accords with our intuitions about divergence, as stated above. Finally, the divergent traces of a renamed process are obtained by renaming from those of the original process. It should be noted that each of these divergence set constructions preserves property (D1).

The failures semantic function has type:

$$\mathcal{F} : \mathrm{CSP} \rightarrow [\mathrm{NEnv} \rightarrow \mathcal{P}(\Sigma^* \times \mathcal{P}(\Sigma))].$$

We have already specified $\mathcal{F}[\![\mu p.P]\!]e$. For the other syntactic constructs, we specify the following clauses. Apart from the need to close up under condition (D2), these definitions are essentially those of [4], and the reader will find further explanation there.

$$\begin{aligned}
\mathcal{F}[\![p]\!]e &= \mathrm{failures}(e[\![p]\!]) \\
\mathcal{F}[\![\mathrm{STOP}]\!]e &= \{ (\langle\rangle, X) \mid X \in \mathcal{P}(\Sigma) \} \\
\mathcal{F}[\![\mathrm{SKIP}]\!]e &= \{ (\langle\rangle, X) \mid \surd \notin X \} \cup \{ (\surd, X) \mid X \in \mathcal{P}(\Sigma) \} \\
\mathcal{F}[\![a \rightarrow P]\!]e &= \{ (\langle\rangle, X) \mid a \notin X \} \cup \{ (\langle a \rangle s, X) \mid (s, X) \in \mathcal{F}[\![P]\!]e \} \\
\mathcal{F}[\![P \sqcap Q]\!]e &= \mathcal{F}[\![P]\!]e \cup \mathcal{F}[\![Q]\!]e \\
\mathcal{F}[\![P \,\Box\, Q]\!]e &= \{ (\langle\rangle, X) \mid (\langle\rangle, X) \in \mathcal{F}[\![P]\!]e \cap \mathcal{F}[\![Q]\!]e \} \\
&\quad \cup \{ (s, X) \mid s \neq \langle\rangle \,\&\, (s, X) \in \mathcal{F}[\![P]\!]e \cup \mathcal{F}[\![Q]\!]e \} \\
&\quad \cup \{ (s, X) \mid s \in \mathcal{D}[\![P \,\Box\, Q]\!]e \} \\
\mathcal{F}[\![P \| Q]\!]e &= \{ (s, X \cup Y) \mid (s, X) \in \mathcal{F}[\![P]\!]e \,\&\, (s, Y) \in \mathcal{F}[\![Q]\!]e \} \\
&\quad \cup \{ (s, X) \mid s \in \mathcal{D}[\![P \| Q]\!]e \} \\
\mathcal{F}[\![P ||| Q]\!]e &= \{ (u, X) \mid \exists s, t.\, (s, X) \in \mathcal{F}[\![P]\!]e \;\&\; (t, X) \in \mathcal{F}[\![Q]\!]e \;\&\; u \in \mathrm{merge}(s, t) \} \\
&\quad \cup \{ (u, X) \mid u \in \mathcal{D}[\![P ||| Q]\!]e \} \\
\mathcal{F}[\![P;Q]\!]e &= \{ (s, X) \mid s \text{ tick-free } \& \, (s, X \cup \{ \surd \}) \in \mathcal{F}[\![P]\!]e \} \\
&\quad \cup \{ (st, X) \mid (s\surd, \emptyset) \in \mathcal{F}[\![P]\!]e \;\&\; s \text{ tick-free } \;\&\; (t, X) \in \mathcal{F}[\![Q]\!]e \} \\
&\quad \cup \{ (s, X) \mid s \in \mathcal{D}[\![P]\!]e \} \\
\mathcal{F}[\![P \backslash a]\!]e &= \{ (s \backslash a, X) \mid (s, X \cup \{ a \}) \in \mathcal{F}[\![P]\!]e \} \\
&\quad \cup \{ (u, X) \mid u \in \mathcal{D}[\![P \backslash a]\!]e \} \\
\mathcal{F}[\![f^{-1}(P)]\!]e &= \{ (s, X) \mid (f(s), f(X)) \in \mathcal{F}[\![P]\!]e \} \\
\mathcal{F}[\![f(P)]\!]e &= \{ (f(s), X) \mid (s, f^{-1}(X)) \in \mathcal{F}[\![P]\!]e \} \cup \{ (s, X) \mid s \in \mathcal{D}[\![f(P)]\!]e \}.
\end{aligned}$$

The next result establishes that our semantic definitions make sense.

THEOREM 1. *All CSP operations defined above are well defined and continuous.*

Proof. Well definedness is easy to show, except for the synchronous parallel operator. In each case we have to establish that the failure set operations and divergence set operations corresponding to the syntactic constructions preserve the properties (N1)–(N5) and (D1)–(D2). Only the proof for the synchronous parallel operator is non-trivial. A full proof may be found in [23] or in the full version of this paper [5]. Continuity proofs are relatively straightforward, along the lines of the proofs given in [4],[2], and [23]. ∎

Since all of our operators are continuous, we can justify our use of least fixed points in defining the meaning of recursive definitions, and we know that these fixed points are explicitly constructible, as was the case in the earlier model.

Examples.

1. The process defined by the recursion $P = (a \to P)$ is denoted $\mu p.(a \to p)$. This process has:

$$\begin{aligned} \mathcal{F}[\![\mu p.(a \to p)]\!]e &= \{(a^n, X) \mid n \geq 0 \ \& \ a \notin X\} \\ \mathcal{D}[\![\mu p.(a \to p)]\!]e &= \emptyset. \end{aligned}$$

2. The recursive term $\mu p.p$ denotes the most nondeterministic process $\perp$, which can do anything at all:

$$\begin{aligned} \mathcal{F}[\![\mu p.p]\!]e &= \Sigma^* \times \mathcal{P}(\Sigma), \\ \mathcal{D}[\![\mu p.p]\!]e &= \Sigma^*. \end{aligned}$$

Note that our notation implies that

$$\begin{aligned} \mathcal{M}[\![\mu p.p]\!]\rho &= \text{CHAOS} \\ \mathcal{N}[\![\mu p.p]\!]e &= \perp. \end{aligned}$$

This is an example in which the two semantics produce distinct results. We should be careful to distinguish between the meanings of terms in the two models. However, we can show that the old semantics and the new essentially coincide except in their treatment of divergence. This is stated precisely as follows. First we need to define an appropriate notion of matching between the environments used in the $\mathcal{M}$ semantics and those used in the $\mathcal{N}$ semantics.

Definition. The operation $\Phi : M \to N$ induces a function $\Phi : R \to \text{Env}$ by:

$$(\Phi\rho)[\![p]\!] = \langle \Phi(\rho[\![p]\!]), \emptyset \rangle.$$

The environments ρ and $\Phi\rho$ can be said to *match.*

LEMMA 1. *If P is a TCSP term, then for all ρ,*

$$\mathcal{N}[\![P]\!](\Phi\rho) \sqsubseteq_N \Phi(\mathcal{M}[\![P]\!]\rho).$$

THEOREM 2. *If P is a TCSP term and ρ an environment such that $\mathcal{D}[\![P]\!](\Phi\rho) = \emptyset$, then*

$$\mathcal{N}[\![P]\!](\Phi\rho) = \Phi(\mathcal{M}[\![P]\!]\rho).$$

Many algebraic properties of processes and these operators can be proved. The identities listed in Table 1 for the failures model are also true in this model (with $\equiv_M$ replaced by $\equiv_N$), except that

$$P \,||\, \text{STOP} \equiv_N \text{STOP}$$

is valid only if $P \not\equiv_N \bot$, as we regard divergence as catastrophic. It is important to remember, then, that not all equivalences remain true in the passage from the failures model to the extended model, because of the superior treatment of divergence in the new model. Additional identities for the new semantics include the following.

$$\begin{aligned} P \,\square\, \bot &\equiv_N \bot \\ P \sqcap \bot &\equiv_N \bot \\ P \,||\, \bot &\equiv_N \bot \\ \bot; Q &\equiv_N \bot \\ \bot \backslash a &\equiv_N \bot \end{aligned}$$

TABLE 2

The fixed point theorem also holds in the new model. We have the identity

$$\mu p.P \equiv_N [(\mu p.P)\backslash p]P.$$

Strictness.

It can be argued [4] that most of the operators introduced so far ought to be *strict*, in that they should preserve divergence. The identities listed in Table 2 reflect this property. An exception is the prefixing operation ($a \rightarrow P$), where divergence of P cannot manifest itself until after the initial occurrence of a; a similar exception is the second argument of a sequential composition, whose divergence cannot come into effect until the first component has terminated. Some further exceptions to strictness will be discussed in the next section, where we define the semantics of some operations introduced in [3,4].

4. Further operators.

It is possible to devise many useful operations, notably some interesting forms of parallel composition. In this section we revise the definitions of a few interesting forms of composition which were described in [3,4], bringing out certain inadequacies in the earlier treatment of divergence and showing that a cleaner treatment is obtained with our new definitions. By redefining the semantics of these operations in this way we achieve a better match with operational intuitions.

1. Mixed parallel composition.

We can define a parallel composition in which two processes operate with named alphabets and are required to cooperate on events common to both of their alphabets, but may progress independently on events belonging solely to their own alphabet. This mixed parallel composition is less restrictive than the *synchronous* version and not as generous as the *asynchronous* form. It is closely related to the *ignoring* operator of [3,4] and to the mixed parallel composition of [2,23]. When P and Q are to run in parallel, with P using alphabet A and Q using alphabet B, the resulting process is denoted:

$$[P_A \|_B Q].$$

Its divergence set and failure set, built up as usual from those of the constituent processes, are:

$$\begin{aligned}\mathcal{D}[\![P_A\|_B Q]\!]e = \{\, uv \mid u \in (A\cup B)^* \ \&\ \text{either } ((u{\restriction}A \in \mathcal{D}[\![P]\!]e \ \&\ u{\restriction}B \in \text{traces}(\mathcal{F}[\![Q]\!]e))\\ \text{or } (u{\restriction}A \in \text{traces}(\mathcal{F}[\![P]\!]e) \ \&\ u{\restriction}B \in \mathcal{D}[\![Q]\!]e))\,\}\\ \mathcal{F}[\![P_A\|_B Q]\!]e = \{\, (u, X\cup Y\cup Z) \mid u \in (A\cup B)^*, X \subseteq A, Y \subseteq B, Z \subseteq \overline{A\cup B},\\ (u{\restriction}A, X) \in \mathcal{F}[\![P]\!]e, (u{\restriction}B, Y) \in \mathcal{F}[\![Q]\!]e\,\} \cup \{\, (u,X) \mid u \in \mathcal{D}[\![P_A\|_B Q]\!]e\,\}.\end{aligned}$$

Here we introduce the notation $u{\restriction}A$ for the trace resulting from u after the removal of all events outside of the set A. We also use $\overline{C}$ for the complement of a set C. According to this definition, the traces u of $P_A\|_B Q$ are built up from events in A and B, and filtering out only those events which belong to A produces a trace $u{\restriction}A$ of P, while filtering out the events in B produces a trace $u{\restriction}B$ of Q. The compound process diverges after performing the sequence u if either P can diverge after $u{\restriction}A$ or Q can diverge after $u{\restriction}B$. Events in A are refused if P refuses them, while Q chooses whether or not to perform the events in B. Events common to A and B can be refused by either process. Events outside of A and B are always impossible.

It is easy to check, given the well-definedness of the synchronous parallel composition [5], that this construction produces a process when applied to processes, *i.e.* that conditions (N1)–(N5) and (D1)–(D2) are preserved. The following *associativity* property can also be proved; see [2] for details.

LEMMA 3. *For all processes P, Q, R, and all sets of events A, B, C,*

$$[P_A \|_{B\cup C} [Q_B \|_C R]] \equiv_N [[P_A \|_B Q]_{A\cup B} \|_C R].$$

In view of this result, this notation generalizes to a parallel composition of more than three processes. Given an indexed collection $V = \{(P_i, A_i) \mid 1 \le i \le n\}$ we will write

$$\mathrm{PAR}(V) = \|_{i=1}^{n} (P_i, A_i)$$

for the parallel composition. Using this notation the mixed parallel composition $[P_A \|_B Q]$ may be rendered $(P, A) \| (Q, B)$. This type of composition can be useful in analysing the deadlock behaviour of networks of parallel processes, as shown in [6].

Another interesting identity concerns the result of hiding an event which is involved in a parallel composition. This identity did not in general hold in the old model, in some cases where hiding the event introduces divergence.

LEMMA 4. *Let A, B be subsets of Σ, let $c \not\in B$, and let $C = A \cup \{c\}$. Then for all processes P, Q,*

$$[P_C \|_B Q]\backslash c \equiv_N [(P\backslash c)_A \|_B Q].$$

This result is important in analysing the effect of hiding internal communications in networks of communicating processes. It enables us to move hiding operators (in some cases) inside a parallel composition. This result is used in [6] to prove some useful results on deadlock analysis.

If we wish to run P and Q in parallel using alphabets A and B, we use the composition $[P_A \|_B Q]$ as above; events in the intersection $A \cap B$ are synchronized and correspond to communications between the two processes. These internal events may be concealed from the environment by applying the hiding operation. Provided this intersection is finite, we can define the process in which these internal communications are hidden as:

$$[P_A \|_B Q]\backslash(A \cap B).$$

This makes sense because hiding is associative. It is convenient to introduce a notation for this composition: we will denote it $[P\ {}_A\!\Leftrightarrow_B Q]$. Now if we wish to extend this to a network of several processes we may do so. The key associativity property is as follows. Provided $A \cap B \cap C = \emptyset$, and provided each of $A \cap B$, $B \cap C$, and $C \cap A$ is finite, we have:

$$[[P\ {}_A\!\Leftrightarrow_B Q]\ {}_{(A\cup B)}\!\Leftrightarrow_C R] \equiv_N [P\ {}_A\!\Leftrightarrow_{(B\cup C)} [Q\ {}_B\!\Leftrightarrow_C R]].$$

This follows from Lemmas 3 and 4.

2. Chaining.

In [3,4] we also defined a form of "chaining", a parallel composition $P \gg Q$ in which all outputs of P are fed into Q as inputs and hidden from their common environment. Assume that all events are communications between processes along named channels. An event consists of two parts m.t, where m is a channel name and t a value. Normally, the channel name "in" is associated with input, and "out" with output. We use the abbreviations

$$\begin{aligned} (?x{:}T \to P(x)) \quad & \text{for} \quad \Box_{t \in T}\,(\text{in}.t \to P(t)), \\ !t \quad & \text{for} \quad (\text{out}.t \to \text{SKIP}). \end{aligned}$$

It is convenient also to allow the abbreviated form $?t$ to stand for the correspoding event. In order to cope with a form of channel naming, we also use the abbreviations:

$$\begin{aligned} (c?x{:}T \to P(x)) \quad & \text{for} \quad \Box_{t \in T}\,(\text{c.in}.t \to P(t)), \\ c!t \quad & \text{for} \quad (\text{c.out}.t \to \text{SKIP}). \end{aligned}$$

We also allow the abbreviated form $c?t$ to stand for the corresponding event. The construct $(c?x{:}T \to P(x))$ represents a process which initially *inputs* on channel c a value for x from the set T (a value of type T); similarly, $c!t$ represents output of the value t along the channel. For example, a simple buffer of type T using input channel *in* and output channel *out* is:

$$B_1 = \mu p.(\text{in}?x{:}T \to \text{out}!x;\, p).$$

The chaining operation can be defined by combining a renaming with the mixed parallel operation and hiding. First we rename the output events of P and the input events of Q so that they become identical events; then we run the renamed versions of P and Q in parallel, using the renamed alphabets. This forces P to synchronize its outputs with the inputs of Q. Finally we hide all events common to these alphabets, which are precisely the internal communications between the two processes. Let α be a label distinct from *in* and *out*. Let swap(α, β) be the alphabet transformation defined:

$$\begin{aligned} \text{swap}(\alpha,\beta)(x) &= x && \text{if } x \notin \alpha.T \cup \beta.T \\ &= \beta.t && \text{if } x = \alpha.t \quad (t \in T) \\ &= \alpha.t && \text{if } x = \beta.t \quad (t \in T). \end{aligned}$$

Then if we put $A = \text{in}.T \cup \alpha.T$ and $B = \text{out}.T \cup \alpha.T$, we can define

$$(P \gg Q) = [\text{swap}(\text{out},\alpha)(P)\ {}_A \Leftrightarrow {}_B\ \text{swap}(\text{in},\alpha)(Q)].$$

As an example of the use of the chaining operation, the result of chaining two simple buffers B_1 together is again a buffer process, $B_1 \gg B_1$, capable of holding at most two values. Several interesting properties of buffer processes built from the chaining operation were discussed in [4]. Most of these carry over without problems to the new model. In particular, we have the identities $(B_n \gg B_m) = B_{n+m}$ for all $n, m \geq 0$.

Interestingly, the version of the chaining operation defined in the failures model can fail to be associative: it is not always true that $P \gg (Q \gg R)$ and $(P \gg Q) \gg R$ denote the same failure set. This property can fail to hold when divergence can arise between two of the processes, so that either $(P \gg Q)$ or $(Q \gg R)$ diverges. Recall that in the failures model divergence is represented by CHAOS; it is not generally true that

$$\text{CHAOS} \gg Q \equiv_M P \gg \text{CHAOS} \equiv_M \text{CHAOS}.$$

Again, the use of CHAOS to represent divergence is unsatisfactory. In the new model the chaining operation is associative. The identities

$$(\bot \gg Q) \equiv_N (P \gg \bot) \equiv_N \bot$$

are true for all P and Q.

LEMMA 5. *For all processes P, Q, R,*

$$P \gg (Q \gg R) \equiv_N (P \gg Q) \gg R.$$

3. Master-slave operation.

In [3,4] we also defined a "master-slave" construction $[P \parallel \text{m}:Q]$, in which the master process P refers to its slave Q by the name m. The communications between master and slave are hidden in this construction. The definition here is similar to the previous version, except that we do not make the construction strict in the "slave" argument. The reason for this is that we do not want a master-slave pair to diverge unless either the master is diverging or the slave has been asked to perform some action and is diverging. In other words, the master's activity will only be affected by a divergence of the slave if the master is actually waiting for a response from the slave. Let $C = T \cup \text{in}.T \cup \text{out}.T$ and let m be chosen to be distinct from *in* and *out*. We define first, for traces u, v a compatibility condition:

$$\text{compat}_{\text{m}}(u, v) \Leftrightarrow v \in C^* \ \& \ u\lceil(\text{m}.C) = \text{m.swap}(\text{in}, \text{out})(v).$$

If u is a trace of the master process, then $u\lceil(\text{m}.C)$ is the sequence of events involving the slave named m. If we interchange the roles of input and output in this sequence we should get a trace of the slave process; this is the essence of the compatibility condition. For two compatible traces u and v, define $[u \parallel \text{m}:v]$ to be the trace $u\lceil(\Sigma - \text{m}.C)$. This is the sequence of events performed by the master process which do not involve the slave. Then we can define the master-slave operation on processes as follows:

$$\begin{aligned}\mathcal{D}[\![P \parallel \text{m}:Q]\!]e = &\ \{\, [u \parallel \text{m}:v]w \mid \text{compat}_m(u,v) \ \& \ u \in \mathcal{D}[\![P]\!]e \ \& \ v \in \text{traces}(\mathcal{F}[\![Q]\!]e) \,\} \\ &\cup \{\, [u \parallel \text{m}:v]w \mid \text{compat}_m(u,v) \ \& \ u \in \text{traces}(\mathcal{F}[\![P]\!]e) \ \& \ v \in \mathcal{D}[\![Q]\!]e \ \& \ v \neq \langle\rangle \,\} \\ &\cup \{\, sw \mid \exists^\infty(u,v).\ u \in \text{traces}(\mathcal{F}[\![P]\!]e) \ \& \ v \in \text{traces}(\mathcal{F}[\![Q]\!]e) \ \& \ \text{compat}_m(u,v) \ \& \\ &\qquad s = [u \parallel \text{m}:v] \,\}.\end{aligned}$$

For the failure set we define:

$$\mathcal{F}[\![P \parallel \text{m}{:}Q]\!]e = \{(s,X) \mid s \in \mathcal{D}[\![P \parallel \text{m}{:}Q]\!]e\} \cup \{([u \parallel \text{m}{:}v], X) \mid (u,U) \in \mathcal{F}[\![P]\!]e \;\&\; (v,V) \in \mathcal{F}[\![Q]\!]e \;\&\; \text{compat}_m(u,v) \;\&\; U \cup \text{m.swap(in, out)}(V \cap C) = X \cup \text{m}.C\}.$$

Thus, the traces of the compound process are built from a master trace and a compatible slave trace; and an event not involving the slave process can be refused if the master process refuses it and there is no possibility of an internal action. On the other hand, an event involving the slave process may be refused if either the slave or the master refuses it.

The version of master-slave operation used in the old failures model had some slight problems, in particular in its behaviour in recursive definitions. For example, in the failures model we have the identity

$$\mu p.[(?x \to m!x) \parallel m{:}p] \equiv_M (?x \to \text{STOP}),$$

although intuitively we can see that there is a possibility of divergence after the first input. In the new model, with the above definition, we do indeed get

$$\mu p.[(?x \to m!x) \parallel m{:}p] \equiv_N (?x \to \bot).$$

Another problem was that in the failures model, the order in which a master process binds his slaves could make a difference in the behaviour of the system. In other words, the following identity does not always hold in the failures model:

$$[[P \parallel m{:}Q] \parallel n{:}R] \equiv_M [[P \parallel n{:}R] \parallel m{:}Q] \quad (n \neq m).$$

Again this deficiency appears when divergence can occur between the master and one of the slaves. In the new model the order in which a master process binds his slaves is irrelevant, and we do have

$$[[P \parallel m{:}Q] \parallel n{:}R] \equiv_N [[P \parallel n{:}R] \parallel m{:}Q] \quad (n \neq m).$$

5. Conclusions.

The revised model of processes described here enjoys the mathematical properties of a complete semi-lattice under the componentwise ordering $\sqsubseteq_N$ introduced earlier. All of the techniques used in [4] to specify and prove properties of processes may be adapted with ease to this setting. In particular, it is possible to use the notions of *constructivity* and *non-destructivity* in the analysis of recursively defined processes. Thus, with minor modifications to fit with the revised definitions of some of the operators, the examples described in [4] and the proofs of their properties described in that paper can be reformulated in the revised setting.

The failures model of communicating processes was introduced in [3,4]. This model was itself an extension of Hoare's earlier *traces* model of processes [13], which was incapable of supporting any reasonable treatment of deadlock properties since it is impossible to represent the ability to refuse to perform an action in a model based solely on sequences of possible actions. Our motives in designing the failures model were therefore driven by a desire to model deadlock satisfactorily. Several other authors have also discovered models which can be related to failures. Milner's CCS [18] is founded on a rather different (more discriminating) notion of *observation equivalence*, and his synchronization trees provide an alternative framework in which our results can be formulated [2]. Our development of the failures model has clearly been strongly influenced by the work of Milner and his colleagues.

As we observed earlier, a model based on failures alone is inadequate for reasoning about the phenomenon of divergence. Problems related to this fact have been pointed out by [23], [12]. This led to the inclusion in [2] and [23] of an explicit and distinguished representation of divergence in the semantics of processes, producing models isomorphic to the one used in this paper. In a similar vein, Hennessy and de Nicola have constructed several models based on synchronization trees augmented by acceptance sets, and they have introduced the notion of *representation trees* [11,12,19,20]. Hennessy has pointed out in [11] that the model known as RT_2 is closely related to a submodel of ours based on extra assumptions on finite branching, although there are subtle differences between the treatments of internal actions in their model and ours. In fact, this submodel with finite branching can be thought of as containing all of the *denotable* elements of our model. Similar observations were made by de Nicola in [19,20], where he suggested an adjustment to the failures model to handle divergence in a more subtle way than was done in that model: this was the *Bounded Refusal Sets* model, and again this model can be seen as an alternative presentation of a submodel of ours. The full model N, as it stands, does allow a (pessimistic) treatment of unbounded nondeterminism, in the sense that many unboundedly nondeterministic processes can be represented in this model but any process will be identified with its closure.

If one focusses solely on the finitely branching submodel of ours, it is largely a matter of taste as to which presentation one prefers, as any theorem provable in one formulation of the model will be adaptable to the alternative settings. This is an observation due to Matthew Hennessy. He has proved in [11] some general results on the congruence of denotational and operational semantics and these can be adapted to our setting to demonstrate that our semantics is indeed in accordance with operational intuitions. It is possible to define an operational semantics for our language based on Milner's *synchronization trees*, extending the definitions of [2,23] and following the lines of the presentations in

[11,12,20,23]. Essentially the idea is that a term denotes a synchronization tree whose arcs are labelled by events or by a special symbol τ denoting an internal event. Recursively defined terms will in general denote infinite trees, and divergence corresponds to the presence of an infinite path of τ arcs. Each syntactic construct of our language then corresponds to an operation on synchronization trees. There is a natural notion of *implementability* of operations on these trees, and all of the CSP operations turn out to be implementable. Moreover, the denotational semantics of this paper can be shown to agree with the operational semantics, a property that failed for the earlier model because of its inadequate treatment of divergence.

Kennaway [15,16] described a model for processes from which failures can be derived [2], but in which the underlying partial ordering is different because of his decision to regard deadlock as disastrous. The notion of *implementation sets*, given in [2,4], is closely related to Kennaway's idea of a nondeterministic process as a set of deterministic processes. We defined a notion of *implementation* for the failures model of CSP. A deterministic process Q is said to *implement* a process P if $P \sqsubseteq_M Q$. For divergence-free processes in the new model the same ideas can be adapted. A divergence-free process can be identified with its set of deterministic implementations,

$$\mathrm{imp}(P) = \{\, Q \mid P \sqsubseteq_N Q \ \&\ Q \,\text{deterministic}\,\}.$$

In the absence of divergence, the CSP operations on processes are fully determined by their effect on deterministic processes. Thus, if $\circ$ is a binary CSP operation (such as $\|$), and if P, Q are divergence-free processes, we have

$$\begin{aligned} \mathcal{F}[\![P \circ Q]\!]e &= \bigcup\{\, \mathcal{F}[\![P' \circ Q']\!]e \mid P' \in \mathrm{imp}(P), Q' \in \mathrm{imp}(Q)\,\} \\ \mathcal{D}[\![P \circ Q]\!]e &= \bigcup\{\, \mathcal{D}[\![P' \circ Q']\!]e \mid P' \in \mathrm{imp}(P), Q' \in \mathrm{imp}(Q)\,\}. \end{aligned}$$

Similar results hold for unary CSP operations. As stated here, these definitions and results apply only to divergence-free processes. It is possible to extend these results to cover all processes, by redefining the notion of an implementation to include only "minimal" divergent processes. We will not discuss this issue here.

Darondeau [8] gave an "enlarged definition of observation congruence" for finite processes which essentially coincides with the failure equivalence [2] induced by focussing on failures; Darondeau's paper only considered finite terms. In [25] a model including acceptance sets in addition to refusal sets was discussed, although this seems not to possess such elegant mathematical properties as the failures model and appears as a result to be less well suited to analysis of deadlock. Olderog [21] introduced a model involving "readiness sets", which are analogous to acceptance sets; again there are connections with failure sets, since a readiness set can be regarded as the dual of a refusal set. The readiness model is based on a slightly different notion of equivalence than the one induced by failures. Broy introduces in [7] a somewhat complicated model in which rather more distinctions between processes are possible; in particular, he chooses not to regard the possibility of divergence as necessarily catastrophic (so that, for instance, $P \Box \bot \neq \bot$ in general in his model). His fixed point theory and operator definitions are made more complicated by this and by the intricate structure of his model.

There are several directions in which we want to develop our techniques and results. In the full version of this paper, proofs are given of some of the most interesting theorems. In [6] we discuss some useful results pertaining to the analysis of deadlock behaviour in networks of communicating processes. It is possible to adapt our semantics to imperative communicating processes such as Hoare's original CSP, in which processes have disjoint local states and can perform assignments to update their own state. An example in this vein is provided by Roscoe's semantics for *occam* [24], which arises from a failure set semantics by adjoining local states and building a "hybrid" semantic model. We plan to adopt similar techniques for CSP in a future paper. This should lead to a semantic model closely related to the linear history model developed by Pnueli, Lehmann and Francez [9], which uses *expectation sets* rather than refusal sets and is based on a different notion of equivalence. Connections with earlier models such as the one described in [10] should also become apparent. We also believe that this should lead us to a semantics supporting a partial correctness analysis which takes deadlock fully and explicitly into account, unlike many existing CSP semantics which have served as the basis for partial correctness reasoning. We hope to be able to make some connections with existing proof systems for CSP, such as those described in [1,17], and with Plotkin's structural operational semantics for CSP [22].

Acknowledgements.

The authors would like to thank C. A. R. Hoare for his many helpful suggestions and discussions, and for his encouragement and guidance during the development of this work. We have been strongly influenced by the work of Robin Milner, Matthew Hennessy and Rocco de Nicola. Discussions with them and with Bill Rounds and Ernst-Rudiger Olderog have been very useful.

6. References.

[1] Apt, K. R., Francez, N., and de Roever, W. P., A Proof System for Communicating Sequential Processes, ACM TOPLAS, Vol. 2 No. 3, July 1980.

[2] Brookes, S. D., A Model for Communicating Sequential Processes, Ph. D. thesis, Oxford University (1983). Available as CMU Technical Report CMU-CS-83-149 and PRG Monograph.

[3] Brookes, S. D., Hoare, C. A. R., and Roscoe, A. W., A Theory of Communicating Sequential Processes, Oxford University Computing Laboratory, Programming Research Group, Technical Report PRG-16.

[4] Brookes, S. D., Hoare, C. A. R., and Roscoe, A. W., A Theory of Communicating Sequential Processes, JACM July 1984.

[5] Brookes, S. D., and Roscoe, A. W., An Improved failures Model for Communicating Processes (full version of this paper), to appear, CMU Technical Report.

[6] Brookes, S. D., and Roscoe, A. W., Deadlock Analysis in Networks of Processes, to appear in Proceedings of the NATO Advanced Seminar on Concurrency, La Colle-Sur-Loup, Springer Verlag LNCS (1985).

[7] Broy, M., Semantics of Communicating Processes, preprint, Institut fur Informatik, Technische Universitat Munchen (1983).

[8] Darondeau, Ph., An enlarged definition and complete axiomatization of observational congruence of finite processes, Springer Verlag LNCS vol. 137, pp. 47-62 (1982).

[9] Francez, N., Lehmann, D., and Pnueli, A., A Linear History Semantics for Communica Processes, Theoretical Computer Science 32 (1984) 25-46.

[10] Francez, N., Hoare, C. A. R., Lehmann, D., and de Roever, W. P., Semantics of nondeterminism, concurrency and communication, JCSS vol. 19 no. 3 (1979).

[11] Hennessy, M., Synchronous and Asynchronous Experiments on Processes, Informati and Control, Vol. 59, Nos 1-3, pp. 36-83 (1983).

[12] Hennessy, M., and de Nicola, R., Testing equivalences for processes, Proc. ICALP 1983, Springer LNCS 154 (1983).

[13] Hoare, C. A. R., A Model for Communicating Sequential Processes, Oxford University Computing Laboratory, Programming Research Group, Technical Report PRG-22.

[14] Hoare, C. A. R., Communicating Sequential Processes, CACM 1978.

[15] Kennaway, J., Formal semantics of nondeterminism and parallelism, D. Phil thesis, Oxford University (1981).

[16] Kennaway, J., A theory of nondeterminism, Springer LNCS vol. 85, pp 338-350 (1980).

[17] Levin, G. M., and Gries, D., A Proof Technique for Communicating Sequential Processes, Acta Informatica 15 (1981).

[18] Milner, R., A Calculus of Communicating Systems, Springer Verlag LNCS 92.

[19] de Nicola, R., Two Complete Sets of Axioms for a Theory of Communicating Sequential Processes, Proc. International Conference on Foundations of Computation Theory, Borgholm, Sweden, Springer LNCS (1983).

[20] de Nicola, R., Models and Operators for Nondeterministic Processes, Proceedings of the Conference on Mathematical Foundations of Computer Science, Springer Verlag LNCS (1984).

[21] Olderog, E-R, Specification-oriented semantics of communicating processes, Proc. ICALP 1983, Springer LNCS 154 (1983).

[22] Plotkin, An Operational Semantics for CSP, W.G.2.2 Conference proceedings (1982).

[23] Roscoe, A. W., A Mathematical Theory of Communicating Processes, Ph. D. thesis, Oxford University (1982).

[24] Roscoe, A. W., A Denotational Semantics for *occam*, Proc. NSF–SERC Seminar on Concurrency, to appear in Springer Lecture Notes series (1984).

[25] Rounds, W. C., and Brookes, S. D., Possible futures, acceptances, refusals and communicating processes, Proc. 22nd IEEE Symposium on Foundations of Computer Science (1981).

[26] Stoy, J. E., Denotational Semantics: The Scott–Strachey Approach to Programming Language Theory, MIT Press, Cambridge, Mass. (1977).

DENOTATIONAL SEMANTICS FOR OCCAM

A.W. Roscoe

Oxford University Computing Laboratory

8-11 Keble Road, Oxford OX1 3QD,

United Kingdom.

ABSTRACT. A denotational semantics is given for a large subset of occam, a programming language for concurrent systems. The semantic domain used is a "failure-sets" model modified to allow machine states to be properly dealt with. The applications of the semantics are discussed briefly, and we see how the natural congruence induced by the semantics allows us to prove simple algebraic laws relating occam programs.

0. <u>Introduction</u> The occam programming language [10] was designed with the philosophy of eliminating unnecessary complexities, thus keeping the language simple and elegant. Fundamental to its design was the idea that the language should have close ties with formal methods of designing and verifying programs. The main aim of this paper is to develop a theory which will allow us to apply existing techniques of program verification to occam, as well as giving us a rigorous mathematical framework for developing new ones.

The main difficulty in developing a useful theory of occam is the fact that it is a concurrent language. Indeed the idea of concurrency is central in occam, making an adequate treatment of concurrency essential in such a theory. There has been a considerable amount of effort expended in recent years in developing theories of concurrency. This subject is rather harder than the study of purely sequential computation, because of the emergence of such phenomena as nondeterminism, deadlock and livelock. Fortunately occam is close in spirit to CSP [6], a language which has been one of the main vehicles for research into concurrency.

Since the problems of dealing with concurrency in isolation are quite considerable, mar authors have chosen to omit several "conventional" programming constructs from the exan ple languages they have used when reasoning about concurrent systems. In particular they have often omitted those constructs, such as assignment and declaration, which dea with a machine's internal state (or store). Several of the most successful theories of concurrency have been based on these "purely parallel" languages. To handle occam we need a theory which, while retaining its full capacity for dealing with concurrency, is extended to handle machine states.

This paper presents one possible approach to this problem by constructing a mathematica model for communicating processes with internal states. As a basis for our treatment c concurrency we take the "failure-sets" (or "refusal-sets") model for communicating proc esses, originally developed as a model for a purely parallel version of CSP. It was introduced in [4], and developed and improved in [3,5,12]. It provides a reasonably simple mathematical structure within which most of the important features of concurrenc are easy to study. The fact that it was developed as a model for CSP makes it well suited to occam. It is necessary to add to the model a mechanism for dealing with the state transformations induced by occam's "conventional" constructs. The framework chosen for this is the well-known idea of regarding a program as a relation between initial and final states. This is sufficient because it turns out that knowledge of intermediate states is not required. One of the aims when putting these models together was that on purely parallel programs the results obtained would correspond closely to the old failure-sets model, and that on sequential programs the results would be relations on states.

The first part of the paper is concerned with the construction of the revised model. The second part shows how it can be used to give a denotational semantics in the style of [11,13,14] to occam. The third section discusses a few applications of these semantics, and derives some algebraic laws relating occam terms.

Throughout this paper $\mathcal{P}(X)$ will denote the full powerset of X (the set of all subsets of X), while $p(X)$ will denote the finite powerset of X (the set of all finite subsets of X). X* will denote the set of all finite sequences of elements of X. <> denotes the empty sequence, and <a,b,...,z> denotes the sequence containing a,b,...,z in that order. If s,t $\in$ X*, then st denotes the concatenation of s and t (e.g. <abc><de> = <abcde>). If s,t $\in$ X* then s $\leq$ t (s is a *prefix* of t) if there is some u $\in$ X* with su = t.

1. Constructing the model Our semantic domain for occam is based on the failure-sets model for communicating processes. The following is a brief summary of its construction; much fuller descriptions and motivations can be found in [3,4,5,12]. The version described here is that of [5].

The failure-sets model has as its only primitives the set Σ of atomic communications between processes. Communications are events which occur when the participating processes agree to execute them. In themselves they have no direction - there is no inputting process or outputting process. Input and output are modelled at a higher level by varying the set of a process' possible communications (an outputting process will typically have one possible communication, while an inputting process will have many). Each process communicates with its *environment*. This might be some other process or processes, or it might be some external observer. No distinction is made between these cases. We will think of a process proceeding by accepting (i.e. communicating) symbols in Σ which are offered by the environment. Only one symbol can be communicated at a time, and only finitely many in any finite time.

A process is modelled as a pair. The first component is a relation between the possible *traces* of the process (the elements of Σ* which are the possible sequences of communications of the process up to some time) and the sets of symbols which the process can refuse to respond to after the traces (*refusals*). A *failure* of a process is a pair (s,X) where the process can refuse to communicate when offered the set X by its environment after the trace s. The first component of our representation of a process is the set of all its possible failures.

The second component is a set of traces. It represents the set of traces on which the process may *diverge*, that is, engage in an infinite unbroken sequence of internal actions. When a process diverges, it not only never communicates with its environment again, but furthermore the environment can never detect that this is so. A diverging process is bad both practically and technically, so it is desirable to differentiate between it and a process which merely stops. (We can imagine the environment being able to detect the absence of internal activity in a process, perhaps via some light on its side. If, in such a state, it does not accept communications offered to it immediately, the environment can deduce that it never will.)

The sets of failures and divergences always satisfy the laws below (see [5]). If our representation of a given process P is $\langle F,D\rangle$ where $F \subseteq \Sigma^* \times \wp(\Sigma)$ and $D \subseteq \Sigma^*$, then

N1) traces(P) ($= \{s \in \Sigma^* : (s,\emptyset) \in F\}$) is nonempty and prefix closed (i.e. traces(P) $\neq \emptyset$, and if $s \in$ traces(P) and $t \leqslant s$ then $t \in$ traces(P));

N2) if $(s,X) \in F$ and $Y \subseteq X$, then $(s,Y) \in F$;

N3) if $(s,X) \in F$ and $Y \cap \{a \in \Sigma : s\langle a\rangle \in \text{traces}(P)\} = \emptyset$, then $(s,X \cup Y) \in F$;

N4) if $(s,Y) \in F$ for each $Y \in p(X)$, then $(s,X) \in F$;

N5) if $s \in D$ and $t \in \Sigma^*$, then $st \in D$;

N6) if $s \in D$ and $X \subseteq \Sigma$, then $(s,X) \in F$.

The failure-sets model N is defined to be the set of all pairs $\langle F,D\rangle$ satisfying these laws.

If $P \in N$ then f(P) will denote the first component of P, and d(P) the second component. There is a natural partial order on N given by $P \sqsubseteq P'$ if and only if $f(P) \supseteq f(P')$ and $d(P) \supseteq d(P')$. If $P \sqsubseteq P'$ then we can naturally think of P' as being more deterministic than P, for it has fewer possible actions. N is a complete semilattice with respect to $\sqsubseteq$; its minimal element is $\langle \Sigma^* \times \wp(\Sigma), \Sigma^*\rangle$ (which represents the completely unpredictable process) and its maximal elements are the *deterministic* processes. These can neither diverge nor have any choice about whether or not to accept any communication.

This model is adequate for modelling the behaviour of programs written in a purely parallel version of CSP. All the operators in CSP translate naturally to continuous functions over N. It is well suited to reasoning about the nondeterminism which arises from distributed systems and to reasoning about deadlock. Axioms N5 and N6 above correspond to the assumption that once it becomes possible for a process to diverge we do not care about its subsequent behaviour. In other words divergence is something to be avoided at all costs. The inclusion of these laws makes for considerable technical simplification at what does not seem to be a very great cost. Since the model has well-defined close links with behaviour, it is a good medium for expressing many correctness properties of processes.

Models whose only primitives are communications can be adequate for giving denotational semantics to purely parallel languages because the only way in which one of two separate parts of a program can influence the behaviour of the other is via communication. One part of an occam program can influence another in two ways. Firstly, it can communicate along channels with its parallel partners. Secondly, it can, by assignment to common variables, influence the behaviour of its successors. Any mathematical model for occam will have to be able to deal with both these methods.

One process can communicate with another at any time before it terminates, but can only pass on its final state when it terminates successfully. (Since the sharing of variables by parallel processes is not permitted, its intermediate states cannot directly affect another process.) Successful termination has previously been modelled in purely parallel models (for example in [4,7]) by the communication of some special symbol: usually ✓ (pronounced "tick"). Thus all successful terminations looked the same.

Perhaps the most obvious way of letting a process pass on its final state is to have not one but many ✓s - one for each possible final state. If this solution were adopted then a large proportion of our alphabet of "communications" would consist of these ✓s. Noting that all elements of Σ have precisely the same status in the construction of N, it does seem rather unnatural to include final states in this way. Besides, there are several specific problems which arise from this treatment.

Firstly the degree of refinement required to correctly model ordinary communication seems inappropriate for the passing on of final states. It is natural to assume that if more than one final state is possible after some trace then the choice of which one is passed on is nondeterministic (i.e. outside the control of the environment). However the model as adapted above would contain elements which offer the environment a choice of final states. This would correspond to the environment controlling the internal workings of the process to a most unlikely degree.

Secondly, if the number of possible states were infinite, there would be problems in defining a continuous sequential composition operator. When a process could terminate in infinitely many different states after some trace, the "hiding" of termination by sequential composition would yield unbounded nondeterminism.

Finally, in a model where termination plays a more important role than before, the technical complexities caused by allowing nonfinal ✓s in traces are unacceptable (as well as being unnatural).

The solution we adopt is similar but avoids these difficulties. First, we remove ✓ from the traces of processes (which thus only contain "real" communications). A single symbol ✓ remains in the alphabet used for refusal sets, indicating that a process can refuse to terminate successfully. The second component is expanded. Instead of just recording the possible divergences, it now also records the possible states which result from successful termination. It becomes a function from Σ^* to $\wp(S) \cup \{\perp\}$, where S is the space of final states and $\perp$ represents possible divergence. Thus each process is now a pair <F,T>, where $F \subseteq \Sigma^* \times \mathcal{P}(\Sigma \cup \{\checkmark\})$ $(\checkmark \notin \Sigma)$ and $T: \Sigma^* \rightarrow \wp(S) \cup \{\perp\}$. Our interpretation of the behaviour of a process $P = \langle F,T\rangle$ is as follows.

(i) F (the failures of P) lists all possible traces of the process, together with all sets of communications which it can refuse on each trace. (So that if a set of communications which is *not* a current refusal set is offered to the process, then it *must* accept some element.)

(ii) One of the possible elements of the refusal sets is ✓ – this indicates that the process may fail to terminate successfully (even though there may be some final states possible for the given trace). Thus it is possible to discriminate between a process which will always terminate successfully and one which may nondeterministically deadloc *or* terminate successfully. Termination *must* take place (if desired by the environment) only when the set {✓} cannot be refused.

(iii) Termination *can* take place on any trace s for which T(s) is a nonempty set of states. When T(s) contains more than one element the choice of which final state occur is nondeterministic. (T will be referred to as the termination component of P.)

(iv) If $T(s) = \bot$, then the process is considered to be broken. We allow the possibilit that it might diverge or do anything else at all.

For a given alphabet Σ and a set S of final states, the **space** Q of all processes is thu the set of all pairs $P = \langle F,T\rangle$ $(F \subseteq (\Sigma^* \times \wp(\Sigma \cup \{✓\})),\ T:\Sigma^* \to \wp(S) \cup \{\bot\})$ which satisfy the following eight laws.

F1) $traces(P)\ (= \{s \in \Sigma^* : (s,\emptyset) \in F\})$ is nonempty and prefix closed;

F2) $(s,X) \in F \ \ \&\ \ Y \subseteq X \ \Rightarrow\ (s,Y) \in F$;

F3) $(s,X) \in F \ \ \&\ \ Y \subseteq \{a \in \Sigma : s\langle a\rangle \notin traces(P)\} \ \Rightarrow\ (s, X \cup Y) \in F$;

F4) if $(s,Y) \in F$ for each $Y \in \wp(X)$, then $(s,X) \in F$;

T1) $T(s) \neq \emptyset \ \Rightarrow\ s \in traces(P)$;

T2) $(s,X) \in F \ \ \&\ \ T(s) = \emptyset \ \Rightarrow\ (s, X \cup \{✓\}) \in F$;

T3) $T(s) = \bot \ \ \&\ \ t \in \Sigma^* \ \Rightarrow\ T(st) = \bot$;

T4) $T(s) = \bot \ \ \&\ \ X \subseteq \Sigma \cup \{✓\} \ \Rightarrow\ (s,X) \in F$.

In the above s,t range over Σ^* and X,Y range over $\wp(\Sigma \cup \{✓\})$.

These laws are just the natural extension of the laws governing N to the revised struct ure.

If $P = \langle F,T\rangle$, then define $f(P) = F$ and $t(P) = T$. We will adopt the conventions that $A \subseteq \bot$ and $A \cup \bot = \bot$ for all $A \subseteq S$, and that $\sigma \in \bot$ for all $\sigma \in S$.

The new model clearly has a great deal in common with the old one. On the assumption that S has no important partial order of its own, Q has a natural partial order:

$$P \sqsubseteq P' \ \Leftrightarrow\ f(P) \supseteq f(P') \ \ \&\ \ \forall s \in \Sigma^*.\ t(P)s \supseteq t(P')s.$$

$P \sqsubseteq P'$ can again be interpreted as meaning that P' is more deterministic than P. With respect to "$\sqsubseteq$", Q is a complete semilattice whose minimal element is $\langle \Sigma^* \times \mathcal{P}(\Sigma \cup \{\checkmark\}), T_\perp \rangle$ (denoted $\perp_Q$), where $T_\perp(s) = \perp$ for all $s \in \Sigma^*$. $\perp_Q$ is the completely unpredictable process; it may diverge immediately. The maximal elements of Q are again the deterministic processes, which are divergence free and never have any internal decisions to make. A process P is deterministic if and only if it satisfies

$$(s,X) \in f(P) \;\Rightarrow\; X \cap \{a \in \Sigma : s\langle a\rangle \in traces(P)\} = \emptyset$$

and $t(P)s \neq \emptyset \;\Rightarrow\; (s,\{\checkmark\}) \notin f(P)$ & $t(P)s$ is a singleton set.

The assumption that all sets of final states are finite corresponds closely to an assumption of bounded nondeterminism. As remarked earlier, this is necessary to make sequential composition easy to deal with. Of course, if the set S of states is finite, this assumption is vacuous.

There is no concept of time in our model. Thus the occam timing constructs (NOW and WAIT) cannot be modelled directly. The other main feature lacking is an analogy of prioritised ALT: there is no way of telling from our model that a process would rather communicate "a" than "b" (say). It seems to be necessary to have a model which includes time before one can handle priority in a fully satisfactory way. One could handle time in the present model by adding a "clock" process to every system which processes communicate with when they want to know the time. Unfortunately this solution does not prove to be fully satisfactory, and forces untidy semantic definitions which are, in some sense, at the wrong level of abstraction. We therefore omit timing and priority from our language, and pose the problem of the introduction of time as a topic for future research.

2. Denotational semantics In this section we see how the model we have constructed can be used to give a natural denotational semantics to a large subset of occam. Having constructed what is essentially a hybrid model, one might expect to be able to adapt work on purely parallel and sequential languages. This does indeed turn out to be the case, as there are few parts of the language which make demands on both aspects of the model.

In the previous section we discussed an abstract set S consisting of states. Nothing was assumed about S except (tacitly) that it did not use the space of processes in its definition (for then we would have required a recursive domain definition) and that it did not carry an important partial order with it. In devising our space of machine states we need to bear in mind the role they play in our model: passing on information from one occam process to its successor. The only way one occam process can influence its successors is by modifying (though assignment or input) the values of variables: it cannot change the binding of identifiers in any other way. Thus our states will be "stores" - functions from locations to storable values. A separate *environment* will be used to map identifiers to locations, constants, channels, procedures and so on.

This distinction between environment and state is a familiar idea in denotational semantics; the way the present model works makes it natural to adopt the same distinction here. The management of environments and states relative to sequential languages is well understood. In translating the idea to occam there is only one place where difficulties arise: we must decide how environments and states behave under the parallel operator. Parallel occam processes do not use shared variables for communication. The can only use global variables in a very restricted way: *either* only one process can use a given variable normally *or* all processes can read (but not write to) it. This idea corresponds to giving each parallel process a distinct portion of the state and reserving the rest as read only for the life of the parallel command. The state will be reconstructed at the end of a parallel construct by the "distributed termination" propert of occam processes - a PAR construct can only terminate when each of its components can terminate (and thus yield its own component of the final state).

In order to construct our model we also need to know the structure of the alphabet of communications between processes. In occam each communication has two components - an element (or word value, the same as a storable value) and a channel. We will thus postulate the existence of sets CHAN and $\mathbb{B}$ of (respectively) channels and elements. The alphabet of communications is then $\Sigma = \{\chi.\beta : \chi \in \text{CHAN},\ \beta \in \mathbb{B}\}$. Note that we make no distinction between "input" and "output" communications. The fact that $\mathbb{B}$ is in practic finite is useful to us, since the semantics of *hiding* (necessary for the correct definition of PAR) are much easier in this case. We will therefore assume that $\mathbb{B}$ is finite. If χ is any channel then $\chi.\mathbb{B}$ will denote the set $\{\chi.\beta : \beta \in \mathbb{B}\}$.

In the conclusion we will indicate how the semantics can be adapted to cope with an infinite $\mathbb{B}$, and also describe a way in which the model Q might be altered to take advantag of the special structure of the occam alphabet.

Our language The version of occam used in this paper differs slightly from the occam of [10]. We have already remarked that we will omit timing and priority. We also omit certain non-central features of occam such as those involving configuration. This particular omission is justified by the argument that since the logical behaviour of a program is independent of its configuration, so also should be its semantics. Minor omissions in the cause of simplicity are BYTE subscription, vector operations (slices) and vectors of constants. An additional atomic process STOP has been added, and the semantics of IF has been altered, to be consistent with the latest releases of occam.

The chief change we make in occam syntax is to insist that parallel processes declare which global channels and variables they want to use. Given the restrictions placed on their use this seems good practice. These restrictions (particularly where components of vectors are concerned) would not otherwise be syntactically checkable. Problems arise with the associativity of PAR (one of the most desirable algebraic laws) if these declarations are not made. Any truly parallel implementation of PAR will need to be able to determine the allocation of global variables and channels at compile-time.

For ease of presentation occam syntax has been linearised in this paper. For example we write SEQ(P_1,P_2,...,P_n) instead of SEQ .

$$\begin{array}{l} P_1 \\ P_2 \\ \vdots \\ P_n \end{array}$$

A detailed formal syntax of occam is given in the occam programming manual [10]. Rather than duplicate the definitions of the subsidiary syntactic domains, we give instead a summary of the differences between the standard occam versions and those of this paper. We give each syntactic domain a name and a notation for its typical element.

Expressions ($e \in$ **Exp**) The syntax of these is the same as in [10], except for the omission of NOW and BYTE.

Vector operations are omitted.

Declarations ($\Delta \in$ Decl) The syntax of declarations is the same except for the omission of BYTE subscription and vectors of constants.

Formal parameter lists ($\Phi \in$ Form) These are the same as in [10].

Guards ($g \in$ Guard) There are no WAIT guards. For brevity all guards are assumed to contain a boolean expression (which could of course be TRUE).

The following are new syntactic domains.

Actual parameter lists ($\Lambda \in$ Act) It is convenient to have a name for these objects, which are just lists of expressions.

Parallel declarations ($U \in$ PD) We insist that a parallel process should declare which global channels it intends to use, dividing them into three categories.
OWNCHAN means that the channel(s) are for internal use by the process.
INCHAN means that the channel(s) are to be used by the process for inputting.
OUTCHAN means that the channel(s) are to be used by the process for outputting.
We also insist that the process declares which global channels it wants to assign to.

parallel.declaration	=	USING({*claim*})
claim	=	OWNCHAN *chan* {, *chan*}
	|	INCHAN *chan* {, *chan*}
	|	OUTCHAN *chan* {, *chan*}
	|	VAR *var* {, *var*}

Processes (or programs) ($P \in$ Proc) The definition of our syntactic domain of processes is given below. The only differences from the domain defined in [10] are those which have already been described.

process	=	STOP
	|	SKIP
	|	*variable* := *expression*
	|	*channel* ? *variable*
	|	*channel* ? ANY
	|	*channel* ! *expression*
	|	*channel* ! ANY
	|	*identifier* (*actual.parameter.list*)
	|	SEQ({*process*})
	|	PAR({*parallel.declaration* : *process*})
	|	ALT({*guarded.process*})
	|	IF({*conditional*})
	|	SEQ *replicator process*
	|	PAR *replicator parallel.declaration* : *process*
	|	ALT *replicator guarded.process*
	|	IF *replicator conditional*
	|	WHILE *expression process*
	|	*declaration* : *process*
replicator	=	*identifier* = [*expression* FOR *expression*]
guarded.process	=	*guard process*
	|	ALT({*guarded.process*})
	|	ALT *replicator guarded.process*
conditional	=	*expression process*
	|	IF({*conditional*})
	|	IF *replicator conditional*

Semantic domains The semantic domains whose existence we postulate are the following.

$\beta \in \mathbb{B}$ the (finite) domain of basic storable values or elements. We assume that each element can be identified with some positive or negative integer.

$\chi \in$ CHAN the domain of channels.

$\lambda \in$ LOC the domain of locations in store.

$p,x \in$ IDE the (syntactic) domain of identifiers.

There is no need in this work to suppose that any of the above domains is partially ordered or contains a "bottom" element. We will, however, need to deal with errors. Given any semantic domain X, we will denote by X^+ the domain $X \cup \{error\}$. If X is partially ordered then "error" will be incomparable with the other elements of X^+. Given a domain X, X^V will denote the domain of vectors of elements of X. We will regard an element of X^V as being a function from $\{0,1,...,n-1\}$ to X for some non-negative integer n (the vector's length). If X has a partial order then vectors of the same length are ordered component-wise, vectors of different lengths being incomparable.

Given this notation we can construct a few semantic domains.

$$S = LOC \rightarrow \mathbb{B}^{+}$$

S is the domain of machine states. Each location is mapped either to a storable value or to error (perhaps indicating that the location is uninitialised).

$$ENV = (IDE \rightarrow D^{+}) \times LSTATUS \times CSTATUS$$

$$D = LOC + \mathbb{B} + CHAN + NP + LOC^{V} + CHAN^{V}$$

$$LSTATUS = LOC \rightarrow \{\underline{x}, \underline{u}, \underline{r/w}, \underline{ro}\}$$

$$CSTATUS = CHAN \rightarrow \{\underline{x}, \underline{u}, \underline{ud}, \underline{in}, \underline{out}\}$$

ENV is the domain of environments. The first component of each environment is a function from identifiers to denotable values (plus error). A denotable value ($\delta \in D$) is either a single location (corresponding to a non-vector variable) or an element (corresponding to a constant) or a channel or a named process (the domain NP will be defined later, when it is used) or a vector of locations (corresponding to a vector of variables) or a vector of channels. The second component of each environment gives the status of each location.

- $\underline{x}$ means that the location is not in the environment's range;
- $\underline{u}$ means that it is in the range but is unused;
- $\underline{r/w}$ means that it is in range and is in normal use *(read/write)*;
- $\underline{ro}$ means that it is in the range but has "read only" status.

The third component of each environment gives the status of each channel.

- $\underline{x}$ means that the channel is not in the environment's range;
- $\underline{u}$ means that it is in the range but is unused;
- $\underline{ud}$ means that it is in use but has not been assigned a direction;
- $\underline{in}$ means that it is in use as an input channel;
- $\underline{out}$ means that it is in use as an output channel.

If $\rho \in ENV$ then ρ_i ($i \in \{1,2,3\}$) will denote its ith component (so that $\rho = \langle\rho_1,\rho_2,\rho_3\rangle$). If $x \in IDE$ then $\rho[\![x]\!]$ will mean $\rho_1[\![x]\!]$; similarly $\rho[\lambda]$ will mean $\rho_2[\lambda]$ ($\lambda \in LOC$) and $\rho[X]$ will mean $\rho_3[X]$ ($X \in CHAN$). If $x \in IDE$ and $\delta \in D^{+}$ then $\rho[\delta/x]$ will denote the environment which is the same as ρ except for mapping x to δ. The corresponding interpretations will be put on $\rho[r/\lambda]$, $\rho[r/X]$ and $\sigma[\beta/\lambda]$.

$A \in Q$ the domain of processes is constructed as in the previous section, using **S** as the set of states and $\Sigma = \{X.\beta : X \in CHAN,\ \beta \in \mathbb{B}\}$ as the alphabet.

A few further semantic domains will be defined later, when they are required.

<u>The semantics</u> We will only give detailed definitions of the "higher level" semantic functions required. The other ones are all fairly standard and should not prove too hard for the diligent reader to define. The main semantic functions are listed below.

$$\mathcal{C} : \text{Proc} \to \text{ENV} \to \text{S} \to \text{Q}$$

This the main semantic function. Given a program segment, an environment and a state it yields an element of Q. In the definitions below all execution errors map a process to the minimal **element** $\bot_Q$ of Q (from the point in its communication history where the error arises). Thus an erroneous process is identified with a diverging one. We are thus allowing that erroneous processes might do anything. There is no reason why more sophisticated semantics could not be devised which allowed for a certain amount of erro recovery, perhaps by introducing extra elements into the semantic domain. Our present approach has the advantage of simplicity, though.

$$\mathcal{F} : \text{Proc} \to \text{ENV} \to \text{S} \to \mathcal{P}(\Sigma^* \times \mathcal{P}(\Sigma \cup \{\checkmark\}))$$

$$\mathcal{T} : \text{Proc} \to \text{ENV} \to \text{S} \to (\Sigma^* \to \wp(\text{S}) \cup \{\sqcup\})$$

These two functions pick out the failure and termination components of $\mathcal{C}[\![P]\!]\rho\sigma$, so that $\mathcal{C}[\![P]\!]\rho\sigma = \langle \mathcal{F}[\![P]\!]\rho\sigma, \mathcal{T}[\![P]\!]\rho\sigma \rangle$.

$$\mathcal{D} : \text{Decl} \to \text{ENV} \to \text{ENV}^+$$

This function carries out the modifications to the environment caused by declarations. When an error occurs the value produced is "error".

$$\mathcal{E} : \text{Exp} \to \text{ENV} \to \text{S} \to \mathbb{B}^+$$

This function evaluates expressions as elements of $\mathbb{B}$. The error element results when something goes wrong (e.g. vector subscript out of bounds). Its definition is completely standard and is omitted.

$$\text{lv} : \text{Exp} \to \text{ENV} \to \text{S} \to \text{LOC}^+$$

$$\text{cv} : \text{Exp} \to \text{ENV} \to \text{S} \to \text{CHAN}^+$$

These are important auxiliary functions which help reduce the number of cases in higher level definitions. lv and cv produce (respectively) the values as locations and channels of expressions which are meant to denote them. They take value "error" when an expression cannot be given the relevant interpretation. lv is defined below, the definition of cv being very similar.

$$\begin{aligned}
\text{lv}[\![x]\!]\rho\sigma &= \rho[\![x]\!] && \text{if } \rho[\![x]\!] \in \text{LOC};\\
\text{lv}[\![x[e]]\!]\rho\sigma &= \rho[\![x]\!](\mathcal{E}[\![e]\!]\rho\sigma) && \text{if } \rho[\![x]\!] \in \text{LOC}^V \text{ and } \mathcal{E}[\![e]\!]\rho\sigma \in \text{dom}(\rho[\![x]\!]);\\
\text{lv}[\![e]\!]\rho\sigma &= \text{error} && \text{otherwise.}
\end{aligned}$$

A few more specialised semantic functions will be defined later, when required.

We will now concentrate on the definition of $\mathcal{C}$, the main semantic function. Each of the clauses is given a brief explanation. Many of the operators used are very similar to ones used over the failure-sets model in giving semantics to CSP. The construction of these is explained in detail in [4,5]. Many of the clauses contain one or more conditions "*provided .....*" which exclude error conditions. When these conditions are not met the value of the clause is always $\bot_Q$. Several clauses are split into separate definitions of $\mathcal{F}$ and $\mathcal{T}$.

$\mathcal{F}[\![STOP]\!]\rho\sigma = \{(<>,X) : X \subseteq \Sigma \cup \{\checkmark\}\}$

$\mathcal{T}[\![STOP]\!]\rho\sigma(s) = \emptyset \qquad$ (for all $s \in \Sigma^*$)

STOP never communicates or terminates. It just refuses everything offered to it.

$\mathcal{C}[\![SKIP]\!]\rho\sigma = skip_\sigma$, where

$$f(skip_\sigma) = \{(<>,X) : \checkmark \notin X\}$$
$$t(skip_\sigma)s = \{\sigma\} \quad \text{if } s = <>$$
$$= \emptyset \quad \text{otherwise.}$$

$skip_\sigma$ is the element of Q which never communicates, but which must immediately terminate successfully in final state σ.

$\mathcal{C}[\![e_1 := e_2]\!]\rho\sigma = skip_{\sigma'}$, where $\qquad$ *provided*

$\sigma' = \sigma[\mathcal{E}[\![e_2]\!]\rho\sigma / lv[\![e_1]\!]\rho\sigma] \qquad \mathcal{E}[\![e_2]\!]\rho\sigma \neq error$

$lv[\![e_1]\!]\rho\sigma \neq error$

and $\rho[lv[\![e_1]\!]\rho\sigma] = \underline{r/w}$

This process also terminates immediately, but modifies its final state to take account of the assignment.

$\mathcal{F}[\![e_1?e_2]\!]\rho\sigma = \{(<>,X) : X \cap \chi.\mathbb{B} = \emptyset\} \cup \{(<\chi.\beta>,X) : \checkmark \notin X \ \& \ \beta \in \mathbb{B}\}$

$\mathcal{T}[\![e_1?e_2]\!]\rho\sigma(s) = \{\sigma[\beta/\lambda]\} \quad$ if $s = <\chi.\beta> \quad (\beta \in \mathbb{B})$

$= \emptyset \quad$ otherwise

where $\chi = cv[\![e_1]\!]\rho\sigma \qquad$ *provided* $\quad cv[\![e_1]\!]\rho\sigma \neq error$, $lv[\![e_2]\!]\rho\sigma \neq error$,

and $\lambda = lv[\![e_2]\!]\rho\sigma \qquad \rho[\lambda] = \underline{r/w}$ *and* $\rho[\chi] = \underline{in}$.

On its first step this process is prepared to communicate anything on channel χ (it cannot refuse any element of $\chi.\mathbb{B}$). After communicating $\chi.\beta$ ($\beta \in \mathbb{B}$) it terminates with β substituted for λ.

$\mathcal{F}[\![e?ANY]\!]\rho\sigma = \{(<>,X) : X \cap \chi.\mathbb{B} = \emptyset\} \cup \{(<\chi.\beta>,X) : \checkmark \notin X\}$

$\mathcal{T}[\![e?ANY]\!]\rho\sigma(s) = \{\sigma\} \quad$ if $s = <\chi.\beta> \quad (\beta \in \mathbb{B})$

$= \emptyset \quad$ otherwise

where $\chi = cv[\![e]\!]\rho\sigma \qquad$ *provided* $\quad cv[\![e]\!]\rho\sigma \neq error$ *and* $\rho[\chi] = \underline{in}$.

This process is the same as the previous one except that it terminates with unchanged state.

$\mathcal{F}[\![e_1!e_2]\!]\rho\sigma = \{(<>,X) : \chi.\beta \notin X\} \cup \{(<\chi.\beta>,X) : \checkmark \notin X\}$

$\mathcal{T}[\![e_1!e_2]\!]\rho\sigma(s) = \{\sigma\} \quad$ if $s = <\chi.\beta>$

$= \emptyset \quad$ otherwise

where $\beta = \mathcal{E}[\![e_2]\!]\rho\sigma \qquad$ *provided* $\quad \mathcal{E}[\![e_2]\!]\rho\sigma \neq error$, $cv[\![e_1]\!]\rho\sigma \neq error$

and $\chi = cv[\![e_1]\!]\rho\sigma \qquad$ *and* $\rho[\chi] = \underline{out}$.

This process communicates the value of the expression e_2 along the output channel denoted by e_1, and then terminates in an unchanged state.

$\mathcal{F}[\![e!\text{ANY}]\!]\rho\sigma = \{(\langle\rangle, X) : \chi.\mathbb{B} \not\subseteq X\} \cup \{(\langle\chi.\beta\rangle, X) : \beta \in \mathbb{B} \ \&\ \checkmark \notin X\}$

$\mathcal{T}[\![e!\text{ANY}]\!]\rho\sigma(s) = \{\sigma\}$ if $s = \langle\chi.\beta\rangle$ $(\beta \in \mathbb{B})$

$= \emptyset$ otherwise

where $\chi = cv[\![e]\!]\rho\sigma$ *provided* $cv[\![e]\!]\rho\sigma \neq$ error *and* $\rho[\chi] = \underline{out}$.

This process communicates any value at all along the output channel denoted by e. The choice of value is nondeterministic. (Note that the process can refuse any *proper* subset of $\chi.\mathbb{B}$.) It then terminates with unchanged state. *This definition would need to be changed if* $\mathbb{B}$ *were infinite, in order to satisfy axiom F4.*

Thus each primitive process has a simple interpretation in the model.

$\mathcal{C}[\![\text{SEQ}(P_1, P_2, \ldots, P_n)]\!]\rho\sigma = \text{skip}_\sigma$ if $n = 0$, and otherwise

$= \underline{\text{seq}}(\mathcal{C}[\![P_1]\!]\rho\sigma, \mathcal{C}[\![\text{SEQ}(P_2, \ldots, P_n)]\!]\rho)$.

Here seq is the function from $Q \times (S \to Q)$ to Q which is defined

$f(\underline{\text{seq}}(A,B)) = \{(s,X) : (s, X \cup \{\checkmark\}) \in f(A)\}$

$\cup \{(su, X) : \exists\sigma'.\ \sigma' \in t(A)s \ \&\ (u,X) \in f(B\sigma')\}$

$\cup \{(su, X) : t(A)s = \bot\}$

$t(\underline{\text{seq}}(A,B))s = \bot$ if $t(A)s = \bot$, or if $s = uv$ where $\sigma' \in t(A)u$ and $t(B\sigma')v = \bot$

$= \bigcup\{t(B\sigma')v : \exists u,v,\sigma'.\ s = uv \ \&\ \sigma' \in t(A)u\}$ otherwise.

If $n = 0$ then $\text{SEQ}(P_1, P_2, \ldots, P_n)$ behaves exactly like SKIP (terminating immediately in an unaltered state). Otherwise process P_1 is run until it terminates successfully, the final state of P_1 being given as the initial state to $\text{SEQ}(P_2, \ldots, P_n)$. Note that P_1 cannot refuse a set X of communications unless it can refuse $X \cup \{\checkmark\}$; otherwise it would be able to terminate (invisibly) and let $\text{SEQ}(P_2, \ldots, P_n)$ take over.

The semantics of ALT are made rather difficult by the presence of SKIP guards. This is because the two types of guard work in quite different ways. We need an extra semantic function which tells us whether any SKIP guard is ready. (In this section b,c and e will respectively denote boolean, channel and other expressions. G will be a typical guarded process.)

$\mathcal{R}[\![b\ \&\ c?e\ P]\!]\rho\sigma = \underline{\text{false}}$

$\mathcal{R}[\![b\ \&\ \text{SKIP}\ P]\!]\rho\sigma = \underline{\text{true}}$ if $\mathcal{E}[\![b]\!]\rho\sigma$ is "true"

$= \underline{\text{false}}$ if $\mathcal{E}[\![b]\!]\rho\sigma$ is "false"

$=$ error otherwise

$\mathcal{R}[\![\text{ALT}(G_1, \ldots, G_n)]\!]\rho\sigma = \overset{n}{\underset{i=1}{\dot{\bigvee}}} \mathcal{R}[\![G_i]\!]\rho\sigma$ where $\dot{\bigvee}$ is the error-strict version of the usual boolean "or".

The clause for replicator guarded processes is similar.

It is convenient to extend the domain of $\mathcal{C}$ to include all guarded processes.

$$\begin{aligned}\mathcal{C}[\![b \,\&\, c?e\ P]\!]\rho\sigma &= \text{stop} && \text{if } \mathcal{E}[\![b]\!]\rho\sigma \text{ is "false"}\\ &= \mathcal{C}[\![\text{SEQ}(c?e,P)]\!]\rho\sigma && \text{if } \mathcal{E}[\![b]\!]\rho\sigma \text{ is "true"}\end{aligned}$$

$$\begin{aligned}\mathcal{C}[\![b \,\&\, \text{SKIP}\ P]\!]\rho\sigma &= \text{stop} && \text{if } \mathcal{E}[\![b]\!]\rho\sigma \text{ is "false"}\\ &= \mathcal{C}[\![P]\!]\rho\sigma && \text{if } \mathcal{E}[\![b]\!]\rho\sigma \text{ is "true"}\end{aligned}$$

where stop = $\mathcal{C}[\![\text{STOP}]\!]\rho\sigma$ (this value is independent of ρ and σ)

provided in each case that $\mathcal{E}[\![b]\!]\rho\sigma$ *can be regarded as a boolean.*

$$\begin{aligned}\mathcal{F}[\![\text{ALT}(G_1,\ldots,G_n)]\!]\rho\sigma = {} & \{(\langle\rangle,X) : \exists i.\, \mathcal{R}[\![G_i]\!]\rho\sigma \ \&\ (\langle\rangle,X) \in \mathcal{F}[\![G_i]\!]\rho\sigma\}\\ & \cup \{(\langle\rangle,X) : \forall i.\, \neg\mathcal{R}[\![G_i]\!]\rho\sigma \ \&\ \forall i.(\langle\rangle,X) \in \mathcal{F}[\![G_i]\!]\rho\sigma\}\\ & \cup \{(\langle\rangle,X) : \exists i.\, \mathcal{T}[\![G_i]\!]\rho\sigma(\langle\rangle) = \bot\}\\ & \cup \{(s,X) : s \neq \langle\rangle \ \&\ \exists i.(s,X) \in \mathcal{F}[\![G_i]\!]\rho\sigma\}\end{aligned}$$

$$\mathcal{T}[\![\text{ALT}(G_1,\ldots,G_n)]\!]\rho\sigma(s) = \bigcup\{\mathcal{T}[\![G_i]\!]\rho\sigma(s) : i \in \{1,\ldots,n\}\}$$

If any SKIP guard is ready then the process may choose (invisibly) to behave like the corresponding guarded process. If no SKIP guard is ready then the process must wait for something to be communicated to **it** along one of the channels of the c?e guards. Note that if none of its boolean expressions evaluates to "true", then $\text{ALT}(G_1,\ldots,G_n)$ is equivalent to STOP.

To allow for the possibility of nested "IF"s we need to adopt a similar technique for conditionals: we define a semantic function to determine whether or not a given conditional is "ready". (In this section C will denote a typical conditional.)

$$\begin{aligned}\mathcal{J}[\![e\ P]\!]\rho\sigma &= \underline{\text{true}} && \text{if } \mathcal{E}[\![e]\!]\rho\sigma \text{ is "true"}\\ &= \underline{\text{false}} && \text{if } \mathcal{E}[\![e]\!]\rho\sigma \text{ is "false"}\\ &= \text{error} && \text{otherwise}\end{aligned}$$

$$\mathcal{J}[\![\text{IF}(C_1,\ldots,C_n)]\!]\rho\sigma = \bigvee_{i=1}^{n} \mathcal{J}[\![C_i]\!]\rho\sigma \qquad \text{(once again } \bigvee \text{ is error-strict),}$$

the clause for replicators being similar.

$$\begin{aligned}\mathcal{C}[\![\text{IF}(C_1,\ldots,C_n)]\!]\rho\sigma &= \text{stop} && \text{if } n=0,\\ &= \mathcal{C}[\![P]\!]\rho\sigma && \text{if } C_1 = e\ P \text{ and } \mathcal{E}[\![e]\!]\rho\sigma \text{ is "true",}\\ &= \mathcal{C}[\![C_1]\!]\rho\sigma && \text{if } C_1 \in \text{Proc and } \mathcal{J}[\![C_1]\!]\rho\sigma = \underline{\text{true}},\\ &= \mathcal{C}[\![\text{IF}(C_2,\ldots,C_n)]\!]\rho\sigma && \text{otherwise,}\end{aligned}$$

$$\text{provided } \mathcal{J}[\![\text{IF}(C_1,\ldots,C_n)]\!]\rho\sigma \neq \text{error}.$$

The only form of recursion allowed in occam is the WHILE loop. The fact that the following definition works, essentially only depends on the fact that <u>seq</u> is continuous in its second argument.

$$\mathcal{C}[\![\text{WHILE } e\ P]\!]\rho\sigma = \Big(\bigsqcup_{n=0}^{\infty} F^n(\bot_{S\to Q})\Big)\sigma, \qquad \text{where } F : (S \to Q) \to (S \to Q) \text{ is the function defined}$$

$$\begin{aligned}F(B)\sigma' &= \underline{\text{seq}}(\mathcal{C}[\![P]\!]\rho\sigma', B) && \text{if } \mathcal{E}[\![b]\!]\rho\sigma' \text{ is "true"}\\ &= \text{skip}_{\sigma'} && \text{if } \mathcal{E}[\![b]\!]\rho\sigma' \text{ is "false"}\\ &= \bot_Q && \text{otherwise.}\end{aligned}$$

In fact it turns out that *all* our operators are continuous, so that there is no reason why these semantics should not be extended to more ambitious forms of recursion. (The failure-sets model has been used to reason about recursions through parallel and hiding operators [4,12].)

The parallel operator is understandably the most complicated to define. The first part of our definition shows how the parallel declarations are used to set up local environments and states for each individual process. The second part shows how the processes interact once they are running. Overall we have

$$\mathcal{C}[\![\mathrm{PAR}(U_1{:}P_1,\ldots,U_n{:}P_n)]\!]\rho\sigma = \mathrm{skip}_\sigma \quad \text{if } n=0, \text{ and otherwise}$$
$$= \prod_{i=1}^{n}(\mathcal{C}[\![P_i]\!]\rho_i\sigma_i, X_i) \;/\; Y.$$

The processes are run in parallel(||) with their respective alphabets (X_i), environment (ρ_i) and states (σ_i). The communications local to the network are hidden (/Y). These items are all defined below.

The following basic semantic functions are not hard to define, but their definitions ar omitted for brevity.

$$\mathrm{inchans} : PD \to ENV \to S \to \wp(CHAN)^+$$
$$\mathrm{outchans} : PD \to ENV \to S \to \wp(CHAN)^+$$
$$\mathrm{ownchans} : PD \to ENV \to S \to \wp(CHAN)^+$$
$$\mathrm{locs} : PD \to ENV \to S \to \wp(LOC)^+$$

These functions extract respectively the sets of input, output and internal channels and locations claimed by a parallel declaration (USING(.)). *To be declared as an input channel by* $\mathrm{inchans}[\![U_i]\!]\rho\sigma$, χ *must have status* <u>ud</u> *or* <u>in</u> *in* ρ; *output channels must have status* <u>ud</u> *or* <u>out</u>; *internal channels must have status* <u>ud</u>; *locations must have status* <u>r/w</u> *If an undirected (*<u>ud</u>*) channel of* ρ *is declared as an input (output) channel by one of the* U_i, *then it must be declared as an output (input) channel by another. In addition, the* U_i *must satisfy the following:*

$$\mathrm{inchans}[\![U_i]\!]\rho\sigma \cap \mathrm{ownchans}[\![U_j]\!]\rho\sigma = \emptyset$$
$$\mathrm{outchans}[\![U_i]\!]\rho\sigma \cap \mathrm{ownchans}[\![U_j]\!]\rho\sigma = \emptyset$$
$$\mathrm{inchans}[\![U_i]\!]\rho\sigma \cap \mathrm{outchans}[\![U_i]\!]\rho\sigma = \emptyset$$
$$\mathrm{inchans}[\![U_i]\!]\rho\sigma \cap \mathrm{inchans}[\![U_j]\!]\rho\sigma = \emptyset \quad \textit{whenever } i \neq j$$
$$\mathrm{outchans}[\![U_i]\!]\rho\sigma \cap \mathrm{outchans}[\![U_j]\!]\rho\sigma = \emptyset \quad \textit{whenever } i \neq j$$
$$\mathrm{locs}[\![U_i]\!]\rho\sigma \cap \mathrm{locs}[\![U_j]\!]\rho\sigma = \emptyset \quad \textit{whenever } i \neq j$$

We define $X_i = \bigcup\{\chi.\mathbb{B} : \chi \in \mathrm{inchans}[\![U_i]\!]\rho\sigma \cup \mathrm{outchans}[\![U_i]\!]\rho\sigma\}$
and $Y = \bigcup\{X_i \cap X_j : i \neq j\}$.

(Note that the above disjointness conditions, which enforce the separation of occam parallel processes, imply that $X_i \cap X_j \cap X_k = \emptyset$ *whenever* i,j,k *are all different.)*

The first component of each ρ_i is the same as that of ρ, and

$$\begin{aligned}\rho_i[\lambda] &= \underline{r/w} \quad \text{if } \lambda \in \text{locs}[\![U_i]\!]\rho\sigma \\ &= \underline{ro} \quad \text{if } \rho[\lambda] \in \{\underline{ro}, \underline{r/w}\} \text{ and } \lambda \notin \bigcup_{j=1}^{n} \text{locs}[\![U_j]\!]\rho\sigma \\ &= \underline{x} \quad \text{if } \rho[\lambda] = \underline{x} \text{ or } \lambda \in \text{locs}[\![U_j]\!]\rho\sigma \text{ for some } i \neq j \\ &\in \{\underline{x}, \underline{u}\} \text{ if } \rho[\lambda] = \underline{u}\text{, subject to } \rho_i[\lambda] = \underline{u} \Rightarrow \rho_j[\lambda] = \underline{x} \text{ whenever } i \neq j.\end{aligned}$$

The last line says that a free location in ρ becomes either free in ρ_i or outside the domain of ρ_i, but that no such location becomes free in more than one ρ_i. If stores are infinite then we will assume that infinitely many free locations are allocated to each ρ_i.

$$\begin{aligned}\rho_i[\chi] &= \underline{ud} \quad \text{if } \chi \in \text{ownchans}[\![U_i]\!]\rho\sigma \\ &= \underline{in} \quad \text{if } \chi \in \text{inchans}[\![U_i]\!]\rho\sigma \\ &= \underline{out} \quad \text{if } \chi \in \text{outchans}[\![U_i]\!]\rho\sigma \\ &\in \{\underline{x}, \underline{u}\} \text{ if } \rho[\chi] = \underline{u}\text{, subject to } \rho_i[\chi] = \underline{u} \Rightarrow \rho_j[\chi] = \underline{x} \text{ whenever } i \neq j \\ &= \underline{x} \quad \text{otherwise.}\end{aligned}$$

If the supply of channels is infinite then infinitely many are allocated to each ρ_i.

$$\begin{aligned}\sigma_i[\lambda] &= \sigma[\lambda] \quad \text{if } \lambda \notin \bigcup_{j \neq i} \text{locs}[\![U_j]\!]\rho\sigma \\ &= \text{error} \quad \text{otherwise.}\end{aligned}$$

This completes the definitions of the local environments and states. The parallel operator ($||$) and hiding operator ($/Y$) defined below are derived from the CSP operators in [5]. (Below, $A_i \in Q$, $X_i \subseteq \Sigma$, $X = \bigcup_{i=1}^{n} X_i$.)

$$\begin{aligned}f(\prod_{i=1}^{n}(A_i,X_i)) = \; &\{(s,S) : \exists Y_1,\ldots,Y_n.\; s \in X^* \;\&\; (s\restriction X_i, Y_i) \in f(A_i) \\ &\quad \& \; S \cap (X \cup \{\checkmark\}) = \bigcup\{Y_i \cap (X_i \cup \{\checkmark\}) : i \in \{1,2,\ldots,n\}\}\} \\ &\cup \{(su,S) : s \in X^* \;\&\; s\restriction X_i \in \text{traces}(A_i) \;\&\; \exists i.t(A_i)(s\restriction X_i) = \bot\}\end{aligned}$$

$$\begin{aligned}t(\prod_{i=1}^{n}(A_i,X_i))s = \; &\bot \quad \text{if there exists } u \leqslant s \text{ such that } u \in X^*,\; u\restriction X_i \in \text{traces}(A_i) \text{ for all } i \\ &\quad \text{and there is some } j \text{ with } t(A_j)(u\restriction X_j) = \bot, \\ = \; &\{\text{join}(\sigma_1,\ldots,\sigma_n) : s \in X^* \;\&\; \sigma_i \in t(A_i)(s\restriction X_i)\} \quad \text{otherwise.}\end{aligned}$$

Here, $s\restriction X$ is the restriction of trace s to the set X, so that

$$\langle\rangle\restriction X = \langle\rangle \qquad \text{and} \qquad \begin{aligned}s\langle a\rangle\restriction X &= s\restriction X && \text{if } a \notin X \\ &= (s\restriction X)\langle a\rangle && \text{if } a \in X.\end{aligned}$$

Given states $\sigma_1,\ldots,\sigma_n$, join$(\sigma_1,\ldots,\sigma_n)$ is the state σ^* such that

$$\begin{aligned}\sigma^*[\lambda] &= \sigma_i[\lambda] \quad \text{whenever } \sigma_i[\lambda] \neq \text{error for some } i \\ &= \text{error} \quad \text{otherwise.}\end{aligned}$$

If σ_i and σ_j map λ to different non-error values the parallel combination is broken from the point of this error. The disjointness constraints of PAR *guarantee that this error cannot arise in occam.*

The parallel operator works by allowing each process to communicate only in its own declared alphabet, and only allowing a given communication to occur when each process whose alphabet it belongs to agrees. Termination can only take place when all processes agree, the final state being formed by joining together the states of the individual processes. As soon as one process breaks or diverges, the whole system is considered broken.

$$f(A/Y) \;=\; \{(s/Y,X) : (s, X \cup Y) \in f(A)\} \cup \{(u,X) : \{s \in traces(A) : s/Y \leqslant u\} \text{ is infinite}\}$$

$$\begin{aligned} t(A/Y)s &= \bot \quad \text{if } \{u \in traces(A) : u/Y \leqslant s\} \text{ is infinite,} \\ &= \bigcup\{t(A)u : u/Y = s\} \quad \text{otherwise.} \end{aligned}$$

If $s \in \Sigma^*$ then s/Y is defined to be $s \lceil (\Sigma - Y)$.

The hiding operator is used to conceal the communications which are internal to the parallel system. The above definition is valid as a continuous function on Q when Y is finite (which is implied by the finiteness of $\mathbb{B}$). When $\mathbb{B}$ is infinite one can no longer separate the parallel (||) operator from hiding (/Y) (see Conclusions).

/Y transforms communications in Y into internal actions which occur automatically. Thus A/Y cannot refuse any set X unless A can refuse $X \cup Y$, as an (internal) Y action might bring the process into a state where it can accept an element of X.

This completes the definition of the parallel operator PAR.

Replicators allow us to construct (using SEQ, ALT, IF, PAR) processes from many similar small processes. Their semantics are of course closely related to those of the constructs they extend. As an example we will show how to deal with replicated SEQ.

$$\mathcal{C}[\![\text{SEQ } x = [e_1 \text{ FOR } e_2]\ P]\!]\rho\sigma = \underline{rseq}(\beta_1,\beta_2,\lambda)(\mathcal{C}[\![P]\!]\rho')\sigma$$

where $\lambda = new\rho \quad \rho' = \rho[\lambda/x][\underline{ro}/\lambda]$, *(see below for definition of* new*)*

$\beta_1 = \mathcal{E}[\![e_1]\!]\rho\sigma, \quad \beta_2 = \mathcal{E}[\![e_2]\!]\rho\sigma$

$$\begin{aligned} \text{and} \quad \underline{rseq}(\beta_1,\beta_2,\lambda)B\sigma' &= skip_{\sigma'} \quad \text{if } \beta_2 \leqslant 0 \\ &= \underline{seq}(B\sigma'[\beta_1/\lambda],\ \underline{rseq}(\beta_1+1,\ \beta_2-1,\lambda)B) \quad \text{otherwise,} \end{aligned}$$

provided none of new ρ, $\mathcal{E}[\![e_1]\!]\rho\sigma$, $\mathcal{E}[\![e_2]\!]\rho\sigma$ *evaluate to error, and each of* β_1, $\beta_2+1, \ldots, \beta_1+\beta_2-1$ *is in* $\mathbb{B}$.

Note that a replicator index is given the status of a read-only variable. This is because it may neither be assigned to nor used in constant definitions.

A declaration introduces a new identifier for the process which follows it. In the semantics this is achieved by modifying the environment.

$$\mathcal{C}[\![\Delta : P]\!]\rho\sigma = \underline{prune}_\rho(\mathcal{C}[\![P]\!](\mathcal{D}[\![\Delta]\!]\rho)\sigma) \qquad \textit{provided } \mathcal{D}[\![\Delta]\!]\rho \neq \text{error}$$

where $\underline{prune}_\rho : Q \to Q$ is defined

$$f(\underline{prune}_\rho(A)) = f(A)$$

$$\begin{aligned} t(\underline{prune}_\rho(A))s &= \bot \text{ if } t(A)s = \bot, \\ &= \{prune_\rho(\sigma') : \sigma' \in t(A)s\} \quad \text{otherwise;} \end{aligned}$$

and $\text{prune}_\rho(\sigma')[\lambda] = \sigma'[\lambda]$ if $\rho[\lambda] \in \{\underline{ro}, \underline{r/w}\}$
$= \text{error}$ otherwise.

The function $\underline{\text{prune}}_\rho$ makes sure that when $\Delta : P$ terminates it does not pass on information local to itself (the contents of locations corresponding to identifiers declared in Δ). The use of $\underline{\text{prune}}_\rho$ improves the set of algebraic laws satisfied by occam.

This completes the definition of $\mathcal{C}$ except for calls of named processes. Before this final clause can be defined we must see how named processes are stored in the environment by declarations. We must therefore see how the function $\mathcal{D}$ is defined. We assume the existence of the following semantic functions.

$$\text{new}: \text{ENV} \to \text{LOC}^+ \qquad \text{newvec}: \text{N} \to \text{ENV} \to (\text{LOC}^{\text{V}})^+$$
$$\text{newchan}: \text{ENV} \to \text{CHAN}^+ \qquad \text{newchanvec}: \text{N} \to \text{ENV} \to (\text{CHAN}^{\text{V}})^+$$

These functions have the job of producing locations or channels (either singly or in vectors) which are unused (i.e. have value $\underline{u}$) in some environment. They give result "error" if the required resource is not available. For example newρ is a location such that $\rho[\lambda] = \underline{u}$, and newchanvec(3)$\rho$ is a vector of three channels, each of which has value $\underline{u}$ in ρ.

$\mathcal{D}[\![\text{VAR x}]\!]\rho = \rho[\lambda/x][\underline{r/w}/\lambda]$ where $\lambda = \text{new}\,\rho$ *provided* $\text{new}\,\rho \neq \text{error}$.

$\mathcal{D}[\![\text{VAR x[e]}]\!]\rho = \rho[\nu/x][\underline{r/w}/\nu[0]]\ldots[\underline{r/w}/\nu[\beta-1]]$
where $\beta = \max(\mathcal{E}[\![e]\!]\rho\sigma_{err}, 0)$ $\quad(\sigma_{err}[\lambda] = \text{error}$ for all $\lambda \in \text{LOC})$
$\nu = \text{newvec}\,\beta\,\rho$ *provided* $\text{newvec}\beta\rho \neq \text{error}$ *and* $\mathcal{E}[\![e]\!]\rho\sigma_{err} \neq \text{error}$.

$\mathcal{D}[\![\text{CHAN c}]\!]\rho = \rho[\chi/c][\underline{ud}/\chi]$ where $\chi = \text{newchan}\,\rho$ *provided* $\text{newchan}\rho \neq \text{error}$.

$\mathcal{D}[\![\text{CHAN c[e]}]\!]\rho = \rho[\nu/c][\underline{ud}/\nu[0]]\ldots[\underline{ud}/\nu[\beta-1]]$
where $\beta = \max(\mathcal{E}[\![e]\!]\rho\sigma_{err}, 0)$ and $\nu = \text{newchanvec}\beta\rho$
provided $\mathcal{E}[\![e]\!]\rho\sigma_{err} \neq \text{error}$ *and* $\text{newchanvec}\beta\rho \neq \text{error}$.

$\mathcal{D}[\![\text{DEF x = e}]\!]\rho = \rho[\beta/x]$ where $\beta = \mathcal{E}[\![e]\!]\rho\sigma_{err}$ *provided* $\mathcal{E}[\![e]\!]\rho\sigma_{err} \neq \text{error}$.

The evaluation of expressions in the state σ_{err} forces them only to use identifiers representing constants (for accessing a location will lead to error).

The denotations of multiple declarations such as VAR x,y are easy generalisations of the above definitions.

$\mathcal{D}[\![\text{PROC p}(\Phi)]\!]\rho = \rho[\pi/p]$, where $\pi = \lambda\langle\rho_2',\rho_3'\rangle.\lambda L.\mathcal{C}[\![P]\!]\langle\mathcal{S}[\![\Phi]\!]\rho_1 L, \rho_2', \rho_3'\rangle$

> $\mathcal{S}$ substitutes the denotations listed in L ($\in$ D*) into the environment component ρ_1, using the identifiers listed in Φ. *If $\mathcal{S}$ fails (because of incorrect length or type) then a call of the procedure produces value $\perp_Q$.*

The bindings of identifiers used in the call of a procedure are the same as those at the point of declaration. However the state and the status part of the environment are as at the point of call. This last detail stops parallel processes accessing illegal variables via their procedures. The denotation of a procedure or named process is thus

$\pi \in NP = (LSTATUS \times CSTATUS) \to (D')^* \to S \to Q \quad (D' = LOC + \mathbb{B} + CHAN + LOC^{v} + CHAN^{v}$

We can now complete the definition of $\mathcal{C}$ by giving the clause for procedure calls.

$\mathcal{C}[\![p(\Lambda)]\!]\rho\sigma = \rho[\![p]\!]\langle\rho_2,\rho_3\rangle(\mathcal{L}[\![\Lambda]\!]\rho\sigma)\sigma$ *provided* $\mathcal{L}[\![\Lambda]\!]\rho\sigma \neq$ error.

Here $\mathcal{L}: Act \to ENV \to S \to (D'^*)^+$ is a semantic function which converts syntactic actual parameter lists into their denotations. If a particular parameter could represent either an element ($\mathbb{B}$) or a location, then the location is chosen. *If the evaluation of any element of* Λ *produces an error (or a named process) then the procedure call breaks* ($\perp_Q$).

This completes the definition of our denotational semantics for occam. It gives an interesting illustration of how the domain Q defined in the first section can be used to model concurrent languages. Our model (sometimes with minor modifications) can cope with many possible extensions to the language. These include more sophisticated value domains, recursive procedure definitions, and additional operators on processes. We will mention a few of the possible additional operators in the conclusion.

3. Applications of the semantics

We now have a mapping from occam to a well-defined mathematical model which is closely related to the behaviour of processes. This section outlines a few uses to which this mapping might be put. No topic is covered in detail; we merely identify some promising areas for future work.

Our model's relationship with process behaviour makes it a natural framework for expressing correctness conditions on processes. Our semantics will then provide a basis for proving correctness. We should therefore look at the type of correctness condition that is expressible by reference to the model, techniques for manipulating these conditions within the model, and methods (formal, and perhaps informal) of proving them of programs.

The most natural types of correctness condition to consider are those which specify that every "behaviour" of a process must satisfy some predicate (related, perhaps, to the environment and initial state). There are essentially three different types of behaviour to consider for a process $\langle F,T\rangle \in Q$. The first consists of the process' *failures* ($(s,X) \in F$); the second consists of its (successful) *terminations* ((s,σ) with $\sigma \in T(s)$); the third consists of its *divergences* (s such that $T(s) = \perp$). The predicate of behaviour should tell us which of each sort of behaviour is acceptable.

Except for specifications which are approximations to final goals one will almost always demand that a process is *divergence-free* (i.e. no divergence is a correct behaviour). Divergence can arise in three distinct ways in our semantics: from a badly constructed WHILE loop; from a PAR construct which becomes livelocked (an infinite sequence of internal communications takes place without any communication with the environment); and from technical errors of diverse sorts (e.g. assigning to a channel identifier).

The first type can be eliminated by familiar methods such as making sure some loop variant is decreased. On its variant becoming zero one can allow a loop *either* to terminate *or* to communicate. This is because an occam WHILE loop can be correct without ever terminating. Proving the absence of livelock in a parallel system will require consideration of the connection structure of that network. Freedom from livelock is established if (for example) no two processes are connected together, each of which has the ability to communicate infinitely without communicating with the external environment of the network. (Properties such as this can be rigorously specified and proved within Q.) A few simple results on the absence of livelock for specific types of network (simple linear arrangements, rectangular arrays and trees) can be found in [12]. Often one will expect the absence of divergence to be a corollary to some more specific correctness proof; sometimes, however, one might find that its proof is a necessary first step.

A second type of behaviour which we will usually wish to eliminate is *deadlock*. A process deadlocks when it comes into a state where it can do nothing at all (neither communicate nor terminate successfully). Deadlock after trace s is represented by the failure $(s, \Sigma \cup \{\checkmark\})$. The usual cause of deadlock will be a badly designed parallel network, where it is possible for the individual processes to reach a state where they cannot agree which communications to perform. Perhaps the best known example of a potentially deadlocked system is *the five dining philosophers* (this was studied relative to the failure-sets model in [5]).

Once again, a proof of deadlock-freedom might be a corollary to some more specific result (such as congruence with some sequential program). On the other hand it is sometimes useful to be able to prove it in isolation. The simple way in which deadlock is represented (as the failure $(s, \Sigma \cup \{\checkmark\})$) makes our model a natural vehicle for studying it. Proofs will depend on the form of the network of connections between processes, and will often be graph-theoretic. A few simple applications of the failure-sets model to this problem will be found in [5,12]. There it is shown, for example, that if the interconnection graph of a network is a tree, then the whole network is free of deadlock if it is locally free of deadlock (in a strictly defined sense). The phenomenon of distributed termination will considerably complicate the connection graphs in occam. It should be possible, though, to separate off the issue of termination, and so only consider the graphs of ordinary communications.

In general our model gives us a rich language for specifying correctness conditions. Specifying which traces and terminations are allowable corresponds to *safety* or *partial correctness*, while divergences and refusal sets enable us to specify *liveness* or *total correctness*. An important topic for future research must be discovering a good formal syntax for useful correctness conditions for occam programs.

Another important topic will be research into formal methods for proving these properties of programs. Our semantics will provide the foundations for justifying such methods (proving them sound and perhaps complete). There are several promising approaches, a few of which are summarised below.

One can regard every program as a logical formula describing the strongest predicate satisfied by all the observations one can make of it. If a program's specification is also a logical formula, describing all allowable observations, then proving a program P meets specification S simply requires the proof of the formula $P \Rightarrow S$. In [9], we show how every occam program may be identified with a predicate describing its traces, refusals, status (waiting, terminated or divergent) and the values (initial and final) of its free variables. The way this was done was based very closely on the semantics presented in this paper, and essentially provides an encoding of our model Q in the predicate calculus. It should be possible to develop this approach into a very useful formal system for proving properties of occam programs.

Our semantics induce a natural congruence on occam: programs P,Q are equivalent if and only if $\mathcal{C}[\![P]\!]\rho\sigma = \mathcal{C}[\![Q]\!]\rho\sigma$ for all ρ,σ. Two programs are thus equivalent if they behave identically under all circumstances. It is convenient to strengthen this congruence a little: we can reasonably regard P and Q as equivalent if $\mathcal{C}[\![P]\!]\rho\sigma = \mathcal{C}[\![Q]\!]\rho\sigma$ for all ρ,σ such that ρ has infinitely many free locations and channels, and $\sigma[\lambda]$ = error whenever $\rho[\lambda] \in \{\underline{u},\underline{x}\}$. These restrictions prevent "naturally equivalent" programs being distinguished for technical reasons. Henceforth, if $P,Q \in$ Proc, then P = Q will mean that P is congruent to Q in this sense. (This relation is indeed a congruence in the sense that if we replace any subprogram P of Q by P' = P to get Q', then Q = Q'.)

The following theorem lists a small selection of the algebraic laws which can be proved relating the constructs of occam.

<u>Theorem</u> The following equivalences all hold between occam programs.

a) $\mathrm{SEQ}(P_1,P_2,\ldots,P_n) = \mathrm{SEQ}(P_1,\mathrm{SEQ}(P_2,\ldots,P_n)) = \mathrm{SEQ}(\mathrm{SEQ}(P_1,\ldots,P_{n-1}),P_n)$

b) SEQ(P,SKIP) = SEQ(SKIP,P) = P

c) $\mathrm{SEQ}(\mathrm{ALT}(G_1,\ldots,G_n),P) = \mathrm{ALT}(G_1;P,\ldots,G_n;P)$

where the guarded processes $G_i;P$ are defined by induction on the structure of G:

(g P');P = g SEQ(P',P)

$(\mathrm{ALT}(G_1',\ldots,G_m'));P = \mathrm{ALT}(G_1';P,\ldots,G_m';P)$

d) WHILE e P = IF(e SEQ(P,WHILE e P), true SKIP)

e) $\mathrm{PAR}(U_1:P_1,\ldots,U_n:P_n) = \mathrm{PAR}(U_1:P_1,U^*:\mathrm{PAR}(U_2:P_2,\ldots,U_n:P_n))$

where U* is the *union* of $U_2,\ldots,U_n$, in other words the parallel declaration which claims all the variables claimed by any of $U_2,\ldots,U_n$; claims as OWNCHANs all OWNCHANs of $U_2,\ldots,U_n$, as well as all channels declared both as an INCHAN and as an OUTCHAN among $U_2,\ldots,U_n$; claims as INCHANs all other INCHANs of $U_2,\ldots,U_n$; and as OUTCHANs all other OUTCHANs of $U_2,\ldots,U_n$.

f) $\mathrm{PAR}(U_1:P_1,U_2:P_2) = \mathrm{PAR}(U_2:P_2,U_1:P_1)$

In [8], this list will be much extended. We will in fact show there that there are enough algebraic laws to completely characterise the semantics of occam, as presented in the present paper. We will construct a *normal form* for WHILE-free programs (every such program is equivalent to one in normal form, but no two distinct normal form programs are semantically equivalent), and give enough laws to transform every such program into normal form. We are therefore able to decide whether any pair of WHILE-free programs are equivalent. The postulate that the value of any program is determined by those of its *finite syntactic approximations* then gives us an infinitary rule for deciding the equivalence of arbitrary programs. (This postulate is a theorem in the denotational semantics of the present paper.) This *algebraic semantics* is closely related to similar work on a purely parallel version of CSP in [3].

Several authors (for example in [1,2] and in [15]) have given Hoare-style axiom systems for similar languages (usually the CSP of [6]). It should be possible to construct such a system for occam. Our semantics will allow the formal analysis of such a system.

Denotational semantics should provide a standard by which to judge implementations of a language. Proving an implementation correct (with respect to our semantics) will probably require one or more intermediate levels of abstraction as bridges. A typical intermediate level would be an *operational* semantics. In [5] there is an operational semantics for CSP which is provably congruent to the failure-set semantics.

4. Conclusions In building our mathematical model and constructing the denotational semantics we have made many decisions. In this section we will discuss a few of these, and see how a few of the restrictions we have imposed might be relaxed.

Most of the major decisions come when constructing the mathematical model: once this is fixed, the semantics of most constructs are determined by their roles in the language. There are several factors which influence the choice of model. It should be at the right level of abstraction; it should have sufficient power to specify desired correctness properties; it should be able to cope with all the constructs of the given language; and it should be as simple, elegant and understandable as possible.

It is possible to do without "states" in the model. Variables could be replaced by parallel processes, created at their points of declaration, with which the "main" processes communicate when they want to read or assign. Because one can use a "purely parallel" semantic model, this approach simplifies model building. On the other hand the semantic definitions become more complex, and the level of abstraction seems wrong. One loses many of the advantages gained from the similarity with the semantics of ordinary languages; in particular, the semantics of a "purely sequential" occam fragment will no longer bear much resemblence to a relation on states. Nevertheless, this approach should lead to a semantics congruent to ours on programs without free variables.

The model Q was devised as a *general purpose* model for communicating processes with state. It is slightly too "rich" for occam, in that an occam process' refusals are really sets of channels, rather that sets of individual communications. The consequence of this is that Q contains rather more types of behaviour than are actually describable in occam (for example a process which is prepared to input any integer *greater than 6* on channel c). One can give a semantics for occam, congruent with our own, into a model where a failure is an element of $\Sigma^* \times (\wp(CHAN) \cup \{\checkmark\})$ rather than $\Sigma^* \times (\wp(\Sigma) \cup \{\checkmark\})$. Thi fact is illustrated by the predicate logic model in [9]. Of course, if occam were extended to include "selective inputs" of the type indicated above, then the reduced model would no longer be sufficiently detailed.

It seems likely that the techniques employed in this paper to combine the models N and $\wp(S \times S)$ into Q would work for other pairs. For example one could simplify the model by using the *traces* model [7] in place of the failures model N. However the semantics wou only be simplified in their "purely parallel" aspects; we would suffer by losing the ability to reason about total correctness properties. If the object language contained jumps, there would be few problems in adapting our model for *continuation* semantics.

In this paper we have been guilty of omitting part of the language, as well as making other simplifying assumptions. The ones which made the construction of the model easie were omission of *timing* and *priority*, and the restriction of the set $\mathbb{B}$ to be finite. T rectify the first two will require future research, probably into timed models for communicating processes. While the final assumption is perfectly realistic, it is unfortunate from a theoretical point of view. The main problem which arises when $\mathbb{B}$ is infini is that the hiding operator (/Y), used in the semantics of PAR, can yield unbounded non determinism (and so discontinuity). However the restricted syntax of occam, for exampl the separation rules for channels under PAR, means that this unbounded nondeterminism cannot actually occur. If one were prepared to make the model Q more technical, perhap by discriminating between input and output communications and restricting the circumstances under which they could occur or be refused, one could construct a satisfactory model for occam with infinite $\mathbb{B}$.

On the other hand our model can cope easily with certain features not present in occam, such as general recursion, more elaborate types, output guards in ALTs, and multiple (simultaneous) assignments. The two final members of this list are useful theoretical additions to occam (see [8]).

Once the main model was decided, the majority of the semantic definitions seemed to follow naturally. Nevertheless there were still a few decisions made, both consciously and unconsciously. An example of such a decision arises in the hiding of internal communication. In this paper the hiding has been incorporated into the definition of the parallel operator: we hide the internal communications of each network as it is constructed. An alternative would have been to hide the channels at their points of declaration. These two alternatives should give identical results for programs with no free variables that are used for internal communication. The version we have chosen does, however, have better algebraic properties. For example, under suitable restrictions on U_1, U_2,

$$SEQ(x := e,\ PAR(U_1{:}P_1,\ U_2{:}P_2)) \;=\; PAR(U_1{:}SEQ(c!e,P_1),\ U_2{:}SEQ(c?x,P_2)),$$

a law which would not hold under the alternative interpretation of hiding.

Acknowledgements I would like to thank Tony Hoare, whose work on occam inspired this research, and who has made many valuable suggestions. I would also like to thank Steve Brookes and everyone else who has commented on the various versions of this work.

References

[1] Apt, K.R., Formal justification of a proof system for communicating sequential processes, JACM Vol. 30, No. 1 (Jan 1983) pp197-216.

[2] Apt, K.R., Francez, N., and de Roever, W.P., A proof system for communicating sequential processes, Trans. Prog. Lang. Syst. 2, 3 (July 1980) pp359 - 385.

[3] Brookes, S.D., A model for communicating sequential processes, D.Phil. thesis, Oxford University, 1983.

[4] Brookes, S.D., Hoare, C.A.R., and Roscoe, A.W., A theory of communicating sequential processes, JACM 31, 3 (July 1984) pp560 - 599.

[5] Brookes, S.D., and Roscoe, A.W., An improved failures model for communicating processes, Carnegie - Mellon Tech. Report 1984. (Appears in an abbreviated form in this volume.)

[6] Hoare, C.A.R., Communicating sequential processes, CACM 21, 8 (August 1978) pp666 - 676.

[7] Hoare, C.A.R., A model for communicating sequential processes, Tech. Report PRG-22, Oxford University Programming Research Group, 1981.

[8] Hoare, C.A.R., and Roscoe, A.W., The laws of occam programming, in preparation.

[9] Hoare, C.A.R., and Roscoe, A.W., Programs as executable predicates, in Proceedings of FGCS 84, North-Holland 1984.

[10] INMOS Ltd., The occam programming manual, Prentice - Hall International, 1984.

[11] Milne, R.E., and Strachey, C., A theory of programming language semantics, Chapman Hall, London, and Wiley, New York, 1976.

[12] Roscoe, A.W., A mathematical theory of communicating processes, D.Phil. thesis, Oxford University, 1982.

[13] Stoy, J.E., Denotational semantics, MIT Press, 1977.

[14] Tennent, R.D., Principles of programming languages, Prentice - Hall International, 1981.

[15] Zhou Chaochen, The consistency of the calculus of total correctness for communicating processes, Tech. Report PRG - 26, Oxford University Programming Research Group, 1982.

Linguistic Support of Receptionists for Shared Resources

Carl Hewitt

Tom Reinhardt

Gul Agha

Giuseppe Attardi

MIT Artificial Intelligence Laboratory
545 Technology Square
Cambridge, Mass. 02139

Abstract

This paper addresses linguistic issues that arise in providing support for shared resources in large scale concurrent systems. Our work is based on the Actor Model of computation which unifies the lambda calculus, the sequential stored-program and the object-oriented models of computation. We show how *receptionists* can be used to regulate the use of shared resources by scheduling their access and providing protection against unauthorized or accidental access. A shared financial account is an example of the kind of resource that needs a receptionist. Issues involved in the implementation of scheduling policies for shared resources are also addressed. The modularity problems involved in implementing servers which multiplex the use of physical devices illustrate how delegation aids in the implementation of parallel problem solving systems for communities of actors.

1 Background

Two computational activities A1 and A2 will be said to be *concurrent* if they do not have a necessary temporal ordering with respect to one another: A1 might precede A2, A2 might precede A1, or they might overlap in time. Concurrency can arise from a variety of sources including the multiplexing of individual processors as well as the interaction of multiple processors. Thus concurrent systems include time sharing systems, multiprocessor systems, distributed systems, and integrated circuits. *Parallelism* is the exploitation of concurrency to cause activities to overlap in time.

For thirty years, the lambda calculus and the sequential stored program models have coexisted as important bases for software engineering. Systems based on the lambda calculus [McCarthy 62, Landin 65, Kahn 81, Friedman and Wise 76, Hewitt and Baker 77 and Backus 78] provide a sound basis for constructing independent immutable objects (functions and functional data structures) that have inherent concurrency which is constrained only by the speed of communications between processing elements. Such systems provide important ways to realize the massive parallelism that will be made possible by the development of very large scale integrated circuits.

Unfortunately, the lambda calculus is not capable of realizing the need in concurrent systems for shared objects such as shared checking accounts which must change their behavior during the course of their lifetimes. Moreover, checking-accounts are good examples of *objects created for open-ended, evolving systems* in that their behavior must be specified independently of the number of teller machines.

While it has been shown that by treating input and output to functions as infinite, continuous streams, functional languages can create objects capable of changing their local states, it is also known that this is only adequate for "closed systems." In an *Open System* (that is, a system which is open ended and continuously evolving, see [Hewitt 83]), the inter-stream ordering is indeterminate and subject to interactive external influences: the Brock-Ackerman anomaly [Brock-Ackerman 81] is an example of a system where one is unable to abstract the arrival order information from the purely functional behavior of a concurrent system, Gul Agha (from forthcoming dissertation 1984).

The stored program computer provides a way to make the required changes through its ability to update its global memory. However the concurrency of the stored program computer is limited as only one access to the memory occurs at a time. The variable assignment command (e.g., SETQ in Lisp or the := command in the Algol-like languages) incorporates this ability in higher level languages with the attendant cost that they become inherently sequential.

In the early seventies, an important step was made toward unifying of the two approaches by developing the concept of *objects*. An object consists of a local state and procedures to operate on it. SIMULA was the first language in the ALGOL family which introduced objects in the form of *class* instances. A class declaration specifies the structure of each object (in term of the variables which constitute its local state) and a set of procedures which can be invoked from outside to operate on the object.

In Lisp, objects are embodied by closures, sometimes called "funargs". A closure is a function plus an environment. The environment keeps the values associated with variables used within the function and represents the local state of the closure. When the closure is invoked, its function is applied in that environment. Closures can modify their states by means of an assignment command.

In the case of truly concurrent systems, however, the assignment command is not suitable as the basis for change of behavior because it doesn't address the problem of scheduling access to a shared object; such access must be regulated so that timing errors can be avoided. To deal with this problem, C.A.R. Hoare

[Hoare 74] proposed an adaptation of the Simula class construct called a *monitor* as an operating systems construct for higher level languages. By imposing the constraint that only one invocation can be active at a time, monitors provide a means for achieving synchronization and mutual exclusion. Monitors retain most of the aspects of sequential programming languages including:

- Use of the assignment command to update variables of the monitor

- Requiring sequential execution within the procedures of a monitor

One of the most criticized aspect of monitors is the use of low level *wait* and *signal* primitives to manipulate the queues of the scheduler of the operating system of the computer. The effect of the execution of such instructions is the release of the monitor by the process presently executing inside of it and transfer of control to some other processes. Thus control "jumps around" inside a monitor in a way which is not obvious from the structure of the code.

Monitors do a good job of incorporating important abilities of the operating system of a sequential computer in a high level language. As an "operating systems structuring concept", monitors are intended as a means of interaction among parts of an operating system. These components are all at the same level, and each bears some responsibility for the correct behavior of the system as a whole. Monitors basically support the ability for processes to synchronize and notify each other when some action is performed on shared data. However, the correct use of the resource, or the consistency of its state when a process leaves the monitor, or the guarantee that each process will eventually release the monitor, cannot usually be established from the code of the monitor alone.

In the context of a distributed system, it seems more appropriate that the responsibility for the use of a shared resource be delegated to a specific abstraction for the resource which regulates its use. It is unreasonable to expect that each user is aware of the protocols to be followed in accessing the resource and that each user will follow them.

Historically we have called the abstractions that have been developed for this purpose *serializers* [Hewitt, Attardi and Lieberman 79a and Atkinson and Hewitt 79]. Serializers solve the problem of scheduling access to shared objects by unifying the notions of *opacity* found in lambda-calculus based systems and *mutability* provided by the assignment command in imperative languages. ***Receptionists*** are an extension of this notion that lend themselves to more modular implementations of larger actor systems.

The purpose of a receptionist is to provide an interface to users for performing operations on a protected resource. The receptionist is responsible for serializing concurrent requests, for scheduling the access to the resource, and for providing protection and ability to recover from failures. Receptionists accept requests for operations and act on behalf of the requesters to carry out such operations. Those requesting service are not allowed to act directly on the resource, a property which we call *absolute containment.*

2 The Actor Model of Computation

The actor model is based on fundamental principles that must be obeyed by all physically realizable communication systems. Computation in the Actor Model is performed by a number of independent computing elements called *actors*. Hardware modules, subprograms and entire computers are examples of things that may be thought of as actors.

A computation is carried out by actors that communicate with each other by *message passing*. Various control structures are hence viewed as "patterns of message passing" [Hewitt 77]. Examples of such communications are electrical signals, parameter passing between subroutines of a program and messages transferred between computers in a geographically distributed network.

Conceptually, one actor communicates with another using a ***mail address***. Mail addresses may be the *targets* of communications and may also be sent as messages within communications. Thus a mail address differs fundamentally from a machine address which has read and write as the defined operations. Mail addresses may be physically implemented in a variety of ways including copper wires, machine addresses and network addresses.

An actor performs computation as a result of receiving a ***communication***. The actor model refers to the arrival of a communication, $\mathcal{K}$, at an actor, $\mathcal{A}$, as an *event*. Symbolically, an Event, $\mathcal{E}$, may be represented:

$$\mathcal{E} = [\mathcal{A} \Longleftarrow \mathcal{K}]$$

As a result of receiving a communication, an actor may produce other communications to be sent to other actors (trivially, this includes itself). In terms of events, this means that an event may *activate* some other events. Events are hence related by an *activation* ordering [Hewitt and Baker 77], and computation occurs between such events.

While processing a communication, an actor can create new actors and can also designate another actor to take its place to receive the next delivered communication.

In summary, an actor, $\mathcal{A}$, can take the following actions upon receipt of a communication:

- It can make simple decisions.
- It can create new actors.
- It can send communications to actors.
- It can specify a replacement actor which will handle the next communication accepted.

Communications received by each actor are related by the *arrival* ordering, which expresses the order in which communications are received by the actor. The arrival ordering of a serialized actor is a total ordering, i.e., for any two communications received by an actor, it always specifies which arrived first. Some form of arbitration is usually necessary to implement arrival ordering for shared actors.

A computation in the actor model is a partial order of events obtained by combining the *activation* ordering and all of the *arrival* orderings. Although the actor model incorporates properties that any physically realizable communication system must obey, not all partially ordered sets of events can be physically realized. For instance, no physically realizable computation can contain two events which have a chain of infinitely many events in between them, each activating the next.

2.1 The Nature of Actor Communication

For some of the recently proposed models of concurrent systems [Hoare 78, Milner 79], the communication mechanism resembles a telephone system —where communication can occur only if the called party is available at the time when the caller requests the connection, i.e., when both parties are simultaneously available for communicating. For the actor model, however, message passing resembles mail service, in that communications may always be sent but are subject to variable delays *en route* to their destinations. Communication via a mail system has important properties that distinguish it from "hard-wired" connections:

- *Asynchrony*: The mail system decouples the sending of a communication from its arrival. It is not necessary for the recipient to rendezvous with the sender of a communication.

- *Buffering*: The mail system buffers communications between the time they are sent and the time they are delivered to the recipient.

We have found the properties of asynchrony and buffering fundamental to the widespread applicability of actor systems; they enable us to disentangle the senders and receivers of communications, thus raising the level of the description.

2.2 Functionality of the Mail System

The implementation of an actor system entails the use of a mail system to effect communication. The mail system transports and delivers communications by invoking hardware modules, activating actors defined by software, or sending communications through the network as appropriate. The mail system provides the following functionality:

- *Routing.* The mail system routes a communication to the recipient over whatever route seems most appropriate. For example, it may be necessary to route the communication around certain components which are malfunctioning. The use of a mail system contrasts with systems which require a direct connection in order for communication to take place.
- *Forwarding.* The mail system must also forward communications to actors which have migrated. Migration can be used to perform computational load balancing, to relieve storage overpopulation, and to implement automatic, real-time storage reclamation.

2.3 Sending Mail Addresses in Communications

An important innovation is that mail addresses of actors can be sent in communications. This ability provides the following important functionalities:

- *Public Access.* The receiver of a communication does not have to anticipate its arrival, in contrast to systems which require that a recipient know the name of the sender before any communication can be received, or, more generally, to systems where element interconnections are fixed and specified in advance.
- *Reconfiguration.* Actors can be put in direct contact with one another after they are created since the mail address of a newly created actor can be sent to pre-existing actors.

In some models, e.g., those which only allow messages composed of elementary data types such as integers, reals and character strings, the mobility of processes is limited. Processes or other nonprimitive objects cannot be transmitted: a limitation which is closely related to an important restriction on the reconfiguration of the system. Reconfiguration is not possible in such systems which require that a process be created knowing exactly the processes with which it will be able to communicate throughout its entire existence.

New actors can be dynamically created as a result of an actor receiving a communication. The creator of an actor is provided with a mail address that can be used to communicate with the new actor. Reconfiguration (see above) enables previously created actors to communicate with the new ones.

2.4 Mathematical Models

Mathematical models for actor systems rigorously characterize the underlying physical realities of communication systems. In this respect, they share a common motivation with other mathematical models which have been developed to characterize physical phenomena. The actor model differs in motivation from theories developed for reasons of pure mathematical elegance or to illustrate the application of pre-existing mathematical theories (modal logic, algebra etc.). The actor model of computation has been mathematically characterized pragmatically [Grief 75], axiomatically [Hewitt and Baker 77], operationally [Baker 78], and in terms of power domains [Clinger 81].

An important innovation of the actor model is to take the arrival ordering of communications as being fundamental to the notion of concurrency. In this respect, it differs from systems such as Petri Nets and CSP which model concurrency in terms of nondeterministic choice (such as might be obtained by repeatedly flipping a coin). The use of arrival ordering has a decisive impact on the ability to deal with fundamental issues of software engineering, such as being able to prove that a concurrent system will be able to guarantee a response for a request received within the mathematical model.

3 The Actor Language Act3

> When you speak a new language you must see if you can translate all of the poetry of your old language into the new one.
>
> (Dana Scott)

A number of languages have been recently developed for concurrent systems. These languages differ in their conception of communication, in what can be communicated, and in their ability to dynamically create new computational agents. Design decisions in Act3 have been determined by the need to provide support for parallel problem solving in our applications. Our applications require that we be able to efficiently create, garbage collect and migrate large numbers of actors from place to place in the network. This circumstance causes it to differ with other languages and systems.

Act3 is an experimental language based on the actor model of computation. Act3 is universal in the sense that any physically realizable actor system can be implemented in it.

3.1 Notation

Act3 generalizes Lisp's syntactic notation for expressions (i.e. each expression is enclosed in parentheses with the elements of the expression separated by white space) by allowing infix operations to be defined. This notation has the advantage that all expressions have a uniform syntax at the level of expression boundaries. This is, however, only a superficial resemblance between Act3 and Lisp. Most of the new semantic notions in Act3 (such as receptionists, delegation, proxies, etc.) are not present in Lisp. Act3 was designed to implement concurrent systems, whereas Lisp was designed and has evolved to implement sequential procedures on a sequential computer.

3.2 Descriptions

Descriptions serve a role in Act3 that corresponds to the role of data types and structures in more conventional languages. Descriptions are used to express properties, attributes and relations between objects. Our description language includes first order logic as a sublanguage.

Data types in programming languages have come to serve more and more purposes in the course of time. Type checking has become a very important feature of compilers, providing type coercion, helping in optimization and aiding in checking consistent use of data. The lack of power and flexibility in the type systems of current programming languages limits the ability of the languages to serve these purposes. Descriptions help overcome these limitations.

We use descriptions to express assumptions and the constraints on objects manipulated by programs in Act3. These descriptions are an integral part of programs and can be used both as checks when programs are executing and as useful information which can be exploited by other systems which examine programs such as translators, optimizers, indexers, etc.

3.3 Communications and Customers

Communications are actors that embody the units of information that are transmitted from one actor to another. There are different kinds of communications, each with possibly different attributes. Act3 provides mechanisms that enable an actor to distinguish between kinds of communications which it receives and to select their attributes by means of simple pattern matching.

A **Request** is a kind of communication which always contains a message and a customer. The notion of customer generalizes the concept of a *continuation*, introduced in the context of denotational semantics [Strachey and Wadsworth 74 and Reynolds 74] to express the semantics of sequential control mechanisms in the lambda calculus. In that context, a continuation is a function which represents "the rest of the computation" to which the value of the current computation will be given as an argument. A customer is actor analogue to a continuation, in that a reply is sent to the customer when the transaction activated by the request is completed.

A `Response` is another kind of communication and can be either a `Reply` or `Complaint`. The first reply received by a customer is usually treated differently than any subsequent reply. In general, subsequent replies will be treated as errors and generate complaints.

This notion of customers subsumes and unifies many less well defined concepts such as a "suspended job" or "waiting process" in conventional operating systems. The ability to deal explicitly with customers unifies all levels of scheduling by eliminating the dichotomy between programming language scheduling and operating system scheduling found in most existing systems.

3.4 Communication Primitives

Act3 provides primitives to perform unsynchronized communication. This means that an actor sending the communication simply gives it to the electronic mail system. It will arrive at the recipient at some time in the future. That is, an actor can transmit and receive communications (continue computing) while communications that it has sent are in transit to their destinations.

Transmitting communications using commands is a very convenient method for spawning more parallelism. The usual method in other languages for creating more parallelism entails creating processes (as in ALGOL-68, PL-1, and Communicating Sequential Processes, etc.). The ability to engender parallelism simply by transmitting more communications is one of the fundamental differences between actors and the languages based on communicating sequential processes.

3.5 Transactions

The notion of an *Event* is now further elaborated to take into account the various communication types:

$$\mathcal{E}_1 = [\mathcal{A} \Longleftarrow (A\ Request\ (With\ Message\ \mathcal{M}\ (With\ Customer\ \mathcal{C})))]$$

describes the reception of a **Request** by some actor, $\mathcal{A}$. Note, that in place of a symbol representing the communication, the communication type and its primary components are specified. As a result of $\mathcal{E}_1$, some computation is performed and, at some later time, a **Reply** is sent to the customer, $\mathcal{C}$, specified in the **Request**.

$$\mathcal{E}_n = [\mathcal{C} \Longleftarrow (A\ Reply\ (With\ Message\ \mathcal{M}))]$$

Events $\mathcal{E}_1$ and $\mathcal{E}_n$ are thus causally related and together comprise a ***transaction***. For a given computation, transactions may encompass sub-transactions. For instance, sending a **Request** to an actor, $\mathcal{F}$, that recursively calculates the factorial of the incoming message might result in a series of events:

$$\mathcal{E}_1 = [\mathcal{F} \Longleftarrow (A\ Request\ (With\ Customer\ \mathcal{C}_1)\ (With\ Message\ 3))]$$
$$\mathcal{E}_2 = [\mathcal{F} \Longleftarrow (A\ Request\ (With\ Customer\ \mathcal{C}_2)\ (With\ Message\ 2))]$$
$$\mathcal{E}_3 = [\mathcal{F} \Longleftarrow (A\ Request\ (With\ Customer\ \mathcal{C}_3)\ (With\ Message\ 1))]$$
$$\mathcal{E}_4 = [\mathcal{F} \Longleftarrow (A\ Request\ (With\ Customer\ \mathcal{C}_4)\ (With\ Message\ 0))]$$
$$\mathcal{E}_5 = [\mathcal{C}_4 \Longleftarrow (A\ Reply\ (With\ Message\ 1))]$$
$$\mathcal{E}_6 = [\mathcal{C}_3 \Longleftarrow (A\ Reply\ (With\ Message\ 1))]$$
$$\mathcal{E}_7 = [\mathcal{C}_2 \Longleftarrow (A\ Reply\ (With\ Message\ 2))]$$
$$\mathcal{E}_8 = [\mathcal{C}_1 \Longleftarrow (A\ Reply\ (With\ Message\ 6))]$$

The top-level transaction begins with $\mathcal{E}_1$ and ends with $\mathcal{E}_8$, whereas $\mathcal{E}_2$ and $\mathcal{E}_7$, $\mathcal{E}_3$ and $\mathcal{E}_6$, and $\mathcal{E}_4$ and $\mathcal{E}_5$ delimit nested sub-transactions.

3.6 Receptionists

Receptionists are actors that can accept only one communication at a time for processing. Communications that arrive while the receptionist is receiving another communication are serviced in the order in which they arrive.

Accepting communications in the order in which they arrive does not involve any loss of generality since a communication need not be acted on when it is accepted. For example, a request to print a document need not be acted on by a receptionist when it accepts the request. The receptionist can remember the request for future action, and, in the meantime, accept communications concerning other activities. Processing of a request can resume at any time by simply retrieving it from where it is stored. The ability to handle customers as any other actors allows receptionists to organize the storage of requests in progress in a variety of ways. Unlike monitors, receptionists are not limited to the use of a couple of predefined, specialized storage structures such as queues and priority queues.

In other languages, which do not support the concept of a customer, the acceptance of a request must be delayed until the proper conditions are met for processing it. This usually requires complicated programming constructs to guard the acceptance of communications.

4 Implementation of a HardCopyServer

Implementing a module to service printing requests for two printing devices provides a concrete example to illustrate the flexibility of receptionists. The following example, see Figure 1, illustrates the implementation of a receptionist

```
(Define (New HardCopyServer
             (With device-1 ≡d-1)
             (With device-2 ≡d-2))
  (New HardCopyReceptionist
       (With device-1 d-1)
       (With device-2 d-2)
       (With pending (A (New waiting-queue)))
       (With device-status-1 idle)
       (With device-status-2 idle)))
```

Figure 1: *Actual Implementation of the HardCopyServer. Note HardCopyServer merely returns a new instantiation of the HardCopyReceptionist.*

that protects more than one resource (in this case two printers).

We have modularized the implementation of the receptionist for a `HardCopyServer` into two kinds of modules:

1. *Receptionists* which provide the external interfaces to the outside world.
2. *Proxies* which deal with the issues of delegated communications for a shared resource.

The `HardCopyServer` is provided with the mail addresses of two devices (which are printers) when it is created. The function of the receptionist is to set up and initialize a `HardCopyServer`. The receptionist has to maintain a fundamental constraint that no device should be idle if there are pending requests. The `HardCopyServer` accepts printing requests and communicates with the printing devices. It maintains records of the status of the printing devices and of pending requests in order to schedule the printers.

We can bind an identifier to a new instance of an actor using the `Define` construct, see Figure 2.

4.1 Receptionist Implementation

A first implementation of the Receptionist provides that print requests submitted to the receptionist will be served in the order in which they are received.

```
(Define Server-64 (New HardCopyServer
                      (With device-1 Dover)
                      (With device-2 LGP)))
```

Figure 2: *Creating an instance of the* HardCopyServer *bound to the identifier,* Server-64.

```
(Define (New HardCopyReceptionist <attributions>)
  (Is-Request <pattern> Do
    (Join p   ;; the current transaction joins p
      (Then Do
        (Release-from p IF  <some-device-is-idle>))
      (After-Released Do ;; the current transaction has been released from p
        <record-starting>          ; device is now busy
        ;;  After delegating the print request to a proxy
        (After <delegate-request>
               <record-stopping>           ; device is now free
               <reply-to-customer>
               ;; the next pending print-request is released
               (Release-From p If <some-device-is-idle>)))))))
```

Figure 3: *Template for implementation of* HardCopyReceptionist

In general, though, requests cannot be served immediately for no printer may be available at that time. Hence, a FIFO queue will be used as appropriate scheduling structure for pending requests. Later, we will evolve this implementation into one which uses a more sophisticated scheduling structure.

Prior to code generation, a "template" program is constructed in Figure 3, which will serve as guide to the actual implementation.

Operationally, the behavior of the HardCopyReceptionist is as follows:

1. A print request arrives and its transaction immediately joins the pending queue.

2. If device is free, the receptionist releases a transaction from the pending queue, although not necessarily the one that just "joined" p.

3. When a transaction is released, the HardCopyReceptionist updates its state to reflect the fact that one of the printers is busy. Concurrently, the print message is delegated to the chosen device.

4. Eventually, a reply is received from the printer causing the receptionist to update its local state to reflect that the device is no longer busy.
5. The reply is forwarded to the customer of the transaction concurrently with releasing another transaction from the pending queue if some device is free.

It is important to understand that the `After` construct frees up the receptionist for other processing while the printers are operating in parallel.

4.2 Actual Implementation

The actual code for the `HardCopyReceptionist` is presented in Figure 4. Readers not interested in studying it may safely skip this and the following subsection.

Act3 is homogeneous; all data are actors. A program in Act3 is a collection of actors that, taken together, specify a behavior for the top-level actor —in this case, `HardCopyReceptionist`. Specifically, the Act3 language is comprised of *commands*, *expressions* and *communication-handlers*.

The terms *command* and *expression* are used in the ordinary semantic sense: Commands are actors whose execution results in some effect, whereas evaluating an expression results in the production of more actors.

Note that Act3 maintains the distinction between *describing* an actor and *creating* it. Basically, expressions of the form:

```
(A <Concept> (With <Att-Relation> <Att-Filler>))
```

are called *Instance-Descriptions*. Evaluating an instance-description results in the creation of an `<A-Expression>` actor whose `<Att-Relation>`s and `<Att-Filler>`s are determined by the encompassing environment.

`<New-Expressions>` have exactly the same syntax, except that the first token must be the symbol, `New`. Evaluating a `<New-Expression>`, however, results in the creation of an instance of the specified actor.

```
(Define (New HardCopyReceptionist
             (With device-1 ≡d-1)
             (With device-2 ≡d-2)
             (With pending ≡p)
             (With device-status-1 ≡ds-1)
             (With device-status-2 ≡ds-2))
 (Is-Request (≡pm Which-Is (A PrintRequestMessage)) Do
   (Join p
    ;;suspend this transaction to wait in queue,p
    (Then Do
          ;;if some device is idle, then resume the next
          ;;request to be processed
        (Release-From p
                 If (∨ (ds-1 Is idle) (ds-2 Is idle))))
    (After-Released Do
     ;;when this transaction is resumed
      (Let (((An IdleDeviceFound
                  (With device-status ≡chosen-device-status)
                  (With device-chosen ≡chosen-device))
             Match
             (Call ChooseIdleDevice
                   (With device-status-1 ds-1)
                   (With device-status-2 ds-2)))
       ;;Call ChooseIdleDevice to bind the Chosen Device
       ;;and the device-status.
       In
       (Become (New HardCopyReceptionist
                    (With chosen-device-status busy)))
       (After (Ask chosen-device pm)
        Cases
        (Is (≡r Which-Is (A PrinterReplyMessage)) Do
         (Reply (Call MakePrintingCompletedReport
                    (With printer-reply r)))
         (Become (New HardCopyReceptionist
                      (With chosen-device-status idle)))
          ;;if some requests are pending
          ;;then resume the next one to continue processing
         (Release-From p
                 If (∨ (ds-1 Is idle) (ds-2 Is idle))))))))))
```

Figure 4: *The complete implementation of the* HardCopyReceptionist.

Communication-handlers are expressions of the form: (Is-Request <Pattern> Do <Commands>) . Note, they contain a <Pattern> which is an expression and a series of one or more <Commands>. In general, commands are preceded by the keywords, Do or In. Besides Is-Request, Is-Reply and Is-Complaint, an Is-Communication handler type is provided for complete generality.

Forms typed in at the top level are "asked to parse themselves", hence, "actor programs" are intrinsically distributed, and, depending upon context, many Act3 constructs can appear as both commands and expressions.

4.3 An Operational HardCopyReceptionist

Act3 is inherently parallel, *i.e.*, concurrency is the default. Communication handlers, commands and sub-expressions may all be evaluated in parallel.

For instance, in the HardCopyReceptionist the Become command executes concurrently with the After command making a new HardCopyReceptionist with device-status-i set to busy. Hence, communications arriving at the HardCopyReceptionist during the interim will have the information that it is not available.

A key part of the above code is the After command which we have duplicated in Figure 5 for scrutiny. The After command works as follows:

1. The HardCopyReceptionist becomes sensitive to incoming communications while (Ask chosen-device pm) is taking place invoking device, chosen-device. In effect, then, the implementation of the HardCopyReceptionist concurrently processes printing requests and guarantees service.

2. After the reply from (Ask chosen-device pm) has been accepted, the bindings of d-1, d-2, p, ds-1 and ds-2, are *bound* to the values they have *when the reply is accepted* which may be different from what they were when chosen-device was invoked. The reply r is processed by the Cases handler in the After command.

3. The processing consists of replying with a printed completed report and then concurrently releases a print request, if any are pending.

```
(After (Ask chosen-device pm)
       Cases
       (Is (≡r Which-Is (A printer-replymessage)) Do
        (Reply (Call MakePrintingCompletedReport
                     (With printer-reply r)))
        (If (non-empty p)
         ;;if some requests are pending,
            (Then Do
              ;;then resume the next one to continue processing
              (Release-From p)))))
```

Figure 5: *Closeup of* **After** *construct as used in the* **HardCopyReceptionist** *example.*

5 Methodology

In the following sections, we present a more thorough treatment of important methodological issues raised by our treatment of the hard copy server presented above.

5.1 Absolute Containment

With receptionists it is possible to implement computational abstractions which have a property called *absolute containment* of the protected resource. This concept was proposed by [Hewitt 75] and further developed in [Atkinson and Hewitt 79] (cf. [Hoare 76], for a similar idea using the **inner** construct of SIMULA). The idea is to send a communication with directions to the receptionist. This, in turn, will pass it to the resource so that it can carry out the directions without allowing the user to deal directly with the resource. An important robustness issue arises with the usual strategy of giving out the resource. It is not easy to recover the use of the resource from a situation in which the user process has failed for any reason to complete its operations.

We have found that absolute containment produces more modular implementations than schemes which actually allocate resources protected by receptionists.

Note that the correct behavior of a receptionist which implements absolute containment depends only on the behavior of the resource and the code for the receptionist which implements the receptionist, not on the programs which call it.

Our `HardCopyServer` implements absolute containment by never allowing others to have direct access to its devices. Thus there is no way for others to depend on the number of physical devices available. Furthermore, no problem arises in retrieving the devices from users who have seized them since they are never given out.

5.2 Evolution

An important consideration in the design of a receptionist is the likely direction in which it will need to evolve to meet future needs. For example, users may decide that smaller documents should be given faster service than larger documents.

A simple scheme for accomplish this is to assign floating priorities to the documents based on their length. The idea is to assign an initial priority equal to the length of the document. When a printer is free, the document with highest priority (i.e. with the smallest priority number) is served next. If a print requisition for a document `d-1` of length n_1 is received when there is a document `d-2` at the rear of pending with priority n_2 which is greater than n_1, then `d-1` is placed in front of `d-2`. In addition the priority of `d-2` is changed to $n_2 - n_1$.

Simply replacing the queues in the original implementation of the hard copy receptionist with floating priority queues will accomplish the desired change.

5.3 Guarantee of Service

In our applications we want to be able to implement receptionists which guarantee that a response will be sent for each request received. This requirement for a strong guarantee of service is the concurrent system's analogue to the usual requirement in sequential programming that subroutines must return values for all legitimate arguments. In our applications, it would be *incorrect* to have implementations which did not guarantee a response to communications received.

If one can prove that each *individual* serialized actor in an actor system will specify a replacement for itself for each communication that it processes, then that actor system is guaranteed to be deadlock free. In general, the proof that a receptionist always designates a replacement might depend on assumptions on the behavior of other actors. In our example, the property of the server was achieved by relying on the well defined behavior of each printer. In cases where such dependencies constitute a partial ordering, a proof can be performed without difficulties. If there are loops in the dependencies, then a more complex analysis is necessary.

Proving a guarantee of service (i.e., every request received will generate a response) is not trivial. Note that it is impossible to prove the property of guarantee of service in some computational models, such as Petri nets and CSP, in which processes communicate via synchronized communication. We consider the ease with which we can prove guarantee of service to be one of the principal advantages of using the actor model of computation in our applications.

We recognize that our conclusions concerning the issue of guarantee of service are at variance with the beliefs of some of our colleagues. These disagreements appear to be fundamental and have their genesis in the inception of the field in the early 1970's. The disagreements can be traced to different hypotheses and assumptions on conceptual, physical, and semantic levels.

- *Conceptual Level.* As mentioned earlier, one of the innovations of the actor model is to take the arrival ordering of communications as being fundamental to the notion of concurrency. In this respect, it differs from systems such as Petri Nets and CSP which model concurrency in terms of nondeterministic choice. Modeling concurrency using nondeterministic choice implies that all systems must have bounded nondeterminism. However, a system, such as our `HardCopyServer` which guarantees service for requests received, can be used to implement systems with unbounded nondeterminism. Actor systems impose a constraint on all implementations that all mail sent must be delivered to the target actor. Whether the target actor ever accepts the communication and acts on it is a separate matter which is not of concern to the mail system.

- *Physical Level.* A careful analysis of the physical and engineering realities leads to the conclusion that guarantee of service can be reliably implemented in practice. Worries about the possibility of implementing guarantee of service have caused others to shrink from constructing theories in which the ability to guarantee service can be proved (e.g., [Dijkstra 77], pg. 77).

- *Semantic Level.* The axiomatic and power domain characterizations of actor systems are closely related and represent a unification of operational and denotational semantics. The axioms which characterize actor computations that are physically realizable are entirely different from those which have been developed by Von Neumann, Floyd, Hoare, Dijkstra, etc. to characterize classical programming languages. The power domain semantics for actor computations developed by Clinger is grounded on the underlying physical realities of communication based on the use of a mail system. It provides a model theory to support proofs in which properties such as guarantee of service can be proved.

One criticism of guarantee of service is that it does not give any indication of when the service will be performed. Of course, this theoretical problem has been with us for a long time since it occurs even for sequential programs. In the case of concurrent systems, we can do somewhat better by transmitting progress reports as the computation proceeds as well as estimates when the request will be accomplished. For example, we can modify the communication handler of our receptionist for the `HardCopyServer` so that it produces a report of the number of print requests queued before the one which has been submitted using the `Report-Status` command, see Figure 6.

The idea for incorporating this modification in our example comes from a suggestion of Hoare [private communication 1981] and is, in fact, similar to the way that the current hard copy server for our laser printer at MIT works. Using such ideas, we can incorporate stronger performance criteria into our mathematical semantics.

```
(Define (New HardCopyReceptionist
              (With device-1 ≡d-1)
              (With device-2 ≡d-2)
              (With pending ≡p)
              (With device-status-1 ≡ds-1)
              (With device-status-2 ≡ds-2))
 (Is-Request (≡pm Which-Is (A print-request-message)) Do
   (Report-Status
     (A Report
        (With no-of-previous-requests (length p))))
   (Join p (With priority (length (document pm)))
          ...)))
```

Figure 6: *The same Excerpt from the* `HardCopyReceptionist`, *incorporating the* `Report-Status` *command.*

6 Concurrency

Concurrency is the default in Act3. Indeed, maximizing concurrency, minimizing response time, and the avoidance of bottlenecks are perhaps the most fundamental engineering principles in the construction of actor systems. The only limitation on the concurrency of a serialized actor is the speed with which the replacement can be computed for a communication received.

Concurrency occurs among all the following activities:

- **Within the activities of processing a single communication for a given serialized actor. The serialized actor which receives a communication can concurrently create new actors, send communications, and designate its replacement (cf. [Ward and Halstead 80] for the application of this idea in a more limited context).**

- **Between the activities of processing a communication for an actor and a successor communication received by the same actor. The ability to pipeline the processing of successive communications is particularly important for an unserialized actor which does not change state as a result of the communication which it has received and thus can easily designate its successor. Another important case occurs where the computation for constructing the replacement can occur concurrently with the replacement processing the next communication using "eager evaluation" [Baker and Hewitt 77]. For example, a checking account can overlap the work of constructing a report of all the checks paid out to the Electric Company during the previous year with making another deposit for the current year.**

Of course, no limitation whatsoever exists on the concurrency that is possible between the activities of two different serialized actors. For example, two separate checking accounts can be processing withdrawals at exactly the same time (within a given frame of reference).

Unlike communicating sequential processes, the commands in a receptionist do not have to be executed sequentially. They can be executed in any order or in parallel. This difference stems from the different ways in which parallelism is developed in the actor model and communicating sequential processes. In the latter, parallelism comes from the combination of sequential processes which are the fundamental units of execution. In the actor model, concurrent events are the fundamental units and sequential execution is a derived notion since special measures must be taken to force the actions to be sequential.

7 Related Work

The work on actors has coevolved with a great deal of work done elsewhere. Important differences have emerged in part because of different motivations and intended areas of application. The driving force behind the our work has been the needs of parallel problem solving systems for communities of actors [Kornfeld and Hewitt 81, Barber, DeJong and Hewitt 83].

The work on Simula and its successors SmallTalk, CLU, Alphard, etc., has profoundly influenced our work. We are particularly grateful to Alan Kay and the other members of the Learning Research group for interactions and useful suggestions over the last few years.

One of our achievements is to unify procedure and data objects into the single notion of an actor. The Simula-like languages provide effective support for coroutines but not for concurrency. Through its receptionist mechanism, Act3 provides effective support for shared objects in a highly parallel distributed environment.

In the area of semantics, parallels can be found with the recent work of Hoare, Milner, and Kahn and MacQueen. From the outset, an important difference between the Actor Model and the process models of Hoare and Milner has been that process models have not allowed direct references to processes to be stored in data structures or communicated in messages. The Actor Model differs in that all objects are actors and all computation takes place via communication.

A fundamental part of the motivation of the work reported in this paper is to provide linguistic support for receptionists in open systems [Hewitt 83]. One of the fundamental properties of open systems is that they do not have well defined global states. In this respect our work differs from previous work on concurrent access to data bases using the notion of ***serizability***.

The only thing that is visible to an actor is the communication which it has just accepted. Other communications which might be on the way will not have been noticed yet. We have deliberately made nothing else visible so that a variety of scheduling procedures can be implemented such as pipes, queues, multiple queues, priority queues, floating priority queues, etc.

8 Future Work

Dealing with the issues raised by the possibility of an actor being a specialization of more than one description has become known as the "Multiple Inheritance Problem". A number of approaches have been developed in the last few years including the following: [Weinreb and Moon 81, Curry, Baer, Lipkie and Lee 82, Borning and Ingalls 82, Bobrow and Stefik 82 and Borgida, Mylopoulos and Wong 82].

Our approach differs in that it builds on the theory of an underlying description system [Attardi and Simi 81] and in the fact that it is designed for a parallel message passing environment in contrast to the sequential coroutine object-oriented programming languages derived from Simula. In this paper we have shown how *receptionists* can be used to regulate the use of shared resources by scheduling their access and providing protection against unauthorized or accidental access. The work in this paper needs to be combined with work on relating descriptions and actions in concurrent systems [Hewitt and DeJong 83] to provide a general framework for addressing problems of multiple inheritance.

Acknowledgments

Much of the work underlying our ideas was conducted by members of the Message Passing Semantics group at MIT. We especially would like to thank Gul Agha, Jon Amsterdam, Jerry Barber, Peter de Jong, Henry Lieberman, Tim McNerney, Elijah Millgram, Chunka Mui, and Dan Theriault. We are indebted to Henry Lieberman for his insistence that the tough problems associated with delegation and proxies can and must be worked through to a satisfactory resolution and for his earlier work on the problem [Hewitt, Attardi and Lieberman 79b].

Our colleagues at the MIT Artificial Intelligence Laboratory and Laboratory for Computer Science provided intellectual atmosphere, facilities, and constructive criticism which greatly facilitated our work.

Conversations with Jean-Raymond Abrial, Ole-Johan Dahl, Jack Dennis, Edsger Dijkstra, David Fisher, Dan Friedman, Stein Gjessing, Tony Hoare, Jean Ichbiah, Gilles Kahn, Dave MacQueen, Robin Milner, Birger Moller-Pedersen, Kristen Nygaard, Jerry Schwarz, Steve Schuman, Bob Tennent, and David Wise have proved to be of great value in shaping our concepts. The first author would like to thank Luigia Aio and Gianfranco Prini and the participants in the summer school on Foundations of Artificial Intelligence and Computer Science in Pisa for helpful comments.

Robin Stanton has provided constructive criticism and great encouragement. Peter Deutsch made valuable suggestions on how to organize the early sections of this paper. Maria Simi, Phyllis Koton, Valdis Berzins, Alan Borning, Richard Fikes, Gary Nutt, Susan Owicki, Dan Shapiro, Larry Tesler, Deepak Kapur and the members of the Message Passing Systems Seminar have given us valuable feedback and suggestions on this paper.

This paper describes research done at the Artificial Intelligence Laboratory of the Massachusetts Institute of Technology. Major support for the research reported in this paper was provided by the System Development Foundation. Major support for other related work in the Artificial Intelligence Laboratory is provided, in part, by the Advanced

Research Projects Agency of the Department of Defense under Office of Naval Research contract N0014-80-C-0505. We would like to thank Charles Smith, Mike Brady, Patrick Winston, and Gerald Wilson for their support and encouragement.

[Atkinson and Hewitt 79] Atkinson, R. and Hewitt, C. Specification and Proof Techniques for Serializers. IEEE Transactions on Software Engineering SE-5 No. 1, IEEE, January, 1979.

[Attardi and Simi 81] Attardi, G. and Simi, M. Semantics of Inheritance and Attributions in the Description System Omega. Proceedings of IJCAI 81, IJCAI, Vancouver, B. C., Canada, August, 1981.

[Backus 78] Backus, J. Can Programming be Liberated from the von Neumann Style? A Functional Style and Its Algebra of Programs. *Communications of the ACM 21*, 8 (August 1978), 613-641.

[Baker 78] Baker, H. Actor Systems for Real-Time Computation. Technical Report 197, Mit Laboratory for Computer Science, 1978.

[Baker and Hewitt 77] Baker, H. and Hewitt, C. The Incremental Garbage Collection of Processes. Conference Record of the Conference on AI and Programming Languages, ACM, Rochester, New York, August, 1977, pp. 55-59.

[Barber, de Jong, and Hewitt 83] Barber, G. R., de Jong, S. P., and Hewitt, C. Semantic Support for Work in Organizations. Proceedings of IFIP-83, IFIP, Sept., 1983.

[Birtwistle, Dahl, Myhrhaug, and Nygaard 73] Birtwistle, G. M., Dahl, O-J., Myhrhaug, B., Nygaard, K. *Simula Begin.* Van Nostrand Reinhold, New York, 1973.

[Bobrow and Stefik 82] Bobrow, D. G., Stefik, M. J. Loops: An Object Oriented Programming System for Interlisp. Xerox PARC, 1982.

[Borgida, Mylopoulos, and Wong 82] Borgida, A., Mylopoulos, J. L., Wong, H. K. T. Generalization as a Basis for Software Specification. Perspectives on Conceptual Modeling, Springer-Verlag, 1982.

[Borning and Ingalls 82] Borning, A. H., Ingalls, D. H. Multiple Inheritance in Smalltalk-80. Proceedings of the National Conference on Artificial Intelligence, AAAI, August, 1982.

[Brock and Ackerman 78] Brock, J. D. and Ackerman, W.B. An Anomoly in the Specifications of Nondeterminate Packet Systems. Tech. Rep. Computation Structures Group None 33-1, M.I.T., January, 1978.

[Clinger 81] Clinger, W. D. Foundations of Actor Semantics. AI-TR- 633, MIT Artificial Intelligence Laboratory, May, 1981.

[Curry, Baer, Lipkie, and Lee 82] Curry, G., Baer, L., Lipkie, D., Lee, B. Traits: An Approach to Multiple-Inheritance Subclassing. Conference on Office Information Systems, ACM SIGOA, June, 1982.

[Dijkstra 77] Dijkstra, E. W. *A Discipline of Programming.* Prentice-Hall, 1977.

[Friedman and Wise 76] Friedman, D. P., Wise, D. S. The Impact of Applicative Programming on Multiprocessing. Proceedings of the International Conference on Parallel Processing, ACM, 1976, pp. 263-272.

[Greif 75] Greif, I. Semantics of Communicating Parallel Processes. Technical Report 154, MIT, Project MAC, 1975.

[Hewitt 75] Hewitt, C.E. Protection and Synchronization in Actor Systems. SIGCOMM-SIGOPS Interface Workshop on Interprocess Communications, ACM, March, 1975.

[Hewitt 77] Hewitt, C.E. Viewing Control Structures as Patterns of Passing Messages. *Journal of Artificial Intelligence 8-3* (June 1977), 323-364.

[Hewitt 83] Hewitt, C.E. Open Systems. Perspectives on Conceptual Modeling, Springer-Verlag, 1983.

[Hewitt and Baker 77] Hewitt, C. and Baker, H. Laws for Communicating Parallel Processes. 1977 IFIP Congress Proceedings, IFIP, August, 1977, pp. 987-992.

[Hewitt and de Jong 83] Hewitt, C., de Jong, P. Analyzing the Roles of Descriptions and Actions in Open Systems. Proceedings of the National Conference on Artificial Intelligence, AAAI, August, 1983.

[Hewitt, Attardi, and Lieberman 79a] Hewitt C., Attardi G., and Lieberman H. Specifying and Proving Properties of Guardians for Distributed Systems. Proceedings of the Conference on Semantics of Concurrent Computation, Vol. 70, INRIA, Springer-Verlag, Evian, France, July, 1979, pp. 316-336.

[Hewitt, Attardi, and Lieberman 79b] Hewitt, C. E., Attardi, G., and Lieberman, H. Delegation in Message Passing. Proceedings of First International Conference on Distributed Systems, ACM, Huntsville, October, 1979.

[Hoare 74] Hoare, C. A. R. Monitors: An Operating System Structuring Concept. *CACM* (October 1974).

[Hoare 76] Hoare, C.A.R. Language Hierarachies and Interfaces. In *Lecture Notes in Computer Science*, Springer-Verlag, 1976.

[Hoare 78] Hoare, C. A. R. Communicating Sequential Processes. *CACM 21*, 8 (August 1978), 666-677.

[Kahn 81] Kahn, K. Uniform--A Language Based Upon Unification which Unifies (much of) Lisp, Prolog, and Act 1. University of Uppsala, March, 1981.

[Kornfeld and Hewitt 81] Kornfeld, W. A. and Hewitt, C. The Scientific Community Metaphor. *IEEE Transactions on Systems, Man, and Cybernetics SMC-11*, 1 (January 1981).

[Landin 65] Landin, P. A Correspondence Between ALGOL 60 and Church's Lambda Notation. *Communication of the ACM 8*, 2 (February 1965).

[McCarthy 62] McCarthy, John. *LISP 1.5 Programmer's Manual.* The MIT Press, Cambridge, Ma., 1962.

[Milner 79] Milner, R. Flowgraphs and Flow Algebras. *JACM 26. No. 4* (1979).

[Reynolds 74] Reynolds, J.C. On the Relation Between Direct and Continuation Semantics. Proceedings of the Second Colloquium on Automata, Language and Programming, Springer-Verlag, 1974.

[Strachey and Wadsworth 74] Strachey, C. and Wadsworth, C.P. *Continuations - A Mathematical Semantics for Handling Full Jumps.* Univeristy of Oxford, Programming Reseach Group, 1974.

[Ward and Halstead 80] Ward, S. and Halstead, R. A Syntactic Theory of Message Passing. *JACM 27, No. 2* (1980), 365-383.

[Weinreb and Moon 81] Weinreb, D. and Moon D. *LISP Machine Manual.* MIT, 1981.

APPLICATIONS OF TOPOLOGY TO SEMANTICS OF COMMUNICATING PROCESSES

William C. Rounds *
Computer Science and Engineering Division
University of Michigan
Ann Arbor, Michigan 48109

1. Introduction

In this paper we point out some general principles which underlie proofs of correctness for communicating processes. We are concerned with those properties of processes which can be defined with reference to the possible finite behaviors of a process. These include *safety properties*: those assertions which say that nothing undesirable will ever happen.

Hoare, Brookes, and Roscoe, in their paper on CSP [HBR], define *buffers* by means of a collection of safety assertions about buffer behavior. They state some general theorems about properties of processes which can be established using a rule of proof called *fixed-point induction*. We generalize these results to a more refined semantic model than theirs. In doing so, we are led to an interesting application of the *compactness theorem* from first-order logic. This result can be interpreted as saying that the so-called Stone topology on a class of mathematical structures is compact. This topology is induced by defining the closed sets to be classes of structures which satisfy every assertion in a given (consistent) collection of assertions. Our structures represent the possible behaviors of a process, and we show that the definition of buffers can be rephrased as a consistent collection of assertions. Therefore the class of buffers is closed. We also prove that the Stone topology is definable by a metric given naturally in terms of Milner's observational equivalence relations. Convergence in the metric is guaranteed by the hypothesis of the rule of fixed-point induction; in fact, this rule is seen to be nothing more or less than the Banach fixed-point theorem for the space in question.

We view this work as a synthesis of the methods of Hoare, Brookes, and Roscoe with those of de Bakker and Zucker [BaZ], and also those of Milner [M]. Our examples confirm the validity of the idea of *specification semantics* in [OH]. Moreover, the suggestions of Smyth [S] are confirmed because the general notions of topology serve as a guide to formulating theorems about all these models.

The paper is organized into four sections, of which this is the first. Section 2 introduces the basic model of processes–the transition system– and presents the logical system used to describe these models. Section 3 is devoted to buffers and CSP. The final section gives

* Research supported by NSF grant BSR–8301022.

another application of the compactness theorem which solves a problem left open in [Rou] concerning transition systems over a countable alphabet.

2. The operational model

The underlying framework for expressing the behavior of processes will be the familiar *transition system.* This is a tuple

$$S = \langle Q, q, \{\xrightarrow{\sigma} : \sigma \in \Sigma \cup \{\tau\}\}\rangle$$

where Q is a countable set of *states*; $q \in Q$ is the *initial state*; Σ is an alphabet of *event names*; τ is a special event, not in Σ, and denoting the *silent transition*. The relations $\xrightarrow{\sigma}$ are binary relations on Q which for each σ event, denote the possible changes of state which may take place during that event. The elements of Σ are called *visible events*. Typically these might represent the instantaneous transmission of a value along a wire or channel. Generally we will compare and combine systems over the same alphabet.

2.1. Operators on transition systems.

There are several familiar ways of combining transition systems to form new ones. We concentrate on those needed in our examples.

2.1.1. Prefixing.

Let $\Delta \subseteq \Sigma$, and let S_σ be a transition system for $\sigma \in \Delta$. then

$$\sigma : \Delta \to S_\sigma$$

is the system with a new initial state q_0, and a transition on σ from this state to the initial state of S_σ for each $\sigma \in \Delta$. (It is presumed that the state sets in question are disjoint.) The event σ is bound in this construction. A simple special case occurs when Δ is the singleton $\{\sigma\}$. This system is denoted $\sigma \to S$.

2.1.2. Synchronized parallel composition.

Again, let $\Delta \subseteq \Sigma$, and let S and T be transition systems over Σ. This time, the alphabet Δ is regarded as specifying a collection of events which must occur simultaneously in S and T. It is called the *synchronization alphabet.* Other events (in $\Sigma \setminus \Delta$) may occur independently in S or T. We define $S \parallel_\Delta T$ to be the system

$$\langle Q_S \times Q_T, \langle q_S, q_T\rangle, \{\xrightarrow{\sigma}\}\rangle,$$

where $\langle q, r\rangle \xrightarrow{\sigma} \langle q', r'\rangle$ iff either

$$\sigma \in \Delta, \quad q \xrightarrow{\sigma} q', \quad \text{and } r \xrightarrow{\sigma} r'$$

or

$$\sigma \notin \Delta, \quad \text{and either } q \xrightarrow{\sigma} q' \text{ with } r = r'$$
$$\text{or } r \xrightarrow{\sigma} r' \text{ with } q = q'$$

Notice that if Δ is empty we get the "shuffle" of the two systems, while if $\Delta = \Sigma$ we get the direct product.

2.1.3. Hiding or concealment.

Often we wish to ensure that an action a is not available to the environment of a process for synchronization purposes. This is accomplished by renaming the event a to be the silent event τ. This operation will be denoted hide_a, and is formally given by letting the $\xrightarrow{a}$ relation be empty and adding those pairs to the $\xrightarrow{\tau}$ relation.

2.1.4. Renaming.

This operation is used in our examples to direct information being sent on a particular channel to some other channel. It is specified by a renaming map $r : \Sigma \to \Delta$. The result of applying this to a transition system is another system over the alphabet Δ which will allow a transition $q \xrightarrow{b} q'$ iff there is some a with $r(a) = b$ and $q \xrightarrow{a} q'$ (the state set of the new system is unchanged.)

2.2. Logic for process description.

We employ a modal logic L of Hennessy and Milner [HM] modified slightly for our present purposes. The formulas of L are defined to be the least set containing the Boolean constants tt and ff, closed under the usual Boolean operations, and under the rule stating that $\langle a \rangle \phi$ and $\langle \Lambda \rangle \phi$ are formulas whenever $a \in \Sigma$ and ϕ is a formula.

Intuitively, the meaning of these modal formulas is that it is possible to execute a single a event and then be in a state satisfying ϕ; or that it is possible to execute a sequence of silent events and then to satisfy ϕ. To explain the semantics precisely we need to define some auxiliary relations. Let the relation $\xRightarrow{\Lambda}$ be the reflexive, transitive closure of the $\xrightarrow{\tau}$ relation. Let the relations $\xRightarrow{a}$, for $a \in \Sigma$, be

$$\left(\xRightarrow{\Lambda}\right) \circ \xrightarrow{a} \circ \left(\xRightarrow{\Lambda}\right).$$

(For $u \in \Sigma^*$ we also have the natural relations $\xRightarrow{u}$.)

We next define the *satisfaction predicate* $\models$. Let S be a system and $q \in Q_S$. The predicate $\models$ is the least relation between Q_S and L satisfying:

$$q \models \text{tt} \quad \text{always;}$$
$$q \models \text{ff} \quad \text{never;}$$
$$q \models \phi \vee \psi \text{ iff } q \models \phi \text{ or } q \models \psi;$$

(Similarly for the other Boolean operations)

$$q \models \langle a \rangle \phi \text{ iff } (\exists q')(q \xRightarrow{a} q' \wedge q' \models \phi);$$
$$q \models \langle \Lambda \rangle \phi \quad \text{similarly.}$$

Definition 2.2.1 (modal rank.)

Let

$$|\,tt\,| = |\,ff\,| = 0;$$
$$|\phi \vee \psi| = |\phi \wedge \psi| = max(|\phi|, |\psi|);$$
$$|\neg\phi| = |\phi|;$$
$$|\langle a\rangle\phi| = |\langle \Lambda\rangle\phi| = 1 + |\phi|.$$

Definition 2.2.2. Let $L(n,\Delta)$ be the set of all ϕ with $|\phi| \leq n$ and modalities $\langle a\rangle$ with $a \in \Delta$. Two states q and r are n-elementarily equivalent iff $\mathrm{Th}_n(q) = \mathrm{Th}_n(r)$, where

$$\mathrm{Th}_n(q) = \{\phi \in L(n,\Sigma) : q \models \phi\}$$

Let E_n be the relation just defined. Let $q\ E\ r$ iff $q\ E_n\ r$ for all n. Similarly let E_n^{Δ} and E^{Δ} be these relations induced by formulas with modalities restricted to Δ.

Example. Consider the two systems

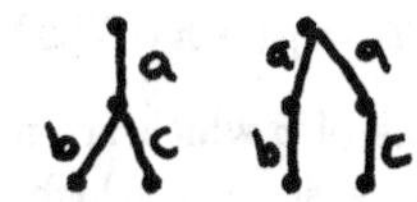

where the initial state is at the root of the tree. These systems are E_1 but not E_2–equivalent.

We also have another useful and closely related definition of equivalence.

Definition 2.2.4. Two states p and q are 0-behaviorally equivalent trivially. They are $(n+1)$-behaviorally equivalent iff for all $\sigma \in \Sigma.\cup\{\tau\}$, and for all p' such that $p \stackrel{\sigma}{\Longrightarrow} p'$, we have

$$(\exists q')(q \stackrel{\sigma}{\Longrightarrow} q' \wedge q' \text{ is n-behaviorally equivalent to } p') \text{ and vice versa.}$$

Let B_n denote the relation of n-behavioral equivalence, and let B be the intersection of all the B_n.

Lemma 2.2.5. If Δ is finite, then among the formulas of $L(n,\Delta)$, there are only finitely many logically distinct ones.

Proof. This is found in [GR]; one merely has to put the formulas of $L(n,\Delta)$ into a normal form.

Lemma 2.2.6. (Master formula theorem for L.) For each finite Δ, and each state q, there is a "master formula" $M\phi(n,\Delta,q)$ such that (i) $q \models M\phi(n,\Delta,q)$, and (ii) for all r, if $r \models M\phi(n,\Delta,q)$ then $r\ E_n^{\Delta}\ q$.

Proof. Let $\theta_1,\ldots,\theta_k$ be the logically distinct representatives of the set of (n,Δ)-formulas satisfied by q. Then we may take

$$M\phi(n,\Delta,q) = \bigwedge_{i=1}^{k} \theta_i.$$

Theorem 2.2.7. If Σ is finite, then $B_n = E_n$ for all n.

Proof. It is easy to show that B_n equivalence implies E_n equivalence. The other direction is by induction on n. This is trivial for $n = 0$. Assume it for n, and let $p\ E_{n+1}\ q$. We want to show $p\ B_{n+1}\ q$. Let $p \stackrel{\sigma}{\Longrightarrow} p'$ and let $\theta = M\phi(n, \Sigma, p')$. Then $p \models \langle\sigma\rangle\theta$. So therefore does q, and Lemma 2.2.6 and the induction hypothesis complete the proof.

Theorem 2.2.8. If Σ is finite, then the E_n relations are congruences with respect to the operations in Section 2.1, except hiding.

Proof. The result is straightforward to show if we use B_n instead of E_n, by induction on n. Applying 2.2.7 then gives the desired conclusion.

The relationship between E_n and B_n is more interesting when Σ is infinite; in this case the relations do not agree. However, we can characterize the distinction as follows.

Definition 2.2.9. For $\Delta \subseteq \Sigma$, let $RUN(\Delta)$ be the transition system with one state q, and a transition $q \stackrel{a}{\Longrightarrow} q$ for each $a \in \Delta$. Let p be a state in an arbitrary transition system over Σ. We define

$$p \parallel \Delta = p \parallel_{\Sigma} RUN(\Delta).$$

This operator disallows any transitions of p which are not in the set Δ. (By the transition system p we understand the transition system in which p occurs, redefined to have p as its initial state.)

Lemma 2.2.10. For any finite Δ, and any $n \geq 0$, we have for all states p and q,

$$p\ E_n^{\Delta}\ q \iff (p \parallel \Delta)\ B_n\ (q \parallel \Delta).$$

Proof. ($\Rightarrow$.) We proceed by induction on n to show that $p\ E_n^{\Delta}\ q$ implies $(p \parallel \Delta)\ B_n (q \parallel \Delta)$ for all p and q. The case $n = 0$ is trivial. Assume the result for n. Let $(p \parallel \Delta) \stackrel{\sigma}{\Longrightarrow} (q \parallel \Delta)$. The proof is the same whether or not σ is visible. We know from Def. 2.2.9 that σ, if visible, is in Δ, and that there is some p' such that $p \stackrel{\sigma}{\Longrightarrow} p'$. Therefore

$$p \models \langle\sigma\rangle M\phi(n, \Delta, p').$$

Since $p\ E_{n+1}^{\Delta}\ q$, there is a state q' such that $q \stackrel{\sigma}{\Longrightarrow} q'$ and $q' \models M\phi(n, \Delta, p')$. By Lemma 2.2.6, $q'\ E_n^{\Delta}\ p'$. By induction hypothesis, $(p' \parallel \Delta)\ B_n\ (q' \parallel \Delta)$. Since $(q \parallel \Delta) \stackrel{\sigma}{\Longrightarrow} (q' \parallel \Delta)$, we have the result for the case $n + 1$.

($\Leftarrow$.) The converse is another induction on n. We show: for all p and q, $(p \parallel \Delta)\ B_n\ (q \parallel \Delta)$ implies $p\ E_n^{\Delta}\ q$. Again the basis is trivial. For the inductive step, assume that $(p \parallel \Delta)\ B_{n+1}\ (q \parallel \Delta)$. The conclusion requires $p\ E_{n+1}^{\Delta}\ q$. This is established by another induction over $L(\Delta, n+1)$ formulas. For each ϕ in $L(\Delta, n+1)$ we must establish

$$p \models \phi \iff q \models \phi.$$

This is clear when ϕ is tt or ff . If ϕ is a Boolean combination of smaller formulas, the result follows easily from the induction hypothesis for those formulas. Suppose, therefore, that ϕ is $\langle\sigma\rangle\psi$. Let $p \models \phi$. Then there is a p' such that $p \stackrel{\sigma}{\Longrightarrow} p'$ and $p' \models \psi$. If σ is visible then of course $\sigma \in \Delta$, and therefore $(p \parallel \Delta) \stackrel{\sigma}{\Longrightarrow} (p' \parallel \Delta)$. This gives a q' such that $(q \parallel \Delta) \stackrel{\sigma}{\Longrightarrow} (q' \parallel \Delta)$, and $(p' \parallel \Delta)\ B_n\ (q' \parallel \Delta)$. The overall induction hypothesis applies, showing that $p'\ E_n^{\Delta}\ q'$. Thus $q' \models \psi$, and so $q \models \langle\sigma\rangle\psi$. The reverse implication is the same, so that we have proved the whole lemma.

Theorem 2.2.11. For any states p and q in a transition system over Σ, $p\ E_n\ q$ iff for every finite $\Delta \subseteq \Sigma$, we have $(p \parallel \Delta)\ B_n\ (q \parallel \Delta)$. The same holds for B and E.

Proof. This is immediate from Lemma 2.2.10.

Theorem 2.2.12. The conclusions of Theorem 2.2.8 hold without the hypothesis of finite Σ.

Proof. We show that E_n is a congruence for synchronized parallel composition, leaving the other operators as an exercise. Let Γ be the synchronization alphabet. Suppose $p\ E_n\ q$. We want: for all r, $(p \parallel_\Gamma r)\ E_n\ (q \parallel_\Gamma r)$. Let Δ be a finite subalphabet of Σ. Then $(p \parallel \Delta)\ B_n\ (q \parallel \Delta)$. These systems can be regarded over the finite alphabet Δ, and so by 2.2.8, we have

$$(p \parallel \Delta) \parallel_\Gamma r \quad B_n \quad (q \parallel \Delta) \parallel_\Gamma r$$

for any r. It is easy to see that

$$(p \parallel \Delta) \parallel_\Gamma r \quad B_n \quad (p \parallel_\Gamma r) \parallel \Delta,$$

so we have the desired conclusion for all finite Δ. Applying 2.2.11 gives the result.

2.3. The metric space of transition systems.

Using the equivalences in 2.2 we can define the distance between two states in a transition system, and therefore also the distance between two transition systems.

Definition 2.3.1. Let p and q be states in a transition system. The E-distance $d_E(p, q)$ is

$$\inf\{2^{-n} : p\ E_n\ q\}.$$

It is easy to check that d_E makes $\mathcal{T}/E$ into a metric space, where $\mathcal{T}$ is the class of (countable) transition systems over some fixed countable alphabet, and $\mathcal{T}/E$ is the quotient by the E equivalence relation. The same remark holds for the relation B. We wish, however, to introduce yet another topological structure on transition systems. This is done by using the *Stone topology* associated with the logic L. The points of this space are the elementary equivalence classes p/E. We choose as a basis for the space the sets of the form

$$\text{Mod}(\theta) = \{\ p/E : p \models \theta\}$$

where $\theta \in L$. This collection of sets is closed under the Boolean operations and so by itself forms a base for some topology. It will be convenient to consider the *closed sets* in this topology, which by definition are of the form

$$\text{Mod}(\Gamma) = \bigcap_{\theta \in \Gamma} \text{Mod}(\theta).$$

If Σ is finite, the Stone topology is the same as that given by the metric d_E.

Theorem 2.3.2. A subset K of $\mathcal{T}/E$ is closed iff it is metrically closed in the E-metric, provided Σ is finite.

Proof. Suppose $K = \text{Mod}(\Gamma)$ for some set of formulas Γ. Let $p_n \in K$ and suppose $d(p_n, p) \to 0$. (The relation E will be suppressed from now on.) If $p \notin K$, then for some $\theta \in \Gamma$, $p \models \neg\theta$. Choose n bigger than $|\theta|$, and p_m so that $d(p_m, p) \leq 2^{-n}$. Then $p_m \models \theta$ and $p_m \models \neg\theta$, a contradiction.

Conversely, let K be a closed set in the metric sense. Define

$$\text{Th}(K) = \{\theta : (\forall s \in K)(s \models \theta)\}.$$

Claim: $K = \text{Mod}(\text{Th}(K))$. The inclusion of left in right is trivial. For the other inclusion, suppose $t \in \text{Mod}(\text{Th}(K))$. We will construct a sequence $s_n \in K$ such that $d(s_n, t) \to 0$, which will prove $t \in K$. Fix the value of n. Consider the formulas $M\phi(n, \Sigma, s)$ as s ranges over K. By Lemma 2.2.5, there are only finitely many logically distinct such formulas. Set

$$\phi_n = \bigvee_{s \in K} M\phi(n, \Sigma, s).$$

Now $s \models \phi_n$ for each $s \in K$, which implies $\phi_n \in \text{Th}(K)$. Since $t \in \text{Mod}(\text{Th}(K))$, we have $t \models \phi_n$. Thus for each n, there is an $s_n \in K$ with $t \models M\phi(n, \Sigma, s_n)$. Therefore $t\ E_n\ s_n$, which implies $d(s_n, t) \to 0$, and the proof is complete.

We can now state and apply the Compactness Theorem for L. Its use will be in the next sections, and principally in Section 4.

Theorem 2.3.3 (Compactness). Let Γ be a subset of L. If every finite subset F of Γ has a countable model (i.e. a p such that $p \in \text{Mod}(F)$), then so does Γ. :

Proof. This proof is given in [GR], where it is shown how to translate L into first-order logic. Only minor modifications to that proof are necessary to deal with silent transitions.

Corollary 2.3.4. If Σ is finite, then the space $\mathcal{T}/E$ with the metric d_E is a compact metric space.

Proof. It is a standard fact from logic that the Compactness Theorem states that the Stone topology is compact. Since the Stone topology agrees with the E-topology, the result follows.

Remark. The compactness theorem itself does not depend on the finiteness of Σ. This will be important in Section 4.

3. Applications to buffer specifications

We present the definition of buffers appearing in Hoare, Brookes, and Roscoe. Their explanation goes roughly as follows. A buffer is a process which accepts messages on its input channel, and emits them in the same order on its output channel. The buffer should not have any other events allowed in its behavior. For the actual specification, we need to impose some structure on the set of events Σ.

Let T be a set of *values*. For example, T might be the set of integers. Let C be a set of *channel names* (e.g., $C = \{$ in, out $\}$.) A pair $\langle c, t \rangle$, to be written $c.t$, denotes the event of passing the message with value t along channel c. For buffer specifications, the channel names will be in the set $\{$ in, out $\}$. We will also use a renaming operator which maps the event $c.t$ to t. This operator is called *restriction* to c, and we write $r(c.t, c) = t$. If an event σ is not in $C \times T$, then $r(\sigma, c) = \sigma$. This operation is extended to strings of events in the usual way.

One other concept is needed about transition systems: for a state q, we define

$$\text{Initials}(q) = \{a \in \Sigma : (\exists q')(q \stackrel{a}{\Longrightarrow} q')\}.$$

Now we can formalize buffers.

Definition 3.1. A *buffer* is a transition system over $\Sigma = \text{in}.T \cup \text{out}.T$, with initial state b, such that for all $s \in \Sigma^*$ and states q such that $b \stackrel{s}{\Longrightarrow} q$, we have

(i.) $r(s, \text{out}) \leq r(s, \text{in})$; ($\leq$ is the prefix relation)
(ii.) If $r(s, \text{out}) = r(s, \text{in})$ then $\text{Initials}(q) = \text{in}.T$;
(iii.) if $r(s, \text{out}) \neq r(s, \text{in})$ then $\text{Initials}(q) \cap \text{out}.T \neq \emptyset$.

The first condition states that outputs appear in the order in which they came in, and that no output appears before it has been input. The second clause states that an empty buffer must be prepared to accept any input in the set T, and the third states that a nonempty buffer must be prepared to output some value in the set T. Note that the condition stating that every value which has come in must eventually come out is not explicitly expressed in this definition; it is possible to input values forever, provided that the buffer has unbounded capacity.

We are going to prove that the class of buffers is a closed set in the Stone topology defined in Section 2. This will have the consequence that the rule of fixed-point induction works to establish properties of buffers. These conclusions appear in [HBR] and [Ros]; what is new here is the topology and the method of proof using logical specifications.

Lemma 3.1.2. Let K be a closed set in the Stone topology, and let $L \subseteq \Sigma^*$. Then the set K_1 of (equivalence classes of) systems p such that for all $s \in L$ and all q such that $p \stackrel{s}{\Longrightarrow} q$, we have $q \in K$, is also closed.

Proof. We know that $K = \text{Mod}(\Gamma)$ for some set Γ of formulas. Let $\langle s \rangle \phi$ be the formula $\langle \sigma_1 \rangle \ldots \langle \sigma_n \rangle \phi$, where $s = \sigma_1 \ldots \sigma_n$, and let $[s]\phi$ be $\neg \langle s \rangle \neg \phi$. Then

$$K_1 = \{[s]\phi : s \in L \text{ and } \phi \in \Gamma\}.$$

Corollary 3.1.3. The set K_1 of processes p such that for all q, if $p \stackrel{s}{\Longrightarrow} q$, then $s \in L$, where $L \subseteq \Sigma^*$, is also closed.

Proof. Let $K = \emptyset$ and let L be replaced by the complement of L in Lemma 3.1.2.

Lemma 3.1.4. The set K_2 of processes q such that Initials$(q) = \Delta$, where $\Delta \subseteq \Sigma$, is a closed set.

Proof. Define

$$\Gamma = \{\langle a\rangle\ \mathrm{tt}\ : a \in \Delta\} \cup \{\neg\langle a\rangle\ \mathrm{tt}\ : a \notin \Delta\}.$$

It is clear that $K_2 = \mathrm{Mod}(\Gamma)$.

Lemma 3.1.5. If Δ is finite, then the set $K_3 = \{q : \mathrm{Initials}(q) \cap \Delta \neq \emptyset\}$ is closed.

Proof. Let Γ consist of the single formula $\langle a_1\rangle\ \mathrm{tt}\ \vee \ldots \vee \langle a_n\rangle\ \mathrm{tt}$, where $\Delta = \{a_1, \ldots, a_n\}$. Then $K_3 = \mathrm{Mod}(\Gamma)$.

Theorem 3.1.6. If T is finite, then the class of buffers over T is closed in the Stone topology.

Proof. This is now immediate from Definition 3.1.1 and the foregoing lemmas.

Remark. Lemma 3.1.5 is false for infinite Δ and the Stone topology. This is the only lemma that fails, however. We shall assume that the event set is finite for the remainder of the section.

3.2. Examples in CSP.

Let c be a channel name. We define the operator $hide_c$ to be the renaming of each $c.t$ event to the silent transition τ, and otherwise the identity. Now let p and q be processes over the buffer alphabet. We define the *chaining* of p and q, written $p \gg q$, as follows. Let c be a new channel name. Let $p(\mathrm{out} \leftarrow c)$ be the process p except that all output events out.t have been renamed to $c.t$. Similarly, let $q(\mathrm{in} \leftarrow c)$ be the process where all input events in.t have been renamed to $c.t$. Then we define

$$p \gg q = hide_c(\ p(\mathrm{out} \leftarrow c) \parallel_\Delta q(\mathrm{in} \leftarrow c)\ )$$

where $\Delta = c.T$. This has the effect of connecting the output of p directly to the input of q, and then hiding the communications on the new channel. It allows the interaction of p with the environment by means of the input channel, and of q with the environment by means of the output channel. One can prove, as do Hoare, Brookes, and Roscoe, that if p and q are buffers, then so is $p \gg q$.

Now we want to consider the effect of recursive applications of the chaining operator. This will allow the definition of buffers with unbounded capacity. First, consider the one-place buffer B1, which inputs a value of type T, then outputs it, and repeats the process. It is easy to describe B1 as a transition system. In CSP, the process B1 would be expressed

$$*(?x.T \rightarrow\ !x).$$

As an example of a recursive definition, consider the equation

$$p = ?x.T \rightarrow (p \gg (!x \rightarrow \ \mathrm{B1}\ )).$$

Let $F(p)$ be the function of p denoted by the right-hand side of this equation. In the notation of Section 2, F would be defined

$$F(p) = \sigma : \mathrm{in}.T \rightarrow S(p,\sigma)$$

where

$$S(p,\mathrm{in}.t) = p \gg (\mathrm{out}.t \rightarrow \mathrm{B1}\ ).$$

Definition 3.2.1. A function F on transition systems is said to be *constructive* iff whenever $p\ E_n\ q$, it follows that $F(p)\ E_{n+1}\ F(q)$.

Lemma 3.2.2. The function F defined above is constructive. Furthermore, if p is a buffer, so is $F(p)$.

Proof. Omitted here, but see [HBR] for some details. It should be noted that the chaining operator involves hiding, which is in general a nonconstructive operation. Special properties of the function F must be used in the proof.

The significance of constructive functions lies in their metric space formulation.

Definition 3.2.3. Let F be a map from a metric space to itself. F is said to be *contractive* iff there is a number α with $0 \leq \alpha < 1$ such that for all x and y,

$$d(F(x), F(y)) \leq \alpha \cdot d(x,y).$$

Corollary 3.2.4. A function F is contractive in the E-metric iff it is constructive.

Now we recall the well-known Banach fixed-point theorem.

Theorem 3.2.5. Let F be a contractive mapping of a complete metric space to itself. Let B be a nonempty closed subset of the space. Suppose further that whenever $b \in B$, we have $F(b) \in B$. Then F has a unique fixed point which also belongs to B.

Putting all the above results together, and remembering that the space $\mathcal{T}/E$ is compact, and therefore complete, we deduce that the function F defined above has a unique fixed point, up to E-equivalence, and this fixed point is also a buffer. Many other examples of recursive constructions of buffers can be found in [HBR], and they can all be treated in this way.

4. A cpo for processes over an infinite alphabet

In [Rou] it is shown that the class of *synchronization forests* forms a complete partial order (in fact, a Scott domain) under reverse set inclusion. A synchronization forest is a collection of synchronization trees, and a synchronization tree is just a transition system whose graph is a tree. It is required in [Rou] that a synchronization forest be closed in the B-metric, and that a synchronization tree be over a finite alphabet with no silent transitions. Here we remove the latter two restrictions on synchronization trees, and we state our results for general transition systems.

One of the technical contributions in [Rou] was the construction of cpo-continuous functions from metrically continuous functions in the topology of synchronization trees. Specifically, it was shown that whenever F is a metrically continuous operation (unary, binary, etc.) on a compact metric space X, then the *direct image* map $\lambda K.F[K]$ is a cpo-continuous operation on the class of all nonempty closed subsets of X, ordered by reverse set inclusion. The topology used in [Rou] was the $\mathcal{B}$-metric topology, which is compact if the alphabet is finite. This topology is *not* compact in the case of an infinite alphabet, and so the question arises about the existence of a suitable extension theorem for the direct image mapping in the infinite alphabet case.

Our approach is to use the weaker Stone topology in order to retain the compactness property of the underlying space. Although this topology is metrizable, it is not necessary to use the metric! The topological definition of continuity (the inverse image of a closed set is closed) will suffice for our application, and in fact is extremely natural when used in conjunction with logical specifications.

As an example, we will use the synchronized composition operator. In what follows, the space X will be $\mathcal{T}/E$ with the Stone topology. Let $\Delta \subseteq \Sigma$ and let

$$F(p,q) = p \parallel_\Delta q.$$

It follows from Theorem 2.2.12 that E is a congruence with respect to this operation, and so F is well-defined on the space $X \times X$.

Lemma 4.1. The function F is a continuous map from $X \times X$ to X.

Proof. Recall that a basis for the topology of X is given by the collection of sets $\mathrm{Mod}(\theta)$, where $\theta \in L$. Let $\mathcal{B}$ be the collection of finite unions of sets of the form $\mathrm{Mod}(\theta_i) \times \mathrm{Mod}(\theta_j)$ as θ_i and θ_j range over L. Then $\mathcal{B}$ is a closed basis for the product space. It suffices to show that the inverse image of a basis set for X is a member of $\mathcal{B}$. We define, for a formula ϕ in L, the set

$$K(\phi) = \{\langle t,u\rangle : F(t,u) \models \phi\}.$$

We are required to show that $K(\phi) \in \mathcal{B}$ for all ϕ. This we do by induction on formulas. The result is clear for $\phi =$ tt , and if it holds for ϕ and ψ then it clearly holds for $\phi \vee \psi$. Consider the set $K(\neg\phi)$. By induction hypothesis, this is the complement of a set in $\mathcal{B}$. Therefore this set can be written as a finite intersection of sets of the form $U_i \cup U_j$, where

$$U_i = \{\langle t,u\rangle : t \models \neg\theta_i\}$$

and

$$U_j = \{\langle t,u\rangle : u \models \neg\theta_j\}.$$

By distributivity, the set can be rewritten as a finite union of sets of the form $U_i \cap U_j$. But

$$U_i \cap U_j = \mathrm{Mod}(\neg\theta_i) \times \mathrm{Mod}(\neg\theta_j),$$

and so $K(\neg\phi) \in \mathcal{B}$.

Finally, consider the case $\phi = \langle a \rangle \psi$. Suppose that $a \in \Delta$. Then

$$F(t,u) \models \langle a \rangle \psi \quad \text{iff} \quad \exists \langle t', u' \rangle : t \stackrel{a}{\Longrightarrow} t', \ u \stackrel{a}{\Longrightarrow} u', \text{ and } F(t',u') \models \psi.$$

Let

$$K(\psi) = \bigcup_{\langle i,j \rangle \in G} \mathrm{Mod}(\theta_i) \times \mathrm{Mod}(\theta_j)$$

where G is a finite set of pairs. Then

$$K(\langle a \rangle \psi) = \bigcup_{\langle i,j \rangle \in G} \mathrm{Mod}(\langle a \rangle \theta_i) \times \mathrm{Mod}(\langle a \rangle \theta_j).$$

Consider the case where $a \notin \Delta$. Then $F(t,u) \models \langle a \rangle \psi$ iff one of two subcases occurs:

$$\exists \langle t', u' \rangle : t \stackrel{a}{\Longrightarrow} t' \text{ and } u \stackrel{\Lambda}{\Longrightarrow} u', \text{ and } F(t',u') \models \psi,$$

or the subcase with the roles of t and u reversed. Let

$$K_1 = \bigcup_{\langle i,j \rangle \in G} \mathrm{Mod}(\langle a \rangle \theta_i) \times \mathrm{Mod}(\langle \Lambda \rangle \theta_j)$$

to account for the first subcase, and

$$K_2 = \bigcup_{\langle i,j \rangle \in G} \mathrm{Mod}(\langle \Lambda \rangle \theta_i) \times \mathrm{Mod}(\langle a \rangle \theta_j)$$

to account for the second. Then $K(\phi) = K_1 \cup K_2$. This completes the proof of Lemma 4.1.

We now state a general extension theorem. The proof is standard.

Theorem 4.2. Let F be a continuous function from a compact Hausdorff space Z to a space Y. Define, for a closed subset K of Z,

$$F[K] = \{F(z) : z \in K\}.$$

Let K_i be a decreasing sequence of closed nonempty subsets of Z. Then the intersection of all the K_i is nonempty, and

$$F\left[\bigcap K_i\right] = \bigcap F[K_i].$$

This result gives us a way to construct continuous functions on the cpo of closed subsets of a compact space like X. For binary operations like parallel composition, we can simply define

$$F(K_1, K_2) = F[K_1 \times K_2]$$

Since the space $X \times X$ is compact, the extension theorem applies with $Z = X \times X$ together with Lemma 4.1 to give cpo-continuous mappings. We have thus generalized the results of [Rou] to the infinite alphabet case.

References

[BaZ] J. W. de Bakker and J. F. Zucker, "Processes and the denotational semantics of concurrency," *Proc. 14th ACM Symp. on Theory of Computing*, 153–158.

[GR] W. Golson and W. Rounds, "Connections between two theories of concurrency: metric spaces and synchronization trees," Tech. Rep. CRL-TR-3-83, Computing Research Laboratory, University of Michigan, 1983 (to appear in *Inf. Control*)

[HM] M. Hennessy and R. Milner, "On observing Nondeterminism and Concurrency," *Proc. 7th ICALP*, LNCS **85** (1980).

[HBR] C. A. R. Hoare, S. D. Brookes, amd W. Roscoe, "A mathematical model for communicating processes," Report PRG-16, Programming Research Group, Oxford (1981). Also to appear in *JACM*.

[M] R. Milner, "A calculus of communicating systems," LNCS **92**, (1980).

[OH] E. Olderog and C. A. R. Hoare, "Specification-oriented semantics for communicating processes," *Proc. 10th ICALP*, LNCS **154** (1983), 561–572.

[Ros] W. Roscoe, "A mathematical theory of communicating processes," D.Phil. thesis, Oxford (1982).

[Rou] W. Rounds, "On the relationships between Scott domains, synchronization trees, and metric spaces," Tech. Rep. CRL-TR-25-83, Computing Research Laboratory, University of Michigan (1983).

[S] M. Smyth, "Power domains and predicate transformers: a topological view," *Proc. 10th ICALP*, LNCS **154** (1983), 662–675.

DENOTATIONAL MODELS BASED ON SYNCHRONOUSLY COMMUNICATING PROCESSES: REFUSAL, ACCEPTANCE, SAFETY

William G. Golson
Department of Computer Science
Rice University
Houston, Texas 77251

Abstract: An improvement to the *failures* model of concurrency is presented. We derive our model from first principles and show it to be a generalization of *failures*. Our approach gives rise to a natural treatment of the *hiding* operation not possible in the *failures* model. In addition, we employ the above technique to construct acceptance-refusal models leading to similar satisfactory treatments of *hiding*.

0. Introduction

One formulation of a denotational semantics for *CSP*-like languages [Hoa] is the *failures* model of Hoare, Brookes and Roscoe [HBR]. Despite the overall success of their approach, the treatment of *hiding* is not completely satisfying. *Hiding*, an operator which entails loss of information, behaves well in the *failures* model when applied to processes of finite character. In the general case, however, *hiding* leads to a greater loss of information than is actually necessary. In this paper we present a model, *failog*, which handles *hiding* smoothly and avoids any such loss.

Our model incorporates a more general notion of process than [HBR] and their model is readily embedded in ours. The distinctions between the two are instructive: [HBR] processes are precisely those *failog* processes which can be represented in a natural way by synchronization trees [Mil]. We feel requiring processes to be representable by synchronization trees is too stong a condition to impose and still obtain an informational preserving treatment of *hiding*. Indeed, under some mild assumptions, we show that no *hiding* operation can both preserve representability and continuity within our model. However, we also show our definition to be optimal in an informational preserving sense: any richer definition fails to be continuous. What we obtain is essentially a *hiding* operation which is more faithful to the operational interpretation of processes as transition systems [HBR], [RoB]. In addition, the usual process operations are continuous in *failog* and all, except *hiding*, preserve representability.

In another vein, the *failog* construction itself is an instance of a technique for generating denotational domains for synchronously communicating processes. The method involves constructing a logic specifying general behavioral characteristics and applying Scott's theory of information systems [Sco] to obtain a domain. The elements of this domain are interpreted over synchronization trees, which provide the underlying semantic models for the logics. To illustrate the technique, we present two additional constructions which take into account events acceptable as well as those refusable. The first, *acrelog*, deals with events that may be accepted, or are possible, while the second, *failsafe*, deals with events that must be accepted, or are safe. We compare these models to the *acceptance-refusal machine* model (*ARM*) of Rounds and Brookes [RoB], which arose as an extension of the *failures* model to treat acceptances. Their model, which handles a wide range of operations but excludes *hiding*, turns out to be a strengthening of the *failsafe* construction: their processes are a proper subclass of the *failsafe* processes representable by synchronization trees. Finally, continuous process operations for both our models are presented, and, as with the *failog* case, *hiding* is treated satisfactorily.

The paper is divided into two parts, with Sections 1 through 5 dealing with the *failog* and *failures* models, and Sections 6 through 10 with the acceptance-refusal models. Proofs are omitted throughout; see [Gol] for details.

1. The Failures Model

The *failures* approach to modeling concurrency [HBR] adopts the nondeterministic transition system as its underlying operational model. Both the state set and alphabet are countable, and empty string transitions are allowed. The alphabet, Σ, represents the collection of observable *events*, indivisible and instantaneous; empty transitions represent hidden, internal actions. A sequence of events, $x \in \Sigma^*$, is referred to as a *trace*, and for two states U and V, the transition relation $U \xrightarrow{x} V$ indicates that, after executing trace x from state U, it is possible to arrive in state V. Naturally, in proceeding from U to V, the transition system may have taken a finite number of empty transitions.

The behavior of the transition system with respect to U is characterized as follows. Let x be executed from state U. After execution, if a subset of events is impossible for the system to do next, either immediately or after any finite number of empty transitions, then the subset is *refusable* by the system at that point. This set of events is a *refusal* set of U *after* x. The behavior of this transition system with respect to U is represented in [HBR] by a suitable collection of trace-refusal set pairs. Let

$$P(U) = \{\langle x,R\rangle \mid x \in \Sigma^*,\ R \in p\Sigma, \text{ and } \exists V\ U \xrightarrow{x} V \text{ where } Init(V) \cap R = \varnothing\}.$$

Here $p\Sigma$ is the collection of finite subsets of Σ, and $Init(V) = \{a \in \Sigma \mid \exists W\ V \xrightarrow{a} W\}$. For $\langle x,R\rangle \in P(U)$, we say that after tracing out x from U, it is possible for the system to be in a state where it must refuse to do every event in R. [HBR] takes the characterization above as essentially defining the external, observable behavior of a process:

Definition [HBR]: A *process* is a relation P over $\Sigma^* \times p\Sigma$ satisfying

(P1) $\langle \Lambda,\varnothing\rangle \in P$ where Λ is the empty string
(P2) $\langle xy,\varnothing\rangle \in P \Rightarrow \langle x,\varnothing\rangle \in P$
(P3) $\langle x,R\rangle \in P \Rightarrow \forall U \subseteq R\ \langle x,U\rangle \in P$
(P4) $\langle x,R\rangle \in P$ and $\langle xa,\varnothing\rangle \notin P \Rightarrow \langle x,R\cup\{a\}\rangle \in P$.

Therefore any process is nonempty (P1) and by (P2) any prefix of any possible trace of P is also possible. By (P3) if R is refusable after x, then so is any subset of R. (P4) stipulates that if xa is not a trace of P but x is, then a must be refusable in every context possible after x.

[HBR] establishes that the set of all processes under reverse inclusion forms a complete partial order (cpo), where $P \supseteq Q$ is interpreted to mean that P is more nondeterministic than Q. The bottom element of the cpo, denoted by *CHAOS*, is the most nondeterministic process: every trace can be executed and every finite set is refusable after every trace. Deterministic processes, those derivable from deterministic transition systems, are the total elements of the cpo. The standard set of concurrent process operations are defined and proven continuous with respect to this model.

Unfortunately, *hiding* in [HBR] destroys too much information. Our consequent efforts to avoid this loss have led to a different approach to the problem. The result is a more general concept of process than [HBR], leading to a domain within which a natural view of *hiding* is well treated and relevant information is preserved.

The remaining sections of this part are organized as follows. The next presents preliminary material concerning information systems. The *failog* model is constructed in Section 3 and Section 4 deals with *hiding*. The fifth section presents the remaining process operations.

2. Information Systems

In [Sco] Scott introduces *information systems* as a means for simplifying the basic ideas underlying the denotational approach to semantics. Within an information system, the denoted objects or elements are represented by the collection of propositions deducible about them. An information system is a structure which deals with consistent collections of propositions and induces a cpo with elements as the denoted objects.

Definition (Information System) [Sco]:

An information system is a structure $(D,\theta,Con,\vdash)$

where	D is a set	(of data objects)
	$\theta \in D$	(the least informative member of D)
	$Con \subseteq pD$	(the consistent sets)
	$\vdash \subseteq Con \times D$	(the entailment relation)

and Con and $\vdash$ satisfy the following properites for $\Gamma \in Con$ and $\varphi,\psi \in D$:

(i) $\Delta \in Con$ for $\Delta \subseteq \Gamma$
(ii) $\{\varphi\} \in Con$
(iii) $\Gamma \vdash \varphi \Rightarrow \Gamma \cup \{\varphi\} \in Con$
(iv) $\Gamma \vdash \theta$
(v) $\varphi \in \Gamma \Rightarrow \Gamma \vdash \varphi$
(vi) $\Gamma \vdash \varphi$ for all $\varphi \in \Delta$ and $\Delta \vdash \psi \Rightarrow \Gamma \vdash \psi$.

The definition requires that (i) subsets of consistent sets are consistent, (ii) each data object forms a consistent set, (iii) adding an object to a consistent set entailing it preserves consistency, (iv) the least informative element is entailed by any consistent set, (v) any consistent set entails its members and (vi) the entailment relation is transitive.

Definition (Elements) [Sco]:

The *elements* of an information system $(D,\theta,Con,\vdash)$ are those subsets Δ of D such that

(i) all finite subsets of Δ are in Con, and
(ii) Δ is closed under entailment:

$$\Gamma \in p\Delta \text{ and } \Gamma \vdash \varphi \Rightarrow \varphi \in \Delta.$$

An element represents a complete consistent informational description and corresponds to a member of a semantic domain. Elements which are contained in no other element (in the sense of set inclusion) are total, otherwise partial. The payoff for formulating a problem as an information system is the following:

Proposition [Sco]:

For any information system, the set of elements with set inclusion forms a cpo.

3. Failog Construction (FAIlure LOGic)

The logic *failog* is defined as follows. We assume Σ is finite throughout.

Definition (*Failog*):

failog formulas are of two types:

Type 1 formulas (T_1):
$tt \in T_1$
$a \in \Sigma \Rightarrow \eta a \in T_1$
$\varphi, \psi \in T_1 \Rightarrow \varphi \wedge \psi \in T_1$

Type 2 formulas (T_2):
$\varphi \in T_1, x \in \Sigma^* \Rightarrow \langle x\rangle\varphi \in T_2$.

Here tt represents the truth constant, ηa is to be read "never a" or "a is refusable", and $\langle x\rangle\varphi$ is to be read "it is possible to execute trace x and have φ be true afterward". We note that formulas of *failog* do not have such forms as $\langle x\rangle\varphi\wedge\langle y\rangle\psi$ or $\langle x\rangle\langle y\rangle\varphi$.

For the semantics we shall use synchronization trees [Mil] as models, taking our arc labels from $\Sigma\cup\{\tau\}$. Σ is the set of visible, observable events and $\tau\notin\Sigma$ represents the internal transition. The outdegree at any node may be countably infinite, a departure from [Mil], and outgoing arcs from any node may have the same label. We define $\longrightarrow$ and *Init* as with transition systems. We will when convenient write $\sum\delta_i S_i$ with $\delta_i\in\Sigma\cup\{\tau\}$ to represent the trees S_i prefixed with δ_i and joined at the root. When we write $S + T$ we mean the tree with S and T joined at the root. For example, $a + b$ represents the tree whose root has two arcs with labels a and b. The tree *nil* consists of just the root.

Definition (*Semantics of Failog*):

Let S be a synchronization tree. Then

$S \models tt$ always
$S \models \eta a \Leftrightarrow a \notin Init(S)$
$S \models \varphi \wedge \psi \Leftrightarrow S \models \varphi$ and $S \models \psi$
$S \models \langle x\rangle\varphi \Leftrightarrow \exists S \xrightarrow{x} S' \models \varphi$.

Here we have used $\exists S \xrightarrow{x} S' \models \varphi$ to abbreviate $\exists S'\ S \xrightarrow{x} S' \wedge S' \models \varphi$. Since $\varphi\in T_1$ means φ is the finite conjunction of zero or more terms of the form ηa, we introduce the notation

$$\eta R = \begin{cases} tt & \text{when } R = \emptyset. \\ \eta a_1 \wedge \ldots \wedge \eta a_n & \text{when } R = \{a_1, \ldots, a_n\}. \end{cases}$$

Since clearly $\eta a \wedge \eta a$ is equivalent to ηa, we shall adopt $\langle x\rangle\eta R$ as our *normal form* for Type 2 formulas.

We proceed next to formulate *failog* as an information system. See [Rou] for a similar construction using a logic due to Hennessy and Milner.

Definition (Failog Information System):

Let $(D, \langle\rangle tt, Con, \vdash)$ be a structure where

$D = \{\varphi \in T_2 \mid \exists S \models \varphi\}$	
$\langle\rangle tt$	is the least informative element
$Con = \{\Gamma \in pD \mid \exists S \models \Gamma\}$	
$\Gamma \vdash \varphi$ iff $\forall S \models \Gamma\ S \models \varphi$	for $\Gamma \in Con,\ \varphi \in D$.

Above we abbreviate by $S \models \Gamma$ the expression $\forall \psi \in \Gamma\ S \models \psi$. Note that only formulas of Type 2 are permitted as data objects. Indeed we have an information system. D is the set of formulas of Type 2 and Con is pD.

Our setting so far is too abstract. As we wish to know more about the concrete structure of *failog* elements, our next goal is to characterize entailment in terms of the constituents of consistent subsets.

Theorem (Failog Entailment Characterization):

For $\Gamma \in Con$:

(E1) $\Gamma \vdash \langle\rangle tt$ always

(E2) $\Gamma \vdash \langle x\rangle tt \Leftrightarrow \exists y \exists \varphi\ \langle xy\rangle \varphi \in \Gamma$

(E3) $\Gamma \vdash \langle x\rangle \eta R \Leftrightarrow \exists U \supseteq R\ \langle x\rangle \eta U \in \Gamma$ $\qquad (R \neq \emptyset)$.

Now we get our characterization of elements by the following:

Theorem: (Failog Elements)

Δ is an element just when

(F1) $\langle\rangle tt \in \Delta$

(F2) $\langle xy\rangle tt \in \Delta \Rightarrow \langle x\rangle tt \in \Delta$

(F3) $\langle x\rangle \eta U \in \Delta \Rightarrow \langle x\rangle \eta R \in \Delta$ $\qquad$ for any $\emptyset \subseteq R \subseteq U$.

As synchronization trees have been adopted as our underlying models of process behavior, we wish to determine exactly when an element completely describes a tree, i.e. is precisely the collection of all propositions true about a specific tree. For example, over an alphabet $\{a,b\}$ the element $\{\langle\rangle tt\}$ completely describes no one tree while

$$\{\langle\rangle tt, \langle\rangle \eta a, \langle\rangle \eta b, \langle\rangle \eta a \wedge \eta b\}$$

completely describes the *nil* tree, up to equivalence. We begin with a definition.

Definition: Δ is *representable* by S just when

$$\Delta = Th(S) =_{df} \{\varphi \in T_2 \mid S \models \varphi\}.$$

The reader who suspects a strong connection between (P1)–(P3) and (F1)–(F3) may expect the following

Theorem (Representation of Failog Elements by STs):

Δ is representable iff

(F4) $\langle x\rangle \eta R \in \Delta$ and $\langle xa\rangle tt \notin \Delta \Rightarrow \langle x\rangle \eta (R \cup \{a\}) \in \Delta$.

A similar result between *bounded* synchronization trees (trees with bounded path length) and *bounded failure* processes (processes which have a finite global bound on their trace length) is established in [Bro].

As it is clear that $<x>\eta R \equiv <y>\eta U$ iff $x=y$ and $R=U$, it is easy to see that the *failures* and *failog* representations are isomorphic under the correspondence

$$<x>\eta R \leftrightarrow <x,R>$$

and that (P1)–(P4) correspond to (F1)–(F4). So we take as our

Definition (*Failog Process*):

A *process* is a relation over $\Sigma^* \times p\Sigma$ satisfying (P1)–(P3). A *full* process also satisfies (P4).

So <*processes*, $\subseteq$> is the cpo induced by the information system. It is a complete lattice, with bottom element $\{<\Lambda,\emptyset>\}$ and top element $CHAOS=\{<x,R> \mid x\in\Sigma^*, R\in p\Sigma\}$. The *failures* model of [HBR] is a complete semilattice with bottom element *CHAOS*, and total elements corresponding to processes representable by the unfolding of deterministic transition systems. Their cpo is precisely <*full processes*, $\supseteq$>.

4. Hiding

Hiding is a process operation which has the effect of internalizing an event, effectively removing it from the observable alphabet. One natural definition for *hiding* applied to synchronization trees is to relabel the appropriate event wherever it occurs with the empty transition τ, that is, we write $S[\tau/b]$ for S after hiding the event b. If we let $P(S)$ be the (full) process represented by S, i.e.

$$P(S)=\{<x,R> \mid \exists S \xrightarrow{x} S' \text{ and } Init(S')\cap R=\emptyset\},$$

then we could try as our canonical definition of *hiding* for full processes

Definition (*Canonical Hiding*):

$$P(S)\backslash_c b =_{df} P(S[\tau/b]) = \{<x,R> \mid \exists S[\tau/b] \xrightarrow{x} S'[\tau/b] \text{ and } Init(S'[\tau/b])\cap R=\emptyset\}.$$

We note that canonical *hiding* is not well defined on arbitrary full processes. As an illustration, let $S=bS_1+bS_2$ where $S_1=a+bS_1$ and $S_2=c+bS_2$ and let $T=bT_1+bT_2$ where $T_1=a+b(c+bT_1)$ and $T_2=c+b(a+bT_2)$. S is a tree with two b^ω-paths, one path having an a branch at every node away from the root, the other path offering c at every node away from the root. T also possesses two b^ω-paths, the first alternating choices of first a then c, the second c then a. It is not difficult to see that $P(S)=P(T)$. However $P(S)\backslash_c b$ is representable by $\tau a+\tau c$ and $P(T)\backslash_c b$ by $a+c$. Therefore canonical *hiding* does *not* preserve failure equivalence, i.e.

$$P(S)\backslash_c b \neq P(T)\backslash_c b.$$

However canonical *hiding* is well defined with respect to failure equivalence on bounded trees:

Theorem: For bounded S,

$$P(S)\backslash_c b = hide(P(S),b) =_{df} \{<x\backslash b,R> \mid <x,R\cup\{b\}>\in P(S)\}$$

where $x\backslash b$ is x with the occurrences of b removed.

This characterization is motivated by

Definition (*Hiding* [HBR]):

$$P\backslash_H b = \{<x\backslash b,R> \mid <x,R\cup\{b\}>\in P\} \cup \{<(x\backslash b)y,R> \mid \forall n\ xb^n\in dom(P) \text{ and } <y,R>\in CHAOS\}.$$

The effect of $\backslash_H$ is to behave like canonical *hiding* in favorable situations and to reduce to *CHAOS* in unfavorable ones. For example, consider the process

$$B^\omega = \{<b^n,R> \mid n\geq 0 \text{ and } R\subseteq\Sigma-\{b\}\},$$

which is representable by the tree with the infinite path b^ω. Now since $B^\omega\backslash_H b=CHAOS$, the knowledge that b can *no longer occur* after it is hidden is lost. Despite this drawback, $\backslash_H$ is continuous with respect to <*full processes*,$\supseteq$> and it is not evident whether alternative definitions are available for this model which satisfy the necessary properties.

In the *failures* model, process operations necessarily must preserve full processhood. For *failog*, operations do not have to preserve fullness and indeed, under some natural assumptions, *hiding* cannot and still be continuous. For example, assume *hiding* both acts canonically on bounded trees and is continuous with respect to <*processes*,$\subseteq$>. Let $\Sigma=\{a,b\}$ and let S be the tree $S=\tau a+\tau bS$. We can write $P(S)=\bigcup P(S_i)$ where $S_0=\tau a$ and $S_{n+1}=\tau a+\tau bS_n$, i.e.

$$P(S) = Cl_\vdash\{<b^m,\{a\}>,<b^m,\{b\}>,<b^m a,\{a,b\}> \mid m\geq 0\}$$

and

$$P(S_0) = Cl_\vdash\{<\Lambda,\{b\}>,<a,\{a,b\}>\}$$

$$P(S_{n+1}) = P(S_n) \cup \{<b^{n+1},\{b\}>,<b^{n+1}a,\{a,b\}>,<b^n,\{a\}>\}$$

$$= \{<b^{m+1},\{b\}>,<b^{m+1}a,\{a,b\}>,<b^m,\{a\}> \mid m\leq n\},$$

where $Cl_\vdash$ closure under $\vdash$. Since *hiding* is assumed canonical on bounded trees,

$$\forall n\ P(S_n)\backslash b = Cl_\vdash\{<\Lambda,\{b\}>,<a,\{a,b\}>\} = P(a).$$

Therefore by continuity $P(S)\backslash b=P(a)$. Consider again the process

$$B^\omega = \{<b^n,R> \mid n\geq 0 \text{ and } R\subseteq\Sigma-\{b\}\} = Cl_\vdash\{<b^n,\{a\}> \mid n\geq 0\}.$$

The only feasible trace in $B^\omega\backslash b$ is Λ, and so if *hiding* preserves fullness, $B^\omega\backslash b=Cl_\vdash\{<\Lambda,\{a,b\}>\}$. As $B^\omega\subseteq P(S)$, by continuity we must have $B^\omega\backslash b\subseteq P(S)\backslash b$; however this relation does not hold.

For our definition of *hiding* we take the canonical part and preserve the knowledge that the hidden event is refusable after any possible trace:

Definition (*Failog Hiding*):

$$P\backslash b = \{<x\backslash b,R> \mid <x,R\cup\{b\}>\in P\} \cup \{<x\backslash b,R> \mid R\subseteq\{b\} \text{ and } x\in dom(P)\}.$$

Note that if P is representable by a bounded tree, then $P\backslash b=P\backslash_c b$, for $<x\backslash b,\{b\}>\in P\backslash_c b$. That this clause makes a positive contribution in the general case is seen from $B^\omega\backslash b=Cl_\vdash\{<\Lambda,\{b\}>\}$ where $B^\omega\backslash_H b=CHAOS$. Note that although $B^\omega\backslash b$ is not full, it contains more informational content than *CHAOS*.

Hiding enjoys the necessary properties:

Theorem: *Hiding* preserves processhood and is continuous with respect to <*processes*,$\subseteq$>.

As we have seen, *hiding* does not preserve fullness, and indeed no definition can be expected to. However, given that a *hiding* operation is to both behave canonically on bounded processes and be continuous, our definition turns out to be optimal:

Theorem: Let $H(P,b)$ be an operator that behaves like canonical *hiding* on bounded trees and is contínous with respect to $\langle processes, \subseteq \rangle$. If $H(P,b) \supseteq P \backslash b$, that is, H contains at least the informational content of $\backslash$, then $H(P,b) = P \backslash b$.

5. Additional Process Operations

We present the usual collection of process operations. Syntactically our language is as follows:

$$P ::= a \mid a \rightarrow P \mid P \text{ or } P \mid P \square P \mid P \parallel P \mid P \parallel\!| P \mid \mu x.F(x) \mid P \backslash a.$$

The language statement a represents the process

$$\{\langle \Lambda, R \rangle \mid R \in p(\Sigma - \{a\})\} \cup \{\langle a, R \rangle \mid R \in p\Sigma\}.$$

All operations, except *hiding*, are as defined in [HBR] and are continuous with respect to the *failog* model and preserve full processhood. The details are straightforward and omitted here. For reference we present the definitions.

Prefixing $\quad a \rightarrow P = \{\langle \Lambda, R \rangle \mid a \notin R \text{ and } R \in p\Sigma\} \cup \{\langle ax, R \rangle \mid \langle x, R \rangle \in P\}.$

Nondeterministic Choice $\quad P \text{ or } Q = P \cup Q.$

Conditional Choice $\quad P \square Q = \{\langle \Lambda, R \rangle \mid \langle \Lambda, R \rangle \in P \cap Q\} \cup \{\langle x, R \rangle \mid x \neq \Lambda \text{ and } \langle x, R \rangle \in P \cup Q\}.$

Intersection $\quad P \parallel Q = \{\langle x, R \cup U \rangle \mid \langle x, R \rangle \in P \text{ and } \langle x, U \rangle \in Q\}.$

Interleaving $\quad P \parallel\!| Q = \{\langle z, R \rangle \mid z \in x \Delta y \text{ and } \langle x, R \rangle \in P \text{ and } \langle y, R \rangle \in Q\},$
where Δ is the string shuffle operator.

Recursion $\quad$ Given a continuous function F, the expression $\mu x.F(x)$ represents the least (with respect to inclusion) process P such that $P = F(P)$.

6. Introduction to Acceptance/Refusal Models of Process Behavior

To our notion of process behavior we wish to incorporate the additional information concerning sets of events acceptable at a certain juncture as well as those events refusable. We investigate two formulations of acceptance: an event set if *acceptable* at a certain point if every event in the set *may* be accepted at that point, whereas an event set is *safe* at a certain point if events in the set *must* be accepted at that point. If a set is acceptable, it may still be possible to deadlock on some of the events due to certain sequences of internal transitions. However safety ensures that an event cannot be refused at that point. Whereas refusability is preserved through internal transitions, acceptability and safety are not, but are rather transitory properties which may no longer hold after internal computations.

We construct two systems, *acrelog* and *failsafe*, reflecting these notions. They turn out to be very closely related, both to each other and to the *acceptance-refusal machine* (*ARM*) model of Rounds and Brookes [RoB]. *ARM* processes are readily seen to be a subclass of the full *failsafe* processes.

The remainder of this part is organized as follows. The *acrelog* construction is presented first, based on a suitable formalization of acceptance, and we characterize representability. Section 8 presents the *ARM* model of [RoB]. The *failsafe* construction, directly motivated as an attempt to reconcile the differences between the *ARM* and *acrelog* models, is developed. In the ninth and tenth sections, the *acrelog* and *failsafe* process operations are presented. *Hiding*, as expected, does not preserve fullness in either case, but it is continuous and preserves processhood.

7. Acrelog Construction (ACceptance/REfusal LOGic)

The *acrelog* construction is defined as follows. Again we assume Σ is finite throughout.

Definition (Acrelog):

acrelog formulas are of two types:

Type 1 formulas (T_1):
$tt \in T_1$
$a \in \Sigma \Rightarrow \eta a \in T_1$ and $\rho a \in T_1$
$\varphi, \psi \in T_1 \Rightarrow \varphi \wedge \psi \in T_1$

Type 2 formulas (T_2):
$\varphi \in T_1, x \in \Sigma^* \Rightarrow \langle x\rangle\varphi \in T_2$.

The readings here are the same as in the *failog* case, with the addition that ρa is to be read "possibly a" or, alternatively, "a is acceptable". Again we use synchronization trees to express our semantics:

Definition (Semantics of Acrelog):

Let S be a synchronization tree. Then

$S \models tt$ always
$S \models \eta a \Leftrightarrow a \notin Init(S)$
$S \models \rho a \Leftrightarrow a \in Init(S)$
$S \models \varphi \wedge \psi \Leftrightarrow S \models \varphi$ and $S \models \psi$
$S \models \langle x\rangle\varphi \Leftrightarrow \exists S \xrightarrow{x} S' \models \varphi$.

We note the following identities: $\rho a \equiv \langle\rangle\rho a$, $\langle x\rangle\rho a \equiv \langle xa\rangle tt$.

As might be expected, *acrelog* is more expressive than *failog*. For example, $\tau+\tau(a+b)$ and $b+\tau(a+\tau)$ are equivalent in *failog* but are distinguishable in *acrelog* by $\langle\rangle(\rho a \wedge \eta b)$.

Since $\varphi \in T_1$ means φ is a finite conjunction of terms of the form ρa and ηb, we shall as before adopt the notations ρA and ηR and write $\langle x\rangle(\rho A \wedge \eta R)$. The preceding can be written without ambiguity as $\langle x\rangle\rho A \wedge \eta R$, a format which we will adopt as our *normal form* for T_2 formulas.

Definition (Acrelog Information System):

Let $(D, \langle\rangle tt, Con, \vdash)$ be a structure where

$D = \{\varphi \in T_2 \mid \exists S \models \varphi\}$
$\langle\rangle tt$ is the least informative element

$Con = \{\Gamma \in pD \mid \exists S \models \Gamma\}$
$\Gamma \vdash \varphi$ iff $\forall S \models \Gamma \; S \models \varphi$ for $\Gamma \in Con$, $\varphi \in D$.

Again only formulas of Type 2 are permitted as data objects. D and Con are characterized as follows:

Lemma: (i) $<x>\rho A \wedge \eta R \in D \Leftrightarrow R \cap A = \varnothing$
(ii) $Con = pD$

The structure, $(D, <>tt, Con, \vdash)$, is readily seen to be an information system. As with *failog*, we characterize entailment:

Theorem (Acrelog Entailment Characterization):

For $\Gamma \in Con$

(AE1) $\Gamma \vdash <>tt$ always
(AE2) $\Gamma \vdash <xa>tt \Leftrightarrow \exists \varphi \exists y <xay>\varphi \in \Gamma$ or $\exists A' \exists R' \; a \in A'$ and $<x>\rho A' \wedge \eta R' \in \Gamma$
(AE3) $\Gamma \vdash <x>\rho a \Leftrightarrow \Gamma \vdash <xa>tt$
(AE4) $\Gamma \vdash <>\rho A \Leftrightarrow \forall a \in A \; \Gamma \vdash <>\rho a$
(AE5) $\Gamma \vdash <x>\rho A \Leftrightarrow \exists A' \supseteq A \; \exists R' <x>\rho A' \wedge \eta R' \in \Gamma$, when $x \neq \Lambda$ and $|A|>1$
(AE6) $\Gamma \vdash <x>\rho A \wedge \eta R \Leftrightarrow \exists A' \supseteq A \exists R' \supseteq R <x>\rho A' \wedge \eta R' \in \Gamma$, when $R \neq \varnothing$.

To better understand the characterization, e.g. (AE4) and (AE5), note that it must account for the following. Suppose $S \models <>\rho a$ and $S \models <>\rho b$. Then $S \models <>\rho a \wedge \rho b$ as $\{a,b\} \subseteq Init(S)$, or both events are possible at the root. However when $x \neq \Lambda$, it does not follow that $S \models <x>\rho a \wedge \rho b$ if both $S \models <x>\rho a$ and $S \models <x>\rho b$.

Our elements are characterized by the following

Theorem (Acrelog Elements):

Δ is an element just when

(A1) $<>tt \in \Delta$
(A2) $<xa>tt \in \Delta \Rightarrow <x>tt \in \Delta$
(A3) $<x>\rho a \in \Delta \Leftrightarrow <xa>tt \in \Delta$
(A4) $<x>\rho A \wedge \eta R \in \Delta \Rightarrow \forall A' \subseteq A, R' \subseteq R \;\; <x>\rho A' \wedge \eta R' \in \Delta$
(A5) $\forall a \in A <>\rho a \in \Delta \Rightarrow <>\rho A \in \Delta$.

As in the *failog* case we say

Definition: Δ is *representable* by a synchronization tree S just when

$$\Delta = Th(S) =_{df} \{\varphi \in T_2 \mid S \models \varphi\}.$$

For *acrelog*, representability of Δ corresponds to the fact that at any point in a synchronization tree an event is either acceptable or refusable:

Theorem (Representation of Acrelog Elements by STs):

Δ is representable $\Leftrightarrow$
(A6) $<x>\rho A \wedge \eta R \in \Delta \Rightarrow \forall a \in \Sigma <x>\rho A \wedge \rho a \wedge \eta R \in \Delta$ or $<x>\rho A \wedge \eta R \wedge \eta a \in \Delta$.

We are now ready to formally define our *acrelog* processes. In order to facilitate what follows, we change our representation in a manner similar to the *failog* case, i.e., we now represent $<x>\rho A\wedge\eta R$ by the triple $<x,A,R>$ with the conventions that $<x>tt$ is represented by $<x,\emptyset,\emptyset>$, $<x>\rho a$ by $<x,\{a\},\emptyset>$, etc.

Definition (Acrelog Process):

An *acrelog process* is a relation over $\Sigma^* \times p\Sigma \times p\Sigma$ satifying (suitably modified forms of) (A1)–(A5). In addition a *full* process also satisfies (A6).

By modified forms, we mean, for example, in the case of (A4):

$$<x,A,R>\in\Delta \Rightarrow \forall A'\subseteq A\ \forall R'\subseteq R\ <x,A',R'>\in\Delta.$$

The cpo induced by the information system, $<$*acrelog processes*$,\subseteq>$, is a complete lattice with bottom element $\{<\Lambda,\emptyset>\}$ and top element

$$\{<x,A,R> \mid x\in\Sigma^*,\ A\in p\Sigma,\ R\in p\Sigma,\ A\cap R=\emptyset\}.$$

8. A Comparison with the ARM Model and the Failsafe Construction

We now compare our construction to the *acceptance-refusal-machine* (*ARM*) model of Rounds and Brookes [RoB]. A primary concern of [RoB] was their *possible-futures* model of process behavior; the *ARM* construction arose as a suitable representation for (equivalence classes of) possible-futures processes in a denotational domain, admitting an array of concurrent operations but omitting *hiding*.

Definition [RoB] (ARM Machines):

An *ARM* is a relation M on $\Sigma^* \times p\Sigma \times p\Sigma$ satisfying

(ARM0) $<x,A,R>\in M \Rightarrow A\cap R=\emptyset$
(ARM1) $dom(M)$ is nonempty and prefixed closed
(ARM2) $\{a\in\Sigma \mid xa\in dom(M)\} = \bigcup\ \{A \mid \exists R\ <x,A,R>\in M\}$
(ARM3) $<x,A,R>\in M,\ A'\subseteq A,\ R'\subseteq R \Rightarrow <x,A',R'>\in M$
(ARM4) $<x,A,R>\in M,\ a\in\Sigma \Rightarrow <x,A\cup\{a\},R>\in M$ or $<x,A,R\cup\{a\}>\in M$.

It is easy to see that an *ARM* relation is just a full *acrelog* process with condition (A5) relaxed. The significance of the difference between these two constructions can be seen in the *failsafe* model below based on safety, a stricter notion of acceptance: a set of events is said to be *safe* after x if it is possible for a process to arrive in a state after x in which no event in the set can be refused. The conditions (ARM0)-(ARM3) (or (A1)-(A4)) characterize the elements *failsafe*. Representability is not (A6) but turns out to be somewhat weaker due to the fact that although any event at any point is either acceptable or refusable, this property no longer holds with respect to safety and refusability. Although [RoB] interprets acceptability similar to *acrelog*, we contend their model is closer in spirit to *failsafe*. Indeed, their processes are a proper subclass of the full *failsafe* processes.

Definition (FAILure/SAFEty logic):

failsafe formulas are of two types:

Type 1 formulas (T_1):
$tt \in T_1$
$a \in \Sigma \Rightarrow \eta a \in T_1$ and $\sigma a \in T_1$
$\varphi,\ \psi \in T_1 \Rightarrow \varphi \wedge \psi \in T_1$

Type 2 formulas (T_2):

$$\varphi \in T_1,\ x \in \Sigma^* \Rightarrow \langle x\rangle\varphi \in T_2.$$

Here σa should be read "a is safe". For the semantics we need some preliminary definitions.

Definitions: (i) a is *immediate* at S if the root of S has an arc with label a.

(ii) $a \in Safe(S) \Leftrightarrow$

$$\forall S'\ S \xrightarrow{\Lambda} S'\ a \notin Init(S') \Rightarrow \exists S''\ S \xrightarrow{\Lambda} S'' \text{ and } S'' \xrightarrow{\Lambda} S' \text{ and } a \text{ is immediate at } S'',$$

that is, any τ-path from S contains a node at which a is immediate.

Definition (*Semantics of Failsafe*):

Let S be a synchronization tree. Then

$S \models tt$ always
$S \models \eta a \Leftrightarrow a \notin Init(S)$
$S \models \sigma a \Leftrightarrow a \in Safe(S)$
$S \models \varphi \wedge \psi \Leftrightarrow S \models \varphi$ and $S \models \psi$
$S \models \langle x\rangle\varphi \Leftrightarrow \exists S \xrightarrow{x} S' \models \varphi.$

Note that $S \models \langle x\rangle\sigma a \Leftrightarrow S \models \langle x\rangle\rho a$ and that $\langle x\rangle\sigma a \equiv \langle xa\rangle tt$. Unlike *acrelog*, $\sigma a \not\equiv \langle\rangle\sigma a$. Safety and acceptance differ when dealing with sets of more than one event. For example if $S=\tau a+\tau b$ then $S \models \langle\rangle\sigma a$ and $S \models \langle\rangle\sigma b$ but $S \not\models \langle\rangle\sigma a \wedge \sigma b$. Of course $S \models \langle\rangle\rho a \wedge \rho b$.

As before we shall adopt $\langle x\rangle\sigma A \wedge \eta R$ as our *normal forms* for Type 2 formulas.

Definition (*Failsafe Information System*):

Let $(D, \langle\rangle tt, Con, \vdash)$ be a structure where

$D = \{\varphi \in T_2 \mid \exists S \models \varphi\}$	
$\langle\rangle tt$	is the least informative element
$Con = \{\Gamma \in pD \mid \exists S \models \Gamma\}$	
$\Gamma \vdash \varphi$ iff $\forall S \models \Gamma\ S \models \varphi$	for $\Gamma \in Con,\ \varphi \in D$.

Only formulas of Type 2 are permitted as data objects. D and Con have the same characterization as in *acrelog*:

Lemma: (i) $\langle x\rangle\sigma A \wedge \eta R \in D \Leftrightarrow R \cap A = \varnothing$
(ii) $Con = pD$

and $(D, \langle\rangle tt, Con, \vdash)$ is an information system.

The entailment characterization is somewhat simpler than *acrelog* as there are no special dispensations for the empty string:

Theorem (*Failsafe Entailment Characterization*):

For $\Gamma \in Con$

(FE1) $\Gamma\vdash<>tt$ always
(FE2) $\Gamma\vdash<xa>tt \Leftrightarrow \exists\varphi\exists y <xay>\varphi\in\Gamma$ or $\exists A'\exists R'$ $a\in A'$ and $<x>\sigma A'\wedge\eta R'\in\Gamma$
(FE3) $\Gamma\vdash<x>\sigma a \Leftrightarrow \Gamma\vdash<xa>tt$
(FE4) $\Gamma\vdash<x>\sigma A \Leftrightarrow \exists A'\supseteq A\ \exists R'\ <x>\sigma A'\wedge\eta R'\in\Gamma$, when $|A|>1$
(FE5) $\Gamma\vdash <x>\sigma A\wedge\eta R \Leftrightarrow \exists A'\supseteq A\exists R'\supseteq R\ <x>\sigma A'\wedge\eta R'\in\Gamma$, when $R\neq\emptyset$.

Theorem (*Failsafe Elements*):

Δ is an element just when

(S1) $<>tt\in\Delta$
(S2) $<xa>tt\in\Delta \Rightarrow <x>tt\in\Delta$
(S3) $<x>\sigma a\in\Delta \Leftrightarrow <xa>tt\in\Delta$
(S4) $<x>\sigma A\wedge\eta R\in\Delta \Rightarrow \forall A'\subseteq A, R'\subseteq R\ <x>\sigma A'\wedge\eta R'\in\Delta$

As (S1)−(S4) are analogous to (A1)−(A4), *failsafe* elements are *acrelog* elements with (A5) removed.

The appropriate notion of representability in *failsafe* must be somewhat more general than for *acrelog*. In *acrelog* it is always the case that at any point an event is either acceptable or refusable. However for *failsafe*, an event can be neither safe nor refusable but rather simply just *possible*, that is, it will eventually become safe. As an example, consider the tree $a+\tau(\tau b+\tau)$. At the root b is neither refusable nor safe.

The representability condition is best motivated by considering for each $x\in dom(\Delta)$,

$$max(x) = \{<A,R> \mid <x>\sigma A\wedge\eta R\in\Delta \text{ and } <A,R> \text{ is maximal}\},$$

i.e., if $<x>\sigma A'\wedge\eta R'\in\Delta$ then $A\subseteq A'$ and $R\subseteq R'$ means that $A=A'$ and $R=R'$. Putting it another way, if $<A,R>\in max(x)$ and $A\cup R\neq\Sigma$, then

$$\forall a\in\Sigma-(A\cup R)\ <x>\sigma A\wedge\sigma a\wedge\eta R\notin\Delta \text{ and } <x>\sigma A\wedge\eta R\wedge\eta a\notin\Delta.$$

Suppose now we have an element $<A,R>$ of $max(x)$ and an event $a\notin A\cup R$. Picture a tree where such a situation holds. The event a must be safe at some point, and at that point R is also refusable, giving us

Theorem (*Representation of Failsafe Elements by STs*):

Δ is representable $\Leftrightarrow$

(S5) $<x>\sigma A\wedge\eta R\in\Delta \Rightarrow \forall a\in\Sigma$ if $<x>\sigma A\wedge\sigma a\wedge\eta R\notin\Delta$ and $<x>\sigma A\wedge\eta R\wedge\eta a\notin\Delta$ then $<x>\sigma a\wedge\eta R\in\Delta$.

Due to (S4), (S5) is equivalent to

$$\forall a\in\Sigma\ \ <x>\sigma A\wedge\eta R\in\Delta \Rightarrow <x>\sigma A\wedge\eta R\wedge\eta a\in\Delta \text{ or } <x>\sigma a\wedge\eta R\in\Delta.$$

We conclude this section with the definition of *failsafe* processes. As before, we change notation, representing $<x>\sigma A\wedge\eta R$ by $<x,A,R>$.

Definition (*Failsafe Process*):

A *failsafe process* is a relation over $\Sigma^* \times p\Sigma \times p\Sigma$ satifying (suitably modified forms of) (S1)−(S4). In addition a *full* process also satisfies (S5).

The cpo induced by the information system, <*failsafe processes*,$\subseteq$>, is a complete lattice with bottom element $\{<\Lambda,\emptyset>\}$ and top element

$$\{<x,A,R> \mid x\in\Sigma^*,\ A\in p\Sigma,\ R\in p\Sigma,\ A\cap R=\emptyset\}.$$

9. Acrelog Operations

The *acrelog* construction admits the usual collection of continuous process operations, including *hiding*. The language syntax is as follows:

$$P ::= a \mid a\to P \mid P \text{ } or \text{ } P \mid P\,\square\,P \mid P \parallel P \mid P \mid\mid\mid P \mid \mu x.F(x) \mid P\backslash a.$$

The language statement a represents the process

$$\{<\Lambda,A,R> \mid A\subseteq\{a\},\ R\in p(\Sigma-\{a\})\} \cup \{<a,\emptyset,R> \mid R\in p\Sigma\}.$$

Like *failog*, all operations except *hiding* preserve full processhood. We present here some of the details for *hiding* and list the rest of the definitions for reference.

Hiding

In *acrelog*, *hiding* cannot be canonical even on bounded trees, in the sense of replacing every occurrence of the event to be hidden by τ, as then *hiding* fails to be continuous. For example, let $\Sigma=\{a,b,c,d\}$ and let $S=ba+bc$ and $T=ba+bc+bd$. Now $P(S)\subseteq P(T)$ but $P(S\backslash_c b)\not\subseteq P(T\backslash_c b)$ because $<\Lambda,\{a,c\},\{b,d\}>\in P(S\backslash_c b)-P(T\backslash_c b)$. So unlike *failog*, *acrelog* can lead to unfavorable situations with bounded processes, for example, where (A5) must be applied after *hiding*.

Definition (*Acrelog Hiding*):

For a process P

$$\begin{aligned} P\backslash b = &\{<x\backslash b,A,R> \mid <x,A,R\cup\{b\}>\in P\} \\ &\cup \{<x\backslash b,A-\{b\},R> \mid R\subseteq\{b\} \text{ and } \exists U <x,A,U>\in P\} \\ &\cup \{<\Lambda,A,R> \mid R\subseteq\{b\},\ b\notin A, \text{ and } \forall a\in A\exists n <b^n,\{a\},\emptyset>\in P\}. \end{aligned}$$

In addition to not behaving canonically on bounded trees, the definition does not preserve full processhood. In S above we have $<\Lambda,\{a,c\},\{b\}>\in P(S\backslash b)$, but neither $<\Lambda,\{a,c\},\{b,d\}>$ nor $<\Lambda,\{a,c,d\},\{b\}>$ is.

Inspecting the definition we see that refusals after *hiding* are treated as in *failog*. The second clause also incorporates the fact that, excluding the hidden event, the number of different events possible in the same context after *hiding* can only grow. Therefore, aside from removing the hidden event if present, *hiding* does not effect acceptance sets. The third clause is necessary to preserve (A5).

Prefixing $\quad a\to P = \{<\Lambda,A,R> \mid A\subseteq\{a\},\ R\in p(\Sigma\text{-}\{a\})\} \cup \{<ax,A,R> \mid <x,A,R>\in P\}.$

Nondeterministic Choice $\quad$ Due to (A5), the *or* operator for *acrelog* is more than just set union. However, the following definition preserves the interpretation of *or* on synchronization trees, that is $P(S)$ *or* $P(T) = P(\tau S+\tau T)$:

$$P \text{ } or \text{ } Q = P\cup Q\cup\{<\Lambda,A\cup A',R\cap R'> \mid <\Lambda,A,R>\in P,\ <\Lambda,A',R'>\in Q\}.$$

Conditional Choice $P \Box Q = \{<\Lambda, A \cup A', R \cap R'> \mid <\Lambda, A, R> \in P \text{ and} <\Lambda, A', R'> \in Q>\}$
$\cup \{<x, A, R> \mid x \neq \Lambda \text{ and } <x, A, R> \in P \cup Q\}$.

Intersection $P \| Q = \{<x, A \cap A', R \cup R'> \mid <x, A, R> \in P \text{ and } <x, A', R'> \in Q\}$.

Interleaving $P ||| Q = \{<z, A \cup A', R \cap R'> \mid z \in x \Delta y,\ <x, A, R> \in P, \text{ and } <y, A', R'> \in Q\}$,
where Δ is the string shuffle operator.

Recursion Analogous to *failog*.

10. Failsafe Operations

Like both *failog* and *acrelog*, the process operations are continuous in *failsafe*. In fact, as (A1)-(A4) are precisely (S1)-(S4) and since satisfaction of (A6) implies satisfaction of (S5), the results from the *acrelog* case carry over to *failsafe* whenever the definitions of an operation coincide. The definitions only differ with *hiding* and *or*. The definition for *or* is the one presented in *failog*.

Hiding

As with *acrelog*, *hiding* cannot be both canonical and continuous, even for bounded trees. Consider the case when $S=a+\tau bc$ and $T=a+\tau(bc+b)$. Clearly, $P(S) \subseteq P(T)$; however $\{a,c\}$ is safe in $P(S\backslash_c b)$ but not in $P(T\backslash_c b)$.

Definition (*Failsafe Hiding*):

For a process P

$$P\backslash b = \{<x\backslash b, A, R> \mid <x, A, R \cup \{b\}> \in P\}$$
$$\cup \{<x\backslash b, A, R> \mid R \subseteq \{b\},\ A \subseteq \{a\} \neq \{b\} \text{ and } \exists U <x, A, U> \in P\}.$$

The additional information represented by the second clause is that events possible after x, other than b, will be possible after $x\backslash b$. (A singleton event set is safe after x iff it is possible after x). Once again, *hiding* is not canonical and does not preserve fullness. The latter becomes evident when considering $B^{\omega}=Cl_{\vdash}\{<b^n,\{b\},\{a\}>\}$, as $B^{\omega}\backslash b=Cl_{\vdash}\{<\Lambda,\varnothing,\{b\}>\}$.

References

[Bro] Brookes, S., (1983), "On the Relationship of CCS and CSP", in *Automata, Languages and Programming*, LNCS 154.

[Gol] Golson, W., (1984), "Denotational Models Based on Synchronously Communicating Processes", Ph.D. thesis, University of Michigan.

[HeM] Hennessy, M. and Milner, R., (1980), "On Observing Nondeterminism and Concurrency", in *Automata, Languages and Programming*, LNCS 85.

[Hoa] Hoare, C.A.R., (1978), "Communicating Sequential Processes", *CACM* 21:8.

[HBR] Hoare, C.A.R., Brookes, S. and Roscoe, A., (1984), "A Theory of Communicating Sequential Processes", *JACM* 31:3.

[Mil] Milner, R., (1980), *A Calculus of Communicating Systems*, LNCS 92.

[Rou] Rounds, W., (1983), "On the Relationship Between Scott Domains, Synchronization Trees, and Metric Spaces", University of Michigan, Computing Research Laboratory Technical Report, CRL-TR-25-83.

[RoB] Rounds, W. and Brookes, S., (1981), "Possible Futures, Refusals and Communicating Processes", *Proceedings of the 22nd FOCS.*

[Sco] Scott, D., (1982), "Domains for Denotational Semantics", in *Automata, Languages and Programming*, LNCS 140.

The ESTEREL Synchronous Programming Language and its Mathematical Semantics

Gérard Berry
Laurent Cosserat

Ecole Nationale Supérieure des Mines de Paris (ENSMP)
Centre de Mathématiques Appliquées
Sophia-Antipolis
06565 VALBONNE
FRANCE

1. INTRODUCTION.

The goal of the ESTEREL project is to develop a real-time language based on a *rigorous formal model*, and actually to develop simultaneously the language, its semantics and its implementation. The present paper presents a reasonably stabilized version of ESTEREL together with its formal structural operational semantics. The language is rather unclassical since it is purely *synchronous*, *deterministic*, and based on a *multiform* notion of time, while all parallel and "real-time" languages such as ADA [3], CSP [19], LTR [1], OCCAM [4], RTL/2 [6], are asynchronous, nondeterministic, and consider only one notion of "absolute" time for their temporal primitives. The mathematical semantics leads naturally to a compiler producing small and efficient finite automata from ESTEREL programs, with possibility of temporal analysis by systems such as Clarke's EMC [14].

Let us first analyze the notion of time in ESTEREL and the synchrony hypothesis. In most "real-time" languages one can write delay instruction with classical temporal units (typically seconds), Hence one can write something like

```
delay 2 s; delay 3 s
```

How does one define what that statement *means*? Is it *equivalent* to the statement "delay 5 s"? The answer to the first question is often not given, and the answer to the second question may very well be negative since usual languages are essentially *asynchronous*. Take for example the OCCAM language, where an external event such as "second" is treated just as an ordinary message (and hence receives a clear semantics). Then the mentioned equivalence has no reason to be true, since messages are treated in a purely asynchronous way: one may expect the equivalence to be "true" if the implementation is "fast enough", but one has no real control on what will really happen. For actual real-time applications that approach is not sufficient, since one wants a program to respond to externally generated input stimuli within a "controllable" delay (see Young's definition or real time in [29]). Although the term "controllable" is vague enough, it is in no way a synonym of "arbitrary" and asynchrony can do little for us here. Temporal statements should be semantically well-defined at least at a "conceptual level" suited to reason about programs, and the validity of their implementation should be really checkable (i.e. one should have a reasonable idea of the actual temporal behavior of the compiled code),

Our goal in ESTEREL is to treat completely these two problems in the rational case, i.e. in the case where there is no dynamic creation of processes. We have no other choice than building a *synchronous* language, in which a delay statements terminates *exactly* when its ending event occurs (at least in the formal semantics). With respect to the equivalence problem, we shall take a rather drastic choice and say that the sequencing operator ";" *takes no time at all*, in other words that our execution machine is infinitely fast. This will generalize to all other ESTEREL constructs: all control transmission inside a program and all simple operations (assignment, addition etc) will "take no time". The only instruction which may take time are the ones *explicitely required to do so*, for example a "delay" statement. A program has no "internal clock", and it simply reacts instantaneously to external stimuli producing itself some stimuli to its output lines, and does *nothing* in absence of external stimuli. The conjunction of the synchrony hypothesis and of the "control takes no time" hypothesis will be called the *strong synchrony hypothesis*. In a strongly synchronous framework, it is obvious that "delay 3 s; delay 2s" is indeed the same as "delay 5 s".

The strong synchrony hypothesis may seem totally unrealistic at first glance, since real machines are of course not infinitely fast. However, we shall see that it is in fact extremely useful and has surprisingly good consequences: it really *simplifies* many problems, and for example allows us to reduce the number of primitives of the language (the hypothesis being necessary to ensure that many useful derived constructs work correctly). It suppresses the need for nondeterminism, which is usually necessary for handling communication between parallel processes but is not so natural in most real-time application. More surprisingly it leads to a truly *efficient implementation* of ESTEREL programs, where the *exact timing* of operation can be measured and where the assumption of having an infinitely fast machine is quite realistic in most practical applications. We shall come back on this point in a moment.

We turn now to the study of the notion of *time*. An essential point is that manipulating only a notion of "physical time" measured in seconds is not enough for most real-time applications. In fact many control algorithms use much more varied notion of time, if one considers a "time unit" as being just a repetitive event of some kind. For example, a mile runner knows four different natural time units: the second of course, but also the step, the meter run and the lap elapsed. All these units are of the same temporal nature, and there is no reason not to write statements such as "delay 3 meter" or "at 3 laps do <action>". Therefore a typical ESTEREL program will look like

```
during 2 LAP do
   every LAP do
      during 100 METER do
         RUN-SLOWLY
      end;
      during 100 STEPS or 50 SECOND do
         every STEP do
            [ JUMP-HIGH || BREATHE-OUT ]
         end
      end;
      WALK-SLOWLY
   end
end
```

The role of the "during" construct (which is actually not really primitive and will be derived from two "upto" and "uptonext" constructs) is to define the *temporal extent* of its body, measured versus the appropriate time unit, the "every" construct being simply a loop over a "during" construct. We leave to the reader to write the above program in a classical language and to discover how complex are the synchronizations it contains. As another example, here is a natural way of specifying an *exact* speed measure:

```
var SPEED : int in
   loop
      SPEED:=0;
      during 10 seconds do
         every METER do
            SPEED:=SPEED+1
         end
      end;
      emit SPEED-MEASURE (SPEED)
   end
end
```

With the strong synchrony hypothesis one can *guarantee* that an exact speed measure will be emitted exactly every 10 seconds. As we shall see in various examples, ESTEREL allows us to write small and elegant programs and to analyze them rigorously.

The next question is obvious: admitting that our strong synchrony hypothesis is reasonable for a specification language, how good is it for a real programming language, how far will our specification be from a real program? We have several answers. The first one is that there are many application in which the difficulty is *not* related to the speed of computation, but only to the complexity of the interaction between signals: this is the case when one wants to control *slow processes*; that case turns out to be quite frequent in practice (an object like a train has intrinsically high time constants; the problem for controlling it is not to write fast programs but *correct* programs). The second answer concerns the way programs are executed. The inefficiency of many parallel languages is due to the fact that programs are executed just as they are written, with an important overhead due to the process handling. In ESTEREL we shall overcome this difficulty by *compiling* a program into a simple and efficient input-output automaton, just as a grammar is translated into an efficient automaton by a parser generator. Then the execution times of apparently complex tasks may really be very low and reasonably close to the theoretical zero of ESTEREL, since all the internal control transmission and process communication corresponding to the treatment of an external event have been compiled into a single state transition. The strong synchrony hypothesis will also prove very useful for avoiding the explosion in the number of states which is the rule in asynchronous formalisms, and is due to the fact that internal control of the program generates states (problem which does not exist in ESTEREL). One could even go further and realize functions specified by ESTEREL programs by hardware components, for which the notion of synchrony makes real sense.

Of course the automata generated by ESTEREL programs could have been written by hand. However, a slight change to an ESTEREL program may induce a deep change in the resulting automaton, which could have been very difficult to do by hand. This is an essential advantage of high-level programming versus hand-coding of automata, which is well-known to users of parser of scanner generators.

Let us now analyze the relation between the language and its semantics. The process of developing a language together with its semantics is now widely admitted and actually used for classical sequential languages. But the situation is not so advanced for parallel or real time languages: on one hand the asynchronous languages we mentioned above were developed mainly on pragmatic grounds, often by adding various synchronization and communication primitives to rather classical sequential languages; on the other hand, many models of parallel computations have been developed in a quite independent way: denotational semantics based on powerdomain constructions [23], Petri Nets [22, 2], process algebras such as CCS, SCCS or MEIJE [20, 21, 9], temporal logics [26]. The relation between models and languages are still not very clear: the models tend to depart more and more from the classical sequential languages models and to become more and more elegant, but they are not so easy to use for giving natural semantics of actual languages or to compare the respective power of possible communication primitives. (although there are for instance some relations between rendez-vous in CSP and CCS [18, 5]). These problems were particularly clear during the development of ESTEREL, since we made the choice of introducing primitives only when their formal semantics were clear, but at the same time lacked good tools for giving the semantics. We actually developed several intermediate versions of the language and semantics

[7, 11, 8], which all contained imprecisions or even mistakes revealed only by a careful analysis of the proposed semantics (and which should now be considered as obsolete). At that time we used the only existing synchronous models, namely Milner's SCCS [21] or Boudol's MEIJE [9] calculi of processes. Our main difficulty was to give natural translation of ESTEREL constructs into SCCS or MEIJE ones. The final solution was obtained when we decided to forget about such translations and to use a *direct structural operational semantics* à la Plotkin [25, 24]. We shall in fact propose three semantics of ESTEREL :

(i) A *static semantics*, the role of which is mainly to check that a program raises no "temporal paradoxes", of the same kind as short-circuits in electricity.

(ii) A *behavioral semantics*, which defines completely the temporal behavior of a program which is correct versus the static semantics. This semantics is suited for studying program behaviors or program equivalences, but not for computing what a program does, in other words for executing the program: it relies on the fact that some fixpoint equations have a unique solution, but does not really give ways of computing that solution.

(iii) A *computational semantics*, which is more complex than the behavioral semantics, but also more effective in the sense that it really allows us to compute what a program does.

A remarkable fact is that the computational semantics we give is really *executable*: once it was fully understood, we were able to write a prototype interpreter of ESTEREL within a few days (using the LELISP/CEYX environment [13]). An even more remarkable fact is that the computational semantics leads directly to a *compiler* from ESTEREL programs to finite states machines, where the states are just program texts and the transitions program execution steps. Once a machine is constructed, one may forget about the programs associated with its states, and replace them simply by state numbers. The finite state machine is then trivially implementable in any classical language. It realizes a sequential implementation of an originally parallel synchronous program.

In section 2 we present the kernel language and its "naive" semantics: we define the notions of signal, event and control, and give the basic instruction set. In section 3 we propose natural extended instructions useful in real programs; the way we define these instructions gives some insight into the ESTEREL programming style. In section 4 we give two examples of ESTEREL programs. Sections 5, 6 and 7 are devoted to the three semantics, namely the static, behavioral and computational semantics. In section 8 we indicate briefly how ESTEREL symbolic evaluators and compilers can be derived from the computational semantics (they will be presented in more details in another paper). The last section indicates the futures research directions of the ESTEREL project.

2. The kernel language.

2.1. Types, variables,expressions and declarations

The treatment of variables and values is quite classical and not very much relevant to what follows, so that we shall give little detail here. We assume given some basic types, say integer, string and boolean, with adequate denotations for their values (the user will be able to introduce its own types in full ESTEREL versions).

The variable declarations have the form

var X: *type*

The expressions are constructed in a completely classical way. They may contain calls to externally defined functions (on data only, not on events).

2.2. Signal and events.

The basic communication unit in ESTEREL is the *signal*. A signal has a *name* and a *type*, which is the type of the values it conveys (later on we shall see that a pure signal can be considered as a signal conveying trivial values).

An *event* is conceptually an *instantaneous and broadcasted flash of information*, where an "information" is formed of possibly many simultaneous signals conveying values. An event is not remanent, so that its information is simply lost in the air if nobody listens to it.

Events may come from the outside of a program (e.g. interrupts) or be internally generated by the "emit *signal*" instruction, see below. We make no difference between these two cases.

We allow to have several simultaneous emissions of the same signal with possibly different values. A typical case is resource allocation, where several consumers may want simultaneously some resource: they send an inquiry message containing their name, the manager of the resource sends an acknowledgement to one of them (i.e. broadcasts a message containing the name of one of them). Another well-known case is local network protocols, where several stations may try simultaneously to use a line.

We have then to determine what values the receivers of such an event will then receive. The idea is taken from Milner [21]. With any signal of type b we associate an associative and commutative operation $*$ of type $b \times b \rightarrow b$. If there are n emitters ($n>0$) emitting n values $v_1, v_2, \ldots, v_n$ then the receivers will receive the value $v_1 * v_2 \cdots * v_n$.

As natural examples, one may send *pure signals* by considering a type b with only one value *triv*, setting $triv * triv = triv$. One may instead emit and receive *sorted lists* of values, a product operation "sortappend" appending and sorting the lists (this amount to gathering all emitters into a list, and is perfectly suitable in the above resource allocation example; sorting the list is normal since we want a deterministic result). One may also say that the product of two objects is a special value "error", so that one will dynamically detect that there was more than on emitter (typical example : local networks protocols).

A signal declaration has the form

signal *name*(*type*,*product*)

where *name*, *type* and *product* are the name of the signal, its type, and the name of its $*$ operation. In the extended language, we shall introduce simpler declarations for pure and single signals (signals having at most one emitter at a time). Signals will usually be named s, s1 etc.

The events will be called E,E',F. They have the following form :

$$s_1^{v_1}.s_2^{v_2}. \cdots .s_n^{v_n}$$

where v_n is the value conveyed by s_n The operations $*$ naturally induce a commutative monoid structure on the set of events : the neutral element 1 contains no signal, and one derives the $*$ product of two events in an obvious way by setting

$$s^{v_1} * s^{v_2} = s^{v_1 * v_2}$$

We shall omit the exponent *triv* for pure signals.

We say that a signal s *belongs* to an event E and write $s \in E$ if s is present in E with some exponent v. We then write $E(s)=v$.

2.3. The discrete time model

The strong synchrony hypothesis naturally lead to a discrete time model: we shall deal with sequences of events, that we shall call *histories* $H=E_1,E_2, \ldots ,E_n, \ldots$ The pair (n,E_n) will be called the n-th *instant* of H. An *input history* for a program will be an history such that only E_1 may contain no signal, i.e. be equal to 1: the idea is that a program will do something only on reception of an event from its environment, except when it is started (in that case it may decide on its own to send signals to its environment). A program P produces an *output history* $H'=F_1,F_2, \cdots ,F_n \cdots$. Conceptually the event F_n is formed by the signals emitted by P at instant (n,E_n) upon reception of the input event E_n. Since reception of E_n and emission of F_n are synchronous, an external observer will observe simply the composite event $E'_n=E_n * F_n$.

One should always remember that a program does nothing "between" input instants.

2.4. The basic instructions and their naive semantics.

We describe informally the basic primitives used for forming the ESTEREL instructions (or terms, or statements). We use an implicit notion of "control flow", and say that an instruction "passes the control" when it terminates and allows other instructions in sequence to proceed. Passing the control always takes no time, in the sense that it takes place in the current instant. If the control reaches the end of a program, i.e. if the whole instruction constituting the program passes the control, then the program does nothing anymore. We say that an instruction "takes no time" if it passes the control at he same instant it receives it, and that it "takes time" otherwise. These notions will be formalized in the mathematical semantics.

We use the letters i, i', i_1 for denoting instructions. We use brackets "[" and "]" to parenthesize instructions in the concrete syntax with usual priority rules, so that ";" has precedence over "||". Comments start with "%" and end at newline. we use the metasymbols *exp* and *boolexp* to range over expressions. For variables, tag labels and signals, we write simply X (or Y), T, s.

We do not give a precise definition of the way a program transforms histories for the moment, this will be done only when when defining the behavioral semantics.

Here is the list of the ESTEREL instructions, which we shall always treat in that order in the naive or in the formal semantics :

nothing
X:=*exp*
emit s(*exp*)
do i upto s(*exp*)
do i uptonext s(*exp*)
i_1; i_2
loop i end
if *boolexp* then i_1 else i_2 fi
i_1 || i_2
tag T in i end
exit T
var X : *type* in i end

2.4.1. The nothing instruction.

This instruction does nothing in no time, and hence passes the control in the same instant. A terminated program will always behave as the nothing instruction, hence does nothing upon reception of any event. Notice that the output history associated with a program containing only the nothing instruction is a sequence of 1's for any input history.

2.4.2. The assignment instruction.

An assignment has the form

X:=*exp*

The computation of the expression and the assignment itself take no time, so that the assignment statement passes the control in the same instant it gets it. (In practice it may be unreasonable to assume that the computation of an expression takes no time - for example if it is a matrix inversion. Then one has to create explicit signals for sending the data to an external program and for receiving the output of that program, not synchronously.)

2.4.3. The emit instruction.

It has the form

emit s(*exp*)

where *exp* is an expression having the required type (given at the signal declaration). An emit instruction always passes the control in the same instant. For emitting two signals s1 and s2 simultaneously, one just writes

emit s1(exp_1) || emit s2(exp_2)

or indifferently

emit s1(exp_1); emit s2(exp_2)

according to the semantics of the operators "||" and ";" described below.

2.4.4. The upto instruction.

It has the form

do *i* upto s(X)

where X is a variable of the appropriate type. The idea is as follows: the upto instruction defines the "end of the world" for its body *i*, which is executed normally upto the first occurrence of s, taking as input all other signals. At the first instant where an s occurs, *i* is killed, X is bound to the current value conveyed by s, the upto instruction terminates and passes the control. By "*i* is killed", we means that *i* is not executed at that instant, and will never be executed anymore. Let us illustrate this behavior on an example. Consider the instruction

```
do
    var X : int in
        every s1(X) do emit s2(X+1)
    end
upto s(Y)
```

where the meaning of the (derived) "every" construct is intuitively obvious. Consider the following input history :

$H_1 = s1^2, s3, s1^3, s1^4 * s^0, s1^5$

The generated output history is

$s2^3, 1, s2^4, 1, 1$

The occurence of s1 in the fourth instant does not provoke an emission of s2 since the reception of s at that instant kills the "every" statement. In that fourth instant, the variable Y is bound to 0, the upto terminates and passes the control in sequence. The occurence of s1 in the fifth instant also provokes no emission since the whole upto statement is now dead.

Consider another history :

$$H_2 = s1^0 * s^0,\ s1^1,\ s1^2 * s^1$$

Th output history is now

1, 1, 1

The every statement is killed in the first instant since s is present, the upto instruction terminates at that instant and binds Y to 0. Hence nothing is emitted.

Three facts need to be enhanced :

(i) An essential choice is that if the signal s is present when the upto instruction receives the control, then the body i is *not executed at all*. In any case when s occurs i is *instantaneously killed* without receiving the control in the corresponding instant. This is necessary for the extended constructs described in the next section (in particular for the "inpresence" and "inabsence" derived instructions).

(ii) The termination of i does *not* provoke the termination of the upto instruction, which simply waits for s.

(iii) There is a "temporal paradox" if i is "emit s(*exp*)", we shall come back on that point in section 5.

To avoid any confusion, let us finally mention that there is no kind of "implicit loop" in an upto instruction. All loops will be constructed explicitely by using the loop instruction.

2.4.5. The uptonext instruction.

Notice that waiting twice in a row for an event with an upto instruction is useless; in the instruction

do i_1 upto s(X); do i_2 upto s(X)

the instruction i_2 will never be executed: i_1 will be killed at the first occurrence of s, but since the sequencing operator ";" takes no time the instruction "do i_2 upto s(X)" will receive the control in the same instant and hence receive also the signal s. It will terminate instantly. Hence we need a way to skip the current instant. This is the purpose of the uptonext instruction, which has the form :

do i uptonext s(x)

It behaves just as the upto instruction, except that an occurrence of s at the instant where it receives the control is *ignored*, so that i is always executed in the instant where the uptonext instruction receives the control. Let us modify the previous example :

```
do
    var X : int in
        every s1(X) do emit s2(X+1)
    end
upto s(Y)
```

The output on history H_1 is the same as before, since an uptonext instruction behaves just as an upto statement if the signal is not present when it receives the control. But the output history on input history H_2 is now

$s2^1, s2^2, 1$

since the occurence of s in the first instant is ignored.

Notice that an uptonext instruction will always "take time", (unless it contains exits, see below). It is actually the only instruction having this property.

The upto and uptonext instructions are used both for synchronization and value communication.

2.4.6. The sequencing instruction.

Sequencing is written as usual :

$i_1; i_2$

The control is passed instantaneously to i_1 when received. It is then passed instantaneously to i_2 when i_1 terminates (if ever).

2.4.7. The loop instruction.

There is a single loop instruction, written

loop i end

Its semantics is obvious: it behaves just as the infinite sequence

i; i; ... ; i; ...

However the body i is not allowed to pass the control instantaneously! (We shall show that this is statically checkable.) Consider what should do instantaneous instructions such as

```
X:=0; loop X:=X+1 end
loop emit s(X) end
```

2.4.8. The conditional instruction.

The conditional is also the usual one :

if *boolexp* then i_1 else i_2 fi

The evaluation of the boolean expression *boolexp* is assumed to be instantaneous, so that either i_1 or i_2 receives the control instantaneously.

2.4.9. The parallel instruction.

It is written as follows :

$i_1 \parallel i_2$

The control is passed instantaneously to i_1 and i_2. The parallel construct terminates exactly when both i_1 and i_2 have terminated. Since the signals are broadcasted, i_1 receives all the signals emitted by itself and by i_2, and conversely. Hence i_1 and i_2 work in the same event environment. We shall freely use the "||" operator as a n-ary one, assuming associativity to the left, and use often brackets for the parallel constructs in order to improve readability.

2.4.10. tag and exit.

The tag-exit mechanism is a central one. It is similar to the catch-throw mechanism in LISP or the failure mechanism in ML [16]. The syntax is as follows for the two instructions tag and exit :

tag T in *i* end
exit T

where an exit can only appear within a tag of the same name (the usual scope rules apply). Again the transmission of control is instantaneous, so that an exit provokes instantaneously the termination of its tag. Of course the exit instruction itself does *not* pass the control in sequence. A tag also terminates when its body terminates. Exits are used for exiting loops, upto or uptonext instructions. They will be of great use for deriving new convenient construct from the kernel ones.

Since we have also a parallel construct, we must be careful to understand how an exit works inside a parallel branch. Here are two examples :

```
tag T in
   [
      emit s1; exit T; emit s2
   ||
      emit s3
   ]
end
```

Here s1 is obviously emitted while s2 is obviously not emitted, and s3 is also emitted : the exits in a parallel branch are treated only "at the end" of the treatment of the whole parallel construct in the current instant.

```
tag T1 in
   tag T2 in
      exit T1 || exit T2
   end;
   emit s
end
```

We have two simultaneous exits. Then the outermost one has precedence, so that the whole program terminates instantaneously, s being not emitted.

2.4.11. Local bindings.

If *decl* is a variable declaration, then

decl in *i* end

is an instruction. The declared variable is local to the instruction, with scope rules as usual. Variables cannot be shared. More precisely, a variable which is modified (by an assignment instruction, an upto or an uptonext instruction) within one branch of a parallel construct must be local to that branch; this is not necessary for a variable which is just read. The following situation is not allowed :

```
var X: int in
   [
      X:=0
   ||
      emit s(X)
   ]
end
```

But the following situation is allowed:

```
var X: int in
    X:=3;
    [
        emit s(X)
    ||
        var X: int
            do nothing upto s(X);
            X:=X+1;
            emit s1(X)
        end
    ]
end
```

Because of the ordinary scope rules, there are in fact two distinct variables named X.

2.5. The ESTEREL programs.

A program is formed of a *sort definition* which defines the signals being input, output, input and output, or local to the program and their types, (keywords "input", "output" or "input output" followed by signal declarations), followed by a closed term (i.e. a term without free variables or free exits). The local events are internal to the program, they will not be emitted to its environment. Example of programs are given in section 4.

The type-checking of expression is classical and omitted here. We shall always assume that programs are well-typed. We shall also assume that a variable is always initialized before being used (this may be statically checked).

3. The extended language.

The kernel language presented in the previous section is not really a language we would like to program in, but rather a set of programming *primitives*. We now present *derived constructs* making life easier. These constructs are just *macros*, so that there will be no need to define their semantics. They make extensive use of the tag-exit mechanism, and work correctly only under the strong synchrony hypothesis. We hope that the way we define extensions will train the reader to the quite unusual style of ESTEREL programs.

The extended ESTEREL language being still in development, several aspects will not be treated completely (in particular modularity).

3.1. Some trivial extensions.

We give the possibility of assigning a value to a variable when it is declared :

var X:=*exp* : *type* in *i* end

stands for

```
var X : type in X:=exp; i end
```

And we give also the possibility of defining constants :

```
const TWO=2 in i end
```

We give the possibility of not binding a variable by an upto or uptonext instruction :

```
do i upto(next) s
```

stands for

```
var X : type in
   do i upto(next) s(X)
end
```

where *type* is the type of s and X is a new variable not contained in *i*.

Finally we allow the user to use an "if-then-fi" statement omitting the else part (which is simply set to "nothing"), and to use a repetition construct of the form

```
repeat exp times i end
```

which is trivially built as

```
tag T in
   var X := exp : integer in
      loop
         if X<=0 then
            exit T
         else
            X:=X-1;
            i
         fi
      end
   end
end
```

where the variable X does not appear free in *i*.

3.2. Pure and single signals.

General signals being a bit heavy to handle, we introduce two special cases as follows:

pure signal s
single signal s(*type*)

Pure signals convey no value, while single signals are restricted to have at most one emitter at a time; hence one may forget about the $*$ operation. The reader should be convinced that the pure and single signal constructs represent only convenient syntactic sugar : pure signals were shown to be a general case of general signals in section 2, and for single signals the operation $*$ needs not even to be defined since the fact that there is no more than one emitter at a time will be shown to be statically checkable in section 5.

3.3. Local signals.

In the kernel language, we did not give the full power of local declarations for signals as we did for variables, since we allowed looal signals to be declared only at the level of a program (the effect being that the signal will not be output to the outside). The reason is that we would have to manipulate a much heavier formalism for the static and dynamic semantics given in the present paper, since we shall arrange the signals of a program into a graph.

A way to introduce local signal declarations at any point in the program is to rename the signal with a new name and to push its declaration at the top of the program; this would not be feasible in a natural way for variables, because we must guarantee that variables are not shared, that constraint making no sense for signals. We shall therefore use freely the following syntax for declaring local signals :

signal s(*type*) in
  i
end

3.4. Waiting for signals.

The following extended statements are obvious:

await s(X) ≡ do nothing upto s(X)
awaitnext s(X) ≡ do nothing uptonext s(X)

There is a sharp difference between await and awaitnext : two await statements in a row behave just as one, since the signal is already present when the second wait statement is activated: Hence "await s; await s" is equivalent to "await s", while "awaitnext s; awaitnext s" will terminate only at the second next occurence of s. Consider also the two programs :

emit s(5); await s(X)
emit s(5); awaitnext s(X)

The first program immediately terminates with X bound to 5. The second program does not immediately terminate, since the signal s emitted by the emit statement is ignored by the awaitnext statement. One has always to remember that an await statement may take no time, while an awaitnext statement always takes time.

As a side remark, we notice that an await statement may be used for exporting the value of a variable which is local to a branch of a parallel construct to the end of that construct :

```
single signal s(int) in
   tag T in
      [
         ...
      ||
         var X : int in
            ...
            emit s(X);
            exit T
         end
      ]
   end;
   await s(Y)
end
```

Since the emission of s(X) is synchronous with the "exit T" statement, the "await s(Y)" statement terminates immediately and binds Y to the last value of the local variable X.

3.5. Temporal loops.

We introduce several forms of temporal loops :

```
do i uptoeach s(X)
```

stands for

```
do i upto s(X);
loop
  do i uptonext s(X)
end
```

similarly

```
do i uptoeachnext s(X)
```

stands for

```
loop
  do i uptonext s(X)
end
```

while

```
every s(X) do i end
```

stands for

```
await s(X);
loop
   do i uptonext s(X)
end
```

and finally

```
everynext s(X) do i end
```

stands for

```
awaitnext s(X);
loop
   do i uptonext s(X)
end
```

To understand why the signal and its variable appear last in the first cases and first in the last cases, just look at when *i* starts and at which value X is bound.

3.6. Testing for the presence or absence of a signal.

These constructs really shows the power of our primitives. Assume that we want to do i_1 only if the signal s is present in the current instant. The instruction is

```
inpresence s(X) do i end
```

Its implementation is

```
tag T in
   do exit T upto s(X);
   i
end
```

where T is not free in *i*. It works as follows: if s is present, then the upto terminates immediately without executing its body "exit T", and *i* starts immediately with X bound to the value of s in the current instant. The whole construct then terminates when *i* terminates. Otherwise the exit statement is indeed executed, and the whole construct immediately terminates. The strong synchrony hypothesis is absolutely essential here. Conversely, one can test for the absence of a signal :

```
inabsence s do i end
```

stands for

```
tag T1 in
    tag T2 in
        do exit T2 upto s;
        exit T1
    end;
    i
end
```

where T1 is not free in *i*. We need two exits: T1 is exited if s is present, which provokes the termination of the whole construct; T2 is exited if s is absent and this provokes the execution of *i*.

3.7. Watchdogs.

A very common problem in real-time programming is to check whether a task has been completed before a signal s occurs, to terminate normally in that case, and to provoke some exception treatment in the abnormal case. This may be programmed as follows :

```
do i watching s(X) abnormal i' end
```

standing for

```
tag T in
    do
        i; exit T
    upto s(X);
    i'
end
```

3.8. Failures

The tag-exit mechanism is obviously close to a classical failure mechanism. However we have given no way of telling why an exit was raised, i.e. of naming exceptions. This is very easily done by using local signals. Here is a syntax for failure handling :

```
trapfailure
    i
    failure F1 do i1
    failure F2 do i2
    ...
    failure Fn do in
end
```

where i may contain statements "failwith Fi". It translates into

```
pure signal F1, F2, ... , Fn in
    tag OK in
        tag FAIL in
            i;
            exit OK
        end;
        [
            inpresence F1 do i1 end
        ||
            inpresence F2 do i2 end
        ||
            ...
        ||
            inpresence Fn do in end
        ]
    end
end
```

all the "failwith Fi" statements in i being replaced by "emit Fi; exit FAIL". Notice that several failures can be handled simultaneously. One may trivially extend this constructs to pass values in failures.

3.9. Operations on signals.

3.9.1. Division of signals.

For the moment we are only able to reference the current or the next occurrence of a signal. But we should also be able to reference any occurrence in the future. Hence we extend the upto and uptonext statements in the following way, s having type b and *exp* type int :

do i uptonext *exp* s(X)

stands for (the value of *exp* being supposed greater than 1)

```
pure signal f, var COUNT:=0 in
    [
        tag T in
            var Y : b in
                everynext s(Y) do
                    COUNT:=COUNT+1;
                    if COUNT=exp then emit f; exit T fi
                end
            end
        end
    ||
        do i upto f
    ];
    await s(X)
end
```

The local signal f is sent for killing *i* at the right instant. Because of the strong synchrony hypothesis, the emission of f is synchronous with the reception of s, and that the last "await s(X)" terminates instantaneously and binds X to the right value.

Now we can define a clock division, producing for example a clock beating the second from a clock beating the millisecond, and being sure that a second is indeed *synchronous* with one millisecond over 1000 :

```
loop
    awaitnext 1000 MS;
    emit S
end
```

And one sees at once how to program arbitrary long delays (actually the meaning of the word "delay" is not quite clear in a synchronous framework : when does a delay start, right now or on the next signal?).

3.9.2. Conjunction or disjunction of pure signals.

It is quite common to wait for some instantaneous conjunction or disjunction of signals. This naturally leads to the introduction of two constructs

```
s1 and s2
s1 or s2
```

We introduce these constructs only for pure signals here. The program

```
do i upto(next) s1 and s2
```

is translated into

```
pure signal s1-and-s2 in
   [
      every s1 do
         inpresence s2 do emit s1-and-s2 end
      end
   ||
      do i upto(next) s1-and-s2
   ]
end
```

which terminates when s1 and s2 occur simultaneously, and similarly the program

```
do i upto(next) s1 or s2
```

expands into

```
pure signal s1-or-s2 in
   [
      tag OK in
         [
            await(next) s1; exit OK
         ||
            await(next) s2; exit OK
         ]
      end;
      emit s1-or-s2
   ||
      do i upto(next) s1-or-s2
   ]
end
```

which terminates at the first occurrence of s1 or s2.

3.9.3. Absolute time.

It is often useful to count signals and define the "absolute time" associated with a signal, for writing instructions such as

```
at 1000 s do i end
```

For this we introduce an absolute time counter in parallel with the whole program. It uses a variable s-COUNT declared globally and initialized to 0. The value of that variable may then be consulted.

```
every s do
   s-COUNT:=s-COUNT+1;
   every s-TIME do
      emit s-TIME-IS(s-COUNT)
   end
end
```

The above "at" instruction translates as

```
var TIME: int in
   tag END in
      every s do
         emit s-TIME;
         await s-TIME-IS(TIME);
         if TIME=1000 then
            i; exit END
         fi
      end
   end
end
```

and the absolute time may indeed be consulted at any instant by

```
emit s-TIME;
await s-TIME-IS(s-count)
```

The syntax for this kind of extended construct has clearly to be polished further on. Notice however that we used two synchronous messages s-TIME and s-TIME-IS to model in fact an asynchronous communication.

3.10. The during instruction

We chose to write

do *inst* upto s(X)

and not

upto s(X) do *inst* end

since the variable X is assigned only at termination of the upto statement. The second form could suggest something different, since X is written before *inst*. But for pure signals the two forms could be considered as equivalent. Using the division of signals just described, we may write

during *exp* s do *inst* end

instead of

do *inst* uptonext *exp* s

(see examples in the introduction).

3.11. Modules.

It is of course necessary to have nice module structures in really useful programming languages. The modular structure we propose for ESTEREL is quite simple. A *module* has formal parameters, which may be constants, variables or signals. The syntax of a module declaration is

module $name(par_1, \ldots, par_n)$ =
    i
in
    i'
end

A parameter declaration may be a classical variable declaration, a constant declaration, or a signal declaration with input/output indication, as in the program sort definition :

```
module FOO (var X:int list, const TWO=2, input output pure signal s) =
    ...
end
```

A module invocation has the form

$name(actual_1, \ldots, actual_n)$

and it works just as a textual copy of the body of the module with syntactic replacement of the formal parameters by the actual ones (the types must match, of course). Hence module invocation may not be recursive, and modules add nothing to the power of the language. They will not be considered in the formal semantics. Of course there are some problems with polymorphic modules etc., but these problems are in no way specific to ESTEREL and they will not be treated here.

4. Some programming examples.

In the examples we make free use of the extended constructs presented in the last section.

4.1. A reflex game.

We want to program a reflex game, working as follows : a game starts by pressing a RESET button, and it will be composed of 10 reflex measures. Each measure starts when the player presses a button A; then after a random time a green lamp lights on, and the player must press as fast as possible a button B.

Then the green lamp is turned off and the reflex time is displayed. A new measure starts when the player presses A again. When the cycle of 10 measures is completed, the average reflex time is displayed after a pause of 3 seconds. There are many exception cases; some of them are simple mistakes and make a bell ring. Some other represent true cheating tentatives or abandons of the game, they turn on a red light and stop completely the game, which waits for a new RESET :

- The player presses B instead of A to start a measure. The bell rings.
- The player presses A during a measure. The bell rings.
- The player presses B too early during a measure, i.e. before the green lamp turns on or just at the same time it turns on. Then the red light turns on and the game is ended (the player cheats!).
- The player does not press A or B within 10 seconds when it is supposed to do so. Then the machines stops the game and turns the red light on (case of abandon).

A last rule is that a new game is started from fresh if the player presses RESET at any time.

```
input pure signal RESET, A, B, MS
output pure signal GREEN-OFF, GREEN-ON, RED-OFF, RED-ON,
                   RING-BELL
output single signal DISPLAY(int) in
   every RESET do
      emit RED-OFF;
      trapfailure
         var AVERAGE:=0 : int in
            % measure loop
            repeat 10 times
               % waiting for A
               do
                  do
                     every B do emit RING-BELL
                  upto A
               watching 10000 MS abnormal failwith END-GAME end;
               % delay and waiting for B; A rings the bell
               [
                  everynext A do emit RING-BELL end
               ||
                  % random delay - B may not be pressed
                  do
                     awaitnext random() MS
                  watching B abnormal failwith END-GAME end;
                  emit GREEN-ON;
                  % waiting for B and displaying the result.
                  var TIME:= 0 : int in
                     do
                        do
                           every MS do TIME:=TIME+1 end
                        upto B
                     watching 10000 MS abnormal failwith END-GAME end
                     emit GREEN-OFF;
                     emit DISPLAY(TIME);
                     AVERAGE:=AVERAGE+TIME
                  end
               ]
            end;
            % final display of the average time
            await 3000 MS;
            emit DISPLAY (AVERAGE/10)
         end
      failure END-GAME do emit RED-ON end
   end
end
```

4.2. A prompting machine.

This quite different example is actually used in the user interface of the prototype ESTEREL compiler. The problem is to send prompts to a terminal at the right moment. The machine is interfaced with a lexical analyzer and a reader; the lexical analyzer sends signals PEEK–CHAR and READ–CHAR to the reader, which gives back a character by sending a signal CHAR(char), after a while (i.e. not synchronously). Our machine uses the fact that signals are broadcasted, and listens to the discussion between the analyzer and the reader.

The prompting mechanism may be armed by a signal PROMPT–ON for reading from a terminal, and disarmed by a signal PROMPT–OFF, for reading from a file. In addition one may emit two prompts PS1 and PS2, as in UNIX: PS1 is emitted at the first line, PS2 is emitted at the following lines, until a signal BACK–TO–PS1 is received (from some other machine driving the lexical analyzer). A prompt should be sent when the program is started and at each PEEK–CHAR or READ–CHAR request following the reading of a carriage return (a carriage return is read each time the reader answers a request READ–CHAR by an answer CHAR(CR), where CR is the appropriate character value). The program is made of three parallel submachines exchanging local signals; the first machine detects when a carriage-return is read, the second machine decides when a prompt should be emitted, the third machine decides which prompt should be emitted.

```
input pure signal PROMPTON, PROMPTOFF, BACK-TO-PS1,
                  READ-CHAR, PEEK-CHAR,
output pure signal PS1, PS2 in
   pure signal CR-READ, SEND-PROMPT in
      [
         % detects when a READ-CHAR is followed by a CHAR(CR)
         var X: char in
            every READ-CHAR do
               await CHAR(X);
               if X=CR then emit CR-READ fi
            end
         end
      ||
         % decides when to emit a prompt
         emit SEND-PROMPT;
         loop
            do % upto PROMPTOFF
               every CR-READ do
                  awaitnext READCN or PEEKCN;
                  emit SEND-PROMPT
               end
            upto PROMPTOFF;
            awaitnext PROMPTON
         end
      ||
         % decides to emit PS1 or PS2
         do
            await SEND-PROMPT; emit PS1;
            everynext SEND-PROMPT do emit PS2 end
         uptoeach BACK-TO-PS1
      ]
   end
end
```

The use of local signals makes programming much more elegant. Moreover, as we shall see later on, it does *not* introduce execution overhead.

5. Signal dependency and the static semantics.

5.1. Signal dependency.

Let us come back on the naive semantics of the upto instruction :

```
do i upto s(X)
```

One terminates instantaneously or one executes *i* according to the presence or absence of the signal s in the current instant. Hence one must know whether s is present or not *before* executing the upto statement; moreover, if s is indeed present, one must know which values were emitted in order to bind properly X. There are basically two cases where these conditions are not met; by analogy with electronics, we call them *oscillations* and *short-circuits*. An oscillation is typically

```
do emit s upto s
```

The signal s should be emitted if not present and not emitted if present, which is clearly a nonsense. Short-circuits have the form

```
signal s(int,'*') in
      emit s(1)
   ||
      var X: int in
         await s(X); emit s(X+1)
      end
end
```

where the signal s is assumed to have type int with the usual multiplication as * operation, see section 2. The "emit s(X+1)" statement if synchronous with the "emit s(1)" statement, according to the strong synchrony hypothesis. It is then impossible to bind sensibly X: if one binds X to the integer 1, then one should also bind X to the integer 1*2=2, hence to the integer 2*3=6 and so on. That divergence problem is very similar to the problem raised in electronics when one plugs the output line of an amplifier directly into its input line.

We want our flow of control to keep a precise "past-to-future" direction even inside an instant, so that we should not be allowed to emit a signal if we have already received it or if we have decided that we shall not receive it. We may have similar situations involving more than one signal :

```
signal s1(int,'*'),s2(int,'*') in
        var X1: int in
            await s1(X1); emit s2(X1+1)
        end
    ||
        var X2: int in
            await s2(X2); emit s1(X2+1)
        end
    ||
        emit s1(0)
    ||
        emit s2(0)
```

and also

```
    do emit s2 upto s1
||
    await s1; emit s2
```

To avoid oscillations and short circuits, we introduce a notion of *dependency* between signals. We say that s2 depends on s1 in two cases

(i) An "emit s2" instruction appearing inside the body of a "do *i* upto s1" statement may be executed in the current instant. In that case we say that s1 *inhibits* s2.

(ii) An "emit s2" statement follows in the same instant the termination of a "do *i* upto s1" statement (which of course has terminated because of the presence of s1 in the current instant). We then say that s1 *causes* s2 (notice that the emission of s2 is synchronous with the reception of s1. For example, when one constructs a clock beating the second by dividing a clock beating the millisecond, the second is caused by the millisecond).

In the dependency analysis, inhibition and causality behave exactly in the same way. Our requirement will be as follows:

The dependency relation between signals must have no cycle

In the first examples, the dependency graph has a cycle containing only s (s inhibits itself in the first case, s causes itself in the second case). In the two last examples, there are cycles through s1 and s2 (s1 causes s2 and s2 causes s1 in the first case, s1 inhibits s2 and s2 causes s1 in the second case).

Short-circuits problems appear only "inside an instant". There is no problem with an instruction like

```
await s1; awaitnext s2; emit s1
```

Here we are certain that the "await s1" and "emit s1" instructions will never appear in the same instant.

5.2. The formalism used for the static semantics.

We now construct the dependency graph on signals in a formal way : this is the main purpose of the *static semantics*, which gives an analysis of all possible behaviors of a program *in the first instant of any of its executions*. The complete causality analysis of a program in all possible input histories will require to use also the dynamic semantics presented in the next sections. We shall not require the dependency graph to be declared by the programmer, and not even to be constant for a given program (i.e. the graphs corresponding to two different instants need not to have any kind of relation with eachother). In practical systems, we shall however allow the user to specify himself dependency relations which must hold at every instant (e.g. that the second is always caused by the millisecond).

As all our semantics, we shall present our static semantics by a set of *structural conditional rewrite rules* à la Plotkin, defining a transition system with transitions of the form

$$<i, D> \xrightarrow{b, L} <G, D'>$$

where :

(i) i is an ESTEREL instruction.

(ii) D is a set of signals, on which the execution of i will depend. That is D is the set of signals of which we must know the status before being able to execute i.

(iii) The termination status b is a boolean indicating whether i may terminate and pass the control in sequence (values *tt* or *ff*). The boolean conjunction and disjunction are written $\cap$ and $\cup$.

(iv) L is a set of tag labels (free in i), which represents the set of exits that i may execute in the first instant.

(v) G is the dependency graph, represented as a set of pairs (s1,s2) where s2 depends on s1.

(vi) D' is the set of signals on which the execution will depend after executing i. The set D' will always contain the set D.

The dependency graph of a program P with body i (removing the event declarations which are irrelevant here) will be obtained by computing a transition of the form

$$<i, \phi> \xrightarrow{b, L} <G, D'>$$

The static semantics will have another role: testing that the body of a loop statement cannot terminate instantaneously. The static semantics will then be undefined (and the rules will show how to output an appropriate error message, not done here).

5.3. The rules of the static semantics.

5.3.1. Axiom of nothing.

A nothing statement terminates instantaneously and does just that :

$$<\text{nothing}, D> \xrightarrow{tt,\,\phi} <\phi, D>$$

5.3.2. Axiom of assignment.

As far as signal dependencies are concerned, an assignment behaves just like nothing :

$$<X{:=}exp\,, D> \xrightarrow{tt,\,\phi} <\phi, D>$$

5.3.3. Axiom of emission.

We record in the graph all generated dependencies (this is the only rule which increments G) :

$$<\text{emit s}(exp), D> \xrightarrow{tt,\,\phi} <\{(\text{d,s}),\ \text{d}\in D\}, D>$$

5.3.4. Rule of upto.

The body i of an upto statement is analyzed by adding the signal s to the given dependency set D, since all emissions it may contain are potentially inhibited by s. This yields as result a graph G and a new dependency set D'. One outputs the facts that an upto statement may always terminate (if the signal is present), that it exits the same tags as its body, that it gives graph G and dependency set D' :

$$\frac{<i, D\cup\{\text{s}\}> \xrightarrow{b,\,L} <G, D'>}{<\text{do } i \text{ upto } s(X), D> \xrightarrow{tt,\,L} <G, D'>}$$

Notice that D' will always contain D and s, so that the dependency on s is transmitted to the instructions which follow in sequence; the rule for upto is the only one to increment D.

5.3.5. Rule of uptonext.

An uptonext does not pass the control in sequence. Besides that, it behaves just as its body.

$$\frac{<i, D> \xrightarrow{b,\,L} <G, D'>}{<\text{do } i \text{ uptonext } s(X), D> \xrightarrow{ff,\,L} <G, D'>}$$

5.3.6. Rules of sequence.

There are two cases, according to the fact that the first instruction may pass the control or not. In the first case one analyzes the second instruction with the dependencies generated by the first one, and one outputs as termination status the status then obtained, as tag set the union of the two tag sets, as graph the union of the two generated graphs, as new dependencies those generated by the second instruction (which always contain those generated by the first one) :

$$\frac{<i_1, D> \xrightarrow{tt,\, L_1} <G_1, D'> \quad <i_2, D'> \xrightarrow{b_2,\, L_2} <G_2, D''>}{<i_1; i_2, D> \xrightarrow{b_2,\, L_1 \cup L_2} <G_1 \cup G_2, D''>}$$

In the second case one outputs simply what was generated by the analysis of the first instruction :

$$\frac{<i_1, D> \xrightarrow{ff,\, L_1} <G_1, D'>}{<i_1; i_2, D> \xrightarrow{ff,\, L_1} <G_1, D'>}$$

5.3.7. Rule of loop.

We give a rule only if the body of the loop may not terminate instantaneously. The loop statement then behaves as its body :

$$\frac{<i, D> \xrightarrow{ff,\, L} <G, D'>}{<\text{loop } i \text{ end}, D> \xrightarrow{ff,\, L} <G, D'>}$$

5.3.8. Rule of conditional.

To be really accurate, the conditional cannot be treated in a simple way. One should study separatedly all possible control paths it generates. However we shall make some approximation here in order to simplify the presentation: we shall union the graphs generated by the two arms of the conditional. This makes incorrect a program such as

```
if boolexp then
      do emit s1 upto s2
else
      do emit s2 upto s1
fi
```

which could perfectly be considered as correct, since there is obviously no communication between the two branches of a conditional. We shall say that a conditional may terminate iff one of its arms may, and output the union of the exits, graphs and generated dependencies :

$$\frac{<i_1, D> \xrightarrow{b_1, L_1} <G_1, D'_1> \quad <i_2, D> \xrightarrow{b_2, L_2} <G_2, D'_2>}{<\text{if } boolexp \text{ then } i_1 \text{ else } i_2 \text{ fi}, D> \xrightarrow{b_1 \cup b_2, L_1 \cup L_2} <G_1 \cup G_2, D'_1 \cup D'_2>}$$

5.3.9. Rule of parallel.

A parallel statement may terminate iff both its arms may. The tags, graphs, and resulting dependencies are obtained by unioning those of the arms.

$$\frac{<i_1, D> \xrightarrow{b_1, L_1} <G_1, D'_1> \quad <i_2, D> \xrightarrow{b_2, L_2} <G_2, D'_2>}{<i_1 \parallel i_2, D> \xrightarrow{b_1 \cap b_2, L_1 \cup L_2} <G_1 \cup G_2, D'_1 \cup D'_2>}$$

5.3.10. Rule of tag.

A tag may terminate iff its body may terminate or generate a corresponding exit. The other exit labels generated by the body are output, the graph and dependency output are those of the body :

$$\frac{<i, D> \xrightarrow{b, L} <G, D'>}{<\text{tag T in } i \text{ end}, D> \xrightarrow{b \cup (\mathrm{T} \in L), L - \{\mathrm{T}\}} <G, D'>}$$

5.3.11. Axiom of exit.

An exit does not pass the control, and generates as exit set L the corresponding singleton :

$$<\text{exit T}, D> \xrightarrow{ff, \{\mathrm{T}\}} <\phi, D>$$

5.3.12. Rules of binding.

A variable binding has no effect w.r.t. the static semantics :

$$\frac{<i, D> \xrightarrow{b, L} <G, D'>}{<\text{var X in } i \text{ end}, D> \xrightarrow{b, L} <G, D'>}$$

5.4. Static correctness.

Definition: We say that a program P is *statically correct (w.r.t. all possible first instants)* if and only if there exists a provable transition of the form

$$<\mathrm{P}, \phi> \xrightarrow{b, L} <G, D'>$$

with G acyclic.

From the form of our rules, one sees easily that the a proof can be computed in a pure top-down way, with at most one rule to apply at any subterm. Therefore there is at most one possible transition from <P,ϕ>. There is no transition if and only if the body of a loop statement may terminate instantaneously. In fact we could have defined the static semantics as a partial function from terms and dependency sets to termination status, tag label set, graph and new dependency set. But we think that the rewrite rule formalism is easier to read anyway.

Our rules are in fact a bit too strong, and we reject also the following program which could be considered as correct :

```
tag T1 in
    tag T2 in
        exit T1 || exit T2 || do emit s1 upto s2
    end;
    do emit s2 upto s1
end
```

Here the graph is {(s1,s2),(s2,s1)} and has a cycle. But the "do emit s2 upto s1" instruction will never be executed because of the presence of "exit T1". There is however not too much trouble to reject programs in which some instruction will never be activated.

Notice finally that we are able to count how many "emit s" instructions may receive the control in the first instant. Hence it is possible to check that a signal declared to be single has indeed at most one emitter.

5.5. An example.

Here is an example of a formal derivation, presented in a bottom-up way. Consider the following program :

```
input pure signal s1,
output pure signal s2, s3,
local pure signal s in
   [
      do nothing upto s1;
      emit s
   ||
      tag T in
         [
            do
               do emit s3 upto s;
               emit s2
            uptonext s3;
         ||
            exit T
         ]
      end
   ]
end
```

We shall give names to the transitions and indicate for any transition the name of its premisses, replacing the horizontal bar we used in rules by a turnstile $\vdash$. Here is a derivation :

a) First branch of the outermost || :

$$\vdash\ T_1 \equiv \langle \text{nothing}, \{s1\}\rangle \xrightarrow{tt,\,\phi} \langle \phi, \{s1\}\rangle$$

$$T_1 \vdash\ T_2 \equiv \langle \text{do nothing upto s1}, \phi\rangle \xrightarrow{tt,\,\phi} \langle \phi, \{s1\}\rangle$$

$$\vdash\ T_3 \equiv \langle \text{emit s}, \{s1\}\rangle \xrightarrow{tt,\,\phi} \langle\{(s1,s)\}, \{s1\}\rangle$$

$$T_2, T_3 \vdash\ T_4 \equiv \langle \text{do nothing upto } s\,1\text{;emit s}, \phi\rangle \xrightarrow{tt,\,\phi} \langle\{(s\,1,s)\}, \{s1\}\rangle$$

b) Second branch of the outermost || :

b.1) First branch of the innermost || :

$$\vdash\ T_5 \equiv \langle \text{emit s3}, \{s\}\rangle \xrightarrow{tt,\,\phi} \langle\{(s,s3)\}, \{s\}\rangle$$

$$T_5 \vdash\ T_6 \equiv \langle \text{do emit s3 upto s}, \phi\rangle \xrightarrow{tt,\,\phi} \langle\{(s,s3)\}, \{s\}\rangle$$

$$\vdash\ T_7 \equiv \langle \text{emit s2}, \{s\}\rangle \xrightarrow{tt,\,\phi} \langle\{(s,s2)\}, \{s\}\rangle$$

$$T_6, T_7 \vdash\ T_8 \equiv \langle \text{do emit s3 upto } s\text{ ;emit s2}, \phi\rangle \xrightarrow{tt,\,\phi} \langle\{(s,s3),(s,s2)\}, \{s\}\rangle$$

$$T_8 \vdash\ T_9 \equiv \langle \text{do} \cdots \text{ uptonext s3}, \phi\rangle \xrightarrow{ff,\,\phi} \langle\{(s,s3),(s,s2)\}, \{s\}\rangle$$

b.2) Second branch of the innermost $\|$:

$$\vdash T_{10} \equiv \text{<exit T, } \phi\text{>} \xrightarrow{ff,\ \{T\}} \text{<}\phi,\ \phi\text{>}$$

c) The innermost $\|$ and its enclosing tag :

$$T_9, T_{10} \vdash T_{11} \equiv \text{<[do } \cdots \text{ uptonext s3 } \| \text{ exit T], } \phi\text{>} \xrightarrow{ff,\ \{T\}} \text{<}\{(s,s3),(s,s2)\},\ \{s\}\text{>}$$

$$T_{11} \vdash T_{12} \equiv \text{<tag T in } \cdots \text{ end, } \phi\text{>} \xrightarrow{tt,\ \phi} \text{<}\{(s,s3),(s,s2)\},\ \{s\}\text{>}$$

d) The body of the program :

$$T_4, T_{12} \vdash T_{13} \equiv \text{<[} \cdots \text{ } \| \text{ tag T in } \cdots \text{ end], } \phi\text{>} \xrightarrow{tt,\ \phi} \text{<}\{(s1,s),(s,s3),(s,s2)\},\ \{s1,s$$

The resulting graph is {(s1,s),(s,s3),(s,s2)}, and the program is statically correct since it has no cycle.

6. The behavioral semantics.

6.1. The formalism of the behavioral semantics.

The behavioral semantics defines the history transformation associated with a program. The key idea is to treat each event separately: let P be a program, let E be some input event for P, which defines the signals coming from the outside world and the values they convey; the execution of P on E will provoke the emission of signals forming an output event F (intented to be used by the outside world) and yield *another program* P_1 which represents the program to be executed at the next instant. This is written

$$P \overset{F}{\underset{E}{\Longrightarrow}} P_1$$

Then it is extremely easy to define the behavior of a program P on a given history $H = E_1, E_2, \cdots E_n, \ldots$, considering the sequence

$$P \overset{F_1}{\underset{E_1}{\Longrightarrow}} P_1 \overset{F_2}{\underset{E_2}{\Longrightarrow}} P_2 \Longrightarrow \cdots \overset{F_n}{\underset{E_n}{\Longrightarrow}} P_n \Longrightarrow \cdots$$

The F_n are the events output from input events E_n.

For example consider the following program P, which "shifts" a signal s1 : a signal s2 is output synchronously with the reception of any occurrence of s1 but the first one, and the value output with s2 is the previous value input with s1 :

```
input single signal s1(int),
output single signal s2(int) in
    var X,Y : int in
        await s1(X);
        everynext s1(Y) do
            emit s2(X);
            X:=Y
        end
    end
end
```

Assume the first input event is $s1^3$. Then one has a transition

$$P \underset{s1^3}{\overset{1}{\Longrightarrow}} P_1$$

with P_1 as follows :

```
input single signal s1(int),
output single signal s2(int) in
    var X:=3, Y : int in
        every s1(Y) do
            emit s2(X);
            X:=Y
        end
    end
end
```

If the second input event is $s1^5$, then one has a transition :

$$P_1 \underset{s1^5}{\overset{s2^3}{\Longrightarrow}} P_2$$

with P2 as follows :

```
input single signal s1(int),
output single signal s2(int) in
    var X:=5, Y:=5 : int in
        every s1(Y) do
            emit s2(X);
            X:=Y
        end
    end
end
```

Notice that in this setting the values taken by the variables are recorded in the program themselves. We shall also use a different setting and work with a global memory σ which associates values with variables, having then transitions of the form

$$<P_1, \sigma_1> \underset{E_1}{\overset{F_1}{\Longrightarrow}} <P_2, \sigma_2> \Longrightarrow \cdots$$

In this new setting the program P_1 above must be replaced by the pair $<P'_1, \sigma'_1>$ where P'_1 is the program

```
input single signal s1(int),
output single signal s2(int) in
   var X, Y : int in
      every s1(Y) do
         emit s2(X);
         X:=Y
      end
   end
end
```

and where σ'_1 associates the value 3 with X. Both techniques have their advantages and their drawbacks : the first technique is more intrinsic and gives a simpler semantics. The second technique is more classical and will be used anyway when we shall compile programs in section 8. Our formalism will actually treat equally well the two possibilities, with only two rules changing from the first one to the second one : the rule of variable declaration, the rule of the parallel construct.

Now we have to describe how an input event transforms a program into another program. This will be done as usual by a set of structural rewrite rules, which will define transitions of the form

$$<i, \sigma, E> \xrightarrow{b, L} <i', \sigma', E'>$$

where

(i) i is the current instruction to treat.

(ii) σ is a *memory state*, defining the current association of values with variables.

(iii) E is the input event.

(iv) b is the *termination status* of i. It is a boolean set to tt if and only if i terminates and passes the control in the current instant (cf. the static semantics).

(v) L is the set of labels of tags actually exited by i (only the labels which are free in i appear in L).

(vi) i' is the *reconfiguration* of i. It represents the new instruction to execute at the next instant.

(vii) σ' is the memory state after the execution of i at the current instant.

(viii) E' is the event output by i (and in particular is the event 1 if i emits no signal). Notice that E' may contain signals which are local to the program, event if i is the body of the program. They will have to be removed in order to get the event F in the $\Longrightarrow$ relation.

The form is more complex than with the $\Longrightarrow$ relation, but this is necessary for the structural induction to work correctly. The position of E and E' is also different this will be justified in the next section.

We shall only treat general signals in the semantics, single and pure signals being just particular cases.

6.2. Two techniques for dealing with the memory.

Before giving the rules, we say how to deal with the memory σ. We shall use two different techniques : the de Bruijn stack technique [10] for the case where we want the relation $\Longrightarrow$ to work with programs only, and the allocation technique, where we want the relation $\Longrightarrow$ to work with program-memory pairs. Both techniques will treat correctly name conflicts, but both will require a preliminary labeling of the occurrences of the variables of a program by integers. In both cases we use the same notations : given a memory σ and a (labeled) variable X^i, the value of σ on X^i is written $\sigma(X^i)$ and the memory obtained by changing the value of σ on X^i to v is written $\sigma[X^i \leftarrow v]$.

6.2.1. The stack technique.

The index of an occurrence of a variable represents its *binding depth*, i.e. the number of enclosing variable declarations upto its own declaration. Here is a correct indexing :

```
var X in
    var Y in
        Y¹:=X²;
        var X in
            Y²:=X¹
        end
    end;
    X¹ := 1
end
```

A memory is simply a stack of cells, with usual push and pop operations. A new cell will be pushed at each new "var" declaration (with initial value $\perp$, the undefined value), it will be popped when the corresponding instruction is treated. The cell associated with a variable in a stack is just given by the index of the variable: X^1 is the top of the stack, Y^2 the cell just before the top and so on. The name of the variable is irrelevant.

Let us call ε the empty stack. Then we shall produce for a program P and an input instant E_1 a transition of the form

$$<P, \varepsilon, E_1> \xrightarrow{b, \phi} <P_1, \varepsilon, E'_1>$$

where the output event E'_1 still contains signals which are local to P. Let F_1 be obtained from E'_1 by removing them. Then the corresponding $\Longrightarrow$ transition will be :

$$P \underset{E_1}{\overset{F_1}{\Longrightarrow}} P_1$$

6.2.2. The global allocation technique.

Given the initial program P we want to study, we allocate a cell for every variable of P, taking care of name conflicts so that different X's correspond to different cells. The index is just the "address" of the cell. The above program could be labeled as follows, allocating the three cells in a natural order :

```
var X in
    var Y in
        Y²:=X¹;
        var X in
            Y²:=X³
        end
    end;
    X¹ := 1
end
```

A cell is then read and written in the obvious way, by indexing the global memory at the right position. The relation $\Longrightarrow$ is then obtained as follows : start initially with a memory *undef* which associates undefined values with variables. Produce the transition

$$<P, undef, E_1> \xrightarrow{b, \phi} <P_1, \sigma_1, E'_1>$$

Remove from E'_1 the local signals, obtaining F_1. Then the relation $\Longrightarrow$ is

$$<P, undef> \underset{E_1}{\overset{F_1}{\Longrightarrow}} <P_1, \sigma_1>$$

and the second step now starts from $<P_1, \sigma_1, E_2>$, producing

$$<P_1, \sigma_1, E_2> \xrightarrow{b_2, \phi} <P_2, \sigma_2, E'_2>$$

Removing the local events from E'_2 to get F_2 this yields

$$<P_1, \sigma_1> \overset{F_2}{\underset{E_2}{\Longrightarrow}} <P_2, \sigma_2>$$

and so on.

6.2.3. Computing expressions.

We assume given a semantics $[\![\,]\!]$ for simple expressions, which for any expression exp and memory state σ defines the value $[\![exp]\!]\sigma$ of exp in σ (see for example [25]). Since the test of proper variable initialization was assumed to be made for all programs, we shall not have to treat the case of expression containing undefined variables.

6.3. The rules of the behavioral semantics.

6.3.1. Axiom of nothing.

$$<\text{nothing}, \sigma, E> \xrightarrow{tt,\ \phi} <\text{nothing}, \sigma, 1>$$

6.3.2. Axiom of assignment.

An assignment modifies the memory in the usual way :

$$<X^i{:=}exp, \sigma, E> \xrightarrow{tt,\ \phi} <\text{nothing}, \sigma[X^i \leftarrow [\![exp]\!]\sigma], 1>$$

6.3.3. Axiom of emission.

The rule is obvious, using the notation of 2.2:

$$<\text{emit s}(exp), \sigma, E> \xrightarrow{tt,\ \phi} <\text{nothing}, \sigma, s^{[\![exp]\!]\sigma}>$$

6.3.4. Rules of upto.

There are two cases, according to the presence of the signal in the current instant. If the signal is present one binds the variable and terminates :

$$\frac{s \in E,\ E(s)=v}{<\text{do } i \text{ upto s}(X^i), \sigma, E> \xrightarrow{tt,\ \phi} <\text{nothing}, \sigma[X^i \leftarrow v], 1>}$$

If the signal is not present, we execute i without passing the control. The exits possibly generated by i are transmitted :

$$\frac{s \notin E, \quad <i, \sigma, E> \xrightarrow{b,\ L} <i', \sigma', E'>}{<\text{do } i \text{ upto s}(X^i), \sigma, E> \xrightarrow{ff,\ L} <\text{do } i' \text{ upto s}(X^i), \sigma', E'>}$$

6.3.5. Rule of uptonext.

An uptonext does not pass the control, and besides that behaves as its body. The reconfiguration becomes an upto statement, according to the naive semantics :

$$\frac{\langle i, \sigma, E\rangle \xrightarrow{b, L} \langle i', \sigma', E'\rangle}{\langle \text{do } i \text{ uptonext } s(X^i), \sigma, E\rangle \xrightarrow{ff, L} \langle \text{do } i' \text{ upto } s(X^i), \sigma', E'\rangle}$$

6.3.6. Rules of sequencing.

The are two cases. In the first one, the first instruction passes the control; this may happen only if it provokes no exit. The second instruction receives the signal emitted by the first one. The event produced is the product of the of events yield by both instructions.

$$\frac{\langle i_1, \sigma, E\rangle \xrightarrow{tt, \phi} \langle i'_1, \sigma'_1, E'_1\rangle \qquad \langle i_2, \sigma'_1, E * E'_1\rangle \xrightarrow{b_2, L_2} \langle i'_2, \sigma'_2, E'_2\rangle}{\langle i_1; i_2, \sigma, E\rangle \xrightarrow{b_2, L_2} \langle i'_2, \sigma'_2, E'_1 * E'_2\rangle}$$

In the second case the first instruction does not pass the control. The rule is obvious :

$$\frac{\langle i_1, \sigma, E\rangle \xrightarrow{ff, L_1} \langle i'_1, \sigma'_1, E'_1\rangle}{\langle i_1; i_2, \sigma, E\rangle \xrightarrow{ff, L_1} \langle i'_1; i_2, \sigma'_1, E'_1\rangle}$$

6.3.7. Rule of loop.

The rule realizes a classical unfolding of the loop. As in the static semantics, it applies only if the body does not pass the control :

$$\frac{\langle i, \sigma, E\rangle \xrightarrow{ff, L} \langle i', \sigma', E'\rangle}{\langle \text{loop } i \text{ end}, \sigma, E\rangle \xrightarrow{ff, L} \langle i'; \text{loop } i \text{ end}, \sigma', E'\rangle}$$

6.3.8. Rules of conditional.

The rule are obvious :

$$\frac{[\![boolexp]\!]\sigma = tt \qquad \langle i_1, \sigma, E\rangle \xrightarrow{b_1, L_1} \langle i'_1, \sigma'_1, E'_1\rangle}{\langle \text{if } boolexp \text{ then } i_1 \text{ else } i_2 \text{ end}, \sigma, E\rangle \xrightarrow{b_1, L_1} \langle i'_1, \sigma'_1, E'_1\rangle}$$

$$\frac{[\![boolexp]\!]\sigma = ff \qquad \langle i_2, \sigma, E\rangle \xrightarrow{b_2, L_2} \langle i'_2, \sigma'_2, E'_2\rangle}{\langle \text{if } boolexp \text{ then } i_1 \text{ else } i_2 \text{ end}, \sigma, E\rangle \xrightarrow{b_2, L_2} \langle i'_2, \sigma'_2, E'_2\rangle}$$

6.3.9. Rule of parallel.

6.3.9.1. Rule for the stack technique.

This is the most interesting rule. The main idea is that each component of the parallel construct receives also the signals emitted by the other component :

$$\frac{<i_1, \sigma, E * E'_2> \xrightarrow{b_1, L_1} <i'_1, \sigma, E'_1> \qquad <i_2, \sigma, E * E'_1> \xrightarrow{b_2, L_2} <i'_2, \sigma, E'_2>}{<i_1 \| i_2, \sigma, E> \xrightarrow{b_1 \cap b_2, L_1 \cup L_2} <i'_1 \| i'_2, \sigma, E'_1 * E'_2>}$$

The termination is the boolean conjunction of the terminations of the components. The exits are obtained by unioning the exits raised by the components. The memory σ does not change, since there are no shared variables and since a branch of a parallel statement in not allowed to modify its free variables. For signals, we do not say at all how to find E'_1 and E'_2, and it is not clear that E'_1 and E'_2 indeed exist or are unique. Hence our rule is in some sense "non-constructive". Our main result will say that we indeed have existence and uniqueness for statically correct programs. The whole purpose of the computational semantics of the next section is to make the rule constructive.

6.3.9.2. Rule for the global allocation technique.

We have just to remember that the variables that i_1 and i_2 may modify are disjoint. Let $L(i)$ be the set of local variables to an instruction i. For two disjoints sets of variables V_1 and V_2, and for σ_1,σ_2 two memory states such that $\sigma_1(X^i)=\sigma_2(X^i)$ for $X^i \not\in V_1 \cup V_2$ Then let $\sigma_1 {}_{V_1}+_{V_2} \sigma_2$ be the memory σ such that $\sigma(X^i)=\sigma_1(X^i)$ for $X^i \in V_1$, $\sigma(X^i)=\sigma_2(X^i)$ for $X^i \in V_2$, and $\sigma(X^i)=\sigma_1(X^i)=\sigma_2(X^i)$ for $X^i \not\in V_1 \cup V_2$. Then the rule is

$$\frac{<i_1, \sigma, E * E'_2> \xrightarrow{b_1, L_1} <i'_1, \sigma'_1, E'_1> \qquad <i_2, \sigma, E * E'_1> \xrightarrow{b_2, L_2} <i'_2, \sigma'_2, E'_2>}{<i_1 \| i_2, \sigma, E> \xrightarrow{b_1 \cap b_2, L_1 \cup L_2} <i'_1 \| i'_2, \sigma'_1 {}_{L(i_1)}+_{L(i_2)} \sigma'_2, E'_1 * E'_2>}$$

6.3.10. Rules of tag.

A tag passes the control if its body does so or if the body executes an exit with the corresponding label and no enclosing exit :

$$\frac{<i, \sigma, E> \xrightarrow{b, L} <i', \sigma', E'> \qquad b=tt \text{ or } L=\{T\}}{<\text{tag T in } i \text{ end}, \sigma, E> \xrightarrow{tt, \phi} <\text{nothing}, \sigma', E'>}$$

Otherwise, i.e. if the body does not pass the control while raising no exit or if the body exits enclosing tags, the tag instruction does not pass the control and removes its label from the tag label set L (if present) :

$$\frac{<i,\sigma,E> \xrightarrow{ff,L} <i',\sigma',E'> \qquad L\neq\{T\}}{<\text{tag T in } i \text{ end},\sigma,E> \xrightarrow{ff,L-\{T\}} <\text{tag T in } i' \text{ end},\sigma',E'>}$$

6.3.11. Axiom of exit.

An exit does not pass the control and raises the exit :

$$<\text{exit T},\sigma,E> \xrightarrow{ff,\{T\}} <\text{nothing},\sigma,1>$$

6.3.12. Rule of variable declaration.

6.3.12.1. Rule for the stack technique.

One pushes a new cell (with initial value $\perp$) for analyzing the body. Then one pops the cell and one retains its value as the current value of the variable by an appropriate assignment (types omitted) :

$$\frac{<i,push(\perp,\sigma),E> \xrightarrow{b,L} <i',\sigma',E'>}{<\text{var X in } i \text{ end},\sigma,E> \xrightarrow{b,L} <\text{var X in } X^1{:=}top(\sigma');\ i',\ pop(\sigma'),E'>}$$

6.3.12.2. Rule for the global allocation technique.

There is just nothing to do :

$$\frac{<i,\sigma,E> \xrightarrow{b,L} <i',\sigma',E'>}{<\text{var X in } i \text{ end},\sigma,E> \xrightarrow{b,L} <\text{var X in } i' \text{ end},\sigma',E'>}$$

6.4. Existence and uniqueness of the behavioral semantics.

Theorem: Let P be statically correct for the first instant. Then the exists one and only one provable transition of the form

$$<P,\sigma,E> \xrightarrow{b,L} <P',\sigma',E'>$$

(where $\sigma=\sigma'=\varepsilon$ with the stack memory allocation and where σ and σ' are the memory states before and after execution with global memory allocation).

The proof is rather technical and omitted here, see [15]. The main difficulty is to show that there is always one and exactly one way of applying the rule of $\|$. The main argument is an induction on the longest path of the graph G produced by the static semantics. Notice that we never chain the arrows $\longrightarrow$, unlike in [24]. An instant corresponds always to a single transition in our formalism. The flow of control may be quite complex inside an instant, and this is exactly reflected in the complexity of the corresponding transition proof.

Hence we can derive the relation $\Longrightarrow$ as in 6.2, provided that the program generated at each step is statically correct for the first instant. This means that any computation step involves the computation of the static and dynamic semantics, in that order.

The fact that there is at most one reduction shows that an ESTEREL program is indeed deterministic: it produces exactly one output history per input history.

6.5. Examples.

In the examples we shall name the transitions we prove and indicate for any transition the names associated with its premisses, as already done in section 5. We show first why static correction is necessary. Consider the incorrect program P :

```
local pure signal s1, s2
[
    do nothing upto s1; emit s2
||
    do nothing upto s2; emit s1
]
```

Then there are two ways to apply the parallel rule to the body of P (we omit obvious deductions and the memory state which is unnecessary here) :

$$T_1 \equiv \langle \text{do nothing upto s1; emit s2, 1} \rangle \xrightarrow{\mathit{ff},\,\phi} \langle \text{do nothing upto s1; emit s2, 1} \rangle$$

$$T_2 \equiv \langle \text{do nothing upto s2; emit s1, 1} \rangle \xrightarrow{\mathit{ff},\,\phi} \langle \text{do nothing upto s2; emit s1, 1} \rangle$$

$$T_1, T_2 \vdash \langle [.. \,\|\, ..], 1 \rangle \xrightarrow{\mathit{ff},\,\phi} \langle [.. \,\|\, ..], 1 \rangle$$

orelse :

$$T_1 \equiv \langle \text{do nothing upto s1; emit s2, s1} \rangle \xrightarrow{\mathit{tt},\,\phi} \langle \text{nothing, s2} \rangle$$

$$T_2 \equiv \langle \text{do nothing upto s2; emit s1, s2} \rangle \xrightarrow{\mathit{tt},\,\phi} \langle \text{nothing, s2} \rangle$$

$$T_1, T_2 \vdash \langle [.. \,\|\, ..], 1 \rangle \xrightarrow{\mathit{tt},\,\phi} \langle [\text{nothing} \,\|\, \text{nothing}], \text{s1} * \text{s2} \rangle$$

Let us now turn to a correct program P :

```
output pure signal s3,
local pure signal s1, s2 in
   [
      [
         emit s1
      ||
         do nothing upto s2;
         emit s3
      ]
   ||
      do nothing upto s1;
      emit s2
   ]
end
```

re s3 is emitted, but the proof of that fact is not immediate : one has to guess at the first branch of the outermost || receives s2, while its second branch ceives s1 and s3, and that for the innermost || the first branch receives s2 $*$ s3 ile the second branch receives s1 $*$ s3. Here is the derivation, which is unique to some step permutation (we again omit the memory state) :

$T_1 \equiv$ <emit s1, s2 $*$ s3> $\xrightarrow{tt,\,\phi}$ <nothing, s1>

$T_2 \equiv$ <do nothing upto s2, s1 $*$ s2> $\xrightarrow{tt,\,\phi}$ <nothing, 1>

$T_3 \equiv$ <emit s3, s1 $*$ s2> $\xrightarrow{tt,\,\phi}$ <nothing, s3>

$T_3 \vdash T_4 \equiv$ <do nothing upto s2; emit s3, s1 $*$ s2> $\xrightarrow{tt,\,\phi}$ <nothing, s3>

$T_4 \vdash T_5 \equiv$ <[$\cdots$ || $\cdots$], s2> $\xrightarrow{tt,\,\phi}$ <nothing || nothing, s2>

$T_6 \equiv$ <do nothing upto s1, s1 $*$ s3> $\xrightarrow{tt,\,\phi}$ <nothing, 1>

$T_7 \equiv$ <emit s2, s1 $*$ s3> $\xrightarrow{tt,\,\phi}$ <nothing, s2>

$T_7 \vdash T_8 \equiv$ <do nothing upto s1; emit s2, s1 $*$ s3> $\xrightarrow{tt,\,\phi}$ <nothing, s2>

$T_8 \vdash T_9 \equiv$ <[[$\cdots$ || $\cdots$] || ...], 1> $\xrightarrow{tt,\,\phi}$ <[[nothing || nothing] || nothing], s1 $*$ s2 $*$ s3>

$\overset{s3}{\underset{1}{\Longrightarrow}} P_1$

nce we emit indeed s3. The resulting program is clearly equivalent to nothing o programs being equivalent if they produce the same output history for any out history[9, 21]).

6.6. Derived rules for derived constructs.

When we introduced the derived constructs in section 3, we said that they should be considered as syntactic macros without semantical meaning. This means in particular that the semantics of the extended language is completely determined by the semantics of the kernel. But, in practice, for analyzing programs it is very cumbersome to always come down to the kernel level. A much better idea is to use the syntactic definition of a construct to *derive* its behavior. For example it is not hard to derive the following rules for the "inpresence" construct :

$$\frac{s \in E \qquad E(s)=l \qquad <i, \sigma[X^i \leftarrow l], E> \xrightarrow{b,L} <i', \sigma', E'>}{<\text{inpresence } s(X^i) \text{do } i \text{ end}, \sigma, E> \xrightarrow{b,L} <i', \sigma', E'>}$$

$$\frac{s \notin E}{<\text{inpresence } s(X^i) \text{do } i \text{ end}, \sigma, E> \xrightarrow{\#,\phi} <\text{nothing}, \sigma, 1>}$$

It would often be preferable to give directly a set of rules rather than an implementation for a derived construct. However the problem of knowing whether a construct defined by a rule is definable from our kernel has not yet been investigated, and has no reason to be simple. See [27] for an analysis of that problem for SCCS and MEIJE calculi.

7. The computational semantics.

7.1. The intuitive idea.

The behavioral semantics is enough for giving the dynamic semantics of any program, but it is not "effective" and therefore does not lead to a natural interpretation mechanism. The computational semantics will do that job. It is a refinement of the behavioral semantics, which uses the information given by the static semantics (and is naturally related to the proof of our main theorem, which we did not give here).

Consider the last program studied in section 6. The causality graph produced by the static semantics is easily seen to be {(s1,s2),(s2,s3)} : s1 causes s2 which in turn causes s3. In the computational semantics we shall use a "wavefront propagation" technique on that graph, resolving first s1, then s2 and finally s3, where by "resolving" a signal s we mean treating the active "upto s" statements. By construction of the graph, we know that there will be no emission of a signal after that signal is resolved, so that we shall correctly decide whether a signal is emitted or not and bind correctly variables to emitted values when the signal is actually emitted. Back to the example, at the first step we freeze all upto statements, so that the only possible instruction to execute is "emit s1". At the second step we can terminate the "do nothing upto s1" statement and hence emit s2. Finally at the third step we can terminate the "do nothing upto s2" statement and emit s3.

7.2. The formalism.

The formalism we use is quite close to the one we used for the behavioral semantics. We manipulate transitions of the form :

$$<i, \sigma, E> \xrightarrow[G,n]{b,L} <i', \sigma', E'>$$

where i, σ, E, i', σ', E', L are just as before, where b has now three values, tt and ff as before and $\perp$ standing for unresolved, and where there are two additional inputs, the causality graph G and the current propagation level n (notice that all inputs are on the left of the arrow and under it, while all outputs are above the arrow or on its right).

We define the depth $depth(G)$ of an acyclic graph G as being the length of its longest path, and the level $level_G(\mathrm{s})$ of s in G as the longest path from s to a root of G.

7.3. The rules of the computational semantics.

We consider only the stack technique for memory, the global allocation technique being left to the reader (it works just as before).

7.3.1. Axiom of nothing.

$$<\mathrm{nothing}, \sigma, E> \xrightarrow[G,n]{tt,\phi} <\mathrm{nothing}, \sigma, 1>$$

7.3.2. Axiom of assignment.

$$<\mathrm{X}^i\!:=exp\,, \sigma, E> \xrightarrow[G,n]{tt,\phi} <\mathrm{nothing}, \sigma[\mathrm{X}^i \leftarrow [\![exp]\!] \sigma], 1>$$

7.3.3. Axiom of emission.

$$<\mathrm{emit\ s}(exp), \sigma, E> \xrightarrow[G,n]{tt,\phi} <\mathrm{nothing}, \sigma, \mathrm{s}^{[\![exp]\!]\sigma}>$$

7.3.4. Rules of upto.

The two first rules apply when the signal can be properly treated. In the first one the signal is present :

$$\frac{level_G(\mathrm{s}) \leq n \qquad \mathrm{s} \in E \qquad E(\mathrm{s}) = v}{<\mathrm{do}\ i\ \mathrm{upto\ s}(\mathrm{X}^i), \sigma, E> \xrightarrow[G,n]{tt,\phi} <\mathrm{nothing}, \sigma[\mathrm{X}^i \leftarrow v\,], 1>}$$

In the second one the signal is not present. One has to take care of the fact that the body of the upto may not be resolved yet; this is the reason of the $\cap$ in the resulting termination flag

$$\frac{level_G(\text{s})\leq n \qquad \text{s}\not\in E \qquad \langle i,\sigma,E\rangle \xrightarrow[G,n]{b,L} \langle i',\sigma',E'\rangle}{\langle \text{do } i \text{ upto s}(X^i),\sigma,E\rangle \xrightarrow[G,n]{ff\cap b,L} \langle \text{do } i' \text{ upto s}(X^i),\sigma',E'\rangle}$$

The last rule applies when the upto cannot be resolved :

$$\frac{level_G(\text{s})>n}{\langle \text{do } i \text{ upto s}(X^i),\sigma,E\rangle \xrightarrow[G,n]{\perp,\phi} \langle \text{do } i \text{ upto s}(X^i),\sigma,1\rangle}$$

7.3.5. Rules of uptonext.

The first rule applies when the body is resolved :

$$\frac{\langle i,\sigma,E\rangle \xrightarrow[G,n]{b,L} \langle i',\sigma',E'\rangle \qquad b\neq\perp}{\langle \text{do } i \text{ uptonext s}(X^i),\sigma,E\rangle \xrightarrow[G,n]{ff,L} \langle \text{do } i' \text{ upto s}(X^i),\sigma',E'\rangle}$$

And the second rule applies when the body is unresolved :

$$\frac{\langle i,\sigma,E\rangle \xrightarrow[G,n]{\perp,\phi} \langle i',\sigma',E'\rangle}{\langle \text{do } i \text{ uptonext s}(X^i),\sigma,E\rangle \xrightarrow[G,n]{\perp,\phi} \langle \text{do } i' \text{ uptonext s}(X^i),\sigma',E'\rangle}$$

7.3.6. Rules of sequencing.

The rules are basically the same as for the behavioral semantics, the second one taking care of the case when i_1 is unresolved :

$$\frac{\langle i_1,\sigma,E\rangle \xrightarrow[G,n]{tt,\phi} \langle i'_1,\sigma'_1,E'_1\rangle \qquad \langle i_2,\sigma'_1,E * E'_1\rangle \xrightarrow[G,n]{b_2,L_2} \langle i'_2,\sigma'_2,E'_2\rangle}{\langle i_1;i_2,\sigma,E\rangle \xrightarrow[G,n]{b_2,L_2} \langle i'_2,\sigma'_2,E'_1 * E'_2\rangle}$$

$$\frac{\langle i_1,\sigma,E\rangle \xrightarrow[G,n]{b_1,L_1} \langle i'_1,\sigma'_1,E'_1\rangle \qquad b_1\neq tt}{\langle i_1;i_2,\sigma,E\rangle \xrightarrow[G,n]{b_1,L_1} \langle i'_1;i_2,\sigma'_1,E'_1\rangle}$$

7.3.7. Rule of loop.

Same rule as in the behavioral semantics, but adding the case where the body is unresolved :

$$\frac{\langle i,\sigma,E\rangle \xrightarrow[G,n]{b,L} \langle i',\sigma',E'\rangle \qquad b\neq tt}{\langle \text{loop } i \text{ end},\sigma,E\rangle \xrightarrow[G,n]{b,L} \langle i';\text{loop } i \text{ end},\sigma',E'\rangle}$$

7.3.8. Rules of conditional.

The rule are again obvious :

$$\frac{[\![boolexp]\!]\sigma=tt \qquad <i_1, \sigma, E> \xrightarrow[G,n]{b_1, L_1} <i'_1, \sigma'_1, E'_1>}{<\text{if } boolexp \text{ then } i_1 \text{ else } i_2 \text{ end}, \sigma, E> \xrightarrow[G,n]{b_1, L_1} <i'_1, \sigma'_1, E'_1>}$$

$$\frac{[\![boolexp]\!]\sigma=ff \qquad <i_2, \sigma, E> \xrightarrow[G,n]{b_2, L_2} <i'_2, \sigma'_2, E'_2>}{<\text{if } boolexp \text{ then } i_1 \text{ else } i_2 \text{ end}, \sigma, E> \xrightarrow[G,n]{b_2, L_2} <i'_2, \sigma'_2, E'_2>}$$

7.3.9. Rules of parallel.

The first rule applies when both sides are simultaneously resolved or unresolved:

$$\frac{<i_1, \sigma, E> \xrightarrow[G,n]{b_1, L_1} <i'_1, \sigma, E'_1> \qquad <i_2, \sigma, E> \xrightarrow[G,n]{b_2, L_2} <i'_2, \sigma, E'_2> \qquad b_1 \cap b_2 \neq \perp \text{ or } b_1 = b_2 = \perp}{<i_1 \| i_2, \sigma, E> \xrightarrow[G,n]{b_1 \cap b_2, L_1 \cup L_2} <i'_1 \| i'_2, \sigma, E'_1 * E'_2>}$$

Notice that the above rule is very different from the corresponding behavioral rule, since E'_1 and E'_2 can now be computed by pure structural induction. This will be also true for the other rules for $\|$, which correspond to the case where one of the arms is resolved and the other arm is unresolved. We need to remember the output termination tag, exit and reconfiguration of the resolved arm. For this we introduce two new operators : ${}^{b_1, L_1}\|$ means that the left arm has been resolved with termination status b_1 and exits L_1, and conversely $\|^{b_2, L_2}$ means that the second arm has been resolved with status b_2 and exits L_2 (in an implementation, this amounts of course to keep appropriate attributes together with the parallel node - one must say that the implementation is obvious here while the rewrite rule formalism is quite heavy). This gives the two rules :

$$\frac{<i_1, \sigma, E> \xrightarrow[G,n]{b_1, L_1} <i'_1, \sigma, E'_1> \qquad <i_2, \sigma, E> \xrightarrow[G,n]{\perp, \phi} <i'_2, \sigma, E'_2> \qquad b_1 \neq \perp}{<i_1 \| i_2, \sigma, E> \xrightarrow[G,n]{\perp, \phi} <i'_1 \;{}^{b_1, L_1}\| \; i'_2, \sigma, E'_1 * E'_2>}$$

$$\frac{<i_1, \sigma, E> \xrightarrow[G,n]{\perp, \phi} <i'_1, \sigma, E'_1> \qquad <i_2, \sigma, E> \xrightarrow[G,n]{b_2, L_2} <i'_2, \sigma, E'_2> \qquad b_2 \neq \perp}{<i_1 \| i_2, \sigma, E> \xrightarrow[G,n]{\perp, \phi} <i'_1 \; \|^{b_2, L_2} \; i'_2, \sigma, E'_1 * E'_2>}$$

Now the rules for the new operators are immediate. Two rules apply when the arm still remains unresolved :

$$\frac{\langle i_2,\ \sigma,\ E\rangle \xrightarrow[G,n]{\bot,\phi} \langle i'_2,\ \sigma,\ E'_2\rangle}{\langle i_1 \ {}^{b_1,L_1}\|\ i_2,\ \sigma,\ E\rangle \xrightarrow[G,n]{\bot,\phi} \langle i_1 \ {}^{b_1,L_1}\|\ i'_2,\ \sigma,\ E'_2\rangle}$$

$$\frac{\langle i_1,\ \sigma,\ E\rangle \xrightarrow[G,n]{\bot,\phi} \langle i'_1,\ \sigma,\ E'_1\rangle}{\langle i_1 \ \|^{b_2,L_2}\ i_2,\ \sigma,\ E\rangle \xrightarrow[G,n]{\bot,\phi} \langle i'_1 \ \|^{b_2,L_2}\ i_2,\ \sigma,\ E'_2\rangle}$$

And the two last rules finally resolve the $\|$ operator :

$$\frac{\langle i_2,\ \sigma,\ E\rangle \xrightarrow[G,n]{b_2,L_2} \langle i'_2,\ \sigma,\ E'_2\rangle \qquad b_2 \neq \bot}{\langle i_1 \ {}^{b_1,L_1}\|\ i_2,\ \sigma,\ E\rangle \xrightarrow[G,n]{b_1 \cap b_2,\ L_1 \cup L_2} \langle i_1 \ \|\ i'_2,\ \sigma,\ E'_2\rangle}$$

$$\frac{\langle i_1,\ \sigma,\ E\rangle \xrightarrow[G,n]{b_1,L_1} \langle i'_1,\ \sigma,\ E'_1\rangle \qquad b_1 \neq \bot}{\langle i_1 \ \|^{b_2,L_2}\ i_2,\ \sigma,\ E\rangle \xrightarrow[G,n]{b_1 \cap b_2,\ L_1 \cup L_2} \langle i'_1 \ \|\ i_2,\ \sigma,\ E'_1\rangle}$$

7.3.10. Rules of tag.

The rules are similar to the behavioral ones, but taking care of an unresolved body :

$$\frac{\langle i,\ \sigma,\ E\rangle \xrightarrow[G,n]{b,L} \langle i',\ \sigma',\ E'\rangle \qquad b = tt \ \mathit{or}\ (b = ff \text{ and } L = \{\mathrm{T}\})}{\langle \text{tag T in } i \text{ end},\ \sigma,\ E\rangle \xrightarrow[G,n]{tt,\phi} \langle \text{nothing},\ \sigma',\ E'\rangle}$$

$$\frac{\langle i,\ \sigma,\ E\rangle \xrightarrow[G,n]{b,L} \langle i',\ \sigma',\ E'\rangle \qquad (b = ff \text{ and } L \neq \{\mathrm{T}\}) \ \mathit{or}\ b = \bot}{\langle \text{tag T in } i \text{ end},\ \sigma,\ E\rangle \xrightarrow[G,n]{b,\ L-\{\mathrm{T}\}} \langle \text{tag T in } i' \text{ end},\ \sigma',\ E'\rangle}$$

7.3.11. Axiom of exit.

$$\langle \text{exit T},\ \sigma,\ E\rangle \xrightarrow[G,n]{ff,\ \{\mathrm{T}\}} \langle \text{nothing},\ \sigma,\ 1\rangle$$

7.3.12. Rule of variable declaration.

$$\frac{\langle i,\ \sigma,\ E\rangle \xrightarrow[G,n]{b,L} \langle i',\ \sigma',\ E'\rangle}{\langle \text{var X in } i \text{ end},\ push(\bot,\sigma),\ E\rangle \xrightarrow[G,n]{b,L} \langle \text{var X in } \mathrm{X}^1 := top(\sigma');\ i',\ pop(\sigma'),\ E'\rangle}$$

7.4. Identity of the computational and behavioral semantics.

Theorem: Let P be a statically correct program with associated graph G. Then for any memory state σ and input event E there exists a unique provable sequence of transitions of the form

$$<\mathrm{P}, \sigma, E> \xrightarrow[G,0]{b_0, \phi} <\mathrm{P}_0, \sigma_0, E_0>$$

$$<\mathrm{P}_0, \sigma_0, E * E_0> \xrightarrow[G,1]{b_1, \phi} <\mathrm{P}_1, \sigma_1, E_1>$$

$$<\mathrm{P}_{k-1}, \sigma_{k-1}, E * E_0 * E_1 * \cdots * E_{k-1}> \xrightarrow[G,k]{b_k, \phi} <\mathrm{P}_k, \sigma_k, E_k>$$

with $k \leq m$, $b_0 = b_1 = \cdots = b_{k-1} = \perp$ and $b_k \neq \perp$. Moreover one has in the behavioral semantics

$$<\mathrm{P}, \sigma, E> \xrightarrow{b_k, \phi} <\mathrm{P}_k, \sigma_k, E_0 * E_1 * \cdots * E_k>$$

The proof is omitted.

8. Compiling ESTEREL programs into automata.

8.1. Symbolic evaluation of ESTEREL programs.

Although the rules of the computational semantics are much more complicated than the rules of the behavioral semantics, they are very easy to implement, and we built rapidly from them a LISP symbolic evaluator for ESTEREL which fits in a few pages. The interpreter is not fast enough for running really in real-time (it needs typically some tenths of a second to evaluate the game program on any input). But it makes possible to make easily experiments and simulations on a program.

8.2. Compiling programs containing only pure signals to finite automata.

The main role of the interpreter is however not to make simulations, but to produce really "compiled code" from an ESTEREL program. We shall do it first for programs containing only pure signals. Let us state a definition and an essential result :

Definition : write $\mathrm{P} \overset{*}{\Longrightarrow} \mathrm{P}'$ if there exists an input history $E_1, E_2, \cdots, E_n$ and an output history $F_1, F_2, \cdots, F_n$ such that

$$\mathrm{P} \overset{F_1}{\underset{E_1}{\Longrightarrow}} \mathrm{P}_1 \overset{F_2}{\underset{E_2}{\Longrightarrow}} \mathrm{P}_2 \Longrightarrow \cdots \overset{F_n}{\underset{E_n}{\Longrightarrow}} \mathrm{P}'$$

Theorem : Let P be a program containing only pure signals. Then there exists only finitely many P' such that $\mathrm{P} \overset{*}{\Longrightarrow} \mathrm{P}'$

As a consequence we can use the symbolic evaluator for producing *all* the possible P' such that P $\overset{*}{\Longrightarrow}$ P', and all the possible transitions from those P', using the fact that there is always a finite number of possible input events. Now we can enumerate these programs : call them P_0=P, P_1, . . . , P_n. The transitions $P_i \underset{E}{\overset{F}{\Longrightarrow}} P_j$ may be equally well seen as transitions $i \underset{E}{\overset{F}{\Longrightarrow}} j$ where i and j are now states of a *finite automaton*. The automaton works exactly as the original program : from state i with input event E it produces an output event F and goes to state j if and only if $P_i \underset{E}{\overset{F}{\Longrightarrow}} P_j$. The essential point is that once we have produced the automaton we can completely forget about the original program, and just execute the state-to-state transitions corresponding to given input events, with emission of the output event to the external world. The automaton may therefore be trivially implemented in any classical *sequential* language. The parallelism and internal communication of the original program have totally disappeared in the "compiling" process.

It is of course important to know whether the automata produced are small or big. Our present experiments tend to show that they are indeed quite small (for example the reflex game automaton and the prompting machine automaton have no more than 4 and 11 states respectively). This is due to the strong synchrony hypothesis, which implies that many things may happen at once in an instant, and in particular that adding many internal communications does not increase the size of the automaton, contrarily to what happens in usual asynchronous mechanisms. Consider for example the two following programs, which both emit s2 every time s1 is received twice :

```
input pure signal s1,
output pure signal s2 in
    await s1;
    loop
        awaitnext s1;
        emit s2;
        awaitnext s1;
    end
end
```

```
input pure signal s1,
output pure signal s2,
local pure signal s3,s4 in
    [
        await s1;
        awaitnext s1;
        emit s3
    ||
        await s3;
        emit s2
    ||
        await s1;
        awaitnext s1;
        awaitnext s1;
        awaitnext s1;
        emit s4
    ||
        await s4;
        loop
            emit s2;
            awaitnext s1;
            awaitnext s1
        end
    ]
end
```

It is obvious that the optimal automaton has two states. Our compiling process indeed produces that automaton directly from the first program. For the second (stupid) program, the automaton produced has 6 states, but the classical minimisation algorithm brings it back to the optimal one : the additional signals and control structure give no state explosion at all.

A more convincing use of internal events for improve the programming style was of course the prompting machine of section 4.

6.3. Compiling general programs.

The above theorem does not hold for general programs handling possibly infinite data types. However we can still compile any program into a finite automaton representing its *control behavior*, associating with each transition a sequential program manipulating a global memory. The sequential program is written with 5 instructions :

(i) assignment X:=*exp* as before.

(ii) An instruction X:=*val*(*s*) assigning to X the values conveyed by an external signal in the current input event.

(iii) An instruction emit s(*exp*) for emitting a signal with some value (list)

(iv) The usual conditional.

(v) A "newstate *n*" instruction which indicates that the current processing is terminated and that the new state is *n*.

We shall give no more details here, since the compiler will be described in a forthcoming paper. We just give the example of a program which emits s2(X+Y) every time it has received two successive signals s1(X) and s2(Y), but only if X+Y is even :

```
input single signal s1(int),
output single signal s2(int) in
    var X, Y : int in
        loop
            await s1(X);
            awaitnext s1(Y);
            if even(X+Y) then emit s2(X+Y) fi;
            awaitnext s1
        end
    end
end
```

The automaton obtained looks as follows :

```
state 0 :
    1  --> newstate 0
    s1 --> X:=val(s1); newstate 1
state 1 :
    s1 --> Y:=val(s1);
             if even(X+Y) then
                 emit s2(X+Y);
                 newstate 0
             else
                 newstate 0
             fi
```

Again that automaton is trivially implemented in any sequential language. Notice that the execution of a transition may be very fast, so that the strong synchrony hypothesis may be met in practice upto a really satisfactory point. Moreover if we have a model of the execution machine we can exactly compute the time taken by transitions, and know if the machine is fast enough for executing the program in a satisfactory way.

We are not forced to allocate globally *all* variables in a program. Remember the stack allocation technique for variables : we keeped the value of a variable *inside* the program by an appropriate assignment. If the data type on which the variable ranges is finite, we can still apply this technique and get a finite automaton without allocation of the variable, transforming so to speak data into control (there is indeed no problem in intermixing the two allocation techniques). A typical use of that method is for protocols: messages between senders and receivers convey generally two kinds of information, the message itself which will naturally be stored in a globally allocated variable, and some control information which is often limited to a finite number of values. Then it is good practice not to allocate the variables which hold that information: it makes the analysis and minimization of the automaton produced both easier and more powerful.

If a program has n input signals, the number of transitions to consider from any state is normally 2^n, since we have to consider all possible input events. However there are often relations between the input signals : two signals may always be synchronous (say millisecond and second) or on the contrary incompatible. We give in the prototype compiler rather crude ways of specifying such facts, and this results in reducing drastically the size of the automata (mainly in the number of transitions to consider). Much work remains to be done there, in particular for expressing such constraints in a general formalism (see in particular [28]), and for taking care of these additional constraints in the static semantics.

As far as automaton analysis is concerned, we have done very succesful experiments with the EMC temporal logic model checker [14]. This will also be detailed elsewhere.

8.4. Interfacing ESTEREL programs.

An ESTEREL program produces an automaton which should be interfaced to the real world. We have little to say here, since the problem is common to all real time languages. The only difference is that the ESTEREL program should *not* be considered as the "master" program as in usual languages, but rather as a "servant". Some master program should decide *when* events have really come from the outside, send them to the ESTEREL program for calculations and state transitions, and transmit to the outside world the emitted signals. This is particularly clear for programs which test for the instantaneous conjunction of two events (resetting a game by pressing two buttons together is a good example). The master must decide when to consider that two external events are simultaneous. Further investigation is obviously needed here.

9. Conclusion.

We intend to develop the present work in four directions :

(i) *Investigating extensions to the language.* The most important one is certainly dynamic creation of processes. There as far as behavioral and computational semantics are concerned, but we will certainly loose the possibility of compiling a program into a finite automata, which was the main idea for making the strong synchrony hypothesis realistic. Hence we have to find some limitations in order to keep fast execution mechanisms. We have also to see if some applications require non-determinism in a natural way.

(ii) *Producing really usable compilers and programming environments.* This work is in progress at the moment. An important issue is separate compilation, but it raises to our opinion no major problem. We should also investigate other means of producing automata than the one presented in section 8, and especially more structural ones.

(iii) *Understanding the proof theory of ESTEREL*, and more generally relating the ESTEREL imperative formalism to non-imperative ones, such as temporal logics or event algebras [28, 12, 17]. The translation to automata is of great help there.

(iv) Making real experiments with ESTEREL programs, by constructing real-time machines and experimenting complex ESTEREL programs on them. Running real programs in real environments should also serve as the main tool for understanding what should be the programming style in a synchronous language such as ESTEREL.

Acknowledgements: we want to thank J-P Marmorat and J-P Rigault who got the original ideas of ESTEREL and participated to the whole project, J. Camerini and B. Nguyen-Phuoc who wrote the first SCCS formal semantics, and F. Boussinot, S. Moisan and R. de Simone for their contributions to the present version.

References.

1. *LTR Manuel Officiel de Référence*, Ministère de la Défense, France (1978).

2. *Net Theory and Applications*, LNCS 84, Springer-Verlag (1979).

3. *Reference Manual for the ADA Programming Language*, CII Honeywell-Bull (1980).

4. "OCCAM Programming Manual," *INMOS Limited* (1983).

5. E. Astesiano and E. Zucca, "Semantics of CSP via Translation into CCS," in *Proc. MFCS 81*, Springer-Verlag, LNCS 116 (1981).

6. J.G.P. Barnes, *RTL/2 Design and Philosophy*, Heyden & Sons Ltd. (1976).

7. G. Berry, J. Camerini, B. Nguyen Phuoc, J.P. Marmorat, and J.P. Rigault, "Quelques Primitives pour la Progammation Temps Réel et leur Sémantique Mathématique," *Proc. Real Time Data Conference, INRIA*, (1982).

8. G. Berry, S. Moisan, and J.P. Rigault, "ESTEREL: Towards a Synchronous and Semantically Sound High Level Language for Real Time Applications," Proc. IEEE 1983 Real-Time Systems Symposium (1983).

9. G. Boudol and D. Austry, "Algèbre de Processus et Synchronisation," *Theoretical Computer Science* **30**, pp.91-131 (1984).

10. N.G. de Bruijn, "AUTOMATH, a Language for Mathematics," in *Lecture Notes prepared by B. Fawcett*, , Les Presses de l'Université de Montreal, Canada, (1973).

11. J. Camerini, "Sémantique Mathématique de Primitives Temps Réel," Thèse de Troisième Cycle, Université de Nice (1982).

12. P. Caspi and N. Halbwachs, "Algebra of Events: a Model for Parallel and Real-Time Systems," RR 285, IMAG, Grenoble (1982).

13. J. Chailloux, M. Devin, and J.M. Hullot, "LELISP: a Portable and Efficient LISP System," *1984 ACM Symposium on LISP and Functional Programming, Austin, Texas* (1984).

14. E.M. Clarke, E.A. Emerson, and A.P. Sistla, "Automatic Verification of Finite State Concurrent Systems Using Temporal Logic Specifications: A Practical Approach," Department of Computer Science Report, Carnegie-Mellon University (Septermber 1983).

15. L. Cosserat, "Sémantique Opérationnelle du Langage Synchrone ESTEREL," Thèse de Docteur Ingénieur, Ecole des Mines de Paris (1984).

16. M. Gordon, R. Milner, and C. Wadsworth, "Edinburgh LCF," Lecture Notes in Computer Science 78, Springer-Verlag (1980).

17. N. Halbwachs, "Modélisation et Analyse du Comportement des Systèmes Informatiques Temporisés," Thèse de Doctorat d'Etat, Université de Grenoble (1984).

18. M.C.B. Hennessy, W. Li, and G.D. Plotkin, "A First Attempt at Translating CSP into CCS," Research Report, Edinburgh University (1980).

19. C.A.R. Hoare, "Communicating Sequential Processes," *Comm. ACM* **21**(8), pp.666-678 (1978).

20. R. Milner, *A Calculus of Communicating Systems*, Springer-Verlag, LNCS 92 (1980).

21. R. Milner, "Calculi for Synchrony and Asynchrony," *Theoretical Computer Science* **25**(3), pp.267-310 (1983).

22. J.L. Peterson, "Petri Nets," *Computing Surveys* **9**(3) (1977).

23. G.D. Plotkin, "A Powerdomain Construction," *SIAM Journal on Computing* **5**(3), pp.452-487 (1976).

24. G.D. Plotkin, "An Operational Semantics for CSP," Research Report, Edinburgh University (1981).

25. G.D. Plotkin, "A Structural Approach to Operational Semantics," Lectures Notes, Aarhus University (1981).

26. A. Pnueli, "The Temporal semantics of concurrent Programs," *TCS* **13**, pp.45-60 (1981).

27. R. de Simone, "Calculabilité et Expressivité dans l'Algèbre des Processus Parallèles MEIJE," Thèse de Troisième Cycle, Université Paris VII (1984).

28. G. Winskel, "Events in Computations," PhD Thesis, Univ. of Edinburgh (1980).

29. S.J. Young, *Real-Time Languages : Design and Development*, Ellis Horwood Publishers (1982).

An implementation model of rendezvous communication

Luca Cardelli

AT&T Bell Laboratories
Murray Hill, New Jersey 07974

Introduction

This paper describes the low-level primitives necessary to implement a particular flavor or inter-process communication. It is motivated by the design of a communication subsystem for a higher-order functional language [Cardelli 84]. Here we try to abstract somewhat from the special characteristics of that language, but the model does not accommodate a wide range of communication schemes.

This communication model is intended to be used on (uniprocessor) personal computers. In this model, processes running on the same processor can share the same address space. If the underlying language is safe, a process can affect other processes only by communication, or by affecting data structures which have been explicitly transmitted. This ensures privacy and data protection even in a shared address space.

Processes running in the same address space can exchange arbitrarily complex objects very cheaply, just by passing pointers. Processes running on different processors communicate through restricted "flat" channels, e.g. character channels. In this case, complex objects have to be encoded to fit into flat channels, and decoded on the other side; the encoding activity may or may not be automatic. In any case there is a semantic difference between exchange of objects in the same address space, where objects are shared, or in different address spaces, where objects are copied.

The basic communication mechanism is rendezvous [Milner 80]: both the sender and the receiver may have to wait until the other side is ready to exchange a message. Both the sender and the receiver may *offer* communications simultaneously on different channels: when a pair of complementary offers is selected for a rendezvous, all the other simultaneous offers, on both sides, are *retracted*.

The scheduling is non-preemptive: a running process will run until it explicitly gives up control (e.g. by attempting a communication); at that point other processes will get a chance to run. We assume a cooperative universe, where no process will try to take unfair advantage of other processes, unless it has some reason for doing so.

Channels and processes can be dynamically created. Channels can be manipulated as objects and even passed through other channels [Abramsky 83, Inmos 84, Milner 82]. Processes are not denotable values; they can only be accessed through channels.

In the following sections, we use the term "pool" rather than "queue" because the latter term implies a particular scheduling policy to which we do not wish to commit ourselves. Note that the relation "being in the same pool" is non-transitive: an object can appear in different pools without implying the equivalence of all such pools.

Channel pools

A communication channel has an *output* pool and an *input* pool. The output pool records all the processes that have offered an output communication on this channel, and the respective output values. The input pool records all the processes that have requested an input communication on this channel. There can be any number of processes in either pool. In the figures, objects in the same pool are connected by a double line.

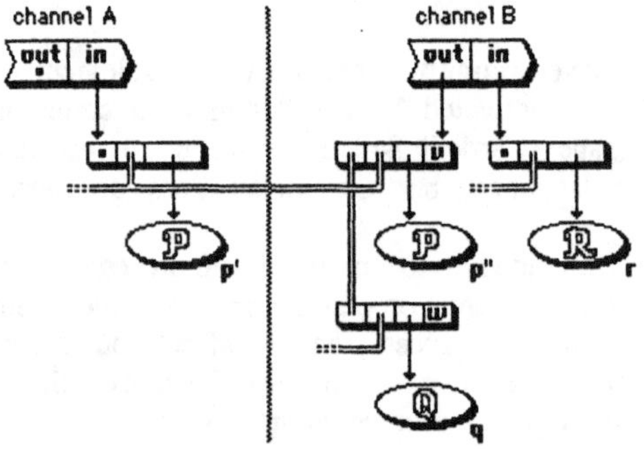

Figure 1: Channel pools

In the above figure, the process P is simultaneously waiting for input on channel A, and for output on channel B (where it is ready to communicate the value v) and possibly on more channels. The simultaneous communication offers of processes are chained across channels into *mutual exclusion* pools; one such pool connects the two instances of P above.

If P is selected for communication on channel A (which could not happen in this situation because the out pool is empty), then P will resume in state p'. If instead P is selected for communication on channel B, it will resume in state p''. In both cases, P is removed from the pool of channels A, B and all other channels in the same mutual exclusion pool.

Two communications are possible on channel B: P with R and Q with R. If Q and R are made to communicate (by exchanging the value w), both Q and R are removed from the channel B pools; Q is resumed in state q and R is resumed in state r. Again, all the simultaneous offers of Q and R are removed from the appropriate channels. Restriction: although a process can be waiting for input and output on the same channel, it cannot be made to communicate with itself because the resumption state would be ambiguous.

Scheduler Pools

A channel is *active* if it has non-empty in or out pools. At any moment, all the active channels are grouped into an *active channel* pool, which is used to select the next communication according to some scheduling policy.

The active channel pool is the primary scheduling structure: processes ready to communicate hang from it until they are activated. However, in some situations, e.g. just after process creation, processes have not had a chance to be inserted into the active channel pool. Such processes are temporarily stored in an auxiliary pool of *ready* processes. Processes in the ready pool have a resumption state; for newly created processes this is just the initial state.

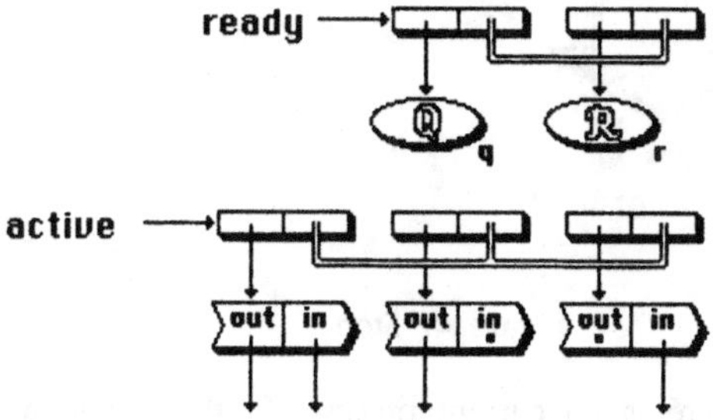

Figure 2: Scheduler pools

State Transitions

The global state of the system is determined by three quantities: the currently executing process (and its current state), the ready process pool and the active channel pool.

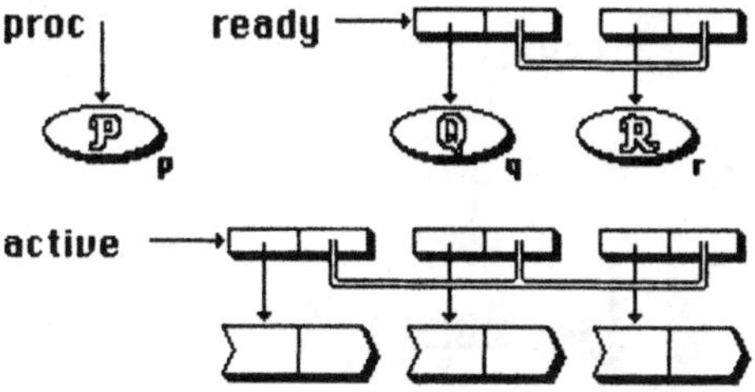

Figure 3: The state

The system evolves by state *transitions* [Plotkin 81]. There are three kind of transitions: (a) internal process transitions, which only affect the internal state of the currently executing process, (b) external process transitions, which affect the ready pool, the active pool or deactivate the current process, and (c) scheduler transitions, which take place when there is no current process. Internal process transitions are not described here (except for an operation which creates new channels), because they are largely independent of the concurrency aspects, but they can be taken to be similar to the ones in [Cardelli 83].

In the figures, a transition is represented as an "old" state, a big arrow with a transition name, and a "new" state. Those parts of the state which are not affected by a transition, are omitted.

Process transitions

There are five concurrency-related operations a process can perform. The first one is **stop**, which kills the currently executing process:

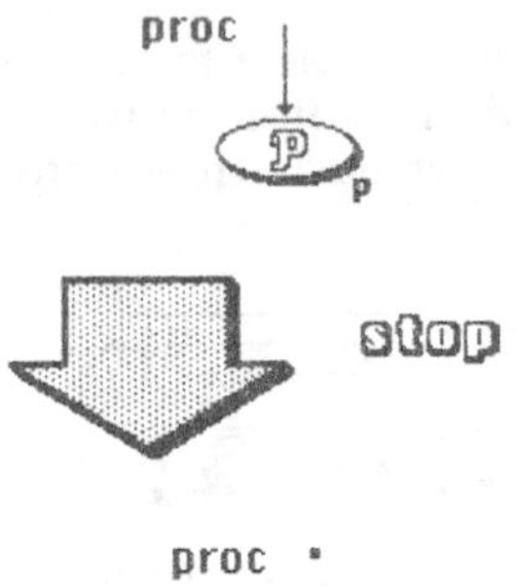

Figure 4: Stop

After a stop operation there is no current process. In this situation the scheduler takes over, as we shall see in the next section. The scheduling discipline ensures that P is not in any pool when it stops. We assume that the channels known by P will be garbage collected, if needed.

A process can create another process by a **start** operation. Given a program Q, a new process is created to execute Q and is placed in the ready pool in its initial state. The current process continues execution. The exact structure of Q is not discussed here; it could be a functional closure, as described in [Cardelli 83].

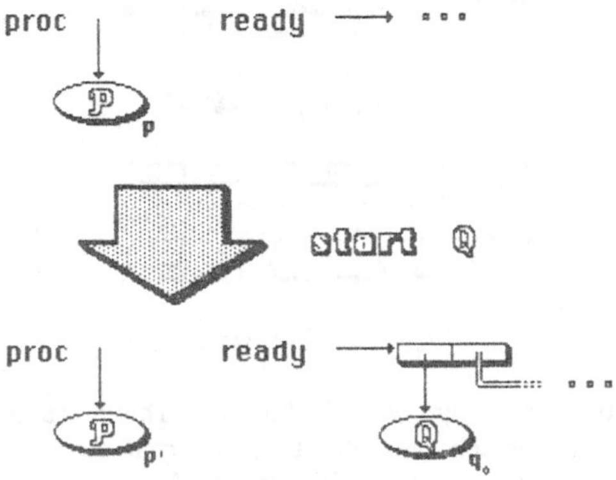

Figure 5: Start

A process can create a new channel by the **channel** operation. New channels are not active, and are placed on the execution stack of the current process.

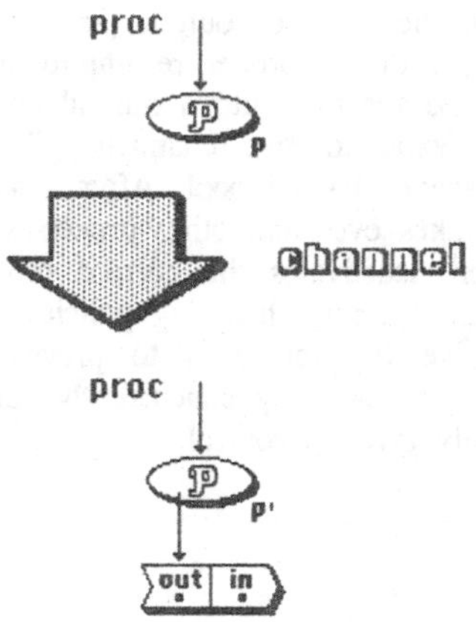

Figure 6: Channel

A process can simultaneously offer communication on a set of channels, with the intent of communicating on exactly one of them as soon as a communication is available. This is done by the **select** operation. There can be any positive number of input and/or output offers (a **select** with zero offers would be equivalent to **stop**). Each offer designates a channel (A, B and C in the example below) and a resumption state (a, b and c) for the process after a communication. Input offers are decorated with a question mark (?) and output offers with an exclamation mark (!) and a value to be communicated.

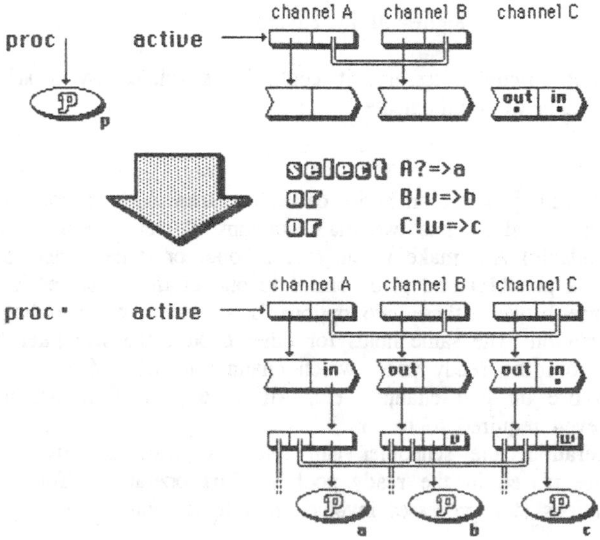

Figure 7: Select

The current process is inserted in the input or output (as appropriate) channel pools of the channels involved in the operation, with the proper resumption state and output value (if appropriate). All these offers are chained together into a mutual exclusion pool, to remember that they were done simultaneously. Some inactive channels (like C above) may become active and are then inserted into the active channel pool. After a **select** operation there is no current process. Hence, the scheduler takes over and other processes get a chance to run.

The following **deactivate** operation deactivates the current process and gives control to the scheduler. It can be useful in some special scheduling policies. For example a **deactivate** can be inserted in loops and recursive function calls to prevent looping processes from locking out everybody else. It can also be used by concurrently running processes which do not need to communicate, to periodically give up control.

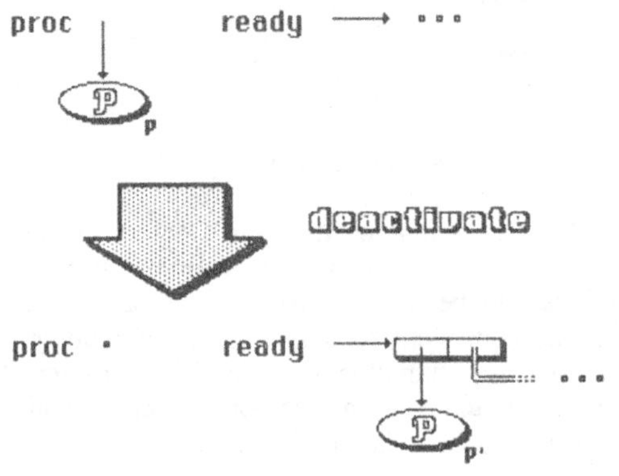

Figure 8: Deactivate

This operation is not strictly necessary; it could be simulated by a **select** on some channel which is always ready to communicate.

Scheduler transitions

When there is no current process, an entity called the *scheduler* gets control and decides who should run next. The scheduler has two major options: it can take a process from the ready pool (if one is available) and make it the current one, or it can select a channel for a communication (if one is possible) and give control to one of the processes involved in the communication. The choice between these two options is a matter of scheduling policy, and depends on the implementation. The same holds for other choices the scheduler has to make: which process to select from the ready pool, which channel to select from the active pool, which communication to fire on that channel, etc. All these possibilities are left open; the scheduling policy is not even required to be fair.

By an **activate** operation, the scheduler can select a ready process to become the current one. Processes are placed in the ready pool by **start** operations (for new processes) and by **rendezvous** operations (for processes involved in output communications, as explained later).

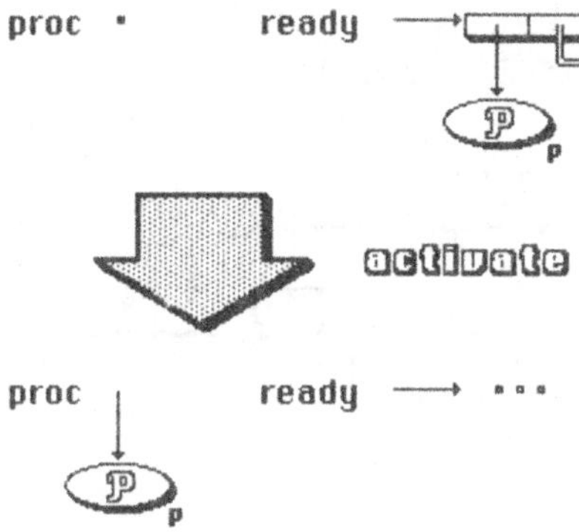

Figure 9: Activate

A **rendezvous** operation causes a communication to happen between two distinct processes, one waiting for input and the other one waiting for output on the same channel (P and Q on channel C in the example below). The process waiting for input (Q, with resumption q) becomes the current process, and the value being communicated (w) is placed on its execution stack. The process waiting for output (P, with resumption c) is placed in the ready pool. These communication offers, and all the ones linked in the same mutual exclusion pools (Pa, Pb and Pc below, and all the ones linked with Qq), are removed from the respective channel pools. Some channels may become inactive (e.g. C), and are then removed from the active pool.

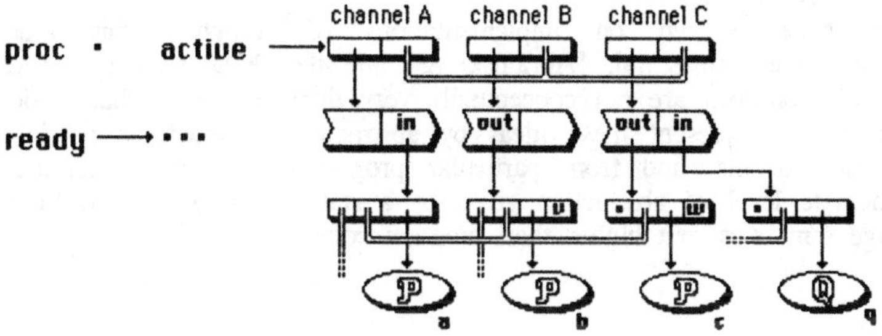

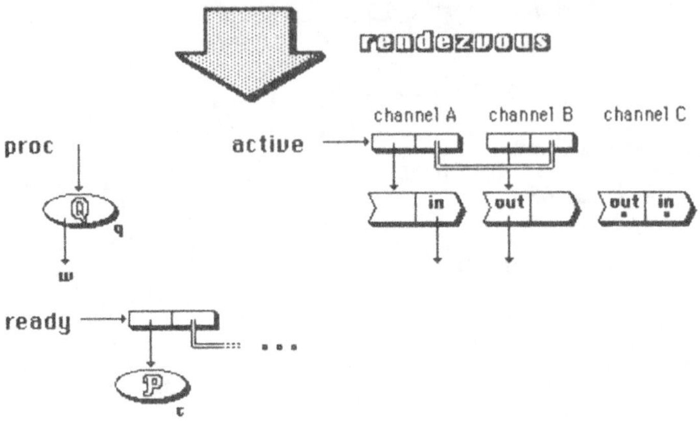

Figure 10: Rendezvous

Hence, the scheduler passes control to a process waiting for input, and eventually will give control to the corresponding process waiting for output, which is temporarily stored in the ready pool.

Conclusions

We have informally presented a set of concurrency-related primitives. They can be used as a basis for the implementation of rendezvous communication mechanisms in programming languages. The method used to describe these primitives can be formalized following [Plotkin 81], as was done in [Cardelli 83].

Several people have worked on implementations of, roughly, this model of communication, for example [Inmos 84], [Abramski 83] and the BCSP system at Oxford. I am confident that their solutions are not conceptually very different from what is described here. The aim here was to present these ideas by abstracting as much as possible from low-level implementation details, and from particular programming language features. The result is this intermediate level of abstraction given by a state transition model, lower than programming language semantics, but higher than program code.

References

[Abramski 83] S.Abramsky, R.Bornat: *Pascal-m: a language for loosely coupled distributed systems*. In *Distributed Computing Systems; Synchronization, Control and Communication*. Ed. Y.Parker, J.P.Verjus, Academic Press, 1983.

[Cardelli 83] L.Cardelli: *The functional abstract machine*. Bell Labs Technical Report TR-107, 1983.

[Cardelli 84] L.Cardelli: *Amber*. To appear.

[Inmos 84] INMOS Ltd.: *occam programming manual*. Prentice Hall, 1984

[Milner 80] R.Milner: *A Calculus of Communicating Systems*. Lecture Notes in Computer Science, n. 92, Springer-Verlag, 1980.

[Milner 82] R.Milner: *Four combinators for concurrency*. ACM Sigact-Sigops Symposium on Principles of Distributed Computing, Ottawa, Canada, 1982.

[Plotkin 81] G.D.Plotkin: *A structural approach to Operational Semantics*. Internal Report DAIMI FN-19, Computer Science Department, Aarhus University, September 1981.

A FULLY ABSTRACT MODEL OF FAIR ASYNCHRONY

- extended abstract -

Philippe DARONDEAU
IRISA
Campus de Beaulieu
F 35042 Rennes Cedex
France

Assuming strong fairness for a CCS-like language, we construct a fully abstract model of the implementation preorder : $p \underset{\sim}{\sqsubseteq} q$ iff for every context $\mathcal{C}$ and for every program $\mathfrak{r}$, no computation of $\mathfrak{r}$ in $(\mathcal{C}(p) \mid \mathfrak{r})$ allows to recognize that q has been replaced by p.

1. THE LANGUAGE

1.1. THE SYNTAX

The language studied here evolved from the pure version of the asynchronous CCS of Milner [M_i 1] . The main alterations are as follows : polyadic guarding operators replace the sum operator, and recursive definitions have been obliterated so that every term is a fully defined program. The limitations due to the latter feature are balanced by the supply of iterators for obtaining cyclic agents and unbounded networks of communicating agents, used much the same way as in pure CCS to simulate Turing machines.

In the sequel, we assume given disjoint sets of complementary <u>action names</u> Δ and $\overline{\Delta}$, ranged over by α resp. $\overline{\alpha}$, such that there exist reciprocal bijections $\alpha \rightleftarrows \overline{\alpha}$. We let <u>Ren</u>, ranged over by π, denote the set of domain finite injections over $\Lambda = \Delta \cup \overline{\Delta}$ such that :

$$(\forall \lambda)\ (\pi\ (\lambda)\ \text{defined} \Rightarrow \pi\ (\overline{\lambda}) = \overline{\pi\ (\lambda)})\ \&$$

$$(\exists n)\ (\forall \lambda)\ (\pi^n\ (\lambda)\ \text{undefined}).$$

Our language is the free term algebra T_Σ for the signature $\Sigma = \bigcup \Sigma_n$, $n \geq 0$ given by:

$$\Sigma_o = \{NIL\} \cup \{<\lambda \Rightarrow \lambda_1 : \lambda'_1 , \ldots , \lambda_n : \lambda'_n> \mid \lambda, \lambda_i, \lambda'_i \in \Lambda\}$$

$$\Sigma_1 = \{<\lambda> \mid \lambda \in \Lambda\} \cup \{ [\pi] \mid \pi \in Ren\} \cup \{ [\lambda \triangleright \pi] \mid \lambda \in \Lambda, \pi \in Ren\}$$

$$\Sigma_2 = \{ | \} \cup \{ <\lambda_1 , \lambda_2> \mid \lambda_i \in \Lambda\}$$

$\Sigma_n = \{< \lambda_1 , \ldots , \lambda_n > \mid \lambda_i \in \Lambda \}$ for $n > 2$.

In Σ_2 for instance, $< \lambda_1 , \lambda_2 >$ denotes a binary guarding operator and $|$ is the asynchronous composition. Let π be the renaming function with domain $\{ \alpha , \bar{\alpha} \}$ such that $\pi(\alpha) = \beta$, then $p\,[\alpha \triangleright \pi]$ is intuitively the unbounded string $p_1 \frown p_2 \frown \cdots \frown p_i \frown \cdots$ of copies of p each of which, once started from the left by an α, may further communicate with its left neighbour by α's (or $\bar{\alpha}$'s) perceived as β's (or $\bar{\beta}$'s). Thus, $p\,[\alpha \triangleright \pi]$ might be specified by the recursive statement $X \Leftarrow \langle\alpha\rangle ((p \mid X)\ [\pi])$, but this is not a Σ-term. Due to the definition of Ren, the possible influence of an agent in $p\,[\alpha \triangleright \pi]$ is confined within an interval of size 2n if π^n is the undefined function. Hence, network iterators $[\alpha \triangleright \pi]$, when applied to finite agents, do not afford a way to program infinite behaviours of finite automata. Opportunately, such behaviours may be rendered by finite compositions of local iterators $< \lambda \Rightarrow \{\lambda_i : \lambda'_i\}_i >$.

A local iterator might be specified by a recursive statement $X \Leftarrow \langle\lambda\rangle(\langle\lambda_1,\ldots,\lambda_n\rangle (\langle\lambda'_1\rangle(X),\ldots,\langle\lambda'_n\rangle(X)))$, but once more, this is not a Σ-term. The power of the language comes from the application of network iterators to finite compositions of local iterators.

1.2. THE OPERATIONAL DEFINITION

A computation is a sequence of communications between the process agents of an insulated system, whose global state is described by a program in T_Σ. In a strongly fair computation, a process who infinitely often has opportunities to communicate with other processes necessarily does so. Communications and actions of programs/processes may be specified together by an axiomatic system, using the following conventions.

- λ ranges over Λ ; $\tau = \bar{\tau} \notin \Lambda$ is the undefined action name, thus $\pi(\lambda) = \tau$ if $\lambda \notin \mathrm{dom}(\pi)$ and $\pi(\tau) = \tau$ for any π in Ren ; μ ranges over $\Lambda \cup \{\tau\}$.
- ID $= \{ \leftarrow , \rightarrow \}^*$ is the set of process identifiers, ranged over by R,S. Arrows have a positional meaning with respect to the asynchronous composition operator $|$.
- E, ranged over by e, is the union $E_1 \cup E_2$ of the sets with respective elements $\{\lambda_R\}$ or $\{\mu_R, \bar{\mu}_S\}$; for $T \in$ ID, T(e) denotes accordingly the set $\{\lambda_{TR}\}$ or the set $\{\mu_{TR} , \bar{\mu}_{TS}\}$.

THE ACTION RULES

$$< \lambda_1 ,\ldots, \lambda_n > (t_1 ,\ldots, t_n) \xrightarrow{\lambda_i} t_i \ , \ i \in \{1\ldots n\}$$

$$\frac{t \xrightarrow{e} t'}{(t|u) \xrightarrow{\leftarrow(e)} (t'|u)} \qquad \frac{t \xrightarrow{e} t'}{(u|t) \xrightarrow{\rightarrow(e)} (u|t')}$$

$$\frac{t \xrightarrow{\lambda_R} t' \ , \ u \xrightarrow{\overline{\lambda}_S} u'}{(t|u) \xrightarrow{\lambda_{\leftarrow R} \ , \ \overline{\lambda}_{\rightarrow S}} (t'|u')}$$

$$\frac{t \xrightarrow{\lambda_R} t'}{t[\pi] \xrightarrow{\pi(\lambda)_R} t'[\pi]} \qquad \text{if} \quad \pi(\lambda) \neq \tau$$

$$\frac{t \xrightarrow{\mu_R \quad \overline{\mu}_S} t'}{t[\pi] \xrightarrow{\pi(\mu)_R \quad \pi(\overline{\mu})_S} t'[\pi]}$$

$$t \, [\, \lambda \rhd \pi \,] \xrightarrow{\lambda} (\, t|t\, [\lambda \rhd \pi]) \, [\pi]$$

if $t = < \lambda \Rightarrow \ \lambda_1 : \lambda'_1 ,\ldots, \lambda_n : \lambda'_n >$ then

$$t \xrightarrow{\lambda} (NIL \mid < \lambda_1,\ldots, \lambda_n > (< \lambda'_1 > (t) ,\ldots, < \lambda'_n > (t)))$$

The operational setting may now be summarized by two definitions.

<u>definition 1</u> For $t \in T_\Sigma$ and $R \in ID$, the set $Act_R(t)$ of t's <u>R-actions</u> is the set $\{\mu \mid (\exists u \in T_\Sigma , \exists S \in ID : t \xrightarrow{\mu_R \, \overline{\mu}_S} u)\}$

<u>definition 2</u> For p_o in T_Σ , the associated set <u>fair</u> (p_o) of <u>fair computations</u> is the set of sequences $(p_i, e_i)_{i \in \omega}$ such that the following conditions are satisfied, letting $\underline{E}_o = \{\emptyset\}$:

1- $(\forall i)\ ((e_i \in E_2\ \&\ p_i \xrightarrow{e_i} p_{i+1}) \vee (e_i = \emptyset\ \&\ p_i = p_{i+1}))$

2- $(e_i)_{i \in \omega} \in (E_2^{\omega} \cup E_2^{*}\ E_o^{\omega})$

3- $(\forall R \in ID)(\exists j)\ \ (\forall k \geq j)\ (Act_R\ (p_k) = \emptyset\ ).$

1.3. THE IMPLEMENTATION PREORDER

Once, we introduce experiments as a kind of projections of fair computations.

definition 3 Given a fair computation

$\mathcal{F} = ((p_i \mid q_i),\ e_i)_{i \in \omega}$, let $\mathcal{F}' = (q_i,\ e'_i)_{i \in \omega}$ where $e'_i = \{\mu_R \mid (\mu_{\rightarrow R} \in e_i)\}$. Set down $|\mathcal{F}'| = \text{l.u.b}\{i + 1 \mid (q_i \xrightarrow{e'_i} q_{i+1})\}$. The right projection $\mathcal{F}_{\rightarrow}$ of $\mathcal{F}$ is the sequence obtained from $\mathcal{F}'$ by erasing pairs $(q_i\ ,\ e'_i)$ for every $i < |\mathcal{F}'|$ such that $e'_i = \emptyset$.

definition 4 For $p\ ,\ q \in T_{\Sigma}$, the set $EXP_q(p)$ of the q-experiments upon p is $\{\ \mathcal{F}_{\rightarrow} \mid (\ \mathcal{F} \in fair(p|q))\}$, and the set EXP(p) of the experiments upon p is $\bigcup\ EXP_q(p)\ ,\ q \in T_{\Sigma}$.

The observation preorder $\lesssim$ may now be given two readily equivalent definitions.

definition 5 $\lesssim$ is the subset of $T_{\Sigma} \times T_{\Sigma}$ such that $p \lesssim q$ iff $EXP(p) \subseteq EXP(q)$.

definition 5' $\lesssim$ is the subset of $T_{\Sigma} \times T_{\Sigma}$ such that $p \lesssim q$ iff $(\forall r \in T_{\Sigma})\ (EXP_r(p) \subseteq EXP_r(q))$.

The implementation preorder generalizes the above to Σ -contexts, defined as 1-hole Σ-terms.

definition 6 For $p,\ q \in T_{\Sigma}$, p implements q $(p \subsetsim q)$ iff $\mathcal{C}[p] \lesssim \mathcal{C}[q]$ for any Σ-context $\mathcal{C}$.

Thus, p implements q iff for every context $\mathcal{C}$ and for every program r, no computation of r in $(\mathcal{C}(p) \mid r)$ allows to recognize that q has been replaced by p.

Results contained in the full paper show that the implementation preorder coincides with the observation preorder. Hence, the following programs "$\tau\ p$" and "$p\ \mid \tau^{\omega}$" are implementation equivalent to p, with $\pi_1(\alpha) = \tau$, $\pi_1(\beta) = \beta'$ for β in the sort of p, and $\pi_2(\beta') = \beta$:

- "$\tau\ \ p$" = $(\langle\alpha\rangle(p) \mid \langle\overline{\alpha}\rangle\ (NIL))\ [\pi_1]\ \ [\pi_2]$

- "$\ p|\tau^{\omega}$" = $(p\ \mid (\langle \alpha \Rightarrow \alpha : \alpha \rangle \mid \langle\ \overline{\alpha}\ \ \Rightarrow\ \overline{\alpha}\ \ :\ \ \overline{\alpha}\rangle))\ \ [\pi_1]\ \ [\pi_2]$.

On account of the above, the model of $\lesssim$ offered in the second half of the paper may well be called a "fully abstract" model of fair asynchrony (Mi 2).

2. THE MODEL

2.1. THE DOMAIN OF HISTORIES

In all the sequel, L denotes a finite subset of Λ such that $L = \overline{L}$, and Sorts is the set made out of the so-called sorts L. The domain of the forthcoming model is built upon $\mathcal{H}$, the set of histories given by the following definition, where we let $L^{\infty} = L^{*} \cup L^{\omega}$, and where $\mathrm{Ult}(\rho)$ denotes the set of actions $\lambda \in \Lambda$ which occur infinitely often in the word $\rho \in L^{\infty}$.

<u>definition 7</u> $\mathcal{H}_L$, the set of <u>L-sorted histories</u>, is the collection of the triples $< \delta, \rho , d >$ which satisfy : $\delta \subseteq L$ & $\rho \in L^{\infty}$ & $(\mathrm{Ult}(\rho) \subseteq d \subseteq L)$ & $(d \cap (\delta \cup \overline{\delta}) = \emptyset)$. $\mathcal{H}$, the set of histories, is the union $\bigcup \mathcal{H}_L$, $L \in$ Sorts. $< \delta ,\mathcal{L}, d >$ and $\{< \delta, \rho , d > \mid \rho \in \mathcal{L} \}$ are equivalent notations for subsets of histories.

<u>hint</u> : let $\mathcal{F} = (p_i , e_i)_{i\in\omega}$ be an "open" computation, that is the left or right projection of some fair computation, then $\mathcal{F}$ may be abstracted into an history $\mathrm{abs}(\mathcal{F}) = <\delta, \rho , d>$ with components as follows : - ρ traces the e_i but ignores communications, i.e. pairs of actions, - δ displays the potential actions of the agents which remain unchanged throughout some subsequence $(p_i)_{i>k}$. - $(d \cup \delta)$ shows the $\lambda \in \Lambda$ which are potential actions of infinitely many p_i in the sequence $(p_i)_{i\in\omega}$.

Histories are provided with prefixing, renaming and composition operators as follows.

<u>definition 8</u> To each action name $\lambda \in \Lambda \cup \{ \varepsilon \}$, we associate the operator λ : from $\mathcal{H}$ to $\mathcal{P}(\mathcal{H})$ such that $\lambda : < \delta , \rho , d >$ is the singleton set $<\delta , \lambda \rho , d >$.

<u>definition 9</u> To each function $\pi \in$ Ren, we associate the function $[\![\pi]\!]$ from $\mathcal{H}$ to $\mathcal{P}(\mathcal{H})$ such that :

$[\![\pi]\!] (<\delta, \rho , d >)$ is the empty subset of $\mathcal{H}$ if $(\rho = \rho' \lambda \rho''$ & $\pi(\lambda) =\tau)$ for some $\lambda \in \Lambda$, or else is the singleton set $< \pi \delta, \pi \rho, \pi d >$.

<u>definition 10</u> Given histories h' and h" in $\mathcal{H}$, let $h' = < \delta' , \rho', d' >$ and $h'' = < \delta'', \rho'', d'' >$, these histories are <u>compatible</u> ($h' \# h''$) iff

1- $\delta' \cap \mathrm{Ult}(\rho'') = \emptyset = \delta'' \cap \mathrm{Ult}(\rho')$

2- $\delta' \cap (\overline{d''} \cup \overline{\delta''}) = \emptyset = \delta'' \cap (\overline{d'} \cup \overline{\delta'})$

The <u>parallel composition</u> $h' \| h''$ of h', h" is either the empty subset of $\mathcal{H}$ if $\neg(h' \# h'')$ or else is the set of histories $< \delta' \cup \delta'' , \rho' \| \rho'' , (d' \setminus \delta'') \cup (d'' \setminus \delta') >$

for $\|$ the operator on words given below.

definition 11 Let words ρ' , ρ'' in L^∞ , their parallel composition $\rho' \| \rho''$ is the set of the words $\rho = \rho_1 \rho_2 \ldots \rho_i \ldots$ for which there exist corresponding factorizations $\rho'_1 \rho'_2 \ldots \rho'_i \ldots$ resp. $\rho''_1 \rho''_2 \ldots \rho''_i \ldots$ of ρ' resp. ρ'' on $(L \cup \{\varepsilon\})$ such that for every i :

- $(\rho'_i \neq \varepsilon \ \& \ \rho''_i \neq \varepsilon) \Rightarrow (\rho'_i = \overline{\rho}''_i \ \& \ \rho_i = \varepsilon)$
- $(\rho'_i = \varepsilon \vee \rho''_i = \varepsilon) \Rightarrow \rho_i = \rho'_i \rho''_i$.

hint : let $\mathcal{F}'$, $\mathcal{F}''$ denote open computations, then abs $(\mathcal{F}') \# $ abs $(\mathcal{F}'')$ holds just in case that there exists some open computation $\mathcal{F}$ with $\mathcal{F}'$ and $\mathcal{F}''$ as respective left and right projections.

hint : the parallel composition of words is a variant of the more classical fair shuffle or fair merge.

Finally, histories are ordered according to the following definition.

definition 12 $\leqslant$ is the order relation on $\mathcal{H}$ such that $<\delta, \rho, d> \leqslant <\delta', \rho', d'>$ iff $(\rho = \rho')$ & $(\delta \subseteq \delta')$ & $((d \cup \delta) \subseteq (d' \cup \delta'))$. We let $\vee$ denote the operator upon $\mathcal{P}(\mathcal{H})$ which sends parts of $\mathcal{H}$ to their greatest subsets of minimal elements.

2.2. THE DOMAIN OF THE MODEL

The domain of our model is not $\mathcal{P}(\mathcal{H})$ but a subset of it, called $\mathcal{K}$, equipped with an ordering $\sqsubset_I$ which does not even ensure the existence of limits of increasing or decreasing chains ! Before going on, let us briefly indicate that henceforth, set extensions of the operators $\lambda :$, $\|$ and $[\![\pi]\!]$ will be used freely with $\mathcal{K}$ or $\mathcal{P}(\mathcal{H})$ as their co-domain. For instance, $[\![\pi]\!](\{h_1, h_2\})$ amounts to $[\![\pi]\!](h_1) \cup [\![\pi]\!](h_2)$.

definition 13 Let $h = <\delta, \rho, d> \in \mathcal{H}_L$, then h is normalized iff $(\forall \alpha \in L)$ $(\alpha \in d \Rightarrow \overline{\alpha} \in d)$

definition 14 $\mathcal{K}$ is the set of the normalized subsets of $\bigcup_L \mathcal{P}(\mathcal{H}_L)$ which do not contain any two $\leqslant$ - comparable histories, and $\sqsubset_I$ is the ordering on $\mathcal{K}$ such that $P \sqsubset_I Q$ iff $(\forall h \in P)(\exists h' \in Q)(h' \leqslant h)$.

2.3. THE EQUATIONS OF THE MODEL

To start with, we associate sets of normalized histories to local iterators.

- let $u_i = \lambda \lambda_i \lambda'_i$, $i \in \{1 \ldots n\}$

- let $\mathcal{L} = (\sum_i u_i)^*$ and for $I \subseteq \{1 \dots n\}$,

  let $\mathcal{L}_I = \bigcap_{i \in I} (\mathcal{L} u_i)^\omega \cap (\mathcal{L}(\sum_{i \in I} u_i)^\omega)$

- for $I, J \subseteq \{1 \dots n\}$, let

$d_{I,J} = \mathrm{sym}\,(\{\lambda\} \cup \{\lambda_i \mid i \in I \cup J\} \cup \{\lambda'_i \mid i \in I\})$,

where $\mathrm{sym}\,(L) = L \cup \overline{L}$, and let

$\delta_{I,J} = \{\lambda_1 \dots \lambda_n\} \setminus d_{I,J}$.

With an additive notation of sets, we define

$\mathcal{M}\,(<\lambda \Rightarrow \lambda_1 : \lambda'_1, \dots, \lambda_n : \lambda'_n>) =$

$< \{\lambda\}, \mathcal{L}, \emptyset > +$

$< \{\lambda_1 \dots \lambda_n\}, \mathcal{L}\lambda, \emptyset > +$

$\sum_i < \{\lambda'_i\}, \mathcal{L}\lambda\lambda_i, \emptyset > +$

$\sum_{I,J} < \delta_{I,J}, \mathcal{L}_I, d_{I,J} >$

Using the above defined constants, we can now state the characteristic equations of the model $\mathcal{N} : T_\Sigma \to \mathcal{K}$, letting $Y(G)$ denote the greatest fixpoint of $G : \mathcal{K} \to \mathcal{K}$ (when such a fixpoint exists).

THE MODEL

$\mathcal{N}(\mathrm{NIL}) = < \emptyset, \varepsilon, \emptyset >$

$\mathcal{N}(<\lambda_1, \dots, \lambda_n>(t_1, \dots, t_n)) =$

$$< \{\lambda_1 \dots \lambda_n\}, \varepsilon, \emptyset > + \check{}\,(\sum_{i=1}^{n} \lambda_i : \mathcal{N}(t_i))$$

$\mathcal{N}(t_1 \mid t_2) = \check{}\,(\mathcal{N}(t_1) \parallel \mathcal{N}(t_2))$

$\mathcal{N}(t\,[\pi]) = \check{}\,([\![\pi]\!]\,\mathcal{N}(t))$

$\mathcal{N}(t\,[\lambda \triangleright \pi]) = Y(\check{F})$ where

$$F(X) = < \lambda, \varepsilon, \emptyset > + (\lambda : [\![\pi]\!]\,(\mathcal{N}(t) \parallel X))$$

$\mathcal{N}(<\lambda \Rightarrow \lambda_1 : \lambda'_1, \dots, \lambda_n : \lambda'_n>) =$

$$\check{}\,(\mathcal{M}(<\lambda \Rightarrow \lambda_1 : \lambda'_1, \dots, \lambda_n : \lambda'_n>))$$

<u>theorem</u> $\mathcal{N}$ is a fully abstract model of T_Σ w.r.t. the observational preorder $\lesssim : \mathcal{N}(t) \subset_I \mathcal{N}(t')$ iff $EXP(\mathcal{C}(t)) \subsetneq EXP(\mathcal{C}(t'))$ for every Σ- context $\mathcal{C}$.

3. SOME CONCLUSIONS

The fair composition of infinitary words (Pa) must be accounted for some way or other in any kind of model of fair asynchrony : we do not see the reason why these models should not be constructed around that central concept, and thus in the frame-work of infinitary languages where greatest fixpoints are generally available. In this paper, we have shown that fully observational models may be obtained this way for communicating programs. It was clear from a long time that conventional traces do not provide an adequate semantics of programs : beside the effective trace, some indication must be given about the alternative actions which are avoided. This is why our histories are triples whose middle element is a trace. The fact that our model has been proven fully abstract w.r.t. the most discriminative observational congruence indicates without any doubt that branching time logic is in-adequate to reason about observable behaviours In our sense, programs p and q are observationally equivalent iff for every r, the set of the possible computations of r in $p|r$ is identical to the set of the possible computations of r in $q|r$. We conjecture that the previous equivalence is strictly included into the testing equivalence of Hennessy and de Nicola (He-1). Compared to Hennessy's study of fair delay operators for synchronous processes (He-2), our work follows a parallel way for the asynchronous case. But we feel that no junction exists between the two ways. An observation congruence suited to fair asynchrony may perhaps be derived from a "synchronous" congruence, but the derived relation cannot coincide with the "asynchronous" congruence which is obtained when considering asynchronous observers only. We feel for instance that the essential properties $p \sim \tau\, p$ and $p \sim p|\tau^\omega$ cannot be caught.

REFERENCES

(He - 1)

Hennessy M, de Nicola R, Testing equivalences for Processes.
Proc. ICALP 83, LNCS 154 - 1983 -

(He - 2)

Hennessy M, Modelling Finite Delay Operators
Report CSR 153-83, University of Edinburgh - 1983 -

(Mi - 1)

Milner R, A calculus of Communicating Systems.
LNCS 92 - 1980 -

(Mi - 2)

Milner R, Fully Abstract Models of Typed
Lambda - Calculi
TCS 4,1 (pp. 1 - 23) - 1977 -

(Pa)

Park D , On the Semantics of fair parallelism
In abstract Software Specifications,
LNCS 86 - 1980 -

ALTERNATIVE SEMANTICS FOR McCARTHY'S AMB

William Clinger
Indiana University

Charles Halpern
University of Toronto

ABSTRACT.

McCarthy's ambiguous operator **amb** is a locally angelic choice operator. A description of its semantics using power domains is much more complex than similar descriptions of globally angelic choice or erratic choice. Operational semantics based on rewrite rules are used here to compare the three kinds of choice. A natural problem shows erratic choice to be less expressive than the angelic forms of choice. Erratic choice and globally angelic choice share a pleasant distribution property that has been proposed as the basis for an algebra of nondeterministic programs. Locally angelic choice does not share this property. Locally angelic choice may play a role in otherwise globally angelic nondeterministic programs similar to the role played by the cut operator in Prolog.

INTRODUCTION.

The three commonly used power domain constructions differ in what they can express about a nondeterministic semantics. Using terminology from [3], the Smyth power domain expresses *demonic* nondeterminism, in which an implementation is required to resolve nondeterministic choices in such a way that every program that might possibly fail to terminate does in fact fail to terminate. The Hoare power domain expresses *angelic* nondeterminism, in which an implementation is required to ensure that every program that might possibly terminate does in fact terminate. The Plotkin power domain expresses *erratic* nondeterminism, in which an implementation may choose at its own convenience whether a program that might or might not terminate does in fact terminate.

The distinction between erratic and angelic nondeterminism provided by the Plotkin and Hoare power domains is too sharp to model the semantics intended for many languages designed to express concurrent computation. In particular the intended semantics of McCarthy's ambiguous choice operator **amb** fits neither the Plotkin nor the Hoare domain, but has thus far been modelled only by a complex melange of the two [3].

As an attempt to develop intuitions in the matter, this paper investigates three alternative operational semantics for a simple functional programming language augmented with a nondeterministic choice operator. One semantics is erratic, another is angelic, and together the two bracket a third semantics that corresponds to the interpretation intended for **amb**.

McCarthy intended that the value of (**amb** E_1 E_2) should be ambiguously the value of E_1 or the value of E_2, with the restriction that if the value of E_1 is undefined then the value of (**amb** E_1 E_2) should be the value of E_2, and vice versa [8]. Thus **amb** is a *locally angelic* choice

Figure 1

Syntax

$I \in \text{Ide}$

$F \in \text{Fun} \quad ::= \quad$ **succ** | **pred** | **ifzero** | **amb** | I
| **(lambda (**$I_1 \ldots I_n$**)** E**)** | **(label** I F**)**

$E \in \text{Exp} \quad ::= \quad$ **0** | I | **(**F $E_1 \ldots E_n$**)**

Numerals

$N \in \text{Num} \quad ::= \quad$ **0** | **(succ** N**)**

operator in the sense that with each choice the implementation is required to choose convergence over divergence for the local subcomputation, but it need not concern itself with whether the entire program converges. Locally angelic choice can be implemented by computing the two alternatives in parallel with synchronization at the level of the amb expression.

If the restriction is dropped, then amb becomes a simple erratic choice operator. Erratic choice can be implemented in many ways, of which the simplest is to choose the leftmost alternative in every case. Such a semantics for the language used in this paper can easily be described using the Plotkin power domain [10].

If on the other hand the restriction on amb is strengthened so that choices are made to cause the entire program to converge rather than merely the local subcomputation, then amb becomes a *globally angelic* choice operator. Globally angelic choice can be implemented in the same way as locally angelic choice except that synchronization occurs only at the program level. A globally angelic semantics for the language used in this paper can easily be described using the Hoare power domain [4].

THE BASE LANGUAGE.

The syntax of the language we use appears in Figure 1. It is a simplified version of Lisp in which all expressions evaluate to natural numbers. Since the language without the choice operator is just barely Turing complete, we sprinkle syntactic sugar throughout our examples for the sake of readability.

The operational semantics of the amb-free portion of the language is described by a set of rewrite rules together with an evaluation rule that governs their application. The rewrite rules appear in Figure 2 and the evaluation rule appears in Figure 3. The evaluation rule leaves no room for choice in the application of the rewrite rules to amb-free programs.

Figure 2

Rewrite Rules

$$\texttt{(pred 0)} \rightarrow \texttt{0}$$

$$\texttt{(pred (succ } N\texttt{))} \rightarrow N$$

$$\texttt{(ifzero 0 } E_1 \ E_2\texttt{)} \rightarrow E_1$$

$$\texttt{(ifzero (succ } N\texttt{) } E_1 \ E_2\texttt{)} \rightarrow E_2$$

$$\texttt{((lambda () } E\texttt{))} \rightarrow E$$

$$\texttt{((lambda (}I \ I_2 \ \ldots \ I_n\texttt{) } E\texttt{) } N \ E_2 \ \ldots \ E_n\texttt{)} \rightarrow \texttt{((lambda (}I_2 \ \ldots \ I_n\texttt{) } E[N/I]\texttt{)} \ E_2 \ \ldots \ E_n\texttt{)}$$

$$\texttt{((label } I \ F\texttt{) } E_1 \ \ldots \ E_n\texttt{)} \rightarrow \texttt{(}F[\texttt{(label } I \ F\texttt{)}/I] \ E_1 \ \ldots \ E_n\texttt{)}$$

after alpha-conversion to avoid capture of bound variables

The semantics is applicative order, meaning that `lambda` functions are strict in all arguments. This change from the power domain semantics in [4] is motivated by the fact that it is much easier to obtain a singular (or call-time choice [6]) semantics using applicative order evaluation than using normal order evaluation. The semantics in [4] can easily be altered to yield a strict semantics.

THE SEMANTICS OF CHOICE.

The semantics is extended to encompass the choice operator by extending the evaluation rule to deal with amb expressions and by setting forth an interpretation of the semantics to cover questions of termination. Interpretation is always necessary for languages with an undecidable halting problem, since the set of nonterminating programs is not axiomatizable. The reason the interpretation can be left tacit for deterministic programs is that there is only one reasonable interpretation – if a program does not yield a proper value then it must be that the program does not terminate. For nondeterministic programs the interpretation should be explicit because there are several reasonable interpretations. For example, both tight and loose nondeterminism are reasonable interpretations of nondeterminism, and it is important to know which is intended [9]. Loose nondeterminism is intended in this paper. The explicit interpretation is also necessary in the operational semantics of this paper because the extended "rule" involves choices that must in general satisfy constraints such as finite delay.

To obtain erratic choice, the evaluation rule is extended to amb expressions by postulating

Figure 3

Evaluation rules

To evaluate a program, rewrite the entire program repeatedly according to the following rule until a numeral is obtained.

To rewrite an expression of the form:

`0`	leave the expression unchanged.
`(succ` E`)`	rewrite E.
`(pred` E`)`	apply one of the rules in Figure 2 to the entire expression if any apply; otherwise rewrite E.
`(ifzero` E_0 E_1 E_2`)`	apply one of the rules in Figure 2 to the entire expression if any apply; otherwise rewrite E_0.
`((lambda (`I_1 ... I_n`)` E`)` E_1 ... E_n`)`	apply one of the rules in Figure 2 to the entire expression if any apply; otherwise rewrite E_1.
`((label` I F`)` E_1 ... E_n`)`	apply the last rule in Figure 2.

a choice between one of the two rewrite rules

$$(\mathtt{amb}\ E_1\ E_2) \rightarrow E_1$$
$$(\mathtt{amb}\ E_1\ E_2) \rightarrow E_2$$

The interpretation is that any numeral derivable from a program according to the extended evaluation rule is a possible result of that program. A program may diverge iff there exists a sequence of choices such that the operational semantics fails to derive a numeral.

To obtain globally angelic choice, the evaluation rule is extended in exactly the same way as to obtain erratic choice, but the interpretation is different. As before, any numeral derivable from a program according to the extended evaluation rule is a possible result of that program. The difference is that under the globally angelic interpretation a program may diverge iff for every sequence of choices the operational semantics fails to derive a numeral.

To obtain locally angelic choice, the evaluation rule is extended to expressions of the form `(amb` E_1 E_2`)` by postulating a three-way choice between

1. rewrite the entire expression according to $(\mathtt{amb}\ N\ E) \rightarrow N$
2. rewrite the entire expression according to $(\mathtt{amb}\ E\ N) \rightarrow N$
3. rewrite both E_1 and E_2

Of course either or both of the first two choices may be blocked if an alternative is not a numeral. The interpretation is that any numeral derivable from a program is a possible result of the program. A program may diverge iff

(1) there exists a sequence of choices such that the operational semantics fails to derive a numeral

and

(2) there is no point at which the first or second choices above become available and neither is ever taken.

This interpretation of divergence incorporates a form of finite delay.

RELATIVE POWER.

The following theorem shows that the set of possible proper answers is the same for all three kinds of choice. This means that all differences between the three kinds of choice have to do with termination.

Theorem. *Every numeral derivable from a program using erratic choice semantics is also derivable using locally angelic choice semantics.*

Sketch of proof: We show that to every derivation using erratic choice there corresponds a derivation using locally angelic choice, by induction on the number of choices in the derivation using erratic choice. In the basis case, the derivations are identical, so suppose that for every erratic choice derivation of a numeral N with fewer than k choices there corresponds a locally angelic choice derivation of N, and let

$$E \rightarrow E' \rightarrow \ldots \rightarrow N$$

be a derivation with exactly k choices. Without loss of generality the very first step involves a choice, so we may assume E and E' are of the forms ——(amb E_1 E_2)—— and ——E_i—— respectively, where $i = 1$ or $i = 2$. Say $i = 1$ for definiteness. Then by the applicative order nature of the semantics, the derivation following the first step will begin with a series of steps that convert E_1 into a numeral N'. Hence the erratic choice derivation, which begins with

$$\begin{aligned} \text{——(amb } E_1\ E_2\text{)——} &\rightarrow \text{——} E_1 \text{——} \\ &\rightarrow \ldots \\ &\rightarrow \text{——} N' \text{——} \end{aligned}$$

corresponds to a locally angelic choice derivation that begins with

$$\begin{aligned} \text{——(amb } E_1\ E_2\text{)——} &\rightarrow \ldots \\ &\rightarrow \text{——(amb } N'\ E_2'\text{)——} \\ &\rightarrow \text{——} N' \text{——} \end{aligned}$$

by the induction hypothesis. ∎

Corollary. *The set of numerals derivable from a program is the same for erratic choice, locally angelic choice, and globally angelic choice.*

Definition. *Suppose a language has two semantics, A and B. Semantics A is* at least as strong *as semantics B iff for every program in the language the following hold:*

1. The possible proper results of the program under semantics B form a subset of the possible proper results of the program under semantics A.
2. If divergence is possible under semantics A, then divergence is possible under semantics B.
3. If divergence is certain under semantics A, then divergence is certain under semantics B.

Definition. *A semantics A is* stronger than *semantics B iff A is at least as strong as B and there exists a program P such that P must converge under A but may diverge under B.*

Corollary. *Globally angelic choice is stronger than locally angelic choice. Locally angelic choice is stronger than erratic choice.*

The last result above is rather technical. The following problem motivates the inclusion of some form of angelic choice in programming languages by demonstrating an important difference between erratic and angelic choice.

The findzero problem. *Given an amb-free description F of a partial function from the natural numbers to the natural numbers, find a numeral N such that (F N) is zero. (If there does not exist such an N, no answer should be given.)*

Clearly the findzero problem can be solved by any Turing-complete language, but for most programming languages the solution involves using the language to construct a complex scheduling interpreter that is then used to interpret a coded form of *F*. We can rule out such complex, non-modular solutions by insisting that the solution be a program scheme into which *F* can be inserted intact. For example, the findzero problem is solved by the globally angelic choice program scheme

```
((lambda (n)
   (ifzero (F n)
           n
           diverge))
 ((label numbers
    (lambda (n)
      (amb n (numbers (succ n)))))
  0))
```

where `diverge` is syntactic sugar for an infinite loop. This solution is modular in the sense that it separates the generation of candidate numbers from their testing, but it does not work using locally angelic choice. The shorter but less modular program scheme

```
((label loop
   (lambda (n)
     (amb (ifzero (F n)
                  n
                  diverge)
          (loop (succ n)))))
 0)
```

works using either locally angelic or globally angelic choice. The fact that locally angelic choice is weaker than globally angelic choice shows up here as a constraint on programming style. In this case locally angelic choice and globally angelic choice are equally efficient, but locally angelic choice can be more efficient than globally angelic choice in cases where the programmer knows a search can be cut off early.

The following theorem shows that erratic choice is fundamentally less expressive than locally angelic or globally angelic choice.

Theorem. *No program scheme under the erratic choice interpretation solves the findzero problem.*

Sketch of proof: First we show that no amb-free program scheme solves the findzero problem. This is corollary to a very general result by Berry concerning the pure lambda calculus [1] [2]. By taking advantage of the applicative order of our evaluation semantics, however, we can obtain the more elementary proof sketched below.

Suppose that $P[F]$ is an amb-free program scheme with scheme parameter F such that P[`(lambda (x) 0)`] yields a numeral N by some derivation D. If the scheme parameter F does not enter into a rewrite sequence in D of the form

$$\text{——}(F\ N)\text{——} \rightarrow \ldots \rightarrow \text{——}0\text{——}$$

then $P[F]$ also yields N when F is

`(lambda (x) (ifzero (=? x N) diverge 0))`

where `=?` returns 0 if its arguments are equal and 1 otherwise. Clearly such a $P[F]$ does not solve the findzero problem. On the other hand if F does enter into such a rewrite in D, then $P[F]$ diverges when F is as above so again $P[F]$ does not solve the findzero problem.

Now if ——`(amb` E_1 E_2`)`—— must converge under the erratic choice interpretation, then so must ——E_1——. Hence if $P[F]$ is any scheme that must converge for all parameters F such that F denotes any function having a zero in its range, then $P'[F]$ must converge for all such parameters where $P'[F]$ is obtained from $P[F]$ by replacing all subexpressions of the form `(amb` E_1 E_2`)` by E_1. Therefore any program scheme under the erratic choice interpretation that solves the findzero problem would yield an amb-free solution, a contradiction. ∎

The findzero problem shows that locally angelic choice is more powerful than erratic choice in an important sense. We know of no similar sense in which globally angelic choice is more powerful than locally angelic choice.

AN ALGEBRAIC PROPERTY.

The erratic choice and globally angelic choice interpretations share a pleasant distribution property that has been proposed as the basis for an algebra of nondeterministic programs [5]. The locally angelic choice interpretation does not share this property.

Theorem. *Under the globally angelic interpretation of* **amb**,

$$(F \ldots (\mathbf{amb}\ E_1\ E_2) \ldots)$$

is strongly equivalent to

$$(\mathbf{amb}\ (F \ldots E_1 \ldots)\ (F \ldots E_2 \ldots))$$

Sketch of proof: By the interpretation associated with globally angelic choice, weak equivalence implies strong equivalence, so it suffices to show that every numeral derivable from the one is derivable from the other and vice versa. Suppose

$$(F \ldots (\mathbf{amb}\ E_1\ E_2) \ldots) \to^* N$$

There are two cases, depending on whether the subexpression $(\mathbf{amb}\ E_1\ E_2)$ is rewritten in the course of the derivation. If it is not, then $(F \ldots E_1 \ldots)$ derives N by an analogous sequence of steps, since no rewrite rule is sensitive to the presence of an **amb** expression in an argument position. Hence

$$\begin{aligned}(\mathbf{amb}\ (F \ldots E_1 \ldots)\ (F \ldots E_2 \ldots)) &\to (F \ldots E_1 \ldots)\\ &\to^* N\end{aligned}$$

On the other hand if $(\mathbf{amb}\ E_1\ E_2)$ is rewritten in the course of the original derivation, then the original derivation must be of the form

$$\begin{aligned}(F \ldots (\mathbf{amb}\ E_1\ E_2) \ldots) &\to^* \text{——}(\mathbf{amb}\ E_1\ E_2)\text{——}\\ &\to \text{——}E_i\text{——}\\ &\to^* N\end{aligned}$$

where $i = 1$ or $i = 2$. Hence

$$\begin{aligned}(\mathbf{amb}\ (F \ldots E_1 \ldots)\ (F \ldots E_2 \ldots)) &\to (F \ldots E_i \ldots)\\ &\to^* \text{——}E_i\text{——}\\ &\to^* N\end{aligned}$$

showing that every numeral derivable from the first expression given the in the theorem is also derivable from the second expression.

To show the converse, suppose

$$(\mathbf{amb}\ (F \ldots E_1 \ldots)\ (F \ldots E_2 \ldots)) \to^* N$$

Then either $(F \ldots E_1 \ldots) \to^* N$ or $(F \ldots E_2 \ldots) \to^* N$. Say $(F \ldots E_1 \ldots) \to^* N$. If E_1 is not rewritten in the course of deriving N, then it is clear that

$$(F \ldots (\mathbf{amb}\ E_1\ E_2) \ldots) \to^* N$$

Otherwise the derivation is of the form

$$\begin{aligned}(F \ldots E_1 \ldots) &\to^* \text{---}E_1\text{---}\\ &\to^* \text{---}N'\text{---}\\ &\to^* N\end{aligned}$$

whence

$$\begin{aligned}(F \ldots (\mathbf{amb}\ E_1\ E_2) \ldots) &\to^* \text{---}(\mathbf{amb}\ E_1\ E_2)\text{---}\\ &\to \text{---}E_1\text{---}\\ &\to^* \text{---}N'\text{---}\\ &\to^* N\end{aligned}$$

▮

Theorem. *Under the erratic interpretation of* **amb**,

$$(F \ldots (\mathbf{amb}\ E_1\ E_2) \ldots)$$

is strongly equivalent to

$$(\mathbf{amb}\ (F \ldots E_1 \ldots)\ (F \ldots E_2 \ldots))$$

Sketch of proof: The proof of weak equivalence is exactly as in the previous theorem. Suppose $(F \ldots (\mathbf{amb}\ E_1\ E_2) \ldots)$ may diverge, and let

$$(F \ldots (\mathbf{amb}\ E_1\ E_2) \ldots) \to x_1 \to x_2 \to \ldots$$

be an infinite sequence of terms obtained according to the extended evaluation rule. If $(\mathbf{amb}\ E_1\ E_2)$ is never rewritten in that sequence, then the same sequence of choices yields an infinite term sequence for $(F \ldots E_1 \ldots)$, which in turn yields an infinite term sequence for

$$(\mathbf{amb}\ (F \ldots E_1 \ldots)\ (F \ldots E_2 \ldots))$$

If on the other hand $(\mathbf{amb}\ E_1\ E_2)$ is rewritten, so that the sequence has the form

$$\begin{aligned}(F \ldots (\mathbf{amb}\ E_1\ E_2) \ldots) &\to^* \text{---}(\mathbf{amb}\ E_1\ E_2)\text{---}\\ &\to \text{---}E_i\text{---}\\ &\to x_j \to x_{j+1} \to \ldots\end{aligned}$$

then

$$\begin{aligned}(\mathbf{amb}\ (F \ldots E_1 \ldots)\ (F \ldots E_2 \ldots)) &\to (F \ldots E_i \ldots)\\ &\to^* \text{---}E_i\text{---}\\ &\to x_j \to x_{j+1} \to \ldots\end{aligned}$$

is an infinite term sequence also.

It is easy to see that if (amb $(F \ldots E_1 \ldots)$ $(F \ldots E_2 \ldots)$) yields an infinite term sequence, then so must $(F \ldots$ (amb E_1 E_2) $\ldots)$. ∎

These two theorems suggest alternative operational semantics for erratic and globally angelic choice in which the theorems are used to float ambs up to the outer level of the expression. By postulating commutativity and associativity for amb, all choices could occur at the program level. The choices would be free in the case of erratic choice, but would be restricted to numerals in the case of globally angelic choice.

We show by example that locally angelic choice does not share the distribution property. The program

```
(ifzero (amb 0 1) 2 diverge)
```

may diverge under locally angelic choice but

```
(amb (ifzero 0 2 diverge)
     (ifzero 1 2 diverge))
```

must converge.

Indeed, the plural (run time choice) semantics in [4] does not share the distribution property even though it uses globally angelic choice. Under the globally angelic plural semantics the program

```
((lambda (n)
   (ifzero n
           (ifzero n diverge 2)
           diverge))
 (amb 0 1))
```

must yield 2 as its result but the program

```
(amb ((lambda (n)
        (ifzero n
                (ifzero n diverge 2)
                diverge))
      0)
     ((lambda (n)
        (ifzero n
                (ifzero n diverge 2)
                diverge))
      1))
```

cannot even terminate.

It appears that singular (call time choice) semantics with erratic or globally angelic choice are the only useful choice semantics to have the distribution property. Erratic choice is of little use to programmers, however. Its main use is in programming language design when efficiency and portability argue against fixing any particular order of evaluation. Among choice semantics that are useful for programming, globally angelic singular semantics is the only one to have the distribution property. What this means will remain unclear until further research has determined the importance of the property.

RELATED WORK.

The original paper on power domains included a semantics for a language with erratic choice [10]. As far as we know, [3] contains the only power domain semantics for locally angelic choice. Power domain semantics for globally angelic choice were considered in [4]. It should be possible to prove the equivalence of our operational semantics with the various power domain formulations, but so far we have been unable to do so.

The term "backtracking" has been applied to globally angelic choice [7], but that term is misleading because backtracking generally implies depth-first rather than breadth-first or parallel search. In [4] I chose the terms "by lazy" and "by need" to refer to locally angelic and globally angelic choice. The confusion that resulted showed my choices to be demonic.

Rewrite rules and operational semantics for locally angelic choice were considered in [11].

Rewrite rules for a variant of FP with globally angelic choice were presented in [5], which takes the distribution property as the fundamental axiom from which the other rules dealing with nondeterminism are derived.

CONCLUSIONS.

Since it allows choices to be resolved arbitrarily at compile time, erratic choice is moderately silly when considered as a programming language construct. Its major justification is the efficiency that can be gained by allowing an implementation to decide on the order of evaluation. For example, the guards of a guarded command may have common subexpressions that make it more efficient to evaluate them in a certain order. For that matter, they may even be evaluated in parallel.

Angelic choice, however, is a genuinely useful programming language construct. Though globally angelic choice is stronger than locally angelic choice in a narrow technical sense, it is not clear how important the difference will be in practice. We need results that compare the expressive power of locally and globally angelic choice. For example, does there exist an algorithm for transforming a program using globally angelic choice into an equivalent program using locally angelic choice?

The distribution law satisfied by globally angelic choice should make it more tractable than locally angelic choice for program transformation systems.

Locally angelic choice is a useful optimization of globally angelic choice when the programmer can show that either alternative is satisfactory, because an early commitment to the result of a subcomputation allows work on other alternatives to be dropped. This use of locally angelic choice reminds us of the use of the cut operator in Prolog.

Though this paper has not considered the possibility, the point at which a program commits to the result of a choice could be intermediate between the local choice expression and the global program. We intend to investigate semantics for languages that permit the programmer to specify for each choice point the scope of its angelicism.

REFERENCES.

[1] H P Barendregt, *The Lambda Calculus: its Syntax and Semantics*, North-Holland, Amsterdam, 1981.

[2] G Berry, "Séquentialité de l'evaluation formelle des lambda- expressions", in: *Proc. 3-e Colloque International sur la Programmation*, Paris, mars 1978 (Dunod, Paris).

[3] Manfred Broy, "A fixed point approach to applicative multiprogramming", lecture notes for the International Summer School on Theoretical Foundations of Programming Methodology, July 1981.

[4] William Clinger, "Nondeterministic call by need is neither lazy nor by name", *Conference Record of the 1982 ACM Symposium on Lisp and Functional Programming*, August 1982, pages 226-234.

[5] A Toni Cohen and Thomas J Myers, "Toward an algebra of nondeterministic programs", *Conference Record of the 1982 ACM Symposium on Lisp and Functional Programming*, August 1982, pages 235-242.

[6] M C B Hennessy and E A Ashcroft, "Parameter passing methods and nondeterminism", *Ninth Annual ACM Symposium on the Theory of Computing*, Boulder, 1977.

[7] J R Kenneway and C A R Hoare, "A theory of nondeterminism", in de Bakker and Leuwen [ed], *Proceedings of the 7th International Colloquium on Automata, Languages, and Programming*, Springer-Verlag Lecture Notes in Computer Science 85, 1980, pages 338-350.

[8] John McCarthy, "A basis for a mathematical theory of computation", in *Computer Programming and Formal Systems*, P Braffort and D Hirschberg [ed], North-Holland, Amsterdam, 1963, pages 33-70.

[9] David Park, "On the semantics of fair parallelism", University of Warwick Theory of Computation Report 31, October 1979.

[10] G D Plotkin, "A powerdomain construction", *SIAM J Computing* 5, 3, September 1976, pages 452-487.

[11] Stephen A Ward, "Functional domains of applicative languages", MIT Project MAC Technical Report 136, September 1974.

Semantics of Networks Containing Indeterminate Operators

Robert M. Keller

Prakash Panangaden

Department of Computer Science
University of Utah
Salt Lake City, UT 84112

Abstract: We discuss a denotational semantics for networks containing indeterminate operators. Our approach is based on modelling a network by the set of all its possible behaviors. Our notion of behavior is a sequence of computational actions. The primitive computational action is an *event*: the appearance or consumption of a token on a data path. A sequence of such events is called a *history* and a set of such histories is called an *archive*. We give *composition rules* that allow us to derive an archive for a network from the archive of its constituents. Causal and operational constraints on network behavior are encoded into the definitions of archives. We give a construction that allows us to obtain the denotation of networks containing *loops* by a process of successive approximations. This construction is not carried out in the traditional domain-theoretic setting, but rather resembles the category theoretic notion of limit. By using this construction, we avoid having to impose any *closure conditions* on the set of behaviors, as are typically necessary in powerdomain constructions. The resulting theory is general and compositional, but is also close to operational ideas making it a useful and flexible tool for modelling systems.

1. Introduction

The denotational semantics of sequential programming languages is by now well understood. For concurrent programming languages or languages with an indeterminate construct, the situation is more complex. Several variant semantic definitions have been proposed. In this paper we discuss a semantics for networks containing indeterminate operators, one based on the notion of *computational events*. Although we intend to compose program modules in a style reminiscent of stream-based functional programs, the word "module" is used in place of "function" to emphasize that not all modules behave as functions on their input histories, but rather may exhibit time-dependent behavior (*indeterminacy*). The networks we consider are similar in spirit to those of Kahn and MacQueen (as well as many other *data-flow* languages, (*cf.* [Davis 82]), in that our networks consist of operators connected by unidirectional data *arcs*. However, we do not assume that all arcs necessarily behave as unbounded FIFO queues. If desired, such behavior can be modeled by the insertion of unbounded queue modules into otherwise delayless arcs, and we shall informally discuss such networks as if there could be arbitrary delay on arcs, knowing that we can perform the mentioned insertion when precision becomes necessary. However, generality is served, and the basic mathematical description simplified, by not universally assuming unboundedness of arcs. Likewise, the FIFO condition may be relaxed.

We base our semantics on the simple, but elegantly-treatable, notion of sets of sequences of computational *events*, where an event is the production or consumption of a data value by a module on one of its associated arcs. The sequences are termed *histories*, while sets thereof are termed *archives*. The *denotation* of a network is simply its archive. This approach will be seen to be adequate for describing networks of both determinate and indeterminate operators, with or without delay, and with or without cycles.

We present *composition rules* for obtaining archives of networks from the archives of their component parts, either atomic or sub-networks. Our rules are similar to a set of rules stated informally by Pratt [Pratt 82]. The chief difference is that this he uses "partially-ordered multisets" of events instead of sequences. Similar uses of partially-ordered sets of events appeared in the appendix of [Keller 78], and in [Brock 81].

The basic idea of archives does not require that behaviors be effectively given. However, toward this end we also introduce a fixpoint approach to the construction of archives. This approach is based on rules for extending a history, called *extension rules*, in which the causality and other operational constraints are encoded. These rules are presented as functions on sets of partial histories and can thus be easily composed. The theory of limits of iterations of such functions involves a departure from the conventional theory of complete partial orders, due to the nature of extensions of histories. We introduce a new construction in which limits are defined ín a style reminiscent of the limit constructions for categories.

2. Archives

Programs or systems in our model are networks. A *network* is a directed graph, each node of which is labelled with the name of a *module* and each arc labelled distinctly (using b,c,d,....). The operational behavior of a network consists of nodes passing values to one another in the direction of arcs which connect the nodes. The *production* or *consumption* of a value y on arc b will be called an *event*, and represented either as <+b,y> in the former case or as <-b,y> in the latter case. Whether an event is a production or consumption will be called the *sense* of the event. When we wish to display an event as part of a sequence of events, we will sometimes use the following vertical notation for readability:

$$\begin{matrix} + & - \\ b & b \\ y & y \end{matrix}$$

We also refer to these events as *+b-events* or *-b-events* or just *b-event* when the sense is clear from context. We refer to the value part of a b-event as a *b-value*. When the particular arc, rather than the value, is of central importance, we may omit the latter as if all values were essentially the same. Here it would be the sequence of arcs on which events occur which is important. We hereafter refer to this as the *neutral-value* case. In many instances, the sense is clear from context, and we omit it too. For example, in the case of discussing a module with arcs b and c directed in and d directed out, we may omit the -'s with b and c, and + with with d.

A *history* of a node is a *sequence* of events which can occur in *one* possible run of the network. For example, one history for a module which produces, on arc d, sums of pairs of values consumed on arcs b and c, might be

```
+ - + - + + - + - + + - + - +
b b c c d c c b b d b b c c d
1 1 3 3 4 2 2 6 6 8 3 3 4 4 7
```

The behavior of this particular module can, of course, be expressed more elegantly as a function, but we are interested in a formalism which encompasses indeterminate operators as well. For example, a *merge* module passes its input values unchanged, rather than adding them, but passes them in some arbitrarily-interleaved order. The following are two possible histories for a merge with the same inputs b, c as above:

```
+ - + + - + + + - + + - + - + + - +
b b d c c d c b c d c c d b d c c d
1 1 1 3 3 3 2 6 2 2 7 7 7 6 6 4 4 4
```

and

```
+ + - + - + + - + + + - + - + + - +
b c b d c d c c d b c b d c d c c d
1 3 1 1 3 3 2 2 2 6 7 6 6 7 7 4 4 4
```

The description of a module can always be given by encapsulating it within a node (which provides labelled arcs with which to describe it), and presenting histories using the labels.

The set of all possible histories is called the *archive* for the module, and characterizes the module, i.e. forms a *denotation* for it. Certain features of potential interest, in particular the "internal state" of the node, may be suppressed in this description of the behavior of a node. For the purposes of the present discussion we assume that the history characterizes all *observable* properties of interest. This notion of observability is admittedly weaker than others that have been used in the CCS framework [Hennessey 82]. In the neutral-value case, a history may be represented as a finite or infinite *arc-sequence*, while an archive may be represented as a *language* (of finite or infinite strings) over the set of arc labels.

Figure 2-1 illustrates the "fork$_{bcd}$" module, which simply copies its input arc values to both of its output arcs. Its archive,

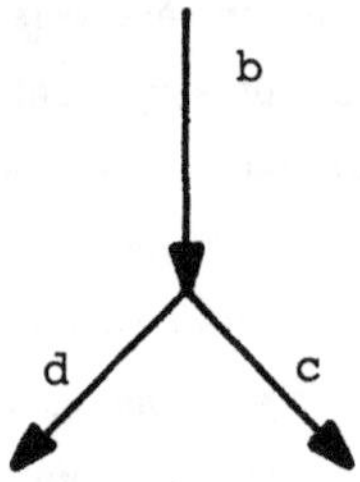

Figure 2-1: Fork module

$$\{\langle -b,v\rangle\langle +c,v\rangle\langle +d,v\rangle \mid v \in V\}^{oo} \cup \{\langle -b,v\rangle\langle +d,v\rangle\langle +c,v\rangle \mid v \in V\}^{oo}$$

indicates that each consumption of a value v (on arc b) is followed by a production of the same value v on arc c and on arc d. (Throughout this paper, if S is a set of sequences, then S^{oo} designates the set of infinite *concatenations* of members of S.)

The inclusion of both b-c-d and b-d-c orders in the archive for the fork module is indicative of the arbitrariness of the ordering between the production of of c and d events. Here, and in what follows, we follow the customary practice of representing *concurrency* by fine-grain interleaving, shown in the form of *sets* of sequences. In doing so we are assuming that the networks we model are asynchronous.

To describe archives of other modules, some additional notation will be useful. For history x and arc b, $\Pi_b(x)$ is the sub-sequence of b-events in x, and $\Pi_{b=v}(x)$ is the sub-sequence of b-events with value v. Similarly, for a set B of arcs, $\Pi_B(x)$ is the sub-sequence of b-events where b is any element of B. Furthermore, $V_b(x)$ is the sequence of b-values in x, in the order they appear, while $\#_b(x)$ is length of that sequence, i.e. the number of b-events in x, and $\#_{b=v}(x)$ is the length of $\Pi_{b=v}(x)$. Finally, $K_b(x)$ is the sequence of events in x which are *not* b-events, and $K_{bc}(x)$ is the sequence of events in x which are neither b-events nor c-events.

We use $\leq$ to designate both the *prefix ordering* on sequences and the numeric ordering on integers. Some relations recur sufficiently often that we give them special names:

equal(b, c, x)

means that $V_b(x) = V_c(x)$, i.e. that the sub-sequence of b and c values in x are the same;

precedes(b, c, x)

means that each c-event in x is preceded by a corresponding b-event, i.e. for every prefix $y \leq x$, we have $\#_b(y) \geq \#_c(y)$; and *leads*(b, c, x)

means that each c-event in x is *immediately* preceded by a corresponding b-event. Thus, *leads*(b, c, x) implies *precedes*(b, c, x), but not conversely.

The *leads* and *precedes* relations are used to capture essential *causal* relationships within histories. For example, if each output event on arc c of a module is produced in response to an input event on arc b, we will have *precedes*(-b, +c, x). Note that if we begin with a sequence having the property *leads*(b, c, x), and insert events other than b- and c- events in arbitrary positions, we shall always have a sequence y such that *precedes*(b, c, y). This phenomenon occurs with some of our operations on sequences.

A module which introduces arbitrary *delay* can be modeled by the insertion of modules δ_{bc}, which with input arc b, and output arc c, and value set V, have the archive

$\{x \in (\{-b, +c\} \times V)^{\infty} \mid$ *equal*(-b, +c, x) and *precedes*(-b, +c, x) $\}$

3. Semantics of Operators and Networks

We now discuss the semantics of various operators and networks. Our discussion centers around rules for composing the archives for operators to obtain the archives of the resulting networks. We consider three types of interconnections between sub-networks, which are sufficient to construct any network: aggregation, serial composition, and loop composition. Of these, the second is a convenience which can be composed from the other two. These rules were first presented in [Keller 83].

The first operation on networks is called **aggregation**. Here we simply lump modules M and N together without connecting them, as shown in Figure 3-1, designating the result by A(M,N).

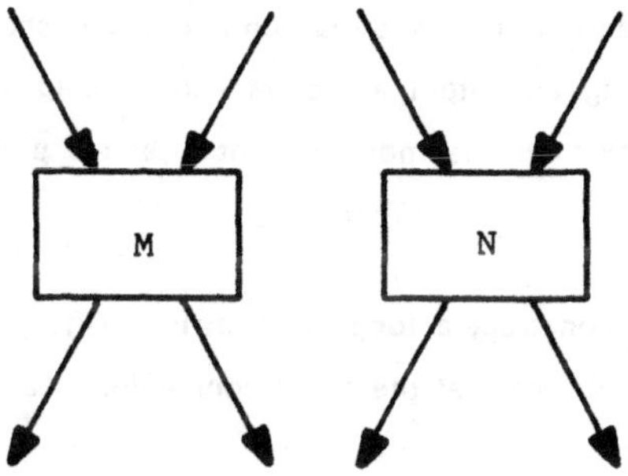

Figure 3-1: Aggregation of networks

The archive-composition rule corresponding to **aggregation** is the "shuffle". To describe the shuffle (designated Δ) more precisely, assume initially that x and y are event sequences over *disjoint* sets of arc labels, B and C. Then

$$x \Delta y = \{z \mid \Pi_B(z) = x \text{ and } \Pi_C(z) = y\}$$

That is, the shuffle of two sequences on disjoint sets of arcs is a set of sequences, such that projecting on the respective sets of arcs gives back the original sequences. We extend this in the natural pointwise fashion to sets,

$$S \Delta T = \cup \{x \Delta y \mid x \epsilon S, y \epsilon T\}$$

In case that the label sets B,C are *not disjoint*, the definition of shuffle is only slightly more complicated. The simplest definition seems to be to force them to be disjoint by *renaming* one set of labels, shuffling as before, then performing the inverse renaming to get the result.

Example To shuffle two events sequences:

$$\begin{array}{cccc} + & + & + & + \\ b & d & b & d \\ 1 & 1 & 2 & 2 \end{array}$$

and

$$\begin{array}{cccc} + & + & + & + \\ c & d & c & d \\ 3 & 3 & 4 & 4 \end{array}$$

We have to rename one of the d's, say that for the second sequence, to d'. Shuffling then gives us, for example,

$$\begin{array}{cccccccc} + & + & + & + & + & + & + & + \\ b & d & c & d' & c & b & d' & d \\ 1 & 1 & 3 & 3 & 4 & 2 & 4 & 2 \end{array}$$

and inverse renaming changes each d' to d.

The next type of interconnection rule is **serial composition**, shown in Figure 3-2, which we designate by $S_{bc}(M,N)$, b being an output arc of M and c being an input arc of N. The archive semantics of serial composition will be more evident after we present the loop interconnection next.

We also need the ability to construct a **loop**, as shown in Figure 3-3, designating the resulting network as $L_{bc}(M)$. It is easy to see that the serial connection is a composition of an aggregation and a loop.

We assume in all the above that arcs of M and N have disjoint sets of labels. Otherwise we can rename them to get this property. It is also clear that connection S can be realized as an aggregation followed by a loop, so if we are treating A and L, we needn't treat S separately.

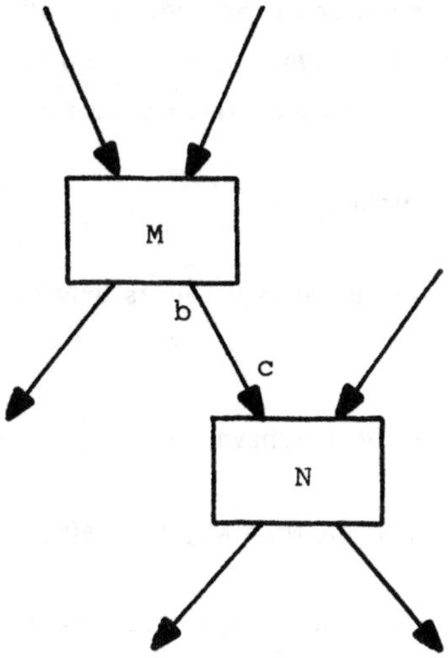

Figure 3-2: Serial composition

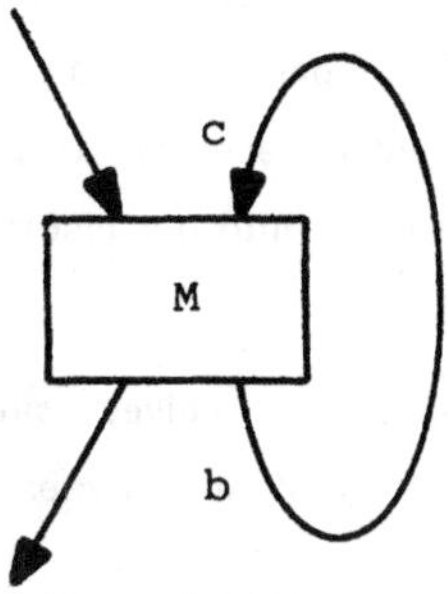

Figure 3-3: Network composition with a loop

Next we give the effect of such compositions on archives. If N is a network, with labels for its unconnected arcs, then Archive(N) denotes the corresponding archive.

Aggregation Rule: Archive(A(M,N)) = Archive(M) Δ Archive(N), where Δ is the shuffle operator.

The validity of the above rule is obvious: since the constituent networks do not interact, every interleaving of their two behaviors is a possible behavior of the result, and conversely.

To describe the effect of the **loop** construct L on an archive, we need to introduce a new cperator M_{bc} where, as usual, b and c are arc signed names.

$$M_{bc}(S) = \{ K_{bc}(x) \mid x \in S \text{ and } \textit{precedes}(b,c,x) \}.$$

Here $K_{bc}(x)$ discards events on arcs b and c, and preserves others. The purpose of the *precedes* condition is to express causality; If b values are fed to c, then in each archive, each -c-event is preceded by a +b-event with the same value. This rationale is summarized as:

Loop Rule: $Archive(L_{bc}(M)) = M_{bc}(Archive(M))$

M_{bc} is called the *matching* operator, because it selects only those sequences in which each c is preceded by a matching b.

According to preceding discussion, we also have

Serial Composition Rule: $Archive(S_{bc}(M, N)) = M_{bc}(Archive(M) \Delta Archive(N))$

The combination $M_{bc}(S\Delta T)$ occurs sufficiently often that is deserves a special notation,

$$S\Delta_{bc}T$$

This *matching shuffle* operator is similar to the operators used by Riddle [Riddle 79] to manipulate event sequences. In his work, special synchronizing symbols are introduced into the event sequences, and shuffling is performed on substrings occurring between matched synchronizing symbols. We also find it necessary to perform restricted shuffling, but we do not need to introduce synchronizing symbols into our history sequences.

Before further illustrating reasoning about archives using the above composition rules, it will be useful to express a few observations about causality, expressed using the *precedes* primitive:

Prefix (*precedes*(b,c,x) and $y \leq x$) imply *precedes*(b,c,y).

Transitivity (*precedes*(b,c,x) and *precedes* (c,d,x)) imply *precedes*(b,d,x).

Antisymmetry If x contains at least one b or c event, not(*precedes*(b,c,x) and *precedes*(c,b,x)).

Example $L_{cb}(fork_{bcd})$ is the network shown in Figure 3-4, with a fork module with the output arc c, connected back to the input arc b. Here we have, assuming the neutral-value case, for any history x, *precedes*(b,c,x), from the definition of the fork archive. But for x to be in $L_{cb}(Archive(fork_{bcd}))$, we also require *precedes*(c,b,x). By antisymmetry, this means that only the null history Λ can be in the resulting archive, i.e.

$$L_{cb}(fork_{bcd}) = \{\Lambda\}$$

Note that the fixed-point theory of Kahn would arrive at this result by starting with the null sequence and applying the fork function, which would give the null sequence back, thereby determining the least fixed-point.

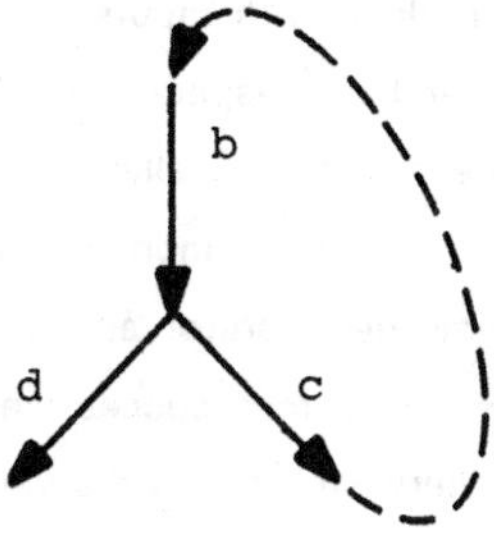

Figure 3-4: Example of a loop network

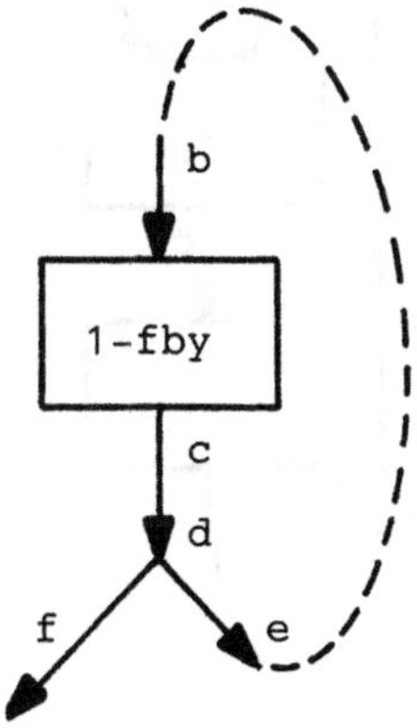

Figure 3-5: Another example of loop composition

Example Here we use a module *1-fby*, the output of which is a 1, followed by a verbatim copy of its input. The archive, with input b and output c, is given by the language (again assuming the neutral-value case)

$$\{c(bc)^{\infty}\}$$

When we compose 1-fby$_{bc}$ with fork$_{def}$ as shown in Figure 3-5, we have

Δ_{cd}(Archive(1-fby$_{bc}$), Archive(fork$_{def}$)) =

$\Delta_{cd}(c\{bc\}^{\infty}, \{def, dfe\}^{\infty}) = \{ef, fe\}\ \{bef, bfe\}^{\infty}$

When we "close the loop", as shown, we are requiring, in each history x, *leads*(e,b,x), which does not additionally constrain the sequences over the previous composition, so the result, after applying $L_{eb'}$ is

$\{f\}^{\infty}$

Example The archive for a *merge* module, with inputs b,c and output d, is simply the shuffle of archives for *identities* with arcs b,d and c,d respectively. This rectifies a prior oversimplification, which lead to the so-called "merge anomaly" [Keller 78]. We consider the network shown in Figure 3-6 and show that there are no causal anomalies in any of the histories of the archive. The network has two operators, a merge operator and an operator called g whose action is as follows: The operator g functions so as to map successive input values to output, in such a way that if the value is 1, it outputs 3, otherwise outputs the value itself.

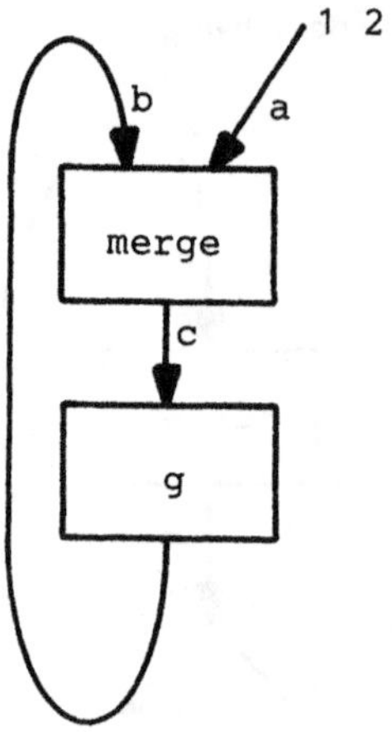

Figure 3-6: The Merge Anomaly Network

One may attempt to define the semantics of the merge operator in terms reminiscent of the functional approach via the following axiom:

> If one input arc contains the stream x and the other contains the stream y then the set of possible output streams is $x \Delta y$.

If one uses this axiom within the successive approximation approach of least fixed point theory, then one obtains output streams which can never be obtained operationally. For example, starting with the input stream 1 2 on arc a, after the second approximation using the above axiom, one might be lead to conclude that the set of possible streams on arc c is

$$\{1\ 2\ 3,\quad 1\ 2\ 3,\quad 3\ 1\ 2\}$$

but the last stream is impossible to obtain operationally. Notice that this anomaly arise because during the iteration *causality* is not imposed. It is the requirement that events in the histories on each arc *match* with each other which has been left out.

We shall now show that the archive composition rules permit the correct derivation of the behavior of the network in question. It is easy to verify operationally that if $\Pi_a(h)$ = 1 2 then for some n,

$\Pi_b(h) = 3^n\ (3\ 2)^{\infty}$ and $\Pi_c(h) = 1\ 3^n 2\ (3\ 2)^{\infty}$

where h is any infinite history from the network archive. We shall now prove that this is indeed true of the network archive, using only properties of the operators in the network and the archival composition rules.

First of all we note that values on the arc c in the network arises from matching events on the output arc of the operator g with the left input arc of the merge operator. The matching requirement is that, in every history, the tokens on the output arc of g precede the corresponding tokens on the input arc of the merge operator. This forces the first c-event to precede the first b-event. This in turn means that the value of the first c-event must appear in response to an a-event. Since we are assuming that the first a-value is 1, it follows that the first c-value is 1. Secondly we observe that since the operator g is determinate, we have

$$V_b(h) = G(V_c(h))$$

where G is the following function on streams:

```
G(x) = if first(x) = 1
       then 3 ^ G(rest(x))
       else first(x) ^ G(rest(x)).
```

Here "^" is the "followed-by" operator, which builds a sequence by adding an element to the front, and "first" and "rest" comprise the inverse of followed-by. Thus there are no b-values equal to 1. From the archive for merge we conclude that

$$V_c(h) = 1\ x\ 2\ y \quad \text{where } V_b(h) = x\ y.$$

Thus we can inset this expression for $V_c(h)$ into the above equation and obtain

$$V_b(h) = 3\ x\ 2\ y.$$

We now have the following equation

$$x\ y = 3\ x\ 2\ y.$$

This forces first(x) = 3, and

$$\text{rest}(x\ y) = x\ 2\ y.$$

Peeling off the first value on each side we get first(rest(x)) = 3. Continuing with this peeling process, we conclude that x is of the form 3^n for some n. When x is completely peeled off the left hand side, we are left with the equation

$$y = 3\ 2\ y$$

which clearly has the solution $y = (3\ 2)^{\infty}$. Thus we have derived the general form of the histories in the network archive and have shown that they agree with the form expected operationally.

4. Extension Rules

In this section, we present a complementary approach to for deriving archives, which corresponds more closely to the traditional [Scott 70] approach to the denotational semantics of sequential programming languages. The key feature of this approach is that the denotations of programming constructs are viewed as functions and the denotations of complex constructs are obtained by ordinary functional composition. We shall view the denotations of operators as functions which act on archives. The actions of these functions on archives is the pointwise extension of their actions on individual histories. The action on a single history inserts new events which correspond to the participation of that operator in the history. Thus these functions are called *extension rules.*

The archive of a network can be constructed by composing the extension rules of the component operators. Networks which contain loops have extension rules obtained by taking fixed points of the (recursive) composition of the extension rules of the component operators. The sense in which a fixed point is taken will be clarified later in this section. We do not use traditional complete partial order theory but give a construction that is similar to the category theoretic notion of a limit. The use of extension rules will mimic the set-theoretic denotational semantics of the preceding sections quite closely

We emphasize at this point that the functions that we will describe in this section are to viewed in the same spirit as semantic functions for sequential languages [Scott 71] and are not to be construed as "implementations" in any sense. Several of these functions have in fact been programmed and executed, but they are not efficient. The role of these functions is to show how one may express the formalism of archives in *constructive* terms.
We now define an *extension rule* as follows:

Definition Let F be an operator and let its archive be A_F. Let I_F be the *input archive,* i.e. the set of all possible input histories to F. I_F consists of all sequences which are serializations of possible events on the input arcs to F. Then the *extension rule* for F, written E_F, is a function from archives to archives which satisfies:

$$E_F(I_F) = A_F.$$

Thus, if I_F is the input archive, then $\Pi_a(E_F(I_F)) = A_F$ where Π_I represents the projection onto the input arcs of F.

Typically an extension rule is used to determine the *part* of the archive that corresponds to a *particular* input history.

An extension rule is required to satisfy several "reasonableness" conditions. These conditions will turn out to be essential in constructing extension rules for networks containing *loops.*

To express these conditions we use the following notation:

"e" will stand for a generic extension rule,

"h" will stand for a generic history,

"$h_1 <= h_2$" means that h_2 extends h_1.

We will also need the following terms:

Definition: An event v, in a history h, is said to be *consumable* by an extension rule e, if it is a production event that appears on the input arc of an operator in the network described by e and there is a history in the archive which contains extends h, as well as containing a consumption event corresponding to v.

Definition: An event v, is said to be *producible* in a history h, by an extension rule e, if there is a history in the archive of the network which extends h and contains v.

We may use the word *"enabled"* to mean either consumable or producible, and *"fired"* to represent the occurrence of the corresponding production or consumption.

The conditions on extension rules e can now be stated:

Monotonicity: The action of e cannot remove an event from a history; in symbols, if $h' \in e(h)$ then $h<=h'$.

Causality: An extension rule can only insert an consumption event after the corresponding production event, and a production event can be inserted only after the consumption events which triggered that production event.

Stability: If a history h, has no enabled events, then e satisfies $e(h) = \{h\}$.

Finite Delay: Within a chain of histories $h_1, h_2, \ldots, h_i, \ldots$ where for each i, $h_{i+1} \in e(h_i)$, no event remains enabled but not fired forever.

Note that monotonicity is not the same as that for partial orders, since embedding is not a partial order, as shall be seen. The finite-delay condition is similar to that of [Karp 69], which is used to show that a suitable notion of taking "limits" of sequences can be defined. It is actually a condition on such limits, rather than a constraint on the *presentation* of the extension rule.

We now present as an example the *extension rule for merge* in which the production of an output event can be delayed indefinitely. It consists of the composition of "consume", an unshown function which inserts the consumption events arbitrarily (consistent with the causality rule) into the history, and "ext", which extends the history

4.1. Extension Rules for Networks With Loops

It is easy to see that serial composition of operators corresponds to functional composition of the extension rules of the operators. The more important issue is to establish the connection between loop composition as expressed as an operation on archives and as an operation on extension rules. The extension rule for a network with a loop is easily *expressed* via a system of recursive equations involving the extension rules of the individual operators in the network.

To show that recursively defined expressions have a well-defined meaning involves introducing a suitable mathematical structure on the set of archives and showing that limits of sequences of approximations can be defined. Normally, the mathematical structure used is that of a complete partial order. However, for our purposes, this structure is not appropriate. We would like our structure to reflect the intuitive idea that histories improve by the *insertion* of new events, which are not necessarily added at the *end* of the histories. Thus we would like to express improvement of histories through the *subsequence* relation rather than prefix. This relation is not a partial order; a simple example is provided by the two sequences $(ab)^{\infty}$ and $(aab)^{\infty}$. The anti-symmetric property does not hold, since these sequences are unequal, yet each may be embedded in the other.

With *sets* of histories the situation is even worse. Even if one does have a complete partial order, subsets of the complete partial order can only be viewed as a complete partial order if one restricts the subsets to be closed in some appropriate sense [Plotkin 76] [Smythe 78]. We would like to be able to work with arbitrary sets of histories, since otherwise operators with different operational behaviors would have the same denotation.

by adding the produced c events. The function ext is defined as follows:

```
ext(h) = if h = [] then { [] }
         else
            if first(h) is a consumption then
              { first(h) ^ y | x ∈ ext(rest(h)) and y ∈ (produce[out(first(h)),x])}
             else
               {first(h) ^ y | y ∈ ext(rest(h)) }
```

where *out* produces the output event corresponding to its argument and *produce* performs insertion of an event in all causally acceptable positions. All functions are assumed to be extended to set arguments in the obvious way. The function *produce* must insert the event in all positions upto the next output event. This ensures that the order of input events on a given input arc is preserved on the output arc. The definition of *produce* is

```
produce[e,h] = if h = [] then {e}
               else
                  if first(h) is an output event then {e ^ h}
                   else
                     {first(h) ^ y | y ∈ produce[e,rest(h)]} U {e ^ h}.
```

The notion of *limit* that we shall define is similar to the category theory notion of limit. Suppose we have an operator *F* which has an input arc c and an output arc b. Let the extension rule for this operator be denoted by E. Now suppose that the arc b is reconnected to the arc c. The extension rule must be modified to identify every reference to a b-event with the corresponding c-event. Let this modified extension rule be denoted by E_{bc}. Whenever E_{bc} is used to extend a given history h, there will be new input events to *F* in the extended history $E_{bc}(h)$. The extension rule E_{bc} must therefore be applied again to the result. Given a particular initial history, h, applying the extension rule E_{bc} may result in several histories. Applying E_{bc} to each history in the resulting set of histories will also yield several new histories.

Let us denote the set containing the original history, h, by S_0, and the sets containing the subsequent extensions by S_1 S_2 ... S_i S_{i+1} ... respectively. As we construct each subsequent extension, we define relations, written R_i, from S_{i+1} to S_i which express which histories in S_i were extended by E_{bc} to yield particular histories in S_{i+1}. Formally, if $h_1 R_i h_2$, then $h_1 \in S_{i+1}$, $h_2 \in S_i$ and $h_1 \in E_{bc}(h_2)$. We refer to such a sequence of sets and relations as the *tower* of E_{bc} *over* h.

The limit of successive iterations of the extension rule E_{bc} applied to h can be defined in terms the *tower of* E_{bc} *over* h. The tower defines a *set of sequences of histories* through the relations R_i. Consider a typical such sequence, h_1 h_2 ... h_i ... with

h_{i+1} R_i h_i for each $i \in N$.

Such sequences of histories satisfy the following property:

Lemma: There exists a function f: N ---> N (N the natural numbers), such that, for every k in N, prefix(k,$h_{f(k)}$)) contains no consumable events or enabled events, furthermore this f can be chosen to be monotonic.

Here prefix(k, x) is the length k prefix of x.

Proof: Suppose h contains no consumable events or enabled events. Then by the stability condition, E_{bc} will leave h unchanged and no history in the tower will have either an consumable event or an enabled event. Suppose that h does contain an consumable event or enabled event. Then there must be a *unique first* such event. By the finite-delay property, at some *finite* point in the tower, this event must be consumed or produced.

Suppose this consumption or production occurs in step t of the tower and the event that was consumed or produced is the *nth* event in this history. Using causality, we can define f(n) = t. Because an extension rule can insert events after their cause,we see that f is indeed monotonic.

Using this lemma, it is possible to construct the following sequence of embeddings:

$$\text{prefix}(1,h_{f(1)}) <= \text{prefix}(2,h_{f(2)}) <= \text{prefix}(3,h_{f(3)}) <= \ \ldots \ \text{prefix}(i,h_{f(i)})$$

However, these embeddings are additionally *prefixes* of one another, so the limit of this sequence does exist and is *unique*. We denote this limit sequence by h^*. By construction, none of the members of the sequence has any consumable or enabled events, so neither does h^*. Thus $e(h^*) = \{h^*\}$ by the stability condition. The limit of the entire tower is obtained by constructing the limit in the above fashion for every sequence of histories in the tower.

Let us call the limit of the tower of E_{bc} over h $E^*_{bc}(h)$. Then E^*_{bc} defines the extension rule for the network with b connected back into c.

The asymmetry between the roles of b and c noted in Section 3 is implicitly present here. The new input events present in the Nth iteration of the extension rule were generated in the $(N-1)^{th}$ iteration. Thus the b-events have two roles: as output events of the $(N-1)^{th}$ iteration and as input events in the Nth iteration. The effect would have been the same as if we had used the original extension rule E with the change that whenever a c-event is inserted, an b-event is also inserted immediately following the c-event. This view of the extension rule shows that it must necessarily construct histories of the form that appear in $L_{bc}(F)$.

5. Conclusions

The denotational approach we have outlined in this paper shares some features commonly associated with operational semantics. In particular, causality constraints are explicitly stated in the definitions of most archives. More importantly, the basic concept on which the theory is built is the computational event, which is a very operational concept. The use of events to define suitable domains for denotational semantics has already been studied in great depth by [Winskel 80]. This closeness to operational ideas makes this formalism a convenient and flexible tool for modelling systems of practical interest, while we retain the advantages of a denotational approach.

Our approach is similar to a variety of other semantic theories for networks containing indeterminate operators. These go under the general name of "trace" domains: a domain is built from sequences of computational actions. As far as we are aware, our theory is the only one using the category theoretic style of limit. Abstract semantics have been given by [Plotkin 76], [Broy 81], and [Abramsky 83]. The Plotkin construction does not handle unbounded indeterminacy or non-flat domains. Our construction does allow us to discuss unbounded indeterminacy, manifested by the merge operator, for example. The Broy construction does not allow one to describe arbitrary sets of possible results, as the sets in his domain constructions are required to satisfy a suitable closure condition. Important recent work on semantics of indeterminate constructs is that of Abramsky. His formalism is explicitly category theoretic; using multi- sets of possible results, he can handle arbitrary sets, unbounded indeterminacy, and power constructions over domains which are not flat.

6. References

[Abramsky 83] Abramsky, S.
Semantic Foundations of Applicative Multiprogramming.
In Diaz, J. (editor), *Automata, Languages and Programming*, pages 1-14. Springer-Verlag, July, 1983.

[Brock 81] Brock J.D.,W.B.Ackermann.
Scenarios:A Model of Non-Determinate Computation.
In J.Diaz, I.Ramos (editor), *Formalization of Programming Concepts, LNCS 107*, pages 252-259. Springer-Verlag, New York, 1981.

[Broy 81] Broy M.
A Fixed Point Approach to Applicative Multiprogramming.
In *Lectures at the International Summer School on Theoretical Foundations of Programming Methodology*. July, 1981.

[Davis 82] A.L. Davis and R.M. Keller.
Dataflow program graphs.
Computer 15(2):26-41, February, 1982.

[Hennessey 82] Hennessey, M.
Synchronous and Asynchronous Experiments on Processes.
Technical Report, University of Edinburgh, September, 1982.

[Karp 69] Karp R. M., Miller R.
Parallel program schemata.
JCSS , May, 1969.

[Keller 78] Keller R.M.
Denotational Models for Parallel Programs With Indeterminate Operators.
In E.J.Neuhold (editor), *Formal Descriptions of Programming Concepts*, pages 337-365. North-Holland, Amsterdam, 1978.

[Keller 83] R.M. Keller.
Unpublished presentation on archives.
June, 1983.
Massachusetts Institute Technology, Applicative Languages Workshop, Endicott House.

[Plotkin 76] Plotkin G.
A Powerdomain Construction.
SIAM J. of Computing 5(3), September, 1976.

[Pratt 82] Pratt V.
On the Composition of Processes.
In *Ninth Annual ACM Symposium on Principles of Programming Languages,* pages 213-223. ACM, January, 1982.

[Riddle 79] Riddle W.E.
An Approach to Software System Behavior Description.
Computer Languages 4:29-47, 1979.

[Scott 70] Scott D.S.
Outline of a Mathematical Theory of Computation.
In *Proceedings of the Fourth Annual Princeton Conference on Information Sciences and Systems,* pages 169-176. 1970.

[Scott 71] Scott D.S., Strachey C.
Towards a Mathematical Semantics for Computer Languages.
Technical Report PRG-6, University of Oxford, 1971.

[Smythe 78] Smythe M.B.
Power Domains.
J. CSS 16:23-36, 1978.

[Winskel 80] Winskel G.
Events in Computation.
PhD thesis, University of Edinburgh, 1980.

Abstract Interpretation and Indeterminacy

Prakash Panangaden

Department of Computer Science
University of Utah
Salt Lake City, UT 84112

Abstract: We present a theory for the semantics of indeterminate operators in a dataflow network. The assumption is made that the language in which the indeterminate operators are written has a construct that allows for the testing of availability of data on input lines. We then show that indeterminacy arises through the use of such an operator together with the fact that communication channels produce unpredictable delays in the transmission of data. Our scheme is to use the notion of hiatons to represent delays as measured *locally*, and then to filter out the hiatons to obtain ordinary streams. This filtering process produces indeterminate behavior at the level of ordinary streams. We indicate how this can be justified using the formalism of abstract interpretation. We show that a particular fairness anomaly does not arise.

keywords and phrases: abstract interpretation, indeterminate operators, hiatons, dataflow networks, fairness.

1. Introduction

We discuss a new approach to the semantics of dataflow networks containing indeterminate operators. The major advantages of our formalism are: (i) we are able to *derive* the denotations of indeterminate operators given their implementation in terms of an imperative language resembling that of [Kahn 77], (ii) we are able to formally realise the assertion that indeterminacy can arise through arbitrary delay in the arrival of data at the nodes of a network, (iii) we are able to recover the standard view of indeterminate dataflow operators through the use of abstract interpretation, (iv) we are able to reason about *fairness* properties of certain indeterminate operators and (v) we do not need to introduce an explicit *oracle* as an additional construct.

The earliest investigation into the formal semantics of networks was carried out by Kahn [Kahn 74] who showed that if the communication between the nodes was restricted to reading from input channels and writing onto output channels then the network would be determinate. [Keller 78] proposed a formalism in which nodes are allowed to test for the availability of data on their input arcs, thus leading to the possibility that some of the nodes are indeterminate when viewed as acting on streams of data tokens. We give a formal semantics to this extended Kahn-Keller language.

Our formalism incorporates two recent developments. The first is the use of a special token called a *hiaton* [Park 82] to represent a delay in the propagation of data. We shall use the symbol τ to represent a hiaton. Thus, a typical stream will contain data values interspersed with τs. The interpretation of such a stream will be clarified in the next paragraph. The virtue of introducing such a special token is that we can give definitions of indeterminate operators on streams as determinate functions on τ-enriched streams. The second recent development that we employ is the idea of an "abstract" interpretation [Mycroft 81] [Mishra 84]. The key idea here is to map the semantic domain onto a (in some suitable sense) simplified domain and to reinterpret the language constructs in terms of the simplified domain.

The technical details of abstract interpretation will be discussed in the next section. We will use abstract interpretations in a slightly non-traditional way. In our case, the original domain will be the domain of τ-enriched streams (τ-streams) and the simplified domain will be the standard domain of streams. Via the abstraction process, the determinate functions over the domain of τ-streams are reinterpreted as indeterminate operators over the domain of standard streams.

In interpreting the τ symbols, we make the following assumptions. Each node has an internal clock which is not synchronized in any way with the internal clock of any other node. The ticks of the clocks mark time periods during which the basic communication actions occur. These basic actions are: read from an input channel, write onto an output channel, and test a channel for availability of data. Thus a τ on the input stream would represent the non-appearance of data on that channel during a cycle. The τ symbols thus convey information about the relative rates of appearance of data at a particular node. The nodes that we model are perfectly determinate with respect to τ-enriched streams, as no additional indeterminate primitives, such as internal choice, are allowed. The meaning of a particular node is defined by a function from τ-enriched streams to streams. The only explicit indeterminate behavior that incorporated at this level is that the channels between nodes insert τ symbols into the output stream in an unpredictable way. Thus, the τ symbols cannot be used to obtain effective synchronization between different nodes. One novelty of our approach is that we have succeeded in incorporating timing considerations into our theory without having to introduce any *global* clock.

The formalism we present may be visualized through the following diagram:

```
OUR VIEW:              NODES                 DATA PATHS
                  are determinate        are indeterminate

                              |
                              | ABSTRACTION (Ignore τs)
                              |
                             \|/
STANDARD VIEW:          NODES                 DATA PATHS
                  are indeterminate      are determinate (in fact are identity)
```

The rest of the paper is organized in the following way. In the next section we discuss the basic formalism of abstract interpretation. In Section 3 we give a simple programming language for writing implementations of the nodes and we give its semantics in terms of τ-enriched streams. In the following section we abstract this interpretation to the domain of ordinary streams and show how indeterminacy arises. The remaining sections are devoted to certain applications particularly to the analysis of fairness. In this context, we are able to show that a particular fairness anomaly does not arise.

2. Abstract Interpretation

Abstract interpretation provides a general framework for the static inference of properties of programs. Typically such inference is of use in program optimization, transformation and (weak) verification (i.e. where termination issues are not addressed). Abstract interpretation was first developed by Cousot & Cousot [Cousot 77, Cousot 81] to aid in the analysis of imperative programs. In this setting, programs are modelled as flowcharts; static inference is expressed as an abstraction of the "collecting interpretation" - the natural lifting of the standard semantics from values to *sets* of values.

In developing the abstract interpretation of applicative programs, Mycroft [Mycroft 81, Mycroft 83] observed that the framework of Cousot & Cousot was useful only for inference schemes which were weakly correct; termination cannot be expressed in their framework. In place of the powerset based formulation as used by the Cousots, a powerdomain based formulation is necessary. This view was further developed in [Mishra 84] where the abstract interpretation of non-flat "stream" domains was considered.

Our use of abstract interpretation is rather different. We use the formalism to show that standard stream-based programming with indeterminate operators can be viewed as an **approximation** to programming with τ-streams, which incorporate a certain degree of timing information. This allows us to pinpoint the phenomenon of indeterminacy as arising from ignoring the explicit timing information and from the fact that the data lines introduce randomness into the relative speeds of transmission of data. Furthermore, our formalism does not introduce oracles as an additional construct, as the abstraction map serves the role of an oracle. Among the advantages of our approach is that it articulates in a precise fashion the relation between indeterminacy and imprecise information about the computational details. This has frequently been expressed in the literature in an intuitive fashion but, has not been captured precisely. Another benefit is that the introduction of explicit delay allows us to reason about *fairness*, something which is very difficult otherwise.

The domains of interest in the present work are the domain of τ-streams, written TS, and the domain of streams. These can be defined as:

TS = stream[integers + τ]

S = stream[integers]

The connection between the two is established by:

Ab: TS --> S

where

Ab: nil = nil

Ab: τ ^x = Abs:x

(Here, and in what follows, ^ represents the infix stream constructor, "followed-by" or "cons", and : represents function application.)

The domain of ordinary streams over a set of data values V is the solution of the recursive domain equation

$$S = [] + V + (V \times S)$$

and has the usual prefix ordering. The domain of τ-streams is the solution of the recursive domain equation

$$TS = [] + (V \cup \{\tau\}) + ((V \cup \{\tau\}) \times TS)$$

once again with the prefix ordering. It is easy to see that the function *Ab* defined above is a continuous map from TS to S.

We cannot use the published accounts of abstract interpretation for our analysis, since the best results available apply only to domains of finite height [Mycroft 83]. We use instead the formalism of [Panangaden 84], which is applicable for general domains. This formalism uses categories, rather than complete partial orders, to model computability concepts. The idea is that the existence of a morphism from an object X to another object Y expresses the fact that X might "improve" to Y. However, approximation is no longer antisymmetric, as there might be morphisms in both directions between two objects. This broadening of the concept of approximation is necessary when dealing with sets of values. The fact that we no longer have a partial order may appear to deprive us of the concept of limits, based as it is on the notion of a least upper bound; in categories we can, however, make use of the theory of direct limits [Arbib 75] to serve this purpose. Using morphisms to express approximation between objects allows us to distinguish *different ways in which two objects may approximate each other*, a distinction crucial to the formalism. Further details may be found in [Panangaden 84].

Given domains D and E and continuous functions from D to E, we wish to extend these functions to "sets of values" in such a way that the extension process (lifting) is continuous and the lifted functions are also continuous. The first step is to redefine the original functions so that they now run from D X ? to D X E, where ? is the one point domain. This is done so that a function can be viewed as mapping a point onto its image in the *graph* of the function, rather than onto its image point in the range of the original function. Given a function $f{:}D \text{ --> } E$ we define $f^g{:}D \times ? \text{ --> } D \times E$ by $f^g(<d, ?>)=<d, f(d)>$. Clearly f^g is continuous and monotonic iff f is. We now define the category **PG**(D, ?); the objects are all subsets of D X ?, the morphisms are *increasing* maps. Similarly, we define the category **PG**(D, E). A function f^g from D X ? to D X E is now extended to a *functor* F from **PG**(D, ?) to **PG**(D, E) in the following way:

1. The action of F on an object X is

   $$F(X) = \{<d, f(d)> \mid <d, ?> \in X\}$$

   The action of F on a morphism κ from X to Y yields a morphism $F(\kappa)$ from F(X) to F(Y) defined by:

   $$\text{if } \kappa(<d, ?>)=<d', ?> \text{ then } F(\kappa)(<d, f(d)>)=<d', f(d')>.$$

The domains D X ? and D X E can be embedded, via the map that takes an element to its singleton set, into **PG**(D, ?) and **PG**(D, E) respectively. In [Panangaden 84] it is shown that these embeddings are continuous. It can also be shown that the lifting of functions to functors yields a functor category, and that approximation of functions from D to E can be reinterpreted as natural transformations between the resulting functors from **PG**(D, ?) to **PG**(D, E).

An abstract interpretation can now be defined in the following way. First "simplified" domains A and B are introduced, then **PG**(A, ?) **PG**(A, B) are constructed in the same way as before. Now the simplification is expressed via abstraction maps γ_1 and γ_2 from **PG**(D, ?) to **PG**(A, ?) and from **PG**(D, E) to **PG**(A, B) respectively. The requirement for an abstraction map to be acceptable is that if a morphism exists from X to Y then it should be possible to find a morphism from $\gamma_{1,\,2}(X)$ to $\gamma_{1,\,2}(Y)$. This is a slightly weaker condition than requiring them to be functors. The abstraction maps should also satisfy a "weak" continuity requirement which is explained in [Panangaden 84].

In our application, we will use TS and S as the domains D and E respectively and S for both A and B. Thus our abstraction ignores the timing information contained in τ-streams. In Section 4 we briefly discuss the formalism sketched in this section as it applies to streams and τ-streams.

3. The Language

We present a simple imperative language for writing implementations of the nodes (operators) in a dataflow network. The language is essentially the same as the language presented in [Kahn 74] with the addition of a construct called "poll" [Keller 78] which tests for the availability of data on the input channels. The communication between nodes is via input and output channels. These channels are viewed as unbounded queues.

A program for a particular node contains a declaration of the input and output channels. The interaction between a node and its channels is carried out by read, poll and write primitives. A read operation on a channel removes a token from that channel and puts the token in the local store. Similarly, a write operation takes a token from the local store and copies it onto the output channel. The poll operation on an input channel is Boolean-valued and returns false when there is no token available, in other words, when the first item in the input stream is a hiaton. We assume that there is always at least a single hiaton on every input channel to start with. The remaining language primitives allow one to manipulate the local store and construct arithmetic and logical expressions in the standard fashion.

The syntax of the language is given by the following grammar:

<program>::=<declarations><body>

<declarations>::=**input channel**:<identifier> | **output channel**:<identifier>

<body>::=<variable declarations><statements>

<statements>::=Λ | <statement>;<statements>

<statement>::=**if**<boolean>**then**<statements>**else**<statements> |

while<boolean>**do**<statements> |

<identifier>:=<expression> |

read from<identifier> **into** <identifier> |

write<identifier> **onto** <identifier>

<boolean>::=**poll** <identifier> | ...

The syntax for expressions and booleans is assumed to be standard.

An example program in this language is shown below [Keller 78].

```
input channel:a,b
output channel:c
variable:x
while true do
if poll a then
    read from a into x;
    write x onto c
    if poll b then
        read from b into x;
        write x onto c
    else
        continue
else
    if poll b then
        read from b into x;
        write x onto c
    else
        continue.
```

This program [Keller 78] implements a fair merge operation. It is clearly a determinate program when viewed as acting on τ-enriched streams, but when viewed as acting on ordinary streams it becomes indeterminate. This particular style of programming language has been implemented by [Tanaka 83] on the Rediflow simulator [Keller 83].

We shall define a meaning function μ for this language assuming that μ is already defined for the purely sequential part of the language. We then give semantics for read, write and poll. The meaning function will map statements to functions from environments to environments. The environment is a function that maps the local variables to values and the input channels to τ-streams and the output channels to ordinary streams. The expressions get mapped to functions from environments to values.

The propagation of values along the data paths is modelled by the extraction of the appropriate output stream from the environment and the insertion of an unpredictable number of delay tokens via a closure operation. Thus, the input to the next node will be a set of possible input streams rather than a single stream. We define the action of a node on a set of possible input streams as the pointwise extension of its action on individual streams. We are suppressing the full mathematical details in this discussion as they would clutter up the formalism. However, in [Panangaden 84] we give the mathematical details involving the categorical collecting semantics.

The semantics of the poll construct is as follows:

μ(**poll** a)(env) = <newenv,val>

where

val = false if first(env(a)) = τ , val = true otherwise

and if val = false then newenv = env(a|-rest(env(a))) else newenv = env.

The modifications to the environment are indicated by the |- symbol, where env(a|-rest(env(a))) means that the binding of a in the environment is changed to be bound to rest of the old binding.

Thus the poll construct essentially detects the presence of hiatons. If there is a hiaton on the channel being polled then the poll operation consumes it, this ensures that poll is in fact time sensitive. The **read** construct is hiaton insensitive, thus it consumes all the leading hiatons from a channel unless it is guarded by a poll operation. The **write** construct will not produce any hiatons at all. The semantics of these constructs are as follows:

μ(**read** a into x)(env) = env(a|-rest(strip_τ(env(a))); x|-first(strip_τ(env(a))))

μ(**write** x onto b)(env) = env(b|-addtoend(env(b), env(x))),

where the addtoend function is defined as:

addtoend(x, y) = rev(y ^ (rev(x))).

It is now easy to see that the action of the merge node is given by the following function:

μ(merge)(env) = if first(env(a)) = τ then f(newenv1) else f(newenv2)

newenv1 = env(a|-rest(env(a)))

newenv2 = env(a|-rest(env(a)), c|-addtoend(env(c), first(env(a))))

f(env) = if first(env(b)) = τ then μ(merge)(env(b|-rest(b))) else
μ(merge)(env(b|-rest(env(b)), c|-addtoend(env(c), first(env(b))))).

The next issue that we discuss is how to derive the meaning of a network of operators given the meaning of the individual nodes. To do so it is necessary to discuss the action of a data line in transmitting a stream from one node to another. In the case of ordinary streams a data line is merely the identity function. On τ-streams, however, a data line causes an unpredictable delay in the transmission of data values and hence causes the insertion of arbitrarily many hiatons. The action of a data line is thus a function from ordinary streams to **sets of** τ-streams. This action is most easily expressed in terms of the inverse of the abstraction map. Recall, from Section 2, that the abstraction map is a map from τ-streams to streams which removes all the hiatons from the τ-stream. The inverse map, therefore, maps a stream to the set of τ-streams that result by arbitrary insertion of hiatons into the stream. Thus the action of a data line on a stream s is simply $\mathbf{Ab}^{-1}$ (s). The action of an operator **O** with input line **a** and output line **b** is thus

$\mathbf{Ab}^{-1}(\mu(\mathbf{O})\ (t))$,
where t is the input τ-stream on **a**.

If the output line **b** is connected to the input line of another operator then its meaning function acts on each member of the set of τ-streams produced by **O**. Thus composition of the meaning functions of operators is effected via the action of $\mathbf{Ab}^{-1}$. This extends in the obvious way to operators that have several input and output lines.

Using $\mathbf{Ab}^{-1}$ as described in the last paragraph allows infinite sequences of hiatons to be appended at the end of the hiatonization of any ordinary *finite* stream. This is acceptable if the stream being hiatonized is "complete", but if we are in the process of iteratively constructing a stream, then we are effectively truncating it by appending an infinite sequence of hiatons at the end. Thus, rather than using $\mathbf{Ab}^{-1}$, we use an operator Δ, called the finite delay operator, to perform the insertion of hiatons. The definition of this operator is as follows: First we define Δ_k:S-->TS as a map that inserts hiatons into a stream in all ways that do not produce sequences of more than k consecutive hiatons. Then $\Delta(s) =_{def} \mathbf{U}_k\ \Delta_k(s)$.

If we wish to describe networks in which the arcs satisfy a finite delay property, we use Δ rather than $\mathbf{Ab}^{-1}$ to effect the connection of nodes in the network. Thus, for example, the action of an operator **O** with input line **a** and output line **b** as a map from τ-streams to τ-streams is

$\Delta(\mu\mathbf{O}(t))$, where t is the τ-streams stream input at **a**.

3.1. Networks with Loops

In networks with loops, the naive discussion of composition given above does not suffice. We need the analog of a fixed point construction to define the limits of iterations through the loops in a network. In this section we describe how such limits can be realized be defining a category of subsets of the domain of τ-sequences.

We introduce some notation in the context of sequential composition. Suppose f and g are two operators and that each has a single input arc and a single output arc. Suppose that the output from f is fed into the input arc of g. Now suppose that the input at f is the stream s. We start by hiatonizing the stream using Ab^{-1} to get $Ab^{-1}(s)$ as the set of τ-streams input to f. For brevity I will call this set s_0. Now suppose that the action of f on s_0 produces the set t_1 defined by t_1 = $\{x|\text{for some } y \text{ in } s_0,\ f(y) = x\}$. The set t_1 consists of ordinary streams rather than τ-streams. Now arbitrary delay must be introduced into the streams in t_1 before they appear at g. To do this we use the finite delay operator, Δ, discussed earlier. Thus the set of τ-streams input at g is s_1 = $\{t|\text{for some } s \text{ in } t_1,\ t \text{ is in } \Delta(s)\}$.

Together with the set s_1, we define a map $\phi_{f,1}$ from s_1 to s_0 which maps each member of s_1 to the element of s_0 which gave rise to it. In general the ϕ maps will be multi-function rather than functions, but for the moment we will pretend that they are functions and note that the arguments go through for the case of multi-functions. The operator g will act on each member of s_1 to produce a new set of streams which after the action of Δ produces a new set of τ-streams s_2. A map, similar to $\phi_{f,1}$ can be defined for the action of g. Now the set s_2, which is the result of f and g acting seqentially, can be given essentially by the maps. We shall use such maps to construct the limits of iterations through a network with loops.

First, note that the collection of all subsets of TS can be made into a category by defining the morphisms to be all *decreasing* maps (in the sense defined by the partial order on TS viewed as a complete partial order). In this category, we can define limits for certain special diagrams which we shall call *spectra*. A spectrum is a diagram consisting of at most countably many objects, indexed by a directed set A, with a morphism, m_{ab} defined from O_a to O_b, between any two objects O_a and O_b which satisfy $a < b$, where $<$ is the partial order of the indexing set, A. The morphisms are required to satisfy $m_{bc} \circ m_{ab} = m_{ac}$. Limits of such diagrams are essentially defined by following all the chains defined by the morphisms and taking limits in the complete partial order TS for each such chain, [Panangaden 84].

We shall illustrate the process of defining the denotation for a network with a loop by considering a network with a single input arc and a single loop. Suppose we break the loop, we then get a network with two input arcs and and an output arc. Let the denotation of this virtual network be the function f. Suppose that there is an input τ-stream t on the input arc and that the initial τ-stream on the virtual input arc of the cut loop is t_0 (usually this will be the empty τ-stream). The action of f on $<t, t_0>$ will yield a set, S^1, of streams. Now we have to iterate the action of f on these streams. First every member of S^1 is hiatonized using the finite delay operator Δ. This then gives a set, T^1, of τ-streams which are input to the next invocation of f. As we construct the sets of successive approximations we will also construct a *spectrum* which we use to define the limit. The first thing to note is that T^1 may contain τ-streams which are not extensions of the original τ-stream, t_0. Thus we take the subset of T^1 which does consist of τ-streams that extend t_0. The complete definition of T^1 is:

$$T^1 = \Delta(f(<t, t_0>)) \quad (t_0)\,\hat{}$$

In addition to constructing T^1, we also define a map, ϕ_1, from T^1 to T^0 ($=\{t_0\}$), by mapping each τ-stream to t_0. This defines the start of the spectrum. The rest of the spectrum can now be defined by induction as follows:

$$T^{n+1} = (\mathbf{U}\ (\Delta(\{x \mid f(<t,y>) = x,\ y \in T^n\})))\ y\,\hat{}$$

where the union ranges over all y in T^n.

The map ϕ_{n+1} from T^{n+1} to T^n is defined by mapping each member in T^{n+1} to the y in T^n that was used in the inductive step.

The "map" is not actually a function, since a particular member of T^{n+1} can arise in many ways by different choices of a y from T^n. The limit construction for a spectrum goes through essentially unchanged for the case that the maps between the members of the spectrum are multifunctions rather than functions.

Thus the denotation of a network with a loop is obtained in three steps; first the loop is cut and the action of the cut network is characterized by a function, the successive approximations are constructed by iterating this function (and the bounded delay operator), and finally the successive approximations are made into a spectrum and the limit is defined via a standard category-theoretic construction.

4. Abstraction in Our Context

In our approach we have two structures to reason about, the domain of timed streams and the domain of ordinary streams. As has been discussed in Section 2, the formal justification of our abstraction is done via the powergraph construction. In other words the domain of τ-streams must be first viewed as a category. We must then show how to abstract to the category of streams.

The category of streams and τ-streams that we use in this section is *not* the same as the categorical structure introduced in the last section to define the denotations of networks with loops. In this section we will not attempt to define how the denotations of networks in general can be reinterpreted in the setting of ordinary streams. Rather, we shall show that the definitions of the individual operators as functions from τ-streams to streams can be reinterpreted as relations from streams to streams through the process of abstraction. In the setting of ordinary streams, the actions of the data paths is trivial. It would of course be preferable to map the entire theory of networks expressed via the τ-streams formalism into a corresponding theory expressed in terms of streams. Such a development would entail broadening the theory of abstract interpretation. A study of such an extended theory of abstract interpretation is underway.

The category **PG**(TS,?) of sets τ-streams is defined in the following way:

Definition 4.1: The category **PG**(TS, ?) has as objects *all* subsets of TS X ?, where ? is the one point domain and TS is the domain of τ-streams. The morphisms are maps between objects that satisfy: if κ is a morphism from X to Y and if $\kappa(x) = y$ then $x <= y$ in the partial order of the domain TS X ?.

Maps from TS to S are modelled by introducing the new category **PG**(TS, S):

Definition 4.2: The category **PG**(TS, S) is defined as: (1) the objects are all subsets of TS X S, (2) the morphisms are *increasing* maps between objects.

First of all, maps from TS to S are reinterpreted as maps from TS X ? to TS X S as described in Section 2. They are then reinterpreted as *functors* from **PG**(TS, ?) to **PG**(TS, S). In [Panangaden 84] it is shown that this process is mathematically well defined, i.e., continuity of the lifted functions is assured and the lifting process is itself continuous.

The abstraction is described as a map from the objects of **PG**(TS, S) to the objects of **PG**(S, S) and another map from the objects of **PG**(TS, ?) to the objects of **PG**(S, ?). The maps in our case are obtained by extending the map **Ab** to sets in the natural pointwise fashion. It is clear that channels define indeterminate functions from S to TS and that these become identity functions under abstraction. More precisely the abstraction map, γ_2, from **PG**(TS, S) to **PG**(S, S) is given by:

$$\gamma_2(X) = \{\langle s_1, s_2\rangle | \langle ts_1, s_2\rangle \epsilon X \text{ and } \mathbf{Ab}(ts_1(ts_1) = s_1.$$

The abstraction map from **PG**(TS, ?) to **PG**(S, ?) is defined analogously.

We now check that these abstraction maps satisfy the acceptability conditions described in Section 2. The fact that **Ab** is continuous is fairly clear from its definition. Suppose that A and B are elements of **PG**(TS, ?). Let f be a morphism from A to B. Can we find a morphism from **fin**(**Ab**(A)) to **fin**(**Ab**(B))? Suppose A contains no infinite τ-stream. Then any element x in A is the prefix of the element f(x) in B. Clearly every non-hiatonic element of x appears in f(x) in this same prefix and thus under abstraction, **Ab**(x) will be a prefix of **Ab**(f(x)). Thus we can certainly define a morphism from **Ab**(A) to **Ab**(B). If A does contain infinite elements then we know that, if x is such an element, that f(x) must equal x and hence after the action of **Ab** we can certainly relate these two elements. Thus **Ab** in fact satisfies a slightly stronger condition than is required for an acceptable abstraction map.

To illustrate the appearance on indeterminacy under the action of abstraction, we shall examine the merge operator of Section 3. The merge operator tests its input arcs for the availability of data in a cyclic fashion. Under the action of **Ab** this testing would not be "visible" and merge would appear to select data from one or other of its input arcs in an indeterminate fashion. However, because the testing is happening in a disciplined fashion, the behavior of the merge operator will be fair.

5. Fairness

In this section we present some preliminary remarks about the application of our formalism to reasoning about fairness. In fact, the original motivation for the introduction of hiatons in [Park 82] was to reason about fairness. One question that naturally arises, now that we can derive the denotations of indeterminate operators, is whether a given node is fair. An obvious answer is the following. Suppose that an operator loops repeatedly over a piece of code in the Kahn-Keller language and suppose that in each loop it tests *every* input channel for available data. Then, when abstracted, the resulting indeterminate operator is fair. Furthermore, if the loop is endless, the operator will be infinity-fair in the sense of [Park 82]. It is now immediately clear that the merge program of Section 3 is fair. This remark is, of course, only indicative of the flavor of possible results in this direction. We are currently working on developing non-trivial *static* tests for fairness properties of programs written in the Kahn- Keller Language.

In [Keller 78] the *merge anomaly* was first introduced. We have recently observed that the same example illustrates a fairness anomaly. Consider a merge operator with its output arc connected back to one of its input arcs. Suppose the stream "ab" is fed in at the remaining input arc. Then, assuming that the operator is fair, the set of possible output streams are $\{a^n b(ab)^{\infty} | n>0)\}$. If we take the "limit", we obtain the possible stream a^{∞}; this corresponds to the situation where the first a cycled through infinitely often before the b token appeared. Thus the resulting network is not fair. We need to express a *finite delay condition* that ensures that this is not possible [Karp 69]. In our framework, we can express the finite delay property required by defining the bahavior of the data arcs on τ-streams via the finite delay operator Δ introduced in Section 3. In terms of our τ-stream formalism, the fairness anomaly cannot occur, and when we abstract the fixed point set resulting from the iteration through the merge operator, we will not have the pathological a^{∞} stream.

6. Conclusions

We have presented a formalism that allows one to derive the behavior of indeterminate operators when they are implemented in a lower level language. Typically, analyses of indeterminacy focus on deriving behaviors of networks from the behaviors of the nodes. We have used a new approach to abstract interpretation that allows us to put our theory on a semantically sound footing and we have illustrated how our theory could be useful for reasoning about fairness.

The key difference between our approach and that of the domain-based approaches [Plotkin 76] is that our formalism allows us to work with sets of possible results that are not required to be closed in any sense. Thus, for example, we are not identifying a set of streams with its convex closure in the domain of atreams as in the Plotkin Powerdomain. Put another way, we are describing situations that correspond to unbounded indeterminacy. Similar results, also based on a category theoretic formalism, but from an completely different viewpoint have been obtained by [Abramsky 83].

Several other applications are also possible. Two directions we are pursuing are to develop static tests for determinacy and for fairness and to study deadlock properties of networks containing indeterminate operators. An interesting observation is that while, typically, abstract interpretation is used for justifying static analysis by simplifying the domain, we have used it in the reverse fashion; that is, we have enriched the standard domain to obtain a useful and interesting model.

7. Acknowledgements

We would like to thank Robert Keller, Uday Reddy, Samson Abramsky, Esther Shilcrat, and especially Prateek Mishra for helpful discussions. This research was supported by a grant from IBM Corporation and by CER grant #MCS-8121750 awarded to the Department of Computer Science at the University of Utah.

8. References

[Abramsky 83] Abramsky, S.
Semantic Foundations of Applicative Multiprogramming.
In Diaz, J. (editor), *Automata, Languages and Programming*, pages 1-14. Springer-Verlag, July, 1983.

[Arbib 75] Arbib M. A., Manes E. G.
Arrows, Structures and Functors.
Academic press, 1975.

[Cousot 77] P. Cousot and R. Cousot.
Abstract Interpretation: A Unified Lattice Model for Static Analysis of Programs by Construction or Approximation of Fixpoints.
POPL IV :238-252, Jan, 1977.

[Cousot 81] P. Cousot.
Semantic Foundations of program analysis.
Prentice-Hall, 1981, pages 303-342.

[Kahn 74] Kahn G.
The Semantics of a Simple Language for Parallel Programming.
In *Proc. IFIP 1974*, pages 471-475. 1974.

[Kahn 77] Kahn G., McQueen D.
Coroutines and Networks of Parallel Processes.
In B. Gilchrist (editor), *Information Processing 77*, pages 994-998. 1977.

[Karp 69] Karp R. M., Miller R.
Parallel program schemata.
JCSS , May, 1969.

[Keller 78] Keller R.M.
Denotational Models for Parallel Programs With Indeterminate Operators.
In E.J.Neuhold (editor), *Formal Descriptions of Programming Concepts*, pages 337-365. North-Holland, Amsterdam, 1978.

[Keller 83] Keller R. M.
Users' Manual for Function Equation Language.
AMPS Technical Memorandum 7, U of Utah, July, 1983.

[Mishra 84] P. Mishra, R. M. Keller.
Static inference of properties of applicative programs.
In *POPL XI, Salt Lake City.* January, 1984.

[Mycroft 81] A. Mycroft.
Abstract Interpretation and Optimising Transformations for Applicative Programs.
PhD thesis, University of Edinburgh, December, 1981.

[Mycroft 83] Mycroft A. and Nielsen F.
Strong Abstract Interpretation Using Powerdomains.
In Diaz J. (editor), *Automata, Languages and Programming,* pages 536-547. EATCS, July, 1983.

[Panangaden 84] Panangaden P., Mishra P.
A Category Theoretic formalism for Abstract Interpretation.
Technical Report UUCS-84-005, University of Utah, May, 1984.

[Park 82] Park D.
The Fairness Problem and Nondeterministic Computing Networks.
In *Proc. 4th Advanced Course on Theoretical Computer Science.* Mathematisch Centrum, 1982.

[Plotkin 76] Plotkin G.
A Powerdomain Construction.
SIAM J. of Computing 5(3), September, 1976.

[Tanaka 83] Tanaka J. and Keller R. M.
S-code Extension in FEL.
AMPS Technical Memorandum 10, U of Utah, July, 1983.

The NIL Distributed Systems Programming Language : A Status Report

Robert E. Strom and Shaula Yemini
IBM Research
Yorktown Hts., NY 10598

Abstract

This paper is a summary of ongoing research activities related to the programming language NIL, a high level language for concurrent and distributed systems developed at IBM Yorktown.

We first present a short summary of the major features of NIL. These include the NIL system model, which is a dynamically evolving network of loosely coupled processes, communicating by message passing; the abstract NIL computation model; and typestate, which is a refinement of type systems allowing a compiler to assume an important subset of program validation.

We then discuss issues related to providing a semantic theory for NIL, and list some general requirements a semantic model should satisfy to be applicable to practical concurrent and distributed systems. We discuss the fit between CCS, which we are studying as a possible candidate for such a semantic theory, and these requirements.

Finally we describe some recent work on transformations which map NIL programs to efficient distributed and parallel implementations.

Introduction

NIL is a high level programming language for distributed systems. The major novel concepts in NIL include

1. the NIL system model, consisting of a dynamically evolving network of loosely coupled processes, communicating by asynchronous message passing. Processes are the single modular building block, supporting both concurrency and data abstraction;
2. typestate, a refinement of type systems, which allows a compiler to assume an important subset of program validation. This subset is sufficient for guaranteeing security, detecting "erroneous programs" (programs whose behavior is undefined by the programming language), and guaranteeing finalization of all resources owned by a program when it terminates;
3. an abstract procedural computation model which hides performance-related and implementation-dependent details, while providing the full power of a general purpose programming language. Performance related details, such as storage layout and physical parallelism, are controlled not by changing the source program, but instead by selecting from a menu of alternative translation strategies supported by NIL compilers.

Language Summary

The NIL System Model

system structure

A NIL system consists of a network of processes. Each process encapsulates private data, its *state*. The state consists of a program counter, and a collection of typed objects, including input and output *ports*, *owned* by the process. Processes may affect one another only by message passing over queued *communication channels*. There is no form of shared data in a NIL system -- all data is distributed among the processes. Each data object is at any time owned by exactly one process, although objects may change ownership by being communicated in messages. Before a process terminates, it is required to finalize any object it owns.

NIL processes are not nested nor is there any other form of statically defined system configuration such as binding by matching port labels. A NIL system is configured by dynamically instantiating processes and linking them by means of dynamically created communication channels between their ports. A communication channel is created when a process A, the owner of an input port P, performs an operation to *connect* an output port Q (also owned by A) to P. Q then becomes a connected output port, also called a *capability*. If A then passes Q in a message received by process B, B will then have the right to communicate over the channel from Q to P. Multiple output ports may be connected to a single input port.

A process always communicates by sending messages to one of its *own* output ports. A process cannot explicitly refer to an external process or port. Thus each process is unaware of the identity of the individual processes comprising the rest of the system. If a new port is created somewhere in the system, another process will not become aware of that port unless it receives a capability to that port by explicit communication. At any point in time, a process sees the rest of the system as a "cloud" whose output and input ports are connected to the given process's input and output ports.

Communication

NIL communication is by *ownership transfer*, in contrast to being by value (copy) or by reference. During communication, the *ownership* of a message is transferred from the process owning an output port to the process owning the input port at the other end of the communications channel.

Both queued *synchronous* ("rendezvous" or "remote procedure call") and queued *asynchronous* ("send without wait") communication are supported. The two forms of communication differ in whether or not the sender of the message waits until the message is returned.

Queued asynchronous communication is initiated by the operation *send*, specifying a message object and an output port object. The ownership of the message is transferred from the process issuing *send* to the process owning the input port at the other end of the communication channel. The sending process no longer has access to the message. The message is queued at the input port until the owner of the input port dequeues it using a *receive* operation. It is possible for the queue to contain more than one message, since the sender may continue to send additional messages through the output port, and since there may be several output ports connected to the same input port. Successive messages sent over a single output port will be received in FIFO order, but no specific order other than a *fair merge* is guaranteed for messages sent over different output ports which arrive at the same input port. An asynchronous message may be of any NIL data type. Typically, a message will be a *record*, which is an aggregate consisting of one or more components (fields) which may be of any data type, including ports, or processes.

Queued synchronous communication is initiated by the operation *call*. This operation builds a *returnable* message called a *callrecord*. A callrecord, like a record, is composed of components (the parameters), which may be of any data type. A call transfers the message through the designated output port to the input port at the end of the channel. The caller then waits until the called process dequeues the callrecord, possibly operates on its components (parameters) and then issues a *return* operation on that callrecord. The return operation causes the callrecord to return to the caller.

Since a call always waits for a return, a queue can never contain more than one callrecord from any given process. All callrecords must have originated at different processes, and since these processes are asynchronous, it is meaningless to talk about the "order" of the callrecords.

A process may wait for messages on any of a set of input ports, by issuing a **select** statement whose alternatives correspond to guarded input ports (only input ports may be guarded). A process in a select statement waits until one of the input ports having a true guard has received a message, at which point it then executes the appropriate select alternative, which will usually dequeue the message. In both synchronous and asynchronous communication, a process owning an input port dequeues the message by issuing a *receive* operation. A typical process body consists of a loop containing one or more select statements.

Note that we use the term "synchronous" here in a different sense than in languages such as CSP [HOA 78] or CCS [MIL 80]. In both NIL's "synchronous" and "asynchronous" communication, there is never any concept of simultaneity of action in two distinct processes, since all communication is queued. We select a queued model of communication because our view of modularity forbids any global properties of a system, in particular a global time. The queued model avoids the need to ever talk about "simultaneity" of events in different processes of a distributed system, and allows each distinct process to have its own local time. The local times of individual processes of the distributed system are partially ordered by *causality*. When a receiver receives a message, the local time of the receiver is *greater* than the local time of the sender at the sending time. The local times of two processes which never communicate either directly or indirectly are incomparable.

Because of the partial order of time, we can only define FIFO ordering for a particular output port's view of the communication, not for all messages sent to a single output port. Similarly, it makes no sense to talk of the "order" of calls made to an input port from distinct processes.

process creation and termination

Processes are instantiated dynamically by a **create** operation specifying the name of a compiled program which the process will execute, and a list of creation-time *initialization parameters*. The initialization parameters constitute a callrecord passed from the creating process to the created process. The initialization parameters will consist of: (1) "in" parameters, typically including a number of bound output ports (capabilities) supplied by the creator to give the created process access to some input ports in the system, and (2) "out" parameters, typically consisting of output ports bound to those input ports owned by the newly created process, on which the created process wishes to receive communication.

Since there is no globally visible environment, a newly created process can only initially see that part of the environment passed in the initial callrecord, and can only export capabilities to those ports of its own which it has returned in the initial callrecord. A process can acquire further capabilities through subsequent communication.

Since a process is itself an object, it has a single owner at each point during its lifetime. Processes terminate upon reaching the end of their program, or may be finalized earlier either by explicit finalization performed by their owner, or as a result of their owner's termination. A process sends an *obituary message* to an owner-determined port upon termination. The owner of a process can thus wait for the process to terminate by waiting for its obituary message. A process can live beyond the lifetime of its owner if its ownership is transferred (i.e., the process itself is sent in a message) to another process.

A typical NIL system will include some processes that do not terminate, i.e., their program includes an infinite repetitive loop. Other processes may represent long-lived data objects, e.g. files, which generally live longer than the programs which use them.

Abstract computation Model

NIL presents the programmer with a simple and abstract computation model, in which all implementation-dependent and performance-related details are transparent.

In more conventional programming languages, e.g., Pascal, C or Ada, features such as dynamically created objects, dynamically changing data structures, very large or long-lived objects, etc., are supported by exposing low-level implementation features through language constructs such as pointers, files, and operating system calls.

In contrast, the NIL programmer is presented with a very simple and abstract set of primitives. For example, in the abstract model seen by the NIL programmer, all objects are created dynamically, arbitrary recursive data structures are supported, and records, variants, and *relations* (described in more detail in the next section) unify all forms of dynamic aggregates such as trees, lists, stacks, queues, sets, and arrays. All communication, whether local or remote, is by message-passing. There is no distinction between "variables" and "file" storage.

This simplicity is not obtained at the expense of expressive power. Rather, the NIL compiler encapsulates both "unsafe" low-level constructs and machine-dependent features in the *implementations* of these abstract language primitives. Thus, pointers, shared memory, the existence of different kinds of storage, multiple processors, different kind of communication media and processor failures, are all encapsulated in implementations of the NIL type families, allowing NIL compilers to exploit these features, while concealing them at the NIL language level.

At the implementation level some objects may be preallocated and some bindings may be performed statically. A relation may be implemented by contiguous storage, i.e., as an array, by a linked structure or a hash table, and if large, may be put on secondary storage. A large relation may even be split among the local memories of multiple processors, or replicated for recoverability. Similarly, multiple processes may be assigned to a single processor, or conversely a single process may be split among multiple processors, with different objects and/or parts of the program of a process (subactions) divided among the processors. Recovery from processor failures may be handled by a combination of compile-time and run-time actions.

In addition to a substantial simplification of the computation model, the abstractness of the language primitives gives NIL a tremendous portability advantage. It enables to incorporate into NIL compilers highly sophisticated mappings, which can exploit target-specific features to achieve highly efficient performance on very different hardware environments.

One of the major focuses of our current research is on designing highly efficient and reliable distributed implementations of NIL systems. We mention some specific results in this area in the last section of this paper.

Types

NIL is a strongly typed programming language. There is a fixed set of *type families* (types and type constructors) in NIL, each of which is associated with a particular set of operations. The type families are:

Scalars Simple integer and booleans are primitive types.

Enumerations The type definition defines a particular set of constants, representing the values of variables of this type.

Records Each record type defines an aggregate of one or more component *fields*, which may have any data type. Records allow groups of objects to be manipulated, e.g. sent and received, as a unit.

Relations Relations contain a variable number of *rows*. Rows are user-defined structured n-tuples of values. The relation type family was designed in accordance with the model of relational databases [COD 70].

Relation definitions may specify *functional dependencies* -- Any valid third normal form relational schema can be expressed as a relation type definition. Relations may be ordered or keyed. Operations are provided to locate, insert, or delete individual rows, or to iteratively operate on an entire relation. Thus relations provide a single type constructor for aggregating data of a uniform type, subsuming arrays, linked lists, sets, queues, stacks, etc.

Variants A variant is an aggregate containing a collection of embedded fields of arbitrary type, which are divided into mutually exclusive *cases*. Variants are used when the type of an object cannot be determined at compile-time, and thus type-checking has to be performed at runtime. The type and typestate rules of NIL guarantee that no field of a variant may be accessed except within a clause in which the case has been explicitly tested.

Ports Ports are either *input* or *output* ports. Port types determine the type of message which may be passed through the port. Operations include creating a communications channel by connecting an output port to an input port of matching type, and sending, calling, or receiving. Since only ports of matching type can be connected to form communications channels, the sender of a message is assured that the receiver is expecting a message of the same type. *All* NIL object types may appear as fields of messages, and thus be transferred between processes.

callrecords A callrecord is a collection of embedded fields which acts as a parameter list for a call. It is distinguished from a record by the following: (1) it contains information which enables the callrecord to return to the originator of the call, (2) some of the fields may not be fully initialized, since they may be **out** parameters, i.e., they are to be initialized by the called process.

Processes The operations on processes are: **create**, creating a new process, and finalizing a process, i.e., forcing the process to terminate.

All NIL object types are first class. If an object can be an operand, then it also has a type, and can appear in all context permitting objects, such as the value of a variable, or as an element in an aggregate or a message.

Control Constructs

NIL includes all the familiar go-to-less structured programming language control constructs: sequential composition, conditionals, loops (while and iterated), and case statements. In addition, there is a select-variant statement to select the case of a variant; a select__event for waiting to receive communication on a set of guarded input ports, selecting non-deterministically from among the input ports which contain a message and whose guard is true, (like guarded commands except that only input ports may appear); and exception handling.

Exceptions

NIL's type families do not specify how data is laid out in memory, or what the actual limit of supposedly unbounded objects such as integers and relations actually is. On any finite implementation, there is always a number, a table, a queue size, which is "too big". The specific cutoff point varies from implementation to implementation. The language therefore allows any operation which may consume machine resources to *raise an exception* thereby notifying the program that it did not compute the expected result. In addition to reaching implementation-dependent resource limits, exceptions can be raised by operations when the expected precondition to the operation is not satisfied, e.g. in an attempt to retrieve a non-existent item from a relation.

When an exception is raised, control transfers to an *exception handler* within the module.

As a result, every program which successfully compiles and loads has a defined result for the execution of every statement. This result may be a normal outcome, and may be an exception, but will never be "undefined and unpredictable".

Typestate

Typestate checking is a fully automated subset of program validation, enabling a NIL compiler (1) to detect and reject "erroneous programs", and (2) to ensure clean termination of processes in all cases.

The *type* of an object determines the set of operations which may be applied to the object. However, not all operations of a type are applicable at all times. For example, an integer variable that has not been bound to a value cannot appear as an operand of an arithmetic operation. Similarly, a message that has not been received should not have its fields operated upon, an output port that has not been bound to an input port should not be used for a send or call, etc.. Such actions not only indicate logic errors that should be corrected; they may also cause the violation of security of other *correct* programs, since in many implementations, they would result in dangling pointers and overwriting arbitrary storage.

Languages permitting erroneous programs to have arbitrary side-effects are *non-secure*, because no part of a system, no matter how simple, can be proven to meet any specification until *every* module in the system has been proven error free. Such languages inhibit modular verification. NIL security is guaranteed at compile-time by a mechanism called *typestate checking*. Because NIL is a secure language, even unverified programs are limited to returning inappropriate results of correct type on their ports.

Typestate is a refinement of the notion of type, which captures the different degrees of initialization of objects. For primitive types, typestate captures whether the object has been created and whether it has been bound to a value; for composite objects, typestate captures to what degree their constituent objects have been initialized.

Each NIL type family has associated with it a set of *typestates*. Each operation of the family has a unique *typestate precondition* for each of its operands, which is the typestate the operand must be in for the operation to be applicable, and a unique *typestate postcondition* for each operand, resulting from the application of the operation. If the operation has both normal and exception outcomes, there may be a different postcondition for each possible outcome.

The typestate information for each family can be represented by a finite state automaton, where the nodes correspond to the typestates of the type family, and the arcs correspond to operations of the type family. User-defined operations, which in NIL correspond to calls, must specify an *interface type* for the corresponding input and output ports. An interface type specifies in addition to the type of each field of the callrecord, the typestate transition resulting from the call. (Interfaces are described in more detail in the following section). The NIL compiler incorporates both the finite state automata and the interface type definitions in order to track the typestate of each variable declared by a process throughout its program.

Typestates of each type family are partially ordered and form a lattice. Intuitively, a higher typestate is associated with a higher degree of initialization. NIL rules require that for each variable, the typestate must be invariant at each statement in a program, independent of the control path leading to that statement. Thus, at control join points such as following a conditional or the end of a block, the typestate is defined to be the greatest lower bound of the resulting typestates of each of the joining paths. Since the compiler tracks the level of initialization of each object, it is able to insert *downhill coercions*, to force the typestate of an object to the greatest lower bound typestate at control join points.

Since typestate tracking enables the compiler to check the consistency of the typestate of each object with respect to the operations applied to it, it enables the compiler to detect and reject "erroneous programs", i.e., programs which in other languages would be compile-time correct, but whose behavior would be undefined, because operations were applied in invalid orders. Additionally, since the compiler tracks the level of initialization of each individual variable and inserts downhill coercions at join points, the compiler effectively performs all that is needed to ensure finalizing all objects owned by a process when it terminates. (The **end** of a program is a join point for which the greatest lower bound for all variables is *uninitialized.*) Thus typestate tracking eliminates the need for expensive run-time garbage collection, as required by other languages which allow dynamic creation of objects.

Typestate-checking thus enables compile-time enforcement of a greater degree of security and finalization in a highly dynamic environment, than that enforced by static scope rules in a static environment. Typestate checking is more fully described in [STR 83a].

Interfaces

Ports are typed by *interface types*. Interface types define the type of message which can travel over the communications channel formed by connecting a matching set of input and output ports. For send interfaces, any message type is permitted. For call interfaces, the message type is in the callrecord type family. The specification of each callrecord type defines not only the type of each parameter, but also the typestate prior to the call -- the *entry typestate*, and and the typestate change resulting from the call -- the *exit typestate* for each possible outcome (normal and each exception).

Interface types, along with all other type definitions, are separately compiled into *definition modules* that may be imported by any NIL program. A caller (sender) program and a receiver program must both be compiled against the same interface type definition for their corresponding ports in order for a binding to be possible. At the call site, the compiler checks that all parameters are in the entry typestate, and assumes all parameters after the call are in the exit typestate. Conversely at the site receiving the call, all parameters are assumed to have the entry typestate, and the compiler checks that they are set to the exit typestate prior to the return from the call.

Differences Between NIL and CSP

Since readers of this paper are likely to be familiar with CSP, we conclude our language summary by highlighting some of the more significant differences between the respective models of concurrency of CSP and NIL. These differences will help to explain why the approaches that have been applied to defining the semantics of CSP (e.g.,[APT 80], [MIS 81]) may not be ideally suited to providing a semantic definition of NIL.

The Program Models

In CSP, one talks about a "program" which is much like the concept of "main program" in more conventional programming languages. The program typically consists of a terminating computation, with a single entry, a single exit, and a logically serial program in between, sped up by the spawning of multiple cooperating processes. CSP processes are a "refinement" of the main program. The programs the created processes will run are determined statically, as are both process bindings and process lifetimes which are determined by standard block structure scope rules. As a result, processes are highly coupled, sharing a common lifetime, and sharing the data of the "original serial program". All processes are expected to terminate when their part of the computation has completed.

In NIL, one talks about a *system* of processes. Each individual NIL process corresponds to a separate logically serial program. Processes are loosely coupled, do not share any data, and each process has an independent lifetime. Each of the processes in a system might be independently communicating with sources external to the NIL system, as well as with other NIL processes within the system. A system thus cannot be viewed as a single main program, with a single entry and a single exit.

A NIL system evolves dynamically. The determination of which processes to create, and what ports bindings to perform is done dynamically, under program control. A system will typically include several non-terminating processes, which are the "core" of the system, in addition to processes which do terminate.

Information hiding

In CSP, the values of variables can be seen by any process at the appropriate level of nesting. Additionally, a process knows the identities of all its peers.

In NIL, all variables are local. No process knows which other processes exist in the system, or how many there are. A process knows only about the rest of the world through the communication channels it has been explicitly given.

Abstractness

The criteria applied to deciding process boundaries in NIL is based solely on software engineering principles: low inter-module coupling, abstraction and information hiding. It is *not* based on exploiting available concurrency.

The software engineering principles turn out to be very well suited to supporting distribution. This is precisely because when interaction between processes is limited to narrow message-passing interfaces, and data is distributed among processes distribution across multiple processors is straightforward. All that remains to be done is is allocating processes to processors, and implementing communication which crosses processor boundaries by physical communication.

However, in some cases it is possible that further parallelization, i.e., implementing a single logical process by multiple cooperating physical processes in the manner of a CSP program, could lead to better performance. In the NIL approach, this further parallelization would be handled at the implementation level, i.e., incorporated into translations supported by the compiler and runtime environment, and would be completely transparent at the NIL language level.

As a result, NIL is more abstract in its treatment of concurrency than is CSP. Whereas in CSP, it is possible to write a vector addition both as a serial loop or as a parallel program, and indeed it is the purpose of CSP to write just such programs, in NIL one may only write the serial loop. The parallel version is, from the NIL perspective, merely an optimized implementation of the same program. The construction of the parallel version belongs, in the NIL view, to the domain of compiler technology and not to programming.

The Communication Models

CSP communication involves "simultaneous" actions at two separate processes: the sender being prepared to send, simultaneously with the receiver wanting to receive. NIL communication is queued.

In CSP, spawned processes communicate results to the parent by updating the state of variables. In NIL, all communication is by message passing, and no two processes ever see the same variables.

In CSP, communication is directed at a particular process, which is known to be part of the system. A NIL process sees the rest of the system only as a set of ports. It knows nothing about the number, structure or identity of the other processes in the system.

If NIL at this point seems to the reader somewhat arbitrary, and therefore of no particular concern to semanticists, we would like to point out the closeness between the NIL model and distributed physical systems. For example, consider hardware systems. A hardware system consists of a collection of individual components, each with a set of pins, (ports) for connecting to other components. Each component hides an internal state. No component can see the insides of other components, nor even the existence of other components -- it "sees" the rest of the system only through its pins. Events are only partially ordered by *causality*: an event in one component, occurring as a result of receiving communication from another component, will be considered to have occurred after the sending event. There is no global notion of time, unless a specific component implementing it, i.e., a clock, which explicitly communicates to all other components to synchronize the local times, is added to the system.

Ongoing Research Activities

NIL's initial design took place between 1978 and 1981. A compiler for the full NIL language (minus real numbers), for a uniprocessor, (IBM 370), was completed early in 1982, and between 1982 and the present, experiments have been conducted in which significant subsystems were written in NIL and in which performance of the compiled code has been measured and enhanced by adding compiler implementation options without modifying the source. We have been very pleased by the results of these experiments, and a new back-end for targets running C/UNIX is currently being written.

Our current research is directed at two separate areas. One is work towards providing a semantic definition of NIL. We expect some features of NIL to simplify the task of providing a complete semantic definition of the language. These include the lack of shared variables, and the existence of typestate checking and exception handling, which eliminate programs whose behavior might otherwise be undefinable. On the other hand, we expect the dynamic nature of NIL systems to make our task harder.

A second research direction, and the one which has been the main focus of our recent work, is that of developing strategies for implementing NIL on various types of distributed system architectures. Developing practical distributed implementation strategies is essential if we are to continue to maintain the abstract level of the NIL computation model.

Below we discuss some of the problems and some results in these two research areas.

Issues in a Formal Semantics Definition of NIL

NIL interface types characterize communication ports by both the type and the typestate transitions for each object in callrecords passed along the port. We would like to be able to augment this information with some form of behavioral specification. Since the only way a process can affect its environment is via communication, it would be desirable to be able to specify the externally observable behavior of a process by relationships among events on its ports.

We would like any semantic model that we apply to be modular, abstract and compositional. *Modularity* implies that the behavior of a process be specifiable independently of any other particular process that may be in the same system. *Abstractness* implies that the process' behavior is specifiable independently of any particular implementation of the process. *Compositional* implies that there are rules for composing multiple individual process' behavior specifications, given a particular connection configuration, to derive the behavior of a system consisting of those processes connected in the given configuration.

Finally, we would like the semantic model to be able to handle the dynamics of the system, though we suspect that this issue might be rather difficult to address.

We became very interested in Milner's CCS [MIL 80] which appeared to be close to what we were searching for. However, when trying to describe NIL semantics using CCS behaviors, we encountered some difficulties. We describe some of these difficulties below, in the hope of motivating enhancements of the basic model and also possibly other semantic approaches that will make it to overcome these difficulties.

- *global time*: As we mentioned earlier, NIL has no concept of global time or simultaneity of events in distinct processes, as it appears in the communication model of CCS. There is only a partial order between the local times of each process. This partial order is determined by causality: The state of a sender sending message M, precedes the state at which the receiver receives M. Events in processes which do not communicate with one another (either directly or indirectly), are incomparable.

  It is possible to model NIL's world lacking action at a distance by inserting a process representing the "ether" within each communication channel and using CCS's instantaneous communication to send and receive from the ether. While this is theoretically possible, it is counterintuitive to model a simpler, relativistic world in which time is local, in terms of a more exotic world in which global time exists, but demon processes contrive to prevent any of the entities in that world from detecting the fact.

- *level of abstraction*: NIL communication is queued. To model this in CCS, one must introduce additional behaviors which implement queues. Modeling queues led to a number of problems. First of all, to model the queue itself it was necessary extend the range of variables to incorporate queues, or to represent sequences as Goedel numbers. This appeared to be much more "operational" than we had wished --- we would prefer to have a set of abstract inference rules which we could apply whenever a pair of processes was connected by a channel. Additionally, concepts like a "fair merge" did not appear to have any simple expression in terms of behaviors.

- *modelling temporal properties*: There are many constructs in NIL for which we would like to be able to express abstract temporal properties such as "a message sent to port p will eventually be accepted by the owner of p", or "a finalized process terminates within a (implementation-dependent) finite amount of time, finalizing all its local objects". A recent attempt by the authors, with Scott Smolka, [SMO 84], to model the fact that cancelled processes eventually stop underscores these problems. Suppose process A is cancelled while it is calling B, which may be calling C. Then if C is deadlocked, an exception may have to be raised in C, to break the deadlock, since it is also a rule of NIL that a callrecord must be returned before a call can terminate. To model this in CCS, it was necessary to add a CCS "register" to process A keeping track of where the currently outstanding callrecord is, and a mechanism to eventually set a "forced" state register in C, to cause breaking the deadlock. This "model" was as complex as any particular implementation of NIL would be, and required modifications to the semantics of "call", "receive", and "select", just to support a simple liveness property of the "cancel" operation. Work in using temporal logic with CCS (e.g., [KAR 83]) may provide some solutions.

- *observational equivalence*: The term "observational equivalence" is somewhat misleading, because it seems to imply that internal states which cannot be detected by experiment and observation from outside the process are ignored. In fact, the notion of observational equivalence depends on the ability to examine the *internal state* of processes. It thus does not mesh well with our requirement for modularity because it does not support information hiding. From the point of view of modularity, an equivalence notion that views processes as black boxes, which can be examined only by performing experiments by exercising a test process, is preferable. The test process itself must be a standard process of the model, which can communicate with the black boxes, but cannot peek inside the boxes to see their internal state.

- *satisfiability*: It is desirable to have also a notion of *satisfiability*, which relates a more detailed behavior -- an *implementation* -- to a more abstract behavior -- a *specification*. Satisfiability is a weaker requirement than equivalence, and can be used to define the concept of equivalence *with respect to a particular specification*. This will allow proving that two behaviors which are not equivalent, either by Milner's stringent definition, or by a more truly observational one, are nevertheless equivalent with respect to a given abstract behavior specification, in that they are both correct implementations of the behavior. Satisfiability is useful not only for proving properties of programs but also for proving properties of implementations of a programming language, e.g., for proving correctness of compilers and interpreters.

Some of these problems seem to be handled by Keller's Archival Approach [KEL 83] which we are currently examining.

Distributed and Parallel Implementation Strategies for NIL

Most of our more recent research is directed at developing sophisticated implementation strategies for NIL programs. It is our conjecture that an effective way to design large systems is to first *specify* the systems as a network of process models written in NIL, and to then implement the systems efficiently by applying a set of *transformations*, reflecting different target-specific implementation strategies, to map the NIL "specifications" into concurrent and distributed realizations.

Our goal is to identify transformations independently of any program to which they may be applied, prove that they preserve the intended semantics and quantify their performance properties. We will thus have at our disposal a library of reusable program transformations that can be applied either individually or composed with other transformations, to obtain efficient distributed implementations.

A straightforward distribution of a NIL system requires only allocating processes to processors, and mapping communication that crosses physical processor boundaries into physical communication. However, if we wish to maintain our high level of abstraction, there are additional issues that must be handled transparently by implementations. One important issue is that of recovery from processor failures. If processes run on different processors which may fail independently, it is necessary to ensure that upon recovery, all processes states are *consistent*, i.e., that all processes have a consistent view of which communication between them has actually occurred and which has not.

We recently developed an asynchronous algorithm for such recovery in a distributed system called *Optimistic Recovery*([STR 84a]). Optimistic recovery can be fully embedded in a compiler and run-time environment for NIL.

Another important problem that may need to be supported in practical implementations is that of scheduling computations of *a single process* in parallel, to better exploit distribution and improve response time. In this context we have identified an interesting new and particularly useful *family* of transformations called *optimistic transformations*. Optimistic transformations allow logically serial computations C1; C2 to be executed in parallel whenever C1's effect on C2 can be guessed in advance with high probability. C2's computation is based on this guess. If the guess is wrong, C2 will have to be undone, but if the probability of a correct guess is sufficiently high, the losses due to undoing computations will be compensated by performance gains due to increased parallelism.

In [STR 84b] we show three examples of "guesses" which can lead to optimistic transformations of practical value: (a) the guess that multiple iterations of a loop will not conflict, (b) the guess that exceptional program conditions will not occur, and (c) the guess that machine failures will not occur. We demonstrate the practicality of synthesizing distributed implementations by composing transformations by presenting an improved distributed two-phase commit protocol derived systematically by composing the above three optimistic transformations.

We expect that many transformations will be fairly general, and therefore that they could be developed independently of individual programs, and made available as part of a compiler system. It is very likely that most of these transformations will be closely related to the obvious entities involved in programs: data and computations. Some of the more obvious transformations are distributing the data among the "sites" of a distributed system, distributing computations among the sites, "paging" data to computations or computations to data whenever the data for a computation resides at a different site from the program, replicating data for high availability, checkpointing for recoverability, etc.. Applications of some of these transformations are already used in current distributed systems, though to our knowledge, these have never been considered as transformations of simpler serial algorithms but rather as special algorithms in and of themselves.

If our conjecture proves to be true, we will have developed a simpler software methodology for designing and implementing distributed systems, by applying reusable transformations to serial, implementation-independent programs, instead of designing a specialized version of each system for each individual target. Our initial results in this area have been encouraging, and we are continuing to pursue this direction.

References

[APT 80] Apt, Krzysztof, Nissim Francez and Willem P. de Roever "A Proof System for Communicating Sequential Processes *ACM TOPLAS*, July, 1980.

[COD 70] Codd, E. F. 'A Relational Model of Data for Large Shared Data Banks', *Communications of the ACM*, vol 13, No 6., June 1970.

[HAI 82] Hailpern, B., *Verifying Concurrent Processes Using Temporal Logic*, Lecture Notes in Computer Science, no. 129, 1982.

[HOA 78] Hoare, C. A. R. 'Communicating Sequential Processes' *CACM* August, 1978

[KAR 83] Karjoth, Gunter 'A Behavioral Description Language for the Formal Treatment of Protocols in Distributed Systems ' *Proc. Protocol Specification, Testing and Verification, iii* North Holland, June 1983

[KEL 83] Keller, Robert M., and Prakash Panangaden, 'An Archival Approach to the Semantics of Indeterminate Operators' Draft Report, University of Utah.

[LAM 83] Lamport, L., 'Specifying Concurrent Program Modules' *ACM TOPLAS* 5:2, April 1983 July 1978.

[MIL 80] Milner, Robin 'A Calculus of Communicating Systems', *Springer-Verlag Lecture Notes in Computer Science* #92, 1980.

[MIS 81] Misra, Jayadev, and K. Mani Chandy 'Proofs of Networks of Processes' *IEEE Transactions on Software Engineering* July, 1981.

[MIS 82] Misra, Jayadev, K. Mani Chandy and Tod Smith 'Proving Safety and Liveness of Communicating Processes with Examples' *Proc. Principles of Distributed Computing* August, 1982.

[PRA 82] Pratt, V. R. 'On the Composition of Processes' *Ninth Symposium on Principles of Programming Languages*, Albuquerque NM, January 1982.

[SMO 84] Smolka, S., "A CCS Semantics for NIL", IBM Research Report, in preparation.

[STR 83a] Strom, R. E., "Mechanisms for Compile-Time Enforcement of Security", *Tenth Symposium on Principles of Programming Languages*, Austin, January 1983.

[STR 83b] Strom, R. E., and Yemini, S. 'NIL: An Integrated Language and System for Distributed Programming', IBM Research Report RC9949.

[STR 84a] Strom, R. E., and Yemini, S. 'Optimistic Recovery: An Asynchronous Approach to Fault Tolerance in Distributed Systems' in proc. FTCS-14, June 1984, also available as IBM Research Report RC 10353.

[STR 84b] Strom, R. E. and Yemini, S., 'Synthesizing Distributed Protocols through Optimistic Transformations' *Proc. Fourth International Workshop on Protocol Specification, Testing and Validation*, Skytop Penn. June 1984, to be published by North Holland, 1984.

ol. 167: International Symposium on Programming. Proceedings, 984. Edited by C. Girault and M. Paul. VI, 262 pages. 1984.

ol. 168: Methods and Tools for Computer Integrated Manufacturing. dited by R. Dillmann and U. Rembold. XVI, 528 pages. 1984.

ol. 169: Ch. Ronse, Feedback Shift Registers. II, 1–2, 145 pages. 984.

ol. 171: Logic and Machines: Decision Problems and Complexity. roceedings, 1983. Edited by E. Börger, G. Hasenjaeger and . Rödding. VI, 456 pages. 1984.

ol. 172: Automata, Languages and Programming. Proceedings, 984. Edited by J. Paredaens. VIII, 527 pages. 1984.

ol. 173: Semantics of Data Types. Proceedings, 1984. Edited by . Kahn, D. B. MacQueen and G. Plotkin. VI, 391 pages. 1984.

ol. 174: EUROSAM 84. Proceedings, 1984. Edited by J. Fitch. I, 396 pages. 1984.

ol. 175: A. Thayse, P-Functions and Boolean Matrix Factorization, II, 248 pages. 1984.

ol. 176: Mathematical Foundations of Computer Science 1984. roceedings, 1984. Edited by M. P. Chytil and V. Koubek. XI, 581 ages. 1984.

ol. 177: Programming Languages and Their Definition. Edited by . B. Jones. XXXII, 254 pages. 1984.

ol. 178: Readings on Cognitive Ergonomics – Mind and Computers. roceedings, 1984. Edited by G. C. van der Veer, M. J. Tauber, T. R. G. reen and P. Gorny. VI, 269 pages. 1984.

ol. 179: V. Pan, How to Multiply Matrices Faster. XI, 212 pages. 1984.

ol. 180: Ada Software Tools Interfaces. Proceedings, 1983. Edited y P. J. L. Wallis. III, 164 pages. 1984.

ol. 181: Foundations of Software Technology and Theoretical omputer Science. Proceedings, 1984. Edited by M. Joseph and . Shyamasundar. VIII, 468 pages. 1984.

ol. 182: STACS 85. 2nd Annual Symposium on Theoretical Aspects f Computer Science. Proceedings, 1985. Edited by K. Mehlhorn. /II, 374 pages. 1985.

/ol. 183: The Munich Project CIP. Volume I: The Wide Spectrum anguage CIP-L. By the CIP Language Group. XI, 275 pages. 1985.

/ol. 184: Local Area Networks: An Advanced Course. Proceedings, 983. Edited by D. Hutchison, J. Mariani and D. Shepherd. VIII, 497 ages. 1985.

/ol. 185: Mathematical Foundations of Software Development. Pro- ceedings, 1985. Volume 1: Colloquium on Trees in Algebra and Programming (CAAP'85). Edited by H. Ehrig, C. Floyd, M. Nivat and . Thatcher. XIV, 418 pages. 1985.

/ol. 186: Formal Methods and Software Development. Proceedings, 1985. Volume 2: Colloquium on Software Engineering (CSE). Edited by H. Ehrig, C. Floyd, M. Nivat and J. Thatcher. XIV, 455 pages. 1985.

Vol. 187: F. S. Chaghaghi, Time Series Package (TSPACK). III, 305 pages. 1985.

Vol. 188: Advances in Petri Nets 1984. Edited by G. Rozenberg with the cooperation of H. Genrich and G. Roucairol. VII, 467 pages. 1985.

Vol. 189: M. S. Sherman, Paragon. XI, 376 pages. 1985.

Vol. 190: M. W. Alford, J. P. Ansart, G. Hommel, L. Lamport, B. Liskov, G. P. Mullery and F. B. Schneider, Distributed Systems. Edited by M. Paul and H. J. Siegert. VI, 573 pages. 1985.

Vol. 191: H. Barringer, A Survey of Verification Techniques for Parallel Programs. VI, 115 pages. 1985.

Vol. 192: Automata on Infinite Words. Proceedings, 1984. Edited by M. Nivat and D. Perrin. V, 216 pages.1985.

Vol. 193: Logics of Programs. Proceedings, 1985. Edited by R. Parikh. VI, 424 pages. 1985.

Vol. 194: Automata, Languages and Programming. Proceedings, 1985. Edited by W. Brauer. IX, 520 pages. 1985.

Vol. 195: H. J. Stüttgen, A Hierarchical Associative Processing System. XII, 273 pages. 1985.

Vol. 196: Advances in Cryptology: Proceedings 1984. Edited by G. R. Blakley and D. Chaum. IX, 491 pages. 1985.

Vol. 197: Seminar on Concurrency. Proceedings, 1984. Edited by S. D. Brookes, A. W. Roscoe and G. Winskel. X, 523 pages. 1985.

This series reports new developments in computer science research and teaching – quickly, informally and at a high level. The type of materia considered for publication includes preliminary drafts of original papers and monographs, technical reports of high quality and broad interest advanced level lectures, reports of meetings, provided they are of exceptional interest and focused on a single topic. The timeliness of a manuscript is more important than its form which may be unfinished or tentative If possible, a subject index should be included. Publication of Lecture Notes is intended as a service to the international computer science community, in that a commercial publisher, Springer-Verlag, can offer a wide distribution of documents which would otherwise have a restricted readership. Once published and copyrighted, they can be documented in the scientific literature.

Manuscripts

Manuscripts should be no less than 100 and preferably no more than 500 pages in length.
They are reproduced by a photographic process and therefore must be typed with extreme care. Symbols not on the typewriter should be inserted by hand in indelible black ink. Corrections to the typescrip should be made by pasting in the new text or painting out errors with white correction fluid. Authors receiv 75 free copies and are free to use the material in other publications. The typescript is reduced slightly i size during reproduction; best results will not be obtained unless the text on any one page is kept withi the overall limit of 18 x 26.5 cm (7 x 10½ inches). On request, the publisher will supply special paper wit the typing area outlined.
Manuscripts should be sent to Prof. G. Goos, GMD Forschungsstelle Karlsruhe, Haid- und Neu-Str. 10–14 Postfach 6380, 7500 Karlsruhe 1, Germany, Prof. J. Hartmanis, Cornell University, Dept. of Computer-Science Ithaca, NY/USA 14850, or directly to Springer-Verlag Heidelberg.

Springer-Verlag, Heidelberger Platz 3, D-1000 Berlin 33
Springer-Verlag, Tiergartenstraße 17, D-6900 Heidelberg 1
Springer-Verlag, 175 Fifth Avenue, New York, NY 10010/USA
Springer-Verlag, 37-3, Hongo 3-chome, Bunkyo-ku, Tokyo 113, Japan

ISBN 3-540-15670-4
ISBN 0-387-15670-4